COLONIAL SPANISH AMERICA

The complete *Cambridge History of Latin America* presents a large-scale, authoritative survey of Latin America's unique historical experience from the first contacts between the native American Indians and Europeans to the present day. *Colonial Spanish America* is a selection of chapters from volumes I and II brought together to provide a continuous history of the Spanish Empire in America from the late fifteenth to the early nineteenth centuries. The first three chapters deal with conquest and settlement and relations between Spain and its American Empire; the final six with urban development, mining, rural economy and society, including the formation of the hacienda, the internal economy, and the impact of Spanish rule on Indian societies. Bibliographical essays are included for all chapters. The book will be a valuable text for both students and teachers of Latin American history.

COLONIAL
SPANISH AMERICA

---

edited by

LESLIE BETHELL

Professor of Latin American History,
University of London

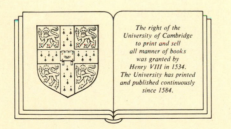

The right of the
University of Cambridge
to print and sell
all manner of books
was granted by
Henry VIII in 1534.
The University has printed
and published continuously
since 1584.

CAMBRIDGE UNIVERSITY PRESS

Cambridge

London   New York   New Rochelle
Melbourne   Sydney

Published by the Press Syndicate of the University of Cambridge
The Pitt Building, Trumpington Street, Cambridge CB2 1RP
32 East 57th Street, New York, NY 10022, USA
10 Stamford Road, Oakleigh, Melbourne 3166, Australia

The contents of this book were previously published as part of
volumes I and II of *The Cambridge History of Latin America*,
copyright © Cambridge University Press, 1984.

© Cambridge University Press 1987

First published 1987

Printed in Great Britain by Woolnough Bookbinding, Irthlingborough

British Library cataloguing in publication data

The Cambridge history of Latin America. Vols. 1 and 2. *Selections*
Colonial Spanish America.
1. Spain – Colonies – America   2. Latin
America – History – To 1830
I. Bethell. Leslie
980'.01   F1410

Library of Congress cataloguing in publication data

Colonial Spanish America.
"Previously published as part of volumes I and II of the Cambridge history
of Latin America"
Includes bibliographies and index.
1. Latin America – History – To 1830.   2. Spain –
Colonies – America – Administration.   3. Latin America –
Economic conditions.   I. Bethell, Leslie.
F1412.C64   1987   980   87-30980

ISBN 0 521 34126 4 hard covers
ISBN 0 521 34924 9 paperback

CONTENTS

MAPS

FIGURES

NOTE ON CURRENCY AND MEASUREMENT

Various units of value and measurement are referred to in the text of the following chapters. It is not possible to give exact equivalents in modern terms, particularly as there were many local variations. The following explanations may prove helpful.

Peso	The silver peso of Mexico in the late eighteenth century was equal to the American dollar or 4*s*. 8*d*.
Real	The peso was divided into eight silver reales or twenty copper reales (*reales de vellón*).
Maravedí	The value of the maravedí varied widely and was often no more than an imaginary division of bigger coins, since for long periods there were no maravedí coins at all. The last ones to circulate, probably in the late seventeenth and early eighteenth centuries, were copper coins, often debased. One such coin was worth 1/34 part of a real de vellón.
Fanega	A dry measure for cacao, wheat, maize, etc. Usually equal to 1.5 English bushels, but there were local variations, e.g. in Mexico, where the fanega of maize could be either 1.5 or 2.5 bushels (or 55 or 90.8 litres).
Quintal	Usually translated as 'hundredweight' and composed of 4 Spanish *arrobas* or 100 *libras*.
Arroba	The Spanish arroba weighed about 11.5 kg (25 lb). The Portuguese arroba weighed 14.5 kg (32 lb).

PREFACE

The Cambridge History of Latin America (*CHLA*) is an authoritative survey of Latin America's unique historical experience during the five centuries from the first contacts between the native peoples of the Americas and Europeans in the late fifteenth and early sixteenth centuries to the present day.

Colonial Spanish America brings together nine chapters from volumes I and II of *The Cambridge History of Latin America* in a single volume which, it is hoped, will be useful for both teachers and students of Latin American history. The first three chapters provide a continuous history of the relations between Spain and America from the end of the fifteenth to the beginning of the nineteenth centuries; the remaining six examine some important aspects of the economy and society of colonial Spanish America: urban development, mining, the hacienda in New Spain, agrarian structures in Spanish South America, the domestic economy and the impact of Spanish rule on Indian societies. Each chapter is accompanied by a bibliographical essay.

Part One

SPAIN AND AMERICA

1

THE SPANISH CONQUEST

THE ANTECEDENTS OF CONQUEST

'Without settlement there is no good conquest, and if the land is not conquered, the people will not be converted. Therefore the maxim of the conqueror must be to settle.' The words are those of one of the first historians of the Indies, Francisco López de Gómara.[1] The philosophy behind them is that of his patron, the greatest of the *conquistadores*, Hernán Cortés. It was this philosophy which came to inform Spain's overseas enterprise of the sixteenth century and did much to make Spanish America what it eventually became. But its success was not inevitable, nor was it attained without a struggle. There are several ways in which an aggressive society can expand the boundaries of its influence, and there were precedents for all of them in medieval Spain.

The *reconquista* – that great southwards movement of the Christian kingdoms of the Iberian peninsula into the regions held by the Moors – illustrated something of the wide range of possibilities from which precedents could be drawn. Fought along the border dividing Christendom from Islam, the reconquista was a war that extended the boundaries of the faith. It was also a war for territorial expansion, conducted and regulated, if not always controlled, by the crown and by the great military-religious orders, which acquired vassals in the process along with vast areas of land. It was a typical frontier-war of hit-and-run raids in pursuit of easy plunder, offering opportunities for ransom and barter, and for more intangible prizes, like honour and fame. It was a migration of people and livestock in search of new homes and new pastures. It was a process of controlled settlement and colonization, based on the establishment of towns which were granted extensive territorial jurisdiction under royal charter.

[1] Francisco López de Gómara, *Historia general de las Indias* (Madrid, 1852), 181.

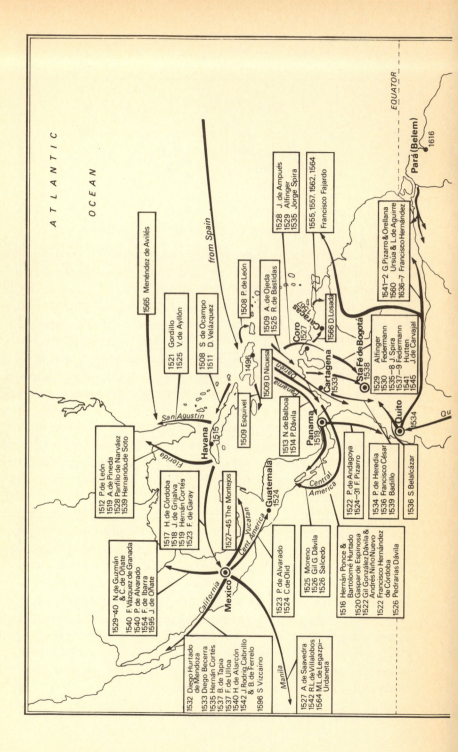

ATLANTIC

OCEAN

from Spain

EQUATOR

Pará (Belém)
1616

1565 Menéndez de Avilés

1521 Gordillo
1525 V. de Ayllón

1508 S. de Ocampo
1511 D. Velázquez

1508 P. de León

1509 A. de Ojeda
1525 R. de Bastidas

1528 J. de Ampués
1529 Alfinger
1535 Jorge Spira

1555, 1557, 1562, 1564
Francisco Fajardo

1541–2 G. Pizarro & Orellana
1560 Ursúa & L. de Aguirre
1636–7 Francisco Hernández

Coro
1527

1496

1509 D. Nicuesa

1566 D. Losada

Cartagena
1533

Sta Fe de Bogotá
1538

1529 Alfinger
1530 Federmann
1535–8 J. Spira
1537–9 Federmann
1541 Hutten
1545 J. de Carvajal

Quito
1534

Darién

Panamá
1519

1513 N. de Balboa
1514 P. Dávila

1509 Esquivel

1515

Havana

San Agustín

1512 P. de León
1519 A. de Pineda
1528 Pánfilo de Narváez
1539 Hernando de Soto

Florida

1517 H. de Córdoba
1518 J. de Grijalva
1519 Hernán Cortés
1523 F. de Garay

1527–45 The Montejos

Yucatán

Guatemala
1524

Cent. America

Central
America

1522 P. de Andagoya
1524–31 F. Pizarro

1534 P. de Heredia
1536 Francisco César
1539 Badillo

1536 S. Belalcázar

1523 P. de Alvarado
1524 C. de Olid

1525 Moreno
1526 Gil G. Dávila
1526 Salcedo

1516 Hernán Ponce &
       Bartolomé Hurtado
1520 Gaspar de Espinosa
1522 Gil González Dávila &
       Andrés Niño
1522 Francisco Hernández
       de Córdoba
1526 Pedrarias Dávila

Mexico

California

1529–40 N. de Guzmán
          & C. de Oñate
1540 F. Vázquez de Granada
1540 P. de Alvarado
1554 F. de Ibarra
1595 J. de Oñate

1532 Diego Hurtado
     de Mendoza
1533 Diego Becerra
1535 Hernán Cortés
1537 B. de Tapia
1537 F. de Ulloa
1540 H. de Alarcón
1542 J. Rodrig. Cabrillo
     & B. de Ferrelo
1596 S Vizcaíno

Manila

1527 A. de Saavedra
1542 R.L. de Villalobos
1564 M L. de Legazpi-
       Urdaneta

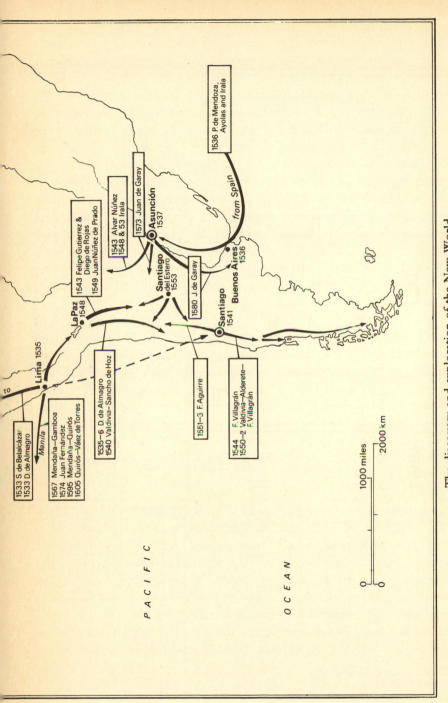

The discovery and exploration of the New World

Source: Francisco Morales Padrón, *Historia general de América* (2nd edn, Madrid, 1975), 336–7.

Map labels:

PACIFIC

OCEAN

1533 S de Belalcázar
1533 D. de Almagro

Manila

1567 Mendaña–Gamboa
1574 Juan Fernández
1595 Mendaña–Quirós
1605 Quirós–Váez de Torres

to

Lima 1535

La Paz 1548

1535–6 D. de Almagro
1540 Valdivia–Sancho de Hoz

1551–3 F. Aguirre

1544 F. Villagrán
1550–2 Valdivia–Alderete—
F. Villagrán

Santiago
del Estero
1553

Santiago
1541

1543 Felipe Gutiérrez &
Diego de Rojas
1549 JuanNúñez de Prado

1543 Alvar Núñez
1548 & 53 Irala

1573 Juan de Garay

Asunción
1537

1580 J. de Garay

Buenos Aires
1536

from Spain

1536 P. de Mendoza,
Ayolas and Irala

1000 miles

2000 km

0

0

To conquer, therefore, might mean to settle, but it might also mean to raid, plunder and move on. Conquest in the first sense gave primacy to the occupation and exploitation of land. In the second sense it conceived power and wealth in a much less static form – in terms of the possession of portable objects, like gold, booty and livestock, and of lordship over vassals rather than ownership of land. Mobility implied adventure, and adventure in a military society enormously enhanced the opportunities to improve one's standing in the eyes of one's fellow men. The desire to 'win honour' and to be 'worth more' (*valer más*) was a central ambition in the status-bound and honour-conscious society of medieval Castile. Honour and worth were most rapidly won with the sword and deserved to be formalized in a grant of higher status by a grateful sovereign. It was in keeping with this tradition that Baltasar Dorantes de Carranza could write of the conquerors of Mexico that, although there were some *hidalgos* among them, they were now 'by presumption' all *hidalgos*, 'because all *hidalguía* originates by its nature in acts of service to the king'.[2]

The reconquista was halted but not terminated by the gradual attainment of its natural limits within the Iberian peninsula itself. The enclave of the kingdom of Granada would remain in Moorish hands until 1492, but otherwise the Christian reconquest of the peninsula was complete by the end of the thirteenth century. As the limits of internal expansion were reached, so the dynamic forces in medieval Iberian society began to look to new frontiers across the seas – the Catalans and Aragonese primarily to Sicily, Sardinia, North Africa and the eastern Mediterranean, the Castilians, like the Portuguese, to Africa and the Atlantic islands.

This expansionist movement of the fifteenth-century Iberians was a reflection both of specifically Iberian aspirations and of more general European aspirations in the later Middle Ages. Fifteenth-century Europe was a society still suffering from the economic and social dislocations caused by the ravages of the Black Death. Labour was in short supply; aristocratic incomes had fallen; monarchs and nobles competed for power and resources. It was a society, too, which felt itself threatened along its eastern frontiers by the menacing presence of Islam and the advance of the Ottoman Turk. It was a restless and relatively

[2] Baltasar Dorantes de Carranza, *Sumaria Relación de las Cosas de la Nueva España* [1604] (2nd edn, Mexico, 1970), 12.

mobile society, at once inquisitive and acquisitive – inquisitive about the world that lay beyond its immediate horizons and acquisitive in its desire for exotic luxuries and foodstuffs, and for gold which would enable it to buy these articles from the East with which it had a permanently unfavourable balance of trade.

The Iberian peninsula, with its proximity to Africa and its long Atlantic seaboard, was geographically well placed to take the lead in a movement of westwards expansion at a time when Europe was being hemmed in along its eastern boundaries. An Iberian maritime tradition had developed, both in the Mediterranean and the Atlantic, where Basque and Cantabrian fishermen had been building up a rich store of experience for the future navigation of uncharted seas. The conquest of Seville in 1248 and the advance of the reconquista to the straits of Gibraltar had given the crown of Castile–León a new Atlantic littoral, whose ports were settled by seamen from Portugal, Galicia and the Cantabrian coast.

Along this seaboard the combination of northern and Mediterranean skills created a race of sailors capable of promoting and taking advantage of advances in ship-construction and navigational techniques. The first Portuguese voyages were made in whatever reasonably suitable craft were available, but by the later fifteenth century the combination of the North European square rig with the Mediterranean lateen sail had produced in the caravel an impressive ocean-going ship, the culmination of a long period of evolution and experiment. Just as the new requirements of Atlantic voyaging helped perfect the caravel, so too they helped to improve the techniques of navigation. Once ships were travelling unknown waters out of sight of land, the old practices of dead-reckoning were no longer adequate, and the Portuguese turned to celestial observation to measure distances and determine latitude, making use of instruments long used by land-based astronomers, the astrolabe and quadrant. These instruments in turn were modified and refined to meet the needs of Atlantic voyagers. The magnetic compass, developed for use in the Mediterranean over the later Middle Ages, made it easier for navigators to take their bearings and plot direction on a chart. Here again Mediterranean experience was harnessed to Atlantic needs, for the Mediterranean region produced the first maritime charts; and the cartographical skills developed in late medieval Italy and transferred to the Iberian peninsula would make it possible to map an expanding world.

With its rich hinterland and its links to the Andalusian port-complex, Seville itself became the maritime and commercial, as well as the agrarian, capital of southern Spain. It served as a magnet to settlers from the interior of the peninsula – those predecessors of the later emigrants to the Indies – and to Mediterranean merchants, especially the Genoese. During the course of the fifteenth century the Genoese settled in growing numbers in Lisbon and Seville, where they glimpsed new possibilities for enterprise and capital at a time when their activities in the Levant were being constricted by the advance of the Turk. In the west they hoped to develop alternative sources of supply for valuable commodities – silks, dyestuffs, and above all, sugar – which were becoming less accessible to them in the east; and they were eager for access to Sahara gold.

It is no surprise, then, to find Genoese capital and skills playing an important, and at times decisive, part in Iberian overseas enterprises of the fifteenth century. The Genoese were well represented in the expeditions to the African coast for slaves and gold, and they actively supported the movement to annex and exploit the islands of the eastern Atlantic – the Canaries, Madeira and the Azores – where they hoped to establish new sugar-plantations.

But the Genoese were no more than one element, although a significant one, in the Iberian overseas movement of the later Middle Ages. Portugal in particular had a strong native mercantile community, which helped place the House of Avis on the throne in the revolution of 1383–5. The new dynasty maintained close ties with prominent merchants and was responsive to their concern for the acquisition of new markets, and of new sources of supply for dyestuffs, gold, sugar and slaves. But Portugal's overseas ventures of the fifteenth century were also guided by other, and sometimes contradictory, interests. The nobility, hit by devaluations of the coinage which reduced the value of their fixed rents and incomes, looked overseas for new lands and new sources of wealth. The princes of the new royal house combined in varying degrees acquisitive instinct with crusading fervour, a thirst for geographical information and a desire to perpetuate their names.

Under the vigorous direction of the royal house, these various motivations combined to produce among the Portuguese an intensive movement towards overseas expansion at a time when Castile had still to take anything more than a first faltering step. The Castilian crown had assumed nominal possession of the Canary islands following the first serious attempt at an expedition of conquest in 1402. But in the face of resistance by the Guanche inhabitants, the conquest lagged; and for much of the fifteenth century domestic troubles and the unfinished business of the reconquista prevented Castile from following in any systematic way the Portuguese example.

By the time of the death of Prince Henry the Navigator in 1460 the Portuguese had penetrated some 1,500 miles down the West African coast, and had pushed outwards into the Atlantic, establishing their presence on Madeira, the Azores and the Cape Verde Islands. Africa was a potential source of slave labour for the sugar-plantations that sprang up in these newly annexed Atlantic islands. Medieval Mediterranean society had devised institutional forms and techniques for trading, enslaving, planting and conquering, and the participation of the Genoese in fifteenth-century Iberian expansion helped ensure the reappearance of these same forms and techniques in the advance down the West African coast and in the island-stepping movement across the Atlantic.

The most characteristic feature of the Portuguese style of expansion was the *feitoria* (factory), the fortified trading-post of the kind established at Arguin or São Jorge de Mina on the African coast. The use of the feitoria made it possible to dispense with large-scale conquest and settlement and enabled the fifteenth- and sixteenth-century Portuguese to establish their presence over large stretches of the globe without the necessity for deep penetration into continental hinterlands. It was a style of settlement which Columbus, with his Genoese background and his Portuguese experience, had come to know well, and which would provide him with an obvious model when he reached the Caribbean islands.

Overseas expansion, however, could mean more than the establishment of trading-posts, as indeed it did for the Portuguese in the Atlantic islands and, later, in Brazil. To establish sugar-plantations, as in the Azores, it was necessary to colonize. Here the cheapest method from the point of view of the crown was to devolve responsibility for settling and developing the territory on a private individual, who would be rewarded with extensive privileges. This system, by which the *donatário*, or lord proprietor, was also the captain and commander, nicely blended the capitalist and military-seigneurial elements of medieval Mediterranean society. It was used by the Portuguese crown in the fifteenth century to develop both Madeira and the Azores, and in 1534 would be extended to the New World when João III divided the Brazilian coastline into twelve hereditary captaincies.

The Castilians, then, could draw upon Portuguese precedents as well as their own experiences in the reconquista, when at the end of the fifteenth century they turned their attention to new worlds overseas. There lay before them a variety of options. They could trade or they could raid; they could settle or move on. The option they chose would be determined in part by local conditions – the ease of occupation, the nature of the resources to be exploited – and in part by the particular combination of individuals and interests which underwrote and controlled the expeditions of conquest.

Much depended, inevitably, on the character of the leader and on the kind of backing which he was able to obtain. The *conquistador*, although highly individualistic, was never alone. He was one of a group under a *caudillo*, a leader, whose capacity for survival would be tested in the first instance by his skill in mobilizing men and resources, and then by his success in leading his men to victory. Cortés' cousin, Alonso de Monroy, master of the order of Alcántara, who distinguished himself in the peninsular conflicts of the fifteenth century, was known as 'supremely fortunate in war' and as one who 'compelled fortune to follow him'.[3] This was the reputation to which Cortés himself aspired, along with every New World caudillo.

The caudillo had at one and the same time to meet the requirements of his backers, and to satisfy the demands of the no less individualistic body of men who had placed themselves temporarily under his command. Tension was therefore built into every conquering expedition – tension about aims and objectives and about the distribution of the spoils. The discipline, such as it was, came on the one hand from the capacity of the leader to impose himself on his men and, on the other, from the collective sense of commitment to a common enterprise.

The long centuries of frontier warfare in Castile helped create that special blend of individualism and sense of community which could one day make possible the conquest of America. The personal pronoun which runs through Hernán Cortés' *Letters* from Mexico is counterbalanced by the confident 'we' of the rank and file who speak through one of their number, Bernal Díaz del Castillo, in his *True Account of the Conquest of New Spain*. But the great expansionist movement which

[3] Alonso Maldonado, *Hechos del Maestre de Alcántara Don Alonso de Monroy*, ed. A. R. Rodríguez Moñino (Madrid, 1935), 24.

carried the Spanish presence across the Atlantic was something more than the massive effort of private enterprise temporarily assuming collectivist forms. For alongside the individual and the collective unit there were two other participants which placed an indelible stamp on the whole undertaking – the church and the crown.

Even when the frontier war against the Moors was carried on largely by autonomous warrior bands, it continued to be conducted under the auspices of church and state. The church provided that moral sanction which elevated a plundering expedition into a crusade, while the state's approval was required to legitimate the acquisition of lordship and land. The land, and the sub-soil, were among the *regalías* belonging to the Castilian crown, and consequently any land acquired through conquest by a private individual became his not of right, but through royal grace and favour. It was for the king, as the supreme lord (the *señor natural*) to control the *repartimiento*, or distribution of lands either won, or to be won, and to authorize colonies of settlement in conquered territory. When the spoils of war came to be divided up, a royal fifth (the *quinto real*) always had to be set aside. Although the *adelantados*, or military governors of the frontier regions, possessed a large degree of autonomy, they were governors for the king.

In these and many other ways the royal presence made itself felt as the reconquista proceeded on its southward advance. Inevitably the effective authority of the crown fluctuated from generation to generation, but kingship itself was central to the whole organization of medieval Castilian society and was accorded an exalted position in that great compilation of Castile's legal tradition, the thirteenth-century *Siete Partidas* of Alfonso X. The vision of a harmonious society enshrined in the *Siete Partidas* is one in which the king, as God's vicar on earth, exercises a constant and active supervision within the framework of the law. It was for the monarch, as the natural lord of this society, to provide good government and justice, in the sense of ensuring that each vassal received the rights and fulfilled the obligations that were his by virtue of his station. A contractual relationship between king and vassals is implicit in this theory: kingship degenerates into tyranny if the king, or his appointed agents, disregard the common weal. The good king, as distinct from the tyrant, sees to it that the evil are punished and the just rewarded. As the dispenser of patronage he recompenses the services of deserving vassals with offices and honours in consonance with a carefully calibrated system by which, at least in theory, every *servicio* by a vassal finds its due compensation in a *merced*, or favour, from the king.

It was this patrimonial society, built around the conception of mutual obligation symbolized by the words servicio and merced, which fell into disrepair in the later Middle Ages, was reconstituted in Castile during the joint reign of Ferdinand and Isabella (1474–1504) and was then carried across the ocean to be implanted in the islands and mainland of America. Ferdinand and Isabella, the Catholic Kings, were the rulers of what was essentially a renovated medieval society. But the nature of their own kingship, although traditional in its theoretical formulations, possessed in practice elements of novelty which made their power more formidable than that of any of their medieval forbears.

Above all, they were the first authentic sovereigns of *Spain* – a Spain consisting of the union, in their own persons, of the crowns of Castile and Aragon. Even though the two crowns remained institutionally distinct, their nominal union represented a striking enhancement of royal power. As kings of Spain, the Catholic Kings had at their disposal, at least potentially, financial and military resources far greater than those which could be mustered by any rebellious faction among their subjects. They could call on deep reserves of instinctive loyalty among subjects weary of interminable civil war. They possessed, in the growing class of *letrados* (university-trained officials) a reservoir of professionally qualified servants whose own interests were best served by maintaining and extending the authority of the crown. Renaissance humanism and a reviving religion with strong eschatological overtones provided ideas and symbols which could be exploited to project new images of the monarchy, as the natural leader in a great collective enterprise – a divinely appointed mission to overthrow the last remnants of Moorish domination and to purify the peninsula of any contaminating elements as a prelude to carrying the gospel to the farthest ends of the earth.

Ferdinand and Isabella possessed the shrewdness and the skill to make the most of these various weapons in their armoury. As a result, the last two decades of the fifteenth century in Castile – where the institutional barriers against the exercise of royal authority were much less strong than those in the crown of Aragon – saw an impressive reassertion and extension of the royal power.

The presence of an intrusive state was to be critical to the whole development of Castile's overseas enterprise. Royal intervention might be actively sought by some and bitterly resented by others, but in both instances the authority of the crown was to be an automatic point of reference for all those engaged in the exploration, conquest and settlement of new lands.

There were already clear indications of this in Castile's first essay in Atlantic conquest and colonization – the occupation of the Canary Islands in the 1480s and 1490s. The Canaries were still only a nominal possession of the Castilian crown when they became an object of dispute between Portugal and Castile in the war of succession that broke out in 1475. Potentially rich in itself, the Canary archipelago was also an obvious base both for raids on the African coast and for Atlantic voyages of exploration of the type being undertaken by the Portuguese. The crown of Castile, engaged in a sharp rivalry with Portugal, therefore had a clear interest in enforcing its claims, and an expedition was sent out from Seville in 1478 to occupy the Grand Canary. This was followed by a new and more successful expedition under the command of Alfonso Fernández de Lugo in 1482; but, although the Portuguese abandoned their claims in the peace treaty of 1479, the resistance of the islanders prevented an easy occupation, and Palma was not subjugated until 1492 and Tenerife a year later. Conquest, as in the Portuguese Azores, was followed by exploitation. The Genoese helped introduce sugar production, and by 1526 there were twelve sugar-plantations on Grand Canary island alone.

The occupation of the Canaries, a natural staging-post on the route to the Indies, illustrated that conjunction of public and private interest which had characterized the reconquista and was also to characterize the enterprise of America. The lordship of the islands belonged to the crown, which therefore had to authorize all expeditions of conquest. The crown on this occasion also participated in the financing of the enterprise, but Fernández de Lugo, named by the crown as adelantado of Las Palmas, made his own private contract with a company of Sevillan merchants. Before an expedition set out, a formal contract, or *capitulación*, was signed between the crown and the commander, along the lines of similar contracts made in the course of the reconquista. By these capitulaciones the crown would reserve for itself certain rights in the territories to be conquered, while guaranteeing specified privileges and rewards to the commander and those who enlisted in his company.

When that obsessive Genoese visionary, Christopher Columbus, finally persuaded Ferdinand and Isabella in 1491 to patronize and support his projected voyage into the Ocean Sea, he therefore found himself caught up in a well-established tradition constituting the relationship between the crown and the leaders of expeditions. To this relationship he brought his own ideas, based on the Portuguese model of charters of donation for those who discovered lands west of the Azores. In the capitulaciones agreed with the Catholic Kings at Santa Fe, outside Granada, in April 1492 he was authorized, following a traditional formula, to 'discover and acquire islands and mainlands in the Ocean Sea' – in fact to 'conquer', in the sense of searching out and occupying desirable land. The crown was willing on this occasion to make a relatively small financial contribution and to provide Columbus with his ships. He was named hereditary viceroy and governor of any new found lands, 'viceroy' being the title conferred by the rulers of medieval Aragon on a deputy appointed to govern territories which the king himself was unable to administer in person. Columbus was also, at his special insistence, created hereditary Admiral of the Ocean Sea. Among the rewards promised him in the event of success was the right to appoint judicial (but not administrative) officials in the area of his jurisdiction, along with 10 per cent of the profits of barter and trade.

On 3 August 1492, when Columbus set sail from the Andalusian port of Palos, it was obviously anticipated that, if he reached the 'Indies', he would establish a Portuguese-style entrepot trade for the benefit of the crown of Castile, based on small garrison settlements. But the news which he brought back on his return to Spain in March 1493 suggested, at least to the crown, the desirability of certain modifications to the original scheme. There was some scepticism as to whether Columbus had indeed reached the East, as he himself insisted. The revelation of what appeared to be new islands and new peoples raised important questions about titles to the land and the treatment of the islanders. Who was to exercise lordship over them, and who was to undertake the salvation of their souls?

The Catholic Kings turned to the papacy, following the precedent set by the Portuguese, who had secured a formal papal donation of rights of sovereignty 'from Cape Bojador towards Guinea and beyond'. From a compliant Spanish pope, Alexander VI, they obtained what they wanted: similar rights in 'all islands and mainlands whatever, found or to be found' in the area beyond a national line of demarcation that was to be formally agreed between the crowns of Portugal and Spain in the treaty of Tordesillas of 1494. Alexander VI's bulls of 1493 might have been regarded as unnecessary in view of the Roman Law principle laid down in the *Siete Partidas* that possession belonged to the first occupiers of the land. But papal authorization gave an extra degree of security to Castilian claims against any attempted challenge by the Portuguese, and raised the enterprise of the Indies to the level of a holy undertaking by linking Castile's exclusive rights to an equally exclusive obligation to win the heathen to the Faith. This missionary enterprise, solemnly entrusted to the crown of Castile, provided it with a moral justification for conquest and colonization which at once reinforced and transcended claims deriving in one form or another from the fact of first discovery.

The crown, having moved to ensure its primacy in the international arena, also moved to ensure its primacy in Columbus's enterprise. The fitting out of the fleet for his return voyage to Hispaniola – a fleet, this time, of seventeen instead of only three ships – was entrusted to the formidable Juan Rodríguez de Fonseca, archdeacon of Seville, and a member of the council of Castile. For the next 23 years, until the death of Ferdinand the Catholic in 1516, Fonseca was to be in effect the supreme director and co-ordinator of Castile's American enterprise, charged with the almost impossible task of ensuring that, at every stage of discovery, colonization and conquest, the interests and authority of the crown were properly upheld. The inclusion on Columbus's second voyage of a deputy of the *contadores mayores* of Castile – the principal financial ministers of the crown – along with a *receptor* to collect all royal dues, and a *veedor*, or inspector of accounts, laid down the precedent for supervision and control by royal officials that was to be followed in future expeditions. Fonseca's men would follow hard on the heels of every future explorer and discoverer, and no captain in the Indies would be able to evade for long the oppressive shadow of the crown.

The 1493 expedition differed also in other important respects from its predecessor. There had been no priest on the first voyage, but this time special emphasis was laid on the conversion of the islanders, and a group of friars, specially selected by Ferdinand and Isabella and led by a Catalan Benedictine, Bernardo Boil, was given responsibility for a missionary enterprise to be undertaken at the crown's expense. Conversion, moreover, implied permanency of occupation, and the whole expedition was geared to the establishment in the Antilles of a long-term Spanish presence. This time, instead of a mere 87 men, Columbus was accompanied by 1,200, including not only soldiers and sailors and gentlemen adventurers but also artisans and agricultural labourers. The emphasis at this stage was on settlement, although *rescate* (barter with the Indian) remained central to the enterprise. A model colony, in fact, was being shipped wholesale from Seville – model except in one critical respect. It included no women.

Already by 1493, then, new elements were coming into play to modify or transform the original enterprise of the Indies as envisaged by Columbus. Trading and exploring remained powerful components of the enterprise; and the establishment of a permanent settlement in the Antilles was closely in line with the Portuguese–Genoese style of overseas activity, as already practised in Madeira and along the West African coast. But the old Castilian reconquista traditions were also tending to assert themselves, encouraged in part by the fact that the newly discovered world of the Antilles appeared heavily settled with a non-Christian population, and one which possessed objects of gold. Amidst the variety of options available to it, Castile was moving towards the one which implied full-scale conquest in the medieval peninsular tradition – the assertion of sovereignty, the establishment of the faith, immigration and settlement, and an extensive domination of land and people. But, as the first Spanish colony in the New World was launched on its precarious career, it was far from certain whether conquest and settlement, or conquest and movement, was the form of conquest that would prevail.

THE PATTERN OF THE ISLANDS

The problem that faced the crown and its agents in Hispaniola prefigured in miniature the problem that underlay the whole Spanish enterprise in America: how to impose stability in a world where almost everything was immediately in flux. Intruding into the new-found Caribbean paradise with their own aspirations, their values, and – not least – their diseases, Columbus and his men were soon on the way to transforming it into a wilderness.

The Spaniards had returned to the Antilles with clear-cut ideas. Above all, they wanted gold. While Columbus himself continued his search for India and the empire of the Great Khan, the bulk of his party established itself in Hispaniola, where it discovered that the first settlement had been wiped out in his absence. A new one, Isabela, was therefore founded on what proved to be an insalubrious site on the northern shore. The settlers, it was assumed, would build a town, plant their crops, establish their livestock and set up a chain of well-defended warehouses, in which the Indians – now subjected to the uplifting influence of Christianity – would meekly deposit large quantities of gold.

This dream was soon shattered. The quantity of gold forthcoming from barter with the Indians proved to be very disappointing, and Columbus, anxious to justify their investment to his sovereigns, tried to supplement the deficiency with another desirable commodity, the Indians themselves. By shipping Caribbean Indians back to Spain for sale as slaves, Columbus posed in acute form a question that was to dominate the history of Spain in America for the next 50 years: the status to be accorded to the indigenous population.

'Barbarians' might, according to the provisions of Roman Law, be legitimately enslaved, and 'barbarian' had come to be interpreted by medieval Christendom as 'infidel'. But although the crown appeared willing to apply this interpretation to the first consignment of Tainos which reached Andalusia, the influence of the theologians led to second thoughts. An infidel was a man who had rejected the true faith, but these new peoples had apparently, if inexplicably, lived in total ignorance of it. They should therefore be classed as pagans and not as infidels, unless, after the gospel was preached to them, they still rejected it. Isabella, counselled by her confessor, Jiménez de Cisneros, suspended the trade. These people were her subjects; and in 1500 the crown declared the Indians 'free and not subject to servitude'. This ruling, apparently decisive, was in fact far from comprehensive. It was still permissible to enslave Indians taken in a 'just war' – a term that proved eminently adaptable as employed in the Caribbean, and, later, on the mainland, embracing as it did anything from 'rebellious' Indians to cannibalistic Caribs. The immediate consequence of the crown's decision was to encourage slave-raiding expeditions against islands of the Antilles still uninhabited by Spaniards, in order to supply the market with 'legitimate' slaves. As the abuses multiplied, so did the revulsion against them, but it was not until the New Laws of 1542, which operated retrospectively as well as for the future, that the enslavement of Indians was definitively, if not universally, abolished.

The rejection, at least in principle, of Indian slavery removed one of the options open to the settlers of Hispaniola, and in consequence exacerbated the problems of survival that were already becoming acute. Disease among the colonists had forced them to move to the southern side of the island, where their new settlement, Santo Domingo, founded by Bartolomé Colón in 1498, was to become the nerve-centre of the Spanish Indies for a generation or more. But the survival of Santo Domingo as a viable settlement depended on the establishment of some equilibrium between colonists who, like all colonists, arrived with exaggerated expectations, and resources which were not only limited but rapidly diminishing.

The Columbus family, enjoying jurisdiction over the islands, proved unequal to the task. As Genoese upstarts they began at a natural disadvantage, and by temperament neither the admiral nor his brothers were equipped to deal with the endemic indiscipline of a bunch of Spaniards whose only thought was for easy wealth. The Columbus era in the West Indies ended definitively with the final return of Diego Colón to Spain in 1524, but already from the mid-1490s the crown was carefully curbing and clipping the family's jurisdiction. The real founder of Hispaniola and, through it, of the Spanish Indies, was Fray Nicolás de Ovando, appointed governor in 1501. An Extremaduran whose political skill and administrative abilities had been displayed in the reform of the military order of Alcántara, he was appointed to bring stability to an island where the settler community was torn by faction and threatened with extinction by shortage of food and of labour.

In the eight years of his government Ovando succeeded in laying the foundations for economic survival and effective centralized control. He began by refounding the city of Santo Domingo itself, destroyed by a cyclone shortly after his arrival in the spring of 1502. Rebuilt on a slightly different site, Santo Domingo became the first real city of the Spanish New World – the one that would first greet the eyes of a whole generation of new arrivals in the Indies, and which would provide the prototype for the towns that would arise in mainland America. In his *Summary of the Natural History of the Indies* (1526), that proud chronicler of Hispaniola, Gonzalo Fernández de Oviedo, would describe it as superior even to Barcelona and all the other Old World cities that he had seen: 'for as it was founded in our times...it was laid out with rule and compass, and all the streets planned on regular lines'.[4] The grid-iron plan, following models already established in Europe – not least the encampment of the Catholic Kings at Santa Fe in Granada – had safely made the transatlantic crossing.

Many of the practices and institutions that were later to be transported to the mainland of America were the direct product of the Ovando

---

[4] Gonzalo Fernández de Oviedo, *Sumario de la natural historia de las Indias*, ed. José Miranda (Mexico, 1950), 88–9.

regime in Hispaniola, which in turn drew on the experiences of the reconquista in Spain and of the conquest of the Canaries. The Spaniards, if they were to be induced to remain, must be given a stake in the island's resources, both natural and human. Hopes of a gold-barter economy had foundered on the shortage of gold, although more might be obtained from the rivers and from mines. This in turn required labour, and Columbus had already introduced a system of forced Indian labour which would help produce tribute for the king and profit for the colonists. Attempts to replace this by voluntary wage-labour proved abortive, as was bound to happen in a society to which the European concept of 'work' was totally alien. The crown, on Ovando's recommendation, therefore approved in 1503 a forced labour system, by which the governor would be free to allocate Indian labour in the mines or the fields, wages being paid by those who received the allocation.

In giving Ovando the power to allocate native labour at his own discretion, the crown had given him the means to shape the island's life to its own requirements. The repartimiento, or distribution of the Indians, was an act of favour by the crown and, therefore, carried with it certain obligations to be fulfilled by the concessionaries. The Indians had to be cared for and instructed in the faith, which meant that they were in effect temporarily 'deposited' or entrusted to individual Spaniards. It was a system which recalled the assignment, or *encomienda*, of Moorish villages to members of the military orders in medieval Spain, and the word encomienda would in due course reappear in this new, American environment, although it would now carry a very different meaning.[5] The New World encomienda included no allocation of land or of rents. It was simply a state assignment of compulsory labour, tied to specific responsibilities towards his Indian charges by the depositary or *encomendero*.

Such responsibilities could not, in theory, be lightly assigned. They must go to those most fitted to exercise them, to the meritorious and the established – and the established man in the Hispanic world was the man of property with an urban residence. His control of the labour supply therefore enabled Ovando to encourage the settlement of the Spaniards in small urban communities, each with its *cabildo*, or town council, on the Spanish model. Indian labour was to be allocated only to *vecinos*, full citizens.

To facilitate the process of allocation, the Indians were also resettled,

---

[5] For further discussion of the *encomienda* system, see chs. 2, 8 and 9 below.

and their *caciques*, or chiefs, made responsible for the supplying of labour to the Spaniards. While some of the labour force consisted of encomienda Indians, other Indians, known as *naborías*, took up service in Spanish households as personal servants. These naborías straddled the dividing line of the harmonious society as planned by Ovando – a society in which Indian and Spanish communities co-existed under the close supervision of the royal governor, with the Indians being introduced to the benefits of Christian civilization and providing in return the labour which was all they had to offer. At the same time Ovando encouraged establishment of cattle-raising and sugar-cultivation, hoping to free Hispaniola society from excessive dependence on that elusive commodity, gold, and to tie the settlers to the land.

Under Ovando, therefore, Hispaniola made the transition from entrepot to colony, but his scheme contained within it the seeds of its own destruction. The formal establishment of forced labour for the Indian population only precipitated a process that was already becoming catastrophic – its total extinction. Within twenty years of the landing of Columbus the population of this once densely-populated island had been all but wiped out by war, disease, maltreatment and the trauma produced by the efforts of the intruders to force it into ways of life and behaviour totally unrelated to its previous experience.

In a desperate attempt to maintain the labour supply, the settlers took to massive raiding of the Bahamas and the deportation of its Lucayo population to Hispaniola. But as more batches of immigrants arrived from Spain in search of a quick fortune, the importation of forced labour from the neighbouring islands could serve as no more than a palliative. The stability sought by Ovando was proving impossibly elusive, and the attempt to impose it by autocratic means provoked fierce resentments against the governor. Setting a pattern that was to be followed time after time in the government of the Indies, local dissidents were able to mobilize influential supporters at court. Ovando was relieved of his office in 1509, the victim of Fonseca and his officials in Hispaniola. Diego Colón, who succeeded him as governor, fared no better. The pretensions of the Columbus family made him a suspect figure to the crown; and in 1511 it moved to curb his powers by establishing a permanent legal tribunal, the *audiencia* of Santo Domingo. The audiencia, modelled on the chancelleries of Valladolid and Granada, was itself to serve as a model for further such tribunals as the Spanish crown extended its control over the mainland of America. The agents of royal government were in future to be held in constant check by the agents of royal justice.

The continuing decline of Hispaniola's indigenous and imported non-white population elicited two distinctive responses, each with major consequences for the future of Spanish America. It provoked, in the first place, a powerful movement of moral indignation, both in the island itself and in metropolitan Spain. The movement was led by Dominicans horrified by the conditions they found on the island on their arrival in 1510. Its first major exponent was Antonio de Montesinos who, in a sermon preached in Santo Domingo on the Sunday before Christmas 1511, denounced the maltreatment of the Indians and refused communion to the encomenderos he held most responsible. Its greatest convert was Bartolomé de las Casas, who in 1514 renounced his encomienda and his commercial interests on the island and devoted the remaining 52 years of a turbulent life to a passionate defence of the Indian subjects of the Spanish crown.

The repercussions of this movement were soon felt at the court of Ferdinand the Catholic, where cynicism about the exploitation of the wealth of the Indies was tempered by an awareness of the obligations imposed upon the crown by a succession of papal bulls culminating in that of 28 July 1508, which gave it a universal *patronato*, or right of presentation to New World benefices, in return for the onerous duties involved in the evangelization of the indigenous population. A new code of legislation was clearly required to protect the Indians from the abuses described in such horrifying detail by Montesinos and his colleagues. The Laws of Burgos of 1512 were an attempt, however ingenuous, to provide this protection, carefully regulating the functioning of the encomienda, an institution not held to be incompatible – in view of the weaknesses and deficiencies of the majority of the Indians – with the principle of Indian liberty which the Laws also proclaimed.

The Laws of Burgos fell dead from the pens of the legislators: there was no authority on the island willing or able to ensure their enforcement. But in 1516, on the death of Ferdinand, the regent Cardinal Cisneros, under the influence of Las Casas, made a fresh attempt to tackle the problem by sending a commission of three Jeronymites to govern the island. The two years' rule of the Jeronymites vividly illustrated the difficulties inherent in pursuing good intentions in the face of unpalatable facts. It was difficult to eradicate abuses and the decline of the native population could not be halted.

Reluctantly conceding that the island economy was unable to survive without forced labour, the Jeronymites concluded that the only solution was to import it from outside, in the form of negro slaves. The institution of black slavery was well known to late medieval Mediterranean society. Portuguese traders had been importing blacks into Portugal from the Barbary coast since the mid-thirteenth century, and the number of black slaves in the Iberian peninsula increased sharply in the fifteenth century as Portuguese penetration down the Guinea coast created new sources of supply. Enjoying an effective monopoly of the trade, Portuguese dealers were extensively supplying the Spanish market from the 1460s. While Lisbon was the city with the largest black population in the peninsula, there were soon substantial numbers of slaves – some of them moors rather than negroes – in many of the major Spanish towns, where they were used in particular for domestic service. Seville, with a total population of around 100,000 in the 1560s, had at that time a slave population of 6,000, the majority of them black.

It is not therefore surprising that black slave labour should have seemed to the Spaniards to offer a natural answer to the problems of Hispaniola. The first shipment of *ladino* (Spanish-speaking) blacks reached the island in 1505 and further consignments followed, until Cisneros banned all shipment on the grounds that the presence of growing numbers of *ladinos* was a cause of serious unrest. But in 1518, after his death and with the blessing of the Jeronymites, shipments began again under the aegis of the crown, with Charles V granting a licence to a member of his Burgundian household to despatch 4,000 slaves to the Indies over the course of eight years. He promptly sold his licence to the Genoese. A new and lucrative transatlantic trade was in the making, as the Old World of Africa was brought in to redress the demographic balance of the New.

The demographic catastrophe that had overtaken the indigenous inhabitants of Hispaniola had another and more immediately potent effect. The island's excess population of Spanish settlers, driven to import labour to ensure its own survival, was also driven for similar reasons to export itself. The urge to wander was in any event instinctive to most of these men, so that necessity and inclination travelled hand in hand. The third and fourth voyages of Columbus in 1498 and 1502–4 had revealed much of the contours of the Caribbean and traced the coastline of Central America and part of Tierra Firme (Venezuela). The admiral's discoveries, like the rich pearl fisheries off the coast of

Venezuela, encouraged others to follow in his tracks. In 1499 Alonso de Hojeda charted the Venezuelan coast as far as the gulf of Maracaibo; in 1504 Juan de la Cosa explored the coast of Darien; and as the radius of explored space around Santo Domingo widened, so the pressures to conquer and migrate increased.

From 1508 the restless colonists of Santo Domingo were reaching out greedily towards the nearby islands. The settlement of Puerto Rico was begun in 1508 and that of Jamaica in 1509. Two years later Diego Velázquez, as the deputy of Diego Colón, embarked on the conquest of what was to be a major prize, the island of Fernandina, or Cuba. This would become a base for voyages of exploration and conquest to mainland America, and its port of Havana, relocated to a sheltered site on the northern coast in 1519, would replace Santo Domingo as the gateway to the Indies.

Disregarding the claims of the Columbus family, the crown was now issuing licences for the discovery and conquest of the rapidly-emerging landmass which appeared to be blocking the route to the East. Juan Ponce de León, the conqueror of Puerto Rico, discovered Florida in 1513, but did not take advantage of the authorization to settle it. More glittering prizes seemed to beckon elsewhere. Along the shores of the Gulf of Darien, barter settlements had been springing up for the *rescate* of gold from the local Indians. In 1513 Vasco Núñez de Balboa, cutting his way across the isthmus, sighted the Pacific Ocean from Darien. Three months before the sighting, orders had already been given in Spain for the despatch of an expedition from the peninsula under the command of Pedrarias Dávila, for the conquest of these mainland regions, now christened Castilla del Oro, the golden land. In the brutal search for gold Pedrarias plundered and terrorized; and in the inevitable clash with Balboa he emerged the victor. Under the direction of Pedrarias, expeditions of discovery fanned out through Central America, most of them making for the Pacific coast, where Pedrarias founded the city of Panama in 1519. In that same year Cortés landed in Mexico, and Magellan sailed on the voyage of circumnavigation that would give Spain, too late, its western sea-route to the East.

With each new forward movement by the Spanish intruders, the radius of devastation was enlarged. As one area after another of Spanish penetration lost its aboriginal population before the steady onward march of disruption, demoralization and disease, so the invaders made frantic efforts to replenish the dwindling native labour force by mounting slave-raiding expeditions to the surrounding region. Raids on the Bahamas and the lesser Caribbean islands to restock the aboriginal population of Hispaniola were followed by raids on Florida and the Gulf of Honduras to restock that of Cuba. Well before Cortés set sail from Cuba, slave-raiders had also been active on the coast of Yucatán. But it was in the period following the occupation of the isthmus of Panama and the discovery and conquest of Peru that slave-raiding became a regular and highly-organized way of life. The disappearance of the Indian inhabitants of the Panama isthmus meant that the Spaniards were left without a labour force to grow the crops, pan the gold and carry the heavy freight that had to be transported across the isthmus for shipment to Peru. To meet their needs, the colonists turned not only to the traditional slave-producing areas of the Caribbean, but also to the densely settled population of lacustrine Nicaragua, where slave-raiding reached a new level of intensity. But everywhere the hope of re-creating a lost Indian population proved illusory. The imported slaves succumbed as rapidly as the local population they had been brought in to replace, and the denuding of one region was not accompanied, as the Spaniards had hoped, by the restocking of another.

The lucrative business of the slave trade did, however, add substantially to geographical knowledge, as raiders explored the coast of Tierra Firme, Panama, Honduras and Florida, and mapped the Bahamas and the Lesser Antilles. It also promoted local trade within the Caribbean and encouraged the first attempts at local ship construction to meet the needs of men who were both raiders and traders. The 'island period' of discovery, conquest and colonization, covering the years 1492 to 1519, culminated, therefore, in a period of intense and accelerating activity, stimulated at once by the initial failure of Santo Domingo to maintain its restless immigrants and by the rapidly expanding prospects for plunder, trade and profit as the landmass of the mainland began to be revealed.

At such a time, and with a frontier in such constant movement, the hopes of persuading natural frontiersmen to strike roots were bound to be defrauded. It was true that Hispaniola, with its growing black labour force, eventually struggled through its difficulties to achieve a modest economic viability, based on the export of sugar and hides. Yet Santo Domingo could never have hoped to retain the pre-eminent position accorded it by Gonzalo Fernández de Oviedo as the capital of

Spain's empire of the Indies. Once the mainland was conquered and settled, it was doomed to find itself on the margin of events. But the whole experience of Hispaniola, its peoples destroyed and its resources squandered in the pursuit of instant gain, stood as a grim warning of the effects of a *conquistador* mentality unrestrained by moral scruple or institutional control. The same process was again being repeated in Pedrarias Dávila's isthmus of Panama. Unless settlement could be more successfully linked to conquest than in the first years of the Spanish Caribbean, then the expeditions now heading for the American mainland would be conquering only to strip bare.

THE ORGANIZATION AND ADVANCE OF CONQUEST

The mainland of Spanish America may be said to have been 'conquered' between 1519 and 1540, in the sense that those 21 years saw the establishment of a Spanish presence throughout large areas of the continent, and an assertion of Spanish sovereignty, more effective in some regions than in others, over those of its peoples who did not fall within the area of jurisdiction allotted to Portugal by the treaty of Tordesillas – an area found to include the recently discovered Brazil. The Iberian peninsula, excluding Portugal, has a surface area of just under 500,000 square kilometres. The surface area of the Americas that fell to Spain in those two decades was two million square kilometres. The crown had some six million subjects in Castile and another million in Aragon; it now acquired – if only fleetingly, before death and destruction took their terrible toll – perhaps 50 million new subjects in the Americas.

Two great arcs of conquest moving outwards from the Antilles accomplished the subjugation of mainland America. One, organized from Cuba between 1516 and 1518, swept through Mexico between 1519 and 1522, destroying the Aztec confederation, and then radiated north and south from the central Mexican plateau. By 1524 the southward movement had extended through present-day Guatemala and El Salvador, but it was another twenty years before the major Mayan centres in Yucatán were brought under some sort of Spanish rule. The northwards advance from central Mexico proved to be an even slower process. Between 1529 and 1536 Nuño de Guzmán, ravaging the Mexican north and the west, carved out the vast kingdom of New Galicia. Exploration continued, with Hernando de Soto setting out in

1539 to explore the North American south-east and Francisco Vázquez Coronado searching in vain for the seven cities of Cíbola in the prairies west of the Mississippi between 1540 and 1542. But the failure of these two expeditions marked the extreme limits of the Spanish advance. The borderlands to the north of New Galicia were left to the slow forward movement of missionary, ranching and mining enterprise; and it was not until 1562–75 that another great region of the Mexican north-west, Nueva Vizcaya, was brought under Spanish rule by Francisco de Ibarra.

The other arc of conquest, starting in Panama, moved briefly upwards in 1523–4 to Nicaragua, and then, after a short pause, took the Pacific route southwards for the conquest of the Inca empire in 1531–3. From Peru the *conquistadores* moved northwards to Quito (1534) and Bogotá (1536), where they met other groups coming down from the coast of Venezuela and Colombia. While an expedition led by Gonzalo Pizarro set out from Quito in 1541 to explore the Amazon basin, other *conquistadores* moved south into Chile, where Santiago was founded by Pedro de Valdivia in 1542. The Chilean conquest petered out in a war of attrition with the Araucanian Indians. On the other side of the continent an expedition from Europe, under Pedro de Mendoza, tried but failed to occupy the Río de la Plata region in 1535–6, and ended by leaving a remote outpost of settlement in Paraguay. Buenos Aires, first founded in 1536 and destroyed in 1541, was refounded in 1580, this time not from Europe but from Asunción.

Even if the marginal areas, whether in northern Mexico or in southern South America, proved refractory, it remains true that the regions with the largest and most settled indigenous populations were brought under Spanish rule within a single generation. How is the extraordinary swiftness of this process of 'conquest' to be explained?

It is in the nature of conquest itself that the voices of the victors resound more loudly than those of the vanquished.[6] This is especially true of the Americas, where a world conquered was so soon to be a world destroyed. It was, in any event, a world of infinite variety, ranging as it did from the densely-settled populations of Mesoamerica and the Andes, through the partially sedentary peoples on the periphery of these regions, to bands of hunters and food-gatherers like those who roamed northern Mexico and the Argentine plains. Among some of these

---

[6] For a fuller treatment of the Indian and the Spanish conquest, see Hidalgo, *CHLA*, 1, ch. 4 and Wachtel, *CHLA*, 1, ch. 6.

peoples, oral traditions and folklore kept alive the story of conquest. Among others, the collective memory was extinguished along with the people themselves. And among a few – most notably the Aztecs and the Mayas, who had evolved systems of writing – the episodes of conquest, kept fresh in song and poetry, were either retailed to friars who wrote them down, or else were recorded in writing by those who, if they had not experienced the conquest itself, had learnt of it from members of their parents' generation.

Given the variety of the peoples, the relative paucity of the sources and the nature of the circumstances in which they were produced, it would be too much to say that the surviving records give us the 'Indian' view of the conquest. But they do provide a series of poignant recollections, filtered through the lens of defeat, of the impact made on certain regions by the sudden eruption of alien intruders whose appearance and behaviour were so remote from normal expectation. The *Relación de Michoacán*, for instance, compiled by a Spanish Franciscan around 1540 on the basis of material gathered earlier from native Tarascan informants, records as follows the Tarascans' impressions of the Spaniards:

When the Indians first saw the Spaniards, they marveled at such strange people who did not eat the same kind of food or get drunk as the Indians did. They called the Spanish Tucupacha, which means gods, and Teparacha, which means big men and is also used to mean gods, and Acacecha, meaning people who wear caps and hats. As time passed they began to call them Christians and to believe that they had come from heaven. They were sure that the Spaniards' clothes were the skins of men such as the Indians themselves used on feast occasions. Some called the horses deer, others *tuycen*, which were something like horses which the Indians made from pigweed bread for use in the feast of *Cuingo* and to which they fastened manes of false hair. The Indians who first saw the horses told the Cazonci that the horses talked, that when the Spaniards were on horseback they told the horses where they were to go as they pulled on the reins.[7]

The shock of surprise created by the appearance of the Spaniards and their horses gave the invaders an important initial advantage. But the doom-laden records of the vanquished, produced under the over-whelming impact of defeat, do not of themselves provide an adequate basis for understanding the Spanish success. By their nature, these narratives move inexorably towards catastrophe, which from the first

[7] *The Chronicles of Michoacán*, trans. and ed. Eugene R. Craine and Reginald C. Reindorp (Norman, Oklahoma, 1970), 87.

is foreshadowed by mysterious portents, like the unexplained burning of temples or the appearance of a strange bird with a mirror in its head. The sense of inevitability adds immeasurably to the poignancy of the tale told by the vanquished, but it remains a tale more likely to reflect the post-conquest perception of an event too vast to be fully comprehended and absorbed, than to provide a reliable assessment of the chances of the Spaniards at the moment of their arrival.

The overwhelming numerical superiority of the indigenous populations would seem at first sight to have offered little chance to small bands of Spaniards linked by only the most precarious of supply lines to their distant bases. But in the early stages of the conquest the complex diversity of those populations worked to the Spanish advantage, even if at a later stage it would pose serious difficulties. Nomadic or semi-sedentary tribes in thinly-populated regions found it difficult to prevent the passage of resolute and heavily-armed Europeans, although the poisoned arrow used in some parts of the Americas took its toll of the invaders. The more immediate problem for the Spaniards was how to conquer and then to hold the areas of greatest interest to them – the areas with large sedentary populations in Mesoamerica and the Andes, where prospects of mineral wealth and a disciplined labour force made conquest worth the effort.

But the very size and character of these Mesoamerican and Andean populations eventually proved to be more of an asset than a liability to the Spaniards. In both the Aztec and the Inca 'empires', a multiplicity of competing tribes had been brought under a form of central control which was more or less resented. This allowed the Spaniards to play off one tribal grouping against another and to turn subjugated peoples against their hated masters. It also meant that, once the central power had been overthrown, the Spaniards in turn found themselves the masters of populations already accustomed to some degree of subservience. The peoples on the periphery of these 'empires', however, and those scattered through the thinly-settled dry lands of the Mexican north or the forest regions of southern South America, proved incomparably more difficult to dominate, especially when they had got the measure of the Spanish style of warfare and mastered the use of gun and horse. Widely dispersed, semi-nomadic, and unused to externally-imposed discipline, they revealed an exasperating capacity to elude or resist whenever the Spaniards attempted to introduce some form of domination. One solution was to leave them to their own devices, and indeed this is what often occurred. But it was not always possible to ignore them, for some tribes, like those of northern Mexico, were found to be inhabiting lands rich in mineral deposits, and others threatened the tenuous supply routes to Spanish outposts of settlement, or created a permanent sense of insecurity on the borders of regions that were lightly occupied.

The characteristics of the host societies in the regions most coveted by the Spaniards provide one major explanation for the success of the conquest and the subsequent occupation. But although the settled nature of the population in these regions, and the degree of central control to which it was already subjected, proved to be assets which the Spaniards were able to turn to account, the fact remains that at many points the invaders were met with heavy military resistance by forces which vastly outnumbered their own.

The horse gave the Spaniards a major advantage, in terms both of initial surprise and of mobility; but Cortés had only sixteen horses with him on his march into the Mexican interior. The invaders also profited immeasurably from belonging to a society with a decisive technological superiority over the societies of the Indies. When a world of iron and gunpowder comes into violent collision with a world of stone, it would seem that the defeat of the latter is foreordained. But the impact of this technical superiority was not quite as clear-cut and unqualified as might appear at first sight. This was partly because the invaders were poorly equipped by the standards of sixteenth-century Europe. Most of Cortés' men were armed with nothing more sophisticated than swords, pikes and knives; and the firearms at his disposal consisted of a mere thirteen muskets, along with ten bronze cannon and four light cannon. Only with the greatest difficulty were these cannon dragged through forests and up mountains; powder was dampened in river-crossings and by torrential rains; and even when it was dry, the rate of fire of muskets could not compare with that of native bows.

Both in Mesoamerica and in the Andes the Spaniards encountered societies accustomed to large-scale warfare, although it was a style of warfare with a different rhythm and ritual to that of the Europeans. Weapons of stone and wood were no match for Spanish steel, and that otherwise lethal weapon, the obsidian-tipped club of the Mexica, known as the *macuahuitl*, would shatter against the helmet and armour of a Spaniard. In a pitched battle on open ground, therefore, the forces of the Aztecs and the Incas, in spite of their vast numerical superiority,

had little hope of overwhelming a combined Spanish force of cavalry
and infantry of as few as 50 men, unless they could succeed in reducing
them to exhaustion. The best hope was to catch small parties of
Spaniards off their guard, or attack them in places where they had no
room for redeployment and manoeuvre.

The Indians had the great advantage of operating in a familiar
environment, to which the Spaniards had still to become acclimatized.
Superior technology served for little when, as so often happened, the
Spaniards were combating the effects of heat and altitude, and the
sickness produced by unfamiliar food and drink. Moreover, heavy
armour proved a liability in these climes, and the Spaniards, in turning
to the quilted cotton armour of the Mexica as a substitute, paid
unwitting tribute to the way in which environmental circumstance
could cancel out technological advantage. Yet the fact remains that the
invaders had at their disposal a vastly superior store of technical
expertise on which to draw in emergencies. This was particularly
apparent in their use of the ship. The ability of the conquerors of Mexico
and Peru to reinforce themselves by sea, and Cortés' domination of
Lake Texcoco by deployment of specially constructed brigantines,
suggest something of the reserves of strength which lay to hand as
Europe embarked on the conquest of America.

Both the character of the societies which faced them and their own
technological superiority created glittering opportunities for European
invaders. But those opportunities still had to be seized, and it is here
that the capacity for organization and improvization of sixteenth-century
Europeans was put to the test. The fact that they failed lamentably
against some of their opponents, like the Araucanian Indians of Chile,
indicates that success of itself was not automatic. Different regions posed
different problems and demanded different responses, and every
expedition or attempt at colonization possessed its own peculiarities.

But while, especially in the early years, there was no uniform
procedure of conquest and colonization, certain patterns tended to
establish themselves, simply because military expeditions required
organization and supplies, and trading expeditions soon found that they
could not dispense with military support. In central Venezuela, which
Charles V's bankers, the Welsers, attempted to colonize between 1528
and 1541, there was, as might have been expected, a strongly commercial

element in the approach to colonization. In spite of this, however, trading expeditions quickly degenerated into slave-raids closely resembling those in the Antilles and Panama.

Yet just as commercial interests found it necessary to resort to military methods, so the *bandas*, the organized warrior bands, could not for long dispense with the services of the merchants. The nearest they came to doing so was in the isthmus region in the years after 1509, when the absence of capital – and of a need for capital so long as short overland expeditions were the norm – made possible the formation of warrior bands, or *compañas*, of a strongly egalitarian character. These warrior companies, based on a prior agreement for equal distribution of the plunder, were well suited to the kind of raiding warfare pursued in the Caribbean, the isthmus of Panama and frontier zones like Venezuela. Indeed they were very much the product of frontier conditions, and it is not surprising that they should have reappeared in a very similar form in Portuguese Brazil in the *bandeiras* which flourished in the late sixteenth and seventeenth centuries. Small, cohesive bodies of men, they possessed, thanks to their horses, the supreme advantage of mobility. Their expenses, apart from the cost of horses, were slight. Firearms, which were costly, and which anyhow rapidly corroded in the humid jungle, were hardly needed against the kind of opposition they were likely to meet. Armed with steel swords, and accompanied by powerful mastiffs, they hunted down the terrified Indians, killing, enslaving and seizing all the gold they could find.

As soon as there was a question, however, of more distant expeditions, especially ones which required ships, more sophisticated forms of organization became necessary. The leaders of potential expeditions then had to resort to merchants or officials with large funds at their disposal, like the *licenciado* Gaspar de Espinosa, the *alcalde mayor* of Castilla del Oro under Pedrarias Dávila, who was a dominant figure in the financing of expeditions from Panama in the early years of the conquest of the mainland.

In the circumstances it was natural that partnerships should be formed – partnerships between the captains themselves and between the captains and investors. In Panama, for instance, Francisco Pizarro and Diego de Almagro formed a profitable partnership in association with Hernando de Luque, whose clerical status did not inhibit his entrepreneurial ventures. Partners would tend to divide their functions, as in the Pizarro–Almagro relationship, where Pizarro provided the military leadership while Almagro recruited followers and arranged for the shipment of men and supplies to fixed points along the route.

Investors demanded as security for their investment the share of the spoils accruing to men who had obtained horses or equipment on credit. Many of the rank and file, therefore, unless they struck exceptionally rich booty, were liable to find themselves permanent debtors either to absentee entrepreneurs or to their own captains. The conquest of America was in fact made possible by a network of credit, which ran by way of local agents and entrepreneurs back to royal officials and rich encomenderos in the Antilles, and still further back across the Atlantic to Seville and the great banking houses of Genoa and Augsburg. But the men who formed the warrior bands were not entirely defenceless. Many of them, pooling such resources as they had, formed their own partnerships within the band, clubbing together to buy a horse and holding together for many years on the basis of mutual trust and an agreed division of the booty.

These private partnerships among the rank and file provided one element of cohesion in the naturally fluid groupings which made up the warrior bands. Regional affiliations, too, helped to provide cohesion, although they could also, on occasions, be a source of sharp divisiveness, as when a new expeditionary force under Pánfilo de Narváez landed on the Mexican coast in May 1520 to challenge Cortés for supremacy. Bernal Díaz observed tartly of the new arrivals: 'as our emperor has many kingdoms and lordships there is a great diversity of people among them, some very brave, and some braver still. We come from Old Castile and are called Castilians, and that captain...and his men come from another province, called Vizcaya. They are called *vizcaínos*, and they speak like Otomi Indians'.[8]

While the regional rivalries in the peninsula were inevitably reflected among the *conquistadores*, it was also true that the predominance of one region in a warrior band could provide a central core of loyalties, linking man to man and the men to their leader. The Extremaduran connection was to be a source of enormous strength both to Cortés and Pizarro. Coming often from a single town or a cluster of towns, the friends, relatives and followers of these two captains formed a unit within the unit, a tightly-knit group based on a shared background,

[8] Bernal Díaz del Castillo, *Historia Verdadera de la Conquista de la Nueva España*, ed. Joaquín Ramírez Cabañas (Mexico, 1944), II, 27.

shared attitudes and a set of close family and personal relationships. To his fellow-Extremadurans, the taciturn and close-fisted Francisco Pizarro was, if not a sympathetic, at least a comprehensible being.

The leaders needed this kind of support if they were to carry their expeditions through to success. From the standpoint of the captains, the conquest of America was something a good deal more complex than the triumph over a demoralized indigenous population of small but determined bands of soldiers, enjoying a decisive technical superiority over their adversaries and impelled by a common dedication to gold, glory and the gospel. Any leader of an expedition knew that the Indians were not his only, nor necessarily his most formidable, opponents. He had enemies, too, in his rear, from the royal officials who were determined to prevent the establishment of independent fiefs or kingdoms in these still unconquered regions to local rivals with an interest in foiling his success. When Hernán Cortés sailed from Cuba in 1519 he did so in defiance of the governor of Cuba, Diego Velázquez, who resorted to every conceivable device to bring about his downfall. Above all, he had enemies in his own camp, from the captains who wanted to step into his shoes to the disgruntled foot-soldiers who planned treachery because their true loyalties lay elsewhere or because they were dissatisfied with the distribution of the spoils.

Leadership, therefore, demanded political as well as military skills of a high order if an expedition were to avoid disintegration from within as well as defeat from without. But the presence of hostile Indians, generally in overwhelming numbers, did force a kind of comradeship even on the uncomradely. In the face of danger and misfortune it was preferable to fight side by side than to die singly; and the prospect of a horrifying death at the hands of heathen enemies proved sufficient to impel a closing of the ranks among men who, for all their personal feuds and grievances, were at least at one in being both Christians and Spaniards. A skilled leader like Cortés knew how to play on the remembrance of shared perils and shared successes to maintain the cohesion and morale of his followers. 'Saint James and Spain' was a battle-cry which could sink all differences in a common cause.

It was a battle-cry at once of defiance and of triumph – the cry of men firmly convinced that they would be the victors. This confidence in their own superiority over enemies who vastly outnumbered them was based, in part at least, on an actual superiority of techniques, organization and equipment. But behind any material factors there lay a set of attitudes and responses which gave the Spaniards an edge in many of the situations in which they found themselves: an instinctive belief in the natural superiority of Christians over mere 'barbarians'; a sense of the providential nature of their enterprise, which made every success against apparently overwhelming odds a further proof of God's favour; and a feeling that the ultimate reward made up for every sacrifice along the route. The prospect of gold made every hardship tolerable. 'I and my companions', said Cortés, 'suffer from a disease of the heart which can be cured only with gold.'[9] They sensed, too, that they were engaged in a historical adventure and that victory would mean the inscribing of their names on a roll-call of the immortals, alongside the heroes of classical antiquity.

The confidence that came from this sense of moral superiority and divine favour was most valuable where it was most needed: in the struggle against their apparently most formidable adversaries, the 'empires' of the Aztecs and the Incas. In the conquest by Cortés of central Mexico between 1519 and 1521, and of Peru by Pizarro between 1531 and 1533, the Spaniards displayed an almost uncanny ability to exploit the weaknesses of their opponents – an ability that itself testified to their own underlying strength.

When Cortés sailed from Cuba in February 1519 with eleven ships carrying 508 soldiers and 110 sailors, he did so with the firm intention of conquering. The two previous expeditions which had reconnoitred the coasts of Mexico and Yucatán, those of 1517 and 1518 under Francisco Hernández de Córdoba and Juan de Grijalva, had been planned only with an eye to exploration and barter. Cortés intended something incomparably more ambitious. Within a few days of his landing on 22 April 1519, he knew that there lived somewhere in the interior a powerful ruler, Montezuma (as he was called by the Spaniards), whose dominion included the peoples of the coastal plain. To a Spanish mind this piece of information suggested a natural strategy: a ruler who himself had dominion over many peoples must himself be brought, by force or by trickery, to acknowledge a yet higher lordship, that of the king of Spain. The supreme objective must therefore be to reach Montezuma – an objective achieved with the hazardous march into the interior and the encounter between Spanish captain and Aztec ruler at Tenochtitlan on 12 November 1519.

[9] Francisco López de Gómara, *Cortés*, trans. and ed. L. B. Simpson (Berkeley, 1964), 58.

Welcomed into the city as guests, the Spaniards were in a position to follow through the strategy of Cortés to its logical conclusion by taking Montezuma into custody and extracting from their unwilling host, turned involuntary guest, a recognition of the sovereignty of the king of Spain.

The alleged *translatio imperii* by Montezuma to Charles V, as described by Cortés in the ingenious tissue of fact and fabrication with which he regaled the emperor in his famous letters, marked the beginning, not the end, of the conquest of Mexico. But it showed decisively where the initiative lay. Cortés had managed to get so far, so fast, because of his extraordinary capacity to size up a situation and turn it to account. To all appearances the Aztec confederation, with a supreme ruler and an organized state structure, represented an incomparably more formidable adversary than any society so far encountered by the Spaniards either in the Caribbean or on the isthmus. But the very degree of organization and of central control from Tenochtitlan created opportunities which Cortés was exceptionally quick to exploit. Mexica domination over the other peoples of central Mexico – a domination which demanded heavy tribute and a constant supply of sacrificial victims – had bred a hatred and resentment which enabled Cortés on his march inland to represent himself as a liberator to the subjugated tribes. This, together with the alliance with Tlaxcala, which the Mexica had never succeeded in subjugating, enabled him to follow a route to Tenochtitlan through relatively friendly territory. It also furnished him with a supporting army from the indigenous population eager for revenge against Montezuma and the Mexica elite.

Montezuma's reasons for allowing Cortés to enter Tenochtitlan will always remain a mystery. He was understandably uncertain about the origin of the intruders and the purpose of their mission, but it is open to question whether, as later came to be suggested by Spanish chroniclers using Indian informants, his reactions were dictated by a conviction that Cortés was none other than the legendary Toltec chieftain, Quetzalcoatl, come out of the east to reclaim his land. It is more probable that he was following towards Cortés and his men the normal behaviour of the Mexica to ambassadors, who traditionally enjoyed immunity, although he may also have believed that by luring Cortés into the interior he would more easily destroy him if this should prove to be necessary. There is no doubt, however, that the cosmological system of the Aztecs, with its fatalistic insistence on the need to propitiate implacable gods by means of human sacrifice, was no match for the confident Christianity of their Spanish opponents. It was a cosmology more likely to inspire its followers with a heroic resignation to death than with a fierce determination to survive; a cosmology, too, which had created a ritualized style of warfare designed to capture the enemy rather than kill him, in order to provide a constant supply of sacrificial victims. Defeat in this highly ceremonial style of war could only discredit the god of war, Huitzilopochtli, the Mexicas' titulary deity, of whom Montezuma was a priest.

By seizing Montezuma, therefore, Cortés had delivered a devastating blow to the political and the religious system of the Aztecs. But this made it more difficult to pursue successfully the next stage of his policy, which was to preserve the administrative and fiscal structure that he had found, keeping Montezuma as a puppet, but effectively replacing his authority with that of the Spaniards. The priestly caste had formed an integral part of the Aztec system, and the Spanish assault on the Aztec deities inevitably constituted a direct challenge to this caste. At the same time, the insatiable Spanish demand for gold created widespread unrest which culminated, after the massacre of the nobility by the future conqueror of Guatemala, Pedro de Alvarado, in a massive popular uprising. Hopelessly outnumbered, the Spaniards successfully fought their way out of Tenochtitlan on the *noche triste*, the night of 30 June 1520, although with heavy casualties. It would take them another fourteen months to recapture the city they left in disarray that night.

The surrender of the last elements of resistance amidst the ruins of Tenochtitlan on 13 August 1521 was as much a triumph for Spanish disease as for Spanish arms. The smallpox carried by a black slave among Cortés' retainers ravaged the defenders of the city and revealed once again what had already become clear from the Antilles: that the inhabitants of the New World would have to pay a heavy price for their centuries of isolation. The conquest of America was a conquest by microbes as well as by men, sometimes running ahead of the main Spanish contingents, at others following in their wake. Especially in densely-populated regions like central Mexico, the part played by epidemics in sapping both the ability and the will to resist goes a long way towards explaining the suddenness and the completeness of the Spanish success.

Yet the collapse of a Mexica empire of some 25 million people in the face of an assault by some few hundred Spaniards cannot be explained purely in terms of external agencies, however destructive. It derived, too, from geological faults within the structure of that empire itself and, in particular, from the repressive nature of Mexica domination over the peoples of central Mexico. Cortés' conquest was as much a revolt by a subjugated population against its overlords as an externally imposed solution. What remains unclear is whether this empire, which was still young and in process of evolution, would, if left to itself, have succeeded in containing and resolving its own internal contradictions. It certainly showed signs of an inner resilience and capacity for adaptation which seem to have been lacking in the Andean civilization that confronted Pizarro, the empire of the Incas.

Pizarro, like Cortés, was able to exploit inner weaknesses and dissensions which happened to be at their worst just at the moment of his arrival. The first firm news of a rich and powerful state to the south had been brought back to Panama in 1523. This encouraged Pizarro and Almagro to organize probing expeditions down the Pacific coast, which provided further evidence of a new kingdom to be conquered. Pizarro himself was in Spain from 1528 to 1530, capitulating with the crown for the governorship of the lands he hoped to conquer and recruiting followers in his Extremaduran homeland. With 180 men and some 30 horses he left Panama in January 1531 on his expedition of conquest. By the time he actually set sail many of his Spanish recruits were dead, struck down by the tropical diseases which carried off such a large proportion of all the new arrivals to the Indies. Only a handful of his followers, therefore, had European military experience. On the other hand, many of them were veterans in the Indies themselves – probably a more useful form of experience in the circumstances. Of these only one or two had been in Mexico. The majority had gained their experience, both of the climate and the Indians, in the Antilles and central America.

The empire that faced him was more tightly organized than that of the Mexica, but the very tightness of its organization served to multiply its internal strains. The Inca state structure, with its insistent and meticulously regulated demand for labour, pressed heavily on the *ayllus*, the village clan communities, creating a subject population that, while docile, was also resentful, especially in the Quito region where Inca rule was relatively recent. As the area of Inca conquest widened, so the problems of central control from Cuzco increased, for all the carefully sited garrisons and the elaborate communications network. This rigid system of uniform control maintained by an Inca ruling caste could only function effectively as long as that caste itself maintained its internal cohesion and unity. But the death of Huayna Capac in 1527 had led to a succession struggle between his sons, Huascar and Atahualpa. The latter was on the way to victory but had not yet consolidated his success at the time of Pizarro's arrival.

Pizarro, like Cortés in Mexico, and like an earlier generation of Spaniards which had sought to profit from the internal feuds of the Nasrid kingdom of Granada, was adept at using these dissensions to further his own purposes. He also used the method employed by Cortés in Mexico and by the *conquistadores* in Central America of making an immediate bid to seize the *cacique* (chief) – in this instance the Inca emperor, Atahualpa.

The emperor, established at Cajamarca in northern Peru, responded to the news of strange invaders in the coastal region in a way that was perfectly natural to a man whose vision of the world had been shaped by the experience of the highlands of the Andes. Those who commanded the mountains effectively commanded the coasts, and beyond the coast lay an impassable sea. As long as the Spaniards remained in the coastal region their presence was not a matter of acute concern to him, because as soon as they moved into the mountain regions they would surely deliver themselves into his hands. Atahualpa therefore made no attempt to molest Pizarro's men as they began their arduous ascent, and the Spaniards still enjoyed the supreme advantage of surprise when they turned on Atahualpa and his retainers on the high plain of Cajamarca on 16 November 1532.

The capture of Atahualpa, like that of Montezuma, was designed to transfer the supreme authority into Spanish hands with a single decisive blow. Then, as in Mexico, the intention was to use the existing administrative structure to channel the profits of dominion to the Spaniards. Although tribute in the Inca empire, unlike that of the Aztecs, consisted entirely of labour, the old imperial system still functioned sufficiently well to produce for the Spaniards as a ransom for Atahualpa the enormous sum in gold and silver of 1.5 million pesos – a treasure far larger than any yet known in the Indies and the equivalent of half a century of European production. Atahualpa's reward, however, was not to be liberty, but judicial murder.

On 15 November 1533 the *conquistadores* captured Cuzco, the heart of the shattered Inca empire. That Pizarro still felt the need for a nominal Inca head of the administrative and military machine which had fallen into his hands is indicated by his selection of Atahualpa's half-brother, Manco Inca, to succeed him. But the smooth transition from Inca to Spanish domination of Peru, which the appointment of a puppet emperor was designed to assist, was made more difficult by a shift in the location of the country's power-centre. Cortés, in deciding to build his new capital of Mexico City on the site of the ruins of Tenochtitlan, succeeded in preserving an important element of continuity between Aztec and Spanish rule. Cuzco, on the other hand, was too high up in the mountains and too remote from the coast to be a satisfactory capital for a Spanish Peru which, unlike its predecessor, would instinctively face towards the sea. In 1535 Pizarro founded his new capital, Lima, on the coast, and by so doing gravely weakened his chances of maintaining control over the Andean highlands.

He weakened them, too, by his failure to keep control over his own subordinates. The growing dissension among the victors over the distribution of the spoils encouraged Manco Inca to rally the remaining Inca forces in a desperate bid to overthrow the Spaniards. The revolt of 1536–7 temporarily jolted but did not halt the process of Spanish conquest. During the year-long siege of the Spaniards in Cuzco, the Indians showed that they had learned something but not enough of the methods of their adversaries. The ceremonial approach to warfare, which had similarly hampered the Aztecs in their opposition to the Spaniards, was so deeply embedded in their mentality that they habitually chose to launch their attacks by the light of the full moon. If the conquest still remained uncompleted once Manco's revolt was suppressed, this was largely because the partisans of Pizarro and Diego de Almagro had diverted their energies to fighting each other. But the impossible geography of the high Andes allowed the continuation of a resistance movement that would have been out of the question in central Mexico. It was not until 1572 that the Inca fastness of Vilcabamba fell to the Spaniards, and isolated pockets of resistance would continue to disturb the sad tranquillity of colonial Peru.

It was precisely because they were centrally organized societies, heavily dependent on the authority of a single ruler, that the empires of Montezuma and of Atahualpa fell with relative ease into Spanish hands. Such vast areas of territory could never have been conquered so speedily if they had not already been dominated by a central power with an elaborate machinery for maintaining control of outlying regions. Both in central Mexico and in Peru the invaders unwittingly found themselves heirs to a process of imperial expansion which did not cease with their arrival. The continuing spread in the post-conquest era of Nahuatl and Quechua, the languages of the Mexica and the Incas, suggests the existence of an inner dynamic within those regions towards a greater degree of unification, which can only have worked to the conquerors' advantage. The *translatio imperii* might be a convenient legal fiction, but it had its justification, in ways of which the Spaniards themselves were only dimly aware, in pre-existing facts.

The very absence in other parts of mainland America of the conditions prevailing in the civilizations of the Andes and central Mexico goes a long way towards explaining the difficulties encountered by the movement of conquest in other areas of the continent. In the Mayan world of Yucatán the Spaniards encountered another sophisticated civilization, but one which lacked the political unity of the Aztec and Inca empires. On the one hand this gave them an opportunity to play the game at which they excelled – that of playing off one community against another. But on the other it slowed down the process of establishing Spanish control because there was no single centre from which to dominate. Francisco de Montejo set out on the conquest of Yucatán in 1527, but in the 1540s the Spaniards still had only a tenuous hold of the region, and the interior was effectively unconquered even after the passage of another century.

No doubt if Yucatán had possessed greater reserves of wealth, the Spaniards would have made more consistently vigorous attempts at conquest. The peripheral regions of America beyond the limits of the great pre-conquest empires all too often proved disappointing in terms of the kind of resources of interest to the Spaniards, as Diego de Almagro discovered to his cost on his abortive Chilean expedition of 1535–7. This did not, however, prevent the despatch of a fresh expedition under Pedro de Valdivia in 1540–1, composed of the disappointed and the unemployed among the conquerors of Peru. Of the 150 members of Valdivia's party, 132 became encomenderos. Their rewards, however, were disappointing in terms of the expectations generated. They lived among an impoverished Indian population which they used for labour services, in particular gold-washing; but by 1560 there was little gold left, and the native population was dwindling. Rescue came in the form of the growing Peruvian market for agricultural produce. Increasingly the Chilean settlers took to farming and ranching, creating for themselves modestly prosperous farming communities in the fertile valleys north of the river Bío-Bío. They suffered, however, from a shortage of native labour and from the proximity of the Araucanian Indians – warrior tribes whose very lack of centralized authority made them dangerously elusive adversaries.

The Araucanians, 'unsophisticated' peoples in relation to those of the settled societies of Mexico and Peru, revealed a much greater degree of sophistication in adapting their fighting techniques to those of the Spaniards. As early as 1553 they inflicted a crushing defeat on the Spaniards at Tucapel, where Valdivia was killed; and by the end of the 1560s they had turned themselves into horsemen and had begun to master the use of the arquebus. The 'Araucanian wars' of the later sixteenth and seventeenth centuries, although they provided the settlers with a supply of labour in the form of enslaved prisoners of war, also imposed a heavy drain on the Chilean economy. From the early 1570s money was having to be sent to Chile from Peru to help with the costs of defence. In these distant regions horses were in short supply and the costs of war material were high; but the abandonment of this remote outpost of empire seemed an impossible option, not least because of its strategic position controlling the straits of Magellan. Madrid was therefore forced to accept the inevitable, establishing from 1603 a standing army of some 2,000 men and making a regular budgetary provision for it. A miniature war of Flanders was in the making – a prolonged and costly frontier war, in which neither Indian nor Spaniard could achieve decisive mastery.

Just as Araucanian resistance checked the southward movement of Spanish conquest and colonization from Peru, so Chichimeca resistance checked its northward advance from central Mexico. The presence of such unsubdued or half-subdued tribes on the fringes of the Aztec and Inca empires created problems for the Spaniards which evaded straightforward solution, but which they could not afford to ignore. The Mixtón rebellion of 1540–1, originating among the still largely unpacified tribes of New Galicia and rapidly spreading southward, illustrated all too alarmingly the constant threat posed by restless frontier regions to the more settled areas of conquest. It also illustrated the limitations of conquest itself, as conceived in purely military terms. By the middle of the sixteenth century the Spaniards had established their presence over vast areas of central and southern America through their military skill and resourcefulness; but the real conquest of America had hardly begun.

THE CONSOLIDATION OF CONQUEST

In view of the extreme contrasts to be found in the levels of 'civility' attained by the different peoples of pre-conquest America, there were bound to be wide variations in the character of conquest from one region to another and in the requirements for the subsequent control of the conquered population. Once the Aztec and Inca empires had been overthrown, it was possible for the Spaniards to consolidate their new regime over vast areas of territory in central Mexico and Peru with remarkable speed. Their task was made easier by the survival of a substantial part of the fiscal and administrative machinery of the pre-conquest area, and by the docility of the bulk of the population, much of it relieved to see its former masters overthrown. It was symptomatic of the success of the Spaniards in establishing their control over the former territories of the Aztecs and Incas that special military measures soon proved to be unnecessary. 'Pacification' – a euphemism employed by Hernán Cortés and adopted as official terminology under Philip II – took longer in Peru, but primarily because the conquerors fell out among themselves. After the Inca rebellion of 1536–7 and the Mixtón war of 1540–1, there was no major Indian uprising in either New Spain or Peru during the Habsburg period, and the Spaniards were so sure of their safety that they never bothered to fortify their cities against possible native revolts.

While the Spaniards were to have considerable success with at least the nominal integration into their new colonial societies of Indians who lived within the boundaries of the pre-conquest empires, they were faced by more intractable problems in other parts of America. Here they often had to deal with tribes and peoples whose way of life seemed primitive by European standards. While some lived in compact villages or in more dispersed settlements, others were simply hunting and food-gathering bands, who had first to be subdued and congregated into fixed settlements before the work of hispanicization could begin.

Some of these peoples, especially the Chichimecas of northern Mexico and the Araucanian Indians of Chile, proved themselves formidable adversaries once they had adapted to Spanish methods of war. Similarly, the Apache Indians of the American plains responded to the approach of the Spaniards by transforming themselves into consummate horsemen and adopting warfare as a way of life.

Spanish success or failure in pacifying these frontier regions would depend both on the habits and culture-patterns of the various tribes with which they came into contact and on the way in which Spaniards themselves approached their task. The missionary would often succeed where the soldier failed; and mission communities, using the weapons of example, persuasion and discipline, scored notable successes with certain tribes – especially those which were neither too nomadic, nor too tightly organized into compact village communities, to be unreceptive to the material advantages and the cultural and spiritual offerings which the mission could provide.

The conquest of America, therefore, proved to be a highly complex process, in which men at arms did not always call the tune. If at least initially it was a military conquest, it also possessed from its earliest stages certain other characteristics which began to predominate as soon as the soldiers had achieved what they could. It was accompanied by a movement aimed at spiritual conquest, by means of the evangelization of the Indians. It was followed by a massive migration from Spain, which culminated in the demographic conquest of the Indies. Subsequently, as more Spaniards settled, the effective conquest of land and labour got under way. But the benefits of this went only in part to the settlers, for hard on their heels came the bureaucrats, determined to conquer or reconquer the New World for the crown. All of these movements produced a conquering society which recalled but failed to reproduce exactly that of metropolitan Spain.

The military conquest of America was achieved by a group of men which was far from consisting entirely of professional soldiers. A comprehensive survey of the background and earlier careers of the *conquistadores* still remains to be undertaken; but an analysis of a list drawn up in 1519 of the encomenderos of the new city of Panama shows that – of the 93 names for which details are available in this select group of 96 *conquistadores* – only half that number were soldiers and sailors by occupation. No less than 34 of the group had originally been peasants or artisans and another ten came from the middling and professional classes in the towns.[10]

There is no reason to think that the Panama group is unrepresentative

[10] See Mario Góngora, *Los grupos de Conquistadores en Tierra Firme, 1509–1530* (Santiago de Chile, 1962), ch. 3.

of the men who conquered America, and it suggests something of the complexity of the transatlantic migratory movement, even in the very first years after the discovery when most of the New World still remained to be won. The *conquista* was from the start something more than a bid for fame and plunder by a military caste looking for new lands to conquer after the overthrow of the Moorish kingdom of Granada. Naturally the military–aristocratic element in peninsular society was well represented in the conquest of America, although the great nobles of Castile and Andalusia were conspicuous by their absence. This is partly to be explained by the determination of the crown to prevent the establishment in the new lands of a magnate-dominated society on the peninsular model. But men with some claim to gentle birth – men from the lesser gentry or *hidalgo* class – were present in substantial numbers throughout the conquest, as was only to be expected. It was not easy for a poor man with pretensions to nobility to survive in the status-conscious world of Castile or Extremadura, as Cortés and Pizarro could testify.

Yet even if the hidalgos formed a minority element, the attitudes and aspirations of this group tended to infuse the whole movement of military conquest. An hidalgo or an artisan prepared to hazard everything to cross the Atlantic obviously did so in the expectation of being able to better himself. In the first years after the discovery the quickest way to self-betterment was participation in expeditions of conquest, which needed the services of men with professional skills – carpenters, blacksmiths, tailors – as long as they would also be prepared to wield a sword when the occasion arose. For these young men, most of them in their twenties and early thirties, the sight of gold and silver brought back from a successful foray opened up visions of a way of life beyond anything they had ever known. The model for this way of life was that provided by the great Castilian or Andalusian magnate, a man who lived to spend. 'All the Spaniards', wrote the Franciscan, Fray Gerónimo de Mendieta, 'even the most miserable and unfortunate, want to be *señores* and live for themselves, not as servants of anyone, but with servants of their own.'[11]

The men, whether professional soldiers or not, who had lived and fought side by side and achieved heroic feats, naturally felt themselves entitled to special consideration by a grateful monarch. *Servicios*, as

---

[11] Quoted by José Durand, *La transformación social del Conquistador* (Mexico, 1953), II, 45.

always, deserved *mercedes*, and what greater servicio could any man render his king than win for him new territories? To have been the first to advance into unconquered regions was a special cause for pride – the 607 men who first accompanied Cortés jealously guarded their pre-eminence against the 534 who only joined him later. But they banded together in a common front against all later arrivals and finally, in 1543, extracted from a reluctant Charles V a statement declaring that the first 'discoverers' (*descubridores*) of New Spain – he avoided the word *conquistadores* – were those who 'first entered that province on its discovery and those who were there for the winning and conquering of the city of Mexico'.

This rather grudging recognition of primacy was as far as the crown was prepared to go. It had set itself against the re-creation of a feudal society in America; and although some *conquistadores* received grants of *hidalguía*, very few, apart from Cortés and Pizarro, received titles of nobility. How, then, were the survivors among the 10,000 or so men who actually conquered America to be rewarded for their sacrifice? The problem was a difficult one, not least because no *conquistador* ever thought his rewards commensurate with his services. From the beginning, therefore, the *conquistadores* were a class with a grievance, although some with a good deal more justification than others.

The struggle for the spoils of conquest inevitably led to sharp inequalities of distribution. When Cortés, for instance, made the first allocation of Mexican Indians to his followers in 1521, the men associated with his enemy, the governor of Cuba, were liable to find themselves excluded. Similarly in Peru there was much bitterness over the distribution of Atahualpa's treasure, with the lion's share going to the men of Trujillo, the followers of Pizarro, while the soldiers who had arrived from Panama with Diego de Almagro in April 1533 found themselves left out in the cold. The Peruvian civil wars, in the course of which Almagro himself was executed in 1538 and Francisco Pizarro assassinated by the Almagrists in 1541, were a direct outcome of the disappointments and rivalries stemming from the distribution of the spoils of conquest, although these in turn were at least partly provoked by personal and regional tensions before the treasure was ever acquired.

Among the recipients of the booty there was also a natural inequality of shares, based on social standing and assumed variations in the value of service. The man on horseback normally received two shares to the infantryman's one, although Hernando Pizarro pronounced revolutionary words on this subject, presumably to encourage his foot-soldiers on the eve of battle with Almagro. He had been informed, he said, that those soldiers who had no horses were slighted when it came to the distribution of land. But he gave them his word that such a thought had never entered his head 'because good soldiers are not to be judged by their horses but by their personal valour... Therefore each one would be rewarded according to his service, because the lack of a horse was a matter of fortune, and not a disparagement of a man's person.'[12] As a general rule, however, the horseman retained the advantage, although even the ordinary foot-soldier could do very well in a major distribution of booty, like Atahualpa's treasure.

The actual rewards of conquest, in the form of spoils, encomiendas, distribution of land, municipal offices, and – not least – prestige, were in fact often very considerable, even if official recognition of service by the crown was grudging or non-existent. Fortunes were made, although they were often as rapidly lost by men who were natural gamblers; and while some of the conquistadores – especially, it seems, those from the better families – decided to return home with their winnings, others hoped to better themselves still further by remaining a little longer in the Indies and never succeeded in leaving them.

It was difficult for these men to settle down. Yet, as Cortés saw very quickly, unless they could be induced to do so, Mexico would be stripped bare and destroyed as the Antilles had been before it. One obvious device, already employed in Hispaniola and Cuba, was to turn soldiers into citizens. This was, in the first instance, a purely legal act. After their landing on the Mexican coast Cortés' men were formally constituted members of what was still a notional corporation, the municipality of Veracruz. Municipal officials were duly chosen from among the captains, and a *cabildo* or town council instituted. Only later did the Villa Rica de Veracruz come to acquire the physical characteristics of a town.

Although the immediate purpose in founding Veracruz was to provide Cortés with a legalistic device for freeing himself from the authority of the governor of Cuba and placing the mainland territories under the direct control of the crown at the request of the soldier-citizens, it provided the pattern for a similar process of municipal incorporation which was followed as the conquering soldiers moved through Mexico.

[12] Quoted by Alberto Mario Salas, *Las armas de la Conquista* (Buenos Aires, 1950), 140–1.

New towns were created, sometimes, as with Mexico City itself, on the site of indigenous towns or villages, and at other times in areas where there were no large congregations of Indians. These new cities and towns were intended for Spaniards, although some of them from the beginning had *barrios* or quarters reserved for the Indians, and most of the others would later acquire them. Based on the model of the Spanish town with its central plaza – the principal church on one side and the town hall (the *ayuntamiento*) on the other – and laid out, wherever possible, on the gridiron plan of intersecting streets used in the construction of Santo Domingo, the New World town provided the expatriate with a familiar setting for daily life in an alien environment.

The soldier turned householder would, it was hoped, put down roots. Each *vecino* would have his plot of land; and land, both in the suburbs and outside the cities, was liberally distributed among the conquerors. But for men who brought from their home country strict views about the demeaning character of manual labour, for those aspiring to seigneurial status, land itself was of little value without a labour force to work it. Although Cortés was initially hostile to the idea of introducing in Mexico the encomienda system, which he and many others held largely responsible for the destruction of the Antilles, he was compelled to change his mind when he saw that his followers could never be induced to settle unless they could obtain labour services from the Indians. In his third letter to Charles V, dated 15 May 1522, he explained how he had been compelled to 'deposit' Indians in the hands of Spaniards. The crown, although reluctant to accept a policy which appeared to threaten the status of the Indians as free men, finally bowed to the inevitable, as Cortés had already done. The encomienda was to join the city as the basis of the Spanish settlement of Mexico and then, in due course, of Peru.

It was, however, to be a new-style encomienda, reformed and improved in the light of Spain's Caribbean experience. Cortés was by nature a builder, not a destroyer, and he was determined to construct in Mexico a 'New Spain' on foundations which would endure. He cherished the vision of a settled society in which crown, conqueror and Indian were linked together in a chain of reciprocal obligation. The crown was to reward his men with Indian labour in perpetuity, in the form of hereditary encomiendas. The encomenderos, for their part, would have a dual obligation: to defend the country, thus saving the crown the expense of maintaining a standing army, and to care for the spiritual and material wellbeing of their Indians. The Indians themselves would perform their labour services in their own *pueblos* (villages), under the control of their own *caciques* (chiefs), while the encomenderos lived in the cities, of which they and their families would become the principal citizens. The type and amount of work performed by the Indians was to be carefully regulated to prevent the kind of exploitation which had wiped them out in the Antilles; but the underlying assumption of Cortés' scheme was that the self-interest of encomenderos anxious to transmit their encomiendas to their descendants would also work to the interest of their Indian charges by preventing callous exploitation for purely short-term ends.

The encomienda was therefore envisaged by Cortés as a device for giving both the conquerors and the conquered a stake in the future of New Spain. The ruling caste of encomenderos would be a responsible ruling caste, to the benefit of the crown, which would derive substantial revenues from a prosperous country. But the encomienda would also work to the benefit of the Indians, who would be carefully inducted into a Christian civility.

As encomiendas were granted through New Spain, Central America and Peru, so this potential ruling caste began to constitute itself. It was drawn from an elite group among the soldiers of the conquest, and its numbers were inevitably small in relation to those of the Spanish population of the Indies as a whole: around 600 encomenderos in New Spain in the 1540s and around 500 in Peru. Living off the revenues produced by the labour of their Indians, the encomenderos saw themselves as the natural lords of the land. But there were in fact profound differences between their situation and that of the nobles of metropolitan Spain. The encomienda was not an estate and carried with it no entitlement to land or to jurisdiction. It therefore failed to become a fief in embryo. Nor, for all their efforts, did the encomenderos succeed in transforming themselves into a European-style hereditary nobility. The crown consistently baulked at the formal perpetuation of encomiendas through inheritance, and in the New Laws of 1542 decreed that they should revert to the crown on the death of the current holder. In the prevailing circumstances this decree was quite unrealistic. In New Spain the viceroy prudently disregarded it. In Peru, where Blasco Núñez Vela attempted to enforce it in 1544, it provoked an encomendero revolt, led by Francisco Pizarro's youngest brother, Gonzalo, who for four years was the master of Peru. In 1548 he was defeated and executed for treason by the *licenciado* Pedro de La Gasca, who arrived armed with a fresh decree revoking the offending clauses in the recent legislation.

Although the crown had retreated, its retreat was largely tactical. It continued to treat the perpetuation of an encomienda in one and the same family as a matter of privilege rather than right, thus depriving the encomenderos of that certainty of succession which was an essential characteristic of European aristocracy. It was able to act in this way with a large measure of success because social forces in the Indies themselves were working in favour of its policy. The encomenderos were a small minority in a growing Spanish population. Even if they gave hospitality and employment to many of the new immigrants, there were many more who felt themselves excluded from the charmed circle of privilege. The deprived and the excluded – many of them building up their own sources of wealth as they acquired lands, and taking to farming and other entrepreneurial activities – naturally looked jealously on the encomiendas and their captive Indian labour. The defeat of Gonzalo Pizarro enabled La Gasca to embark on a large-scale reassignment of encomiendas; and the ability to reassign encomiendas, whether forfeited by rebellion or vacated by death, became a decisive political instrument in the hands of succeeding viceroys. On the one hand it could be used to satisfy the aspirations of non-encomenderos, and on the other it served as a means of curbing and restricting the encomienda itself, since every encomendero knew that, if he antagonized the crown and its representatives, there were a hundred men waiting to step into his shoes.

At the same time as the crown was struggling against the hereditary principle in the transmission of encomiendas, it was working to reduce the degree of control exercised by encomenderos over their Indians. Here its most decisive move was to abolish in 1549 the obligation of the Indians to perform compulsory personal service. In future the Indians would only be liable to payment of tribute, the rate of which was set at a figure lower than that which they had previously paid to their lords. Inevitably the law of 1549 was more easily decreed than enforced. The transformation of the encomienda based on personal service into an encomienda based on tribute was a slow process, accomplished more easily in some regions than in others. In general the older style of encomienda, with the encomendero as the dominant local figure, drawing heavily on labour or tribute or both, was more liable to survive in the marginal regions, like Yucatán or southern Mexico, the Andean highlands, or Chile. Elsewhere, the encomienda was being transformed during the middle decades of the century, under the pressure both of royal officials and of changing economic and social conditions. Encomenderos with only poor villages in their encomiendas found themselves in serious straits as tributes dwindled along with the indigenous population. The wealthier encomenderos, reading the signs aright, began to use their wealth to diversify and hastened to acquire land and to build up agricultural estates before it was too late. There was money to be made from the export of local products, like cacao in Central America, and from the production of grain and meat to feed the growing cities.

While the crown remained deeply suspicious of the encomenderos as a class, the encomienda as an institution had its supporters, and ironically their numbers and influence tended to increase as the encomenderos were gradually stripped of their coercive powers and became little more than privileged crown pensioners. When the New Laws attempted to abolish the encomienda, the Dominicans of New Spain, traditionally less well disposed to the institution than the Franciscans, declared themselves in its favour. The crown was technically correct in stating in a decree of 1544 that 'the purpose and origin of the encomiendas was the spiritual and temporal well-being of the Indians'; and by this time there was a strong conviction among many of the missionaries in the New World that the lot of the Indians would be even worse than it already was without the fragile protection still afforded them by the encomienda.

This conviction reflected a deep disillusionment with the results of an enterprise which had begun amidst such high hopes a generation earlier. By the middle years of the sixteenth century the movement for the spiritual conquest of America had begun to falter, as a result of deep divisions over strategy and discouragement over failures. The discouragement was so great partly because the original expectations of the first missionaries to mainland America had been pitched so high, for reasons which had less to do with New World realities than with Old World preconceptions.[13]

The evangelization of America was conducted in its opening stages by members of the regular orders, as distinct from the secular clergy. The first missionaries to reach Mexico were Franciscans, the 'twelve

[13] For further discussion of the evangelization of Spanish America, see Barnadas, *CHLA*, I, ch. 14.

apostles' under the leadership of Fray Martín de Valencia, who arrived in 1524. They were followed two years later by the Dominicans, and then by the Augustinians in 1533. By the middle years of the century there were some 800 friars in Mexico and another 350 in Peru. The mendicants also gave Mexico its first bishop and archbishop (1528–48), the Franciscan Fray Juan de Zumárraga, a distinguished representative of Spain's Christian humanist tradition.

Among the first generation of mendicant missionaries in the New World were many who had felt the influence both of Christian humanism and of the apocalyptic and millenarian Christianity which was such a vital element in the religious life of late fifteenth- and early sixteenth-century Europe. Fray Martín de Valencia, for one, seems to have been influenced by the twelfth-century mystic, Joachim of Flora, with his prophecies of the coming of a third age of the Spirit. Those who set out from Spain to convert the Indians saw themselves as entrusted with a mission of special importance in the divine scheme of history, for the conversion of the world was a necessary prelude to its ending and to the second coming of Christ. They also believed that, among these innocent peoples of America still uncontaminated by the vices of Europe, they would be able to build a church approximating that of Christ and the early apostles. The early stages of the American mission with the mass baptism of hundreds of thousands of Indians, seemed to promise the triumph of that movement for a return to primitive Christianity which had so repeatedly been frustrated in Europe.

Very soon, however, the doubts which had always been entertained by some of the missionaries began to rise insistently to the surface. At first it looked as though the Mexican Indians possessed a natural aptitude for Christianity, partly, perhaps, because the discrediting of their own gods by defeat in war had created a spiritual and ceremonial vacuum which predisposed them to accept the leadership of the friars as the holy men of a conquering race. The simple instruction in the rudiments of Christianity given by the missionaries, their use of music and pictures to explain their message, and their mobilization of large groups of Indians to construct the great fortress-like convents and churches which changed the architectural landscape of central Mexico in the immediate post-conquest decades, all helped to fill the void left by the disappearance of the native priesthood and by the collapse of the routine of ceremonial labour governed by the Aztec calendar.

But although the rate of conversion was spectacular, its quality left much to be desired. There were alarming indications that Indians who had adopted the new faith with apparent enthusiasm still venerated their old idols in secret. The missionaries also came up against walls of resistance at those points where their attempts to inculcate the moral teachings of Christianity conflicted with long-established patterns of behaviour. The virtues of monogamy, for instance, were not easily conveyed to a society which saw women in the role of servants and the accumulation of women as a source of wealth.

To some of the missionaries, especially those of the first generation, these setbacks served as an incentive to probe more deeply into the customs and beliefs of their charges. Where the first instinct had been to obliterate all vestiges of a pagan civilization, an attempt now began to examine, record and inquire. The Dominican Fray Diego Durán argued that 'a great mistake was made by those who, at the beginning with great zeal but little wisdom, burnt and destroyed all their ancient paintings, for we are now left so unenlightened that they can practise idolatry before our very eyes.'[14] It was in accordance with this line of reasoning that the great Franciscan, Fray Bernardino de Sahagún, devoted his life to the recording and understanding of a native culture that was being rapidly swept away. Many of his colleagues struggled with success to master the Indian languages and to compile grammars and dictionaries. The realization that true conversion required a profound understanding of the evils to be extirpated provided an impetus, therefore, to important linguistic studies, and to ethnographical inquiry which often, as with Sahagún, showed a high degree of sophistication in its controlled use of native informants.

This was truer, however, of Mexico than Peru, where the unsettled conditions of the post-conquest period delayed the work of evangelization, which in some areas was not systematically undertaken until the seventeenth century. Already by the middle of the sixteenth, at a time when the first missions were establishing themselves in Peru, the humanist generation of mendicants was passing into history. In the succeeding generation there was less curiosity about the culture of conquered peoples and a corresponding tendency to condemn instead of seeking to understand. This was encouraged by some spectacular failures which helped to cast doubt on the original assumptions about

[14] Diego Durán, *Historia de las Indias de Nueva España y islas de Tierra Firma*, ed. José F. Ramirez, 2 vols. (Mexico, 1867–80), II, 71.

the Indian aptitude for Christianity. The Franciscan college of Santa Cruz de Tlatelolco, founded in 1536 to educate the children of the Mexican aristocracy, was a natural object of suspicion to all those Spaniards, whether lay or cleric, who were hostile to any attempt to place the Mexican on the educational level of the European, or to train him for the priesthood. Any backsliding by a student of the college, like Don Carlos of Texcoco, who was denounced in 1539 and burnt at the stake as a dogmatizer, therefore served as a convenient pretext for undermining a movement which took as its axiom that the Indian was as rational a being as the Spaniard.

Inevitably the prophecies of disaster proved to be self-fulfilling. The Indians, forbidden to train as priests, naturally tended to look on Christianity as an alien faith imposed on them by their conquerors. They took from it those elements which suited their own spiritual and ritualistic needs and blended them with elements of their ancestral faith to produce beneath a simulated Christianity an often vital syncretic religion. This in turn merely served to confirm the belief of those who argued that they must be kept in permanent tutelage because they were unready to take their place in a European civility.

The often exaggerated ideas about the spiritual and intellectual capacity of the Indians held by the first generation of missionaries therefore tended to give way by the middle decades of the century to a no less exaggerated sense of their incapacity. The easiest response was to regard them as lovable but wayward children, in need of special care. This response came all the more naturally to the friars as they saw their monopoly over the Indians endangered by the advent of the secular clergy. It was encouraged, too, by a genuine fear for the fate of their Indian charges in the rapidly changing conditions of the mid-sixteenth century. As the humanist vision of the first missionary generation faded, and it seemed increasingly improbable that the New World would become the setting for the New Jerusalem, the friars struggled to preserve what still remained by congregating their flocks in village communities where they could be better shielded from the corrupting influences of the world.

It was a less heroic dream than that of the first missionary generation and no less inexorably doomed to failure. For profound changes were occurring in the demographic composition of Spanish America as the number of immigrants multiplied, while that of the indigenous population diminished.

By the middle of the sixteenth century there were probably around 100,000 whites in Spanish America. The news of the opportunities for a better life in the New World encouraged a growing number of Spaniards to take ship from Seville to America, with or without official licence to emigrate. In a letter home characteristic of those written by the emigrants to the Indies, Juan de Robles wrote to his brother in Valladolid in 1592: 'Don't hesitate. God will help us. This land is as good as ours, for God has given us more here than there, and we shall be better off.'[15]

Although the Indies were officially the exclusive possession of the crown of Castile, no sixteenth-century law is known which prohibited inhabitants of the crown of Aragon emigrating to them, although Aragonese, Catalans and Valencians do seem to have been excluded in law, if not always in practice, from holding posts and benefices in Castile's overseas possessions. Emigrants from Navarre, which was officially incorporated with the crown of Castile in 1515, were in a stronger legal position. But the overwhelming number of emigrants came from Andalusia, Extremadura and the two Castiles, with the number of Basques increasing as the century progressed.

Some of these emigrants went to join relatives who had already emigrated, others to escape from conditions which, for one reason or another, had come to seem intolerable at home. Several of those on the losing side in 1521, when the revolt of the Comuneros was crushed, made their way surreptitiously to the New World; and the same was true of those whose Jewish ancestry prejudiced their chances of success at home, although there were stringent regulations to prevent the emigration of Jews and *conversos*. It is hard to believe that the emigration of all seven brothers of St Teresa of Avila was entirely unconnected with the fact that their family was of *converso* origin.

In the early years, as might have been expected, the movement of emigration was overwhelmingly masculine. But, in order to encourage settlement, the crown insisted that all *conquistadores* and *encomenderos* should be married, and this produced a growing number of female emigrants. If women represented 5 or 6 per cent of the total number

---

[15] Enrique Otte, 'Cartas privadas de Puebla del siglo XVI', *Jahrbuch für Geschichte von Staat, Wirtschaft und Gesellschaft Lateinamerikas*, 3 (1966), 78. For a selection of these letters in translation see James Lockhart and Enrique Otte, *Letters and people of the Spanish Indies. The sixteenth century* (Cambridge, 1976).

of emigrants in the period 1509–39, they were up to 28 per cent in the 1560s and 1570s. But the shortage of Spanish women in the first years of conquest naturally encouraged mixed marriages. Baltasar Dorantes de Carranza, writing of the *conquistadores* of Mexico, explains that 'because in those fifteen years when the land was won Spanish women did not come to it in any quantity', some of the *conquistadores* did not marry at all, while others married Indians.[16] This was especially true of Indian women of royal or noble blood, with the sons of these unions, known as *mestizos*, succeeding to their fathers' estates. But the rapid growth of *mestizaje* in the Indies was less the result of formal marriage than of concubinage and rape. During the sixteenth century, at least, the mestizo offspring of these unions tended to be assimilated without excessive difficulty into the world of one or other of the parents. Although the crown was soon expressing concern about their way of life, it was only in the seventeenth century, as their numbers multiplied, that they began to constitute something of a distinctive caste on their own.

It was not only the whites, however, who were transforming the ethnic composition of the population of the Indies. There was also a strong current of African immigration, as black slaves were imported to swell the labour force. Coming to outnumber the whites in the Antilles, they also constituted a significant minority group in Mexico and Peru. The offspring of their unions with whites and Indians – known as *mulattos* and *zambos* respectively – helped to swell the numbers of those who, whether white or hybrid, increasingly preoccupied the authorities by their obvious rootlessness. The Indies were on the way to producing their own population of the voluntary and involuntary idle, of wastrels, vagabonds and outcasts, which seemed so threatening to the ordered and hierarchical society constituting the sixteenth-century European ideal.

The presence of this shiftless population could only add to the forces already bringing about the disintegration of the so-called *república de los indios*. In spite of the strenuous efforts of many of the friars to segregate the Indian communities, only in the remoter regions, where the Spaniards were sparsely settled, was it possible to keep the outer world at bay. The proximity of cities established by the conquerors; the labour demands of encomenderos and the tribute demands of the crown; the encroachment of Spaniards on Indian lands; the infiltration of whites

---

[16] Dorantes de Carranza, *Sumaria Relación*, 11.

and mestizos; all these elements helped to undermine the Indian community and what remained of its pre-conquest social organization.

At the same time as it was being subjected to these powerful pressures from without, the *república de los indios* was also succumbing to a demographic catastrophe. The smallpox epidemic during the course of the conquest was only the first of a succession of European epidemics which ravaged the indigenous population of mainland America in the succeeding decades. The incidence of these epidemics was uneven. Peru, with a more sparsely settled population, seems to have escaped more lightly than Mexico, which was particularly hard hit in 1545–7. All through America the coastal regions proved especially vulnerable and here, as in the Antilles, Africans tended to replace an Indian population which had succumbed almost in its entirety.

European diseases struck a population which was disorientated and demoralized by the experiences of the conquest. Old patterns of life had been disrupted, the precarious balance of food production had been upset by the introduction of European crops and livestock, and European demands for labour services had pressed the Indian population into unaccustomed work, often under intolerably harsh conditions. Although there were some signs of successful adaptation, particularly by the Indians in the region of Mexico City in the period immediately following the conquest, it is not surprising that many Indians should have found the shock of change too great and have lost the will to live. The survivors appear in contemporary accounts as a passive and listless people, seeking escape from their woes in narcotics and intoxicants – pulque-drinking in Mexico and coca-chewing in the Andes.

If the pre-conquest population of central Mexico fell from 25 million in 1519 to 2.65 million in 1568, and that of Peru fell from nine million in 1532 to 1.3 million in 1570, the demographic impact of European conquest was shattering both in its scale and its speed.[17] No preconceived plans, either for the salvation or for the exploitation of the Indians, could hope to withstand intact the effects of such a drastic transformation. By the middle of the sixteenth century Spanish America was a very different world from the one that had been envisaged in the immediate aftermath of conquest.

The assumptions about the wealth to be derived from the conquest of the Indies had taken for granted the existence of a·large and docile

[17] For further discussion of the demographic collapse, see Sánchez-Albornoz, *CHLA*, II, ch. 1.

indigenous population producing labour services and tribute for the
conquerors. Inevitably, the totally unexpected decline of this population
forced sharp readjustments both of policy and behaviour. From the
mid-sixteenth century, the struggle intensified between settler and
settler and crown and settler for a larger share of a shrinking labour
supply. The discovery of rich silver deposits in the 1540s in both Mexico
and Peru and the beginning of large-scale mining operations meant that
priority was bound to be given in the distribution of Indian labour to
mining and ancillary activities. The abolition of the encomienda of
personal service following the decree of 1549 deprived encomenderos
of their Indian workforce, which could then be mobilized for necessary
public services by means of repartimientos organized by royal officials.

At the same time as less Indian labour was becoming available for
private individuals, large areas of land were being left unoccupied as
a result of the extinction of its Indian owners. This coincided with a
rapidly growing need for land among the settler community to satisfy
the dietary requirements of an expanding Hispanic population congregated in the cities, which remained addicted to its traditional habits
and tastes. It wanted meat and wine, and it preferred white bread to
maize. Encomenderos and other influential and wealthy settlers therefore
petitioned the crown with success for grants of land (*mercedes de tierras*)
on which they could grow wheat (more costly to produce than maize
and requiring a greater acreage to provide a comparable yield) and raise
European livestock (cattle and sheep). While Hispanic America was to
remain an essentially urban civilization, there were already strong
indications from the middle of the sixteenth century that the basis of
this civilization was likely to be dominion of the countryside by a
handful of great proprietors.

By the end of the first generation of the conquest it was already clear
that new and distinctive societies were coming into being in the new
world of the Spanish Indies. The conquerors, having moved in, had
taken control of the land and the people; and if they had destroyed on
a massive scale, they were also beginning to create. They brought with
them a belief which was gradually gaining ground in sixteenth-century
Europe: that it was within the capacity of man to change and improve
the world around him. 'We found no sugar mills when we arrived in
these Indies', wrote Fernández de Oviedo, 'and all these we have built
with our own hands and industry in so short a time.'[18] Hernán Cortés,
exploiting the vast estates that he had acquired for himself in the valley

---

[18] Fernández de Oviedo, *Historia general y natural de las Indias* (Madrid, 1959), I, 110.

of Oaxaca, showed that the conqueror also had the ambitions of the
entrepreneur.

The kind of society which the conquerors and immigrants instinctively
set out to create was one that would approximate as nearly as possible
to the society they left behind in Europe. As a result, the fate of the
subjugated peoples was itself pre-ordained. They would be transformed,
in so far as this could be achieved, into Spanish-style peasants and
vassals. They would be made to conform to European notions about
work and incorporated into a wage-economy. They would be
Christianized and 'civilized', to the extent which their own weak
natures allowed. It was not for nothing that Cortés christened Mexico
New Spain.

One of the most striking characteristics of Spain itself, however, was
the increasingly powerful presence of the state. For a time, after the
death of Isabella in 1504, it had seemed that the work of the Catholic
Kings in strengthening the royal authority in Castile would be undone.
The revival of aristocratic factionalism threatened more than once to
plunge Castile back into the disorders of the fifteenth century. But
Ferdinand of Aragon, who survived his wife by twelve years, man-
oeuvred skilfully to preserve the authority of the crown. Cardinal
Jiménez de Cisneros, who acted as regent after the death of Ferdinand
in 1516, displayed similarly effective gifts of command, and Charles of
Ghent, Isabella's young grandson, inherited in 1517 a country at peace.

But the peace was precarious, and the initial events of the new reign
did nothing to make it more secure. Charles' election as Holy Roman
Emperor in June 1519, two months after the landing of Cortés in
Mexico, and his subsequent departure for Germany, served to precipitate
a revolt in the cities of Castile against the government of an alien and
absentee king. The revolt of the Comuneros (1520-1) drew deeply on
the constitutionalist traditions of medieval Castile and, if it had
triumphed, would have imposed institutional restraints on the development of Castilian kingship. But the defeat of the rebels on the
battlefield at Villalar in April 1521 left Charles and his advisers free to
re-establish and extend the royal authority without serious impediment.
Under Charles, and still more under Philip II, his son and successor
(1556-98), an authoritarian and increasingly bureaucratic government
was to make its presence felt at innumerable points in the life of Castile.

It was inevitable that this growing assertiveness of the state would also have its impact on Castile's overseas possessions. The aspirations to state intervention had been there from the beginning, as the capitulaciones between the crown and would-be conqueror bore witness. But the process of conquest itself could all too easily slip out of royal control. Time and distance played into the *conquistadores'* hands, and, if Cortés showed more deference than many in his behaviour towards the crown, this was because he had the vision to realize that he needed powerful supporters in Spain and the wit to appreciate that it could pay to explain, so long as one acted first.

But the Emperor Charles V, like Ferdinand and Isabella before him, had no intention of allowing his newly-acquired realms to slip from his control. In New Spain Cortés saw himself systematically displaced by royal officials. An audiencia, on the model of that of Santo Domingo (1511), was established in Mexico in 1527, under what proved to be the disastrously self-seeking presidency of Nuño de Guzmán. This first attempt at royal control created more evils than it cured, but the period of government from 1530–5 by the second audiencia, composed of men of far higher calibre than the first, made it clear that there would be no place for its conqueror in the New Spain of the bureaucrats.

Cortés went relatively gracefully, but in Peru the establishment of royal control was not achieved without a bitter struggle. The pretext for the revolt of the Pizarrists from 1544–8 was the attempt to enforce the New Laws; but behind it lay the unwillingness of men of the sword to accept the control of men of the pen. It was symbolic that the rebellion was crushed, not by a soldier but by one of those officials trained in the law who were the prime object of *conquistador* hostility. The *licenciado* Pedro de La Gasca triumphed over the Pizarrists because he was above all a politician, with the skill to exploit the divisions within the *conquistador* community between the encomenderos and the foot-soldiers who coveted their possessions.

In New Spain from the 1530s, in Peru from the 1550s, the day of the *conquistador* was over. A new, administrative conquest of the Indies was getting under way, led by the audiencias and the viceroys. New Spain acquired its first viceroy in 1535, in the person of Antonio de Mendoza who served until 1550; and Peru, where an audiencia was established in 1543, began to settle down under the viceregal government of another Mendoza, the marquis of Cañete (1556–60). Gradually under the rule of the first viceroys, the controlling apparatus of royal authority was clamped down on the new societies that the *conquistadores*, the friars and the settlers were in process of creating. The Indies were beginning to take their place within the capacious institutional framework of a world-wide Spanish monarchy.

2

SPAIN AND AMERICA BEFORE 1700

The Emperor Charles V adopted as his emblematic device the pillars of Hercules decorated with scrolls bearing the motto: *Plus Ultra*. When the device was first invented in 1516 it was essentially a humanist conceit designed to suggest that there would be no limits to the power and dominions of the young Charles of Ghent; but increasingly, as more and more of the New World was discovered and subjected to his rule, the device acquired a special kind of geographical appropriateness as the symbol of global empire.

Spain's conquest of America created the possibility of the first genuinely world-wide empire in human history, as Hernán Cortés was characteristically quick to perceive when he wrote to Charles from Mexico that it now lay within his power to become 'monarch of the world'. Indeed, for Cortés, impressed by the might of Montezuma, Mexico constituted an empire in itself: 'one might call oneself emperor of this kingdom with no less glory than that of Germany, which, by the Grace of God, Your Sacred Majesty already possesses'.[1] For Charles V and his advisers, however, there could be only one empire in the world, the Holy Roman Empire; and even after Spain and the Empire were separated on the abdication of Charles in 1556, Philip II respected this convention by retaining the style of 'king of Spain and the Indies'. Yet it became increasingly obvious that America had added a new, imperial dimension to the power of the king of Spain. Philip II and his successors might officially be no more than kings of the Indies, but that great chronicler of the New World, Gonzalo Fernández de Oviedo, had

---

[1] Hernán Cortés, *Letters from Mexico*, ed. A. R. Pagden (Oxford, 1972), 48 (second letter, 1520).

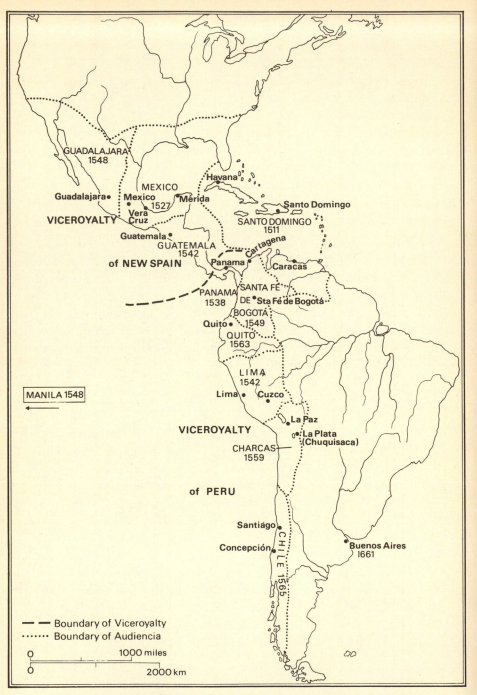

Viceroyalties and audiencias in the sixteenth and seventeenth centuries
Source: Francisco Morales Padrón, *Historia general de América* (2nd edn, Madrid, 1975), 391.

written of 'this occidental empire of these Indies' as early as 1527,[2] and the recurrent appearance, especially in the seventeenth century, of the phrase *imperio de las Indias*, and even of *emperador de las Indias*, testified to an underlying consciousness of American empire.

If the phrase *imperio de las Indias* had difficulty in acquiring wide general acceptance before the coming of the Bourbons, this was partly because the Indies were conceived as forming part of a wider grouping which was known as the Spanish monarchy, the *monarquía española*. In this agglomeration of territories, acquired either by inheritance or by conquest and owing allegiance to a single ruler, most states were equal, but some were more equal than others. Castile came to enjoy an effective predominance in the monarchy, and from the beginning the Indies stood in a special relationship to Castile. Alexander VI's *Inter Caetera* of 1493 vested the government and jurisdiction of the newly found lands, not in the kings of Spain but in the kings of Castile and León. Consequently, the Indies were to be regarded as the possession of Castile and to be governed, where appropriate, in accordance with the laws and institutions of Castile. This implied that the benefits of conquest were to be reserved for Castilians – a convention flouted, when it suited his purposes, by Ferdinand of Aragon, but which gave sixteenth-century Castile an effective monopoly of New World offices and trade. It also meant that the parliamentary and representative institutions which were central to the political life of the crown of Aragon would not be allowed to reproduce themselves in the new American territories.

The intimate association of Castile and the Indies was reflected in the crown's employment of Juan Rodríguez de Fonseca, of the council of Castile, to handle Indies affairs in the first years of discovery and conquest. The rapidly increasing volume of business, however, meant that what originally began as the work of one highly efficient administrator and a small group of assistants would soon have to acquire an institutional form. The pressure was felt first in the organization of the fleets to Hispaniola, and in 1503 the *Casa de la Contratación* – a trading-house comparable to the *Casa da India* in Lisbon – was established in Seville. It was soon responsible for organizing and controlling the passage of men, ships and merchandise between Spain and America. The sweeping regulatory powers conferred by the crown on the officials of the Casa during the next few years established a pattern

---

[2] *Sumario de la natural historia de las Indias*, ed. José Miranda (Mexico, 1950), 272.

of trade and navigation that was to last for a century and a half, and convert Seville into the commercial centre of the Atlantic world.

By channelling all the American trade into Seville, the crown was seeking to ensure a maximum degree of control over what was expected to be a highly lucrative enterprise, to the benefit of its own finances and of a Castile which claimed monopolistic rights over the newly discovered lands. It was only by the exercise of rigorous control over sailings that undesirable elements could be kept out of America, and the American trade – or so it was hoped – be kept in native hands. Time would show, however, that a controlled trade had a way of producing its own form of uncontrolled infiltration, and that the undoubted organizational advantages of monopoly had to be set against the no less undoubted disadvantages of putting enormous power in the hands of a small group of strategically placed officials.

These officials were concerned essentially with the mechanics of the Indies trade – with the equipping of fleets, the licensing of passengers and the registration of silver. Policy towards the Indies was formulated at a higher level; and here again the growing pressure of business forced institutional developments which replaced the informality of the Fonseca regime with a formal bureaucratic apparatus. In the early years the monarchs would turn for advice on Indies affairs to Fonseca or to a handful of members of the council of Castile; but in 1523 a new council came into being, independent of the council of Castile – the council of the Indies. Given the peculiar structure of the Spanish monarchy this was a logical development. A conciliar organization, with distinctive councils responsible for the distinctive states and provinces of the monarchy, was the best means of combining plural interests with unified central control. Taking its place alongside the councils of Castile and Aragon, the council of the Indies provided the formal machinery for ensuring that the affairs of the Indies were regularly brought to the attention of the monarch, and that the monarch's wishes, embodied in laws, decrees and institutions, were duly transmitted to his American possessions.

Royal government in America was therefore royal government by consultation, in the sense that the king's decisions were reached on the basis of *consultas* – the written records of conciliar debate, issuing in a series of recommendations – which would be sent up to him by his council of the Indies. The councils were nominally attendant on the person of the king and only in 1561 found their permanent home in the royal palace in Madrid, which from that year became the seat of the court and the capital of the Monarchy. Of all the councils, that of the Indies was the one furthest removed in time and space from the area of its jurisdiction, although even this was not far enough for some. According to Sir Francis Bacon, 'Mendoza, that was viceroy of Peru, was wont to say: That the government of Peru was the best place that the King of Spain gave, save that it was somewhat too near Madrid.'[3] Royal officials in the Indies, theoretically at large in the great open spaces of a great New World, in practice found themselves bound by chains of paper to the central government in Spain. Pen, ink and paper were the instruments with which the Spanish crown responded to the unprecedented challenges of distance implicit in the possession of a world-wide empire.

Inevitably this style of government by paper brought forth its own breed of bureaucrat. Of the 249 councillors of the Indies from the time of its foundation until 1700, all but a handful – and these in the seventeenth century rather than the sixteenth – were *letrados*, men trained in the law at the universities, although members of the nobility were strongly represented among the 25 presidents of the council over the same period. Very few of the letrado members of the council seem to have had any American experience – only seven in the best part of 200 years occupied posts in one of the American *audiencias* before promotion to the council.[4] Most of them had spent their careers in judicial or fiscal posts in the peninsula itself, and inevitably they tended to see the problems of the Indies through the prism of their peninsular experience. Their formation and outlook was legalistic; they thought in terms of precedents, of rights and of status; and they saw themselves as the exalted guardians of the king's authority. This made for careful rather than imaginative government, more inclined to regulate than to innovate, although now and again an outstanding president like Juan de Ovando (1571–5) would inject life into a naturally slow-moving system and reveal gifts of creative organization which had an impact thousands of miles away.

Once the objectives of government in the Indies were determined, however, and its structure settled – and this was largely achieved by the middle of the sixteenth century – the sheer problems of distance tended to ensure that routine would prevail. Routine has its own

---

[3] *The works of Francis Bacon*, ed. J. Spedding (London, 1859), VII, 130–1.
[4] See J. L. Phelan, *The kingdom of Quito in the seventeenth century* (Madison, 1967), 135.

defects, but judged by the criterion of its ability to maintain a fair degree of public order and a decent respect for the authority of the crown, Spanish government in sixteenth- and seventeenth-century America must be accounted a remarkable success. After the collapse of the Pizarrist rebellion in the 1540s and a conspiratorial flutter in Mexico City in 1566 around the person of Don Martín Cortés, the son of the conqueror, there would be no further direct challenge to the royal authority by a settler community often bitterly resentful of the mandates of Madrid. This high degree of quiescence is in part a reflection of the sense of deference to the crown inculcated from one generation to the next; but it is primarily to be attributed to the character of a system which was all too successful in its almost obsessive determination to prevent the excessive concentration of power at any single point. There was no need to challenge the royal power directly when an indirect challenge could be successfully mounted by playing on the weaknesses of a system in which power was so carefully dispersed.

The diffusion of authority was based on a distribution of duties which reflected the distinctive manifestations of royal power in the Indies: administrative, military, judicial, financial and religious. But often the lines of demarcation were not clearly drawn: different branches of government would overlap, a single official might combine different types of function, and there were endless possibilities for friction and conflict which was likely to be resolved, if at all, only by the lengthy process of reference to the council of the Indies in Madrid. But these apparent sources of weakness might in some respects be regarded as the best guarantee of the survival of rule from Madrid, since each agent of delegated authority tended to impose a check on the others, while at the same time the king's subjects in the Indies, by playing off one authority against another, were left with adequate room for manoeuvre in the interstices of power.

In the first years of the conquest the principal representatives of the crown in the Indies were the *gobernadores*. The title of governor, usually combined with that of captain-general, was given to a number of the early *conquistadores*, like Vasco Núñez de Balboa, appointed governor of Darien in 1510. The *gobernador*, like the *donatário* in Portugal's overseas territories, was given the right to dispose of Indians and land – clearly a major inducement to undertake further expeditions of conquest. The governorship was therefore an ideal institution for extending Spanish rule through the Indies, particularly in remote and poor regions like Chile, where the rewards of conquest were otherwise exiguous. Since the crown had firmly set itself, however, against the creation of a race of feudal lords in the Indies, the days of the governorship seemed to be numbered. Appointments were made short-term – from three to eight years – and came to be non-hereditary. This principle was firmly established once Columbus' grandson, Luis Colón, was finally induced in 1536 after long and complicated legal proceedings to renounce the family claim to a hereditary governorship, retaining only the purely honorific hereditary title of Admiral.

Governorships, however, did not disappear from the Indies once the conquest was completed. They had proved their usefulness as an institution for administering and defending outlying regions. Instead of being abolished, therefore, they were permitted to survive; but, like other institutions which succeeded in surviving the transitional stage of conquest, they were gradually bureaucratized. The new breed of governors of the post-conquest period were administrators, not *conquistadores*, and they had judicial as well as administrative and military functions. Thirty-five provincial governorships existed at one time or another in the sixteenth and seventeenth centuries – the number was not constant because of mergers and boundary changes. They included among their number Guatemala, Costa Rica, Honduras and Nicaragua in Central America; Cartagena, Antioquia and the New Kingdom of Granada, which was governed from 1604 by the presidents of the audiencia of Santa Fe; Popayan, Chile, Paraguay, from which Río de la Plata was separated in 1617 to form a new governorship; and in New Spain, Yucatán, Nueva Vizcaya and Nuevo León. Hernando de Soto, who died on the banks of the Mississippi in 1542, was joint governor of Cuba and Florida, as also was Pedro Menéndez de Avilés from 1567 to 1573; thereafter Florida became a separate governorship. The Philippine Islands, whose conquest was begun in 1564 by their first governor, Miguel López de Legazpi, also constituted an American governorship, dependent on New Spain.

In spite of the survival of the governorships, the most important administrative unit in the Indies was to be not the governorship but the viceroyalty. Columbus had held the title of viceroy, as had his son Diego Colón; but with Diego it became purely honorific and was lost to the family on the death of his widow. It was in 1535 that the viceroyalty was revived as an effective institution, when New Spain was created a viceroyalty and Don Antonio de Mendoza was appointed its first viceroy. In 1543 Blasco Núñez Vela was named viceroy of a second viceroyalty, that of Peru. New Spain and Peru, with their capitals in Mexico City and Lima, were to be the only American viceroyalties under the Habsburgs. The Bourbons added two more: the viceroyalty of New Granada in 1717, with its capital in Santa Fe de Bogotá, and that of Río de la Plata, with Buenos Aires as its capital, in 1776.

The New Laws of 1542 institutionalized the new viceregal system of government: 'the kingdoms of Peru and New Spain are to be ruled and governed by viceroys who represent our royal person'. The viceroy, therefore, was the king's *alter ego*, holding court in his viceregal palace, and carrying with him something of the ceremonial aura of kingship. He combined in his person the attributes of governor and captain-general, and he was also, in his role as president of the audiencia, regarded as the principal judicial representative of the crown. The immense prestige of the post, and the lucrative possibilities that it appeared to offer, naturally made it highly attractive to the noble houses of Castile. In practice the crown, always suspicious of the ambitions of the grandees, tended to reserve it for cadet members of the great families or for titled nobles of middling rank. Don Antonio de Mendoza, the first viceroy of New Spain (1535–49) and one of its greatest, was the sixth of the eight children of the marquis of Mondéjar by his second marriage and had served at court and on a diplomatic mission to Hungary before being raised to his New World eminence at the age of 40.

The length of Mendoza's service was exceptional – once the system was established, a viceroy could reasonably expect a six-year term of office. But this might not prove to be the end of his viceregal functions in the Indies. Of the 25 men sent out from Spain to serve as viceroys of Mexico between 1535 and 1700, nine went on to become viceroys of Peru. The experience gained by these viceroys in the government of the Indies should have made their voices immensely valuable in the highest councils of the monarchy on their return to Spain; but surprisingly it was not until 1621 that a former viceroy of the Indies, the marquis of Montesclaros (viceroy of New Spain 1603–6 and of Peru 1606–14) was given a seat in the highest of all councils, the council of state.

The American viceroyalties, for all their apparent attractiveness, all too often turned out to be a source of disappointment to their occupants, ruining their health, or their reputation, or both. The count of Monterrey, so far from making a fortune, died in office in Peru in 1606 and had to be buried at the king's expense. Don Martín Enríquez de Almansa, viceroy of New Spain from 1568 to 1580, explained for the benefit of his successor that:

although they imagine in Spain that the post of viceroy here is a very easy one, and that there cannot be much to do in these new lands, my own experience and the work I have had to undertake have disabused me of this. You will discover the same, for the viceroy here is responsible for all those duties which are shared out at home among several different people.[5]

One of Enríquez's predecessors, Don Luis de Velasco (1550–64), described his working week. On Mondays and Thursdays the mornings were devoted to receiving delegations of Indians accompanied by their interpreters and to drawing up a list of points to be discussed with the audiencia, which he attended in the afternoon. In the evening, from eight to ten, he despatched government business with his secretary. On Tuesdays and Fridays he attended the discussion of suits in the audiencia in the morning and from one o'clock until three despatched religious business and gave audiences to Spaniards – something he had to be ready to do at any time in the week. He then went on to discuss financial business with the treasury officials. Wednesday mornings were also set aside for hearing Indians and Wednesday evenings to the business of Mexico City.

And all the rest of time is taken up with reading letters from prelates, friars, *alcaldes mayores*, *corregidores*, and other individuals who are in a position to provide information. This is an immense labour, and when ships arrive or leave the work is trebled. And the hardest work of all is to fill the *corregimientos* and *alcaldías mayores*, and to search for the right people for offices, and to put up with the *conquistadores* and their children with all their documents and their demands that they must be saved from starving. There are two hundred posts and two thousand people who want them.[6]

The woes of a viceroy, however, did not finish here. His hands were tied from the beginning by the instructions which he received from the king on appointment, and he was always receiving new orders from Madrid, many of them totally inapplicable to the situation in which he found himself. Don Antonio de Mendoza wrote in despair that in his fifteen years as viceroy of New Spain there had been three major changes in the system of government, and that the members of the council of

[5] *Los virreyes españoles en America durante el gobierno de la Casa de Austria*, ed. Lewis Hanke (Biblioteca de Autores Españoles, CCLXXIII, Madrid, 1976), I, 203.   [6] *Ibid.*, 128–9.

the Indies were like doctors who assumed that they were not curing the patient unless they were always bleeding and purging him.[7]

Mendoza and his successors found themselves hemmed in at every point by the vast and growing body of laws and decrees relating to the Indies. These came in varying types and possessed varying degrees of solemnity. The weightiest of all orders from the crown was the *provisión*, which bore the king's name and titles, and was sealed with the chancellery seal. The provisión was in effect a general law relating to matters of justice or government – the New Laws, containing 54 articles relating to the organization of government and to the treatment of the Indians, were in fact provisiones. The document more commonly used was the *real cédula*, starting with the simple words *El Rey* followed by the name of the recipient. It communicated in the form of an order a royal decision based on a recommendation of the council of the Indies, and was signed *Yo el Rey*. In addition to the provisión and the cédula, there was also the *auto*, not directed to any recipient, but embodying the decisions of the council of the Indies or the audiencias.

Already by the late sixteenth century there was an enormous corpus of laws and provisions relating to the Indies. In 1596 Diego de Encinas published a compilation of some 3,500 of them, but the need for a proper codification was becoming increasingly obvious. Juan de Solórzano Pereira, a distinguished jurist on the council of the Indies, did the fundamental work in the 1630s, but it was not until 1681 that the great four-volume *Recopilación de las Leyes de Indias* finally appeared in print. The laws printed in these tomes were more reliable as a guide to the intentions of the crown in Madrid than as an indication of what actually happened in America; but the very fact of their existence was bound to enter the calculations of the governors and the governed alike as they went about their daily life in the Indies. Every viceroy knew that his enemies would seek to use non-compliance with some law or royal order as a charge against him. He knew, too, that his every action was scrutinized by the official guardians of the law, the *oidores*, or judges, of the audiencia.

During the sixteenth century ten audiencias were set up in the New World. In the Viceroyalty of New Spain: Santo Domingo (1511); Mexico (1527); Guatemala (1543); Guadalajara (1548). In the Viceroyalty of Peru: Panama (1538); Lima (1543); Santa Fe de Bogotá (1548); Charcas (1559); Quito (1563); Chile (1563–73; refounded 1606).

[7] *Ibid.*, 58.

Between them, these audiencias accounted for some 90 posts at the level of president, *oidor* and *fiscal*. The thousand men who occupied them during the two centuries of Habsburg rule constituted the elite of Spain's American bureaucracy. Viceroys came and went, while there was no fixed limit on the tenure of the oidores, who consequently provided an important element of administrative as well as judicial continuity. While the audiencias were intended to be the supreme judicial tribunals in the New World, seeing to the proper observance of the laws of the Indies, they also acquired certain attributes of government, especially by virtue of the New Laws. In particular, the audiencias of Mexico and Lima assumed the functions of government in the interim between the departure of one viceroy and the arrival of the next, while the presidents of lesser audiencias might act as governors and captains-general of the area of their audiencia's jurisdiction. Their governmental duties, either in a direct or an advisory capacity, gave the audiencias of the New World an extra degree of influence which was not enjoyed by their originals in the Iberian peninsula, where the chancelleries were confined to purely judicial functions. Enjoying direct communication with the council of the Indies, where they could count on a sympathetic hearing from their fellow-letrados, the oidores were well placed to bring viceroyal irregularities to the attention of the king.

The oidores, however, like the viceroys, were carefully held in check by a crown congenitally suspicious of its own appointed officials. There were strict regulations governing their style of life, and everything possible was done to preserve them from contamination by their environment. They were not supposed to marry a woman from the area of jurisdiction of their audiencia, nor to acquire landed property or engage in trade. This attempt to turn them into Platonic guardians, judging and governing without the distraction of local ties and pressures, was inevitably doomed to failure, not least because their salaries were so often inadequate. But the crown, if it set an impossibly high ideal, showed no serious expectation that the ideal would be realized. On the contrary, it acted on the assumption that human failing was endemic and legislated against this unfortunate state of affairs by ensuring that the activities of the oidores, like those of all its officials, should be subjected to careful scrutiny. Independent judges were sent out to conduct *visitas*, or visitations of inquiry, into given areas or into the activities of a given set of officials, while every official was subject to a *residencia* at the end of his term of office, which would allow aggrieved parties to bring charges and state their case before the presiding judge.

Viceroys, governors and audiencias formed the upper level of secular administration in the Indies. The areas of jurisdiction over which they ruled were subdivided into smaller units, which went under different names. In New Spain they were known either as *alcaldías mayores* or *corregimientos*, and in the rest of the Indies as *corregimientos*. Some of the more important *alcaldes mayores* and *corregidores* were appointed by the crown, the lesser ones by the viceroys. They were appointed for a limited term of office, and the more important ones at least were not supposed to be local landowners or *encomenderos*. Their area of jurisdiction was based on a city or town, but extended – as it did in Castile itself – into the surrounding countryside, so that corregimientos were essentially large districts with an urban centre.

The emphasis of local government on the town was characteristic of life in the Indies as a whole. From the standpoint of the law, even those Spanish settlers in the Indies who lived in the countryside existed only in relation to their urban community. They were *vecinos* (citizens) of the nearest urban settlement, and it was the town which defined their relationship to the state. This was very much in line with the traditions of the Mediterranean world; and, in spite of the growing importance of the large estate in Spanish America, rural settlements never quite attained the importance they enjoyed in Brazil, although here too the cities enjoyed the preponderant influence.

Each town had its town council, or *cabildo*, a corporation which regulated the life of the inhabitants and exercised supervision over the properties in public ownership – the communal lands, woods and pastures and the street colonnades with their market stalls – from which much of its income derived. There were great variations in the composition and powers of the cabildos through the cities and towns of Spanish America, and the institution of the cabildo itself changed over the course of the centuries in response to changing social conditions and to the growing financial distress of the crown. Essentially, however, it was composed of judicial officials (*alcaldes*, who were lay judges, and presided over the cabildo, whenever the corregidor was not present) and *regidores*, town councillors, who were responsible for municipal provisioning and administration and represented the municipality in all those ceremonial functions which occupied such a substantial part of urban life.

The cabildos, as might have been expected from the pattern of municipal government in metropolitan Spain, were, or soon became, self-perpetuating oligarchies of the most substantial citizens. In the early years of the conquest, governors and captains would nominate alcaldes and regidores, some of them for life. Where elections occurred, the right of election tended to be confined to the more prominent citizens; and, as from the days of Philip II the crown increasingly resorted to the sale of public office, so the balance between elected and hereditary office-holders tilted towards the latter, reducing still further any 'popular' element which had originally existed in municipal life. Sometimes a *cabildo abierto* – an open cabildo – was held, which allowed for a wider representation of citizens to discuss matters of urgent concern, but by and large city governments were closed corporations which, by their character, were more representative of the interests of the urban patriciate than of the generality of the citizens.

The desirability of a seat in the cabildo varied greatly, according to the wealth of the town, the powers of its officers and the perquisites to be expected. There must have been many towns like Popayán, one of the most typically 'colonial' towns in present-day Colombia, where for long periods the elective positions were left unfilled. With the governor of Popayán responsible for the principal functions of government, the duties of the cabildo were largely confined to choosing minor municipal officials. The financial benefits of office were limited, and the obligations – largely honorific – could be time-consuming.[8]

A cabildo, however, was not only an institution of local self-government and a corporation in which the rivalries of the principal local families were played out. It also formed part of that larger structure of authority which reached upwards to audiencias, governors and viceroys, and thence to the council of the Indies in Madrid. It was only by operating within this structure and resorting to lobbying and petitioning that the urban patriciates could hope to exercise any influence over governmental action and decree, for no other constitutional outlets were available to them. In 1528 Mexico City unsuccessfully petitioned Charles V for a vote in the Cortes of Castile. Periodic suggestions were made thereafter either for representation of the cities of the Indies in the Castilian Cortes, or for regional meetings in the Indies themselves of representatives of the leading towns. But the

[8] See Peter Marzahl, 'Creoles and government: the cabildo of Popayán', *Hispanic American Historical Review*, 54 (1974), 636–56.

sixteenth-century Castilian crown set its face firmly against such dangerous constitutionalist tendencies. America had been conquered and colonized at a time when the thrust in metropolitan Spain was towards the theoretical and practical enhancement of royal sovereignty, and the Indies, as virgin territory, provided opportunities for the assertion of the presence of the state to a degree that was not possible even in Castile, where constitutionalism, however mortally wounded, had not yet expired.

The power of the state was all the greater in the Indies because of the extraordinary concentration of ecclesiastical power in the hands of the crown. This derived originally from precedents already established in the church of Granada, along with the rights accruing to the Castilian crown under the papal bulls conferring upon it the responsibility for the evangelization of the newly discovered lands. By a bull of 1486 the papacy had given the crown the _patronato_, or right to present to all bishoprics and ecclesiastical benefices in the Moorish kingdom of Granada, which was then on the point of reconquest. Although nothing was said in the bulls of 1493 about presentation, the Catholic Kings took Granada as their model; and in 1508 the position was regularized when Ferdinand secured for the rulers of Castile in perpetuity the right to organize the church and present to benefices in their overseas territories. A bull of 1501, amplified by further bulls in 1510 and 1511, had already vested in the crown the tithes collected in the Indies, so that the newly established church was also assured of permanent endowment, raised and managed in conformity with the wishes of the crown.

The effect of the patronato was to give the monarchs of Castile in their government of the Indies a degree of ecclesiastical power for which there was no European precedent outside the kingdom of Granada. It allowed the king to represent himself as the 'vicar of Christ', and to dispose of ecclesiastical affairs in the Indies on his own initiative, without interference from Rome. Indeed, no papal nuncio was allowed to set foot in the Indies or have any direct communication with it; and all documents passing in either direction between Rome and the New World needed the prior approval of the council of the Indies before being allowed to proceed to their destination. The crown's ecclesiastical power in the Indies was, in effect, absolute, with theoretical rights buttressed by a total control of patronage.

The church in the Indies was by nature and origin a missionary or teaching church – a fact which made it natural that the religious orders should take the lead in the work of evangelization. But, as the first pioneering work was accomplished, the mendicants, powerful as they were, found their ascendancy challenged by a secular clergy based in the towns and operating within the framework of a now well-established institutional church. In the later sixteenth century other religious orders were allowed to join the original three orders of Augustinians, Franciscans and Dominicans; and the Jesuits, who founded their Province of Paraguay in 1607, were to play an especially important part in missionary work in the remoter areas and the frontier regions. The frontier mission indeed became one of Spain's most effective colonial institutions along the fringes of empire, whether in Paraguay, the eastern fringe of the Andes, or northern Mexico. But by 1574, when the crown's *ordenanza del patronazgo* set a firm limit on the work of the regular clergy and brought them under episcopal control, it was clear that, at least in the urbanized areas, the heroic missionary age was officially at an end.

The agents used by the crown to bring the missionary church to heel were the bishops, a considerable proportion of whom, especially in the first decades, were themselves drawn from among the regular clergy. The first New World diocese, that of Santo Domingo, was founded in 1504; the first mainland diocese, Sant María de la Antigua of Darien (later transferred to Panama) in 1513. By 1536 there were fourteen dioceses; in 1546 Santo Domingo, Mexico City and Lima were raised to archbishoprics; and by 1620 the total number of archbishoprics and bishoprics in Spanish America was 34. The occupants of these sees were in effect royal functionaries who, in addition to their spiritual duties, exercised an important influence, both direct and indirect, on civil life. The dividing line between church and state in Spanish America was never sharply defined, and clashes between bishops and viceroys were a constant feature of colonial life. It was symptomatic that Juan Pérez de la Serna, archbishop of Mexico from 1613–24, came into conflict first with the marquis of Guadalcázar and then with his successor, the marquis of Gelves – two viceroys who could hardly have been more dissimilar in their temperaments and policies.

The bishops, like the letrados who staffed the audiencias, were metropolitan rather than local in their affiliations, although Philip III (1598–1621) recognized local aspirations to the extent of appointing 31 creoles to American bishoprics. In selecting from among the religious orders he also showed a preference for Augustinians over Franciscans and Dominicans. The latter in particular had been very strongly represented in the sixteenth century – of the 159 occupants of bishoprics in the Indies between 1504 and 1620, 52 were Dominicans.[9] This high proportion of Dominicans, many of them friends or followers of Las Casas, suggests a determination on the part of the sixteenth-century crown to enforce its pro-Indian policies as far as possible against the pressures exercised by encomenderos and settlers. For a time, indeed, the crown appointed bishops as official *protectores* of the Indians – an experiment that proved unsatisfactory because, as Juan de Zumárraga, the first bishop of Mexico, unhappily discovered, the duties of the post were ill-defined and led to endless conflicts of jurisdiction with the civil authorities. But, if it was found necessary to transfer these duties to civil functionaries, the crown remained heavily dependent on the episcopate for supervising both the material wellbeing and the spiritual progress of the Indian community.

In the early years of Spanish rule the bishops had in their hands an important instrument of control, over settlers and Indians alike, in the inquisitorial powers that were vested in them. A number of unfortunate cases, however, raised the whole question of whether the Inquisition, as a device for preventing Judaizing and heresy, was an appropriate means of ensuring the orthodoxy of the Indians; and in 1571 these were finally removed from all inquisitorial jurisdiction and placed under the direct control of the bishops where matters of faith and morals were concerned. At the same time, the Holy Office began establishing its tribunals in the New World – in Lima (1570), Mexico City (1571) and a third in Cartagena in 1610 – to guard the faith and morals of the settler community, whether against corruption by sexual delinquents, or against contamination by the numerous *conversos* who had managed to slip into America and by foreigners peddling their dangerous Lutheran heresies. In due course this New World Inquisition, secretive, arrogant and ruthless, like its Old World original, came into conflict not only with the secular and regular clergy, but also with the episcopate. Here, as elsewhere with the church in America, there were too many competing organizations and interests for it ever to become a monolithic institution.

It is this fragmented character of authority, both in church and state, which is one of the most striking characteristics of Spanish colonial

---

[9] See Enrique Dussel, *Les Evêques hispano-americains* (Wiesbaden, 1970), for a statistical survey of the American bishops in the sixteenth and early seventeenth centuries.

America. Superficially the crown's power was absolute, both in church and state. A stream of orders issued from the council of the Indies in Madrid, and a massive bureaucracy, both secular and clerical, was expected to put them into effect. But in practice there was so much jockeying for power between different interest groups – between viceroys and audiencias, viceroys and bishops, secular clergy and regular clergy, and between the governors and the governed – that unwelcome laws, while deferentially regarded because of the source from which they emanated, were not obeyed, while authority itself was filtered, mediated and dispersed.

The presence of the state, therefore, while all-pervasive, was not all-commanding. The certainties of Madrid were dissolved in the ambiguities of an America where to 'observe but not obey' was an accepted and legitimate device for disregarding the wishes of a supposedly ill-informed crown. In fact the crown was extraordinarily well informed, in the sense that a vast quantity of written information flowed in from across the Atlantic – information that was often, no doubt, a year or more out of date, but which reflected the widest possible range of views, from those of the viceroy's inner circle to the humblest Indian community. A system under which 49,555 sheets of paper could be used in the course of a visita into the activities of a single viceroy of Peru is not one that can be described as suffering from a dearth of facts.[10]

Well-informed administration of its overseas territories became, indeed, almost an end in itself for the crown, especially in the reign of Philip II with his inclinations towards planned and orderly government. Juan de Ovando, one of the officials who most closely reflected the spirit of Philip II's regime, concluded after conducting a visitation of the council of the Indies in 1569–70 that it still lacked sufficient information about the lands it governed, and during his relatively brief tenure of the presidency of the council in the early 1570s he set out to remedy this deficiency. Detailed questionnaires were sent out to officials in the Indies about the region and peoples subjected to their charge (a device that was also employed in Castile), and the responses, as they came in, were carefully ordered and summarized. In 1571 the post of *cronista de las Indias* (official chronicler and historiographer of the Indies) was established, and the first holder of the post, Juan López de Velasco,

[10] See Lewis Hanke, 'El visitador licenciado Alonso Fernandez de Bonilla y el virrey del Perú, el conde del Villar', in *Memoria del II Congreso Venezolano de Historia* (Caracas, 1975), II, 28.

produced on the basis of the *relaciones* sent in by the officials a *General Description of the Indies* which represents the first comprehensive statistical survey of Spain's American possessions.

Professionalism for its own sake is always liable to be a feature of government when the bureaucrats take control. But all imperialists need an ideology, whether they recognize the need or not. Sixteenth-century Castilians, imbued with a deep sense of the need to relate their enterprises to a higher moral end, had to articulate for themselves a justification for their government of the New World which would set their actions firmly in the context of a divinely ordained purpose. The silver of the Indies, which it was the crown's object to exploit to the maximum in order to enhance its revenues, was itself seen as a gift of God which would enable the kings of Castile to fulfil their world-wide obligations to uphold and propagate the Faith. Empire, therefore, was sanctioned by purpose; and empire in the Indies was regarded as a sacred trust, the character of which was summarized by the great seventeenth-century jurist, Juan de Solórzano y Pereyra in his *Política Indiana* [1648]. The Indians, he wrote, 'because they are so barbarous... needed somebody who, by assuming the duties of governing, defending and teaching them, would reduce them to a human, civil, social and political life, so that they should acquire the capacity to receive the Faith and the Christian religion'.[11]

But by what right could Spaniards wage war on Indians, subject them to their rule and reduce them to a 'human, civil, social and political life'? Although the juridical question of Castile's right to subjugate the Indies might seem to have been largely resolved by the papal bulls of donation, the confrontation between Europeans and the numerous and very diverse peoples of the Indies raised a host of problems, moral as well as juridical, which were at once so new and so complex that they were incapable of being summarily disposed of by a stroke of the papal pen. In principle, the doctrine of *compelle eos intrare* – 'Go into the highways and hedges, and compel them to come in' (Luke xiv. 23) – might seem justification enough for a forcible reduction of a pagan people to Christianity. But it did not need a high degree of moral sensitivity to appreciate that there was something ludicrously inadequate about confronting the Indians, before engaging them in battle, with a reading of the *requerimiento*, the document drafted in 1513 by the jurist, Palacios

---

[11] Book I, chap. ix, 119.

Rubios, which briefly expounded the history of the world since Adam and called on uncomprehending hearers who knew not a word of Spanish to submit to the authority of the church and the kings of Castile.

Uneasiness over the requerimiento merged with the more generalized concern over the ill-treatment of the Indians once they submitted or were conquered, to provoke an intensive and wide-ranging debate throughout the first half of the sixteenth century on the question of Spanish titles and Indian subjection. It was conducted in the convents and universities of Castile, but its repercussions were felt both at court and in the Indies, ruled as they were by legislation which would be shaped by the arguments of the victorious party.

In view of the vitality of Aristotelian and Thomist thought in the intellectual life of sixteenth-century Spain, it was inevitable that all claims to government in the Indies should be subjected to critical scholastic scrutiny. Already in 1510 the Scottish Dominican, John Major, had argued on Aristotelian grounds that infidelity was insufficient cause to deprive pagan communities of the right to property and jurisdiction, which belonged to them by natural law. This Aristotelian doctrine was at the heart of the great series of lectures, the *Relectio de Indis*, delivered by the Spanish Dominican, Francisco de Vitoria, at Salamanca university in 1539. If civil authority was inherent in all communities by virtue of reason and natural law, neither pope nor emperor could justifiably claim world-wide temporal dominion over-ruling and annulling the legitimate rights of non-Christian communities. By a daring stroke, therefore, Vitoria had undermined the justification for Spanish rule in the Indies on the basis of papal donation. Equally, he rejected titles based on alleged rights of discovery and on the unwillingness of Indians to accept the Faith.

In the circumstances it is not surprising that a stern rebuke was issued in November 1539 against 'those theologians who have called in question, through sermons or lectures, our right to the Indies...' Vitoria's arguments could only be a grave embarrassment to the emperor at a time when other European states were challenging Castilian claims to exclusive American dominion. He did not, however, go so far as to leave his sovereign without a fig-leaf to cover his nakedness. He was prepared to concede that the pope, by virtue of a 'regulating' authority, could charge a Christian prince with the mission of evangelization and that this charge was binding on his Christian colleagues. But it was not binding on the Indians themselves, and it carried with it no entitlement for war or conquest. How then could Spanish domination of the Indies, which was after all a *fait accompli*, be justified? Vitoria's answers, although impressively reasoned, were not entirely comfortable. If, as he argued, there was a law of nations, a *jus gentium*, embracing all mankind, the Spaniards had the right to trade with and preach the gospel to the Indians, and the Indians were bound to receive them peaceably. If they refused to do so, then the Spaniards had just cause for war. While this doctrine might perhaps be adequate justification for Spaniards in their relations with the Indians, it was less useful to them in their relations with other European powers. If there was indeed a world community in which all peoples had freedom of movement and trade, it was not immediately apparent why Europeans other than Spaniards should be rigorously prevented from setting foot in the Indies. It is not, therefore, surprising that later Spanish apologists of empire should have preferred to fall back on the argument of prior discovery, buttressed by claims of a Christianizing and civilizing mission formally entrusted to Castile.

Vitoria's arguments, as he himself ruefully accepted, had long since been overtaken by facts, and they remained at a level of theoretical abstraction which inevitably reduced the impact of their radical message. But they illustrate the difficulty inherent in the formulation of any coherent theory of empire, and suggest why the Spanish crown tended to fall back on a set of attitudes and responses rather than purveying any clear-cut 'imperialist' ideology. As long as Spain's dominion over the Indies was to all intents and purposes unchallengeable by its European rivals, facts in any event spoke louder than words, although this did not preclude considerable defensiveness in the face of international public opinion – a defensiveness suggested by the official replacement in 1573 of the word 'conquest' by 'pacification'.

There were, however, in Vitoria's rather hesitant justification of Castile's title to the Indies, a number of arguments which might be put to use by the crown. In particular he hinted at the idea of a possible right of tutelage over the Indians if they were demonstrated to be irrational beings in need of guidance. But what kind of tutelary control should be exercised over them, and, above all, who should exercise it?

For Bartolomé de Las Casas, waging his bitter campaign against the maltreatment and exploitation of the Indians by the Spanish settlers, there could be only one answer. The crown, and the crown alone, had jurisdiction over the Indians, by virtue of the bulls of 1493. This jurisdiction, which was tied to the missionary enterprise, could not be delegated to other Spaniards or transferred by means of encomiendas to private individuals. Las Casas, in fact, was advocating a form of tutelary kingship, which would provide the necessary conditions for the conversion of the Indians but would not deprive them of the rights of property and of government by their own rulers that belonged to them by virtue of natural law.[12]

In the circumstances of the late 1530s and the 1540s such arguments were well calculated to appeal to the crown. If the emperor was concerned on one front with the international challenge to his government of the Indies, he was still more concerned by the internal challenge represented by the encomenderos as a potential feudal aristocracy owning Indian serfs. The settlers threatened both his own authority and, by their scandalous treatment of the Indians, the evangelizing mission that was the *raison d'être* of Spanish rule. That the Indians were being cruelly abused was clear not only from the violent denunciations of Las Casas himself, but also from letter after letter that arrived from the Indies – from Archbishop Zumárraga, from Viceroy Mendoza, and from the licenciado, Vasco de Quiroga, that New World admirer of Sir Thomas More, whose *Utopia* provided a model for the Indian communities that he would establish in the Valley of Mexico and beside Lake Pátzcuaro in his diocese of Michoacán.

The agitation about the wellbeing of the Indians was reaching a climax at the time when Charles V returned to Spain after two years' absence in 1541. Along with reports of the factional struggles between Pizarrists and Almagrists in Peru it helped create a climate in which a radical re-thinking of royal policy in the Indies became a matter of urgency. The councillors of the Indies, suspected of being in the pay of the encomenderos, were not to be trusted, and the emperor, therefore, turned to a special *junta* to advise him on the encomienda question. It was this junta which produced the New Laws of 20 November 1542 – laws which, if implemented, would have realized Las Casas' ideals by abolishing all forms of personal service and transforming encomienda Indians into direct vassals of the crown.

The explosive reaction of the New World settlers forced the emperor to retreat. But the campaign against the New Laws was waged not only in the Indies themselves, but also at court, where the settlers' lobby

---

[12] For Las Casas and his writings about the treatment of Indians, see ch. 1 above.

worked hard to bribe and influence the royal councillors, and where Cortés and his friends organized a formidable opposition to the Las Casas group. They needed an effective publicist, however, and they found one in the great Aristotelian scholar, Juan Ginés de Sepúlveda, whose *Democrates Alter*, written in 1554–5, was circulated in manuscript around the councils, although it failed to secure a licence for publication. In his treatise Sepúlveda raised a question that was fundamental to the whole problem of government in America: that of the rational capacity of the Indians. John Major had argued in 1510 that they lived like beasts and that consequently, in accordance with Aristotelian principles, their natural inferiority condemned them to servitude. It was this line of reasoning which Sepúlveda pursued, although with greater difficulty than Major, because the discovery of the Mexican and Andean civilizations had revealed the existence of peoples with a capacity for political and social organization impressive even to European eyes. Sepúlveda, however, from the safe distance of Castile, did his best to remain unimpressed. The Indians, it was clear, were a people naturally inferior to the Spaniards, and as such were properly subject to Spanish rule.

Sepúlveda was arguing not for the enslavement of the Indians, but for a form of strict paternalistic control in their own best interests. This was an argument for tutelage, exercised, however, by the encomenderos and not by the crown. The *Democrates Alter* was, in fact, advocating government by a natural aristocracy drawn from the settler community and, as such, was bound to be anathema to the royal authorities. Equally it was anathema to Las Casas, who had hurried back to Spain from his Mexican diocese of Chiapas in 1547 in a desperate bid to shore up the anti-encomendero policy which he saw collapsing in ruins around him. In April 1550 the crown responded to the storm of protest unleashed by Las Casas and his fellow-Dominicans by ordering a temporary suspension of all further expeditions of conquest in the New World, and by summoning a special meeting of theologians and councillors to consider the whole question of the conquest and conversion of the Indians. In the great debate staged at Valladolid in August 1550 between Las Casas and Sepúlveda, the 76-year-old bishop of Chiapas launched into a five-day public reading of his new treatise *In Defence of the Indians*, in the course of which he challenged Sepúlveda's theory of Spain's civilizing mission.[13]

---

[13] Bartolomé de Las Casas, *In defense of the Indians*, trans. Stafford Poole (DeKalb, Illinois, 1974), 171.

Although the Sepúlveda–Las Casas debate was superficially concerned with the justice of military conquest, it really reflected two fundamentally opposed views of the native peoples of America. Within the Aristotelian framework in which the debate was conducted, proof of 'bestiality' or 'barbarism' would serve as justification for the subordination of Indian to Spaniard. It was this which made it so important for Las Casas to prove that the Indians were neither beasts nor barbarians. But, for all the violence of the disagreement, there was a certain unreality about it in the sense that Las Casas, even as he questioned the benefits conferred on Indians by Spaniards, did not really doubt Spain's mission in the Indies. Where he differed from Sepúlveda was in wanting that mission pursued by peaceful means rather than coercion, and by the crown and the missionaries rather than the settlers.

The members of the junta, not surprisingly, were divided in their reactions, with the jurists apparently supporting Sepúlveda and the theologians leaning towards Las Casas. The latter may be said to have 'won' in the sense that the ban on the publication of the *Democrates Alter* was upheld. The stringent new conditions laid down in Philip II's new ordinances of 1573 for the procedures to be followed in future conquests in the Indies may also be seen as an expression of the crown's determination to prevent a repetition of the atrocities against which the bishop of Chiapas had fulminated year in and year out. But the age of conquest, even under the euphemism of 'pacification', was largely at an end by the time the ordinances were issued; and Las Casas lost the battle he most wanted to win – the battle to rescue the Indians from the clutches of the Spaniards.

He did, however, win another and more dubious victory, this time in the court of international public opinion. The 'black legend' of Spanish brutality pre-dated Las Casas, as it also pre-dated, at least in some form, any major European preoccupation with news from America. But Las Casas' devastating denunciation of the behaviour of his compatriots in his *Brief Account of the Destruction of the Indies*, first published in Spain in 1552, was to provide, along with Girolamo Benzoni's *History of the New World* (Venice, 1565), a repository of horror stories which Spain's European enemies would plunder to advantage. French and Dutch translations appeared in 1579 and the first English edition in 1583, as the antagonism between the Spain of Philip II and the northern Protestants mounted to its climax. The lurid engravings of Theodore de Bry reinforced the written word with a visual image of Spanish atrocities against innocent Indians which was to impress a crude stereotype of Spanish imperial rule on the minds of generations of Europeans.

Inevitably, the assault on Spain's record in the Indies provoked an apologetic literature in response and helped create that sense of Spain as a beleaguered fortress defending Christian values which itself became an important element in the Castilian national consciousness. Measured by the legislation which emerged from the discussions of the council of the Indies, the record of sixteenth-century Spain in America was in many respects remarkably enlightened. Strenuous efforts were made to protect the Indians from the grosser forms of exploitation, and there was a genuine if misconceived attempt on the part of crown and church to introduce the inhabitants of the Indies to what was automatically assumed to be a higher way of life. But the gulf between intention and practice was all too often hopelessly wide. Metropolitan aspirations, deriving as they did from different interest groups, all too often tended to be mutually incompatible; and over and over again the best of intentions foundered on the rock of colonial realities.

COLONIAL REALITIES

When the first viceroy of Mexico, Don Antonio de Mendoza, handed over the government to his successor, Don Luis de Velasco, in 1550, he made clear the existence of a fundamental incompatibility between the crown's desire to protect the Indians, and its desire to increase its revenues from the Indies. The crown was genuinely concerned to preserve the so-called *república de los indios*, threatened as it was by the depredations of unscrupulous settlers who took advantage of the 'innocence' of the Indians and their ignorance of European ways. On the other hand, the crown's perennial shortage of money naturally drove it to maximize its revenues from the Indies by every means at its command. The bulk of these revenues derived directly from the Indies in the form of tribute, or indirectly in the form of labour producing goods and services yielding a dividend to the crown. At a time when the size of the Indian population was shrinking catastrophically, the attempt even to preserve tribute rates at the levels set in the immediate post-conquest period was likely to be a source of growing hardship to Indian communities, while there was also a diminishing amount of labour available for distribution. Any attempt, therefore, to augment the Indian contribution could only disrupt still further a república de los indios which increasingly appeared doomed to destruction as a result of the impact of conquest and population decline.

The payment of tribute, in specie or in kind, or in a combination of the two, was obligatory on the Indians under Spanish rule almost from the conquest until its abolition during the wars of independence at the beginning of the nineteenth century. Paid either to the crown or to the encomenderos, tribute occupied a central place in Indian life as an inescapable imposition, harshly discriminatory in that only Indians were liable. In New Spain in the 1550s the tribute had to be reassessed in the light of the patent inability of dwindling Indian communities to pay their allotted share, and the same process occurred in Peru during the viceroyalty of Don Francisco de Toledo (1568–80), that austere servant of an austere royal master. All nobles other than caciques (chiefs) and their eldest sons now lost their tax exemption, and the same occurred for other groups lower down the social scale which, for one reason or another, had until now escaped tribute. The inevitable result of this was to accelerate the levelling process already at work in the Indian communities and to undermine still further their already weakened structure.[14]

The organization of tribute collection was placed in the hands of a new breed of officials, the *corregidores de indios*, who were making their appearance all over the more densely-settled areas of Spanish America from the 1560s. These corregidores de indios, who held appointment for only two or three years, were designed as the crown's answer to the encomenderos. Either Spanish-born Spaniards, perhaps drawn from the entourage which each viceroy brought with him from home, or else creoles (Spaniards born in the Indies) without land or encomiendas of their own, they would, it was hoped, prove reliable agents of the crown, in a way that the encomenderos, with a direct interest in the Indians under their charge, could never be. The new *corregimientos*, however, tended to have many of the defects of the old encomiendas, together with new ones of their own. The duties of the corregidor de indios included not only tribute collection but also the administration of justice and the organization of the labour supply for public and private works. Dependent on a small salary drawn from Indian tribute he naturally used his brief tenure to make the most of the enormous power with which he suddenly found himself vested. There was little to prevent him from

[14] For a further discussion of Indian tribute, see ch. 9 below.

making his own private extortions as he organized the tribute and directed part of the work-force into enterprises of benefit to himself. Where the encomendero had tended to rely on the traditional indigenous authorities to get his wishes obeyed, the corregidor, living like a lord among the Indians, had his own little army of officials, whose activities undercut those of the caciques, and so reduced still further their influence among their own people.

The very officials, therefore, who were intended to watch over the interests of the traditional república de los indios were themselves among its most dangerous enemies. But it is the operation of the labour system under the supervision of the corregidores de indios which most vividly reveals the inherent contradictions in the crown's Indian policies. In theory the Indians were supposed to lead segregated lives. Spaniards, other than royal officials, were not allowed to live among them, and they in turn were not allowed to live in Spanish cities, unless in specially reserved *barrios*. But, while strenuous attempts were being made to confine them to a world of their own, they were also being inexorably drawn into a European labour and money economy. This was a natural consequence of the abolition of personal labour services for the encomenderos in 1549. With slavery forbidden, and the service-encomienda tending to be replaced by the tribute-encomienda, alternative methods had to be devised for mobilizing Indian labour. The viceroys of the second half of the sixteenth century encouraged a wage-labour system to the best of their ability, but with the Indian population diminishing rapidly they also found it necessary to resort to coercion in order to save the fragile economic life of the Indies from collapse. There was nothing new about forced labour in either Mexico or Peru. It had existed before the conquest as well as after it, but it was reorganized in the 1570s on a systematic basis, although with regional variations inspired by earlier regional practices. Conscripted Indian labourers were ruthlessly wrenched from their communities and drafted to the fields, to public works, to the *obrajes*, or textile workshops, for the production of wool and cotton cloths and, above all, to the mines. Efforts were made by the crown in the early seventeenth century to legislate against the worst abuses of the labour system, but without much success. In so far as the deployment of labour was at least more tightly controlled, this was facilitated by the vast reorganization of the declining Indian population which had taken place in both New Spain and Peru during the second half of the sixteenth and the first decade of the seventeenth centuries. Under the so-called policy of *congregaciones* and *reducciones*, Indians scattered through the countryside had been congregated into larger settlements where they could be more easily governed and Christianized.

By the beginning of the seventeenth century the old-style república de los indios, based on structures inherited from the pre-conquest period, was in a state of advanced disintegration and the assumption which had governed the crown's policy towards the Indians in the first post-conquest decades – that the old Indian polity could be preserved without major changes – had lost all validity. The pressures to incorporate the Indians into the life and the economy of the new colonial society – even while still attempting to keep them at arm's length from the vigorous new world of settlers, mestizos (half Indian-half Spanish) and mulattos (half African-half Spanish) – were simply too powerful to be resisted. Those Indians who moved to the cities to become servants and employees of the Spaniards, were gradually assimilated and Hispanicized. Outside the Spanish cities, however, a new world was in process of formation. Paradoxically the establishment of the new corregimiento de indios and of the reducciones gave a new lease of life to the república de los indios, although it was now a república of a very different style from that of the immediate post-conquest period. The Indians congregated into settlements did in fact assimilate certain elements of Christianity; they appropriated for their own use European techniques, plants and animals and entered the monetary economy of the surrounding world. At the same time they preserved many of their indigenous characteristics, so that they remained genuinely Indian communities, conducting their own lives under the supervision of royal officials but through their own largely autonomous municipal institutions. The more successful of these Indian munici-palities developed their own forms of resistance against encroachments from outside. Their *cajas de comunidad*, or community chests, allowed them to build up financial reserves to meet their tribute and other obligations. They learnt how to secure their lands with legal titles and how to engage in the petitioning and lobbying techniques which were essential for political survival in the Hispanic world. As a result, these indigenous communities, consolidating themselves during the seventeenth century, came to act as breakwaters against the engulfing tide of the large estate, or hacienda, which swept around them without ever quite submerging them.

The separate development of the *república de los indios*, ministering to the needs of the *república de los españoles* without forming a part of it, implied the development of Spanish America itself as two worlds, indigenous and European, linked to each other at numerous points but preserving their distinctive identities. Between them, belonging wholly neither to one nor the other, were the mestizos, rapidly increasing in numbers and acquiring during the course of the seventeenth century some of the characteristics of a caste. But, inevitably, in this tripartite society now in process of constitution it was the república de los españoles which dominated.

Within the Hispanic community, although the crown had triumphed over the encomenderos, it was incapable of preventing the establishment of what was in practice, although not in name, a New World nobility. This nobility differed in important ways from that of metropolitan Spain. Whereas Castilian society was divided between taxpayers (*pecheros*) and those who, by virtue of their noble status, were exempt from taxes, all the Hispanic population of the Indies was tax-exempt, and therefore stood in an aristocratic relationship to the tribute-paying Indian population. Consequently the elite among the creoles (*criollos*)[15] – those of Spanish blood who were native to the Indies – was not distinguished by any special fiscal privileges. Nor, unlike its metropolitan equivalent, did it possess any rights of jurisdiction over vassals, since its attempt to transform encomiendas into fiefs had failed. It lacked, too, any substantial titular differentiation. The crown was extremely sparing of titles for creoles; and in 1575 it withdrew from the encomenderos certain honorific privileges associated with the status of *hidalgo* in Castile, although in 1630, under the pressure of its financial needs, it changed its policy and authorized the viceroys to put privileges of *hidalguía* up for sale in the Indies. Similarly, that other perquisite of many Spanish nobles and hidalgos, membership in one of the great military orders of Santiago, Calatrava and Alcántara, was largely unavailable to

---

[15] Although the term 'creole' is commonly used in modern historical writing to describe the sixteenth- and seventeenth-century colonists, *criollo* does not seem to have been in common use at that time. The Indies-born settlers spoke of themselves as 'Spaniards' and were referred to as such in official documents. It is, however, noticeable that the renegade English Dominican, Thomas Gage, who travelled extensively in Mexico and Guatemala between 1625 and 1637, refers on a number of occasions to 'Creoles' or the 'Creole faction'. See *Thomas Gage's Travels in the New World*, ed. J. Eric S. Thompson (Norman, Oklahoma, 1958), 105, 127. On this question, see Lockhart, *CHLA*, ii, ch. 8.

the conquerors and first-generation settlers. Only sixteen of them became members of these orders in the sixteenth century. Here again, however, there was a major change in the seventeenth century, during the course of which 420 creoles were granted membership.

The greater inclination of the crown in the seventeenth century than in the sixteenth to respond to the creoles' eager demand for honours was an obvious reflection of its pressing financial problems, which in one area after another would make it sacrifice what had once been tenaciously held policies for the sake of immediate fiscal advantage. But it also reflected social changes in the New World itself, as a creole elite consolidated itself in spite of the unwillingness of the crown to concede it formal recognition.

By the end of the sixteenth century this elite was a composite one, based on old settlement, new wealth and influential connections. The *conquistadores* – the natural aristocracy of the Indies – seem to have been strikingly unsuccessful in meeting the first challenge confronting all aristocracies, the establishment of a dynastic succession. In 1604 Baltasar Dorantes de Carranza said that there were only 934 living descendants of the 1326 conquerors of Mexico; and, even if several names were omitted, it is clear that the conquerors, at least as far as legitimate children were concerned, had been a demographically unfortunate group of men. Of those who surmounted the demographic hazard, many fell at the next fence. It was only a very small group among the conquerors – a group drawn largely from among the captains and the men on horseback – which acquired wealth and substantial encomiendas. These would live in major cities, like Mexico City or Puebla, while their former comrades, many of them fallen on bad times, would settle down to relatively obscure lives in small settlements remote from the main urban centres.

This small group of successful *conquistadores* was joined by a number of the early settlers who, for one reason or another, prospered in the new environment. It was a particular advantage, for instance, to have influential relatives at court, as did the Ruiz de la Mota, the Altamirano and the Cervantes Casaus families in New Spain, and so to have access to sources of patronage. Royal officials, and especially treasury officials like Alonso de Estrada, Rodrigo de Albornoz and Juan Alonso de Sosa, with large sums of money at least temporarily at their disposal, married their families into those of the leading settlers of New Spain. So, too, did members of each new viceregal entourage and the judges of the audiencias, in spite of the crown's attempts to keep them segregated. The outgoing viceroy of New Spain in 1590, for example, reported to his successor that the *fiscal* of the audiencia of Guadalajara had married his daughter without receiving a royal licence, and that the audiencia had sprung to his defence when an effort was made to deprive him of his office.[16]

As the century proceeded, this nucleus of leading families assimilated further elements, especially from among those who had made their fortunes in mining. Carefully planned matrimonial alliances, in which the rich widows of encomenderos played a decisive part, produced a network of interlocking families, which resorted to the Castilian system of *mayorazgos*, or entails, to prevent a dispersal of family wealth.

Inevitably, the consolidation of local oligarchies proved easier in some areas of the Indies than in others. Much depended on the biological chance of family survival and on the degree of wealth locally available. In a provincial backwater like Popayán, encomiendas were poor, local landowning families failed to establish entails, and there was a rapid turnover in the urban patriciate – apparently only one of its twenty principal families at the end of the seventeenth century went back in the male line to the first generation of settlers. Elsewhere, however, and especially in the viceroyalties of New Spain and Peru, a number of leading families, benefiting from their close associations both with the viceregal administration and with influential figures in metropolitan Spain, built up for themselves a formidable power base in their local regions.

The process by which this was done still has to be charted in detail; but as far as New Spain is concerned, the viceroyalties of the two Don Luis de Velasco, father and son, seem to have been the critical periods. The second Don Luis himself had a creole upbringing, living in Mexico as a boy and young man during his father's tenure of the viceroyalty from 1550–64. In due course he became viceroy himself, from 1590–5, and again from 1607–11, and then returned to Spain, where, with the title of count of Salinas, he was president of the council of the Indies until 1617, the year of his death. This long and close Velasco connection with the creole elite appears to have given it wide opportunities to secure lucrative privileges and consolidate its hold over major offices not reserved for Spaniards. Links with well-placed officials, for instance, could sway decisions in major lawsuits, and especially lawsuits for the

16 *Los virreyes*, I, 281.

control of that most precious commodity in a dry country, the water supply. Possessing irrigated lands in well-chosen areas, members of the elite monopolized the grain-provisioning of the cities, where they and their relatives occupied *regimientos* and *alcaldías* and used their influence to control the world of local politics.

Inevitably the ties of kinship and interest which linked this increasingly entrenched creole oligarchy to sectors of the viceregal administration and also to nobles and high officials in metropolitan Spain, made it potentially difficult for Madrid to pursue with any consistency policies which tended to conflict with the oligarchy's wishes. The strengthening of the New World oligarchies, too, coincided with a weakening of the central government in Madrid following the death of Philip II in 1598; and this weakening in turn gave new impetus to the consolidation of oligarchical power that was already occurring as a result of local conditions. For the Indies, as for Spain itself, the reign of Philip III (1598–1621) was a period in which the late king's vision of a just society governed by an upright monarch in the interests of the community as a whole, was tarnished by the success of special interest groups in securing the commanding positions of power. In this respect the Mexican viceroyalty of the marquis of Guadalcázar (1612–21) was characteristic of the reign. Government was lax, corruption rampant and collusion between royal officials and a handful of leading families led to the further enrichment of a privileged few.

Once the oligarchies were established in the Indies, it proved virtually impossible to loosen their hold. There was one abortive attempt to do so in New Spain at the beginning of the reign of Philip IV in 1621, by a zealous viceroy, the marquis of Gelves, who was sent out from Spain with a specific mission to reform the system. Within a short period of his arrival in Mexico City in the autumn of 1621 Gelves had managed to alienate almost every influential section of the viceregal community. This was partly the result of his own political ineptitude, but it also reflected the strength of the vested interests which felt themselves threatened by his reforming projects. During the interim between the departure of Guadalcázar and the arrival of Gelves, government had been exercised by the audiencia under the presidency of Dr Vergara Gaviria. The judges, having acquired a taste for power, were reluctant to surrender it. They were also deeply involved with the local landowners who controlled Mexico City's grain supply and who had forced up the price of maize and wheat to artificial levels. In attempting to lower prices and bring the racketeers to book, Gelves inevitably arrayed against him some of the most powerful figures in the viceroyalty, including the audiencia of Vergara Gaviria. Simultaneously he rode roughshod into a world where angels feared to tread – that of the Mexican ecclesiastical establishment – and alienated one party after another, including Juan Pérez de la Serna, the archbishop of Mexico. He also antagonized the mercantile community and the *consulado* of merchants of Mexico City by attempting to put a stop to the contraband trade and raising a forced loan. There was always an acute shortage of liquid capital in the viceroyalty, whose economy depended on the smooth functioning of an extremely elaborate system of credit. By defying the merchants and by insisting that royal officials should pay tribute money directly into the royal treasury, instead of retaining it for a time in their own hands and using it for interesting entrepreneurial operations, he undermined the credit system on which Mexico's mining economy depended and plunged the viceroyalty into an economic crisis.[17]

It is not, therefore, surprising that the personal clash between viceroy and archbishop should have escalated into a full-scale confrontation between Gelves on the one hand and on the other an alliance of royal officials, high clerics and local oligarchs, whose own sectional rivalries were suddenly and dramatically swallowed up in their common fury at the activities of an over-zealous reformer. On 15 January 1624, after days of mounting tension in Mexico City, crowds manipulated by the anti-*gelvistas* attacked the viceregal palace, and forced the unhappy Gelves to flee for refuge to a Franciscan priory. The audiencia took over the government; Madrid sent out a new viceroy; and although, in order to save face, Gelves was ceremoniously restored to office for a day after his successor's arrival, nothing could alter the fact that a viceroy had been driven from office by a powerful combination of local forces determined to thwart the policies which he had been instructed by Madrid to implement.

Although there was to be another uprising in Mexico City in 1692, provoked by temporary shortages of wheat and maize, the Mexican 'tumults' of 1624 represented a more dramatic challenge to the authority of the crown in the Indies than any other it had to face in the seventeenth century. But, if at other times and in other parts the drama was less spectacular, the same underlying forces were at work.

[17] For a further discussion of mining in Mexico and Peru, see ch. 5 below.

Oligarchies were in process of establishing themselves through the Indies, in the more developed areas and the frontier regions alike, and were evolving effective forms of resistance to the commands of a distant royal government. The growing power and self-confidence of these oligarchies was one of the major if least easily documented elements of change in what was in reality a continually changing situation. For the relationship between Spain and the Indies was never a static one, from the original moment of conquest to the extinction of the Spanish Habsburgs on the death of Charles II in 1700. Each party to the relationship had its own internal dynamic, which at once affected, and was affected by, developments in the other. Nor did the relationship exist in a vacuum. Instead, it existed within a wider framework of international interests and rivalries, from which neither the aspirations of the metropolis nor the realities of life in the New World could for any length of time be detached.

THE CHANGING RELATIONSHIP BETWEEN SPAIN AND THE INDIES

Charles V, having renounced his earthly titles, died in his Spanish retreat of Yuste in 1558. In dividing his inheritance between his brother, Ferdinand, who succeeded him in the imperial title and the German lands of the Habsburgs, and his son, Philip, to whom he left Spain, Spanish Italy, the Netherlands and the Indies, he was in effect recognizing the failure of the great imperial experiment which had dominated the history of Europe during the first half of the century. In the end he had been defeated by the multiplicity of challenges which faced him – the rise of Lutheranism in Germany, the rivalry of France, the perennial threat from the Turks in central Europe and the Mediterranean – and by the sheer scale of the enterprise on which he had embarked. Distances were too large, revenues never large enough; and when the Spanish crown defaulted on its obligations to the bankers in 1557, the 'bankruptcy' was that of a whole imperial system which had hopelessly overdrawn its credit.

Philip II's inheritance was, at least in theory, more manageable than that of his father, although the Netherlands were already assuming the appearance of an exposed outpost in a northern Europe increasingly attracted by the doctrines of Luther and Calvin. At the start of Philip's reign the most pressing need was for a period of retrenchment in Spain, where Castile was showing the strain of its heavy contributions to the emperor's finances. In leaving the Netherlands for Spain in 1559, Philip II was acknowledging the realities of the day – that Spain was to be the heart of his dominions, as was, within Spain, Castile.

In a reign of some 40 years, Philip succeeded in imposing the stamp of his own character on the government of the Spanish monarchy. A deep concern with the preservation of order and the maintenance of justice; an austere approach to the duties of kingship, which he looked upon as a form of slavery; a profound mistrust of his own ministers and officials, whom he suspected, usually with good reason, of placing their own interests above those of the crown; a determination to be fully informed on every conceivable topic, and a corresponding tendency to lose himself in minutiae; and a congenital indecisiveness which imposed still further delays on a naturally slow-moving administrative machine – these were to be the hallmarks of the regime of Philip II. He gave his dominions firm government, although the effectiveness of the royal orders and decrees pouring forth from Madrid and the Escorial was inevitably diminished by distance and blunted by the opposition of competing local interests. He succeeded, too, in saving his dominions from heresy, with the exception of the Netherlands, where revolt broke out in 1566. To the world at large his power and authority seemed overwhelming, especially after he had completed the unification of the Iberian peninsula in 1580 by securing his own succession to the throne of Portugal. But against these achievements must be set the strains imposed on the monarchy, and especially on Castile, by almost unremitting war.

The hopes of peace which accompanied Philip's return to the peninsula in 1559 were dashed by the revival of the Mediterranean conflict with the Turks. The 1560s proved a difficult and dangerous decade, as Spain concentrated its resources on the Mediterranean front, only to find itself embroiled simultaneously in northern Europe with the revolt of the Netherlands. After the great naval victory of Spain and its allies at Lepanto in 1571, the war with Islam moved towards a stalemate; but a new battlefront was developing in northern Europe as Spain found itself challenged by the forces of international Protestantism. During the 1580s the struggle of the northern provinces of the Netherlands to retain their freedom from Spain broadened out into a vast international conflict, in which Spain, as the self-proclaimed defender of the Catholic cause, attempted to contain and defeat the

Protestants of the north – the Dutch, the Huguenots and the Elizabethan English.

It was inevitable that this northern struggle should extend into the waters of the Atlantic, for it was here that Spain seemed most vulnerable to its enemies and here that the greatest prizes stood to be won. While the empire of Charles V had been a universal empire, at least in the eyes of its apologists, it had always been in essence a European empire, although with an increasingly important American extension. The *monarquía española* inherited by his son was, in contrast, to develop the characteristics of a genuinely transatlantic empire, in the sense that the power and fortunes of the Spain of Philip II were directly related to the interplay between the metropolis and its transatlantic possessions. During the second half of the sixteenth century the possession of overseas empire became a critical determinant of power relationships within Europe itself, and was seen as such by the enemies of Philip II as they pondered on what seemed to them the unique advantages accruing to him from his dominion of the Indies. As the interdependence of Spain and the Indies became more marked, so the determination of the north Europeans to challenge the Iberian monopoly of the New World increased; and their challenge in turn had its own consequences for the character of the Spanish-American connection.

It was as a silver empire that Spain and Europe saw the Indies. Before the discovery of Mexico, specie exports from the Indies consisted entirely of gold, but in the 1520s silver made its first appearance. American silver production for the next two decades was still small in relation to the European output: the silver mines in the Habsburg hereditary lands produced nearly four times as much silver as the Indies between 1521 and 1544. In the later 1540s and 1550s, however, these proportions were reversed as a result of the discovery and early exploitation of the rich silver deposits of Mexico and Peru. The great silver mountain of Potosí in Peru was discovered in 1545. In the following year large deposits were found in Zacatecas in northern Mexico and then further large deposits to the south at Guanajuato. After the introduction into Mexico in the mid-1550s and into Peru around 1570 of the amalgamation process for refining silver with mercury, massive increases in production led to a dramatic increase in silver exports to Europe.

The economic and financial life of Spain and, through it, of Europe, was heavily dependent on the regular arrival of the fleets from the Indies, with their new consignments of silver. Once the silver arrived in Seville and was registered at the *Casa de la Contratación*, it was released for a variety of purposes. The king's share – probably some two-fifths of the total consignment – deriving from the *quinto*, or fifth part of all production, and from the yield of any taxes collected in the Indies, was used to meet his domestic and international commitments, for which he was perennially in arrears.

The contribution of the Indies to the royal exchequer was at first sight less spectacular than contemporary obsessions might suggest. An English member of parliament in the 1620s was only repeating a commonplace of the age when he referred to the king of Spain's 'mines in the West Indies, which minister fuel to feed his vast ambitious desire of universal monarchy'.[18] In reality, the crown's American revenues, although four times as large in the 1590s as in the 1560s, represented only about 20 per cent of its total income at the end of Philip II's reign. But this 20 per cent was, in fact, crucial for the great enterprises of Philip's later years – the struggle to suppress the revolt of the Netherlands, the naval war against the England of Elizabeth and the intervention in France. It was precisely because it consisted of liquid capital in the form of silver, and was therefore in keen demand by the bankers, that it formed such an attractive part of the revenues. It was on the strength of the silver remittances from America that the king could negotiate with his German and Genoese bankers those large *asientos*, or contracts, which kept his armies in pay and tided over the difficult period before a new round of taxes replenished the royal coffers.

The remainder of the silver reaching Seville belonged to private individuals. Some of it consisted of remittances from colonists to friends and family at home. Some of it was brought back by returning *indianos* – those who had made their fortunes in the Indies and came back to lead a life of suitable ostentation at home. But a large proportion took the form of payments for commodities that had been shipped in earlier fleets sailing to the major American entrepots, Veracruz, Cartagena and Nombre de Dios. In so far as these commodities were of Spanish origin, the payments had a Spanish destination. But as Spain itself proved increasingly incapable of meeting the needs of a developing American market, so the non-Spanish share in the Seville trade grew, and much

---

[18] L. F. Stock, *Proceedings and Debates of the British Parliaments respecting North America* (Washington, D.C., 1924), I, 62.

of the silver automatically passed into the hands of foreign merchants and producers. Both through foreign participation in the transatlantic trade and through the mechanism of the asientos, 'Spanish' silver was dispersed throughout Europe, so that any marked fluctuation in the New World remittances had widespread international repercussions. Times of *largueza*, or easy money, in Seville were times of international business confidence, but when the Sevillans sneezed, western Europe shivered.

The second half of the sixteenth century, although it began with a recession (1555–9) and was punctuated by years of misfortune, was in general a long period of expansion in the Indies trade. From the early 1590s to the early 1620s, the trade, while no longer expanding, remained at a high level of activity, but from the 1620s both the volume and the value of the trade began moving sharply downwards. By 1650 the great age of the Sevillan Atlantic was over, and as Cadiz began to replace Seville as Europe's gateway to America, and more and more foreign vessels forced an entry into Spanish American waters, new patterns of transatlantic trade began to form themselves.

Within the fluctuating boundaries of this transatlantic trade, Spain's economic relationship with its American possessions underwent important changes. In the first half of the sixteenth century the economies of Castile and of the settler communities springing up in the New World were reasonably complementary. Castile and Andalusia were able to provide the settlers with the agricultural products – oil, wine and grain – which they required in bulk, and simultaneously the growing demand in the Indies also served as a stimulus to a number of Castilian industries, especially the cloth industry. By the 1540s, however, problems were already arising. There was increasing complaint in Castile about the high price of domestic manufactures, particularly of textiles, and a tendency to blame this on exports to the Indies. In 1548 and again in 1552 the Castilian Cortes urged the crown to prohibit the export of home-made cloths to America. The crown successfully resisted the pressure from the Cortes to exclude Castile's textiles from its own overseas markets, but it is clear that the American connection, while initially acting as an encouragement to certain sectors of Castilian industry, was also creating problems to which the relatively unsophisticated Castilian economy had difficulty in responding.

It was not only a question of the ability of Castilian industry to increase supply to meet a growing American demand, but also one of how to produce, for both the domestic and the American markets, at internationally competitive prices. The high prices which were a source of such vociferous complaint among Castilian consumers in the mid-sixteenth century were high not only in relation to prices in Castile at the beginning of the century, but also in relation to those of foreign imports. There is no single explanation of the inability of Castilian manufacturers to remain internationally competitive, but a central place must be accorded to the influx of precious metals from America into an economy starved of specie – an influx whose effects were felt first in Castile and Andalusia before extending over Europe in a kind of ripple effect. It was, appropriately, a Spaniard, Martín de Azpilcueta Navarro, who first, in 1556, clearly related the high cost of living to the inflow of bullion from the Indies: 'We see by experience that in France, where money is scarcer than in Spain, bread, wine, cloth, and labour are worth much less. And even in Spain, in times when money was scarcer, saleable goods and labour were given for very much less than after the discovery of the Indies, which flooded the country with gold and silver.'[19]

The inflation of prices which undercut Spain's international competitiveness was a disturbing counterbalance to the visible assets of empire – to the manifest prosperity of the fast-growing city of Seville and to the rising revenues of the crown. The assets of empire, however, were for a long time more easily perceived than its disadvantages, and the veneer of prosperity helped to conceal the detrimental consequences to Castile of major changes that were occurring in the pattern of transatlantic trade during the second half of the sixteenth century. Until the period 1570–80 the agricultural products supplied by Castile and Andalusia constituted the dominant exports from Seville; but as the Indies began to develop their livestock production and to grow more and more of their own wheat, the demand for Spanish produce began to decline. Its place in the cargoes was taken by manufactured goods, which found a ready outlet. Some of the manufactures originated in Spain, but from around the 1580s foreign articles appear to have taken the lead over Castilian goods in the shipments – a clear indication of the inability of Castilian industry to adapt itself to the new and more sophisticated market requirements of the Indies. There was a growing demand among the settlers for European luxury articles of a type that Spain failed to produce; a demand, too, as the Indies developed their

[19] Marjorie Grice-Hutchinson, *The School of Salamanca* (Oxford, 1952), 95.

own production of cheaper lines in textiles, for high quality silks and cloths.

In the years after 1567, when trading links were first established between Mexico and the Philippines, the merchants of Peru and New Spain found it increasingly advantageous to look to the Far East rather than to metropolitan Spain for the supply of these high quality textiles. The rapid growth of the oriental trade – of textiles, porcelain and other luxuries from China – entailed a trans-Pacific diversion by way of Acapulco and Manila of large quantities of American silver which would otherwise have had a transatlantic destination. In 1597, for instance, the volume of the silver sent from Mexico to the Philippines exceeded the value of Mexican transatlantic trade for that year. The attempts of the crown to restrict the Philippines trade to one Manila galleon a year, and to prevent the re-export of Chinese goods from Mexico to Peru by prohibiting in 1631 all trade between the two viceroyalties, resulted in large-scale contraband: the Indies could not be indefinitely confined within an exclusively Hispanic system designed primarily to meet the wishes of the merchants of Seville.

If, then, the economies of Castile–Andalusia and the Indies complemented each other reasonably well until around the 1570s, there was thereafter a divergence which no amount of Spanish protectionist legislation could entirely prevent. The Indies simply had less economic need than they once had of metropolitan Spain; but Spain, on the other hand, had a great and growing need of the Indies. Like an addict, it had become dangerously dependent on regular injections of American silver to maintain the expansive style of life to which it had grown accustomed.

When the silver could not be obtained in the form of payment for Castilian products, it had to be raised by other means: through the manipulation of customs dues, the introduction of some form of taxation and the resort to a variety of fiscal expedients. The white population of the Indies was not subjected to direct taxation; but the Castilian sales-tax, the *alcabala*, was introduced in New Spain in 1574 at a rate of 2 per cent, and in Peru in 1591. From the last decades of the sixteenth century the crown also attempted to raise its American revenues by selling land, or else the titles to land already illegally settled (a form of sale known as *composición de tierras*). It collected cash from the legitimization of mestizos, from 'voluntary' donations and from monopolies. It also had recourse to a practice which was to have important social and administrative repercussions – the sale of offices, which yielded an annual revenue of 38,000 ducats (the annual salary of a viceroy of Mexico was 20,000 ducats, and of a viceroy of Peru, 30,000). As long as these were minor administrative or notarial offices this practice in itself did no great harm, although this was less true of the sale of regimientos in the cities, which accelerated the process whereby municipal power was concentrated in the hands of closed oligarchies. But it also involved the unnecessary multiplication of offices, with large numbers of new posts being created, especially in the seventeenth century, in response to the needs of the government rather than the governed. The result was the creation of a large and parasitic bureaucracy, looking on its offices as an investment ripe for exploitation. The presence of yet another layer of intermediaries with its own interests to protect, only served to hamper still further the implementation of orders from Madrid.

The combination of rising output in the mines with these new devices for extracting money from the settler population brought a large increase in the crown's American revenues in the later years of Philip II. If the crown was receiving an average of a million ducats a year from the Indies in the 1570s, the figure stood at two and a half million in the 1590s. The increase, however, failed to save the crown – which had already defaulted on its debts in 1575 – from another 'bankruptcy' in 1596. Expenditure consistently outran income as Philip II committed himself to the enormous military and naval enterprises of the last years of his reign.

For these enterprises more and more silver was required from the Indies. But Philip II's involvement in northern Europe also had the paradoxical effect of keeping silver *in* the Indies – silver with which to pay for their defence against raids by his northern enemies. Both contraband and piracy had been a fact of transatlantic life ever since regular sailings were established between Spain and the Indies; and the seizure by a French corsair off the Azores in 1523 of part of the Mexican booty sent home by Cortés was no more than an unusually spectacular example of the dangers to which the *carrera de Indias* was increasingly exposed.[20] Ships from Seville began sailing in convoys from the 1520s, and from the 1560s a regular convoy system was definitively established. This system, although expensive, justified the outlay. Over a century and a half, the

[20] For a full description of the *carrera de Indias*, see MacLeod, *CHLA*, I, ch. 10.

treasure fleets fell victim to enemy attack on only three occasions – in 1628 when the Dutch admiral, Piet Heyn, captured the fleet in the Bay of Matanzas off the coast of Cuba, and in 1656 and 1657 when Admiral Blake attacked it once in Spanish waters and once off the Canaries.

The defence of the fleets, however, proved more feasible than the defence of the Indies themselves. The area to be defended was simply too large and too sparsely inhabited by Spaniards. As Spain's European enemies came to identify the source of Spanish power as the silver of the Indies, so their ambition grew to cut Spain's transatlantic lifelines and to establish their own settlements in the Caribbean and on the American mainland. One possible response by the Spaniards was to found new settlements of their own in regions vulnerable to attack. It was the attempt by the Huguenots in 1562 to found a colony in Florida which prompted Spain to establish its own permanent settlement of San Agustín in 1565. But this was a policy that could not be uniformly adopted: every new outpost posed its own problems of supply and defence, and its isolated defenders were all too likely to be driven by the sheer necessities of survival into contraband trade with the same foreign interlopers whose incursions they were supposed to prevent.

The fiasco that overtook John Hawkins at San Juan de Ulúa in 1568 showed that, as the possessing power, Spain enjoyed very considerable advantages in American waters against expeditions mounted by its European rivals. But as the Protestant offensive developed, and first the English and then, in the seventeenth century, the Dutch turned their attention to the Indies, so an over-extended Spanish empire became increasingly conscious of its vulnerability. It was Drake's Caribbean raid of 1585–6 which first compelled the Spaniards to plan the defence of the Indies on a systematic basis. In 1586 Philip II sent out the Italian engineer, Juan Bautista Antoneli, to review the defences of the Caribbean. In the light of his report, elaborate fortifications were constructed for the protection of the principal ports – Havana, San Juan de Ulúa, Puerto Rico, Portobelo and Cartagena. The effectiveness of the new defence system was demonstrated by the discomfiture of the Hawkins–Drake expedition of 1595, but the cost of building and maintaining fortifications inevitably entailed a heavy burden on royal revenues in the Indies.

Philip II's accession to the throne of Portugal in 1580 represented initially an accretion of Spanish strength. It gave him an additional fleet; a new Atlantic seaboard, with a first-class port in Lisbon; and, in Brazil, a vast new dominion. But it was followed by the incursion of the Dutch into South American waters for the first time, acting as carriers for the Portuguese; and from the end of the sixteenth century Dutch shippers were showing an unhealthy interest both in the Brazil trade and in the Caribbean, to which they turned in search of salt. The twelve-year truce of 1609–21 between Spain and the United Provinces had little effect on the new-found interest of the Dutch in the possibilities of America. Their infiltration of the Brazil trade continued; and in 1615 a Dutch expedition, following Drake's route through Magellan's Strait, moved up the Pacific coast on its way to the Moluccas. The appearance of the Dutch in Spain's Pacific waters showed that a vast unguarded coastline was henceforth no longer immune from attack. Fortifications had to be constructed at Acapulco, and the prince of Esquilache, viceroy of Peru from 1614 to 1621, embarked on a costly programme of coastal defence – too costly at a time when Spain was becoming seriously preoccupied by the deteriorating position of the Habsburgs in Central Europe.

In 1617 and 1618 the Spanish council of finance was complaining bitterly about the decline in the crown's share of the silver remittances from the Indies and blamed this decline on the retention of large sums by the viceroys of Mexico and Peru. Much of this money was being used to improve defences against corsair attacks, and Peru also bore the additional burden of subsidizing to the tune of 212,000 ducats a year the interminable war against the Araucanian Indians of Chile. The figures for remittances to Seville bear out the ministers' complaints. Where Philip II was receiving two and a half million ducats a year in the 1590s, the figures in the later years of Philip III barely reached a million, and in 1620 they dropped to a mere 800,000 ducats.[21]

The costs of imperial defence, therefore, were soaring at a time when the crown's receipts from the Indies were dwindling, and when the Seville trade itself, in which Spain was playing a diminishing part, was beginning to show signs of stagnation. Consequently, the early seventeenth century appears as a critical period in the relationship between Spain and the Indies. The balmy days of easy silver appeared to be drawing to a close, and there was a growing awareness in Castile of the costs of empire rather than its benefits. As the Castilians of the reign of Philip III embarked on a great debate about what they were beginning to perceive as the decline of their country, it is therefore not

[21] J. H. Elliott, *The revolt of the Catalans* (Cambridge, 1963), 189–90.

surprising that the role of the Indies should have been brought into the discussion. What benefits, after all, had the Indies conferred on Castile? For Martín González de Cellorigo, writing in 1600, the psychological consequences of empire had been disastrous for his countrymen, creating false illusions of prosperity and persuading them to abandon pursuits which would have made them richer than all the treasures of the Indies.[22]

At a time when the wealth of states was increasingly being measured by the number of their inhabitants, there was also a growing pre-occupation with the demographic consequences for Castile of emigration to the Indies. The Mexican-born Rodrigo de Vivero y Velasco, writing in the early 1630s with firsthand knowledge of conditions on both sides of the Atlantic, was one of the many seventeenth-century Spaniards to lament the high rate of emigration to the Indies: 'at the present rate Spain will be denuded of people and the Indies run the risk of being lost, because they are receiving many more people than they can conveniently take'.[23] He described the large number of passengers making the crossing without a licence, buying their passages from ships' captains in San Lúcar, Cadiz or Seville for twenty or 25 ducats with as much ease as if they were buying bread or meat. This stream of emigrants, perhaps on average 4,000 a year over the course of the seventeenth century, helped to create in the Indies themselves a floating population of unemployed, who constituted a constant source of worry to the authorities. But from the Spanish side of the Atlantic the problem seemed even more serious, for the Indies, instead of yielding up their treasures for Castile, were draining it of its lifeblood.

The sense of disillusionment about the value of the Indies stood in sharp contrast to the sixteenth-century assumption that the conquest of America was a special signal of God's favour for Castile. The degree to which attitudes had changed can be gauged by the fact that in 1631 the principal minister of the crown, the count-duke of Olivares (whose family estates in Andalusia exported wine to the Indies), wondered aloud at a meeting of the council of state whether its great conquests had not 'reduced this monarchy to such a miserable state that it might fairly be said that it would have been more powerful without the New World'.[24] A statement like this, even if made in a passing moment of

---

[22] *Memorial de la política necesaria y útil restauración a la república de España* (Valladolid, 1600), 15v.

[23] *Du Japon et du bon gouvernement de l'Espagne et des Indes*, trans. and ed. Juliette Monbeig (Paris, 1972), 93.

[24] Archivo General de Simancas, Estado, legajo 2332, *consulta* of 7 September 1631.

exasperation, suggests a kind of emotional distancing which may itself have played a part in changing the relationship between Spain and the Indies in the seventeenth century. On both sides of the Atlantic there was a gradual drawing apart, a first weakening of the ties of natural affinity between the metropolis and its overseas dominions.

Yet Castile never needed the Indies more than it needed them after the accession of Philip IV in 1621, when the truce with the Netherlands expired, and Spain found itself once again saddled with enormously heavy European commitments. Spain's new involvement in a conflict that threatened to extend over Europe was bound to increase its dependence on its American possessions. Threatened by the collapse of the Castilian economy under the fiscal pressures of war, the regime of the count-duke of Olivares (1621–43) set out to exploit and mobilize the resources of the various states and provinces of the Spanish monarchy, including the American viceroyalties. The disastrous Gelves government in Mexico constituted a first attempt to reverse the trend of declining revenues. Comparable efforts were also made to increase the crown's income in Peru. In 1626 Olivares launched an elaborate scheme for sharing the burdens of defence. By this scheme, known as the Union of Arms, each part of the monarchy was to guarantee to contribute a stipulated number of paid men over a fifteen-year period. It was agreed in Madrid that it was not practicable to demand soldiers from the Indies. Instead, the council of the Indies proposed in 1627 that Peru should make an annual contribution of 350,000 ducats and New Spain 250,000, the money to be devoted to the fitting out of a naval squadron for the protection of Atlantic shipping.

It proved almost as difficult to introduce the Union of Arms in the Indies as it did in metropolitan Spain, where Portugal and the states of the crown of Aragon showed themselves more conscious of the costs than the benefits of the scheme. The count of Chinchón, appointed viceroy of Peru in 1627 with the assignment of introducing the Union, found good reasons to prevaricate, and it was only in 1636 that the project began to get under way with a doubling of the alcabalas from 2 per cent to 4 per cent and comparable increases in the customs dues. In New Spain the alcabalas were also raised to 4 per cent for the same purpose in 1632, and then again to 6 per cent in 1639, this time to finance a project which had long been under discussion in Spain and the Indies – the creation of a special fleet, the *armada de barlovento*, to police the sealanes of the Caribbean.

The 1620s and 1630s, therefore, may be seen as a period of new and intensified fiscalism in the Indies, just as in Spain itself and in Spain's European territories. Increased taxes, forced gifts and loans, and the sale of rights, privileges and offices – these were the hallmark of the Olivares years on both sides of the Atlantic, as the government in Madrid struggled to sustain its gigantic military effort and to save Castile from collapse. The Indies were being called upon to bear the costs of their own defence, while simultaneously they were also expected to contribute more to the central exchequer.

But how far were Spain's American territories capable in these years of responding to Madrid's intensified demands? At least for New Spain there are clear indications that the 1620s were a time of economic difficulties. In part this was the result of Gelves' heavy-handed attempts at reform, with their disastrous impact on confidence and credit. But this was also a decade of unusually bad climatic conditions, reflected in a run of poor harvests, heavy mortality among livestock, and, in 1629, disastrous flooding in Mexico City caused by the overflow of the waters of Lake Texcoco. Mine-owners, too, were reporting increasing production problems, with labour in short supply and once-rich veins being worked out. On the other hand, the Zacatecas mines, which may have been responsible for as much as a third of the total Mexican production at this period, continued to produce at high rates until the mid-1630s, when they moved into a period of decline that lasted 30 years. In the Potosí silver mines of Peru, production, although it never reached the peaks it had attained in the late sixteenth century, kept up reasonably well until the 1650s, aided in part by Madrid's willingness to give Peru priority over New Spain in the allocation of mercury exports from Europe which helped to supplement the faltering native supplies from the mines of Huancavelica.

To keep the mines producing, however, was an increasingly costly business. This was partly because labour was scarce in many mining regions, and because easily accessible deposits which had produced such a rich yield in the sixteenth century were now nearing exhaustion. But it also reflected the declining value of silver itself in Europe, where its abundance had lowered the value of a silver *peso* relative to gold. In Spain the legal gold–silver ratio, which had stood at 10.11 to 1 in the early sixteenth century had moved to 15.45 to 1 by the mid-seventeenth.[25] The mining economies of the New World, therefore, were less

[25] Earl J. Hamilton, *American treasure and the price revolution in Spain, 1501–1650* (Cambridge, Mass., 1934), 71.

remunerative to the producers than in earlier years; and while the economic life of both Peru and New Spain was being diversified in the seventeenth century by the development of local agriculture and industry, the transitional phase through which the economies of both viceroyalties were passing left them highly vulnerable to the kind of arbitrary fiscalism to which they found themselves subjected during the Olivares years.

In demanding large *donativos*, or in appropriating, as in Peru in 1629, one million *pesos* from the mercantile community, the crown was fatally undermining confidence, removing specie from circulation in regions where it was generally in short supply, and playing havoc with the credit system by which local and transatlantic transactions were conducted. In the circumstances, it is not surprising that merchants in the New World, finding their silver subject to appropriation by the crown either at home or on its arrival in Seville, showed a growing unwillingness to subject it to the hazards of the Atlantic crossing. As a result, the delicate mechanism of the *carrera de Indias*, the sea link between Spain and the New World, began to approach breakdown in the 1630s. If substantial sums were still arriving in Seville for the crown, private individuals were now holding back, and consequently there was less money available in Seville for investment in the next outgoing fleet. In 1640 – that fatal year for Spain itself as both Catalonia and Portugal rebelled against the government in Madrid – no treasure-fleet put in at Seville. The crown's excessive fiscal demands had brought the transatlantic system to the point of collapse.

During those middle decades of the century, from the 1630s to the 1650s, it seemed indeed as if the Spanish monarchy as a whole was on the verge of disintegration. The monarchy was so extended, its lines of communication so fragile, its limited resources under such intense pressure from the strain of a war being fought simultaneously on several fronts, that there was reason to fear that one part after another would break off, or succumb to enemy attack. Although, under Philip II, the international conflict had extended into the waters of the Atlantic, the New World of America had remained on the margin of the struggle. Under his grandson, however, European rivalries took on a global dimension, in which the Americas found themselves in the front line of attack. The English settlements in North America in the years following the Anglo-Spanish peace of 1604 had already shown that hopes of maintaining an Iberian monopoly of America were illusory; but it was the aggressiveness of the Dutch in the years following the expiry of the twelve-years' truce in 1621 which revealed the true scale of the problem of defence that now confronted Madrid.

In 1624 an expedition organized by the newly founded Dutch West India Company seized Bahia in Brazil. A joint Spanish–Portuguese expedition dislodged the Dutch in the following year, but it represented a major effort for the Spanish war machine, difficult to repeat at a time when resources were heavily committed in Europe. In 1630 the Dutch launched their second invasion of Brazil, and this time, although Olivares planned a counter-attack, it had to be postponed from one year to the next. During the 1630s, therefore, the Dutch were able to consolidate their hold over the sugar-producing regions of north-eastern Brazil, and the new armada, finally dispatched from Lisbon in 1638, accomplished nothing of note before dispersing after an inconclusive encounter with a Dutch fleet in Brazilian waters in January 1640.

The inability of the Spanish crown to save Pernambuco from the Dutch had major repercussions in the Iberian peninsula. The union of the Spanish and Portuguese crowns in 1580 had never been popular in Portugal, but one of the arguments in its favour was that it enabled the Portuguese to draw on all the resources of Spain for the defence of their own overseas dominions. This argument, already disproved in the East Indies in the earlier years of the century, was now disproved also for what had become Portugal's most lucrative overseas territory, Brazil. Simultaneously, Portuguese merchants, who had profited from the union of the crowns to move into Spanish America and especially into the viceroyalty of Peru, found themselves subject in the 1630s to mounting hostility and discrimination from Spaniards and creoles. By 1640, therefore, it was becoming obvious to the Portuguese mercantile community that the union of the crowns was no longer offering the advantages that had once made it relatively acceptable; and this in turn predisposed many of them to accept the *fait accompli* of 1 December 1640, when the duke of Braganza was declared king of an independent Portugal.

The secession of Portugal was another crippling blow to the *carrera de Indias*, undermining still further the confidence of Seville, and depriving it of investments from Lisbon which it could ill afford to lose. Moreover, at the same time as Brazil was being lost to the monarchy, it was also suffering further losses in the Caribbean. Here once again it was the Dutch who gave the lead. Dutch fleets in Caribbean waters in the later 1620s provided a cover behind which the English and French could move in to occupy the unpopulated or sparsely populated islands of the Lesser Antilles. In 1634 the Dutch established themselves permanently in Curaçao, and by the early 1640s – with Tortuga, Martinique and Guadalupe overrun by the French, with the English in Barbados, St Christopher and Antigua, and Dutch trading posts established in the islands off the Venezuelan coast – the Caribbean was becoming a European lake.

The Spaniards responded as best they could. The *armada de barlovento* at last went into operation in 1640, but was not as effective as its advocates had hoped, partly because it frequently had to be diverted to escort the transatlantic convoys. The colonists themselves succeeded in repulsing a number of attacks, and the mainland and the principal islands were successfully defended with the assistance of strengthened and reconstructed fortifications. But the capture of Jamaica by the English in 1655 was symptomatic of the major change that had occurred in the Caribbean during the previous half-century. Direct links between Spain and Jamaica had virtually ended twenty years earlier, in 1634. In effect, then, Spain was now concentrating its diminishing resources and abandoning remote outposts which it had become prohibitively expensive to maintain. This policy worked, in the sense that Spain emerged from its mid-century troubles with its 'empire of the Indies' still very largely intact. What had gone for all time, however, was its New World monopoly. This fact was tacitly recognized in the peace settlement of Münster in 1648 ending Spain's 80 years' war with the Dutch – a settlement which allowed the Dutch to remain in possession of such territories as they actually occupied, although forbidding them to trade with the Spanish Indies. In 1670 it was recognized on a more significant scale in the Anglo–Spanish treaty of Madrid, by which Spain effectively accepted the English argument that it was not prior discovery but genuine occupation and settlement which gave title of possession.

The relationship between Spain and the Indies, then, underwent a decisive change as a result of the international conflict of the 1620s to 1650s. Spain itself was disastrously weakened; the Caribbean was internationalized and turned into a base from which illicit trade could be conducted on a large scale with mainland America; and the colonial societies of the Indies found themselves thrown back on their own resources, not least in the area of military organization.

The task of defending the Indies from enemy attack had traditionally devolved upon the encomenderos, who were expected to take to arms if a hostile fleet were sighted. But, as the encomienda itself lost its institutional effectiveness, so the encomenderos ceased to constitute a satisfactory defence force, and by the seventeenth century the crown found it more advantageous to appropriate a proportion of the revenues of their encomiendas for the upkeep of paid men. Although professional soldiers were imported from Spain to serve in the viceregal guards and to man the coastal fortifications, the growing irregularity and inadequacy of these troop reinforcements meant that garrisons tended to be dangerously undermanned, and the colonists became aware that there was little hope of salvation unless they saved themselves. Urban militias and voluntary levies therefore played an increasingly important part in the defence of the Indies as the seventeenth century progressed. The viceroyalty of Peru, for instance, responded to Captain Morgan's attack on the isthmus of Panama in 1668–70 with a general mobilization. The failure of Olivares' scheme for a Union of Arms throughout the monarchy had driven the settler population of the Indies to develop the art of self-defence.

Militarily, then, as well as economically, the ties between the Indies and metropolitan Spain were at least temporarily loosened by the dramatic weakening of Spain itself during the middle decades of the century. Yet at the same time the Indies were being subjected to intensified fiscal pressures and to the whole top-heavy weight of Spanish bureaucratic control. This seventeenth-century combination of neglect with exploitation could not fail to have a profound influence on the development of the New World societies. It created opportunities for the local oligarchies, profiting from the crown's weakness, to consolidate still further their domination of life in their communities by acquiring through purchase, blackmail or encroachment extensive areas of land. If for New Spain, and, to a lesser extent, for Peru, the seventeenth century was the century of the formation of the *latifundia*, the great landed estate, this was not unrelated to the temporary weakening of royal control in the Indies. Nor, for that matter, was the development of what was to be another permanent phenomenon of life in Latin America, rural *caciquismo*. In the political and administrative context of the seventeenth century there were innumerable opportunities for the local magistrate to transform himself into the local boss.

Latifundismo and *caciquismo* were both to some extent the products of metropolitan neglect. A third long-term product of the age was the growth of *criollismo* – the sense of a separate creole identity – which reflected that other facet of seventeenth-century life in the Indies, metropolitan exploitation. Relations between creoles and new-comers from Spain, the so-called *gachupines*, had never run entirely smooth. There was resentment on one side, contempt on the other. The resentment came from those innumerable pinpricks which new arrivals from the homeland inevitably administer to colonials with ambivalent feelings about the mother country. It came, too, from the frustrations of a mercantile community chafing beneath the constraints of Seville's exercise of its monopoly. Most of all it came from the fact that so many of the offices, and almost all the best offices, in church and state, were reserved for Spaniards.

The religious orders in particular were bitterly divided by peninsular–creole rivalries. It was in order to dampen these rivalries that the system of the *alternativa* came increasingly to be adopted in the seventeenth century. Under this system the provincial government of the religious orders alternated between native-born Spaniards and creoles. But the alternativa itself could be a cause of bitterness, as it was among the Peruvian Franciscans in the 1660s when the Spaniards, now heavily outnumbered by the creoles, secured a papal decree imposing the system in a bid to safeguard their own position. The truth was that each new creole generation felt itself one step further removed from metropolitan Spain, and therefore increasingly reluctant to accept the kind of tutelage implicit in the relationship between the mother country and its colonies.

But the ties of kinship, interest and culture linking the metropolis to the settlers of the Indies were all-pervasive and not easily broken. The developing urban culture of the Indies was, and remained, heavily dependent on that of Spain. Although Mexico City acquired a printing press in 1535, and other presses were established in the sixteenth and seventeenth centuries in Lima, La Paz, Puebla and Guatemala, most of the local production was reserved for books used for the evangelization of the Indians. For their culture the settlers depended on the printing presses of Spain; and it is an indication of the closeness of the ties and the remarkable speed of transmission to even the most distant outposts of the monarchy that in 1607, three years after the publication of the first part of *Don Quixote*, the knight of La Mancha and his squire made their first American appearance in a *fiesta* held at Pausa in Peru.[26]

While Spanish books and plays kept the settlers in touch with the latest intellectual trends in Madrid, the Dominican and Jesuit colleges that sprang up through the New World provided a traditional Hispanic education. In 1538 the Dominican college of Santo Domingo was raised to the status of a university, modelled on that of Alcalá de Henares. Mexico City and Lima acquired their own universities in 1551. Their statutes, privileges and curricula were borrowed from Salamanca, as Francisco Cervantes de Salazar, professor of rhetoric in Mexico, proudly pointed out in an imaginary dialogue of 1554 in which a visitor was shown the principal sights of the city.[27] The metropolitan-style scholastic education which the sons and grandsons of the first *conquistadores* and encomenderos received in their native universities was at once a symbol of social standing and an indication of their participation in a wider cultural tradition which knew no Atlantic frontier.

Yet, even as Hispanic culture sought to reproduce itself overseas, it was subjected to subtle changes. These occurred first in the vocabulary of the settlers, which soon included words of Indian origin – *cacique*, *canoa*, *chocolate*. New kinds of sensibility struggled to express themselves through traditional artistic and literary forms; and there was a growing sense of territorial attachment among the Spaniards of the Indies to their own New World – an attachment which began to find literary expression in works like the *Grandeza Mexicana*, the long poem of Bernardo de Balbuena, published in 1604.

During the seventeenth century the indications multiply that the creoles had embarked on the long search to establish their own identity. The growing popularity of the cult of the Virgin of Guadalupe in New Spain, for example, was a means of proclaiming that Mexico was a distinct and separate entity, without yet going so far as to break the links of loyalty to the crown and the Spanish homeland. If any one symbol can be found to illustrate the new-found sense of a distinctive historical community in New Spain it is the triumphal arch erected in Mexico City in 1680 for the entry of the new viceroy, the marquis of La Laguna. For the first time on a triumphal arch of this kind the gods and emperors of the Aztecs were displayed. Once the pre-Hispanic past

---

[26] See F. Rodríguez Marín, *Estudios Cervantinos* (Madrid, 1947), 573–96.
[27] *México en 1554 y Túmulo Imperial*, ed. Edmundo O'Gorman (Mexico City, 1963), 22 (diálogo primero).

could be used by descendants of the *conquistadores* as a means of self-identification before a metropolitan Spaniard, it is clear that at least one part of colonial society had crossed a major psychological divide.

By 1700, therefore, when the Habsburg dynasty which had ruled Spain and the Indies for the best part of two centuries was finally extinguished, the Bourbons found themselves entrusted with a legacy which did not lend itself to easy management. During the sixteenth century the crown, for all its failures, had succeeded in keeping a surprisingly tight control over the new, post-conquest society that was developing in the Indies. As in metropolitan Spain itself, however, by the end of the reign of Philip II the strains were beginning to tell. The crown's financial necessities, brought about by its heavy expenditures in the pursuit of an immensely ambitious foreign policy, were everywhere forcing it into compromises with local communities and privileged social groups. The Indies were no exception. Here, as in Castile or Andalusia, offices were put up for sale, tacit bargains struck with local elites, and the state, even if still intrusive, was visibly in retreat.

During the seventeenth century the crisis in metropolitan Spain deepened; and if this entailed fresh attempts at a crude exploitation of the Indies for the benefit of the metropolis, it also meant expanded opportunities for the increasingly confident and assertive oligarchies of America to turn to their own advantage the desperate needs of the state. The constraints within which those oligarchies operated remained the same as they had been in the sixteenth century. Everything still had to be officially resolved by reference to Madrid. But within those constraints there was a growing latitude for independent manoeuvre. A swollen bureaucracy in the Indies afforded endless opportunities for bending the rules to suit local needs; a remote and bankrupt crown could generally be bought off when it interfered too officiously in the details of the relationship that was developing between the settler elite and the Indian population. In the Indies, just as in the other parts of Spain's global monarchy, the seventeenth century was pre-eminently the age of aristocracy.

The system which the eighteenth-century Bourbons found established in Spain's American possessions was, then, a system which might best be described as self-rule at the king's command. The oligarchies of the Indies had achieved a kind of autonomy within the wider framework of a centralized government run from Madrid. It was a system which fell far short of the aspirations of Charles V and Philip II, but one which also left the Indies still heavily dependent on the Spanish crown. Reflecting a tacit balance between metropolis and the settler communities, it provided stability rather than movement; and its principal victims, inevitably, were the Indians themselves. It enabled Spanish America to survive the calamities of the seventeenth century and even moderately to prosper; and, in spite of foreign depredations, Spain's American empire was still largely intact when the century drew to a close. It remained to be seen whether so comfortably flexible a system could survive a new kind of rigour – the rigour of eighteenth-century reform.

3

BOURBON SPAIN AND ITS AMERICAN EMPIRE

If the decadence of Spain was to provide students of politics from Montesquieu to Macaulay with manifold occasion for the display of liberal irony, the practical consequences of that decline still haunted the Bourbon statesmen who laboured to rebuild the ramshackle patrimony bequeathed by the last Habsburgs. As to the sheer prostration of the country at the end of the seventeenth century, there can be little doubt. The reign of Charles II, *el hechizado* (1664–1700), proved an unmitigated disaster, a bleak chronicle of military defeat, royal bankruptcy, intellectual regression and widespread famine. By 1700 the very population had fallen by at least a million below its level under Philip II. About the only qualification to this image of pervasive decay offered by recent research is that the nadir of the crisis occurred during the 1680s. It was during that decade, when a series of bad harvests brought famine to Castile, that the first steps were taken to resolve the financial problems of the monarchy, through the partial repudiation of the heavy burden of debt inherited from previous reigns. At the same time the progressive inflation caused by repeated debasement of the currency was halted by a return to gold and silver as the standard of value. Then again, there is evidence to suggest that Catalonia and Valencia exhibited signs of economic revival well before the advent of the new dynasty. None of which, however, should in any way obscure the fact that Spain had lost her industries and was reduced to exporting agricultural produce in return for foreign manufactures. In colonial trade, Cadiz acted as a mere entrepot for the exchange of American bullion for European merchandise.

No matter how desperate the condition of the economy might appear, it was the enfeeblement of the crown which threatened the survival of the country. Defeated by France in the struggle for mastery in Europe, the Habsburg state then fell prey to internal foes. With the accession of Charles II, a near imbecile, the territorial aristocracy extended their seigneurial jurisdiction over entire districts and towns, and dominated the central councils of the monarchy. The famous *tercios*, once the finest troops in Europe, declined into local militia raised and commanded by the nobility. Then again, the talented elite of lawyers, on whom the Catholic kings and immediate successors relied to manage the kingdom, had degenerated into a mere *noblesse de robe* recruited from six *colegiales mayores*. The Estate Assemblies of the kingdom of Aragon had successfully resisted the imposition of taxes on the scale that had proved so ruinous for Castile. Throughout the peninsula both tax-collection and the supply of arms and victuals to the army were farmed out to private contractors, prominent among whom were several foreign merchants. In short, whereas elsewhere in continental Europe dynastic absolutism had come to base its newfound power on a standing army and a fiscal commissariat, in Spain the monarchy had suffered a progressive loss in authority.

The eventual price of an enfeebled crown was civil war, foreign invasion and partition of the dynastic patrimony. For the long-awaited death of Charles II in 1700 precipitated a general European war in which the succession to the Spanish throne figured as the chief prize. The court's choice of Philip of Anjou, grandson of Louis XIV, enjoyed widespread support in Castile, where his French troops were welcomed. But the Habsburg contender, Archduke Charles of Austria, was backed by Great Britain, Holland, Portugal, the provinces of Catalonia and Valencia and a considerable part of the Castilian aristocracy who feared that the new dynasty would strip them of their power. In the ensuing civil conflict the peninsula served as a battlefield, with Madrid taken and re-taken by the opposing forces before French troops ensured the final Bourbon victory.

The relatively passive role played by Spain in the war which decided its fate became fully apparent at the Peace Treaty signed in 1713 at Utrecht. For, in compensation for his renunciation of the Spanish throne, the Austrian emperor received the Low Countries, Milan, Sardinia and Naples. The king of Savoy was awarded Sicily. Worse yet, Great Britain retained Gibraltar and Minorca, and obtained the *asiento* for a period of 30 years. Under this clause Britain enjoyed a monopoly right to introduce African slaves throughout the Spanish empire and, in addition, secured the right to despatch an annual ship with 500 tons of merchandise to trade with Spain's colonies in the New World. Finally, Sacramento, a settlement on the east bank of the Río de la Plata, ideally located for contraband, was ceded to Portugal, Britain's faithful ally. If the treaty stripped Spain of its European possessions which had embroiled the monarchy in constant warfare, the breach in its monopoly of colonial trade was to prove a potent source of future conflict.

The accession of Philip V under challenge of civil war and foreign invasion enabled his French advisors to lay the foundations of an absolutist state with remarkable rapidity. The uprisings in Catalonia and Valencia allowed the revocation of their privileges. Henceforth, with the exception of Navarre and the Basque provinces, all Spain was subject to much the same range of taxes and laws. Equally important, Philip followed the example of his grandfather and excluded the aristocracy from the high councils of state. Although the grandees were eventually confirmed in possession of their lands and private jurisdiction, they no longer influenced the direction of crown policy. Similarly, the creation of Secretariats of State reduced the traditional *Consejos* to advisory and judicial functions. Then again, as early as 1704 the old system of *tercios* armed with pikes was replaced by French-style regiments equipped with muskets and bayonets. A corps of royal guards for service in Madrid, separate units of artillery and engineers, together with the formation of a class of career officers – all these reforms marked the beginnings of a new army. To finance this force, fiscal experts drafted in from abroad succeeded in doubling revenue from a mere five million pesos to $11\frac{1}{2}$ million by 1711, a feat largely accomplished by close scrutiny of accounts, a reduction in official places, a repudiation of previous debts, and the incorporation of the kingdom of Aragon into a common fiscal system. With the arrival in 1714 of Elizabeth Farnese of Parma as Philip's second wife, the pace of reform noticeably slackened. Moreover, Elizabeth squandered the hard won resources of the new monarchy in mere dynastic adventures conquering Italian fiefdoms for her two sons. As a result of the Family Pacts with the French Bourbons, signed in 1733 and 1743, the Peace of Utrecht was partially overturned. The price paid by Spain in these wars has yet to be assessed. As late as 1737 the English ambassador, Sir Benjamin Keene, described the country as 'destitute of foreign friends and alliances, deranged in its finances, whose army is in a bad condition, its navy in a worse, if possible, and without any minister of heat.'[1] The accession of Ferdinand VI (1746–59) marked the abandonment of dynastic ambition in favour of a policy of peace abroad and retrenchment at home. The termination of the British *asiento* in 1748 followed by a Treaty of Limits with Portugal (1750), which fixed the frontiers of the viceroyalties of Peru and Brazil, removed potential sources of international friction. However, it was only with the advent of Charles III (1759–88) that Spain at last acquired a monarch actively committed to an entire programme of reform. Although Charles III's renewal of the Family Pact in 1761 brought defeat to Spain in the last stages of the Seven Years War, the rest of his reign was marked by a remarkable increase in prosperity both in the peninsula and the colonies, and for a brief period Spain once more figured as a European power.

If the ambitions and personalities of the Bourbon monarchs undoubtedly influenced the direction of policy, nevertheless, it was the ministerial elite who introduced what amounted to an administrative revolution. Indeed, it remains an open question as to whether the history of these years should be written in terms of kings or of ministers. In particular, the record of José de Patiño (1727–36) and the marquis de la Ensenada (1743–54) as Secretaries of State, has yet to be clearly assessed. The count of Floridablanca (1776–92) and the other ministers of Charles III, built upon the work of these men. As yet we lack any rounded characterization of this administrative elite. Although some aristocrats still attained high office – the count of Aranda is an example – the majority of ministers were impoverished gentry or commoners. It is striking that in the reign of Charles III most ministers appointed after 1766 were *manteistas*, lawyers who had failed to enter the socially prestigious *colegios mayores* at Valladolid, Salamanca and Alcalá. In contrast with contemporary England, or with Habsburg Spain, the Bourbons relied on a service nobility, bestowing titles on its trusted servants, both as reward and to strengthen their authority.

Although it is customary to view the Spanish *Ilustración* as part of the European Enlightenment, it must be remembered that most of its leading figures were public servants, actively engaged in the governance of their country. Small wonder that Jean Sarrailh defined its approach

---

[1] Quoted in Jean O. Maclachlan, *Trade and peace with old Spain, 1667–1750* (Cambridge, 1940), 101.

as '*dirigiste et utilitaire*'. Haunted by the past glory and recent decline of Spain, distressed by the glaring contrast between the growing prosperity and power of France and England and the weakness and impoverishment of the peninsula, alarmed by the inertia of Spanish society – these men all looked to the crown for remedy. The absolutist state was the essential instrument of reform. As a result provincial interests or corporate privileges were regarded with deep suspicion. Whereas under the Habsburgs, Mariana could debate the justice of tyrannicide and Suárez insist on the contractual basis of government, in the Age of Enlightenment their works were banned as subversive. By contrast, the theory of the Divine Right of Kings became virtual orthodoxy in official circles. In short, the servants of enlightened despotism did not forget the source of their power.

If, with the new emphasis on royal authority, the aristocracy were simply excluded from the councils of state, by contrast the church came under severe attack. The regalist tradition in canon law, with its insistence on the rights of the national church against the claims of the papal monarchy, and its assertion of the ecclesiastical role of the king as vicar of Christ, won a signal victory at the concordat of 1753 in which the papacy ceded to the crown the right of appointment to all clerical benefices in Spain. Equally important, the Erasmian tradition, once so influential, flowered anew among the party in the church known as Jansenists. In 1767 the Jesuit Order, the chief bastion of the Counter-Reformation and the sworn defenders of the papacy, were expelled from Spanish dominions. In general, the religious orders were seen as more of a burden on society than as spiritual fortresses. Behind this entire approach was to be found the influence of France, an uneasy blend of seventeenth-century Gallicanism and Jansenism.

The main concern of the administrative elite, however, was the great problem of economic progress. How was Spain to recover its former prosperity? A favourite answer lay in the promotion of science and useful knowledge. The government launched a national census which compiled a vast array of statistics dealing with all aspects of economic life. More to the point, canals and highways were constructed to open up new routes for trade. And, just as in the seventeenth century France and England, confronted by the commercial hegemony of Holland, had brought in protective measures to defend and encourage their shipping, industry and trade, now the ministers of the Bourbon dynasty in Spain consciously attempted to apply much the same set of policies to liberate the peninsula from its dependence on the manufactures of northern Europe.

The starting point for any interpretation of eighteenth-century Spanish mercantilism is *Theórica y práctica de comercio y de marina*, a lengthy tract first circulated in 1724 and then published with official sanction in 1742 and again in 1757. Its author, Jerónimo de Ustariz, a ministerial protégé of Patiño, accepted 'the decadence and annihilation of this monarchy' quite simply as 'a punishment for our negligence and blindness in the organization of trade'. It was ill-considered tariffs and excise duties which had destroyed domestic industry and rendered the peninsula dependent on manufactures imported from abroad. Remedy could only come from a close study and application of 'the new maxim of State', or, as he elsewhere put it, '*la nueva política*' of France, England and Holland, countries whose trade had increased at the expense of Spain. Although obviously conversant with the *arbitristas*, the Spanish advocates of reform in the previous century, Ustariz sought practical guidance in Huet's *Commerce d'Hollande* (he had secured a Spanish translation), the French tariffs of 1664–7, and the English Navigation Laws. In particular, he praised Colbert as 'the most zealous and skilful minister concerned with the advance of trade and shipping that Europe has ever known'. His actual recommendations were simple: he insisted that tariff rates must always distinguish between primary produce and elaborated goods; that imported merchandise should always pay higher duties than exports of native manufactures; and that where possible internal excise should be eliminated. The premise behind these recommendations was that wise regulation of tariffs would release the productive energy of Spanish industry. More positively, he advocated an active procurement policy in respect of equipment, munitions and uniforms for the armed forces, so that all these supplies should come from Spanish workshops and foundries. The main goal here was the creation of a strong navy, its ships built, armed and outfitted in royal arsenals. Thus, if 'the establishment of manufactures in Spain (is) the chief measure on which the restoration of the monarchy is to be based', an essential prerequisite was an expansion in the armed might of the crown.[2]

---

[2] Gerónimo de Ustariz, *Theórica y práctica de comercio y de marina* (3rd edn, Madrid, 1757); quotations taken from pages 4, 46, 96, 238.

The failure of government either to change the methods of agricultural production or to develop manufacturing industry has become the subject of lively debate. The great achievement of the new dynasty was, however, the creation of a bureaucratic, absolutist state, dedicated to the principle of territorial aggrandizement. The revival in the authority and resources of the monarchy clearly preceded the awakening of the economy. Indeed, there are grounds to suggest that much of the economic renewal, at least in its first stage, derived from the necessities of the armed forces and the court. The furnishing of uniforms and munitions for the army, the construction of warships in naval arsenals, the reliance on domestic iron foundries for canon, the provision of luxury textiles and tapestries for the court, and the sheer concentration of consumption in Madrid attendant on the increase in revenue – the most summary catalogue attests to the all-pervasive impact of government expenditure. As yet, however, little is known about the administrative revolution which lay behind the new-found vitality of the state. But if colonial practice be any guide, the chief innovation lay in the reliance on career officials, both military and civilian, subject to regular appraisal and promotion, who lived off fixed salaries instead of gratuities or the fees of office.

At the head of the new regime stood the ministries, the Secretariats of State, Exchequer, Justice, War, Navy and the Indies, which replaced the old Habsburg councils as the chief source of executive action. In the first years several of these offices were grouped together under one powerful minister, so that it is not clear when each secretariat acquired a permanent body of officials. At the provincial level the intendant was the key figure, the symbol of the new order. Employed at the start for specific tasks, it was only in 1749 that these officials were appointed throughout Spain, charged with responsibility for the collection of taxes, the commissariat of the army, the promotion of public works and the general encouragement of the economy. In its reliance on a salaried fiscal bureaucracy the Spanish monarchy in certain measure advanced well beyond the practice of contemporary France where sale of office and tax farmers continued to dominate the financial system until the Revolution. The new type of official certainly proved his worth, since public revenue rose steadily from a mere five million pesos in 1700 to about 18 million in the 1750s, only then to climb to an average 36 million pesos in the years 1785–90. It is in these figures that we find the secret of Spain's political revival.

As in any dynastic state the first call on the budget was the royal family and the court. If estimates as to the construction cost of the three new palaces at Madrid, Aranjuez and La Granja are not available, in 1787 the overall expenditure of the 'royal house' came to five million pesos, a sum equal to 15 per cent of all revenue. By contrast, the much vaunted programme of public works obtained only one-and-a-quarter million pesos. The major item in the budget was the armed forces, which absorbed some 60 per cent of all public revenue, a figure which, if war expenses were included, would undoubtedly rise yet further.

Although the formation, expansion and maintenance of a standing army and a permanent navy were objects of prime concern for the Bourbon state, remarkably little information is as yet available about the organization and operation of these forces. By all accounts it was José de Patiño, first as intendant at Cadiz and later as secretary of state, who was chiefly responsible for the building of warships in royal arsenals. Then, the War of Jenkins' Ear (1739–48) drove the marquis de la Ensenada to extend the programme, so that in the years 1741–61 Spain launched no less than 54 ships of the line, armed with 3,688 cannon. By the close of the reign of Charles III, the navy boasted a fleet of 66 ships of the line supported by the usual assortment of frigates and packet boats.

If the concentration on naval power sprang from the strategic necessities of empire, the scale of the land forces reflected the overseas ambitions of the dynasty. By 1761 the regular army numbered nearly 60,000 men, divided into 50,445 infantry, 5,244 cavalry, 1,329 artillery-men and 2,758 troops stationed in the North African garrisons. Recruitment was by levy, a system which avoided the reliance on foreign mercenaries found in other armies of the day. Moreover, at least a third of the officers were commoners, in many cases promoted from the ranks, so that only the regiments of royal guards had much pretence to social prestige. Nevertheless, it was the formation of this officer corps, men of some education, accustomed to discipline and dependent on royal service for their livelihood, which provided the dynastic state with indispensable agents of government. Foreign travellers commented that the highest provincial authority was vested in the captains general, the commanders of the regional brigades, to whom intendants and other civilian magistrates were subject.

If Frederick the Great of Prussia once assessed Spain as a European power of the second rank, comparable with Austria and Prussia, in part it was because the Italian wars of Philip V had demonstrated that the armed might of the monarchy was sufficiently restored to allow it to carry forward the territorial aggrandizement which that enlightened king defined as the guiding principle of the absolutist state. Stripped of its European possessions by the Treaty of Utrecht, Spain, however, now depended on its vast American empire to ensure it a place in the Concert of Europe. In the New World the Bourbon state proved remarkably successful both in safeguarding its frontiers and in the exploitation of colonial resources. The revival of Spanish power during the reign of Charles III in large measure derived from the efflorescence in trade with the Indies, and from the increased revenue which it yielded.

THE REVOLUTION IN GOVERNMENT

Although both Alberoni and Patiño are credited with the view that the key to Spain's revival was to be found in the New World, the Italian adventures of Elizabeth Farnese prevented these statesmen from effecting much change in the American empire. Similarly, if José del Campillo y Cossío, Secretary of the Treasury, Navy and Indies (1741–3), drew up a comprehensive programme of reform designed to overhaul the entire system of imperial trade and government, his term of office was dominated by the demands of war in both Europe and the Indies. Only in 1754, with the appointment of Julián de Arriaga as Secretary of the Navy and Indies, was the empire at last governed by a minister with American experience (he had served as Governor of Caracas) who had few other administrative tasks to distract his attention. Until then all the emphasis in ministerial circles had been on Europe: the creation of a new system of government and the provisioning of the Italian wars had absorbed virtually all the energy of the administrative elite.

Yet this preoccupation with the Old World had led to a remarkable erosion of imperial power in America. Indeed, during the first decades of the eighteenth century Spain did little more than rebuff foreign incursions into its territory and consolidate its possession over threatened frontiers. To understand the magnitude of the task it is necessary to return to the bleak years of the 1680s. For it was in that decade that the Portuguese established the colony of Sacramento on the estuary of La Plata and the French pushed southwards from Canada to found New Orleans. At much the same time English and French buccaneers burnt

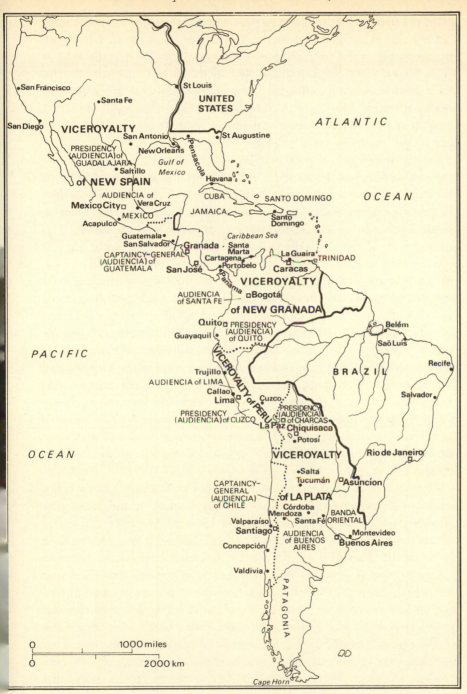

Spanish America *c.* 1790

and ravaged their way across the isthmus to raid the shores of the Pacific. Panama City, Cartagena, Veracruz and Guayaquil were all eventually captured and sacked by these freebooters. In New Mexico the Pueblo Indians rose in rebellion and expelled both settlers and missionaries from a province under effective occupation for almost a century. So weak had Spain become that during the War of Succession it was necessary to beg the protection of French warships to escort the treasure fleet home from Veracruz.

Equally important, in each province of the empire, government had come to be dominated by a small colonial establishment, composed of the creole elite – lawyers, great landlords and churchmen – a few long-serving officials from the peninsula and the great import merchants. At all levels of the administration sale of office was prevalent. The management of the mint, the collection of *alcabalas* (the excise duties) and the very maintenance of the *alcaldes mayores* and *corregidores* (the district magistrates) were all farmed out to merchants of the viceregal and provincial capitals who controlled the import trade and the issue of credit. It was the clergy, both secular and religious, rather than the formal delegates of the crown, who exercised true authority within society, acting as the intellectual and spiritual leaders of the elite and as the counsellors and guardians of the masses. As in the last decades of Habsburg rule in Spain, the crown's power to tap the resources of society was limited by the absence of effective military sanctions. If the new dynasty was to profit from its vast overseas possessions, it had first to recapture control over colonial administration and then to create new institutions of government. Only then could it introduce the economic reforms.

The catalyst of change was war with Great Britain. Spain's tardy entrance into the Seven Years War (1756–63) brought immediate defeat with the British capture of Manila and Havana. Moreover, if at the subsequent peace treaty, these ports were returned, Spain had to cede Florida to Britain and once more hand back Colônia do Sacramento to Portugal. The acquisition of Louisiana from France was but poor compensation for the loss of that ally's support on the mainland. It was at this point that the ministers of Charles turned to the reform programme elaborated in Campillo y Cossío's *Nuevo sistema de gobierno económico para la América* (1743), a manuscript in circulation since 1743 and published in 1762 as the second part of Bernardo Ward's *Proyecto económico*. There they found advocacy for a return to the Habsburg practice of a general visitation, to be followed by the introduction of permanent intendancies. The text also contained warnings about the excessive power and wealth of the church. If his proposals in the political sphere often consisted of the application in America of reforms already introduced in Spain, their implementation proved more drastic in its effects. For the administrative revolution in the empire was inaugurated by soldiers and officials despatched from the peninsula. Small wonder that it has been called the Reconquest of the Americas.

The first step in this programme was the provision of adequate military force, as a safeguard both against foreign attack and internal uprisings. The fall of Havana and Manila in 1761 and the virtual elimination of French power from the mainland signalized the magnitude of the threat from abroad. Once peace was declared, Alejandro O'Reilly, Spain's leading general, was despatched to Cuba to inspect the defences and to organize a local militia. The following year, an inspector-general, Juan de Villalba, arrived in New Spain, at the head of two regiments sent from Europe, charged with a similar task of raising a reserve army of militia. In 1768 a regiment of regular troops was stationed for permanent duty at Caracas. As a result of this activity, an official report of 1771 estimated there were 42,995 soldiers of different categories stationed across Spanish America, with 4,851 men in Cuba, 2,884 in Puerto Rico and 4,628 at Buenos Aires. Not all provinces were so blessed. In New Granada the *comunero* rebellion in 1781 surprised the viceregal authorities with only 75 regular soldiers outside the port garrison at Cartagena. Then again, it was only after the Tupac Amaru rebellion in Peru (1780–1) that the crown sent out two regiments for duty in that viceroyalty. Here is no place to describe the history of the colonial army. Suffice it to say that, by the close of the century, local recruitment and transfers meant that the overwhelming majority of the men in the ranks were native Americans and that a good proportion of the officers, from captain down, were creoles. Numbers depended on local resources. If New Spain eventually boasted an army of 9,971 men, divided into four regiments of infantry and two of dragoons, by contrast Peru managed with a force of 1,985 and Chile had but 1,249 men mainly engaged on frontier duties. It was the circle of fortresses in the Caribbean which still required soldiers from Europe, with the insalubrious port of Cartagena maintaining a garrison of 2,759.

This emphasis on military strength yielded considerable returns. In

1776 an expedition of 8,500 men crossed the Río de la Plata, took Sacramento for the third and last time, and expelled the Portuguese from the entire east bank province, a victory ratified at the Treaty of San Ildefonso (1778). Soon after, in the War of American Independence (1779–83), another force invaded Pensacola, the coastal strip adjoining Louisiana, an initiative which led to the subsequent British cession of that territory, together with Florida. Similarly, in Central America the fortress of Omoa was recaptured and the British settlements along the Mosquito coast finally eliminated. At much the same period expeditions were mounted in New Spain to ensure effective possession of the northern provinces of Sonora, Texas and California. In this drive to secure the frontiers of its American empire, the Bourbon monarchy at last displayed the expansive enterprise of a true imperial power.

Alongside the recruitment of colonial regiments maintained on a permanent footing went the organization of numerous militia units. Admittedly, at times these forces had more reality on paper than on the parade ground, but, despite criticism and occasional disbandment, they eventually proved their worth. For if the 50,000 men allegedly enrolled in the Peruvian reserve army were rarely to be found in uniform, by contrast the 22,277 troops raised in New Spain were reasonably well-armed and disciplined. Elsewhere in Buenos Aires it was the militia which successfully repelled the British invasions of 1806–7. Equally important, the distribution of military titles and legal privileges was viewed as a decisive means of arousing the loyalty of the creole elite. Indeed, a traveller observed of the upper classes in Venezuela: 'At present they seek an epaulette with as much avidity as they did formerly the tonsure.'[3] Moreover, the existence of the militia provided the colonial state with armed sanctions against popular unrest.

The monarchy asserted its power over the church in dramatic fashion when in 1767 Charles III followed the example of Portugal and decreed the expulsion of all Jesuits from his dominions. It was, of course, a measure which warned the church as to the necessity of absolute obedience. For the Jesuits were notorious for their independence of episcopal authority, their intransigence over the payment of ecclesiastical tithes, their devotion to the papacy, their extraordinary wealth and their skill in litigation with the royal bureaucracy. In Paraguay they had established a virtual state within a state, governing over 96,000 Guaraní

[3] F. Depons, *Travels in South America during the years 1801–1804*, 2 vols. (London, 1807), I, 361.

Indians protected by their own armed militia. Elsewhere, in Sonora and the Amazonian provinces of Quito, the order operated a series of mission stations. Equally important, in all the principal towns of the empire, Jesuit colleges educated the creole elite. Moreover, unlike other religious orders, they preserved relative harmony between their American and European members. All in all, the Jesuits exercised formidable influence in colonial society, an influence supported by the wealth which accrued from the efficient management of entire chains of haciendas located in every major province. When Charles III listened to his Jansenist ministers and decreed the expulsion, the loyalty of his colonial subjects was strained to the utmost, as there sailed for Italian exile over a thousand American Jesuits, the very flower of the creole elite.[4] Thereafter, in 1771, Provincial Church Councils were summoned in Lima and Mexico with the aim both of tightening clerical discipline and of emphasizing royal authority over the church. But although any number of reforms were projected, little came of this regalist activity. The religious were subjected to a general inspection. Convents of nuns were exhorted to introduce communal dining. The jurisdiction of ecclesiastical courts over probate of intestate property was terminated. Legal appeals from church courts were admitted by the audiencias with growing frequency. More important, in criminal cases, the very principle of clerical immunity from all royal jurisdiction was challenged, and a handful of priests were actually imprisoned. Then again, an attempt was made to regulate the collection of tithes. By and large, however, although these measures certainly embittered the priesthood, they achieved remarkably little in the way of real change.

More far reaching and effective was the radical reform in civil administration. In 1776 a new viceroyalty was established with its capital at Buenos Aires, covering the vast area now occupied by Argentina, Uruguay, Paraguay and Bolivia. The result was a dramatic shift in the geo-political balance of the continent. For, with its commercial monopoly already broken by the opening of the trade route via Cape Horn, Lima, the former capital of the entire empire in South America, suffered a severe loss in status. The inclusion of Upper Peru in the new viceroyalty, designed to provide Buenos Aires with the fiscal

---

[4] For a discussion of the expulsion of the Jesuits from Brazil, see Mansuy-Diniz Silva, *CHLA*, I, ch. 13, and Alden, *CHLA*, II, ch. 15.

profits of Potosí, prepared the way for the permanent political division of the Andean zone. Elsewhere, the changes were less radical in their impact. The viceroyalty of New Granada, created in 1739 to ensure the defence of Cartagena and the coast, was further buttressed by the introduction of a captain-general at Caracas, assisted by an intendant, who was responsible for the government of the Venezuelan districts. Finally, in the north of New Spain, a comandant-general was appointed to superintend the defences and administration of the entire frontier region, his freedom of action, however, limited by continued financial dependence on revenue remittances from the central Mexican treasury.

Charles III, adopting Campillo's proposal, also revived the ancient Habsburg remedy for colonial misrule, the *visita general*. Moreover, so successful was José de Gálvez as visitor general to New Spain (1765–71) that first Peru (1776) and then New Granada (1778) were subjected to a similar review of the machinery of government. Through the establishment of the tobacco monopoly and a reorganization of alcabala collection, Gálvez secured an immediate increase in revenue remittances for Madrid. Steps were also taken to raise silver production through tax exemptions and reductions in the costs of monopoly materials such as mercury and gunpowder. Gálvez superintended the expulsion of the Jesuits; brutally suppressed the popular uprisings against this measure; and then led an expedition to pacify and settle Sonora. The reward for this remarkable display of administrative energy was a seat on the Council of the Indies, followed by his life-long appointment as Secretary of the Indies (1776–87). It was Gálvez who was mainly responsible for the creation of the viceroyalty at Buenos Aires and the despatch of his protegé, Juan Antonio de Areche as visitor-general of Peru. Like his protector, the count of Floridablanca, this poor Malagueño lawyer was a *manteista*, whose services to the crown were rewarded with the title of marquis of Sonora. As imperious as he was ambitious, Gálvez drove through the revolution in colonial government with single-minded tenacity. Judged from the perspective of Madrid, the results were impressive. But the price was alienation of the creole elite. For Gálvez made no secret of his contempt for the abilities of American Spaniards. During his term of office he became renowned both for his implacable nepotism – his brother and nephew succeeded as viceroys of New Spain – and for his preference for peninsular Spaniards to the exclusion of creole candidates in all branches and levels of colonial government.

Small wonder that one high-placed critic could prophesy: 'Gálvez has destroyed more than he has built...his destructive hand is going to prepare the greatest revolution in the American Empire.'[5]

Nowhere was the impact of the new policies more evident than in the changing composition of the audiencias, the high courts of justice, whose judges counselled the viceroys on all important questions of state. For the reign of Philip V had been characterized by the perpetuation of all the worst abuses of the last Habsburg. In the years between 1687 and 1712 and again during the 1740s, places on the American audiencias were offered for sale to any qualified bidder. As a result, wealthy creole lawyers purchased judgeships on an unprecedented scale, so that by the 1760s the audiencias of Mexico, Lima and Santiago de Chile had a majority of American Spaniards, men related by descent or through marriage to the landowning elite of these capitals. It was during the 1740s that this policy reached a climax when of a total 66 judicial appointments, 39 places were sold, with some two-thirds of the 36 creoles obtaining office through purchase.[6] True, once Arriaga became minister a virtual ban on all further creole appointments was enforced, but it was left to Gálvez to reverse this unforeseen legacy of past abuse. In 1776–7, he moved decisively to enlarge the membership of most audiencias, and then, through a determined policy of transfer, promotion and retirement, to break the creole predominance. Of the 34 appointments made in these two years, only two went to American Spaniards. By the end of his term as Secretary of the Indies creoles comprised between a third and a quarter of the judges in American audiencias, a proportion which was maintained until 1810.

Along with this renewal of peninsular control, there went a revived insistence on promotion between and within audiencias, a system which had been interrupted by sale of office. Once again, it became the rule for judges to start as *alcaldes del crimen* or as *oidores* in lesser courts, such as Guadalajara or Santiago, and then to transfer to the viceregal courts of Lima or Mexico. In 1785–6 new audiencias were created at Caracas, Buenos Aires and Cuzco. The legal advisors of both intendants and viceroys were now also included within the scale of promotion. Equally important, Gálvez created a new judicial post of *regente* to replace the

---

[5] Quoted in D. A. Brading, *Miners and merchants in Bourbon Mexico, 1763–1810* (Cambridge, 1971), 39.

[6] Mark S. Burkholder and D. S. Chandler, *From impotence to authority: the Spanish crown and the American audiencias 1687–1808* (Colombia, Miss., 1977), 104–8, 157, 170, 196.

viceroys as presidents of the audiencias. The system was completed by the transfer of regents and some senior oidores to the Council of the Indies, which for the first time in its long history now came to include a large proportion of members with official experience in the American empire. Here, then, we observe the formation of a true judicial bureaucracy, its autonomy from colonial society based on recruitment in Spain.

The centre-piece of the revolution in government was the introduction of intendants, officials who embodied all the executive, interventionist ambitions of the Bourbon state. To assess the importance of this measure, it has to be remembered that in the sphere of local government the practice of the early Bourbons marked a deterioration rather than an improvement over the past. Since 1678 the district magistracies – alcaldes mayores and corregidores – had been up for sale in Madrid. Although these officials were still charged with the collection of Indian tributes, the new dynasty had curtailed their salaries, or, in the case of New Spain, made no further payment. In consequence, since the fruits of justice and other fees did not provide a subsistence, many magistrates engaged in trade, distributing merchandise and livestock on credit and issuing cash in advance for produce such as cochineal, indigo and cotton. Illegal in the first instance, in 1751 these *repartimientos de comercio* were finally recognized by the crown on condition that the viceregal authorities compile a tariff of prices and values of goods for distribution. In operation for the most part in zones of Indian settlement, where magistrates often enjoyed a virtual monopoly in trade, the repartimientos often provoked great popular unrest. For most corregidores had but five years in which to recoup the cost of their office and repay the great import houses of Lima and Mexico who supplied them with cash and merchandise. In effect, therefore, the judicial authority of the crown was both purchased and employed for the safeguard and furtherance of mercantile profit.

Once more, it was José de Gálvez who was responsible for radical improvement in this ill-conceived system of government. In 1768, with the collaboration of Viceroy Croix of New Spain, he presented proposals for the outright abolition of both alcaldes mayores and repartimientos and their replacement by intendants. The district magistrates, so he argued, both oppressed the Indians and defrauded the crown of tribute monies. The premise behind his paper, elaborated in subsequent debate, was that if the Indians were liberated from the coercive monopoly of the alcaldes mayores and corregidores, they would freely enter the market as producers and as labourers. His opponents, however, asserted that without repartimientos de comercio the Indians would retreat into a subsistence economy or simply renege on all obligations of credit. In any case, the overseas provinces of the empire were too backward to warrant the intervention of intendants, who would prove both costly and ineffective. Despite the introduction of one intendant in Cuba in 1763, it was not until Gálvez became Secretary of the Indies that any further progress was achieved. The floodtime of reform came in the 1780s, starting in 1782 with the appointment of eight intendants in the viceroyalty of La Plata, followed two years later by another eight in Peru and crowned by the establishment in 1786 of twelve intendancies in New Spain. Elsewhere, Central America was allotted five of these officials, Cuba three, Chile two and Caracas one, with New Granada and Quito left exempt.

Recruited from a combination of military men and fiscal officials, with the overwhelming majority peninsular Spaniards, the intendants met with but qualified success and in no sense fulfilled the expectations of the reformers. For the introduction of a range of provincial governors did not correct the deficiencies in local government. At the district level the alcaldes mayores and corregidores were replaced by subdelegates, who were expected to subsist on 5 per cent of tributes and the fruits of justice. As a result, these officials were either selected from the local elite or else were obliged to engage in trade, even if the great import houses no longer offered financial support. It was in the provincial capitals that the reform made its greatest impact. For here the intendants were at their most active, paving streets, building bridges and prisons and suppressing popular disorders. Assisted by a legal advisor and treasury officials, the intendant was living proof of the new executive vigour of the monarchy. Liberated from its former dependence on mercantile credit, colonial administration was immeasurably strengthened by the appointment of career bureaucrats, who by reason of their peninsula background, preserved their independence from the society they governed.

In the capitals of Lima, Buenos Aires and Mexico, Gálvez installed *superintendentes subdelegados de real hacienda*, officials who relieved the viceroys of all responsibility in exchequer matters. In addition, a central finance committee was set up to supervise the activity of the intendants and to review all questions arising from the collection of revenue. It should be emphasized that the appointment of superintendents was designed to reduce the powers of the viceroys, which Gálvez thought far too extensive. His idea was to establish a troika system, with regents heading the judiciary, superintendents the exchequer and intendants, and the viceroys retaining civil administration and the military. In the event, a series of disputes over questions of revenue led to the abolition of the office of superintendent in 1787 after the death of Gálvez. The prestige of the viceroys was too great to be so easily diminished. Moreover, the extraordinary expansion in all branches of government, when taken with the new reliance on the army, all served to augment the effective authority of the king's alter ego. That most viceroys after the accession of Ferdinand VI were career officers in the armed forces further illustrates the nature of the new colonial state.

If the intendants were less effective than anticipated, in part it was because the system of revenue had been largely reformed before their arrival. The key innovations were the appointment of a salaried fiscal bureaucracy and the establishment of new crown monopolies. Hitherto, the collection of excise duties, the *alcabalas*, had been farmed out (for an annual contracted sum) to the *consulados*, the merchant guilds and their provincial delegates. The treasuries, situated at ports or in mining camps, only administered the customs duties and the tithe levied on silver production. But in 1754 the alcabalas of Mexico City were entrusted to salaried officials and in 1776 the same system of direct administration was applied throughout the colony. Henceforth all the leading towns were blessed with a local director and accountant of excise, assisted by a band of guards. The same system was introduced into Peru during the *visita* of Areche and thereafter extended across the empire. The other great innovation occurred in 1768 with the creation of the tobacco monopoly in New Spain. The area of planting was severely restricted and all growers were obliged to sell their produce to the monopoly, which both manufactured the cigars in its factories and distributed them via a network of salesmen and their assistants in the chief towns. At its peak the tobacco monopoly in New Spain had a turnover of nearly eight million pesos, employed a workforce of over 17,000 and yielded net profits of nearly four million pesos. Moreover, if in other provinces of the empire receipts never attained such heights – in Peru the monopoly only sold tobacco – it certainly formed a major source of additional revenue. It was only, therefore, in the more rigorous scrutiny and collection of Indian tributes, where increase in returns easily exceeded any expansion in population, that the intendants and their subdelegates played any perceptible role.

In effect, the appointment of a salaried bureaucracy, supported by an extensive army of guards, enabled the Spanish monarchy to reap an extraordinary fiscal harvest from the expansion in economic activity effected by its reforms in commerce and its encouragement of colonial exports. Once more, it was New Spain which was pacemaker, with treasury receipts rising in the course of the century from three to 20 million pesos, the increase largely concentrated in the years 1765–82, when the gross budget leapt from six to $19\frac{1}{2}$ million pesos. It is significant that Indian tributes only contributed about a million pesos to this grand total, compared with the $4\frac{1}{2}$ million provided by the silver tithe, mint charges and mercury monopoly, and the four million profits accruing from the tobacco monopoly. In all, once fixed charges and monopoly costs had been deducted, there remained about 14 million pesos of which four million were retained for the maintenance of government and the military costs of the northern frontier. The remaining ten million pesos were shipped abroad, either to finance the fortresses and garrisons of the Caribbean, the Philippines and North America, or else remitted directly to Madrid. No other colony was as profitable to its metropolis as New Spain. By 1789 gross receipts in Peru amounted to no more than $4\frac{1}{2}$ million pesos, with the 1.2 million pesos supplied by the silver mining industry closely matched by the 920,000 pesos of Indian tributes. By contrast, in New Granada customs duties of 1.3 million were the largest item in a total budget of 4.7 million, with the tobacco monopoly accounting for 953,000 pesos and Indian tributes a derisory 166,000 pesos. Similarly, despite the still numerous Indian population of Upper Peru, the bulk of fiscal receipts in the viceroyalty of La Plata – a total $3\frac{1}{2}$ million – derived from the mining industry and customs duties. Clearly, in most areas of the empire, it was the export economy which yielded the highest returns to the crown.

In these estimates of revenue are to be found the true significance of the changes in colonial government. In effect, the administrative revolution created a new absolutist state, based, as in Europe, on a standing army and a professional bureaucracy. This state was dedicated, as much as its counterparts in the Old World, to the principle of territorial aggrandizement, albeit chiefly at the expense of the Portuguese

in South America and of roaming Indian tribes in North America. But
it differed from its European exemplars in that it failed to form any true
alliance, founded on common interest, with the leading sectors of
colonial society. The influence of the church, hitherto the chief bulwark
of the crown, was attacked. The economic power of the great import
houses was undermined. But if the standing armies provided armed
sanctions against popular unrest, the titles and provileges offered by the
militia were a poor substitute for any real share of profits or power.
In short, the price of reform was the alienation of the creole elite.
Nevertheless, judged from the perspective of Madrid, its rewards were
considerable. If, as we shall see, the economic revival of the peninsula
in no way matched the opportunities presented by growth in colonial
trade, the administrative revolution allowed the crown to reap a
remarkable fiscal profit. Once again, it is New Spain which offers the
best measure of change. Whereas in the years 1766–78 only 3.94 million
pesos of the total 11.93 million pesos legally exported from New Spain
were on the king's account, in the period 1779–91 no less than 8.3
million pesos of the total 17.2 million consisted of revenue remitted to
the Caribbean colonies or Madrid. By this time, up to 15 per cent of
the royal budget derived from the colonies, leaving to one side the
monies raised from customs duties at Cadiz. It is in these figures, rather
than in the dubious claims for peninsula industry and exports, that we
encounter the true basis of the revival of the monarchy. In the last resort,
the fiscal profit of empire and the commercial monopoly were more
important to the Spanish state than were the commercial returns to the
Spanish economy.

EXPANSION OF COLONIAL TRADE

The revival of the colonial economy, as much as that in the peninsula,
derived from the application of mercantilist policies. The authoritative
text here was Campillo's *Nuevo sistema de gobierno económico para la
América* (1743). For the starting point of his analysis was a direct
comparison of the high profits which accrued to Great Britain and
France from their Caribbean sugar islands with the derisory returns of
Spain's vast mainland empire. To remedy this sorry state of affairs he
advocated the introduction of *gobierno económico*, by which term he clearly
meant the doctrines and measures associated with Colbertian
mercantilism. In particular, he called for the termination of the Cadiz

commercial monopoly and the system of periodic fleets. In America land was to be distributed to the Indians and both silver mining and agriculture encouraged. Above all else, Campillo viewed the colonies as a great untapped market for Spanish industry: its population, especially the Indians, were the monarchy's treasure. But, to increase colonial demand for Spanish manufactures, it was necessary to incorporate the Indians into society by the removal of malign monopolies and to reform the prevailing system of government. It was also necessary to destroy colonial industry. Throughout his text, Campillo was at pains to assert the supremacy of public interest over private profit, a distinction embodied in the contrast he drew between 'political' trade and 'mercantile' trade.

If reform came but slowly it was because the War of Succession and the subsequent Peace of Utrecht threw open the empire to foreign shipping and contraband. In effect, throughout the first half of the eighteenth century, Spain was engaged in a desperate battle to regain control over colonial commerce. Contraband was rife. Yet the great import houses of Mexico and Lima still sought to restrict the flow of merchandise from the peninsula in order to safeguard their monopoly profits. If Spain was to benefit from its American possessions, it was thus necessary first to oust foreign manufactures and contraband from their dominant role in the Atlantic trade and then to dislodge the mercantile confederacy from its commanding position within the colonies.

At the outset the commercial performance of Spain was lamentable. In 1689 it was estimated that of 27,000 *toneladas* of merchandise legally despatched to Spanish America, only 1,500 originated in the peninsula. The bulk of exports from Cadiz consisted of manufactured goods shipped in from France, England and Holland. Even the fiscal yield from customs duties was undercut by the high incidence of contraband trade in the Caribbean and from Sacramento. Indeed, with the War of Succession the last of the barriers against interlopers crumbled, for in 1704 ambassador Amelot obtained permission for French merchant ships to enter the Pacific and trade freely with Peru and Chile. In the period 1701–24 at least 153 French trading vessels visited these coasts and in 1716 alone some 16 ships brought such an abundance of European merchandise that the markets remained glutted for years to come.

Faced with this open challenge to Spanish commercial monopoly, the authorities in Madrid desperately tried to restore the old system of periodic fleets sailing from Cadiz, with the trade fairs at Portobelo and Veracruz serving as the only legal points of entry for imported merchandise. For South America this decision implied the continued closure of the route via Cape Horn and severe restriction on landings at Buenos Aires. For New Spain the old system had never entirely broken down, since in the crucial years 1699–1713 at least five convoys had reached Veracruz. Moreover, the transfer of the fair in 1720 to Jalapa meant that transactions could now be conducted in a pleasant hill town just above the port. By contrast, only one fleet set out for Tierra Firme and the subsequent fair at Portobelo proved quite disastrous for the Lima merchants who purchased goods, owing to the influx of cheap French goods.

If diplomatic pressure eventually secured the exclusion of French ships from colonial ports, there was no way of escape from English traders. For the South Sea Company enjoyed the legal right, conceded at the Treaty of Utrecht, to despatch an annual merchantman to Spanish America (see above, p. 391). Since the goods it carried avoided both customs duties at Cadiz and the internment charges attendant on the delayed departures of the official convoys, the Company could easily undercut the high prices of the Spanish monopolists. In consequence, the English ship effectively ambushed the trade fairs held at Portobelo in 1722 and 1731 and at Jalapa in 1723 and 1732. Indeed, in the last fair at Portobelo about half the nine million pesos sent from Lima went directly into the coffers of the South Seas Company. The Cadiz shippers who had accompanied the fleet were either ruined or else obliged to linger in the colonies for years to come, awaiting purchasers for their costly goods. It was precisely this commercial disaster which led to the suppression of the Tierra Firme fleet. In addition, the volume of merchandise sold at Jalapa in 1736 was decidedly below previous levels.[7] It was no chance matter, therefore, that hostilities arose from Spanish attempts to prevent English contraband.

The War of Jenkins' Ear (1739–48) marked a watershed in the development of colonial trade. For Vernon's destruction of Portobelo put an end to any further hopes of reviving the Tierra Firme fleet. Henceforth all legal trade with the Caribbean islands and South America was by *registros*, individual ships sailing under licence from Cadiz. Equally important, the Cape Horn route was opened and more ships

[7] Geoffrey J. Walker, *Spanish politics and imperial trade 1707–1789* (London, 1979, *passim*).

were allowed to disembark at Buenos Aires. With the marked fall in prices, the European commerce of the entire Peruvian viceroyalty increased, bringing Chile and the zone of the Río de la Plata into direct trade with Spain. Indeed, since the British fleet was none too successful in its blockade, the very years of war witnessed a certain expansion. The other great benefit brought by war was the end of licensed interloping. At the peace treaty of 1750 the South Seas Company renounced both the asiento and the right to an annual trader in return for payment of £100,000. At last, after four decades, Spain had regained unrestricted exercise of its commercial monopoly over the American empire.

An important element in the revival of Spanish trade during the middle decades of the century was supplied by the Royal Guipuzcoa Company of Caracas which Patiño had established in 1728 with exclusive rights of trade between San Sebastian and Venezuela. Authorized to maintain coast boats to put down contraband, in 1729 the company outfitted no less than eight warships and raised a small army after the outbreak of hostilities with Great Britain. Thereafter, the curve of exports rose markedly, with shipments of cacao increasing more than threefold in the years 1711–20 and the 1760s. Moreover, whereas in the first period most cacao went to New Spain, in the latter decade the peninsula took 68 per cent of all shipments. Although the monopoly exercised by the company grew steadily more irksome to the Venezuelan population, it was not until 1780 that the crown first opened the colony to other traders, and then five years later dissolved the company. The success of this Basque venture led ministers to sponsor a series of other companies, of which the most important were the Habana Company (1740) created to handle the export of tobacco from Cuba and the Barcelona Company (1755) to trade with the other remaining Caribbean islands. But as none of these bodies were granted a monopoly of trade they soon foundered.

If for South America and the Caribbean the 1740s ushered in a new epoch, by contrast in New Spain the vested interests of the *consulados*, the merchant guilds of Cadiz and Mexico, prevailed on the crown to restore the fleet system. As a result, six great convoys sailed for Veracruz in the years 1757–76. But although the revived system brought security to the peninsula traders, the lion's share of profits, so critics alleged, went to the *almaceneros*, the great import merchants of Mexico City. At the Jalapa fair it was these men, often with over 100,000 pesos to spend, who dominated transactions, since the Cadiz shippers, faced with storage charges and forbidden further entrance up-colony, were clearly at a disadvantage, with more reason to sell than the *almaceneros* had to buy. Whatever the balance of profit, the system obviously worked to the detriment of both Spanish producers and Mexican consumers, since the volume of merchandise was limited in the interest of high prices. This revival of the fleet system for New Spain – by far the most prosperous of the colonies – demonstrates the nature and power of the vested interests against which the administrative elite had to battle. If foreign interlopers had at last been expelled from colonial ports, the further expansion of Spanish commerce now depended on a direct challenge to the great merchant houses of Mexico and the shippers of Cadiz.

The catalyst of change, once more, was war with Great Britain when Spain's tardy entrance into the Seven Years War led to the capture of Manila and Havana. Equally important, the British occupation of Havana promoted a remarkable increase in Cuban exports. The necessity to reform, both administrative and commercial, was only too evident. In consequence, in 1765 the Caribbean islands were thrown open for trade with the nine leading ports of the peninsula. At the same time the absurd practice of assessment of customs duties by cubic volume of merchandise, known as *palmeo*, was replaced by a 6 per cent *ad valorem* duty on all exported goods. The success of these measures made possible the promulgation in 1778 of the famous decree of *comercio libre*, which finally abolished the Cadiz staple and the fleet system. Henceforth trade between the chief ports of the empire and the peninsula was conducted by individual merchant vessels. The few restrictions which applied in New Spain were removed in 1789 and the Caracas company monopoly abolished in 1780. At the same time customs duties at Cadiz were lowered and preference given to Spanish manufactures.

The period from the declaration of comercio libre to the opening of the British naval blockade in 1796 turned out to be a brief golden age for colonial commerce. Within a decade registered exports tripled. Once the War of American Independence (1779–83) was concluded, unheard of quantities of European merchandise inundated colonial ports. In the one year of 1786 no less than sixteen ships entered Callao bringing goods worth 22 million pesos, at a time when the annual purchase of Peru was little more than five million pesos. The short-term result of this influx was, of course, a commercial crisis. Throughout the empire prices tumbled and profits dwindled as markets were saturated with imports. Many merchants went bankrupt and others cut their losses by withdrawing from transatlantic trade, preferring to invest their capital in agriculture and mining. Bullion drained out of local circulation as great sums were shipped abroad to finance the rising tide of European imports. Small wonder that consulados from Chile to Mexico clamoured for the crown to limit the influx of merchandise by a return to the old system of restricted entry. Ruin threatened their members. But the viceroys who investigated the matter, in particular Teodore de Croix in Peru and the count of Revillagigedo in New Spain, rejected these pleas out of hand. Echoing Campillo, they insisted that public interest should not be confused with the private profits of a handful of merchants. The expansion in trade, they said, had brought great benefits both to the colonial consumer and to Spanish industrialists. Moreover, in the case of Mexico, if the old almaceneros had now invested their capital in mining and the purchase of estates, this was all to the good, the more especially since their trading role had been taken up by a new breed of merchant, men content with a relatively small profit on a more rapid turnover of goods. More generally, statistics were assembled to demonstrate that the increase in the import bill was more than matched by the rising curve in silver production. That these years did in fact witness an extraordinary efflorescence of colonial exports, there can be little doubt. The rapid growth of Buenos Aires is testimony of the efficacy of the new policy.

Few things impress posterity more than the conviction of success and the servants of Charles III were not slow to boast of their achievements. In the course of a standard memorandum on the export of flour from Mexico to Cuba, the treasury *fiscal*, Ramón de Posada, after referring to Spain's former splendour and subsequent decadence, exclaimed: 'It was reserved for the superior wisdom and august protection of Charles III to initiate the splendid enterprise of recovering that former happiness.' But if the unhappy experience of the Hispanic world in the early nineteenth century led historians of that epoch to accept these claims at face value, recent research has greatly modified the traditional image. Above all, it is the role of the peninsula within the commercial system which has been brought into question. In his remarkable survey of registered trade between Cadiz and America for the years 1717–78, Antonio García-Baquero González has found that whereas the royal navy was constructed in Spanish arsenals, by contrast the merchant fleet

sailing from Cadiz was mainly composed of vessels purchased from
abroad. Although locally owned, only 22 per cent of the ships were built
in Spain, with another 4.2 per cent coming from colonial yards. Equally
important, it appears that most of the merchants at Cadiz were little
more than commission agents for foreign traders resident in the city.
The census of 1751 compiled on the instruction of the marquis de la
Ensenada listed 162 merchants from abroad as against 218 native
traders. Yet the Spaniards only accounted for 18 per cent of the declared
income of the trading community, the French clearly being the leaders
with 42 per cent of the total. Moreover, whereas over a fifth of the
foreign merchants enjoyed incomes ranging from 7,000 to 42,000 pesos
a year, only two Spaniards figured in this bracket. Further confirmation
of the limited range of their financial operations can be found in their
investments, which largely consisted of houses and property in the city
of Cadiz.

If the monopolists of Cadiz turn out to be mere intermediaries working
for a commission, it should come as no surprise to learn that in the same
period the contribution of Spanish industry to colonial exports was
derisory. True, measured by volume, peninsula produce occupied 45
per cent of cargoes bound for America, but it consisted of wine, brandy,
oil and other agricultural commodities. Measured by value, the
metropolitan share drops dramatically. On the most generous
calculation, Spanish goods shipped by the 1757 fleet to New Spain
accounted for 16 per cent of the total cargo value. In short, in colonial
trade, Spain figured as a primary producer with little in the way of
elaborated goods for export.[8] Elsewhere, we learn that for the years
1749–51 the royal factories of Guadalajara and San Fernando, which
produced quality woollen cloth, exported no more than twelve *toneladas*
out of an estimated output of over 10,000.

But what of the years after 1778? Certainly statistics were published
which showed that about 45 per cent of exports to the colonies
emanated from within the peninsula. The nascent cotton textile industry
of Catalonia, its machinery bought in England, competed effectively in
American markets. Here indeed was an industry whose growth in large
measure derived from colonial trade. The projects of Ustariz and
Campillo here yielded a rich harvest. But it must be emphasized that

---

[8] Antonio García-Baquero González, *Cádiz y el Atlántico 1717–1778*, 2 vols. (Seville, 1976), 1,
235–7, 309, 319, 326–30, 489–95.

as late as 1788 Cadiz still accounted for 72 per cent of all shipments to the American empire, and if Barcelona had raised the value of its exports from a mere 430,000 pesos before comercio libre to 2.79 million pesos in 1792, nevertheless it still only supplied 16 per cent of all colonial exports. Not that the importance of the American markets should be minimized, since in Barcelona, as elsewhere in Spain, trade with Europe depended on wine and other agricultural produce. The problem is that if Catalan cotton goods were shipped direct from Barcelona to the colonies, how was it possible for Cadiz to register some 45 per cent of its exports, measured by value, as Spanish produce? In fact, there is evidence of widespread contraband and simple re-labelling.[9] Insofar as the bulk of registered exports, measured by value, consisted of textiles, it follows from what we know of Spanish industry that the over-whelming proportion of these goods came from abroad. Indeed, even Catalan cottons and Valencia silks were not exempt from the charge of being French goods bearing a Spanish stamp.

On the other side of the Atlantic the stress on export-led growth stands in less need of revision. Here evidence is certainly partial and clusters about the last years of the century; nevertheless, there can be little doubt that the eighteenth century witnesses a remarkable expansion in overseas trade with Europe. Provinces such as Chile and Venezuela, hitherto neglected and isolated, were now brought into direct contact with Spain through the opening of new trade routes. At the same time, the mining industries situated along the cordilleras of the Sierra Madre and the Andes experienced a dramatic revival in their fortunes. The traditional basis of the expansion in transatlantic trade requires emphasis. In the years 1717–78 bullion still accounted for 77.6 per cent of the assessed value of all shipments from the New World registered at Cadiz, the remainder of the cargoes consisting of tobacco, cacao, sugar, indigo and cochineal. With the promulgation of comercio libre the pace of economic activity gathered momentum, with the coasts and islands of the Caribbean yielding an ever greater harvest of tropical produce. Yet, in the 1790s, bullion shipments still supplied over 60 per cent of the value of colonial exports to the peninsula, a calculation which does not include the monies despatched on the king's account.

By this period the leading province within the American empire was New Spain, with registered exports averaging over 11 million pesos in

[9] Barbara H. Stein and Stanley J. Stein, 'Concepts and realities of Spanish economic growth 1759–1789', *Historia Ibérica* (1973), 103–20.

the years 1796–1820. Silver accounted for 75.4 per cent of value and
cochineal 12.4 per cent, with sugar providing what remained. The
Andean zone was characterized by a similar reliance on bullion to finance
its overseas trade, with an overall production of over nine million pesos
flowing directly out of the ports of Lima and Buenos Aires. For if the
latter port, raised to the condition of a viceregal capital, could boast
of exports worth five million pesos in 1796, only one-fifth was supplied
from the pampa estancias in the form of hides, jerked beef and horns;
the remainder consisted of coin sent down from the Potosí mint. In Chile
the story was much the same, with gold and silver supplying 856,000
pesos of total exports worth a million, as against 120,000 pesos brought
in by copper. Further north in Colombia, gold comprised 90 per cent
of the exports valued at two million. In Central America, however,
indigo shipments from Guatemala brought in 1.2 million pesos, a sum
close to the 1.4 million pesos earned by Mexican cochineal and far in
excess of the 250,000 pesos which was the estimated annual produce
of the silver mines of Honduras. Dyestuffs apart, it was the growth in
sugar, cacao and tobacco which challenged the predominance of bullion
in Spain's Atlantic commerce. By the 1790s the value of exports from
Venezuela had mounted to over three million pesos, distributed
between cacao, indigo and coffee. But the great success story of these
last years of the century was Cuba, where alongside the traditional
cultivation of tobacco, sugar production expanded dramatically after the
revolution in Saint-Domingue (1789–92). If at the start of the 1790s
exports were valued at over three million pesos, by the years 1815–19
they averaged about 11 million, a total equal to the silver exports of
New Spain.

One last comment is necessary. In the middle of the eighteenth
century, Campillo had pointed to the Caribbean sugar islands as the
yardstick by which to measure the commercial performance of the
Spanish empire. As yet we lack any general survey of colonial trade,
a task rendered all the more difficult by the frequent wartime blockades
which interrupted the regular flow of shipping. By way of international
comparison, it is perhaps helpful to recall that in the years 1783–7 Great
Britain imported from her West Indian islands produce worth
£3,471.673 a year, a sum equivalent to 17.3 million pesos. Similarly, by
1789 exports of sugar, cotton and coffee from Saint-Domingue were
valued at 27 million pesos and another source estimated the total value
of produce shipped from the French West Indian islands at 30½ million

Table 1 *The Spanish Balance of Trade in 1792*
(millions of pesos)

(i) *The Peninsula*						
Exports	19.84	Imports	35.74	Deficit	15.9
(ii) *Trade with Colonies*						
Exports			Imports		Deficit	
National goods	11.15		Bullion	21.01		
Foreign goods	10.32		Produce	15.91		
Total	21.47		Total	36.92	15.45	

Source: José Canga Argüelles, *Diccionario de Hacienda*, 2 vols. (Madrid, 1833), 1, 639–45.

pesos. These figures provide a perspective on the Bourbon achievement. For, if the available statistics for all the provinces of the Spanish empire in the New World are put together, the grand total for exports in the early 1790s does not exceed 34 million pesos. Corroboration for this figure can be found in a contemporary balance of trade for 1792 described as the best known year for Spanish commerce (see Table 1).

To generalize from one year's trade at a time of violent fluctuation could easily mislead. Moreover, the table fails to elucidate the relation between peninsula and colonial trade, although the presumption must be that the great proportion of Spanish imports were re-shipped to the colonies and that the peninsula's deficit on the external trading account was met by the despatch of American bullion. But the degree to which colonial trade actually subsidized Spain's commercial balance of payments is not made clear. At the same time, the table omits any entry of the shipments of bullion arriving from the New World on the king's account, which is to say that it fails to take into consideration the fiscal profits of empire. Measured by past performance, the Bourbon revival was decidedly respectable, but, if judged on an international scale, the commercial expansion appears far less impressive.

THE EXPORT ECONOMIES

Whereas the peninsula derived but modest benefit from the revival in Atlantic trade, many of the American colonies were born anew. To sharpen our perspectives on Bourbon achievement, it is necessary to turn to the past. Viewed for the purpose of comparison, the Habsburg monarchy in the New World appears as a successor state raised on foundations built by the Aztec confederacy and the Inca empire. That it was the free labour and tribute of the Indians which allowed the encomenderos and missionaries to create an overseas equivalent of Spanish society within little more than a generation goes without dispute. What requires emphasis is that the pre-hispanic political experience continued to determine the organization of colonial society well into the seventeenth century. The Inca reliance on labour levies as against the Aztec preference for tributes decisively influenced viceregal policy. If Potosí came to act as a magnet for the entire imperial economy, it was largely because Viceroy Toledo summoned a vast annual migration of over 13,000 Indians to work in the mines of the great peak. The failure of the Mexican mining industry to emulate its Andean rival demonstrates that no matter what the importance of Spanish technology, the decisive agent in the rapid expansion of production was the massive input of labour provided by the *mita*. In short, Inca precedent allowed Toledo to mobilize the peasantry in the service of the export economy. By contrast, in New Spain labour drafts were recruited in the immediate locality of each mine, with the result that much of the industry came to rely on free workers and African slaves. The mainspring of the Habsburg trading system was the revival of a command economy in the Andean highlands.

By the eighteenth century, however, the regional balance of commercial activity had shifted away from the Mesoamerican and Andean cultural heartlands out towards frontier zones once inhabited by roving tribes or down to the tropical coasts and islands of the Caribbean and Pacific. The pampas of the Río de la Plata, the farmlands of Central Chile, the valleys about Caracas, the plantations of Cuba, the mines and haciendas of Mexico north of the river Lerma – these were the regions of rapid growth in both population and production. The workforce consisted either of free wage-labourers recruited from the casta (half-caste) or creole community, or, alternatively, of slaves imported from Africa. In contrast to the Habsburg period when the crown furnished the supply of labour, it was now merchants and entrepreneurs who advanced the cash necessary for the purchase of slaves or the payment of wages. The old command economy only survived in the mita at Potosí and in the infamous *repartimientos de comercio*, where royal authority was employed to coerce the Indian peasantry into either consumption or production of trade goods. Even here, it can be argued that the key element was the advance of cash by the merchant backers of the magistrates.

To stress the shift in the regional location of production for export might suggest that the removal of all legal barriers to commerce between the leading ports of the peninsula and the American empire played a decisive role in the opening of new lines of trade. But it would be false to suppose that mere arrival of merchandise from Europe could stimulate local agriculture or mining. As the British experience after American Independence clearly demonstrated, the greater availability of manufactures in American ports did not of itself evoke a matching supply of exports. Although Bourbon statesmen were swift to hail the expansion in Atlantic trade after comercio libre as the result of crown policy, the bureaucracy here, as elsewhere, simply took credit for other men's toil and ingenuity. The decisive agent behind the economic growth of the Bourbon epoch was an entrepreneurial elite composed of merchants, planters and miners. It was a relatively small group of colonial businessmen, in part peninsula immigrants, in part creoles, who seized the opportunities afforded by the opening of new trade routes and the fiscal inducements offered by the crown. These men readily adopted new technology where it proved feasible and did not hesitate to invest large sums of capital in ventures which at times needed years to yield a profit. The emergence of this elite is all the more extraordinary if we pause to consider that in the peninsula the merchant community were mainly content to act as intermediaries for foreign traders and offered small challenge to the hegemony of the territorial aristocracy. By contrast, in the New World merchants actively backed the development of both mines and plantations and at times invested their capital in production for export.

The showpiece of the Bourbon age was undoubtedly the Mexican silver-mining industry.[10] As early as the 1690s the mid-seventeenth century depression was overcome as mintage attained its former peak of over five million pesos. Thereafter, output rose steadily to reach 24 million pesos by 1798, with the 1770s registering the most rapid increase owing to new discoveries and fiscal incentives. Through this quadrupling of production in the course of a century the Mexican

---

[10] For a further discussion of mining in Spanish America in the eighteenth century, see ch. 5 below.

industry came to account for 67 per cent of all American output of silver and Guanajuato, the leading centre, equalled the production of the entire viceroyalty of either Peru or La Plata.

The Spanish crown played a central role in promoting this dramatic resurgence. The dependence of the Mexican refining mills on the royal mine at Almadén for mercury to purify their silver meant that without the thorough-going renovation of this ancient mine (where, in fact, output soared from a mere 2,000 cwt to over 18,000 cwt) the industry would have remained hamstrung. Equally significant, the visitor-general, José de Gálvez, halved the price of this indispensable ingredient and increased the supply of gunpowder, another royal monopoly, cutting its price by a quarter. At the same time, he initiated the policy of granting tax exemptions and reductions for renovations or new enterprises of high risk, which required heavy capital investment. While he was minister of the Indies, Gálvez established a mining court to head a guild which exercised jurisdiction over all litigation within the industry. A new code of mining law was introduced and the court was made responsible for a central finance bank to sponsor investment and renovations. This battery of institutional reforms was rounded off in 1792 with the foundation of a mining college staffed in part by mineralogists brought in from Europe. The magnificent neo-classical palace which housed the court and its college expressed the central importance of Mexican silver mining within the Bourbon empire.

In no sense, however, do government measures offer a sufficient explanation of the eighteenth-century silver bonanza in New Spain. By this period the population of the colony was on the increase so that recruitment of a workforce through the provision of wages offered few difficulties. Indeed, Mexican mineworkers, for the most part mestizos, mulattos, poor creoles and migrant Indians, formed a free, well-paid, highly mobile, often hereditary, labour aristocracy who in most camps obtained a share of the ore in addition to their daily wage. But the decisive element in the expansion was to be found in the activity and collaboration of merchant-capitalists and miners, who displayed both skill and tenacity in ventures which on occasion required years of investment before striking rich. The industry was sustained by an elaborate chain of credit reaching from the silver banks and merchant-financiers in Mexico City to local merchants and refiners in the leading camps who in turn backed the actual miners. The tendency over the course of the century was for individual mines to become larger and in the smaller camps for an entire lode to be dominated by one great enterprise.

The scale of operations and the time expended was often extraordinary. It took over twenty years before the famous count of Regla benefited from his investments at the Veta Vizcaína in Real del Monte, owing to the necessity of driving a drainage adit 2,881 yards underneath the lode. With the enormous profits that followed Regla purchased a chain of haciendas and at the cost of nearly half a million pesos constructed the great refining mill that still stands as his monument. By far the greatest enterprise, however, was the Valenciana at Guanajuato which by the 1790s employed over 3,000 workers. With four shafts and a multitude of work tunnels reaching out across the lode, the Valenciana resembled an underground city. The octagonal central shaft with a circumference of 32 yards and a depth of over 600 yards, was a stone-lined construction, serviced by eight mule-drawn whims, which cost over a million pesos to cut and face. In the scale of its workforce and investment, there can have been few enterprises in Europe equal to the Valenciana.

That Government incentives were not sufficient to revive an ailing industry was demonstrated by the example of Peru. For in the Andean highlands the revival of mining was slow and limited. It was not until the 1730s that the industry began to recover from the depression of the previous century. But from a low point of about three million pesos, production only edged forward to just over ten million pesos in the 1790s, a figure only briefly sustained, and which included both viceroyalties of Peru and La Plata. The basis of this revival was the emergence of new camps, such as Cerro de Pasco which relied on wage labour, and the survival of Potosí, through the labour subsidy of the mita. The crown applied much the same measures as in Mexico – the mercury price was reduced, a technical mission despatched and a mining guild and court established. But certain key elements failed to materialize. The inability of the administration at Huancavelica to expand production – in fact after 1780 it declined – placed severe limits on the quantity of mercury available to the Andean industry, since New Spain always enjoyed preferential rights on all imports from Europe. Equally important, most mines remained small, employing but a handful of workers. The Andean industry lagged far behind its northern rival in the application of available technology. Behind this limited response to the new opportunities for profit created by government initiative lay a shortfall in capital for investment. The great merchants of Lima had lost their dominant position in South American trade and lacked the resources to emulate their counterparts in Mexico. Their rivals in Buenos Aires made no attempt to invest in the Andean industry. Thus, although by the end of the eighteenth century the mines of Upper and Lower Peru produced as much silver as in the reign of Philip II, recovery derived not from any new concentration of capital or labour, but rather from new discoveries and the mere survival of past endeavours. At the same time, bullion remained the only export of any consequence and the purchasing power generated by the industry still sustained a wide range of inter-regional commerce.

Apart from the tropical plantations worked by slaves, the remaining export trades relied on merchant capital, which financed a variety of producers ranging from Indian villagers and mestizo smallholders to Chilean miners and *estancieros* of the Argentine Pampas. Cochineal production in southern Mexico was promoted by repartimientos de comercio, which in this case simply meant cash disbursed by the district magistrate half a year in advance of the crop. If the great import house of Mexico City withdrew from these operations after repartimientos were prohibited by the Intendancy Code of 1786, local merchants in Oaxaca and Veracruz continued to lay out their monies in this trade. The same mercantile domination can be observed in the indigo trade of Central America, where the merchants of Guatemala City advanced credit both to smallholders and to landowners, with the result that through foreclosure merchants became directly involved in production for export. In Central America, therefore, the two dyestuffs were mainly procured through the collaboration of smallholders and merchant capital, with or without the intervention of the crown.

In the southern cone, in Chile and along the Río de la Plata, the merchants of Buenos Aires and Santiago financed the estancieros of the Pampas and the miners of the Chilean north. Both gauchos and mineworkers received a wage, even if the bulk of their clothing and drink often came from stores managed by their employers. It is difficult to ascribe any decisive cause for the growth of exports in these regions other than the simple opening of trade routes via the Río de la Plata and Cape Horn, combined with an increase of population sufficient to provide a workforce. Such expansion as occurred was important for the local economy, if as yet without much weight in the international market. The export of hides from Buenos Aires mounted rapidly from about 150,000 at mid-century to nearly a million by its close, as prices rose from six to twenty *reales* a quintal. The mining industry in Chile was largely the creation of the eighteenth century, with the overall value of its gold, silver and copper rising from an average 425,000 pesos in the 1770s to nearly a million pesos by the 1790s.

The other main lines of the export trade in Spanish America consisted of tropical produce from the Caribbean and Colombian gold. The workforce in all these areas was mainly provided by the import of slaves from Africa. In Colombia the gold placer workings in Popayán and Antioquia were operated by miners who employed relatively small gangs of slaves, their ventures financed by local merchants. Mintage at Bogotá rose from 302,000 pesos in 1701 to over a million pesos by the early 1790s, supplemented by an increase at the Popayán mint from an average 423,000 pesos in the years before 1770 to nearly a million pesos by 1800. Despite the failure of the crown to introduce intendancies in New Granada, its overseas trade equalled in value the export produce of the southern cone.[11] Yet more successful was its neighbour Venezuela, where cacao production mounted steadily across the century as annual exports rose from just under 15,000 *fanegas* in the years 1711–20 to over 80,000 *fanegas* by the 1790s. The plantations which grew cacao were owned by the great families of Caracas who formed a planter aristocracy. The workforce consisted of African slaves who by the turn of the century comprised an estimated 15 per cent of the total population. The long years of neglect prior to the establishment of the Caracas Company had permitted the development of an extensive native population, mulattos, mestizos and isleños from the Canaries. Beyond the coastal mountain valleys lay the great plains of the interior from which came the dried beef and the 30,000 mules shipped across the sea to the islands of the Caribbean.

The phoenix of the late Bourbon period was Cuba. For although the island had produced sugar and tobacco since the sixteenth century, it was only after the British occupation of Havana in 1762 that it seriously sought to emulate the pattern of production found in the French and British possessions. The crown took decisive action to promote the

[11] For these figures see A. J. Macfarlane, 'Economic and political change in the viceroyalty of New Granada with special reference to overseas trade 1739–1810' (Ph.D. dissertation, London University, 1977).

sugar industry through an increased importation of slaves, generous grants of land to planters and permission to import cheap flour from the United States. Between 1759 and 1789 the number of sugar mills rose from 89 to 277 and in much the same period production tripled. But then, with the revolution on Saint-Domingue and the subsequent destruction of its plantations, the Cuban industry entered a period of rapid expansion and technical change as both prices and profits soared. The planter aristocracy and the Havana merchants were if anything more entrepreneurial than their Mexican counterparts, alert to technical innovation, adopting steam-power for their mills and Tahitian strains of sugar for their plantations. In the last resort, however, the boom depended on the massive purchase of African slaves, whose numbers rose from nearly 86,000 in 1792 to some 286,000 in 1827, with annual arrivals after 1800 amounting to 6,670. If Cuba did not participate in the Insurgency after 1810, it was in good measure because the servile element by then comprised almost a third of the entire population. Within a generation Cuba had created an economic system and society more reminiscent of Brazil than of the remainder of Spanish America. Smallholders still dominated the cultivation of tobacco, but were increasingly at the mercy of the great planters who enjoyed the support of the colonial administration. The returns here were remarkably high. If exports were valued at about five million pesos in the 1790s, within just over another decade they had attained 11 million and hence equalled the registered overseas trade of New Spain. By then Havana had become the second city of Spanish America with over 70,000 inhabitants.

No matter how dramatic or rapid the economic transformation wrought in Spanish America by the importation of slaves or the investment in deep-shaft mining, the technological basis of that development remained thoroughly traditional. The purchase of a few steam engines did not effect an industrial revolution. Here a comparison between the two great colonial industries may prove instructive. For, despite the emergence of great capitalist enterprises, both silver-mining and sugar-growing remained trapped within a stage of production in which human muscle was the chief source of energy both for the extraction of ore and the cultivation of cane. Moreover, despite what were at times remarkable concentrations of manpower, all enterprises – mines and mills – were governed by much the same set of costs. As Professor Moreno Fraginals has argued, the great Cuban sugar mills, the *ingenios*, were simply quantitative amplifications of the previous range of small mills. Similarly, in New Spain, a great refining mill merely aggregated a larger number of crush-mills (*arrastres*) under one roof. In both cases the increase in scale of operations brought little, if any, qualitative change. Whether the organization of production became more efficient is another question. A study of the sugar plantations of Morelos found that between the sixteenth and late eighteenth century there was a fourfold increase in productivity calculated on the ratio of output as against the number of workers and draught-animals employed. Much the same sort of improvement occurred in North Atlantic shipping during this period. Without any significant change in maritime technology, a continuous improvement in organization allowed smaller crews to handle larger cargoes and spend much less time in port.[12] A similar process undoubtedly occurred in Mexican silver-mining where the unification of entire lodes under one management rendered drainage less haphazard. Improvements in refining spread from one camp to another. Nevertheless, in the last resort, both sugar-growing and silver-mining depended on a seemingly endless replication of the units of production, without any significant reduction in costs either from technical innovation or from increase in the scale of operation.

One last comment seems appropriate. By 1789 the produce shipped from the French colony of Saint-Domingue came close to equalling the value of the exports of the entire Spanish empire in the New World. This remarkable feat sprang from the deployment of a slave population of over 450,000 consisting in great part of young men imported directly from Africa. The entire colony was obviously geared for production for Europe. Clearly, if the export earnings of the $14\frac{1}{2}$ million inhabitants of Spanish America barely exceeded the output value of a single island in the Caribbean, it was because the bulk of its population found occupation and sustenance in the domestic economy.

THE DOMESTIC ECONOMY

The strategic weight and high profit of the Atlantic trade captured the attention of both contemporary statesmen and subsequent historians. By contrast, the humdrum transactions of the domestic American

---

[12] Manuel Moreno Fraginals, *The sugar mill, the socio-economic complex of sugar in Cuba 1760–1860* (New York, 1976), 40; Ward Barrett, *The sugar hacienda of the Marqueses del Valle* (Minneapolis, 1970), 66–70, 99–101; Douglass C. North, 'Sources of productivity change in ocean shipping 1660–1850', *Journal of Political Economy*, 76 (1968), 953–67.

market passed virtually unnoticed, with the result that entire cycles of
economic activity, both industrial and agricultural, have sunk into
oblivion. Yet all the available evidence attests to the existence of a
lively circle of exchange which at the lower end consisted of barter
arrangements within or between villages, at its middle reaches centred
on the urban demand for foodstuffs, and in its most profitable lines
involved long-distance, inter-regional dealings in manufactures, livestock and tropical cash-crops. Well before the Bourbon heyday, several
frontier provinces were aroused into production by market demand
exerted from the viceregal capitals within the New World. In particular,
the emergence of a colonial textile industry bore witness to the strength
of the internal economic revival which preceded the epoch of export-
led growth. What recent research has demonstrated beyond dispute,
however, is that the mainspring of this economic growth and prosperity
was the increase of population. The eighteenth century witnessed a
significant, though limited and uneven, recovery of the Indian population in Mesoamerica and to a lesser extent in the Andean highlands
together with an explosive growth of the American-Spanish (creole) and
casta (half-caste) population throughout the hemisphere but especially
in formerly peripheral areas like Venezuela, New Granada, Chile,
Argentina and Mexico north of the river Lerma. It has been estimated
that by 1800 the American empire possessed a population of $14\frac{1}{2}$ million
compared with Spain's population of $10\frac{1}{2}$ million.[13]

The bulk of this colonial population found employment and support
in agriculture. In the eighteenth century many Indian villages, possibly
the majority, still possessed sufficient land to support their inhabitants.
Such was certainly the case in Oaxaca, Yucatán, highland Michoacán,
large areas of Puebla, Huancavelica, Jauja and the region surrounding
Lake Titicaca, to mention only those provinces for which data is to
hand. Most Indian communities produced the bulk of their own
foodstuffs and clothing. Their exchange of goods rarely extended
beyond the locality and production for the market was limited, although
the tendency of Indian villages to remain entrenched within their local
peasant economy had been challenged and in part broken by the
demands of the crown for tribute and labour service, by the invasion
of community lands by the great estate and by the infamous repartimientos de comercio.

In contrast the great estates were geared from the outset to the market

---

[13] For a full discussion of the population of Spanish America at the end of the colonial period,
see Sánchez Albornoz, *CHLA*, 11, ch. 1.

economy and in particular to production for towns. Most plantations, it is true, catered for European demands, although in both Peru and New Spain the sugar industry also supplied domestic markets. Stock raising estancias, however, served largely domestic markets; only hides from Argentina were sent to Europe in any great quantity. Yet with the exception of the extensive sheepfarms of the Andean *puna*, they were mostly located in frontier zones several hundred miles away from their markets. Thus, each year over 40,000 mules were driven from their breeding grounds in the Argentine pampas to the trade fair at Salta and from there distributed across the Andean highlands. Similarly, the great flocks of Coahuila and Nuevo León supplied Mexico City with mutton (over 278,000 *carneros* a year by the 1790s) and wool for the mills at Querétaro. Chile despatched tallow and horns to Lima and Venezuela shipped 30,000 mules across the Caribbean. In these frontier zones, the workforce, be they called *guachos*, *llaneros* or *vaqueros*, were free workers, attracted by wages paid either in cash or kind, and, unlike African slaves on sugar plantations, themselves provided a significant market for the produce of colonial industry. The haciendas which produced cereals and other basic foodstuffs for the network of provincial capitals, mining camps and ports dealt in low-priced bulky commodities for which the market was limited by the cost of transport. In so far as the expansion of the export economy caused an increase in urban population, it also entailed an extension in the cultivation of basic foodstuffs. At the same time, the domestic sector maintained its own rhythm of production with prices fluctuating in response to seasonal and yearly variations in supply, which, in the short term at least, bore little relation to any changes in the international economy.

The tendency on haciendas was to rely on a small nucleus of resident peons and to hire seasonal labour from neighbouring villages or from the estate's own tenants. For in Mexico it has been shown that many landowners threw open a considerable part of their land to tenants in return for rents paid either by cash, in kind, or through provision of labour. By contrast, in Chile erstwhile tenants were converted into *inquilinos*, a service tenantry under obligation to supply the landlord with labour. Similarly, in Peru the *yanaconas*, or resident peons, were paid mainly by the lease of land for subsistence cultivation.[15] Only in New Spain was a balance maintained between peons, at times bound to the estate by debt, and the tenants and sharecroppers paying rent and supplying seasonal labour.

The development of the great estate was thus accompanied by the emergence of a new peasantry composed of mestizos, mulattos, poor Spaniards and acculturated Indians. The degree of subordination to the landlord varied from province to province. Certainly, in many parts of Mexico, along the Peruvian coast and on the Chilean frontier the first settlers who occupied small farms were bought out and reduced to the condition of tenants and sharecroppers. Even in these areas, however, important nuclei of smallholders survived, so that both the Valley of Putaendo in Chile and the Bajío in Mexico housed entire clusters of minifundia. Elsewhere, in Antioquia and Santander in New Granada most of the countryside was occupied by small proprietary farmers. Much the same was true in Arequipa in Peru or Costa Rica in Central America, or in the tobacco-growing districts of Cuba. This new peasantry at times competed with the great estate, at times was thrust into dependence on its operations. But across the empire it was the same social group which was largely responsible for the demographic increase and the economic growth of the frontier regions which played such an important role in the Bourbon revival.

Alongside this variegated pattern of production in the countryside there existed a considerable range of industrial activity, both rural and urban. To start with, most Indian villages were accustomed to spin and weave their own cloth, be it woollens in the Andean highlands or cottons in Mesoamerica. They also made their own pottery. Admittedly, at the other end of the social scale, the Hispanic elite paraded in finery imported from across the Atlantic, drank Spanish wines and brandy and fed off ceramic ware made in China and Europe. But there was also an extensive class of families resident in the leading towns, the mining camps and in frontier regions who relied on colonial industry to supply their apparel and other items of domestic use. As early as the sixteenth century large workshops called *obrajes* had been established in America to cater for the growing demand for cheap cloth, a domestic market which flourished by reason of the sheer cost of transatlantic shipping. In addition to these enterprises, however, there also emerged a certain range of cottage manufacture, especially for cotton cloth, which also catered for the urban market.

As yet there is insufficient evidence for any rounded survey of the structure and cycles of colonial industry and commerce during the eighteenth century. The story is decidedly complex. For it must both assess the deepening impact of the Atlantic trade and also register the decisive shifts in the balance of regional exchange within the American empire. The starting point of any analysis lies in the middle decades of the seventeenth century when the crisis in silver production and the failure of the Seville fleet system promoted the expansion of a domestic economy catering for the growing Hispanic and casta population. By all accounts the seventeenth century was the golden age of the *obrajes* of Puebla and Quito, the epoch when their fine woollen cloth commanded a wide distribution across the entire empire. Even at this stage, however, marked differences existed between the two industries, since whereas in Puebla the *obrajes* were situated within the city and operated with an assorted workforce of African slaves, sentenced criminals and apprentices retained through debt peonage, in Quito the *obrajes* were all located in the countryside, built on the great sheep-farms or in Indian villages, with a workforce recruited from the estate peons or operated by a village mita to meet tribute obligations.

The vitality of this American economy is further demonstrated by the growth of exports from Chile and Venezuela. From the 1680s the *hacendados* of central Chile started to ship considerable quantities of wheat to Lima, with the assessed volume rising from 11,556 fanegas in 1693 to 87,702 fanegas in 1734, this latter figure accounting for 72 per cent of all exports. Similarly, cacao shipments from Venezuela started in the 1660s, with annual cargoes rising from 6,758 fanegas to 14,848 fanegas in the decade 1711–20, with New Spain absorbing all but a tenth of these exports. In short, the prostration of Spain, when combined with the steady growth in colonial population, allowed the emergence of a distinctively American economy based on long-distance, inter-regional exchange of foodstuffs, bullion and manufactures, with Mexico City and Lima acting as the dominant centres within this trading network. It was at this period that the pattern was set for the eighteenth century. In South America, cloth came from Quito, brandy and sugar from the coastal valleys of central Peru, wheat and tallow from Chile, coca and sugar from the semi-tropical valleys close to Cuzco, mules from the Argentine pampas, mercury from Huancavelica, with bullion from Potosí providing the mainspring for this vast internal market. Much the same exchange prevailed in New Spain, with *tierra adentro*, the northern interior, supplying bullion, meat, hides and wool in return for cloth and tropical produce.

It must be emphasized, however, that the flow of internal trade changed dramatically during the Bourbon period. In the first half of the eighteenth century renewed competition both from Europe and other colonial centres undermined the prosperity of the textile industry of Puebla and Quito to the point where their *obrajes* ceased operation. In South America the opening of the new sea routes via Cape Horn sharply reduced the prices of imported cloth. At the same time, new *obrajes* situated in the countryside were opened in Cajamarca and Cuzco, the workforce recruited either by landlords or by corregidores as a means of collecting tribute. The success of these establishments over Quito presumably derived from their greater proximity to their markets. Much the same replacement occurred in New Spain where the industry at Puebla was destroyed by competition from Querétaro, which, by reason of its location at the edge of the Bajío, was better placed to purchase its wool from the great estancias of Coahuila and Nuevo León and to supply its market in the mining towns of the north. By 1790, Querétaro, with a population of over 30,000, had become a leading manufacturing centre, since the textile industry employed at least 3,300 workers divided between eighteen *obrajes* which produced fine woollens, ponchos and blankets and 327 workshops (*trapiches*) which mainly wove coarse cottons. The rise of these new centres drove Quito and Puebla to find alternative markets or start new lines of manufacture. By the 1780s Quito had turned from producing quality cloth for Lima to weaving coarse woollens for the market in New Granada. By contrast, Puebla succeeded in recapturing a measure of prosperity through specializing in the fine *rebozos* or shawls, cottons with a handsome silken sheen.[14] At this stage, the industry was dominated by a small group of merchants who purchased the cotton from Veracruz, put it out for manufacture by a numerous class of independent weavers, and then despatched the finished cloth for sale in Mexico City. It is estimated that in the years 1790–1805 Puebla annually supplied the capital with over one million pounds of cloth.

Shifts in the regional exchange of agricultural produce were less dramatic or pronounced than in textiles. Once again, Puebla suffered, with its outlets for flour severely reduced by reason of competition from

---

[14] G. P. C. Thomson, 'Economy and society in Puebla de los Angeles 1800–1850' (D.Phil. dissertation, Oxford University, 1978); Robson B. Tyrer, 'The demographic and economic history of the Audiencia of Quito: Indian population and the textile industry 1600–1800' (Ph.D. dissertation, University of California, Berkeley, 1976).

Table 2 *Value of New Spain's annual production, c. 1810*
(millions of pesos)

Agriculture	106,285	(56)
Manufactures	55,386	(29)
Mining	28,451	(15)
Total	190,122	(100)

the Bajío in the markets of Mexico City and from the United States in Cuba. At much the same time, Venezuelan cacao was diverted from New Spain, so that by the 1790s greatly increased annual exports of over 80,000 fanegas went almost entirely to the peninsula. But this shift in the flow of trade offered an opportunity for the coastal province of Guayaquil which now captured the Mexican market, with overall production rising from 34,000 fanegas in 1765 to over 150,000 in 1809. Similarly, the concentration of tobacco growing in Veracruz provided an opening for Cuba to meet the demands of the Mexican market. In the southern cone the Atlantic trade was imposed over and above the internal pattern of exchange without much apparent distortion, since although in Chile bullion soon constituted the chief value of exports, wheat and tallow shipments to Lima still continued to expand in volume despite a falling price curve. In the Río de la Plata the remarkable increase in the export of hides in no way undercut the breeding of mules for the Andean highlands.

To strike the balance between the transatlantic and American sectors of the colonial economy is a hazardous task. The secretary of the Veracruz consulado provided estimates, recently revised, for the overall value of Mexican production, broken down by sectors.[15]

These figures must be treated with caution, since they are simple extrapolations from an assumed minimum consumption of the population and in no sense express the value of goods actually entering the market. One general point may be advanced. Whereas tropical plantations with their servile labour force generated relatively little

[15] José María Quirós, *Memoria de estatuto. Idea de la riqueza que daban la masa circulante de Nueva España sus naturales producciones* (Veracruz, 1817). See also Fernando Rosenzweig Hernández, 'La economía novo-hispánica al comenzar del siglo XIX', *Ciencias políticas y sociales* 9 (1963), 455–93.

demand for local produce, by contrast the mining sector provided an extensive market for both agriculture and domestic industry. To take a well-known case, in Guanajuato with about 55,000 inhabitants by the 1790s, about half the working population were employed in the mines and the refining mills. The remaining half consisted of artisans and servants. Less than two days' journey away lay the city of Querétaro, where the textile industry and the tobacco monopoly factory also provided support for an equally large number of workers and artisans. Both these cities offered a valuable market for local agriculture. Without the export of silver a great part of this exchange between town and country and between regions and cities would have disappeared, leading to a partial evacuation of urban centres in favour of agriculture. It is doubtful whether the shift to quality textiles attendant upon any decline in the transatlantic exchange of silver for European cloth could have compensated for the loss of a mass market in the cheaper lines of textiles and for foodstuffs. Clearly, the export sector generated high profits and made possible capital accumulation on a scale unimaginable in the domestic economy. Yet much of this capital was subsequently invested in the purchase and development of landed estates which survived through production for the domestic market.

Although some historians have taken up the contemporary lament that the flood of imports after comercio libre drained the continent of its circulating currency, it must be emphasized that without any increase in bullion shipments to Europe mining production inevitably would have fallen in consequence of inflation caused by an over-abundance of silver. Thus the Bourbon epoch constituted a relatively brief period of equipoise between the external and domestic sectors of the economy in which, if the rising curve of silver production certainly helped to finance the revival of the military power of the crown and allowed the colonies to import great quantities of fine cloth from Europe, it also generated a considerable range of employment which in turn created a lively market for domestic industry and agriculture. Indeed, it was the existence of this complex and variegated internal economy which allowed the emergence of an equally complex and distinctive colonial society.

THE LAST YEARS OF EMPIRE

In 1788, the count of Floridablanca, chief minister for more than a decade, had presented a general report, in which he celebrated the success of Spanish arms in the recent war against Great Britain. He hailed the threefold expansion in colonial trade and the doubling of customs revenue which followed the declaration of comercio libre. Public credit stood so high that the debts incurred during the War of American Independence had been funded by the new Bank of San Carlos through the emission of *vales*, bonds which circulated at face value. The programme of public works, in particular the construction of highways and canals, was a source of special pride. This image of a strong enlightened government actively promoting the prosperity of its subjects, both in the peninsula and America was not diminished by the accession of Charles IV (1788–1808), since, with first Floridablanca, and then the count of Aranda guiding the king, no change was evident until 1792. True, in colonial administration a certain loss in executive momentum became apparent, after the death of Gálvez, when in 1787 the ministry of Indies was first divided into two departments and then in 1792 virtually abolished, with its functions distributed among the various ministries, leaving only the Council of Indies exclusively responsible for the American empire. But at the level of colonial administration, the rule of the count of Revillagigedo as viceroy of New Spain (1789–94) and Fray Francisco Gil de Taboada y Lemos as viceroy of Peru (1790–6) marked the apogee of enlightened despotism in the American empire.

But the Bourbon revival of the Spanish monarchy always had depended on the protection afforded by the balance of power in Europe. No matter how effective they were in frontier warfare or auxiliary action, neither the Spanish fleet nor the Spanish army were any match for their chief opponents in the Old World. In 1793 the crown unwisely joined the continental coalition against the revolutionary regime in France, only to suffer outright defeat as French troops swept across the Pyrenees. By the close of 1795 Spain was forced to make peace and obliged both to renew the traditional alliance and to cede Santo Domingo. The consequences of this reversal proved incalculable, since the British fleet now imposed a rigorous naval blockade. In 1798 alone 186 ships leaving Cadiz were commandeered. Thereafter, apart from the brief but invaluable peace of Amiens (1802–4) all trade between Spain and the empire was suspended until the French invasion of 1808 lifted the siege of its ports. Confronted with the seizure of their ships or years of inactivity, many, if not most, of the leading merchant houses in Cadiz were forced into liquidation. At the same time, the commercial crisis led to a dramatic fall in revenue, so that with the budget already deranged by the high costs of the war against France, the treasury plunged headlong into debt. As the sum of *vales* in circulation grew rapidly, public credit collapsed. All hopes of any immediate recovery were brought to an end with the defeat and destruction of the Spanish fleet at Cape St Vincent (1798) and Trafalgar (1805). The loss of Trinidad to Great Britain and the cession of Louisiana to Napoleon offered further confirmation of Spain's impotence. Moreover, these years of international humiliation were accompanied by a marked deterioration in the quality of government at home. Since 1792 Manuel Godoy, an ex-guardsman and the queen's favourite, presided as chief minister over a regime mainly characterized by incompetence and corruption. Leading figures of the old administrative elite such as Floridablanca and Jovellanos were subject to confinement. Small wonder that many enlightened public servants welcomed the advent of Joseph Bonaparte as a means of achieving reform.

For the American empire the enforcement of the British blockade offered damning proof of the inability of Spain to protect the interests of its colonial subjects. In Mexico silver production plummeted as mercury stocks ran low and several mines were obliged to suspend operations. However, stocks at Almadén grew apace, so that with the peace of Amiens (1802) over 80,000 cwt of mercury were quickly shipped to Veracruz, enough to guarantee four years' production. If the impact of the blockade was less severe than might have been anticipated, it was largely because in 1797 permission was granted for neutral shipping to enter colonial ports, a freedom which was renewed in the years 1805–7. Throughout this period contraband was rife. Although French goods were effectively barred from the Atlantic, British merchandise now flooded into Spanish America, either as contraband from the West Indies or through the intervention of American traders. At the same time Cuba enjoyed the exceptional right to deal directly with the United States, exporting sugar in return for flour and other goods. Then again, the very restrictions imposed by the blockade afforded a certain measure of protection for colonial manufactures, which in some provinces enjoyed a last boom before their final eclipse.

Yet this very success of the colonies in preserving their prosperity despite the commercial rupture with the metropolis obviously brought into question the value of the imperial link. If Great Britain had now replaced France as the chief source of imports for Spanish America, why should its goods be shipped to the New World via the port of Cadiz merely to provide a fiscal profit for the crown? The estancieros of Buenos Aires and the planters of Venezuela all stood to gain from direct access to world markets.

Furthermore, it must be remembered that the revolution in government launched by Gálvez and his associates had provoked a series of popular uprisings. In New Spain the establishment of the tobacco monopoly, the formation of the militia and, more important, the expulsion of the Jesuits led to urban riots and open revolt. Only the previous arrival of veteran regiments from the peninsula allowed Gálvez to suppress the movement with unprecedented severity. In 1780–1 the application of much the same set of measures – the more efficient collection of alcabalas, the rigorous supervision of tribute payments and the restrictions on tobacco cultivation coupled with higher prices – set off widespread revolts in both New Granada and the Andean highlands. In southern Peru, José Gabriel Condorcanqui, a local cacique, took the name of Tupac Amaru, the last Inca emperor, as a means of rallying the Indian peasantry against the colonial regime. Only the vigorous defence organized by its creole bishop saved Cuzco from assault and capture. It required expeditionary forces from Lima and Buenos Aires to suppress a rebellion which stretched from Cuzco to La Paz. By contrast, in New Granada the *Comunero* uprising was defused by the skilful negotiation of the archbishop and interim viceroy, Antonio Caballero y Góngora, who cancelled the more unpopular fiscal decrees and granted amnesty to the leaders of the movement. The common theme in all these popular rebellions was resentment against the new taxes imposed by the Bourbon state. But whereas in Mexico the wealthy creoles co-operated with Gálvez to defeat the rebels, in Peru several caciques assisted Tupac Amaru in his venture and in New Granada the local dignitaries allowed themselves to be pressganged into revolt so as best to control the outcome. In short, no matter what the degree of popular mobilization, it was the involvement and leadership of the creole elite which was the decisive agent.

Traditional loyalty to the crown was eroded by the Bourbon attack on the church. For the expulsion of the Jesuits was followed by a series of measures designed to abrogate ecclesiastical jurisdiction and autonomy. The Code of Intendants contained clauses which entrusted the collection of the tithe to juntas controlled by royal officials, an innovation which met such a flurry of clerical protest that it had to be cancelled. Yet in 1795 the crown suspended the total immunity from civil courts hitherto enjoyed by the priesthood and decreed that in cases of grave crime clerics could be tried by royal magistrates. Not for nothing did the bishop of Michoacán warn the crown in 1799 that similar attacks on ecclesiastical privilege in France had so weakened the influence of the church as to allow the *philosophes* to go unchallenged in their plans to change society. Echoing Montesquieu, he declared that if the nobility and church were undermined, then the fate of the monarchy was in doubt. Undeterred and in urgent quest for revenue, in 1804 Godoy introduced the consolidation or amortization decree, by which all ecclesiastical property had to be sold and the receipts deposited in the royal treasury, which henceforth would be responsible for the payment of interest on the capital. Despite the chorus of protest from all leading institutions in New Spain, Viceroy José de Iturrigaray, a venal protégé of Godoy, hastened to implement a measure which dealt a grievous blow not merely to the church, whose income was threatened, but also to the landowning class on whose estates most ecclesiastical capital was invested in the form of annuities and chantry funds.

The campaign against ecclesiastical jurisdiction and property should not be construed simply as a mere assault on corporate institutions which had grown too wealthy or become unduly privileged. The attack on the church signalled the imminent demise of the traditional authority of the crown. For priests throughout the empire had always preached obedience to monarchy as a divine commandment. Their residence at the Escorial, which housed monastery, palace and sepulchre, had invested the Catholic Kings with a sacral aura. But the Bourbon dynasty slowly dissipated the moral and political capital bequeathed by their Habsburg predecessors. Although the Divine Right of Kings was still sedulously purveyed, the doctrine was increasingly detached from its natural background in scholastic theology and baroque sensibility. By the close of the eighteenth century the works of Suárez and Vitoria lay unread: the Hispanic world now looked to France for its inspiration, albeit as much to the France of Bossuet and Port Royal as of Montesquieu and Raynal. The cycle of baroque architecture which had dominated the towns and churches of Spanish America since the late sixteenth century was brought to an abrupt end in the 1790s with the promulgation of the neo-classic as the only acceptable style. At one stroke past glories became an antique embarrassment. The clergy themselves were as much affected by the new climate of opinion as their opponents. Whereas in the first decades of the Bourbon era devotional exercises and liturgical celebration still flourished, the emphasis later changed to practical morality, good works and education. In short, the administrative elite who served enlightened despotism undermined the institutions and the culture which had revered monarchy as a mandate from heaven.

Viewed within the context of Spain's position in the European Concert, the revolution in government and the expansion in the export economy was a desperate rearguard action hastily devised in Madrid first to avert British expropriation of Spain's overseas possessions and then to exploit their resources to strengthen the monarchy. If the measures met with apparent success, the price was the permanent alienation of the creole elite. For the ancient constitution, all the more powerful for being unwritten, which had presumed consultation over taxation and a consonance of interest between king and people was broken asunder by the new reliance on executive decree and military sanction. The vogue in Madrid for the terms metropolis and colonies brought small comfort to territories which formerly had been defined as the overseas kingdoms of a universal Christian monarchy. For many American Spaniards the economic prosperity of these years, so often engineered by peninsular bureaucrats for the benefit of *gachupín* merchants, was no consolation for exclusion from public office. At the same time the establishment of the chief institutions of absolutist monarchy in the leading provinces of the empire provided the creole elite with sufficient machinery of state to assure any future independence. When in 1807 Viceroy Iturrigaray assembled an army of over 15,000 men in the hills above Veracruz to guard against a British assault, he assembled a force recruited in New Spain, led in large part by creole officers and entirely financed by revenue raised in the colony. Similarly, it was the urban militia rather than the regular garrison which repelled the British invasion at Buenos Aires in 1806–7. The reconquest of America had alienated the colonial establishment yet fortified its economic position and provided it with an army and a bureaucracy. With traditional loyalties quite eroded, and the example of the Thirteen Colonies before it, small wonder that, when news arrived of the abdication of Charles IV, the creole elite at once sought a voice in the governance of their countries.

Far from being the natural culmination of 300 years of colonial development, the late Bourbon era was an Indian summer, a fragile equipoise, easily broken asunder by changes in the balance of power in Europe. Once more, the peninsula served as a battlefield for contending armies of British and French troops. But whereas in the War of Succession colonial society had remained somnolent and indifferent, in 1808 when French bayonets made Joseph Bonaparte king of Spain, the creole elite in most provinces of the empire demanded representative juntas to provide a legal basis for government. Events in Europe thus provided the occasion rather than the cause of political upheaval in America. Two years later, when the Cortes met at Cadiz, charged with the task of framing a constitution for the entire monarchy, the overseas provinces either called for immediate autonomy or burst into open revolt.

Part Two

COLONIAL ECONOMY AND SOCIETY

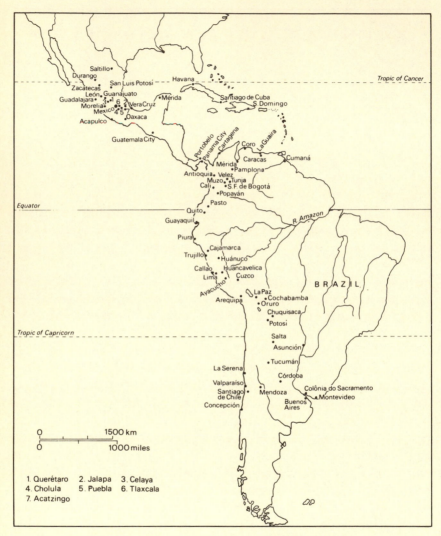

The cities and towns of Colonial Spanish America

4

URBAN DEVELOPMENT

THE URBAN IDEA

Like much of Spanish American colonial history, the region's urban development has two prehistories: one indigenous, the other peninsular Spanish. The *conquistadores* found many populous urban centres in Mesoamerica and, less markedly, in the central Andes. The Aztec capital of Tenochtitlán, with at least 150,000 and perhaps 300,000 inhabitants, became a Spanish viceregal capital. Eight more cities surrounded Lake Texcoco, while outlying centres of regional importance included Cholula, Tlaxcala, Tzin Tzun Tzan, Cempoala, and various sites in Yucatán and Guatemala. In the Inca realm the capital at Cuzco, while lacking the commercial importance of Tenochtitlán, had more than 100,000 inhabitants and exercised political sway over various centres along the Incaic *camino real*, some of pre-Incaic origin: Quito, Cajamarca, Jauja, Vilcas, Huánuco, and Bonbón. These urban hierarchies, in turn, were successors to earlier settlement complexes oriented towards centres at Teotihuacán, Monte Albán, Tajín, the Maya cities, Chan Chan, and Tiahuanaco.

Although the Spaniards converted some Indian cities like Tenochtitlán, Cholula, and Cuzco to their own uses, more pervasive influences on the European settlement scheme were the spatial distribution and village structure of the Indian populations. Indeed, if one were to carry the urban history of Spanish America only up to the late sixteenth century, the continuities with pre-conquest society would deserve a dominant emphasis. On a longer view, however, the political, social, and economic determinations of European rule, taken with the detribalization, relocation, and severe mortality of the Indian population, introduced many new vectors of change. The following treatment, then, begins with European antecedents for urban development in the Indies. Pre-conquest patterns and their transformations are considered later.

Perhaps because Spanish America was for so long thought of as a predominantly agrarian realm, its urban history lay neglected until recently. Two noteworthy exceptions are books by an Argentine and a Peruvian, Juan A. García's sociological study of colonial Buenos Aires, *La ciudad indiana* (Buenos Aires, 1900), and Jorge Basadre's historical analysis of urban–rural relations in Peru, *La multitud, la ciudad y el campo en la historia del Perú* (Lima, 1929). It was not social and institutional aspects, however, but a controversy over physical form that finally brought Spanish American urban history to international scholarly attention. Since the 1940s the origins of the familiar chessboard layout with its spacious central plaza and monumental architecture have received detailed investigation. By now this research on the 'classic' Spanish American city plan has gone well beyond tracing formal precedents for design and has begun to reconstruct institutional and cultural process. Three groups of hypotheses that have emerged yield a convenient approach to our general topic.

First, some have emphasized that Spanish overseas colonization was part of a large imperial design made possible by the prior consolidation of the Spanish nation state. The gridiron plan for cities, while impractical for the irregular townscape of late medieval Spain, was invoked to rationalize the appropriation of vast overseas territories. Geometric layout was emblematic of the imperial will to domination and a bureaucratic need for order and symmetry. On this interpretation, the paradigm for Spanish overseas urbanism is taken to be the rectangular plan for Santa Fe de Granada, founded by the Catholic Monarchs in 1491 for the final siege of the Moors in southern Spain. The inspiration for this grid planning some have traced to ancient sources, notably Vitruvius, many of whose precepts for the ideal city reappear in the Spanish colonization ordinances of 1573.[1] Others hold that Santa Fe and the towns of the Indies found their pedigree in the regular layout of medieval bastide towns of southern France and north-eastern Spain. Still others point to the increasing influence of

[1] 'Ordenanzas de descubrimiento, nueva población y pacificación de la Indias, dadas por Felipe II en 1573', published in facsimile by Spain's Ministerio de la Vivienda (Madrid, 1973). For a partial English translation see D. P. Crouch, D. J. Garr and A. I Mundigo, *Spanish city planning in North America* (Cambridge, MA, 1982), 1–23.

Italian Renaissance or neoclassical planning on New World city building during the sixteenth century and later.

A second viewpoint reminds us that the Spanish conquerors and settlers were untutored in matters of urban design and could scarcely have been conversant with elegant styles of ancient, medieval, or neo-Roman origin. Their urban solutions were pragmatic, producing improvised and jumbled mining towns, cramped fortified seaports, and straggling rural hamlets as well as spacious and regular administrative centres. When geography and circumstances permitted, the grid was a natural, uncomplicated solution for practical leaders charged with making unequivocal land grants to contentious and ambitious settlers. The generous grid and plaza were congenial to the vastness of the territories newly annexed to Christendom. This solution, some conjecture, may even have echoed the grandeur of the Indian ceremonial sites, and E. W. Palm has suggested that the monumental form of the Aztecs' Tenochtitlán caught the attention of European planners through its influence on the 'ideal city' of Dürer.

Finally, some argue that while Spanish settlers made inevitable concessions to circumstance, and while Spanish legislators were aware of classical precedents, new town planning was ultimately a form of cultural expression ensconced in a matrix of traditions. Urban form in America was consonant with certain medieval Spanish treatises that in turn owed much to St Thomas Aquinas' *On the governance of rulers*. Gabriel Guarda in fact claims that the Spanish colonizing ordinances of neo-Vitruvian origin were less widely enforced than those of Thomist–Aristotelian inspiration. On this argument, urban form draws attention not on aesthetic or functional grounds but as a manifestation of social philosophy. We are reminded that whatever the constraints of place and circumstance, a town founding was a liturgical act sanctifying newly appropriated land. More than a mere exercise in cartography, urban design was the vehicle for a transplanted social, political, and economic order and exemplified the 'mystical body' that was central to Iberian political thought.

What began as a debate over the genealogy of urban design has evolved into a discussion of larger historical process, and our three sets of hypotheses turn out to be reconcilable. To be sure, certain propositions have been disproved, for instance that the Spanish grid plan was ubiquitous and unvarying or that neo-Vitruvian and Italian Renaissance theories were widely influential. But a large view shows that the rationalist, imperial, neo-Roman tradition was not incompatible with the Ibero-Catholic, Aristotelian one. Indeed, the two were intertwined from at least the era of the thirteenth-century legal code, *Las Siete Partidas*. It is moreover clear that this complex tradition made constant accommodation in the Indies to the predatory and populist spirit of the conquest; to economic and geographic imperatives; and to the presence of Indians and Africans, who together, despite their high mortality rates from disease and maltreatment, remained many times more numerous than the European population. One way to understand Spanish American cities, then, is to place the 'idea of a city' that came from Europe in dialectical relation with New World conditions of life.

At the close of the Middle Ages the Iberian city ideal drew from assorted classical and Christian sources that had been fused and reinterpreted since the thirteenth century. Prominent ingredients were: (1) the Greek notion of the polis, an agro-urban community based not on a 'covenant' among consenting individuals but on a 'political' entity of functionally integrated groups; (2) the imperial Roman notion that the municipality (*civitas*) was an instrument for 'civilizing' rural peoples and that *civitates* were the constituent parts of empire and, even more grandly, of a universal City of Mankind; (3) the Augustinian notion of a City of God or City of the Beyond that opposed a paradigm of Christian perfection to the sordid strivings and sins of the earthly city; (4) the chiliastic vision of an Edenic city of gold or terrestrial paradise that might be discovered in distant lands, or else a prospective city of poverty and piety that might arise under churchly guidance among overseas peoples newly consecrated to apostolic humility.

Save for the vision of a city of gold widely shared by the *conquistadores*, only jurists, theologians, and missionaries entertained these notions of urban community in explicit detail; yet the large premises on which they rested infused the mindset of settlers and city-builders. This cultural commitment stands in relief when compared to that of the New England Puritans. The Puritan congregation, or 'city upon a hill', did, to be sure, retain certain medieval principles of social subordination. All relations save those between parents and children, however, were voluntary and dependent on a covenant between contracting parties. The community had no 'corporate' identity in the sense that it was antecedent, or superior, to the contractual arrangements of its members. Each private conscience therefore bore extraordinary responsibility for preserving the purity of the 'bond of marriage' between God and the congregation.

While its members remained sinless, the community was an embodiment, not an imperfect replica, of the divine order. Moreover, those who emigrated from a parent community could found new congregations and initiate an independent relation to God. The Spanish American township, by contrast, had corporate identity in a system of empire that rested on hierarchies of urban and village units. Internally the town was composed of ethnic and occupational groups also knit by loosely hierarchical criteria. The urban unit was a microcosm of a larger imperial and ecclesiastical order, and responsibility for its proper functioning lay not with private consciences but with the discretion of bureaucratic, latifundiary, and ecclesiastical notables. The assumption of a 'sinless' community was relegated to chiliastic visions or to mission communities, like those of Jesuits and Franciscans, that served as exemplars or paradigms.

This complex vision of the urban community drew substance from Spanish institutional developments of the Middle Ages. Only in northern Spain along the pilgrimage route to Santiago de Compostela do we find the intrusion, starting in the eleventh century, of the 'communal' form of municipal organization that answered the mercantile preoccupations of travellers from across the Pyrenees. The municipal experience that was to shape Iberian overseas colonization was forged not here but in central Spain during the slow resettlement of lands taken from the Moors. On the meseta of León and Castile the term *burgués*, with its commercial implications, was rarely used and does not figure in the *Siete Partidas*. A propertied townsman was commonly a 'citizen' (*civis*), 'householder' (*vecino*), or 'decent man' (*omo bueno*). Monasteries and private persons accomplished the early resettlement, often under crown supervision. Later, control passed to municipal councils of the former Moorish realm, military orders, and nobles. Groups of free settlers received lands under stipulated conditions and privileges. A full-blown 'communal' municipal regime failed to develop, and the urban administration that managed rural activities was encompassed within the framework of the state. Towns were agro-urban units, and the commercial sector, so prominent in north-western Europe, vied here with military, ecclesiastical, agricultural, and pastoral interests.

In his *Tractado de República* (1521) the Spanish Trinitarian friar Alonso de Castrillo set forth symptomatic views on cities and citizenship. Addressing the crisis of the *comuneros* revolt of 1520–1, Castrillo criticized both the 'foreign' design for empire attributed to the entourage of Charles V and the excesses of the *comunidades* that opposed it – a tension between imperial strategy and local interest that had already appeared in Spain's new Caribbean settlements. Seeking a middle ground between absolutism and revolutionary constitutionalism, Castrillo reminded readers that the city was the noblest of human assemblages and that a kingdom was properly composed of cities, or 'republics', hierarchically arranged. Within cities, qualified citizens were to manage public affairs. Of the three classes of townsmen – nobles (*caballeros*), merchants (*mercaderes*), and artisans (*oficiales*) – only the first embodied civic virtues. Merchants were corrupted by private greed, while artisans were confined to horizons of private need. What Castrillo prophetically feared was a confluence of the cupidity of a few and the indigence of the many that would endanger the welfare of the republic.

THE URBAN STRATEGY

The 'Castilian' plan for urban development was not immediately asserted on Hispaniola, scene of the Spaniards' initial colonization effort in America. The early towns – including the ill-fated La Navidad of Columbus' first voyage, Isabela, founded on the second, and the subsequent mid-island chain of centres reaching the primitive south-coast city of Santo Domingo – had irregular plans and were akin to the fortified commercial 'factories' of the Italians in the Mediterranean and the Portuguese in Africa. Columbus himself frequently cited the Portuguese example. In a few years two things were clear: first, that the southern coast was more favourable than the northern for communication with Spain, control of the interior, and the staging of expeditions to Tierra Firme; second, that to use the inland chain of factories for tribute collection was not a viable social or economic strategy. Isabela, abandoned in about 1500, was by the 1520s a haunted ruin whose knightly inhabitants were said to salute the unwary visitor by doffing their heads along with their hats.

To remedy the bungled administration of the first decade, Nicolás de Ovando was dispatched to Santo Domingo as governor with instructions to found new settlements giving heed to natural features and population distribution. He was told that Christians should henceforth be clustered in municipal centres, thus setting the precedent for the segregation of Spanish *villas* from Indian *pueblos*. Ovando arrived in April 1502 with 2,500 settlers. When after two months a hurricane destroyed his capital, he resited it on the right bank of the Ozama to improve communications with the interior. The new city plan was the first instance of geometric layout in America. Soon Ovando devised a master scheme for a network of *villas* on Hispaniola, fifteen of which received the royal coat of arms in 1508. Some were sited in the west and south-east to control Indian labour; others were located near the gold deposits or in zones suited for agriculture and ranching. Santo Domingo city was the capital, main port, and terminus of roads to the north and west. For founding a town 50 vecinos seem to have been an average number. Certain towns received hospitals in a scheme of regionalized medical assistance. As co-ordinator of the plan, Ovando selected urban sites, controlled municipal appointments, and determined the disposition of lots (*solares*) around the plazas.

By the end of his term Ovando governed a European population of 8,000–10,000. He had created the underpinning for an integrated regional economy and promoted the island as a base for Caribbean exploration. Yet by the time he returned to Spain in 1509 his plans had gone awry. Proper roads were not built, and his decision to abolish the inept system of tribute collection, eliminate the caciques, and allocate the Indians to encomenderos, the mines, and the crown hastened the decline of the native population. By the mid sixteenth century the settlements were desolate, and the north–south route established by the Columbus brothers had prevailed over Ovando's plan for east–west integration. This was to mean evacuation of the northern and western settlements in 1605–6 and eventual cession of western Hispaniola to the French.

In Cuba the governor, Diego Velázquez, chose seven urban sites that were plotted (1511–15), like those of Hispaniola, to profit from regional economic opportunities. Here, contrary to the case of Santo Domingo, Havana was relocated from the south to the north coast once the conquest of Mexico accentuated the importance of the northern shipping route. Eventually Havana overtook Santiago, the early capital, and was designated the rendezvous for Spain's Caribbean convoys.

The Caribbean phase of conquest saw the triumph of the municipal unit as an agro-urban instrument for colonization, and Ovando's experience informed the crown's elaborate instructions of 1513 to Pedrarias Dávila for colonization of Castilla del Oro.[2] By now the obstacles to the establishment of a prosperous network of centres were apparent: the lack of serviceable roads, the swift depletion of mineral

[2] Royal instruction of 1513 to Pedrarias Dávila, 'Ynstrucción para el governador de Tierra Firme, la qual se le entregó 4 de agosto DXIII', in M. Serrano y Sanz (ed.), *Orígenes de la dominación española en América* (Madrid, 1918), cclxx–xci.

resources, the decimation of the native population, and the lure of expeditions to the mainland. The drawbacks to regional planning under the close supervision of a crown-appointed bureaucrat were also evident. In both Hispaniola and Cuba assemblies of procurators soon appeared to assert municipal prerogatives. Although the crown would always oppose consolidation of a third estate, juntas of town procurators were convoked sporadically throughout Spanish America in the sixteenth century. In practice the procurator found his most effective role as a municipal representative at court who could bypass bureaucracy and petition the crown directly for redress of grievances.

The classic example of how municipal notables might choose their own caudillo and, through him, place themselves in vassalic relationship to the crown was the action of Hernán Cortés and his companions in repudiating the authority of their immediate superior, Diego Velázquez, at the start of the Mexican campaign. The so-called 'first letter' of Cortés, dispatched from the Rica-Villa of Veracruz on 10 July 1519, related to the crown that whereas Velázquez had wanted the expedition only to secure gold and return straightaway to Cuba, 'to all of us it seemed better that a town should be founded there in the name of your Majesties with a justiciary and council, so that in this land your Majesties might possess overlordship'. Cortés was 'well pleased and content' to designate *alcaldes* and *regidores* who in turn appointed him chief justice and *alcalde mayor*, completing the process of legitimation.[3]

These two branches of town government – *justicia* officered by *alcaldes* or magistrates and *regimiento* by *regidores* or councillors – had Castilian precedents. In the fourteenth century the crown curbed municipal liberty by converting these offices into prebends (*regalías*). In America the crown in principle controlled the *regimientos* but made concessions to the settlers with respect to *justicia*. Given the immense territory and diverse circumstances of the New World, the crown could not fully implant the Castilian system and was forced to accept various formulas to reconcile its interests with those of *conquistadores* and settlers. Although the municipality was conceived as embedded in the structure of the state, and the cabildo was in part bureaucratized, the regalist idea also permitted concession of *regimientos* in perpetuity. Cabildos enjoyed considerable autonomy during the early years, and those in outlying areas continued to do so after the higher structures of royal government were imposed.

[3] In J. B. Morris (ed.), *5 Letters of Cortés to the emperor* (New York, 1962), 1–29.

In the fourth book of his *Milicia y descripción de las Indias* (1599) an experienced New World caudillo, Bernardo de Vargas Machuca, offered a manual for town founders.[4] The settlers should reassure the Indians of their peaceful intentions, he advised, at the same time haggling over peace terms and exploiting tribal rivalries. The Indians should be encouraged to build houses sited conveniently for missionary purposes. The town itself should stand at the heart of its region to facilitate provisioning and military sorties. The site should be level and bare, not in a dangerous hollow, and close to water and firewood. To found the town Spaniards and Indian chieftains should erect a tree trunk, and the caudillo should sink his knife in it and proclaim his right to rule and punish, with the proviso that the town might later be rebuilt at a more suitable place. He would then declare:

I hereby found this community in the name of his Majesty, and in his royal name I shall protect it and keep peace and justice among all its inhabitants, Spaniards, conquerors, settlers, residents, and outsiders, and all its native population as well. I shall administer even-handed justice to the poor and the rich, to the humble and the exalted, and I shall protect their widows and orphans.

The caudillo would then brandish his sword, challenge any opponent to a duel, slash bushes at the site to establish possession, and place the community under royal jurisdiction. A cross should then be erected at the site of the future church, Mass said to impress the Indians, and the caudillo's cabildo appointments announced.

This done, the caudillo was to have the justices swear to keep order in the king's name, and soldiers desiring residence were to pledge to protect the townsmen. Citizens would then erect temporary tents and shacks on the plaza, which was to be rectangular but conform to the terrain. From it eight streets, each 25 feet wide, were to lead outward, creating blocks 200 by 250 feet divided into four lots. The church, cabildo, and gaol were to face the plaza, with remaining central lots assigned to the caudillo and chief officials. After earmarking space for *conventos*, hospitals, a slaughterhouse, and a butcher's shop, the caudillo was to allot land to householders. The Indian caciques should then provide workers to construct public buildings, level the open spaces, and plant crops under armed supervision of the Spaniards, who would need a stockade for emergency refuge. Adjoining residences of

---

[4] B. Vargas Machuca's instructions to town founders are in book 4 of his *Milicia y descripción de las Indias* [1599] (2 vols., Madrid, 1892).

Europeans should be connected by back doors or low walls in the event of a call to arms. With the town laid out, soldiers should reconnoitre the environs, bring Indian villages under Christian tutelage, assess economic possibilities, and compose reports for the cabildo with copies for higher officials. Further advice concerns colonization of new centres from the original nucleus; allotment of encomiendas according to the merits of the Spaniards and the suitability of the Indians; a warning to caudillos that, although entitled to a quarter of the land, they should not bite off more than they could chew; and the need to stimulate the Indians' self-interest by allowing them weekly markets, encouraging them to produce European commodities, and winking at their occasional pilferage. 'The Indian is thus made content, is better controlled, and gives twice as much service.'

Understandably, the historical experience that informed Vargas Machuca's instructions did not always exhibit so high a degree of formalism and calculation. A Jesuit's report of 1620 claimed that the founding of Asunción in the 1530s had been 'more by marriage than by conquest'. As the Spaniards were proceeding up the Paraguay river, he recounted, the local Indians

asked them who they were, whence they came, where they were going, and what they wanted. The Spaniards told them. The Indians replied that they should go no farther and that because they seemed like decent people they would give them their daughters to make them relatives. This pledge seemed fine to the Spaniards, and they stayed here.[5]

Yet for all their textbook character, Vargas Machuca's precepts contain three points that deserve emphasis: first, the wide discretionary powers enjoyed by caudillos and the hierarchical principle by which they rewarded followers; second, the umbrella of royal and ecclesiastical authority over any new municipal enterprise; third, the role of urban centres in appropriating territory and recruiting native peoples for the economic needs of the settlers and for the political and 'civilizing' purposes of empire. As time passed, personalist leadership gave way to control by municipal notables, often exercised outside the formal cabildo mechanism. Historians were once agreed that this regional oligarchical rule, supplemented by *cabildos abiertos* in occasional times of stress, made the municipality the only arena for effective self-government by creoles. This view draws attention to the considerable

[5] 'Informe de um Jesuíta anônimo' in J. Cortesão (ed.), *Jesuítas e bandeirantes no Guairá (1549–1640)* (Rio de Janeiro, 1951).

autonomy of local patriciates in outlying areas, but it exaggerates the discontinuity between the grass roots and superstructure of government. Creoles in fact attained positions of authority in the royal bureaucracy, while the towns themselves were not hermetic enclaves but a locus of tension between local ambition and imperial design. That is, the claims of a hinterland on those who would appropriate its produce and Indian labour competed with the claims of church and the state, sweetened by prebends and franchises, that aimed to win compliance from the notables and absorb the agro-urban unit within a scheme of empire.

Because the economy and society of colonial Spanish America are often described as archaic and resistant to change, one sometimes forgets that in the space of two generations after the Caribbean phase of conquest a few thousand Spaniards established an urban design for a continent and a half that has largely prevailed to this day. Indeed, by 1548 urban control centres, coastal and inland, had been created from the Mexican plateau south as far as Chile. Many of them are now familiar as modern national capitals: Mexico City, Panama City (resited in 1671), Bogotá, Quito, Lima, La Paz, Asunción, and Santiago. Caracas was founded in 1567 while Buenos Aires was founded permanently in 1580 after an ephemeral settlement in 1535–41. The broad reach of the settlement pattern reflected the colonizers' need for centres of control over prospective Indian workers and tributaries. Without Indians, the adage ran, there are no Indies. After the initial experiments, the commercial enclaves that characterized Portuguese, English, and Dutch overseas expansion were abandoned in the Spanish Indies in favour of direct appropriation of mineral and agricultural resources. In the words of Constantino Bayle:

The *conquistadores* were like the Roman legionaries who became colonists on leaving the wars, using lands distributed to reward their military efforts. The object of their campaigns to subdue native peoples was to establish themselves in the provinces, found cities, and work out ways to live comfortably as in Spain. Hence they did not stop at the coasts, and most of their foundings were mediterranean, where the fertility of the soil promised full compensation for their efforts. Division of land among the settlers was thus a necessary, indispensable complement to the municipality.[6]

As the chronicler López de Gómara put it, 'who fails to settle fails to conquer properly, and if the land is not conquered the inhabitants will not be converted'.

[6] Constantino Bayle, *Los cabildos seculares en la América Española* (Madrid, 1952), 85–6.

Colonization, then, was largely a labour of 'urbanization', that is, a strategy of settlement nucleation for appropriating resources and implanting jurisdiction. Urbanization taken in its simple demographic sense – designating population clusters that grow more swiftly than surrounding regions – is difficult to quantify for sixteenth- and seventeenth-century Spanish America even if one limits attention to towns of Europeans. To begin with, enumerations from the period are generally for vecinos, that is, householders controlling retinues or encomiendas rather than simple residents (*habitantes* or *moradores*) and transients (*estantes*), and the ratio of vecinos to *moradores* and to Indians varied greatly from place to place. Second, by the time the Spaniards' urban hierarchies were in place, the decline of the Indian population – rural, village, and urban – had become so precipitous as to render meaningless the usual measures, or significance, of urbanization and deurbanization. By using such tallies as are available, however, and by establishing weighted indices for urban functions, it is possible to draw certain conclusions about urban development for the period of roughly 1580 to 1630 (a time when the Indian population of central Mexico dropped from about two million to some 700,000). During this span it appears that larger administrative cities grew faster than smaller ones. Admittedly incomplete data indicate that in centres of over 500 vecinos at the terminal dates the number of vecinos had increased by 6.7 times, while in those of 100 to 500 vecinos it had risen by only one-third. The steadiest growth was in the larger bureaucratic centres provided with services, manufactures, and cultural resources. More dramatic growth occurred in favoured ports (Havana, Callao), mining towns (Potosí, Oruro, Mérida in New Granada, San Luis Potosí), and intermediate agricultural centres (Atlisco, Querétaro, Santiago de los Valles). Economic activities, however, tended to have only regional impact or else to be oriented to Spanish mercantilist design. The larger urban pattern was better defined at this time as a 'scheme' of cities than as a complex of interconnected urban 'systems'.[7]

The municipal strategy for appropriating resources derived from the Roman legal principle, revived in late medieval Spain, that separated the public and private domains, vesting in the crown rather than in the king as feudal lord the right to dispose of natural resources, including

[7] See J. E. Hardoy and C. Aranovich, 'Urbanización en América Hispana entre 1580 y 1630', *Boletín del Centro de Investigaciones Históricas y Estéticas* [*BCIHE*] (Universidad Central de Venezuela, Caracas), 11 (1969), 9–89.

land, by *merced real* or *gracia*. An early, idealistic policy statement appeared in a cedula of 1518 that allocated farmlands and urban lots to colonists and their heirs forever 'in ample quantity according to the willingness of each to cultivate them'. The cedula assumes a municipal unit as the distributive agent and accents the social or political concerns of the crown. These concerns were not to prevail against the predatory and personalistic character of colonization, and eventually they had to vie with the crown's own economic and fiscal interests in formulating land policy.

Spanish law gave grounds for three principal types of land grant. One was the *capitulación* that empowered an expedition leader to found towns and distribute lands, contingent on effective occupation for four to eight years. Second was a grant of vacant lands in accord with codified decrees stipulating, for example, that town founders could not be proprietors in existing towns, that prospective founders must guarantee the presence of at least thirty vecinos, and that new towns should be laid out on four leagues of land and be distant by five leagues from previous centres. Later, as the royal treasury became depleted and as better land near towns and along roads was appropriated, the crown increasingly favoured the exchange value of land against its use value. In a cedula of 1591, which Ots Capdequí calls an 'agrarian reform', lands not specifically conceded were to revert to the crown for a third type of disposal, sale by auction. Even then, a cabildo might arrange a collective land title for itself as a juridical person or, in the event of auction, appear as a single bidder and then redistribute the land under free title. The crown's early ideal of independent farm colonies was eclipsed by concentrated landholdings in privileged locations under competition that worked against latecomers and the impecunious. Crown income from land sales could not be fully realized given the difficulties of systematic surveying and title clearance and the fact that judges, trained in Justinian law, were reluctant to enforce policies that threatened outright ownership. In a second 'agrarian reform' the crown, by an *instrucción* of 1754, tried to reassert control over land sales and *composiciones*, prescribed leniency in handling Indian claims, and required legalization of land titles acquired after 1700. By then, however, the *de facto* territorial arrangements of the cabildos strongly resisted change.

What persisted, of course, was not a rigid design but a set of tendencies. Many of the original foundings proved ephemeral because of faulty site selection; disasters such as earthquakes, volcanic eruptions, or disease; Indian attacks; deficient natural resources and economic possibilities; or simply the lure of new prospects. The founders of Jauja, Peru, stipulated that their first site would be used only until a more suitable one was identified. Some towns were refounded six or more times. Nueva Burgos in New Granada has been called a 'portable' city, carried from place to place on its people's backs as they searched for a site where the Indians would leave them in peace to sow their fields. Some towns became apples of discord for competing caudillos, who might wrest control from one another and redistribute choice land to favourites. Other towns commandeered vast jurisdictions far beyond their capacity to settle them. Buenos Aires laid claim to much of modern Argentina, Quito to all of modern Ecuador and part of Colombia, Asunción to land in a hundred-league radius.

The study of seventeenth-century Tunja shows how a regional settlement plan might ramify and become consolidated.[8] Founded in 1559, Tunja was second in importance only to Bogotá in the New Granada highlands. The act of founding justified the site as offering 'caciques and Indians and available land to sustain the Spaniards'. By 1623 the city had 476 buildings, including twenty churches and convents but only seven 'public buildings or industries'. The population included 3,300 adult Spanish males and an indeterminate number of Indians, blacks, and mixed-bloods. City officials came from the 70 or more families of encomenderos occupying tile-roofed dwellings that might boast two storeys around interior patios and display stone trimming and coats of arms. Humbler Spaniards – merchants, master craftsmen, artisans – lived in cramped, thatch-roofed dwellings. Non-Europeans and half-castes were generally burden-bearers, living in *bohíos* outside the city plan.

Commerce took place on three levels. The fifteen leading merchants imported fine cloth and modest luxuries from Spain. Regionally, these and lesser merchants traded throughout New Granada, using the city's 30 horse and mule teams to export farm and ranch products, blankets, sandals, leather goods, and flour. Twice-weekly *tiangues* provided a local market for local produce and for the Indians' cotton blankets and pottery. Analogous three-tiered systems have been described for New Spain. The larger cities of Yucatán had long-distance merchants (*mercaderes*), usually immigrants well connected with the encomenderos; retail tradesmen (*comerciantes*), creoles or sometimes mestizos who

[8] V. Cortés Alonso, 'Tunja y sus vecinos', *Revista de Indias*, 25, 99–100 (1965), 155–207.

supplied local commerce and dealt with the countryside; and *tratantes*, often mestizos, Indians, or mulattos, who trafficked with the Indian communities. Similarly Querétaro's trade functioned at three levels: the first in the hands of factors from Mexico City, the second having a provincial radius and providing credit for industry and agriculture, and the third serving the city's retail outlets.

In the case of Tunja, the rudimentary state of manufacturing and finance and the agrarian orientation of the patriciate suggest that trade was secondary in the functional definition of the city. More decisive were the lines of political fealty and control. The social hierarchy represented in Tunja's concentric rings of architectural style symbolized other hierarchies, spatially extended but always centring on the plaza. Political functions loosely corresponded to the three levels of commercial activity. First, Tunja was a point of shifting equilibrium between the claims and favours of church and empire and the separatism of the encomenderos, many of them descended from the mutinous soldiers of Pizarro. If nine of the largest encomiendas belonged to the crown, it was also true that Tunja's encomenderos comprised the most powerful patriciate of New Granada and the only one to resist seriously the royal tax levies of the 1590s. Second, the city was the administrative base for surrounding towns colonized from Tunja, some of them 100 miles distant. Third, Tunja was the control centre for 161 encomiendas representing villages of 80 to 2,000 Indians.

Tunja usefully illustrates how superimposed schemes of dominion might intersect to produce a hierarchically ordered pattern of colonization. It also brings to the fore two aspects of Spanish American urban history – interethnic relations and commercial activity – that are a key not only to urban society but also to the formation of interurban settlement patterns.

TOWNS AND INDIANS

A central goal of Spanish settlement policy was the creation of two 'republics', one of Spaniards and one of Indians. The term 'republic' implied an agro-urban polis composed of functionally integrated social and occupational groups that was inserted into the structure of empire while enjoying a modicum of self-government, or at least self-administration. Although the notion of two republics suggests co-equality and, for the Indians, officially signified protective armature against exploitation, the republic of Indians became a euphemism for a regime of detribalization, regimentation, Christianization, tribute, and forced labour. What appeared in practice, moreover, was not implantation of the polis in the vision harboured by Las Casas but urban nucleation as designated by the terms *pueblos de españoles* and *pueblos de indios*. A cedula of 1551, later picked up in the *Recopilación*, ordered that 'the Indians be reduced to pueblos and not live divided and separated by mountains and hills, deprived of all spiritual and temporal benefits'. As the study of Central America makes clear, the towns of Spaniards and Indians were far from comparable. The arrangement of dwellings in the former reflected a social hierarchy, and the *plaza mayor* with its distinctive ecclesiastical, administrative, fiscal, and commercial structures identified the locus and functions of authority. In Indian towns, where social distinctions had been effaced or drastically simplified, residential location was not indicative of social or political ranking, while the plaza was but a 'vaguely defined vacant space dominated by a church, its sole architectural distinction'.[9]

The implications of Spanish colonization for the native peoples of New Spain are reasonably clear. On the eve of conquest large urban concentrations like Tenochtitlán were rare, and Indians generally lived in small, often contiguous settlements. Larger settlements had a market, temple, and residences for priests and nobles with outlying clusters for commoners. These were often fortified and located at elevations as wartime retreats for the adjacent population. Other centres were primarily ceremonial, inhabited only by priests. In many regions small dependent clusters of a few houses each were widely dispersed throughout the farmlands.

For a generation after conquest devastating epidemics, particularly of smallpox and mumps, had a far more punishing effect on the Indian population, especially those in populous centres and lowland areas, than did Spanish settlement schemes. A few strategic cities like Tenochtitlán were appropriated and rebuilt by the conquerors. The preferred sites for new towns, however, were precisely the valley regions that the Indians had regarded as less defensible or convenient. During these years the Spaniards imposed their urban vision less by relocation than by institutional redefinition. The pre-conquest Valley of Mexico was

[9] S. D. Markman, 'The gridiron town plan and the caste system in colonial Central America', in R. P. Schaedel, J. E. Hardoy, and N. S. Kinzer (eds.), *Urbanization in the Americas from its beginnings to the present* (The Hague, 1978), 481.

divided into numerous culturally and linguistically united 'city states'. These were formed of a central community of several thousand inhabitants organized by family groups (*calpullec*), where the local ruler (*tlatoani*; plural, *tlatoque*) resided, and its satellite communities composed of a single *calpulli* that controlled landholding. This city state, or *altepetl*, was larger than a hamlet and smaller than a river basin; it was, in Lockhart's words, 'less an urban complex than the association of a group of people with a given extended territory', and the word *altepetl* signified originally 'water and hill'. Upon this structure of lineage groups the Spaniards projected Iberian political nomenclature. That is, the central community became a *cabecera* subdivided into wards or *barrios*, while outlying clusters became *estancias* or *sujetos*. The whole settlement complex might become known as a pueblo, even though it quite lacked the close-knit structure and physical form associated with the Spanish prototype. The so-called pueblo in turn was wrenched from its position in Aztec imperial tribute organization and inserted into a European administrative hierarchy of *partidos* and, above them, *provincias*. Indian leaders soon learned the new rules and began vying to acquire privileges for their *cabeceras* or else to have their *sujetos* raised to *cabecera* status. By and large the dispersed pre-conquest settlement pattern endured to about 1550 and was even extended by the flight of Indian groups to remote places. What the Spaniards had managed was to accommodate a peninsular institution, encomienda, to an existing settlement pattern and an existing system for extracting tribute and labour. *Pueblos de españoles* were established incrementally as control centres, while the *tlatoque*, to whom Spaniards applied the Caribbean name *caciques*, served as intermediaries for new masters. A sizeable amount of the Indian labour made available was deployed to construct public works, churches, convents, and administrative headquarters for Mexico City and the *pueblos de españoles*.

This modified pre-conquest pattern inevitably yielded to the more sharply nucleated design that was the early preference of the Spanish crown. A demographic cause was the severe mortality of the Indian population, which made corporate life in dispersed centres unviable and called for the consolidation of survivors in accessible and manageable clusters. After the epidemic of 1545–8 royal orders explicitly commanded that natives be congregated in European-style pueblos near religious houses. Acceptance of this policy was assisted by the sometimes conflicting ambitions of ecclesiastics and encomenderos, both concerned to bring their wards under close supervision. The friars were the most successful agents of Hispanicization and Christianization, accomplished through large-scale creation of new towns, whether by merging existing centres or congregating scattered populations. Towns were named or renamed after Catholic saints; Indians were appointed to minor church offices; and municipal rituals, fiestas, and sodalities introduced Indians to the Christian calendar. Whether under the friars or under *corregidores*, Spanish municipal forms, the cabildo and its component offices, were widely introduced. By 1560 most of the original *cabeceras* had been moved to lower-lying, level sites and many Indians dispersed in remote areas were being relocated in new *cabeceras* and *sujetos*.

After another disastrous time of plague (probably typhus) and famine in 1576–81 the crown intensified the programme of forced congregation, urged on by clerics and encomenderos. As the new relocation strategy designed for most of New Spain took effect in 1593–1605, thousands of place-names vanished and the Spanish grid design with its broad plaza became a familiar sight. Enforced urbanization, however, met strong countercurrents. First, congregation made Indians more vulnerable to contagious disease. Second, Spanish appropriation of rural holdings abandoned by the Indians created a new productive institution, the hacienda, and these began to replace Indian towns as suppliers for the growing populations of the larger urban centres. Workers suffering from hunger and oppressive tribute schedules were drawn off to the greater security of hacienda labour, often in debt bondage. Thus the corporate structure of Indian municipalities atrophied as their economic life became precarious and control passed to hacendados and royal officials. The latifundium–large city binomial that was for centuries to govern settlement patterns and economic flows in large areas of Spanish America was swiftly taking shape. These new sources of organization for labour and the economy assisted the transition from a pre-conquest economic system to one that meshed more directly into the European mode of agro-pastoral, mining, and manufacturing production based on peonage and wage labour.

The great silver strike at Zacatecas in 1546 posed special problems of settlement, for this important site was at the centre of the north-central plateau that stretched north from a border along the Lerma river and was dominated by the bellicose, semi-nomadic Chichimeca tribes. Early efforts to protect traffic along the silver highways, to create defensive towns, and to tranquillize the Indians with guarantees for colonization all met with failure, although towns of future importance like Celaya, León, and Saltillo date from the 1570s. Not until after 1585 was a workable pacification policy devised, involving development of an effective mission system under the friars and relocation of sedentary Indians, notably the Tlaxcalans, to establish model agricultural communities. Zacatecas itself grew to a population of 1,500 Spaniards and 3,000 Indians, blacks, and mestizos by the early seventeenth century. Around the straggling layout of the core city, Indian townships grouped by 'nations' of origin soon took shape.

Although lacking monumental centres, the Chibcha settlements of the Bogotá *sabana* were similar to those of Mesoamerica.[10] Land occupation was dispersive and based on household groups (*utas*) organized into *sivin*, and these in turn into communities headed by a *sijipena* who became the Spaniards' cacique. The conquerors' policy of forced nucleation after 1549 met strong resistance, and by 1600 three-quarters of the 100 or so Indian settlements of the *sabana* were still intact. *Mestizaje* and Hispanicization of caciques were longer delayed than in Mexico. Spanish livestock were more effective than royal policy in forcing Indians to relocate and release land for use by the Europeans. Chessboard settlements became more common in the seventeenth century, although Indians preferred to remain on their scattered plots, leaving the towns as a scene for intermittent religious and fiscal functions and an eventual place of residence for whites and the racially mixed.

In its effects on Indian settlement patterns, the colonization of Peru was also analogous to the Mexican case, although differences in geography and resources, indigenous institutions, and pragmatic conquest solutions created significant variations. A central feature of the imposed urban system was that while the Spaniards occupied and rebuilt Cuzco, the Inca capital, their own capital was located at Lima on the coast. At the same time the mining boom of Potosí, far up in the highlands, brought that city a population vastly exceeding those of its Mexican counterparts. By 1557, twelve years after the discovery of silver, 12,000 Spaniards were counted; by 1572 the population had risen to 120,000 persons of all races, and by 1610, on the eve of decline, to 160,000, a figure which, if accurate, made Potosí the largest city in the hemisphere. Unlike Mexico–Tenochtitlán, Cuzco lost its function of political and cosmological integration as the 'umbilicus' of the Incaic

[10] J. A. and J. E. Villamarín, 'Chibcha settlement under Spanish rule, 1537–1810', in D. J. Robinson (ed.), *Social fabric and spatial structure in colonial Latin America* (Ann Arbor, 1979), 25–84.

world and became a point of linkage between two new poles of attraction. The Spaniards' predilection for the coastal zone and above all for Lima strongly conditioned what Wachtel calls the spatial 'destructuring' of the Andean realm.

At the regional level the Spaniards encountered again dispersed settlement with landholding managed by lineage groups (*ayllus*) under supervision of lords or *curacas* who became the caciques or go-betweens. The impact of the European market economy, however, may well have been more severe in Andean than in Mesoamerica. For here, pre-conquest exchange of products among regions of diverse climate depended not on market dealings but on the control of microhabitats at different altitudes by clusters of kin groups in a system of what have been called 'vertical archipelagos' – a solution also present in at least rudimentary form among the Chibcha. In opposition to these delicate networks of complementary production the Spaniards imposed their notions of land as a commodity, of tributary exaction, and of nucleated urbanization enhanced by all the accoutrements of European town life. Such policies received their prime impetus from the viceroy Francisco de Toledo (1569–81), nicknamed the Peruvian Solon, who ordered, for example, that 16,000 Indians of Condesuyo province be resettled from 445 villages into 48 *reducciones* and that 21,000 Indians of Cuzco be brought from 309 villages into 40 *reducciones*.

For Central America it is possible to trace the long-term erosion of the dichotomy between Spanish and Indian towns caused by race mixture and economic change. With miscegenation the original ethnic stocks produced intermediate groups of mestizos, mulattos, and zambos which by the late colonial period were collapsed into an indeterminate sector of *pardos* or *ladinos*. Towns, both Spanish or Indian, commanding productive hinterlands and favourably located for trade attracted all ethnic groups, becoming *pueblos de ladinos*. If isolated Indian towns, especially those of Dominican and Franciscan origin, stagnated and kept their early features, many others, for example in the indigo zones of the Pacific coast, drew mixed populations. Such centres became architecturally transformed with arcades around the plazas and monumental ecclesiastical and civic architecture. Similarly, a lively Spanish centre like Santiago de los Caballeros attracted an ethnically mixed population, accommodated in a progressively extended official *traza*. Some Spanish towns, on the other hand, never prospered and lost their regional dominance. On the Bogotá *sabana* the *pueblos de indios*, or *resguardos*, were increasingly infiltrated by whites, mestizos, and a few *pardos* and blacks, a change often signalized by the conversion of *resguardos* into *parroquias*. Breakdown of ethnic segregation has also been described by Marzahl for the Popayán region of modern Colombia, where latifundia and mining attracted many non-Indians to formerly Indian settlements. In the city itself the Spanish population mixed increasingly along the social scale with artisans and small farmers of Indian and half-caste extraction.

As this last example suggests, the 'two republics' principle was applied internally to biethnic cities as well as to systems of central places and satellites. Even a town like Querétaro, where Indians, blacks, mestizos, and Spaniards were mixed in the original residential pattern, eventually developed Indian barrios that preserved Indian languages, mores, and family habits. The classic case of segregation is Mexico City, where the central *traza* was laid out comprising some thirteen rectangular blocks in each direction and surrounded by four L-shaped, irregularly planned Indian barrios governed by Indian officials and providing a workforce for the central city. Inevitably, boundaries dissolved as miscegenation occurred and as the ratio of Indians to whites shifted from ten to one in the mid sixteenth century to one to two in the late eighteenth. On various occasions Indian–mestizo conflicts broke out, notably the riots of 1624 and 1692, and attempts were made to restore the original dichotomous arrangement. After the 1692 uprising a commission that included the eminent scholar Carlos Sigüenza y Góngora reported on 'inconveniences from Indians living in the centre of the city' and the need to congregate them in 'their barrios, curacies, and districts, where they should be organized for their better governance without being admitted to the central city'. The documents spoke of the 'insolent freedom' of Indians in the city, who abandoned their homes, impeding civil and churchly administration and tribute collection and filling 'this republic' with 'lazy, vagabond, useless, insolent, and villainous people', disposed to crime and 'confident in the impunity assured by their very anonymity and obscurity'. Blame was ascribed to both sides. First, the Indian barrios were infiltrated by blacks, mulattos, and mestizos, who were wayward, dishonest, thieving, gambling, and vicious and who either corrupted the Indians or forced them to find other sanctuary. Second, Spaniards living in the *traza* were willing to protect renegade Indians so as to rent them a room, or a shack, a relation cemented by *compadrazgo* ties sheltering 'the impudent behaviour that tries our patience'.[11] The trend towards ethnic mixture, both biological and spatial, was clearly beyond reversal. The city's new ecclesiastical and civil subdivisions of the late eighteenth century paid lip service to Indian segregation but did nothing to restore it.

Recent research on Antequera in the Oaxaca valley stresses the city's role in cultural integration throughout the colonial period.[12] A city census of 1565 identified ten ethnic categories of Indians, seven of them of the Nahua group, distributed within the *traza*, at its fringe, in the satellite community of Jalatlaco, or on near-by farms. Gradually these cultural identities dissolved as Indian barrios lost their ethnic character, native languages fell into disuse, the distinction between Indian nobles and commoners disappeared, and non-Indians took residence in Jalatlaco. Indians originally considered as *naborías*, or a source of labour 'in the city', became proletarianized urban Indians who were 'of the city'. The proliferation of mixed-race groups, the intermingling of white creoles and *castas* across the occupational hierarchy, and – after the region's economic upturn of the 1740s – the increased importance of economic as against ethnic status norms all went far towards effacing the distinction between colonized and colonizer.

On a broad view, it is clear that larger towns in the conquest period were a scene of extensive racial mixing among Europeans, Africans, and Indians, especially given the shortage of Spanish and African women. Subsequent stratification and conversion of racial groups into *castas*, it has been suggested by C. Esteva Fabregat, favoured 'both social separation and the relative sexual self-sufficiency of each ethnic group or *casta*'. A third stage saw the erosion of the system of *castas* at the very time that popular nomenclature for the increasing variety of racial combinations was undergoing baroque multiplication. In large cities particularly, this process was hastened by cityward migrations, political restlessness, and economic changes that undermined the corporate structures of society and nurtured a new psychology of malaise and aggressiveness. The suspension of ethnic categories in favour of a broad distinction between respectable folk and the populace, *gente decente* and *la plebe*, was an urban phenomenon reflecting a crisis of authority, a weakening of social controls, and increased assertiveness among the 'popular' sectors. In his study of 'crowds' in Peruvian history, written

[11] 'Sobre los inconvenientes de vivir los indios en el centro de la ciudad', *Boletín del Archivo General de la Nación* (Mexico), 9/1 (1938), 1–34.
[12] J. K. Chance, *Race and class in colonial Oaxaca* (Stanford, 1978).

Table 1 *Ibero-American population c. 1789 by ethnic group and place of residence*

	Residents of 'urban' places			Residents of 'rural' places			Group totals	
	no. in 000s	% of urban pop.	% of total ethnic group	no. in 000s	% of rural pop.	% of total ethnic group	no. in 000s	% of total pop.
Indians*	1,728	36.8	22.0	6,132	65.3	78.0	7,860	55.8
Whites	1,670	35.6	51.8	1,553	16.5	48.2	3,223	22.9
Mestizos	666	14.1	64.4	368	3.9	35.6	1,034	7.3
Mulattos	419	8.9	39.1	653	7.0	60.9	1,072	7.6
Negroes	214	4.6	23.7	688	7.3	76.3	902	6.4
Totals	4,697	100.0	33.3	9,394	100.0	66.7	14,091	100.0

* Excludes *indios bárbaros*.
Source: Adapted from C. Esteva Fabregat, 'Población mestizaje en las ciudades de Iberoamérica: siglo XVIII', in F. de Solano (ed.), *Estudios sobre la ciudad iberoamericana* (Madrid, 1975), 599. Table contains rounding errors.

in 1929, Jorge Basadre posited an eighteenth-century transition from the religious and 'aulic' crowds who swarmed Lima's streets as spectators and celebrants to crowds that, although still 'prepolitical', were of a more frustrated and menacing disposition. The analogue in Mexico City was the urban culture of *leperismo*, publicized in foreigners' travel accounts and named for the racially indistinct *lépero*, who was pictured as insolent, vagrant, aggressive to women, and given to vice and assaults on property.

Using statistics from Alcedo's *Diccionario de América* of 1789, an attempt has been made to specify the racial composition of towns throughout Spanish America. Of the 8,478 settlements tabulated, 7,884 are considered as primarily rural pueblos, while 594 *ciudades, villas*, and mining centres, 7 per cent of the total, are claimed as having significant 'urban' functions based on commerce, services, and industry. This division does not yield a rural–urban split in the modern sense, for many so-called 'urban' centres were small and all of them included rural residents. Still the population distribution by this conjectural criterion reinforces the suggestion that the urban setting was the prime habitat for whites and racially mixed groups (see table 1). First, only 20–25 per cent of the Indians and blacks resided in urban places; second, whites and mestizos comprised 20 per cent of the rural population and 50 per cent of the urban; third, mulattos were about equal to blacks in rural places and almost double their number in urban ones.

Some have suggested that ethnic identification gave way to class identification in larger cities and even to an embryonic 'class consciousness' of the poor. This claim seems excessive when we recall that the class consciousness even of industrial workers in twentieth-century Latin American cities is problematical. It is more plausible to say that the mid eighteenth to mid nineteenth century was a time of absolute, if not necessarily relative, urban population growth and, especially during the independence movements, a relaxation of social controls that encouraged the urban poor to adopt contumelious attitudes towards constituted authority.

A generation after the conquest the native peoples of New Spain and Peru came to realize that they had lost primary identifications with their multifarious array of ethnic groups and were reduced to a common stratum of 'Indians'. Similarly, the variegated phenotypes of the late colonial urban *castas* lost social significance and were absorbed into an indistinct *plebe*. In both cases homogenization of the dispossessed marked the failure of the old ecclesiastical and juridical ideal of social 'incorporation'. The feeling this kindled was a common sense of disinheritance rather than a sense of common cause.

TOWNS AND COMMERCE

The contrast has more than once been made between the commercial impetus of the late medieval towns of north-west Europe and characteristic agro-administrative functions of colonial Spanish American towns. The first were points of crystallization for early forms of commercial capitalism; the second were centrifugal points of assault on the land and its resources. The first were seedbeds for a new economic and legal order; the second were vehicles for an established imperial order.

The contrast becomes less stark when one recognizes that, in time, commercial development gathered momentum in the Indies as local markets grew, marketable commodities were identified, and opportunities for overseas trade expanded. Even so, these trends did not undermine the old order and bring into being a new 'bourgeoisie' with a distinctive ideology. The merchant guilds (*consulados*) of large cities, even though they were closed groups with corporate *esprit*, were, in the words of Veitia Linaje's *Norte de la contratación de las Indias occidentales*, 'helped, protected, and favoured by the Kings and their Ministers'. In towns based on mixed economies like Arequipa and Popayán elites were resourceful at shifting the brunt of their economic involvements about among trade, mining, and agriculture as conditions changed. Colonial Havana, rendezvous port for homegoing fleets, was not a mercantile but a service city, with its port functions at the mercy of the erratic schedule of the fleet system. To compensate Havana for its utility to the mercantilist scheme the crown recognized the agrarian interests of its notables by granting their cabildo – one of only two so privileged in the Indies – the right to distribute land directly without royal approval.

In general, Spanish immigrants were favoured throughout the Indies over creoles in commercial careers, but their capital was often re-channelled into rural holdings and gifts to the church. Medellín, it appears, was an exception, given the narrow possibilities there for acquiring productive land; here sons tended to follow fathers into mining or trade, which offered high-status occupations.[13] But for Mexico City after the 1590s, although there are examples of two-generation merchant families, circulation of the merchant elite rather than consolidation was the norm.[14] Even in the outstanding 'commercial' city of late colonial Buenos Aires, where agricultural land beyond suburban *quintas* was not yet attractive to investors, merchants, it seems, did not create a stable class. Not only did their sons prefer ecclesiastical, military, and bureaucratic careers, but the institutions for business ventures were so rudimentary, and so vulnerable to inheritance laws, that commercial enterprises rarely survived beyond a generation.[15] Other cities in zones of quickening growth were still less progressive. Late colonial Caracas, the traveller Depons found, was more a workshop than a trade centre; the function of an exchange, of paper money, of discounting were all unknown. Havana, despite the economic impetus imparted by sugar exports after 1760, had no permanent banks until the 1850s. The Guayaquil of 1790, with cacao exports soaring, was a small city of 8,000 'with little in the way of financial institutions or, indeed,

[13] A. Twinam, 'Enterprise and elites: eighteenth-century Medellín', *HAHR*, 59/3 (1979), 444–75.
[14] L. S. Hoberman, 'Merchants in seventeenth century Mexico City: a preliminary portrait', *HAHR*, 57/3 (1977), 479–503.
[15] S. M. Socolow, *The merchants of Buenos Aires, 1778–1810* (Cambridge, 1978).

specialized commercial houses'.[16] A study of the credit market in eighteenth-century Guadalajara exemplifies what one means by the archaic financial capacity of Spanish American cities.[17] Here credit was largely controlled by the church, particularly in the early part of the century, with a lending potential derived from bequests left for masses, convent dowries, *cofradías*, tithe collection, and income from real estate. With such funds, the church could lend on a regular basis, while individuals – merchants, priests, widows – would lend but once or twice in a period of decades. Capital circulated within a small group of businessmen and clergy, reaching the hinterland through hacendados. That the money market achieved no great momentum in late colonial times is attested by the fact that the 892,000 pesos' worth of loans reported for Guadalajara in the 1760s had dropped to 773,000 by the decade 1801–10.

Yet if no Amsterdam or Philadelphia sprang up in the Indies, an important strand of the urban story features the varied commercial activity that gathered in volume to ratify, extend, or reorient the primitive design of empire and the contingent solutions of conquest. Because of the size of the stage on which it was played, the most dramatic episode was the rise to commercial hegemony of penurious Buenos Aires, favoured by strategic location but isolated by Spanish mercantilist policy, at the expense of Lima, the City of Kings and commercial capital of the southern viceroyalty.

Writing of the 'trade, splendour, and wealth' of Lima, the contemporary observer Bernabé Cobo, in his *Historia de la fundación de Lima*, gave little impression of a city where class structure, norms of behaviour, and economic decisions were powerfully shaped by commercial imperatives. He spoke, to be sure, of 'the tremendous volume' of its business and trade as 'the capital, emporium, and permanent fair and bazaar' of the viceroyalty and nearby regions. Most of the city's population made subsidiary incomes from commerce with Europe, China, and New Spain. Yet private wealth was attracted to extravagant consumption. Lima's four or five modest coaches at Cobo's arrival in 1599 had, 30 years later, become over 200, trimmed in silk and gold and worth 3,000 pesos or more apiece, a sum equal to half the annual income

---

[16] M. L. Conniff, 'Guayaquil through independence: urban development in a colonial system', *The Americas*, 33/3 (1977), 401.

[17] L. L. Greenow, 'Spatial dimensions of the credit market in eighteenth century Nueva Galicia', in Robinson, *Social fabric*, 227–79.

from an entailed estate (*mayorazgo*). Even the most affluent, with
fortunes of 300,000 or 400,000 ducats, suffered 'toil and anguish' to
maintain 'this empty pomp'. Persons worth as little as 20,000 were held
as poor. A large fraction of the city's wealth was displayed in furnishings
and jewellery; even the indigent possessed a gem or a gold or silver
plate. Lima's total stock of jewels and precious metals was calculated
at 20 million ducats, with the investment in slaves at 12 million – and
this exclusive of finery, tapestries, and articles of worship. So widespread
were luxurious habits of dress that one could scarcely distinguish social
groups. Merchants in Spain, where sumptuary laws applied, were
delighted at this distant outlet for silks, brocades, and fine linens. The
bulk of the city's fortunes were sunk in real estate (farms, vineyards,
sugar mills, ranches), *obrajes*, and encomiendas. Yet the total income
yielded by its fifteen or so *mayorazgos* was far exceeded by the million
ducats that flowed annually in salaries to ecclesiastics, bureaucrats, and
the military.

Buenos Aires, abandoned in 1541, was finally refounded in 1580 as
an Atlantic outlet for the inland settlements. Through their procurator
in Madrid the townsmen complained of the poverty of the region and
the lack of gunpowder, cloth, and wine for Mass. Trade with Upper
Peru was disallowed because Tucumán could supply it with agro-pastoral
products from a shorter distance. Accordingly, Spain authorized trade
between Buenos Aires and Brazil (then under the Spanish crown), first
(1595) for the import of slaves to expand agricultural production, then
(1602) to allow exports to Brazil of flour, dried beef, and tallow. Because
the Brazilian market was limited, merchants made their larger profits
on the re-export of slaves and tropical produce to Tucumán. Soon a
well-to-do class appeared, inflated by Portuguese immigrants. Bridling
at the threat to its fiscal interests, the crown abolished the Brazil trade
in 1622, limiting Buenos Aires to a yearly traffic with Spain of two 100-ton
ships. The possibilities for contraband, however, doomed to failure this
precarious design of maintaining a strategic outpost on the Plata estuary
while restraining its commercial development. Acarete du Biscay visited
the port in 1658, as he recalls in his *Account of a voyage up the Rio de la
Plata, and thence over land to Peru* (London, 1698), to find a town of 400
earthen houses thatched with cane and straw and defended by only a
small earthen fort of ten guns, using twelve-pound ammunition or less,
and three 50-strong companies, captained by the vecinos and usually
undermanned because soldiers were 'drawn by the cheapness of Living

in those parts to desert frequently'. The houses, all of one storey, had spacious rooms, courtyards, and adjacent orchards and gardens. Beef, game, and fowl were cheap and plentiful, and while only 'the Savages' ate ostriches, their feathers made effective parasols for all. Better houses were 'adorn'd with Hangings, Pictures, and other Ornaments and decent Moveables' and served by many black, Indian, and mixed-blood servants. 'All the wealth of these Inhabitants consists in Cattle, which multiply so prodigiously in this Province, that the Plains are quite cover'd with 'em.' In the harbour Acarete found no less than 22 Dutch ships, each laden with some 14,000 hides bought for less than a crown apiece and saleable in Europe for five times as much. By now cattle were being sent to Peru as well; but although the cattle trade was profitable, the 'most considerable' merchants were 'they that Traffick in European Commodities'. The transfer of customs collection from Córdoba north to Salta and Jujuy in 1676 signalled Buenos Aires' domination of the whole Platine market.

Lima's merchants opposed a strong Buenos Aires–Tucumán regional economy that threatened their commercial sway over Upper Peru. They refused to buy cattle at the Salta fair and tried to corner the Charcas market through factors who intercepted produce from Buenos Aires and set their own price. Gradually, however, northern Argentina, Charcas, and even Chile fell from Lima's commercial control. The simple fact was that Buenos Aires was a more viable port than Lima-Callao. The expensive fleet system was not needed here; fewer pirates attacked ships, and less seaweed clogged their hulls at this latitude; shipments overland from Buenos Aires were cheaper and less troublesome than via Panama; contraband was less controlled at Buenos Aires, and *porteños* could pay with silver that had escaped the royal fifth; finally, after 1680 Sacramento was available as an immense warehouse. During the British *asiento* from 1713 to 1739, contraband opportunities increased, sales of hides and tallow jumped, and British commercial methods were learned. Population figures tell the story. While Lima's inhabitants remained steady at 55,000–60,000 for a century after 1740, those of Buenos Aires rose from 11,000 to 65,000. The elevation of the latter to a viceregal capital in 1776 authenticated commercial realities.

The Lima–Buenos Aires case exemplifies commercial forces that reshaped the settlement pattern of the whole southern continent and would eventually shift its economic axis from the Pacific to the Atlantic coast. Such forces, however, took hold also at the regional level, affecting the destinies of second-rank agro-administrative centres. Although the elite of Santiago de Chile drew its power and prestige primarily from landowning and political careers, the city's merchant interests managed to dominate producers in Chile's three main regional economies – those of Santiago, La Serena, and Concepción – to retard the growth of the last two and subordinate them to a commercial system that was centred on Santiago and oriented towards foreign suppliers and consumers.[18] In the Popayán region the early urban system underwent drastic redefinition, caused locally by changing mining locations and the shift from Indian to African slave labour, and externally by the rise of Cartagena as a port of entry (displacing Buenaventura) and the growth of textile manufactures in the Quito area. In the seventeenth century many centres became ghost towns, leaving Popayán, Pasto, and Cali as the urban mainstays. Popayán took the lead not by virtue of administrative rationalization from above – for its region was riven by cross-cutting civil, ecclesiastical, fiscal, and military jurisdictions – but by virtue of a privileged location for trade, mining and agro-pastoral pursuits, which in turn helped to consolidate its political role.[19]

In Mesoamerica Mexico City is the historic centre of bureaucratic, commercial, financial, and industrial dominance. Over the centuries it has internalized transformations that in South America are best exemplified successively in three cities: Lima (era of colonial mercantilism), Buenos Aires (era of commercial capitalism), and São Paulo (era of industrial, financial, and technological development). Yet the geography, resources, and settlement patterns of New Spain resisted such pervasive forms of spatial organization as Buenos Aires, São Paulo, and, most notably, Montevideo eventually imposed on their respective hinterlands. As James Lockhart has said, the Westernization of colonial Mexico did not occur in neatly concentric stages, 'since activity from the capital leapt great distances to areas of interest, leaving closer ones relatively isolated and unaffected'. It is possible to trace the growth of local resistance to the determination 'from without' of spatial organization and route patterns. It is true that economic and administrative requirements of the mother country reoriented the pre-Hispanic settle-

[18] M. Carmagnani, *Les mécanismes de la vie économique dans une société coloniale: le Chili (1680–1830)* (Paris, 1973).

[19] P. Marzahl, *Town in the empire: government, politics and society in seventeenth century Popayán* (Austin, 1978).

ment patterns of the central plateau or, in mineral and ranching zones, asserted themselves directly. Thus, wrote Moreno Toscano and Florescano:

some Mexicans imagined the system as a huge mouth located in Spain and nourished by a wide conduit running from Mexico City to Cadiz via Jalapa and Veracruz which, in turn, was fed by lesser channels from the centres and cities of the interior. The route system linking centres and cities faithfully replicated that scheme.[20]

Yet this polarized pattern contained internal tensions and exceptions. Puebla, founded as a consolation prize for poorer Spaniards, soon attracted encomenderos, acquired an Indian workforce, and became a leading distribution centre for agricultural produce. The accretion of administrative, commercial, religious, and (as a textile producer) industrial functions allowed it to organize its own hinterland and on several counts resist domination by the capital. A similar case was Guadalajara, with its administrative, commercial, and educational functions. Another rivalry was that between the Veracruz merchants, who distributed imports via the Jalapa fair and were linked to Oaxaca and the Gulf coast's agricultural producers, and the Mexico City merchants, who sought control of the import trade and pressed for a route to the coast via Orizaba and bypassing Jalapa. Finally, there is the case of the Bajío, a prosperous agricultural and mining region supporting a network of specialized towns that resisted domination by either of the largest cities, Guanajuato or Querétaro. Here was an instance, unique for Mexico, of a complex, internally integrated regional economy. In its external relations it supplied agricultural products and raw materials to Mexico City while sending manufactures to northern Mexico in exchange for raw materials. Resulting profits were accumulated locally and not drained off to the capital.

In time, even modest agro-administrative centres became commercial catalysts for immediate hinterlands. For example, the original controls of taxation, forced labour, and administration emanating from Antequera over the Indian communities of Oaxaca were gradually complemented by trade involvements as market demands and cash reserves exerted their power. The city's growing need for pulque and other farm and ranch commodities not only increased rural production but

---

[20] A. Moreno Toscano and E. Florescano, 'El sector externo y la organización espacial y regional de México (1521–1910)', in J. W. Wilkie, M. C. Meyer and E. Monzón de Wilkie (eds.), *Contemporary Mexico* (Berkeley and Los Angeles, 1976), 67.

attracted village Indians to permanent or seasonal urban residence. Administration and regulation were no longer the rationale for Antequera's existence. According to William Taylor, 'trade, commerce, and manufacturing assumed new importance, and the city and countryside of the central valleys had begun to form a stronger regional system'.[21]

Urban places became important centres for the commercialization of Spanish American society and institutions, but ineffective vehicles for diffusing full-blown 'capitalism'. The spread of commercial impetus from cities and *pueblos de españoles*, for example, coexisted with 'commerce' for control and spoliation, as instanced by *corregidores* in their notorious practice of foisting useless merchandise at inflated prices on vulnerable Indian communities. Commercial activity was orchestrated within a framework of mercantilist design, patrician status objectives, and prebendary administration. Urban merchants failed to form a coherent and enduring 'class'. Lacking developed instruments and institutions for credit and financial accrual, they were adept at keeping open their options for social advancement and for orienting their progeny to alternative careers. Mario Góngora prefers to call the Chilean merchants a 'trading' (*negociante*) element, not a truly mercantile one, who pursued a *cursus honorum* that was 'part of an aristocratic, as opposed to mercantile or bourgeois, society'. Port cities, so often seedbeds for commercial innovation, were only intermittently active (Portobelo, the early Havana); or they served as stevedores to bureaucratic capitals (Veracruz, Callao, Valparaíso); or their commercial leadership was reinforced by core administrative, ecclesiastical, and service functions (Cartagena, Buenos Aires, Montevideo, the later Havana). In the 1690s the traveller Gamelli Carreri described Acapulco, with its makeshift houses of wood, mud, and straw, as a 'humble village of fishermen', not an emporium for trade with Guatemala, Peru, and the Orient and port of call for the Manila galleons. When ships from Peru arrived their merchants, carrying millions of pesos for Oriental finery, had to lodge in the miserable shacks of the town's mulattos.[22]

Cities were bastions of the Spanish political order and not conspicuous centres of innovative ideology and programmatic institutional change. This helps account for the diffuse quality of lower-class protest in the

[21] W. B. Taylor, 'Town and country in the valley of Oaxaca, 1750–1812', in I. Altman and J. Lockhart (eds.), *Provinces of early Mexico* (Berkeley and Los Angeles, 1976), 74.

[22] Gamelli Carreri's impressions of seventeenth-century Mexican cities are in *Las cosas más considerables vistas en la Nueva España* (Mexico, 1946).

late colonial years and for the decentralization of political structures after independence and the flow of power to the rural domain. Even so, it would be misleading to conceive of the colonial urban system simply, in the imagery quoted above, as a huge mouth located in Spain and fed by conduits running through the urban hierarchies of the Indies. Semi-autonomous subsystems took shape, sometimes strong enough to challenge the imperial prescription. Their vigour derived, however, not from a 'capitalist' ethic but from their success at regional replication of the Spanish metropolitan design, a process referred to by such expressions as 'interiorization of the metropolis' or, more tendentiously, 'internal colonialism'. A classic example of how the city's 'developmental' role was conceived is the proposal of a Mexico City magistrate for the 'illness' of Hispaniola. In 1699 the *oidor* F. J. de Haro y Monterroso advocated that the capital of Santo Domingo be transferred to a central inland site, assembling the population of a score of scattered villages and receiving the royal bureaucracies, the university, and the colleges. 'The Court is the image of the heart', he wrote, 'and like it should be located virtually in the centre so that justice and assistance may be rendered with the greatest uniformity and dispatch.' Under such conditions,

the Church, Tribunals, and Communities draw everything with them. Merchants, students, and claimants throng the highways: their trips increase the welfare of many; neighbouring places benefit from consumption of their produce, and the Royal Treasury profits from the numerous inns and markets.[23]

The advice was never taken (although a similar proposal appeared as late as 1858 in the Constitution of the Dominican Republic), but it expresses a symptomatic view of the city as a patrimonial centre destined simultaneously to stimulate, control, and hierarchize the forces making for economic change.

LATE COLONIAL CHANGE

From the mid eighteenth century until the era of national independence 75 years later the urbanization of Spanish America can be related to three

[23] 'Medidas propuestas para poblar sin costo alguno (de) la Real Hacienda de la Isla de Santo Domingo', in E. Rodríguez Demorizi (ed.), *Relaciones históricas de Santo Domingo* (Ciudad Trujillo, 1942), 345–59.

Table 2 *Populations of larger Spanish American cities as a percentage of respective 'national' populations in selected years*

4 largest cities of Argentina	24	(1778)	14	(1817)
4 largest cities of Venezuela	15	(1772)	10	(1810)
3 largest cities of Chile	16	(1758)	9	(1813)
3 largest cities of Cuba	35	(1774)	22	(1817)
2 largest cities of Peru	8	(c. 1760)	7	(1820)
largest city of Mexico	2.9	(1742)	2.2	(1793)
largest city of Uruguay	30	(1769)	18	(1829)

general trends: faster population growth, Bourbon reform policies, and economic changes.

Having held somewhat steady at very roughly ten million inhabitants for a century or more, the population of the region rose to perhaps double that number by about 1825. Natural increase occurring with improved health conditions and the recuperation of Indian populations greatly assisted the upturn. So too did immigration. The eighteenth-century data so far collected, whether for European immigration or for European-born residents in America, are too deficient to allow a sequel to Mörner's perhaps conservative estimate of 440,000 Spanish transatlantic migrants for the period 1500–1650. Certainly a steady flow continued. For imports of African slaves Curtin's estimated yearly averages of 3,500 for the period 1601–1760 show a rise to 6,150 for 1761–1810.

General population growth contributed to urban growth, whether large cities, small towns, or fresh nuclei in frontier areas. When, however, we compare population increases in large cities with increases in what were to become the respective national territories, we find that the urban share declined during the decades before independence. The totals that supply the percentages in table 2 are sketchy, but the cumulative tendency is persuasive. Figures for several secondary centres corroborate this decline. From 1760 to 1784 the population of Trujillo, in coastal Peru, dropped from 56.5 per cent to 48.1 per cent of the provincial total,[24] while the three leading towns of central highland Ecuador – Latacunga, Ambato, and Riobamba – slipped from 9.6 per

[24] K. Coleman, 'Provincial urban problems: Trujillo, Peru, 1600–1784' in Robinson, *Social fabric*, 369–408.

cent (1778) to 4.6 per cent (1825) of the regional population, a trend associated here with natural disasters, economic depression, and the independence wars.[25]

The sources of population growth just reviewed explain in part the pattern of lagging urbanization. The decrease in Indian mortality rates was registered primarily in rural areas, where most of the Indians lived. Higher imports of African slaves went largely to rural areas; in fact, more than half the slaves introduced to Spanish America during 1774–1807 went to Cuba, with its burgeoning sugar economy. Spanish immigration, which may have fallen from earlier levels, presumably favoured urban centres, but here, as noted, data are weak. The uprooting of Indian communities, proletarianization of rural workers, and poverty in some of the mining areas swelled internal cityward migrations; but urban health conditions reduced their impact on urban growth. There were a minimum of 124,000 deaths from epidemics in Mexico City in the eighteenth century and 135,000 in Puebla. The 1764 smallpox epidemic in Caracas killed perhaps one-quarter of its population of 26,340.

If scattered statistics fail to show net urban growth, the Bourbon era did witness qualitative urbanization in the form of urban services, city planning, and elegant neoclassical public construction. The long-standing policy of urban nucleation was revived, particularly for colonization and frontier defence. Generally, in fact, Bourbon reform measures tended to favour decentralization of urban systems.

Mexico City received a new aqueduct, mint, custom house, and school of mines, and the Academy of San Carlos. The Alameda was doubled in length, shaded *paseos* were laid out, and the city's policing, paving, and street lighting were improved. Lima offered a cleaner slate for such modernization after its devastating earthquake of 1746. In towns throughout the Platine viceroyalty royal officials restored cathedrals, paved streets, improved drainage, and built schools, hospitals, aqueducts, bridges, granaries, and theatres. Santiago de Chile saw a wave of public construction and urban redesign after the 1760s, crowned by the work of the Italian architect, engineer, and urbanist Joaquín Toesca, who designed the cathedral, the Casa de Moneda, and the retaining walls of the Mapocho river. Dismayed by the rudimentary state of

[25] R. D. F. Bromley, 'The role of commerce in the growth of towns in central highland Ecuador 1750–1920', in W. Borah, J. Hardoy, and G. A. Stelter (eds.), *Urbanization in the Americas: the background in comparative perspective* (Ottawa, 1980), 25–34.

communications in their realm, viceroys assigned to New Granada after 1739 did what they could to improve the road system centring on the capital; in the 1790s Bogotá received its first police force, public cemetery, theatre, and newspaper.

The work of creating new towns was conspicuous in the increasingly productive regions of Chile and north-west Argentina, after 1735 under an expressly created Junta de Poblaciones and, from 1783 to 1797, under supervision of the intendant of Córdoba, the Marqués de Sobremonte. The new towns policy aimed to assemble dispersed rural populations in towns and villages and to bring Indians into *reducciones* or racially mixed centres. In addition to the foundings, some towns were reorganized or even rebuilt and resettled while others, like Concepción, were moved to new sites. The purposes envisioned were to bring schooling and administrative control to rural people, improve productivity, catechize Indians, and strengthen defences against hostile Indians. In all, some 80 new towns took root. Similar initiatives were taken in New Granada, two notable ones being a town founded in 1753 exclusively for convicts and named for Saint Anthony, patron saint of delinquents, and authorization for a community of runaway blacks to choose their own officers and to exclude white residents save for a priest. Distinctive among the frontier settlements in the Interior Provinces of northern Mexico were the 21 missions established in California between 1769 and 1823 and the new-style *presidios* which, as projected under a *reglamento* of 1772, anticipated the future boundary between Mexico and the United States. Although far from modern by European standards of the times, the *presidio* was greatly expanded over the primitive guard posts in the Chichimeca territory of two centuries before. It was now a spacious compound, hundreds of feet along a side, and enclosed by angular bastions and salient gun platforms. *Presidios* became internment centres for hostile Indians but also attracted, in addition to soldiers' families, those of whites, mestizos, and pacified Indians who sought protection and markets for their produce. By 1779 that at San Antonio, Texas with its surrounding *villa* contained 240 military, including families, and 1,117 civilians.

The creation of new towns, missions, and *presidios* had a combined effect of urban nucleation and systemic decentralization. Selectively it amounted to a new surge of conquest and settlement. This 'decentralization' of the late Bourbon period, however, was not the policy idealized by modern planners whereby local centres receive increased authority in day-to-day decision-making. Rather it was a policy aimed at dissolving emergent New World hierarchies and submitting the component parts to metropolitan control. Thus in New Spain after 1760 the intendant system was designed to increase royal power at the expense of corporations and privileged persons. Creation of twelve new administrative entities dependent on royal power rather than local elites interposed between Mexico City and local districts a series of subcapitals enjoying new administrative, judicial, and fiscal functions. In weakening viceregal power the crown achieved centralization by ostensible decentralization. Simultaneous commercial reforms broke the trade monopoly of Mexico City, favouring merchants in Veracruz and Guadalajara, who received their own *consulados* in 1795.

If the late Bourbon decades produced challenges to the older administrative capitals, they favoured accretion and consolidation of functions in hitherto peripheral centres. In the case of Buenos Aires, already discussed, the city's elevation to viceregal status recognized its prior control of a commercial hinterland. In its course towards primacy at the other end of the continent Caracas was more dependent on official reinforcement. On the eve of independence Humboldt observed that Venezuela's wealth was not 'directed at one point' and that it had several urban centres of 'commerce and civilization'. Over the centuries, however, Caracas, with certain marginal advantages of climate and location, had been favoured by successive increments of bureaucratic and cultural functions. The city's evolution can be seen as a complex interaction of economic advantage, political favour, and bureaucratic monopoly. After 1750, in John Lombardi's words, 'Caracas' centrality was created by the Spanish imperial government to serve the economic and military needs of that dying empire'. By a series of administrative decisions from 1777 to 1803 Caracas became seat of the new captaincy general, an *audiencia*, an intendancy, a *consulado*, and an archbishopric. Caracas' effective political control of Venzuela was still problematical; its communication with even nearby rural zones was precarious; other cities were more strategically placed for overseas trade. Yet the accrual of administrative functions gave the city a magnetic force that outlasted the turmoil of independence and the economic and political divisiveness of the early republican decades to ensure its pivotal role is national integration after 1870.

An important source of change for settlement patterns was the growing production for export made possible by expanding metropolitan markets and by the larger, faster ships employed in ocean trade. Port cities that were not merely 'stevedores' but themselves commanded productive hinterlands became particularly active: the sugar port of Havana, the cacao port of Guayaquil, the agro-pastoral port of Buenos Aires. Many inland towns also prospered, as did Antequera, which profited from the cochineal trade and a revived textile industry to evolve after 1740, in J. K. Chance's words, 'from a small, inward-looking agro-town into a highly commercial export centre of considerable size'. Though one might catalogue many more urban loci that responded to agricultural, mining, industrial, and commercial stimuli, we will here restrict ourselves to some broad generalizations about the pervasive effects of commercialization on patterns of settlement.

The eighteenth century witnessed an intensification and specialization of agro-pastoral production for foreign markets that has continued up to modern times. This trend signified many changes in the mode of production: a shift from labour-intensive to more technified, rationalized, and capital-intensive systems; a redirection of profits from consumption to productive infrastructure; new needs for intermediaries, credit facilities, and suppliers in urban centres; and, except for slave-based plantations, a shift from a workforce subject to paternalistic or coercive controls to a deracinated and underemployed 'rural proletariat'. These changes had various implications for urban development. Strategic maritime ports became more active. Larger cities prospered from financial and commercial activity. Patriciates were attracted to urban centres of power, providing a clientele for amenities and improved services. In rural areas, however, the export economies failed to strengthen settlement networks as they had the power and resources of privileged cities. New amenities and services went to latifundia, not to small towns. Commodity flows followed export channels, leaving regional urban networks weak. Traditional villages and *resguardos* were disrupted but not replaced by small commercial towns. Rural workers released from traditional settings who were not absorbed into peonage gained spatial mobility and entered the money economy, but as underemployed migrants, as members of the urban *lumpen*, or as residents of impoverished, makeshift villages. Woodrow Borah has described the impromptu late colonial rural clusters as being frequently 'a thickening of settlement at an existing crossroads, rancho, or hacienda', adapted to existing irregular roads and trails without resort to a formal grid.

The trends just indicated were not yet pre-emptive, and the patterning effects on urban systems of commodity exports, the rise to primacy of selected capitals, and proletarianization of rural workers were not to take more definitive hold until the era of national integration and accentuation of export dependency in the late nineteenth century. A modern planner transported to late Bourbon Spanish America might well have applauded the urban decentralization and colonization policies of the crown. He would have approved of the flourishing manufactures in regions outside the chief administrative centres, such as the Bajío, the Socorro region of New Granada, and the interior cities of the Platine viceroyalty. He would have noted that the rise in exports was accompanied in many places by higher levels and greater diversity of production for domestic consumption and thus by growing integration of economic regions. He would have been refreshed by the climate of intellectual inquiry and concern for applied science to be found in the urban environment. He might in fact have ventured to infer that large areas of Spanish America had embarked on modern economic 'development'. Whatever its basis for the Bourbon years, such a prognosis would not have held good for the early decades of independence. The independence wars themselves damaged productive facilities and many urban centres. As the new nations took form, the city-based bureaucracies of empire were dismantled, and political structures, particularly in the larger countries, were elaborated from provincial bases where wealth and power were more readily reconstituted. The achievements of domestic manufacturing were virtually cancelled by cheap foreign imports as the large cities became commercial headquarters for what have controversially been called new 'informal empires'. Statistically, the 'deurbanization' already discussed for the eighteenth century continued well into the nineteenth; but its causes and significance were in many ways altered by the independence wars and their aftermath.

5

MINING

'Gold is the loftiest and most esteemed metal that the earth brings forth...Among other virtues which nature has bestowed on it, one is singular – that it comforts the weakness of the heart and engenders joy and magnanimity, takes away melancholy, and clears the eyes of cloudiness...'[2] So wrote a Spanish goldsmith half a century after the conquest of New Spain. Cortés perhaps spoke with less cynical intent than is often thought when he told Montezuma's messenger, 'I and my companions suffer from a disease of the heart which can be cured only with gold'.[3] But it was not so much gold as silver that awaited Spain in America. The accumulated gold of centuries was looted during the two decades, 1520–40, which saw the Spanish military conquest of Middle and South America. Thereafter, though gold was mined in varying and often substantial amounts, silver predominated in both volume and value produced.

[1] This chapter concerns the mining of precious metals: silver and, to a lesser extent, gold. Base metal ores, despite their common occurrence in Spanish America, were little exploited during the colonial period. The central Andes, particularly Charcas, was the region best endowed with such ores, and probably the most active in copper, tin and lead production. Copper was also produced in Chile and in Cuba, particularly in the sixteenth century, and in New Spain at various mines in Puebla, Jalisco and Michoacán. The iron supply was almost entirely imported from Spain. Indeed it generally seems to have been cheaper to import base metals than to produce them in America. An abundance of pearls was discovered around the island of Margarita, off the Venezuelan coast, during the early exploration of the Caribbean, but was depleted in the early decades of the sixteenth century. The emerald mines of eastern New Granada, however, which the Spanish learned of in the sixteenth century, continue to produce today.

   In this chapter, colonial provincial names have been used. Thus New Spain corresponds to modern Mexico, New Granada to Colombia, Quito to Ecuador, Peru to Peru more or less as it presently exists, Charcas to highland Bolivia, Río de la Plata to central and northern Argentina.

[2] Juan de Arfe y Villafañe, *Quilatador de la plata, oro y piedras* (Valladolid, 1572; facsimile reproduction, Madrid, 1976), fo. 23v.

[3] Francisco López de Gómara, *Cortés. The life of the conqueror by his secretary* (Berkeley and Los Angeles, 1966), 58.

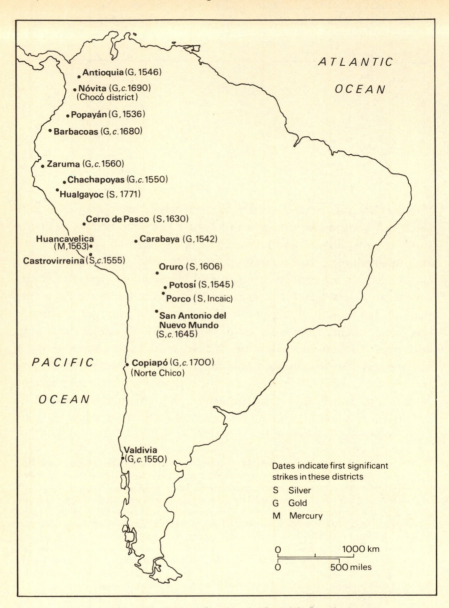

ATLANTIC

OCEAN

• **Antioquia** (G, 1546)

• **Nóvita** (G, *c.* 1690)
(Chocó district)

• **Popayán** (G, 1536)

• **Barbacoas** (G, *c.* 1680)

• **Zaruma** (G, *c.* 1560)

• **Chachapoyas** (G, *c.* 1550)

• **Hualgayoc** (S, 1771)

• **Cerro de Pasco** (S, 1630)

Huancavelica
(M, 1563) •

Carabaya (G, 1542)

Castrovirreina (S, *c.* 1555)

• **Oruro** (S, 1606)

• **Potosí** (S, 1545)

• **Porco** (S, Incaic)

• **San Antonio del
Nuevo Mundo**
(S, *c.* 1645)

PACIFIC

• **Copiapó** (G, *c.* 1700)
(Norte Chico)

OCEAN

Valdivia
• (G, *c.* 1550)

Dates indicate first significant
strikes in these districts

S   Silver
G   Gold
M   Mercury

0   1000 km

0   500 miles

Centres of major mining districts in Spanish South America

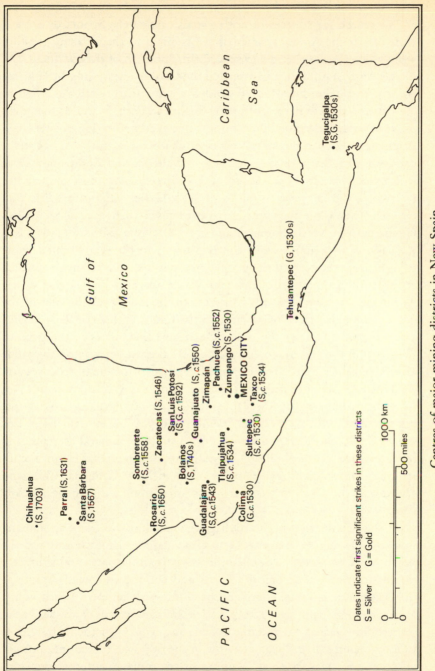

Chihuahua
(S, 1703)

Parral (S, 1631)

Santa Bárbara
(S, 1567)

Sombrerete
(S, c.1558)

Zacatecas (S, 1546)

San Luis Potosí
(S, G, c.1592)

Guanajuato (S, c.1550)

Rosario
(S, c.1650)

Bolaños
(S, 1740s)

Zimapán

Pachuca (S, c.1552)

Zumpango (S, 1530)

Guadalajara
(S, G, c.1543)

Tlalpujahua
(S, c.1534)

MEXICO CITY

Colima
(G, c.1530)

Sultepec
(S, c.1530)

Taxco
(S, c.1534)

Tehuantepec (G, 1530s)

Tegucigalpa
(S, G, 1530s)

Gulf of Mexico

Caribbean Sea

PACIFIC OCEAN

Dates indicate first significant strikes in these districts

S = Silver   G = Gold

1000 km

500 miles

Centres of major mining districts in New Spain

The search for sources of both metals carried the Spaniards far and wide across the Americas, contributing much to the amazing rapidity with which they explored and settled their portion of the continent. On the promise of gold they first settled the Caribbean; finding little in the islands, they were lured on by golden visions to the Isthmus, then to New Spain, then to Peru. Both New Spain and Peru, as well as the north of New Granada, yielded gold booty. But even before Pizarro received Atahualpa's golden ransom, New Spain had begun to reveal her silver deposits, with discoveries about 1530 at Sultepec and Zumpango, close to Mexico City. In 1534, Taxco and Tlalpujahua were in action; and by 1543–4 the far western mines of New Galicia (Espíritu Santo and others). Then came the great northward silver rush: Zacatecas (1546), Guanajuato (*c.* 1550), Sombrerete (*c.* 1558), Santa Bárbara (1567), San Luis Potosí (*c.* 1592), to mention but a few. In the rear Pachuca came to light in 1552. Not all these were prosperous or even much worked at first; but the pattern of deposits was made clear in a few decades. The same was true in South America. In the late 1530s the first of the great goldfields of New Granada, in the Cauca and Magdalena basins, were located; by 1541 the gold of central Chile; in 1542 the gold of Carabaya in the eastern central Andes. By then silver was on the scene also: Gonzalo Pizarro worked the old Inca deposits at Porco by 1538. And the richest silver strike of them all, at nearby Potosí, came in 1545, to be followed by many lesser finds in Charcas. In Peru, Castrovirreina, discovered about 1555, was the first of numerous substantial strikes. For most of colonial times, however, Peru's greatest mineral contribution to the empire was not bullion, but mercury, discovered at Huancavelica in 1563. Other silver strikes were made in New Granada, Chile and Honduras, but proved trivial in comparison with those already described.

As the rich districts began to disgorge metal, towns grew up in many inhospitable regions – coastal New Granada, highland Charcas and the north Mexican plateau, for example – where only sparse and primitive populations had lived before. Roads and commerce spread rapidly as new economic circuits, energized by mining, developed. Cloth, wine, and iron from Spain, slaves from Africa, silks and spices from the Orient – these flowed into the mining towns; and to pay for them streams of bullion, mainly silver, began to flow in the opposite directions. But not all commerce was external. Mining also stimulated internal development: grain cultivation in the Bajío and Michoacán, wine making on

the Peruvian coast and in Chile, cattle and mule raising in the Río de
la Plata provinces, textiles in Peru and Quito; and everywhere freighting
and craftwork. Very few large regions escaped the influence of the
bullion flows.

Nature, in the guise of Tertiary orogenesis, had provided the wide
dispersal of mineral wealth that gave rise to these currents. During the
uplift of the Andean and Mexican ranges in the Tertiary age, rock
fissures in many regions were filled with metallic minerals, among them
those of silver. Far from all the resulting silver veins were rich, but
enough were so to make the silver-mining centre a characteristic
settlement over much of New Spain and the Andes. The veins were
often formed at great heights – up to 15,700 feet at Potosí, for example
– and mining settlements were therefore also high. Almost all were
above 10,000 feet in Peru and Charcas, and between 6,000 and 8,000
in New Spain. Gold, conversely, was normally mined at lower levels,
since most of it lay in alluvial deposits below the ranges from which
it had been removed by hydraulic action. Many such deposits lay in rain
forests, which presented their own difficulties of access and living
conditions. Gold, by its chemical nature, appeared as native metal or
as an alloy; not so silver, which was only occasionally found in a native
state, but rather in compounds resulting from its reaction with other
substances. Some of these compounds were useful ores. A brief account
of the formation and nature of these will serve as a useful introduction
to colonial mining and refining techniques.

The initial silver ores deposited in rock fissures from sources deep
in the earth are known as hypogene or primary ores. These are normally
sulphides. They may be rich – at Guanajuato they were – but frequently
are not; and most of the great Spanish American silver centres drew
their wealth from hypogene ores that had been enriched. This might
happen in two ways. First, the action of descending water oxidized the
hypogene sulphides, usually converting them into silver chloride
(cerargyrite), which contains a higher proportion of silver. This
enrichment by oxidation ceased, however, at the water table, since below
it there was no free oxygen. But enrichment did continue below the
water table through a second process – a rather complex one named
secondary supergene enrichment, which produced sulphides of a higher
silver content than that of the hypogene sulphides. Put simply, the effect
of these processes was to create a zone of rich ores somewhat above
and below the water table: silver chloride above, and sulphide below.

The difference between the two ore types was well known to colonial miners. The chloride ores were called *pacos* in the Andes and *colorados* in New Spain (the redness or brownness implicit in these names coming from the limonite, or blended soft iron oxides, generally found in the oxidized zone). *Pacos* were, for example, the common ores of the Potosí mountain, which was well oxidized 1,000 feet downwards from its summit. Chlorides were generally easy to refine by smelting or amalgamation. Sulphides were universally known as *negrillos*. Though they might be enriched through the supergene process, their sulphur content caused many problems of refining. In general, then, miners could expect increasing yields with depth, down to and beyond the water table, which generally lay at several hundred feet. But the chlorides, above the water table, were more profitable because easily refined. Once a mine dipped below the water table, not only intractability of ores but also flooding presented problems. There was then good reason to seek shallower chlorides elsewhere. The cyclical output of some districts was perhaps the result of a pattern of events deriving from the nature of the ore deposits, which may be summarized in this way: initial discovery of rich chlorides – output rises; deeper workings with some flooding and occurrence of sulphides – output levels off; further flooding and predominance of sulphides – output falls; new prospecting, revealing further shallow chlorides – output rises; and so on.

EXTRACTIVE TECHNIQUES

'Observing the working of mines in New Spain in general...one is surprised to find still in its infancy an art which has been practised in America for three centuries...'[4] So wrote the German traveller and mining engineer, Alexander von Humboldt, of the mining of silver ore in early nineteenth-century New Spain. He found powder wasted, workings made larger than necessary for adequate ventilation, and above all a lack of communication between different mine levels and shafts, which prevented the use of trolleys and animals to extract ore. Ore extraction was doubtless a less sophisticated and efficient process than the subsequent refining. But some qualification of Humboldt's judgement must be made.

The colonial silver miner normally attacked a vein with an open pit,

---

[4] Alexander von Humboldt, *Ensayo político sobre el reino de la Nueva España* (Mexico, 1966), 365 (book 4, ch. 11).

then burrowed deeper in search of particularly rich concentrations of ore. This procedure, which led to twisting, narrow tunnels, was sometimes called in New Spain the *sistema del rato* (meaning the 'opportunistic system', but later translated into English, wrongly but graphically, as the 'rat-hole system'). It persisted in small mines throughout, and indeed beyond, colonial times. The *sistema del rato* has been blamed for many colonial mining problems. But the method arose naturally and had certain advantages. It developed because the early miners were mostly amateurs. There were insufficient professionals initially in America to instil good underground practices into the thousands of individual prospectors who roamed the mining districts. And the crown did nothing to encourage rational exploitation of ores – rather, indeed, the opposite. It was anxious to maximize royalties on refined metals, and held that freedom of prospecting and extraction would lead to maximum production. Furthermore, laws limiting the size of claims to some 110 by 50 yards brought a proliferation of small mines, hardly worth exploiting carefully. Finally, the availability of Indian labour militated against good planning of workings: rather than cut special vertical shafts, for example, to extract ore with winches, it was cheaper to use the *sistema del rato* and employ labourers to carry out material through the resulting serpentine passages. This was particularly true in the early decades, when Indian labour was plentiful; by the later sixteenth century it was growing scarcer and dearer, and the signs of rationalization in workings that are visible by then probably resulted in part from this contraction of the labour supply.

The first notable improvement and rationalization of underground workings came with the cutting of adits (*socavones*): slightly rising tunnels driven from the surface to intersect the lower galleries of a mine. Adits provided ventilation, drainage and easy extraction of ore and waste. An adit was obviously most advantageous when driven into concentrated workings, cutting several mines at one blow. Such concentration existed at the peak of the Potosí mountain; so it is not surprising to find an adit begun there in 1556, nor that by the early 1580s there should have been nine in operation. In New Spain, even the great centres lacked such concentration of ores and mines. Nevertheless, Potosí's Mexican namesake, San Luis Potosí, used an adit to excellent effect in the early seventeenth century to exploit its main source of ores, the Cerro de San Pedro. Adits were by then a standard part of subterranean technique, and remained so. Adits also served to consolidate workings into larger systems. Miners began to pursue such consolidation by the mid-seventeenth century, buying adjacent claims and linking them with adits and galleries. The scale of these integrated workings grew with time, and was remarkable in some cases by the late eighteenth century, when large mining companies appeared. These might have numerous partners whose capital financed extensive under-ground workings. Here the Valenciana enterprise at Guanajuato stands as the supreme example – 'an underground city', according to one historian.[5] This was precisely the mine that Humboldt criticized. But, with its masonry-reinforced galleries, its many faces, its vertical shafts (especially the great octagonal San José shaft, 1,800 feet deep by 1810, and 33 feet across), the Valenciana was a far cry from the early 'rat-holes'. Large-scale integration occurred elsewhere in Mexico, but was rarer in South America, for reasons not yet elucidated.

Three other, more purely technological, developments in extraction may be mentioned. By the late sixteenth century pumps (*bombas*) were occasionally used for draining mines. These were probably lift, force or rag and chain pumps on the patterns shown in book VI of Agricola's *De re metallica*, a work consulted by Spanish American miners.[6] Some at least of the pumps built were human-powered. Water was also lifted in large hide bags, which could be dragged up sloping tunnels, whereas pumps required special vertical shafts. Animal-powered whims were possibly used for this task. Whims were the second notable technological development. By the eighteenth century in New Spain they had become a common means of extracting both water and ore, though they appear less frequent in the Andean mines. As mine workings grew, whims became more powerful. In the great Valenciana shaft no fewer than eight whims operated simultaneously. These were driven by mules or horses. Steam power did not reach Spanish America until the second decade of the nineteenth century. The third technological advance demanding comment is blasting. Its first European use was in Germany in 1627; but exactly when it was adopted in America is unclear. There is rather uncertain evidence for it at Huancavelica by 1635, and unequivocal evidence for it in the Potosí district in the 1670s. In the eighteenth century blasting was a standard technique and probably contributed

---

[5] D. A. Brading, *Miners and merchants in Bourbon Mexico, 1763–1810* (Cambridge, 1971), 287.

[6] Georgius Agricola, *De re metallica* (Basle, 1556), Eng. trans. Herbert Clark Hoover and Lou Henry Hoover (London, 1912).

much to the revival of Spanish American silver production in the first half of the century and to the extraordinary boom of the second.

The practices described so far were applicable to vein mining for gold, though such workings were far smaller than the typical silver mine. Gold vein mines were, moreover, unusual; the main examples occurred in the highlands of New Granada. Most gold came from alluvial deposits, from which it was extracted by placering techniques.

PROCESSING

Silver ore was broken up at the mine to eliminate useless material accompanying it. The resulting concentrate was then ready for processing, which was normally accomplished by amalgamation in a refinery known in New Spain as an *hacienda de minas* and in the Andes as an *ingenio*. The amalgamation refinery was a complex plant. Typically it consisted of a large walled square containing storerooms, stables, a chapel, accommodation for owner and workers, machinery to crush ores, tanks or paved courts to amalgamate them, and vats to wash them. Refineries were usually gathered in mining towns where they could take advantage of concentrated services and supplies, such as labour, crafts (especially carpentry and smithery), and food. Around 1600 Potosí, then at its zenith, had some 65 refineries; and New Spain a total of some 370. At any moment in colonial Spanish America there were probably 400–700 refineries operating, the number varying with prevailing conditions of boom or depression.

At the refinery the concentrated ore was milled to a fine, sand-like consistency, to ensure maximum contact between the silver minerals and mercury during amalgamation, and hence the maximum yield of silver. A stamp mill was the normal means of milling – a simple but massive machine consisting of a number of heavy iron-shod stamps (commonly six to eight of them) which were lifted in turn by cams fixed to a heavy rotating shaft, and allowed to fall on to a stone bed sometimes equipped with iron mortar blocks (see fig. 1). Each stamp shoe weighed up to 150 lb. Sometimes double mills were built, in which a single shaft extended on both sides of a central, vertical water-wheel. The total number of stamps in this case might reach sixteen.

Stamp mills were driven by water, or by horses or mules. (Human-powered mills existed at Potosí in the early 1570s, but quickly

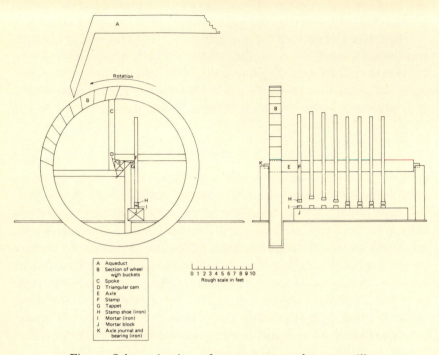

A   Aqueduct
B   Section of wheel
        with buckets
C   Spoke
D   Triangular cam
E   Axle
F   Stamp
G   Tappet
H   Stamp shoe (iron)
I   Mortar (iron)
J   Mortar block
K   Axle journal and
        bearing (iron)

0 1 2 3 4 5 6 7 8 9 10
Rough scale in feet

Fig. 1. Schematic view of a water-powered stamp mill

disappeared because of their inefficiency.) The choice of power source
depended on local circumstances. Much of New Spain, for instance,
lacked water enough to drive machinery, while many Andean districts
were too barren to sustain the necessary animals. Thus, around 1600,
only about a third of Mexican mills were water-powered, and these were
mostly in central New Spain, a wetter region than the northern plateau;
while in Potosí at the same time hardly any animal-driven mills
remained, owing to lack of pasture and the consequent building of dams
and aqueducts that provided water for year-round milling. Records
from Potosí in the 1570s suggest, furthermore, that in general water-
driven mills were more productive per unit of capital and labour
employed in them than those driven by animals. For an equal capital
investment in plant, a water-driven mill crushed over twice the quantity
of ore in a day that an animal-powered mill would process, while the
productivity of labour (the amount of ore milled per Indian worker per

day) was perhaps five times higher in the water-driven mill. Mining districts well supplied with water were therefore at a distinct advantage.

Other types of milling devices existed – for example, the ancient machine consisting of a large stone disc rolling on its edge over a circular stone bed; but the stamp mill, with its large capacity, rapidly prevailed in the major districts. Its design was already well established in Europe when extensive ore processing began in America, and is clearly illustrated in book VIII of Agricola's *De re metallica*. If further pulverization of ore were required, another device might be used, variously known as a *tahona*, *arrastre* or *arrastra*. This simple apparatus consisted of a stone bed enclosed by a low circular wall, with one or more hard, heavy stones suspended from a beam pivoted on a post at the centre of the bed. Animals pulled the beam around, dragging the stone over the bed. Ore placed on this was ground to a fineness which, according to Humboldt, was unequalled in any European mining centre. Nevertheless the *tahona*, though a design known from earliest colonial times, seems to have been used mainly in eighteenth-century New Spain – and not in all centres there. Its absence in other times and places remains to be explained.

Once crushed, ore was ready for amalgamation. This slow but sure process sustained the great edifice of silver production, because it allowed cheap refining of the great masses of low-yielding ore available in Spanish America. Debate continues over the identity of the originators of the process in America, and indeed over whether it was an original invention there at all. The general view is that the 'inventor' was Bartolomé de Medina, a Spaniard from Seville who, with some German technical advice, pioneered the technique in New Spain in the early 1550s. It is generally accepted that though the principle of amalgamation had been known since classical times, its first use on an industrial scale came in the New World. It was so used in several Mexican centres in the late 1550s, and in the central Andes from 1571 – the delay there possibly resulting from the later discovery of the Andean mines and the consequent later availability in them of good smelting ores, which made amalgamation unnecessary for a time.

The classic amalgamation procedure in America took place on a *patio* – a large, flat, stone-paved surface, sometimes roofed. On this, according to one account, milled ore (*harina*) was piled in heaps (*montones*) of some 2,000–3,500 lb; then common salt was mixed in at the rate of $2\frac{1}{2}$–3 lb per 100 lb (*quintal*) of ore. Other reagents might also be used. The commonest was roasted copper pyrites (*magistral*), added at the rate of 8–12 lb per *montón*. Then mercury was squeezed out over the ore through the weave of a sturdy cloth bag in the proportion of 10–12 lb per *montón*. Finally water was added, and the heap spread out to form a *torta* up to 90 feet across. Combination of silver and mercury now proceeded by chemical affinity, helped by much agitation. For most of colonial times Indians did this, paddling bare-legged through the muddy concoction; only in the 1780s were they replaced by horses or mules. After some time, normally six to eight weeks (though extremes of three weeks to five months occurred, depending on refining skill, ambient temperature and the nature of the ore) the refinery supervisor (*azoguero* or *beneficiador*) would determine by assay that the maximum possible fusion of silver and mercury had occurred, and the mixture was shovelled into a washing apparatus, commonly a large vat (*tina*) fitted with a paddle rotated by animal or water power. Water was then passed through the vat, carrying off waste while the heavy amalgam (*pella*) settled. The *pella* was then packed into a sock-like canvas bag, which was twisted to expel free mercury. Final separation of silver and mercury occurred by volatilization under a metal or clay hood, heat being applied to the *pella* from below, causing the mercury to vaporize. The hood itself was cooled so that the vapour condensed on the inner surface and metallic mercury was recovered.

The *patio* process was the standard technique in New Spain from the early seventeenth century on. Before then amalgamation was performed there in wooden troughs (*canoas*). In the Andean centres the *patio* was hardly, if ever, used. Generally in the Andes, refiners employed stone tanks (*cajones*) for amalgamation, each large enough to take 5,000 lb of ore and often, at least in the sixteenth century, built on vaulting so that a fire could be made beneath them. This moderated the low temperatures of the high Andes, accelerating amalgamation. After about 1600, however, and possibly because of the growing scarcity and cost of fuel, artificial heating died out, and refiners used only the sun's warmth.

The chemistry of amalgamation is complex. According to Modesto Bargalló, the modern authority on colonial refining, the basic equations are (in the case of silver sulphides):

$$CuSO_4 + 2NaCl \rightarrow CuCl_2 + Na_2SO_4$$
$$CuCl_2 + Ag_2S \rightarrow 2AgCl + CuS$$
$$2AgCl + nHg \rightarrow Hg_{\hat{n}-2}Ag_2(\text{amalgam}) + Hg_2Cl_2$$

while other subsidiary silver-yielding reactions take place simultaneously.[7] Colonial refiners were, of course, ignorant of these chemical processes. Their knowledge was purely empirical. Rapidly there emerged from experience a series of accepted steps to be followed if ore were of this or that appearance, or if mercury took on this or that colour during amalgamation. These practices, often effective, were the outcome of continual experimentation. Far from all of this was fruitful; but a few important discoveries did emerge, the most profitable of them being that of the utility of *magistral*, copper sulphate obtained by roasting pyrites. This substance, as is clear from the equations just given, was an integral part of amalgamation, especially in the processing of sulphide ores. Its value may well have been discovered in Potosí in the 1580s. If so, the practice of adding *magistral* spread quickly, since it clearly was present in northern New Spain before 1600, where it notably improved yields. Before then Mexican refiners had probably relied, unknowingly, on whatever natural copper sulphate their ores contained, with erratic results.

No other single innovation in refining was as effective as *magistral*. But small adjustments of amalgamation to local conditions took place constantly throughout Spanish America, with positive results. And when the crown in the late eighteenth century sent to America German experts to teach the latest amalgamation method (that of the Baron von Born, which was in fact an elaboration of the *cazo y cocimiento* (vat-boiling) technique of the seventeenth-century Charcas refiner Alvaro Alonso Barba), the Germans were finally obliged to concede that the traditional American processes were best, in American circumstances. Indeed, one of the Germans, Friedrich Sonneschmidt, after long experience in New Spain, wrote in an excess of enthusiasm, 'It is not to be expected that there will ever be found a method by which all varieties of ore can be refined, having expenses lower than or even equal to those required by the *patio* beneficiation'.[8] The method, he said, was slow. But it could be set up almost anywhere; needed little water; used simple and quickly-made apparatus and tools; had techniques rapidly taught even to the ignorant. If Sonneschmidt had travelled to the Andes, he could have said much the same of refining methods there.

---

[7] Modesto Bargalló, *La minería y la metalurgía en la América española durante la época colonial* (Mexico, 1955), 194.

[8] Quoted in Modesto Bargalló, *La amalgamación de los minerales de plata en Hispanoamérica colonial* (Mexico, 1969), 505.

The absolute efficiency of the colonial amalgamation processes – the proportion of the total silver content of the ore that they actually extracted – is unmeasurable, since the only estimate available of the ores' content is that made by the refiners themselves, and that they calculated according to the results amalgamation itself gave them. Nevertheless, an impression of amalgamation's essential ability – that of handling large amounts of poor ore – is conveyed in the fact that refiners could apparently break even with ores yielding only 1½ oz of silver from each 100 lb of concentrate treated with mercury.

A secondary, but remarkably persistent and useful, refining technique was smelting. Here the Spanish borrowed initially from native technology, at least in the central Andes, where Indian miners had progressed beyond the primitive fire-setting techniques used by the native Mexicans and other Andean Indians to obtain certain metals, notably gold, silver, and copper. In Peru and Charcas true smelting had developed. First the ore was crushed under a *maray*, a boulder with a curved base, which was made to rock to and fro; then it was smelted in a small furnace, conical or pyramidal in shape, often only about three feet high. The sides were pierced with many air-holes through which the wind could blow when the furnace was placed in some exposed place. With llama dung or charcoal as fuel, the temperatures generated were sufficient to smelt ores. This was the famous *wayra* (Quechua: 'air') of the Andes; and in furnaces of this sort all silver was produced at Potosí until the arrival of amalgamation in 1571.

Europe, nevertheless, provided the dominant smelting technology, much of it introduced by German miners sent in 1528 by the Fugger banking company to the Caribbean islands and Venezuela. The crown had requested these experts for the improvement of mining and metallurgical skills in America, till then signally lacking among early settlers. Some of these Germans may have moved on to New Spain; others certainly arrived there in 1536, settling at Sultepec, where they built milling machines and furnaces. The basic smelting device was the Castilian furnace, an ancient design consisting of a hollow vertical column about three feet square and four to six feet high, built of stone or adobe. Its sides were pierced for bellows and the drawing of slag and molten metal. Ore, crushed by hand or in a mechanical mill, was packed into the furnace with charcoal. Bellows were essential; in any large establishment they were worked by water or animal power through gears and cranks. Smelted silver usually lacked purity, containing lead occurring in the ore, or that had been added as flux. So further refining was performed by cupellation, normally in a reverberatory furnace, though the Castilian type would serve.

Smelting persisted more strongly through colonial times than has been thought. It was the preferred technique of the poor individual miner or of the Indian labourer who received ore as part of his wage. A small furnace with hand bellows (a *parada de fuelles*) was cheap to make; hundreds of them sprang up in and around mining towns. But large-scale smelting also survived the coming of amalgamation, and particularly flourished when mercury was short, when new strikes of very rich ore were made, and where fuel was abundant. These conditions led, for example, to an important resurgence of smelting in parts of New Spain in the later seventeenth century.

Processing of gold consisted merely of separating the pure metal from whatever material it was found in – sand or gravel in streams and terraces, or some type of rock in veins. Panning or ground sluicing were the basic techniques in the first case. In the second, milling was necessary and could be done by hand or in a stamp mill. Amalgamation might then follow, to gather the gold from the crushed vein material. Gold often occurred in conjunction with silver ores, amalgamation of which then produced an alloy of the two metals. The preferred means of separating them, certainly until mid-colonial times, was the nitric acid method.

RAW MATERIALS

The processing of silver ores required a variety of raw materials, some of them in limited supply. Salt, essential for amalgamation, was easily obtained, either from salinas (in northern New Spain or in the central Andes) or, as in other parts of New Spain, from coastal deposits. Pyrites, from which *magistral* was prepared, occurred commonly enough in the silver districts. So did lead, which was needed as a flux for smelting (though much ore contained enough natural lead for the purpose). Iron, used in machinery and occasionally, in pulverized form, as a reagent in amalgamation, came wholly from Spain, but nevertheless was rarely scarce or excessively dear.

Rather less plentiful were wood and water. Wood was the basic construction material and fuel. Trees were consequently stripped quickly from areas around large mining centres, in some of which – the high Andes and the dry Mexican plateau – they can never have been plentiful. Timber then had to be brought in at high cost over great distances. In late sixteenth-century Potosí, the wooden axles for stamp mills, twenty feet long and twenty inches square, were brought from lower Andean valleys 100 miles or more off. Placed in Potosí they cost 1,300–1,650 pesos, as much as a medium-sized house. Wood or charcoal were also needed to fire furnaces; and charcoal makers ranged many miles from the mines, using scrub where no trees remained.

Water was essential for washing refined ores, and very desirable as a power source. With ingenuity – small dams and animal-driven washing vats – the supply could be stretched everywhere sufficiently to make washing possible. But only in some areas was water power possible – notably in central New Spain and in some parts of the Andes. By 1600 Potosí drew almost all its power from water, but only after some 30 dams with interconnecting canals had been built to store the summer rainfall.

A more crucial substance than any of these was mercury. Nearly all the mercury used in Spanish America came from three sources – in order of volume supplied, Almadén, in southern Spain; Huancavelica, in highland central Peru; and Idrija in the modern Yugoslavian province of Slovenia, then within the Austrian Habsburg domains. Trivial amounts also came now and then from China and various minor Spanish American deposits. In general, Almadén supplied New Spain, Huancavelica supplied South America, and Idrija was tapped when the first two proved inadequate.

Viewed broadly, the mercury supply met demand from silver mining (amalgamation of gold was inconsequential in comparison) in two of the three colonial centuries. In the sixteenth century Huancavelica, an all-but-virgin deposit, boomed; and Almadén's output grew quickly up to about 1620. And in the eighteenth century Almadén, as the result of the discovery of a massive ore body in 1698, so far surpassed its previous performance that it more than compensated for the weakness of Huancavelica. But in the intervening period, for much of the seventeenth century, there was a shortage of mercury, especially in New Spain. This resulted from low output at Almadén (caused by depletion of known ores and inefficient refining), and from a generally weaker showing at Huancavelica than that of the sixteenth century (caused by similar difficulties, compounded by problems of labour supply).

The resulting shortfall was in part met with mercury from Idrija, which was sent to America in substantial quantities from 1621 to 1645

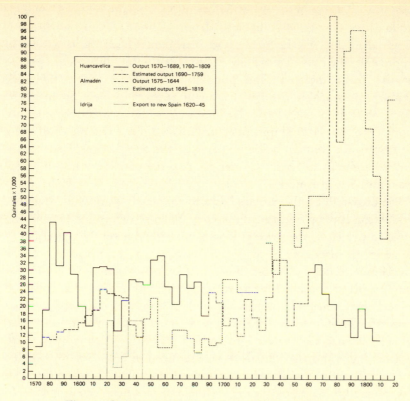

Fig. 2. Quinquennial mercury production, 1570–1820

Sources: **Huancavelica, 1570–1789:** Guillermo Lohmann Villena, *Las minas de Huancavelica en los siglos XVI y XVII* (Seville, 1949), 452–5; **1690–1759** (estimates): Manuel de Mendiburu, *Diccionario histórico-biográfico del Perú*, vol. 6 (Lima, 1933), 454–5; **1760–1809:** John R. Fisher, *Government and society in colonial Peru. The intendant system, 1784–1814* (London, 1970), 257. **Almadén, 1575–1644:** A. Matilla Tascón, *Historia de las minas de Almadén*, 1: *Desde la época romana hasta el año 1645* (Madrid, 1958), 107, 111, 121, 122, 137, 171, 182; **1645–1819** (estimates): M. H. Kuss, 'Mémoire sur les mines et usines d'Almadén', *Annales des Mines*, septième série, Mémoires, 13 (1878), 149–50. **Idrija, 1620–45:** exports to New Spain: P. J. Bakewell, *Silver mining and society in colonial Mexico, Zacatecas, 1546–1700* (Cambridge, 1971), 256. There were also substantial exports of Idrija mercury to Spanish America after 1786, in amounts still to be determined.

(see fig. 2). This mercury went mainly to New Spain, while Almadén's production was largely diverted from there to Peru, which was favoured in this way because up to then it had been the larger silver producer of the two viceroyalties. The crown found difficulty in paying for the Idrija mercury, and purchases ceased in 1645. 'German' mercury, presumably from Idrija, again appears in New Spain in the 1690s, as indeed does Peruvian mercury, which was imported until about 1730. But large shipments from Idrija did not resume until 1786, the result of a contract made in 1785 for the supply of 10,000–12,000 *quintales* annually to Spanish America. This mercury went to both New Spain and South America.

The crown not only exercised as close a control as possible over the production and distribution of mercury, but also determined the selling price. In principle, the price at a particular mining centre was equal to the sum of production costs and freight to that place; but the government tended to assess these to its own advantage. It is true that mercury prices show a downward trend throughout colonial times, as refiners petitioned constantly for reductions and the crown made concessions to the argument that low mercury prices would more than pay off in increased silver production. But the decline was slow. Between 1572 and 1617 the price was reduced in New Spain from 180 to 82.5 pesos. But no further reduction came until 1767, when the price was lowered to 62 pesos. In 1778 a final cut was made, to 41 pesos. In the Andes the price was consistently higher, perhaps because of large freight costs in the mountains, despite the relative closeness of Huancavelica to the silver centres. At Potosí the price fell from 104.25 pesos in the late sixteenth century to 97 in 1645, there to remain until dropping to 79 pesos in 1779 and 71 in 1787. Only in 1809 did mercury become almost as cheap in Peru, at 50 pesos, as it had normally been in New Spain in the late 1700s.

The general surge of silver output in the late eighteenth century, especially in New Spain, coincides closely with reductions in the price of mercury. This cannot be wholly fortuitous, and suggests that earlier reductions would have been profitable for the crown, especially once Almadén began to produce plentifully after 1700.

LABOUR SYSTEMS

Mining rested on Indian labour. Blacks, slave and free, had a part, but a small one except in gold mining, where they provided much of the workforce. The closest white men came to physical mining labour was prospecting; in general they were supervisors and owners. Mestizos could be found at physical mining tasks by the eighteenth century, but the more Spanish they appeared, the rarer they were in such jobs.

The standard labour systems of colonial times supplied mining with its Indian workers: in general chronological order of appearance, these were encomienda, slavery, draft, and hire for wages. The earliest colonial mining, placering and pit excavation for gold in the Greater Antilles before 1500, was performed by Indians whom Columbus distributed to settlers in an early and harsh form of encomienda. Enslaved natives of the Lesser Antilles and the Spanish Main were quickly added. And then, as the aboriginal population collapsed, not least under the demands of gold mining, black slaves were brought in. Meanwhile the use of Indians in encomienda and slavery for mining spread to Middle and South America as these were taken. The advancing conquest naturally yielded slaves, as everywhere there were some natives who resisted doggedly and so found themselves accounted justly enslaved when captured in war. So, for example, Cortés was able to employ some 400 Indian slaves in his Tehuantepec gold deposits in the 1540s.

Drafted Indian labour followed encomienda, but no clear line can be drawn between the two systems. In both viceroyalties draft labour for mining was extensively organized by the late 1570s, under the name *repartimiento* in New Spain and *mita* (Quechua: 'turn') in Peru. But the beginnings of these systems long antedate the 1570s. By 1530 in Guatemala, for instance, Spanish settlers and officials simply obliged gangs of nominally free Indians to wash gold for fixed periods. And by 1549, encomienda Indians being sent to Potosí by their masters from all parts of Peru and Charcas referred to their stay at the mines as mita – a set span of six or twelve months after which they were replaced by another group, and returned home. Their use of the Quechua term clearly indicates their association of this work for the Spanish with the mita imposed previously by the Incas, a draft for various sorts of public work, including mining. The Aztecs had operated a draft (*coatequitl*) also in their domain. The existence of these native antecedents doubtless facilitated the Spaniards' creation of drafts.

Gradually, over the mid sixteenth century, draft labour superseded encomienda and Indian slavery in mining. As the military phase of conquest passed, the supply of Indians taken in just war fell; and simultaneously laws limiting Indian slavery were more firmly enforced. Meanwhile draft labour began to present attractions to the crown and many settlers, since its fundamental effect was to remove Indians from the wide and largely arbitrary control of the encomenderos and make them available to the growing number of non-encomenderos among the Spanish. In this the crown perceived both a gratifying curtailment of the encomenderos' wealth and political power, and a more productive use of the shrinking Indian workforce. Officially organized drafts also gave the crown a chance to fulfil other purposes: first to create a salaried native workforce in America, for another distinction between official draft and encomienda was that drafted Indians should receive wages; second to limit the length of time that Indians worked, since drafts were assigned for specific though varied periods, according to local labour needs.

The largest, most highly organized, most famous, and – in common estimation – infamous, of all mining drafts was the mita of Potosí. Here it may stand as a model for other drafts in both New Spain and South America, though all varied in details. The Potosí mita and its harshness are usually made the personal responsibility of the Peruvian viceroy who created the system, Don Francisco de Toledo. But Toledo acted under general royal instructions to force Indians into mining – instructions that gave him such qualms of conscience that he hesitated for over two years before grasping the nettle. It was finally in late 1572, as he travelled from Cuzco to Potosí on his general inspection of Peru, that he began organizing the mita, instructing the leaders (*curacas*) of the high Andean towns to send able-bodied men to Potosí. The area finally designated for supplying workers was enormous, extending some 800 miles from Cuzco in the north to Tarija in the south, and a maximum of 250 miles across the width of the Andes; though only sixteen of the 30 provinces in this area were included, those excepted being mainly the lower and warmer ones whose inhabitants were feared too susceptible to disease if sent to the cold and height of Potosí. From the sixteen contributing provinces about 14 per cent (a seventh) of the tribute-paying population (males between eighteen and 50) were to go each year to Potosí for one year. According to the census Toledo made, this would provide enough labour for Potosí, about 13,500 men a year. This number was the *mita gruesa*, which, once in Potosí, was divided into three parts, each called the *mita ordinaria*, which worked by turn one week on and two off. So at any moment about 4,500 mita labourers (*mitayos*) were active in the draft.

Toledo then distributed the mitayos among mines and refineries according to their size and need, a process repeated thereafter by many incoming viceroys, and set daily wage rates: for interior mine work, 3.5 reales; for carrying ore to refineries, three reales; for refinery work, 2.75 reales.[9] The real worth of these wages is hard to estimate, as many prices, including those of the Indians' staples, maize and potatoes, are unknown. The week's wage of the mine mitayo would buy, however, about 30 lb of wheat flour. This may seem substantial; but a contemporary estimate put the cost of an Indian's journey to Potosí and one year's residence there at 100 pesos, while the total wage of a mine mitayo for seventeen weeks of six days was about 45 pesos. The normal work week soon fell, however, from six to five days. Sunday was a day of rest, or one, according to Spanish observers voicing the conventional criticism of Indians, of drunken idleness. On Monday, Indian officials from each province assembled the new week's *mita ordinaria* for distribution. Work began on Tuesday morning, continuing non-stop until Saturday night. Toledo's regulations specified a dawn-to-dusk workday; but mine owners soon began forcing mitayos to cut and haul ore by quota, set high so that rest and food had to be snatched when possible, above or below ground.

The mita clearly exposed the Indian to overwork, despite the legal safeguards created by crown and officials. Evidence suggests that wages were paid. But the labour burden grew, particularly as the Andean native population fell and a worker's turn came round more frequently than every seven years. In extreme cases by 1600, mitayos were having to spend every other year in Potosí. The mita itself clearly contributed to the depopulation, accelerating an existing decline by causing people to flee the provinces from which the draft was taken, by inclining some mitayos to stay in Potosí to seek anonymity amidst the town's large Indian population, and by disrupting the rhythms of agriculture and family life. Yet further abuses followed from the greater burden of

---

[9] There were eight reales to a peso. Here, and elsewhere in this chapter, the peso referred to is the *peso de a ocho* (known in New Spain as the *peso de oro común*) worth 272 maravedís.

labour. Those Indians able to do so bought themselves out of the mita by hiring replacements, or paying their own *curacas* or employers the cash necessary to do so. Many miners in the seventeenth century liked this practice of cash payments in lieu of labour, for if a mine were exhausted or a mill dilapidated, the sum the mitayos paid to avoid working might be greater than the value of the silver they would produce if they were working. To these cash payments the Spaniards gave the cynical title *indios de faltriquera* – 'Indians in the pocket'. This common practice was illegal, as was the equally common custom of including the mitayos assigned to a mine or mill in any sale made of these. The law strove to uphold the theoretical freedom of the Indian; but the mitayo was often treated – as when he was made part of a sale transaction – as a near-slave, while being deprived of the material benefits of slavery and of exemption from tribute.

Second to the Potosí mita in numbers of Indians drafted was the mita of Huancavelica, also created by Toledo. It drew, in the early 1620s, some 2,200 Indians a year, about a sixth of those sent to Potosí. But the Huancavelica mitayos may well have suffered more severely than those of Potosí, on account of the extreme hazards of those mercury mines: toxic vapours and soft, shifting rock. Elsewhere smaller drafts existed – for example, for gold production in Chile in the late sixteenth and early seventeenth centuries; for gold in Quito from, apparently, the sixteenth century; for silver in New Granada from the early 1600s; and for silver in New Spain from the mid 1500s.

The iniquities of the drafts were not ignored by the crown; and, indeed, despite the political and economic attractions that draft labour offered the crown, its imposition was much debated in Spain since it contradicted the fundamental principle that the Indians were free. Generally, however, the view that the public good required drafting Indians into mines prevailed. Abolition came only in 1812, though there were earlier attempts to bring it about, as for instance in a notable royal order of 1601 directed to New Spain, only withdrawn after remonstrations from the viceroy that such a step would mean disaster. But the crown did maintain its opposition – cancelling, for example, the assignment of 500 mitayos to Oruro by viceroy Esquilache in 1617. Other cases could be cited.

In the 1601 order the crown stated its desire for a voluntary workforce in mining. And indeed, voluntary labour by Indians in all types of production had from the beginning of colonial times been the ideal. But the natives' unfamiliarity with the work expected of them, with money wages, and their natural attempts to escape the heavy tasks placed on them (interpreted by the Spanish as inborn idleness) went against voluntary labour. There was always, however, some trace of it, originating in native society itself. In the Caribbean cultures the Spanish found the naboría, 'a commoner who was the direct dependent of a noble and who therefore did not participate fully in the general community obligations and privileges'.[10] To a similar social type in New Spain the Spaniards transferred the same name (later hispanized to *laborío*). In Inca lands the yanacona occupied much the same position. Indians of these sorts quickly shifted their allegiance to the new conquering Spanish lords, while growing numbers of other Indians who were in origin plain commoners imitated them, seeing advantages in being the direct personal dependants of Spaniards rather than their more remote servitors in encomienda. Naborías and yanaconas quickly turned to a wide range of tasks in early colonial society, for many of which they received wages, becoming the first wage labourers. Among their characteristic occupations was mining so that, for example, immediately after the discovery of the Zacatecas and Potosí ores in the mid 1540s there were naborías and yanaconas, respectively, working the mines, mixed with Indian slaves and encomienda labourers.

This early element of wage labour in mining grew quickly, for two reasons. First, mining demanded skills which, once acquired, were highly valued. An owner was willing to reward well an Indian who had learned ore-cutting or refining skills as a draft labourer, and would pay wages high enough to make permanent mining work attractive. Well before 1600 professional groups of Indian miners and refiners existed in the main centres. Second, many major mining districts existed in areas where the original native population was unsuitable for encomienda or draft, either because it was too sparse or too rebellious. Such was the case in northern New Spain, where mines were worked largely by wage labourers from the start. Figures for the composition of the Mexican mining labour force taken from a report of about 1597 show the importance of wage labour by then. The total force was 9,143 men, of whom 6,261 (68.5 per cent) were naborías, 1,619 (17.7 per cent) were draft (repartimiento) workers, and 1,263 (13.8 per cent) were black slaves. Also striking is that fact that all the repartimiento workers were

---

[10] Ida Altman and James Lockhart (eds.), *Provinces of early Mexico* (Berkeley and Los Angeles, 1976), 18.

in central Mexico, none in the west and north – the reason being that only in the centre had the native population been of sufficient density and sophistication to be organized into drafts. It was this population, moreover, that sent most of the naborías to the north and west.

A similar situation existed in Potosí. There, in 1603, some 11,000–12,000 workers were active at any one moment, of whom only about 4,500 were from the *mita ordinaria*. The rest were hired men (*mingas*). Undoubtedly many *mingas* were from the two-thirds of the *mita gruesa* that were 'off duty' (*de huelga*); but there is clear evidence that a permanent corps of *mingas* existed in Potosí by this time, consisting largely of mitayos who had stayed on after their year of draft. Their pay was up to five times that of the mitayo: for mine workers, 88 reales a week as opposed to seventeen. The cash wage of skilled ore cutters, who were normally salaried, was augmented in both Potosí and New Spain by ore which they took from the mines, legally or otherwise.

Wage labour was clearly the prevalent form of employment in the large mining districts from the late sixteenth century onwards. Earlier systems did not wholly disappear, especially in remote or unimportant districts: encomienda in seventeenth-century New Granada, even slavery on the northern frontiers of New Spain, where the fight against raiding Indians continued to yield legal slaves. But the waged worker became the norm, especially in New Spain, where growth of mining from the late seventeenth century generated such demand for skilled workers that by the late eighteenth labour costs comprised up to three-fourths of the total expenses in some enterprises. Draft survived in New Spain, but barely. In central Andean districts the mita remained more in evidence, supplying Potosí and Huancavelica with useful cheap labour until late colonial years; while informal (and strictly illegal) lesser drafts were probably organized by local government officials to aid other mines. But wage labour predominated here also. By 1789 only 3,000 came to Potosí in the *mita gruesa* – yielding a *mita ordinaria* of 1,000. But in 1794 the total Potosí workforce was 4,070 in mines and 1,504 in refining – figures suggesting that over three-fourths of workers were then salaried. Wage labour in the lower Peruvian districts in the late eighteenth century was also important.

Almost 14 per cent of Mexican mining labourers were blacks at the close of the sixteenth century – a by no means negligible proportion.

But, except in lowland gold-mining, this proportion can have been rarely exceeded. Many of the great silver districts were at considerable height, 8,000 feet or above; and it was a common opinion that blacks could not do heavy work and survive long in such cold, thin air. While the strict truth of this remains unclear, it certainly seems that at great heights black slaves could not perform heavy underground work efficiently enough to provide a return on their purchase price and maintenance. So at Potosí, for example, blacks were not put to underground tasks. They may have been employed in refining; but were normally found as craftsmen, typically carpenters and smiths, making and servicing tools and machinery, or as personal servants of miners and refiners – signals of success. At the lesser heights (6,000–8,000 feet) of the Mexican districts, some blacks did work below ground. At Zacatecas there are scattered references to black ore cutters (*barreteros*). But here again, surface tasks were far more common. An observer of Zacatecas in 1602 remarked: 'the blacks are mostly occupied in attending to milling and blending [with mercury] and washing the ores'.[11] Crafts also occupied many blacks in the Mexican mines.

The reportedly high mortality and low productivity of blacks in highland silver mining worked against the crown's frequent schemes to replace draft Indian labour with African slaves. But in tropical lowland gold mining, the opposite was true: blacks proved resistant to disease and capable of hard labour, while Indians perished (particularly highland Indians transplanted into the tropics, but also lowland Indians subjected to unaccustomed levels of work). A further difficulty with the lowland Indians was that they were generally lacking in economic and political integration, and so could not be easily organized into a labour force. Lowland gold mining was therefore the province of black workers. The greatest concentration of these undoubtedly occurred in eighteenth-century New Granada, where in 1787 the three main gold provinces (Antioquia, Popayán and the Chocó) held some 17,000 blacks, many of them in mining. Far from all were slaves by that time. In the Chocó in 1778, for instance, 35 per cent of a total of 8,916 blacks were free; by 1808, 75 per cent. The only major lowland gold region in which blacks did not predominate was Chile. There, in the sixteenth century, Indians, both slave and encomienda, worked the deposits; and in the eighteenth-century revival of gold, the labour force was heavily

---

[11] Alonso de la Mota y Escobar, *Descripción geográfica de los reynos de Nueva Galicia, Nueva Vizcaya y Nuevo León* (MS 1605?, Guadalajara, 1966), 68.

mestizo, there existing by that time a large mixed population willing
to work in mining for lack of other employment opportunities.

LABOUR CONDITIONS

As is clear enough from the foregoing account, working conditions
in mining and refining were always uncomfortable and often dangerous.
Below ground the least unpleasant job belonged to the most highly
skilled workers – the *barreteros*, who, with crowbars (*barras*), wedges
and picks, prized ore from the veins. This certainly demanded hard
physical effort in cramped, often hot, and always ill-ventilated and ill-lit
conditions. But far worse was the role of beasts of burden assigned to
the unskilled men who carried ores to the surface; and *barreteros* were
better rewarded, with both higher wages and the opportunity, sometimes
licit and sometimes not, to take pieces of rich ore for themselves. The
lot of the carriers (*tenateros* in New Spain, *apires* in the Quechua-speaking
Andean regions) was grim. Using a variety of receptacles for the ore
– rush baskets, hide buckets (*tenates*), sacks, or even, in early Charcas,
llama-wool blankets – they clambered through twisting passages often
no wider than a man's body. Ascents were negotiated with steps hacked
in the rock, or with steep ladders made from notched tree trunks or
strips of hides strung between poles. As the workings grew, large
cavities developed within them, with drops severe enough to kill a man
if he fell. Loads were heavy. Mine owners demanded a certain rate of
extraction even though ordinance forbade it. Difficult as it is to believe,
there is good evidence that *tenateros* in late colonial New Spain carried
300 lb on their backs. Working in darkness, often by the light of a single
candle tied to the front man's forehead or little finger, the carriers were
exposed to grave risks. Many fell to their deaths or to a severe maiming;
just how many cannot be known. Nor was physical injury the only risk.
In the high Andean mines, especially, changes of temperature between
the lower workings and the surface might cause illness. At Potosí, for
instance, even before 1600, some mines were 600 feet deep, and hot at
that level. After coming up with his load, the *apire* emerged at almost
16,000 feet into freezing temperatures. Respiratory disease was the
frequent outcome, often exacerbated by dust in the workings, especially
after blasting was introduced. Falls and disease were a greater risk than
collapses of workings, which, though they certainly happened, were
apparently not common.

Gold and mercury mining held their particular hazards. Since most gold workings were placers in low, wet areas, labourers in them were exposed to tropical diseases. They also often had the discomfort of working long spells in water. Far more unpleasant and dangerous, though, was mercury mining at Huancavelica – fortunately for workers the only permanent mercury mine in America. Clearly this was the most noisome and dangerous of all mines. The country rock surrounding the ores was soft and unstable, so that here collapses were common. But, worse, the workings were often filled with poisonous gases, which made labour in them particularly hazardous.

Refining also had its dangers, of which two were severe. Stamp mills produced much dust, which must inevitably have caused silicosis. And at various stages of amalgamation workers were exposed to mercury poisoning: in the blending of mercury with the ore, when the Indians were treading the mixture, bare-legged; in the distillation of mercury from the *pella*; and in the roasting of washings to recover mercury. In the latter two processes, attempts were made to trap and condense the mercury vapour, but some escaped.

SOCIAL REPERCUSSIONS

For both individuals and communities engaged in it, mining had profound social effects. To the immigrant from Spain or the poor colonist, mining offered a quick, if perilous, short cut to social distinction. The lucky few dozen, for example, who struck it rich in northern New Spain in the second half of the sixteenth century became figures of national prominence. In lordly style they put their fortunes and extensive entourages at the king's disposal, leading the fight against the nomadic northern tribes; assembled great estates from which they exported beef on a grand scale to central New Spain; married high – one of the founders and first miners of Zacatecas married a daughter of the viceroy Velasco I; another, a daughter of Cortés and doña Isabel Montezuma. Mining wealth brought not only social eminence, but political authority. For instance the greatest miner of late seventeenth-century Potosí, the Galician Antonio López de Quiroga, in his later years dominated the local governments of southern Charcas by placing his blood relations and sons-in-law as corregidores of various districts. Naturally, though, having elevated a man to high social and political places, mining might then cast him into the abyss. If the vein were lost, or workings suddenly flooded, then a mine would swallow silver as swiftly as it had previously disgorged it. Creditors closed in, seizing land, houses, belongings. Few families, indeed, remained prosperous in mining for more than three generations.

For the Indian, too, mining could bring profound social change. Most radical was the shift from rural to urban living that mining often imposed, a shift from traditional agricultural communities to sizeable Spanish-dominated towns. This translation was forced upon many Indians by a labour draft; but once having made the move, some decided to stay, so that from the late sixteenth century there was a corps of professional miners in the larger centres, working for wages and tending to adopt Spanish habits. They bought Spanish-style clothes and perhaps preferred wine to pulque or chicha. In doing so, they gradually lost their Indian identity and passed into the mestizo category, in culture if not in genetic type. This proletarianization and acculturation of Indians was not, of course, unusual in colonial towns, since these were the focus of Spanish presence while the countryside remained predominantly Indian. But the mining towns contributed especially strongly to the process because they drew such large numbers of Indians, because they offered relatively high buying power to the waged worker, and not least because they were almost the only Spanish settlements in several large regions – for example, northern New Spain, the Charcas altiplano, or northern Chile.

Whatever gain an individual Indian might have seen in settling in a mining town, the aggregate effect of mining on the native community was often grave. It is hard to gauge how much loss of Indian population mining caused, because other destructive forces were at work at the same time, and conditions varied from place to place. So, for example, the most severe fall in the Mexican Indian population appears to have happened before mining became widespread in New Spain. On the other hand, it is clear enough that the demands for gold production made of the natives of the Greater Antilles in the early colonial decades were a prime cause of their near annihilation by the mid-sixteenth century; and that two centuries later much the same happened in the central Chocó of New Granada, whose Indian population declined from over 60,000 in 1660 to 5,414 in 1778, as it was put first to washing gold, and then to providing food, housing and freighting for mines worked by blacks. The worst dislocation of Indian communities, although it cannot yet be described in numbers, probably occurred in the area serving the

Potosí mita, simply because this was the largest mining draft of all. The 13,500 mitayos assigned normally took their families with them when they left home for their year in Potosí. At a conservative estimate, therefore, some 50,000 people moved in and out of Potosí each year. Village agriculture was disrupted as people departed; reserves of food were depleted to sustain them on the journey, which from distant regions might last two months; many never returned home. Just how many died as a direct result of mining and refining will probably never be known. The proportion remaining in Potosí each year is also hard to judge; but an early seventeenth-century estimate that there were some 37,000 non-mita Indian males in the town suggests that it was large. Besides those who stayed, there were countless others who moved to isolated places in the mita area, or completely out of it, to escape the draft – with further ill effects for their original communities.

MINING AND THE STATE

Mining paid a substantial royalty directly to the crown; in stimulating trade it indirectly yielded sales taxes and customs dues; Indian tributes came quickly to be paid in kind; and it did certainly add dynamism to many parts of the colonial economy. So it is no surprise that kings displayed avid interest in the industry's fortunes. In principle the crown would have maximized its profit from mining by working the mines itself. Though this was too large an undertaking for general implementation, it was to a degree realized. By law in the sixteenth century a portion of any new vein was reserved for the crown. This requirement fell into neglect in New Spain, but was observed in Peru and Charcas, where such royal mines were leased out. On the refining side, there were in Potosí in the 1570s at least two royal refineries, run by salaried administrators. In mercury production the crown always preserved a direct interest. Ownership of both the Almadén and Huancavelica deposits remained totally in the king's hands, though until 1645 at Almadén and 1782 at Huancavelica the mines were actually worked by contractors from whom the crown bought the mercury at a negotiated price. After these dates the government did work the mines directly itself, with poor results at Huancavelica, though remarkably good ones at Almadén after 1700. In addition the crown monopolized the distribution of mercury and determined its selling price to refiners.

The vast gold and silver deposits of America, though, were beyond the scope of direct royal operation. Instead the crown, invoking its ancient right of universal ownership of precious metal deposits, demanded a royalty on production while conceding free prospecting and usufruct of ores to Spanish subjects. This procedure relieved the government of production costs while encouraging active prospecting. After being set initially at up to two-thirds of output, the royalty was fixed in 1504 at a fifth – the famous *quinto real*. To this was shortly added an assay charge of 1–1.5 per cent. Further royalty reductions were often made in later years, however, in attempts to stimulate mining, some of them going to as little as a twentieth. In time the basic rate became a tenth (*diezmo*). The first broad concession of this was made to Mexican miners in 1548 – temporarily at first but repeated until it became customary. Merchants and other non-miners or refiners bringing silver for royalty payment were still to pay a fifth. But this distinction proved impracticable, and by the mid seventeenth century little *quinto* was being collected on silver in New Spain.

In the Andean mines, however, the standard levy remained a fifth well into the eighteenth century. Some earlier concessions of *diezmo* were made to specific mines when a stimulus seemed necessary (for example, to Castrovirreina in 1621 and to Nuevo Potosí in 1640). But in the great mines of Charcas, Potosí and Oruro, despite their obvious decline, the full fifth was maintained until 1736. Then, finally, a standard *diezmo* was introduced in Peru and Charcas. Further cuts were made by Bourbon reformers after 1770 to encourage Mexican production. Several entrepreneurs attempting to revive old mines received total exemption from royalty until they recovered the cost of their efforts. Zacatecas, among others, benefited greatly from this policy. Research to date has not revealed any such concessions to Andean miners.

Royalties on gold long remained at a full fifth, being cut to a tenth in New Spain in 1723 and a twentieth in Guatemala in 1738. In the Andes, however, *quinto* was levied until 1778 – when a general reduction for all Spanish America was ordered: 3 per cent to be taken in the colonies and a further 2 per cent on arrival of gold in Spain. With its power to adjust royalties the Crown could and did exercise a powerful influence over mining. Royalty cuts were often followed by growth in production, and may sometimes have been foolishly delayed, as in the case of Potosí. Refusal to lower the rate probably cost the crown income that would have accrued from increased production. Similarly the Crown's attempt to profit from its control of mercury distribution by setting a price which, as has been seen, was often above cost, undoubtedly reduced silver output and hence many tax revenues.

Taken together, indeed, the crown's possession of three statutory powers over mining – control of royalty, control of mercury distribution and price, and power to assign or remove draft labour – does lend the industry something of the air of state enterprise. Administrators – viceroys, *audiencias* and treasury officials – clearly tended to see it in this light, regarding miners and refiners perhaps not as employees, but certainly as a special category of servants, of the crown. The miners themselves naturally resented governmental controls over their occupation, for example protesting at royalty rates or labour decrees; while trying, usually without success, to profit from their special standing, as when they played on their close connection with the crown to try to get subsidized supplies of black slaves.

In general, crown policy towards mining lacked co-ordination, creating uncertainty among miners. Some policies had distinctly adverse effects, as in the case of excessive royalty rates. The notable exception to this was the Bourbon mining policy implemented after 1770, which aimed to increase bullion production through a whole range of stimuli. Some were obvious: cheaper mercury; exemption from royalties for specially enterprising miners; creation of royal banks to buy silver from miners with coin, so saving them the heavy discounts charged by private buyers of raw silver; creation of banks to finance the industry; attempted improvement of mining and refining techniques through education, in the form of mining 'missions' of European experts – mostly not Spanish – trained in new techniques; and in New Spain a successful technical college specializing in mining, where teaching began in 1792. More subtle measures were also essayed in an attempt to raise the status and hence the attraction of mining. In both New Spain and Peru a mining guild on the pattern of the patrician merchant guilds was created. In particular miners were now to have a high privilege hitherto reserved for the great corporations of Spanish America, the church and the merchants: their own courts in Mexico City and Lima, which would remove mining litigation from the public forum of the Audiencias. Furthermore, mining law itself was modernized, with sixteenth-century ordinances finally being cast aside. In 1783 a new code appeared, drawn up by the Mexican mining court in consultation with the crown; and this code, modified to meet local conditions, became law in both Peru and the Río de la Plata viceroyalty in 1794.

This ensemble of reforms was certainly not responsible alone for the late eighteenth-century resurgence of mining. Indeed in Peru it seems to have been quite ineffective; and in New Spain several of its components (for instance the finance bank) failed. Nevertheless some part of the late colonial Mexican boom must be attributed to the Bourbon changes. And certainly these royal efforts to stimulate bullion production were the most comprehensive and cogent of any made in colonial times.

CAPITAL

No question is more important for an understanding of the functioning of mining than that of capital – its sources, cost and availability in different times and places. But for no question are manuscript sources scarcer and more enigmatic. Except for the case of late colonial New Spain, knowledge of mining capital is hardly more than generalized guesswork.

Early silver production by smelting required little capital investment: ores were generally near the surface, and the main piece of refining equipment, the furnace, could be built for almost nothing. Similarly, early gold mining in placers using Indian labour required a minimum of spending; though later gold production, in placers with black slaves, or by vein mining and the use of crushing mills, did demand investment in labour and plant. But this investment was not on the scale needed in amalgamation of silver. Here mines soon became deep, often demanding expensive adits; refining required a large set of buildings; powerful crushing mills were essential; and some power source had to be established, either a stock of animals or a water supply; a stock of mercury was needed. Prices of all these varied in place and time; but generally speaking a refining hacienda was among the most costly items exchanged in the colonies, on a par with estates, large town houses and ships. In early seventeenth-century Zacatecas and Potosí an *hacienda de minas* might cost, depending on size and condition, from 10,000 to 50,000 pesos.

To judge from the case of Potosí, the initial capital needed for amalgamation may not, contrary to expectation, have been difficult to assemble. In the previous smelting stage of refining, much ore had been mined that was then discarded as too poor for smelting, but which yielded great profits when amalgamated. Small, cheap machines sufficed initially to crush it, and profits were ploughed back in the form of larger mills able to handle growing amounts of less rich ores. At Potosí in the first six years of amalgamation (1571–6), 30–40 per cent of silver production after tax was probably used to build new refineries alone.

If no new finds of good ore were made, this stage of autonomous financing characteristically lasted two or three decades in any district. Then, as the better ores were depleted, the search began for external sources of credit to finance prospecting, adits, repair of machines, purchase of animals, and so on. The source commonly tapped was the merchant community in the mining centres. And so enters the scene that ubiquitous figure in Spanish American mining, the *aviador* (supplier of goods and credit). The appearance of aviadores was a wholly natural development. The first of them were general merchants who gave credit to the miners on supplies in the normal course of business. Soon they were also lending cash. In repayment they took refined but unminted silver, since most mining centres were too far from mints for refiners to take their silver in for coinage. The aviador therefore also became a buyer (*rescatador*) of raw silver. The aviador–rescatador naturally charged interest on his loans; but how much is so far impossible to tell. Receiving his payment in uncoined silver, he had to cover mintage charges on it as well as freight to the mint. In some cases he may also have paid the royalty. Silver producers constantly denounced the usury of aviadores, and indeed it often seems that aviadores prospered while miners went bankrupt. On the other hand, they doubtless had to absorb many bad debts, and they too suffered failures. The number of prosperous aviadores in any centre at any moment was probably no greater than the number of prosperous silver producers.

As the *avío* (supply and credit) system matured, a hierarchy of dealers developed. At its apex were the silver merchants (*mercaderes de plata*), who normally lived in the cities containing mints: in New Spain, Mexico City alone; in South America, principally Potosí but also Lima from 1683. Similar gold merchants existed in eighteenth-century New Granada, and probably earlier. There were perhaps no more than a dozen or two such merchants in each city. Their business was to buy up unminted silver at a discount with coin, have it minted, buy more silver, and so on, taking their profit from the discount. Their source of uncoined silver might be the refiners themselves, but more usually was the aviadores–rescatadores in mining towns. These in turn would buy from lesser district merchants as well as from refiners. Much of the credit loaned locally stemmed from the funds of the central *mercaderes de plata*.

The silver merchants are figures of the seventeenth century and later. By the eighteenth their businesses had in a few cases developed in New Spain into something resembling banking. The Fagoaga family in Mexico City traded at this level, giving extensive credit on account to important miners, and also taking in loans at 5 per cent interest from private institutions and persons. Even in prosperous eighteenth-century New Spain, however, there were never more than three such banks operating concurrently. As the eighteenth century progressed, miners and refiners tried setting up their own credit institutions to avoid the alleged rapacity of the merchants. This was done in 1747 in Potosí, for example, with some degree of success, especially when in 1752 the credit company expanded its activity beyond mere lending and began to buy silver for coinage from the producers. Later in the century, when the crown organized the mining guilds of New Spain and Peru, these were assigned funds to be lent to producers. Financial mismanagement combined with political opposition to limit severely the guilds' success as financiers. The crown did also, however, from about 1780 begin to establish its own funds for purchasing silver (*bancos de rescate*) in regional treasury offices, so freeing refiners to a degree from dependence on merchants for coin. Direct merchant financing of mining nevertheless continued to predominate until the end of colonial times. In the Andean districts local aviadores seem to have supplied most of it. In New Spain the large merchant houses of the capital were the source of much finance, especially after the implementation of the 1778 Free Trade law, which undermined their control of overseas commerce and caused them to seek other investments for their funds.

SILVER PRODUCTION

The most reliable source for gold and silver production is the record of royalty receipts kept by the treasury offices. The main town of a large mining district normally had its own office, and new ones were created when an important new district emerged or an old one grew notably. Another source, but one more distant from the actual production of metal, is the mintage record. Here the drawback is that not all bullion was minted, except perhaps after 1683, when coinage became obligatory. So in general royalties are preferable as indicators of output. How much bullion escaped paying them cannot be known; much clearly did. But the royalty accounts give at least a minimum estimate of production and

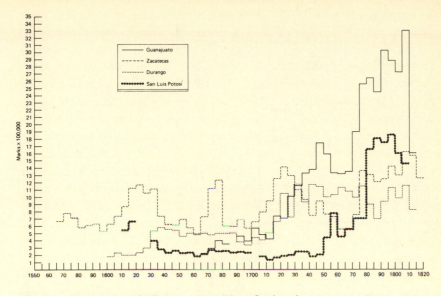

Fig. 3*a*. Quinquennial silver output, New Spain: the great northern mines,
1565–1820

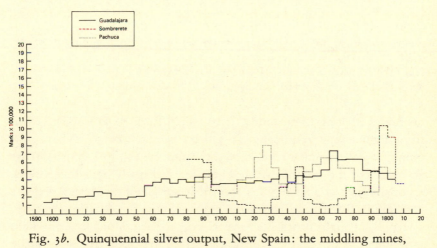

Fig. 3*b*. Quinquennial silver output, New Spain: the middling mines,
1595–1810

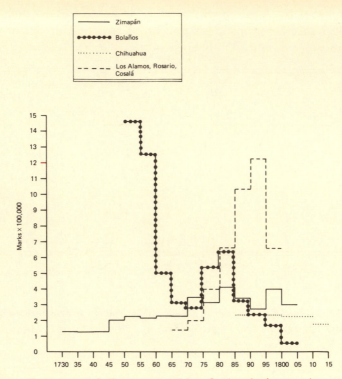

Fig. 3*c*. Quinquennial silver output, New Spain: the lesser mines, 1730–1815

Sources for Figs. *3a*, *3b* and *3c*: **Zacatecas, 1565–1719,** and **Sombrerete, 1681–1719**: Bakewell, *Silver mining and society*, 246, 250. All other data here are from the treasury accounts of the mining centres shown in these figures – accounts being prepared for publication by Professor John J. TePaske.

do reflect its long-term trends. It is mainly from royalty records that the accompanying graphs (figs. 3–5) have been prepared.[12] They show quinquennial output for most of the major silver-producing districts and some of the gold districts. There are still many gaps to be filled, especially for the gold regions and the lesser silver districts. Adequate series of royalty receipts before the 1550s are rare, the American treasury system being in the process of formation up to then. Much interpolation, interpretation of data, and pure conjecture are necessary to estimate early production. A careful calculation from treasury ledgers in the Archive of the Indies was made by Haring, who modified and reduced

---

[12] The author is most grateful to Professor J. J. TePaske for supplying him, before their publication, with transcriptions of Mexican and Andean treasury accounts from regional treasury offices.

earlier estimates by Adolf Soetbeer and W. Lexis.[13] According to Haring, allowance being made for evasion of royalties, the quantities of gold and silver produced in Spanish America up to 1560 were:

Region	Pesos (1 peso = 272 maravedís)	Equivalent in marks of silver (1 mark = 2,380 maravedís)
New Spain:		
gold	5,692,570	650,579
silver*	26,597,280	3,011,429
Peru and Chile	28,350,000	3,240,000
Charcas	56,000,000	6,400,000
New Granada	6,081,000	694,971
West Indies and Tierra Firme	17,000,000	1,942,857
Totals	139,720,850	15,939,836

* The accounts did not permit separation of gold and silver output except in the case of New Spain.

In a later investigation, Jara managed to separate gold and silver output in Peru and Charcas from 1531 to 1600.[14] These figures contain no correction for royalty evasion.

Period	Gold (millions of maravedís)	Silver (millions of maravedís)	Total (millions of maravedís)	Equivalent of total in marks of silver (of 2,380 maravedís
1531–5	1,173	1,016	2,189	919,748
1536–40	325	371	696	292,437
1541–5	547	235	782	328,571
1546–50	406	4,371	4,777	2,007,143
1551–5	363	3,050	3,413	1,434,034
1556–7	52	1,439	1,491	626,471
1562–5	120	2,224	2,344	984,874
1567–70	65	2,106	2,171	912,185
1571–5	13	1,748	1,761	739,916
1576–80	181	7,930	8,111	3,407,983
1581–5	109	12,218	12,327	5,179,412
1586–90	56	14,463	14,519	6,100,420
1591–5	11	14,281	14,292	6,005,042
1596–1600	23	14,024	14,047	5,902,100

[13] C. H. Haring, 'American gold and silver production in the first half of the sixteenth century', *Quarterly Journal of Economics*, 29 (1915), 433–79.

[14] Alvaro Jara, 'La curva de producción de metales monetarios en el Perú en el siglo XVI', in *Tres ensayos sobre economía minera hispanoamericana* (Santiago de Chile, 1966), 93–118.

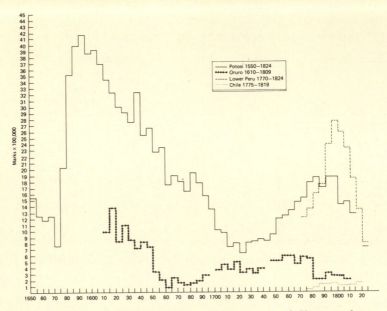

Fig. 4. Quinquennial silver output, Chile, Peru, and Charcas: the great mines, 1550–1824

Sources: **Potosí, 1550–1735,** and **Oruro, 1610–1715:** P. J. Bakewell, 'Registered silver production in the Potosí district, 1550–1735', *JGSWGL*, 12 (1975), 67–103; **Potosí, 1736–89:** Potosí, Casa Nacional de Moneda, Cajas Reales MS 417. **Lower Peru, 1770–1824:** John R. Fisher, *Silver mines and silver miners in colonial Peru, 1776–1824* (Monograph Series no. 7, Centre for Latin American Studies, Liverpool, 1977), 124–5. **Chile, 1775–1819:** Marcello Carmagnani, *Les mécanismes de la vie économique dans une société coloniale: le Chili (1680–1830)* (Paris, 1973), 309.

Both Haring and Jara show clearly that in the first decade or so after conquest the bullion from a region was not so much mine output as booty. Large accumulations of gold, in particular, were seized in New Spain, New Granada, and Peru. Many gold deposits, especially in New Spain and Peru, had long been worked by the native peoples and were already partially depleted when the Spanish took them over. So gold production often trended downwards in the sixteenth century, except where the Spanish located new or little-tapped deposits, as in New Granada. Conversely, silver production tended to rise, since deposits

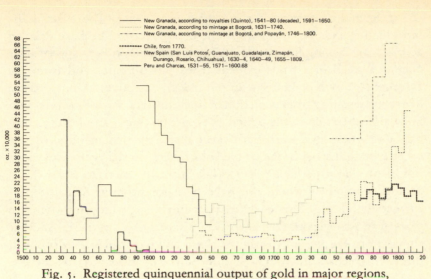

Fig. 5. Registered quinquennial output of gold in major regions,
1530–1820

Sources: **Peru** and **Charcas, 1531–55, 1571–1600:** Alvaro Jara, 'La curva de producción de metales monetarios en el Perú en el siglo XVI', *Tres ensayos sobre economía minera hispanoamericana* (Santiago de Chile, 1966), 93–118. **New Granada, 1541–80, 1591–1740:** Germán Colmenares, *Historia económica y social de Colombia, 1537–1719* (Medellín, 1973), ch. 5; **New Granada, 1746–1800:** Vicente Restrepo, *Estudio sobre las minas de oro y plata de Colombia* (4th edn, Bogotá, 1952), 197. **New Spain, 1630–4, 1640–9, 1655–1809:** treasury accounts of San Luis Potosí 1630–, Guanajuato 1665*–, Guadalajara 1670–, Zimapán 1735*–, Durango 1745–, Rosario 1770*–, and Chihuahua 1800–, being prepared for publication by Professor John J. TePaske. (Dates here, if asterisked, refer to the foundation of the town's treasury office; if not asterisked, to the first significant appearance of gold in the accounts of the office in question.) **Chile, 1770–1819:** Carmagnani, *Les mécanismes de la vie économique*, 367.

had previously been at most lightly exploited, and yielded well to new technology. It was probably in the late 1530s in New Spain and in the mid 1540s in the central Andes that the value of silver production first exceeded that of gold; and this continued for the rest of colonial times in those areas. In others, notably New Granada and Chile, gold always predominated. After the 1540s (at the latest) the total value of gold produced in Spanish America was always inferior to the value of silver.

Amalgamation ensured the ascendancy of silver. The effect of its introduction into New Spain cannot be appreciated because detailed accounts are lacking for the 1550s. But its influence in Peru and Charcas once it arrived in 1571 is evident from Jara's figures and from the enormous growth of Potosí's output (see fig. 4 above). After a period of decline resulting from depletion of smelting ores, Potosí's production grew almost sixfold in the period 1575–90, reaching, around 1592, not only its highest level ever, but a level exceeding that achieved by any other mining district in the whole colonial era. In the years 1575–1600 Potosí produced perhaps a half of all Spanish American silver. Such profusion of silver would not have been forthcoming without con-current abundance of mercury from Huancavelica, which in those same years was also yielding as never again (see fig. 2, p. 121). Another stimulant to Potosí was clearly the cheap and plentiful labour supplied through Toledo's mita. But without amalgamation little of the ore extracted by the mitayos could have been refined profitably. Potosí's main rival in this pre-1600 period was probably the Zacatecas district in New Spain (see fig. 3a above), though Pachuca and Taxco may have been very close also. Specific information on their production is not yet available. By 1600, however, Potosí had entered on a 130-year decline, interrupted occasionally, but not arrested, by new strikes in the district. The easily accessible ore concentration in the peak of the Potosí mountain became increasingly depleted in the seventeenth century, so that the Potosí industry developed into something far more diffuse than before, extending over much of southern Charcas. By 1660, 40 per cent of the silver paying royalties in Potosí originated in the district mines (though later this proportion did fall again somewhat). Oruro is not considered here as part of the Potosí district, as it had its own treasury office almost from the moment it became important (1606–7). It was possibly the second South American producer after the Potosí district in the seventeenth century, though it too suffered from ore depletion. Output series are not available for mines in Peru, nor elsewhere in South America, but indications are that they were comparatively poor.

Potosí and Oruro suffered no substantial mercury shortage in the seventeenth century, despite Huancavelica's erratic performance (see fig. 2). This, however, was at New Spain's expense. Huancavelica having faltered after 1595, the crown at length decided from 1630 to divert much of Almadén's output from New Spain to the Andean mines, which were by far the larger producers. Mercury for New Spain was bought from Idrija, but not in large enough amounts to keep the supply at previous levels. And New Spain was further deprived when the Idrija purchases were stopped in 1645. Mexican silver output thus fell from the 1630s, especially as the mercury shortage coincided with ore depletion in some districts. (The great exception was the Durango district, in which new strikes at Parral actually brought increased output in the early 1630s.) The downward trend in New Spain continued until the 1660s, when it was checked by an unexpected development: the revival of smelting. This is clear in the Zacatecas royalty records from 1670 and certainly had begun well before that. In the 1670s, 60 per cent of the Zacatecas district's output was smelted. The main centre for this was Sombrerete, which produced so prolifically that in 1681 it was allotted its own treasury office. By then the rest of the Zacatecas district had also widely converted to smelting, producing 48 per cent of its silver by that method between 1680 and 1699. After 1700 smelting continued to be commonplace in New Spain, as these figures show:

District	% output smelted in 1720s	% output smelted in 1760s
Guadalajara	26 (1730s)	8 (1770s)
Guanajuato	35 (1730s)	27 (1770s)
Pachuca	27	23
San Luis Potosí	86 (1730s)	54
Sombrerete	68	33
Zacatecas	c. 30	30
Zimapán	90 +	94 (1795–9)

This notable return to smelting after a long predominance of amalgamation was evidently a response to the shortage of mercury from 1630 onwards. But explaining the success of this reversion will require more research. There is no apparent improvement in smelting technique; so high-grade ores must have been found in large quantities to allow profitable smelting on so large a scale. How was the necessary prospecting and expansion of existing mines financed after a long period of falling output? Possibly the answer lies in an acceleration of underground exploration through blasting.

Blasting must certainly be among the causes of the immense, ubiquitous and almost uninterrupted growth of silver output in eighteenth-century New Spain.[15] It is the one known radical innovation in the production process. Also conducive to greater output was the growing size and orderliness of workings, a trend glimpsed in the seventeenth century and now reinforced by the spread among at least some miners of a more rational and methodical approach to mining and its problems. While this cannot be quantified, the change may well have been fundamental to Mexican mining's success in the eighteenth century; it is only necessary to compare the cool, reasoned and precise accounts of their enterprises given by mid-eighteenth-century miners with the jumbled and often unintelligible ramblings of their counterparts a century earlier. Behind the great eighteenth-century Mexican boom lay also abundance of mercury and of labour. The table just given shows that smelting, though common after 1700, tended to decline with time. One reason for this was clearly the enormous growth of mercury production at Almadén, finally relieving the shortage that began in the 1630s. Even this abundance, however, failed to match demand in the late 1700s, so again Idrija mercury was bought, on a contract made in 1785 for the supply of 10,000–12,000 *quintales* annually to Spanish America. This mercury appeared in many Mexican centres in 1786. Plentiful mercury was matched with plentiful labour, as New Spain's population grew, doubling, in fact, over the second half of the eighteenth century (2.6 million in 1742 to 6.1 million in 1810). It is perhaps particularly significant that the population of the intendancy of Guanajuato, in which the most remarkable mines of the late eighteenth century lay, more than tripled in the 1742–1810 period. While no general study of mining wages exists in that century (or in any other for that matter), it is a reasonable supposition that this notable population growth tended to restrain wage increases, if nothing more – to the miners' advantage. This suggestion is supported by the overall stability of wages observed for Zacatecas after 1750 and by the apparent fall of workers' wages at Guanajuato in the final decades of the century. Mexican output was further augmented from about 1770 onwards by the governmental policies already described: reductions in mercury price, royalty concessions, improvements in the miner's status, and the introduction of education in mining, engineering, and geology. Some of these measures encouraged increased investment in mining, which resulted in larger and better-planned workings. And to these stimuli

---

[15] See ch. 3 above.

may possibly be added a growing demand for silver. This question needs closer examination; but it is arguable that the growth of population drove up demand for imported goods, which in turn increased demand for silver, the main export, to pay for them.

The great Valenciana mine at Guanajuato exemplifies many of the developments of late colonial Mexican mining. It was without a doubt the largest single mine ever worked in colonial Spanish America, employing at its peak over 3,300 underground workers and between 1780 and 1810 yielding 60–70 per cent of the total output of Guanajuato, itself the unchallenged silver capital of New Spain (see fig. 3*a*). The Valenciana owed its success to immense capital investment of the sort that the crown's fiscal encouragement of mining set out to evoke. Over a million pesos were spent on three great vertical shafts, which allowed cheap extraction of ore and acted as foci for numerous spacious galleries. Even these shafts ultimately proved inadequate, so that after 1800 another, the San José, was sunk. By 1810 this had reached a depth of nearly 1,800 feet. Its diameter of 33 feet permitted simultaneous operation of eight animal-driven hoists. The Valenciana was an enterprise of unprecedented horizontal integration. No single mine had previously possessed so many great shafts, nor such a multiplicity of galleries. There was also considerable vertical integration: the Valenciana partners ran refineries handling part of the ore coming from the mine. The rest they sold to independent refiners. Other enterprises in Guanajuato, however, carried vertical integration further still.

By the first quinquennium of the nineteenth century, according to Humboldt, New Spain was producing some 67.5 per cent of Spanish American silver – a proportion confirmed by the partial information shown in figs. 3*a*, 3*b* and 4, above.[16] This was the apogee of output. After 1805 disruption of the mercury supply by war, the crown's own increased fiscal pressure on New Spain, and finally damage by insurgents in 1810–11, brought production tumbling down.

The history of eighteenth-century Andean silver mining is less known, especially before 1770, than that of New Spain. For Potosí and Oruro in this period, there is hardly any more information available than the bare production figures. Neither has Peruvian mining in the first two-thirds of the century received attention. It seems, nevertheless, that the 1700s brought a larger recovery of Andean silver mining than has

[16] *Ensayo político*, 425 (book 4, ch. 11).

been thought. Potosí's output almost tripled from 1720 to 1780; the mines of Peru boomed remarkably after then (fig. 4). Potosí and Oruro may have benefited from blasting, and both certainly responded to the reduction in royalty from a fifth to a tenth in July 1736. Added to this was a clear though erratic growth in mercury supply from Huancavelica between 1700 and 1770 (fig. 2). After that Huancavelica slumped, but mercury was imported frrom Almadén and Idrija, so that the mines of Peru, and probably those of Charcas also, did not suffer shortage. The remarkable vigour of the Peruvian mines after 1770 may indeed owe much to abundance of mercury. Beyond this, as in New Spain, there was eighteenth-century population growth with its probably depressive influence on labour costs. And in Peru the late eighteenth century also witnessed an increased injection of capital into mining, resulting in improved workings. Although Peruvian enterprises remained far smaller than those of New Spain, investment did bring useful below-ground changes, most notably in the form of new drainage adits at Cerro de Pasco, which emerged as the most dynamic centre. This enlarged capital flow originated, it would seem, among the merchant community of Lima; though the funds were not invested directly, but reached miners through local aviadores. The new investments may reflect a growth in demand for silver caused by the separation of Peru from Charcas with the latter's incorporation into the new Río de la Plata viceroyalty in 1776. With their traditional source of silver cut off, since Charcas' output now had to be exported through Buenos Aires, the Peruvian merchants perhaps felt impelled to develop mines closer to home. The fall in Peruvian output after 1805 had general causes similar to those operating in New Spain, and a particular reason in the increasing depth and consequent flooding of the Cerro de Pasco workings after 1812.

In this discussion of production, one important but elusive influence has so far been omitted: the value of silver. This is elusive because price and wage series for colonial times are still rare, so that variations in the buying power of silver are scantily known. It is clear, though, that prices (as measured in silver) rose steeply in the late sixteenth and early seventeenth centuries in many places, in an inflation that owed much precisely to high silver production. This loss of value undoubtedly contributed to seventeenth-century declines in silver output. Later in the seventeenth century, prices may have been more stable, at least in New Spain; and may have continued so in the eighteenth. Such stability would have encouraged mining revival. The movement of the European bimetallic ratio tends to reinforce these suggestions: 1500–50 – *c.* 10.5:1; 1600 – *c.* 12:1; 1650 – *c.* 14:1; 1700 – *c.* 15:1; 1760 – *c.* 15:1. That is, until the mid seventeenth century, silver rapidly depreciated in terms of gold; after that the ratio remained steady.

GOLD PRODUCTION

Our knowledge of gold output is less extensive and secure than that of silver production, and is likely to remain so since gold, being much the more valuable, presented still greater temptations than silver to the royalty evader (and the smuggler). Royalties and mintage are therefore slighter indicators of real production of gold than they are for silver. For lack of others, though, these records have been used to prepare fig. 5, which shows output in four major gold regions for at least parts of the colonial era: New Spain, New Granada, Peru and Charcas, and Chile. These were certainly the areas that produced most gold. New Granada was first among them. For a few decades after settlement, several mainland areas – southern New Spain (Colima, Tehuantepec), Central America (Honduras), southern Quito (Zaruma), east central Peru (Carabaya), south central Chile (Valdivia), to mention only the most important – yielded plentiful gold. But only New Granada had deposits extensive enough to permit constantly growing output in the sixteenth century; and then, after a seventeenth-century slump, a still greater boom in the eighteenth. The leading sixteenth-century district in New Granada was Antioquia, between the Cauca and Magdalena rivers in the north. It was worked with encomienda and black slave labour, decline coming in the seventeenth century as the Indian population fell to disease and as the vein gold of Buriticá and placers in the rivers were worked out. The eighteenth-century boom owed much to the Chocó – the rain-forested Andean slopes facing the Pacific in central New Granada. Here river gravels rich in gold were extensively worked with black slaves and freedmen from the 1670s on. In several other areas of New Granada, notably Popayán in the south, there was also substantial gold mining.

In Chile, gold production seems to have become negligible by the mid seventeenth century, but revived again in the 1690s, climbing steadily in the eighteenth century. The reasons for this revival were the need for exports to balance Chile's trade, and the growth of a poor mestizo section of the population which, seeking some means of support, turned to small-scale gold mining in the centre north (Norte Chico).

Another major eighteenth-century gold region was northern New Spain, where gold often occurred in conjunction with silver ores. Recent investigation shows that San Luis Potosí was the first north Mexican district to yield much gold, beginning in the early decades of the seventeenth century. Between 1630 and 1635 it produced some 100,000 oz. Significant gold output began in the following districts, all northern except Guadalajara, at about the date indicated: Guanajuato (1665), Guadalajara (1670), Zimapán (1735), Durango (1745), Rosario (1770), and Chihuahua (1800). The growth of Mexican production, as shown in fig. 5 (which does not take account of any mines in the centre or south), was doubtless stimulated by royalty reductions, from a fifth to a tenth (*c.* 1720), and thence to 3 per cent (1778).

Few aspects of colonial life remained untouched by mining. Gold and silver gleamed in the eyes of conquerors and explorers. 'Great difficulty can be foreseen... in its satisfactory settlement and growth as long as there are no mines to stimulate the greed that will carry forward and facilitate the whole business', wrote the viceroy of New Spain in 1601 of the current Spanish advance into New Mexico, clearly having in mind the overall pattern of sixteenth-century Spanish settlement in America.[17] He predicted well. New Mexico remained a sparsely populated, poor and neglected section of the empire in large part because it revealed no significant bullion sources. Even New Mexico, though, counted heavily on mining for its existence, finding a market for animal and vegetable products in the silver towns of northern New Spain. Other regions of the empire poorly endowed with precious metals stood in similar relation to the mining zones (Quito to Peru, Tucumán and Buenos Aires to Charcas), with the exception of Paraguay, which suffered such extreme geographical isolation that even the immense market opportunities of Charcas failed to induce a flow of trade.

The conquest, exploration, settlement and exploitation of Spanish America were all spurred on by the prospect of mining; and mining determined to a remarkable degree the internal economic arrangement of the colonies. It had a scarcely less profound influence on internal political and administrative structure, since precious metal production led to the accumulation of wealth and population in regions that

[17] Archivo General de Indias, Mexico 24, Conde de Monterrey to king, México, 2 August 1601.

otherwise would have been of no weight. It is hardly necessary to stress further the social consequences of mining: the mobility, both upward and downward, to which mine owners were subject; the disruption of Indian communities and displacement of their people to distant regions; the frequent acculturation of these people in essentially Spanish mining towns to the ways of the colonizers. Nor should it be forgotten that many of these towns hold remarkable examples of colonial art and architecture. The great churches of the mining centres, particularly of those that flourished in eighteenth-century New Spain, are equally reminders of colonial mineral wealth and monuments to the successful miners whose patronage built them.

The external consequences of mining are, of course, almost beyond measure, since silver and gold were the foundation of the wealth that Spain drew from her American empire – wealth that excited the eager envy of other European states. The proportion of mining royalties in total royal income from America has not been calculated; nor would the figure have much interest, since bullion production also provided the cash in which all other taxes and duties were paid. Nor is the proportion by value of bullion in total exports from Spanish America known, though it must have been high – well over 75 per cent in most periods. Spain's rivals were naturally well aware of this gleaming current flowing across the Atlantic, and sought by various means to tap it in its course or at its source. Corsairs, particularly the English, had notable success in sixteenth-century raids in the Caribbean. In 1628 the Dutch West India Company dealt a spectacular blow to Spain by seizing the treasure fleet from New Spain off Cuba, though its reported plan (conceived in an excess of ambition and ignorance of geography) to seize Potosí from the Brazilian coast was beyond realization. More practical and successful was the strategy pursued strongly by the French and English in the eighteenth century of drawing off Spanish American wealth through commerce, some licit, but most not. Finally, independence opened the fabled mining regions themselves to direct foreign access. The flood of English capital into Mexican and Andean mines in the 1820s and '30s is a commonplace of nineteenth-century Spanish American history. But success was elusive. Steam power, Cornish miners, and English expertise were not readily transplanted. As the confident ventures collapsed, their disconsolate stockholders were made only too aware of America's recalcitrance in yielding up her precious metals, and of the magnitude of Spain's achievement in overcoming it.

6

THE HACIENDA IN NEW SPAIN

ECONOMIC TRANSFORMATION

The first revolution to transform the land in Mesoamerica was the invention in prehistoric times of agriculture itself. The second revolution took place some decades after the conquest, when the brutal decline in the native American population coincided with the Spaniards' penetration of the land and the propagation there of European plants and animals. The swiftness with which this process occurred may perhaps be explained by the previous acclimatization of European flora and fauna in the Canary Islands and the Caribbean. The mainland itself offered many different ecological zones for 'the reproduction of plants and animals. As early as the middle of the sixteenth century, the valleys of Puebla–Tlaxcala and the basin around Mexico City surprised the traveller with their diversified agricultural landscape, where maize, beans, squash, and peppers alternated with wheat, barley, and European vegetables and fruits.

European grain spread to the irrigated highlands south of Puebla (Atlixco, Tepeaca) and north of Mexico City (Tlalnepantla and Huehuetoca), and then on from there, pushing back the Chichimeca frontier (San Juan del Río, Querétaro). By the end of the sixteenth century, wheat and maize gilded the black soil of the Bajío and were harvested around Morelia and Guadalajara in the west and Oaxaca in the south. Within a relatively short period of time grain transformed the traditional landscape of the native countryside, opening up many hundreds of kilometres of fertile land to cultivation. Wheat farming introduced Spanish techniques of cultivation, such as the plough, the yoke, and

* Translated from the original Spanish by Dr Richard Boulind; translation revised by Clara García Ayluardo and the Editor.

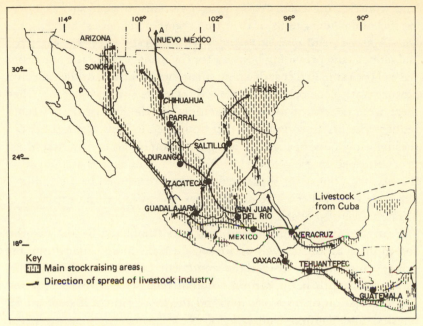

The spread of livestock economy in Mexico and Central America during
the colonial era

Source: Robert C. West and John P. Augelli, *Middle America: its lands and
people,* © 1966, p. 287. Reprinted by permission of Prentice-Hall, Inc.,
Englewood Cliffs, N.J.

irrigation, bringing them into permanent use in New Spain. By the
mid-seventeenth century, the former wastelands of the Bajío had been
converted into the most important, prosperous, and modern agricultural
area of New Spain.

Another vehicle of great transformation in the physical as well as the
social environment was sugar-cane. It was introduced into the *tierra
templada* and *tierra caliente* south of the capital (valley of Cuernavaca and
Atlixco) and into the lowlands of Veracruz from the 1530s, and a few
years later it was also cultivated in the temperate valleys of Michoacán,
New Galicia, and Colima. A crop demanding sun, water, and extensive
flat land, sugar-cane also required heavy investment if the cane's juice
was to be transformed into sugar crystals. Hence, from the first, the
exploitation and processing of sugar-cane was associated with the
powerful magnates. Hernán Cortés was one of the pioneers of sugar-cane
in Cuernavaca and in the Veracruz lowlands. He set the example for
other encomenderos and for rich officials who spent large sums buying

land, constructing extensive irrigation systems, importing machinery for the rudimentary mills of the more complex refineries, building the *casas de prensas*, and *casas de purgar*, where the cane juice was extracted and refined, and providing housing for the managers and the numerous slaves. The estimated cost of a new sugar mill at the end of the sixteenth century was 50,000 pesos or more; it is therefore surprising that by then there were dozens of mills in operation. By the end of the sixteenth century, the first agro-industry that flourished in New Spain produced the highest volume of sugar in the Spanish dominions in America. Much of it remained in New Spain; as P. Acosta commented at the end of the century, 'the sugar that is retained and consumed in the Indies is almost beyond belief'. The rest of what was produced on the coast of Veracruz went to Spain.

European occupation of land was also stimulated by the demand for tropical products such as tobacco, cacao, indigo, dyewood and other plants, which from the second half of the sixteenth century onwards came to be grown on a commercial scale. However, it was the importation of livestock that had the most violent impact on the physical and cultural landscape of New Spain. Arriving from the Antilles, they followed in the tracks of other conquerors of the land. Among the many surprises which awaited the settlers, none had so great an impact as the way cows, horses, sheep, goats, pigs, mules, and donkeys multiplied in prodigious numbers, populating New Spain within a few years. In the two decades following the conquest, European livestock spread rapidly across the whole Valley of Mexico and across the valleys of Toluca, Puebla, Tlaxcala, Oaxaca and Michoacán. In these areas, densely populated by Indians using traditional farming methods, the European animals invaded and destroyed the open-field cultivation system, transformed arable land into pasture, dislocated the pattern of settlement, and reduced the Indians' sources of food. It is true that the Indians soon incorporated pigs, sheep, goats, and chickens into their nutritional system; but, on the whole, they lost rather than gained by the changes that transformed their relationship to the environment.

Cows, horses, and mules had a less adverse effect in the tropical lowlands, where epidemics had already decimated the Indian population, allowing the animals to find nourishing year-round pasture and grasses by the marshes and rivers. These conditions changed the coastal plains of Veracruz and the Pacific into areas of *ganado mayor*, as the Spaniards called estates where cattle, horses, and mules were bred. Even more

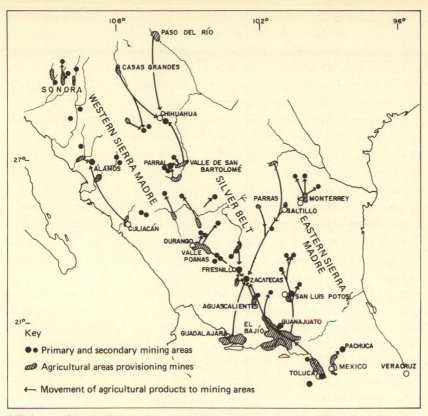

Mining and agriculture in northern New Spain: seventeenth and eighteenth centuries

Source: Robert C. West and John P. Augelli, *Middle America: its lands and people*, © 1966, p. 298. Reprinted by permission of Prentice-Hall, Inc., Englewood Cliffs, N.J.

attractive for both *ganado mayor* and *ganado menor* (lesser stock, i.e. sheep and goats) were the prairies of the north, opened up by settlements of miners. From 1540, the herds followed the northward route of the silver prospectors and, after 1550, overflowed into the semi-arid plains north of the Bajío. From the Valley of Mexico livestock migrated into the valley of Toluca, took possession of the Chichimeca country around San Juan del Río and Querétaro, reached into the north-east, where they populated the territories of San Miguel, Dolores, San Luis de la Paz, and Valles, and multiplied on the plains to the north of Zacatecas in Durango, Parral, and Chihuahua. In all these new territories at the end of the sixteenth century there were already hundreds of thousands of sheep, goats, cows, and horses. A vast new area of land was incorporated into the economy. Stock raising, agriculture and (most importantly) silver mining, attracted successive waves of white, Indian, and black settlement in these territories, and completed the process of colonization and the integration of the economy.

The spread of livestock led to the introduction of Spanish techniques of grazing – common use of lowland, hill, and wilderness pasture – and of the *mesta*, or guild of stock-breeders. This body prescribed rules for the pasturing, migration, and branding of livestock and for the resolution of disputes. A new technique for the breeding and selection of animals, the *rodeo*, was also developed in New Spain. This was a system for rounding up the yearlings annually to brand them and to choose which were to be sold or slaughtered.

These new activities created the man on horseback, the cowboy, who, together with the miner and the missionary, was one of the central figures in the colonization of the north. At the same time wagons and carts drawn by oxen, horses, or mules brought about a revolution in transportation, shortening distances and making the moving of merchandise and produce easier. These animals were the first non-human locomotive power used in New Spain, allowing transportation of equipment for milling and crushing minerals and for pressing and processing sugar. Cattle and goat hides engendered a healthy export trade and furnished articles needed for the extraction and transportation of mineral ores. Sheep's wool made possible the manufacture of textiles and clothing, which came into general use amongst whites, Indians, and mestizos. Since beef was cheap and abundant, the Spaniards and creoles of the north became consumers of it, while pig, chicken, lamb, and goat meat quickly transformed the eating habits of the native population. Some idea of the quantitative change in the physical landscape of New Spain after a century of Spanish colonization is given by Lesley B. Simpson, who estimated the head of cattle in 1620 at 1,288,000 (equalling the figure for the Indian population at that date), while sheep and goats taken together reached the incredible figure of eight million head.

The evangelizing friar was another agent of the great transformation of New Spain's ecology. Franciscan, Dominican and Augustinian missionaries, later joined by Jesuits and Carmelites, were active in introducing and adapting plants, animals, and agricultural and irrigation techniques. Every mission, convent, monastery, or Indian village that they founded saw the planting of European-type orchards with orange, lemon, and pear trees and grape-vines, vegetable gardens with new types of vegetables, and a system of dikes, aqueducts, ditches, and dams which extended the cultivated area and increased the seasonal supply of the fruits of the earth. In the centre and south of New Spain, the missionaries helped the speedy incorporation of these plants, animals, and techniques into the material culture of the settled Indians. In the north, these innovations were adopted by the mission towns, remote and isolated little settlements which were turned into self-sufficient units practising subsistence agriculture (wheat, maize, beans, garden, and orchard crops), stock raising, and cattle, sheep, and goat grazing as well as manufacturing their own textiles, clothing, soap, and artisan products. Between the middle and the end of the sixteenth century, the Dominicans, Augustinians, and Jesuits also built up their own sugar haciendas and cattle and sheep estates.

LAND DISTRIBUTION

Although in the days following the capture of the Aztec capital Cortés seized some of the best lands for himself and his soldiers, mainly those that had belonged to the state or to military or religious officials, the Spaniards were not interested in agriculture. At this stage, native food production was more than enough to satisfy demand. At first, only Cortés himself and a few others sowed European seeds on this fertile soil. They harvested the crops irregularly and with difficulty and frequently abandoned farming for other more profitable activities. Moreover, this type of cultivation lacked precise boundaries and had neither fixed equipment nor regular workers. Later, with the intention of interesting the *conquistadores* in agriculture and of limiting the size of estates, Cortés distributed plots of land called *peonías* to all foot soldiers participating in the conquest and *caballerías* (tracts five times larger than *peonías*) to all horsemen, but without significant success.

The first regular distributions of land were made by the *oidores* (judges) of the second *audiencia* (1530–5). Following the tradition of the *Reconquista* in Spain, and with the purpose of stimulating the 'safekeeping and preservation of the land', they empowered the *cabildos* (town councils) of the new towns and villages to give grants of land to anyone wishing to settle there permanently. Thus the *cabildos*, and

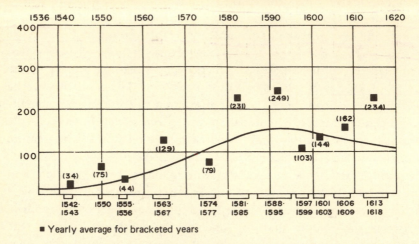

Fig. 6. *Caballerías* of agricultural land granted to Spaniards, 1536–1620

Source: L. B. Simpson, *Exploitation of land in central Mexico in the sixteenth century* (Berkeley and Los Angeles, 1952), 8.

later the viceroys, gave new settlers patents as *vecinos* (householders), with the right to a plot of land on which to build a house and plant a garden together with a grant of one or two *caballerías* to 'break and cultivate the soil'. Moreover, the new towns received an allowance for common lands and pastures. This was the model adopted for Puebla de los Ángeles, founded in April 1531, the first township of farmers who ploughed and cultivated the soil without encomienda Indians. It was later extended to the new towns founded in the north, and made general from 1573 by the New Laws of Settlement. For their part, the settlers undertook to live in the new town and promised not to sell their *caballerías* of land before ten years (later reduced to six) had elapsed, and not to transfer the land to any church or monastery or to the clergy.

From the mid sixteenth century the Spaniards' lack of interest in land and in agricultural activities suddenly changed; they now began to petition for extensive land grants. The distribution of *caballerías* of arable land became generalized, the area of a *caballería* being fixed at just under 43 hectares. To the end of the century there was a steady increase in grants of *caballerías* (see fig. 6). Two periods of extensive land distribution, 1553–63 and 1585–95, were linked to the great epidemics of 1545–7 and 1576–80 which decimated the Indian population. The

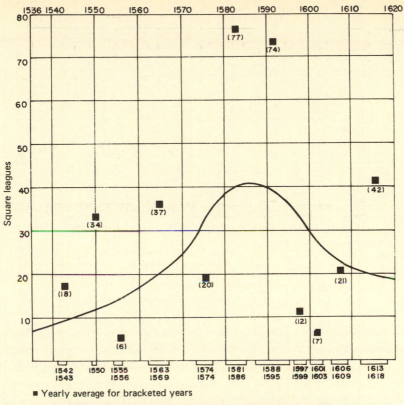

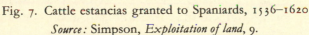

Fig. 7. Cattle estancias granted to Spaniards, 1536–1620

Source: Simpson, *Exploitation of land,* 9.

subsequent programmes for resettling the remaining Indians in *congregaciones* released thousands of hectares to be retained by the crown or distributed to Spanish settlers. According to the estimates of Lesley Simpson, between 1540 and 1620 redistribution was brought about by the granting of 12,742 *caballerías* of arable land to Spaniards, and of 1,000 to Indians; that is, some 600,000 hectares in all. (The *fundo legal* limited the size of each new Indian village to a maximum area of 101 hectares, as first specified in a viceregal order of 1567.) Village land was to be distributed as follows: one portion was reserved for the nucleus of the village, that is, the houses, gardens and personal plots of the inhabitants; another portion was reserved for the communal land and other areas where agricultural and stock-raising activities took place;

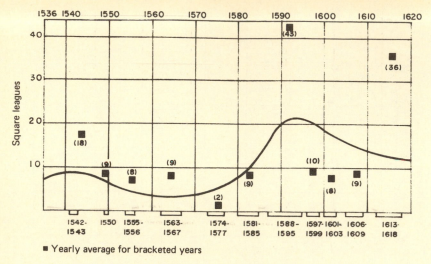

Fig. 8. Sheep estancias granted to Spaniards, 1536–1620

Source: Simpson, *Exploitation of land*, 10.

another consisted of untilled areas (hillside, woodland, grassland, and other areas for animal grazing and for the cultivation of wild fruits and plants); and the fourth and most important portion was divided into individual lots for each head of family to have as private property, but with so many limitations that, as in the pre-Hispanic age, it constituted only a right to the use of the land and in no way implied ownership in fee simple as conceived in Roman law.

The change in land use caused by stock raising, which from 1560 was encouraged by the crown, the viceroys, and the *cabildos* was no less massive or radical. Even though there is documentation of the granting of *asientos* or *sitios* (small farms) and later *estancias de ganado mayor* or *estancias de ganado menor* from 1530, it was not until 1567 that ordinances were enacted explicitly characterizing the area and the nature of such grants (see figs. 7, 8, and 9). François Chevalier, in his masterly analysis of the long process that began with the multiplication of herds and ended with the formation of the great ranching estate, observes that the latter was established in New Spain between 1560 and 1600, although it did not yet have the territorial characteristics of the later hacienda or latifundium. According to Simpson's calculations, by 1620 the grants of *estancia de ganado mayor* (each equal to one square league) had created

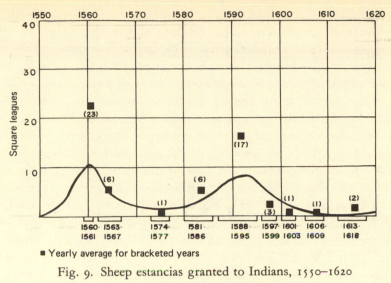

Fig. 9. Sheep estancias granted to Indians, 1550–1620

Source: Simpson, *Exploitation of land,* 11.

a newly cleared space of 2,576 square leagues. *Estancias de ganado menor* (each covering 0.44 of a square league) for the grazing of sheep and goats already came to 1,801 square leagues. A large part of this vast land area was not cultivated or devoted to stock raising at once, but its grant to private owners strengthened and greatly accelerated the massive agricultural transformation which was being brought about. Hundreds of new settlers benefited and a new group of landowners was created which was almost always antagonistic to the great encomenderos, who also benefited from land distribution and with whom they vied for land, workers, and markets.

The crown's decision to make a massive distribution of land and to divide it amongst many recipients institutionalized the original chaotic process of land settlement and gave the landowners stability precisely at the moment when the discovery of the mines, the expansion of settlement, and the decay of native agriculture made it necessary to create new sources of food production. This demand and the offering of grants of *caballerías* and estates attracted old and new settlers who lacked prior resources into the new agricultural towns which from 1560 onwards were established in the Bajío and further north, largely to supply the mining areas. Likewise, the rise in food prices and the abundant availability of land stimulated the formation of haciendas and mixed ranches (combining arable farming and stock-raising) which surrounded the cities and administrative capitals of the centre and south of the country. Under these stimuli, the livestock hacienda began to enclose within its boundaries wandering herds of cows, sheep, goats, and horses which, according to medieval Spanish tradition, were allowed to graze freely on wastelands and even to run on the farmlands after the harvest to feed on the stubble. In New Spain, this custom led to the recognition of pastureland, woodland, and land covered with stubble as land for common use. Out of this sprang a long series of complaints by Indian cultivators at the invasion of their open fields by herds of livestock. Such litigation was subsequently carried on by Spanish farmers themselves and was moderated only when territorial limits were set to livestock haciendas in 1567. Viceroys Luis de Velasco (1550–64) and Martín Enríquez (1568–80) also promulgated severe enactments to reduce the damage that livestock were causing, particularly in areas of native settlement. In Toluca and Tepeapulco, where Indians and livestock were concentrated in direct opposition to one another, fences were set up to stop animals trampling the seedbeds. Dates were also set to restrict the seasons of transhumance and of grazing on the stubble. Livestock owners were required to employ a set number of herdsmen on horseback to bar livestock from invading arable land. During these years, a policy was adopted which curtailed the grants for livestock estates in the basically Indian communities of the centre and south, but which gave them away freely in the newly colonized areas, both in the north and along the coast. In the north, these great unfenced spaces were covered with scrub, in the south they were savanna and woodlands. Stock-pens were situated far away from the pastures and the shack-like buildings where the estancieros (blacks, mulattos or mestizos), but not the owners, lived. In most cases, the herds grazed on wasteland and on the land left over between estates. Sometimes they took up an enormous space for the simple reason that nobody claimed it.

In the sixteenth century, occupying land without legal title was the most common way of extending one's property. This illegal occupation began to be regularized between 1591 and 1616, when the crown laid down new procedures for acquiring land. The most important measure was an ordinance of 1591 under which all irregular possessions of land purchases made illegally from the Indians, and land covered by a defective title could be regularized by means of a *composición* (a fee paid to the treasury). Between 1600 and 1700 most of the great haciendas of arable land, the livestock estates, and the large properties acquired by the church were regularized by this process. Thus in little less than a century the Spanish crown began and completed a vast programme of land redistribution which set the pattern for the later development of agriculture and landholding in the colony.

LABOUR

The hacienda attained stability when it succeeded in creating its own system for attracting, keeping, and replacing workers. It needed a little more than a century to achieve this, by means of constant struggle with the Indian community, the chief supplier of human energy at that time.

From 1521 to 1542, the encomenderos had free use of the labour power that the encomienda Indians gave them. The pre-existing native systems for the production of goods and the rendering of services were left unmodified. Under the encomienda, the Indian retained his bonds with the village and the people to which he belonged, setting up a temporary relationship with the encomendero, consisting in seasonal, unspecialized work. Because of its political character, this relationship was one of vassalage and did not involve any salary. Indians in encomienda were fed by what their community produced The communities also had to defray the costs of the worker's removal from his village of origin to the place where his services were rendered. In sum, encomienda Indians continued to be peasant producers, residing in their villages and performing a multiplicity of compulsory but temporary tasks for the encomendero. However, this system aggravated the exploitation of the Indians, since the rural villages and families had to produce what they needed for their own subsistence and reproduction, as well as a surplus to be transferred to the encomenderos, without receiving any benefit in exchange.

This situation began to change when the crown assessed the difference between the revenue the Indians paid in tribute and the revenue that agriculture, cattle-raising, and mining were beginning to furnish. However, as these activities needed a settled, permanent workforce that the encomienda could not provide, the Spaniards turned to slaves, both Indian and African. The initial exploitation of placer gold

mining, silver mines and sugar mills thus encouraged the formation of
a significant slave population in New Spain, which by 1550 had come
to make up the permanent labour force of these activities. In 1548,
Indian slavery was forbidden and many of the freed Indians became the
first *naborías*, or wage-earners, who lived and worked permanently on
the haciendas and the mines in exchange for pay. It was, however,
African slaves who more often became the permanent workers, especially
in the critical years from 1570 to 1630, when the native population
plummeted. By 1570 there were already some 25,000 African slaves in
New Spain, and it is estimated that between 1595 and 1640 over 100,000
more arrived.

African slaves formed an important part of the permanent labour
force, but the development of agriculture, cattle raising and mining in
New Spain would have been impossible without large numbers of
seasonal workers, who could only be Indians. In order to break the
encomenderos' monopoly of Indian labour the crown in 1549 ordered
the abolition of personal services under the encomienda and in 1550
directed Viceroy Velasco to institute a system where Indians were to
hire themselves out for a wage to Spanish enterprises. If they did not
volunteer, the authorities should force them to do so. This draft labour
system, known as *repartimiento* or *coatequitl*, became general from 1568
onwards and continued until about 1630.

During the greater part of the year, each Indian village was compelled
to contribute between two and four per cent of its active work force, and
ten per cent during the weeding and harvesting seasons. This percentage
of workers was distributed in weekly shifts, so that each worker served
an average of three to four weeks each year, in periods four months
apart. The Indians were to be well treated, and they were only to do
the work assigned to them at the time of hiring. In exchange, they were
to be paid a daily wage, which, between 1575 and 1610, varied from
half a real to a real and a half (1 peso = 8 reales). Between 1550 and
1560, it was also decreed that instead of paying tribute in many different
products tribute should be paid only in two forms: in money or in kind,
preferably in agricultural products, i.e. maize or wheat. Since the only
way for the Indians to obtain money to pay the tribute was by working
in the mines, on the haciendas, and in public services, this decree came
to be another way of forcing them into employment in Spanish
enterprises.

As all later history was to show, the Indians would not have consented to leave their communities and their traditional methods of production had they not been forced to do so, since neither the monetary wages nor other attractions in Spanish enterprises were any improvement over the way of life they enjoyed in their communities. The adoption of the new working system brought about radical changes in the Indian villages, principally because before the conquest and under the encomienda system the Indian used to produce his subsistence, as well as the surplus exacted by his overlords, in the same space and by the same methods of production. The new system of forced repartimiento meant that the work to produce his means of subsistence was performed in his village and much of the surplus labour had to be done elsewhere under different conditions of production. Under the repartimiento, it was the Spanish authorities, not the native communities, who determined the time of compulsory work and the wages, working conditions, and distribution of the workforce. These communities no longer had complete control over the organization of surplus labour. Moreover, when the repartimiento began, the natives were forced to work in specialized sectors of the Spanish economy (mining, agriculture, ranching) and with foreign means of production. Nonetheless, the peasant community did not remain apart from the new production process; on the contrary, it incorporated itself into it, with specific charges and functions.

Under the repartimiento system, the Indian village undertook the task of producing, with its own resources, the labour force required by the Spanish enterprises and of providing the seasonal workers required by the different haciendas, mines, public works, and the growing activities of the religious orders. This massive transfer of workers to the Spanish economy reduced the capacity for self-sufficiency that the native community had previously enjoyed. The constant flow of workers prevented the communities from producing for their own consumption, and this increased their dependence on goods produced by the Spanish economy. Thus, in order to replace the production of the Indians who went to work for the Spaniards, the Indian communities were forced to demand more work and increased production from their remaining members to compensate for the imbalance. However, a large part of that production had to be sent to the Spanish market, on the one hand, to obtain the income needed to make cash payments required from the communities as tribute, and, on the other, to buy goods they had ceased to produce or which political coercion on the part of their overlords forced them to purchase.

By the end of the sixteenth century and the early decades of the seventeenth, hacendados were beginning to oppose the forcible allocation of Indian workers by the *corregidores* (district magistrates) and to petition for the right to hire them in a 'free market' without interference from the authorities. They claimed that the Indians should be 'free to work for whomsoever they please and in any activity they choose, and to go to those employers who offer them the best conditions'. The owners needed more workers if they were going to cope with the demand of new and wider markets calling for a constant supply of agricultural and animal products that the Indian villages themselves could no longer satisfy, doubly weakened as they were by the demographic catastrophes and by the drain of workers. Hacendados began to keep Indian workers on their estates and pay them wages. In 1632, the crown ratified this new system of labour when it decided to suppress the compulsory repartimiento of agricultural workers and approved their hiring themselves out voluntarily in return for a day-wage. This decision benefited the great landowners, who had greater access to credit and more financial resources available and could make advances in clothing and money to workers to attract them and thus win the intense struggle for the scarcest of all resources. On the other hand, small and medium landowners saw themselves obliged to increase their own families' efforts, or to set up forms of joint production such as sharecropping or co-partnerships. By these means the owners of the great farming and stock-raising haciendas had, for the first time, a permanent non-slave workforce available throughout the year. The territorial expansion of the hacienda was consolidated by the acquisition of these workers, who from 1630 onwards settled down and multiplied within the boundaries of the hacienda, forming a resident peonage; that is, a body of workers who in practice had virtually no freedom of movement.

Under the new system, the crown not only lost the power by which it had hitherto been able to have its own official allocate and distribute the workforce, but it also, in effect, handed the workers over to the hacendados without any protection. From then on, the owners progressively became masters, legislators, judges, and magistrates over the hacienda residents. The hacienda ceased to be a simple 'arable farm' or 'stock-raising estate', as sixteenth- and early seventeenth-century documents term it, and became a self-contained unit of production. It was henceforth a permanently inhabited territorial area, with both fallow and cultivated lands, granaries in which the products of the harvest were kept, houses for the owners and their managers, shacks for the workers, small craft workshops, and toolsheds.

The conversion of the hacienda into a permanent economic and social unit engaged in the production of foodstuffs for the nearest urban and mining markets did not, nevertheless, assure it easily available permanent workers. The chief difficulty continued to be the absence of a labour market, since Indians who could have provided it had their own means of subsistence and shared in a peasant culture that was based on the corporate organization of the Indian village. Moreover, there were no sedentary Indian villages in the north whose inhabitants could be compelled to work on Spanish enterprises. Agricultural estates, stock-raising haciendas, and mines had to begin by having thousands of sedentary Indians sent to them from the south, by purchasing African slaves, and by enslaving hundreds of nomadic natives. Later on, the prosperity of the mines and the expansion of the haciendas that fed them attracted a continuous flow of rootless men, 'mestizos', a product of ethnic and cultural cross-breeding. Farming and livestock haciendas, as well as the mining and urban areas, were the crucibles in which New Spain's new population was forged. In the seventeenth century, the permanent workers on the livestock haciendas of the north and of the sugar haciendas in the coastal and tropical lowlands were African slaves, mulattos, creoles and mestizos, men without any secure position in either of the Indian or Spanish poles into which society was divided. However, they did have the necessary cultural adaptation to handle the new techniques and the new economic situation. Thus they became foremen and supervisors of work in the field, well qualified and trusted, and forefathers of a new generation of workers. However, studies now available show that even in the north, with its greater labour mobility, the most usual way to attract workers was to advance them money or clothing on future wages and that the most common way of retaining them was to go on lending them money, so as to keep them permanently indebted and legally tied to the hacienda. This was the system of debt peonage.

The Bajío was nearer to the nucleus of sedentary native peasants but, as a colonization zone, it bordered upon areas with unsubdued Indians.

Hacendados there also felt compelled to offer more attractions to permanent workers, giving them an additional weekly maize ration and putting into effect the system of cumulative debt. However, in contrast to the livestock haciendas, which mostly needed permanent workers, their biggest problem was that of having considerable numbers of seasonal workers available for the sowing, weeding, and harvesting seasons. In the seventeenth century, the hacendados of the Bajío solved this problem by renting out part of their lands to the peasants, under an agreement whereby the latter undertook to work for the hacienda on seasonal tasks. This solution was followed in many agricultural frontier zones, and also in the native centre and south. It gave rise to the existence of the so-called *arrimados* (squatters) and sharecroppers, and to forms of land tenure which in reality concealed labour relationships, as in the case of debt peonage and the *tienda de raya*, the hacienda store where wages were paid in kind. Thus the owner employed his most abundant and cheapest resource, land, to attract the scarcest and costliest resource, seasonal labour. In the majority of farming haciendas, the annual payroll constituted the biggest single running expense.

In the centre and the south, most of the haciendas drew their basic force of permanent workers from individuals of mixed Indian, African, and European blood. The worker received no wages but instead open credits allowing him to receive money loans and clothing, or alternatively compensation in kind, such as extra maize rations, housing, and the use of a small plot of land to cultivate within the boundaries of the hacienda. Besides these methods, hacendados had other ways of retaining workers compulsorily. One of the methods most generally employed was the obligation landowners undertook of paying the annual tribute of resident workers to the royal treasury officials, or of paying the fees that the workers owed the parish priest for marriages, funerals, and baptisms. These practices strengthened debt peonage; in Puebla and Tlaxcala the former practice was used as a pretext to keep workers permanently in the status of 'registered' bondsmen on the hacienda. Other forms of labour relations common in seventeenth- and eighteenth-century central Mexico were withholding all or part of the monetary wages (as in the case of several haciendas 'indebted' to their workers), refusing to accept the tender of payment of the worker's debt so that he could leave, manipulating the payroll in favour of the hacendado, and entering into collusive arrangements with royal officials and Indian caciques to retain workers without due cause. All in all, everything known to date about the means used to attract and retain permanent workers in the haciendas indicates the absence of a free labour market, and the prevalence not so much of a money wage as of means of subsistence (loans, food rations, housing, and the right to use hacienda land). It is also important to note that the permanent workforce of the haciendas did not draw as many members from Indian peasant villages, which maintained their own means of production and had a self-sufficient corporate economy, as from racially mixed groups which from their inception did not have the right to any land.

The pressure that the haciendas of the centre and south exerted on the Indian villages fell upon seasonal workers: it aggravated conflicts as markets expanded and as a bigger volume of production was needed, since this meant an increased demand for unskilled seasonal labour. The Indian villages eluded this pressure as long as they kept the balance between the area of their productive land and the size of their population. However, when land was no longer sufficient to support the population, individuals had to emigrate to the haciendas, the mines, or the cities. So one of the hacendados' principal strategies for acquiring workers was, precisely, to seize the lands of the Indian communities. Another, which the Spanish crown employed from the mid sixteenth century onwards, was to require the Indians to pay tribute in money: this necessarily compelled them to seek at least seasonal employment in Spanish enterprises. In the seventeenth and eighteenth centuries, this pressure increased, because religious fees also had to be paid in cash and, furthermore, because the Indians were coerced into buying merchandise from the *alcalde mayor* (district magistrate). This imposition, also known as *repartimiento*, was the cause of several native insurrections.

Even when continued emigration of workers progressively reduced the communities' capacity for self-sufficiency and compelled them to depend more on outside sources, most of the villages of the centre and south peacefully acquiesced in the relationship imposed on them by this system of domination. In areas where workers were scarcest, they even turned it to their own advantage, requiring landowners to grant them access to woods, quarries, and water supplies that the hacienda had appropriated for itself, in return for providing the hacienda with labour during the sowing, weeding, and harvesting seasons. In other cases, the landlord 'leased' a portion of his land to the Indian communities in return for seasonal workers. The landowners also set up a system of seasonal enlistment of workers, using a recruiter or contractor who visited the villages and, with the connivance of Indian caciques and governors, made up gangs of workers for the haciendas.

In this way, the system of domination gave the Indian villages the costly task of begetting and feeding the future labour force, as well as the obligation to train it in agrarian skills and make it available for the sowing and harvesting seasons. In return, the workers were offered a cash wage barely sufficient for them to meet the tribute, and to pay for the Spanish merchandise which the *alcalde mayor* made them buy. The means of subsistence which actually kept the seasonal workers alive came from their own work on plots of land within their native communities. Similarly the peons, or permanent hacienda workers, produced the major part of their own subsistence, since the maize rations or the plots of land that the landlord assigned to them within the hacienda, together with the labour of other members of their families, made up their true means of support. Thus a major part of the haciendas' economic success was a result of the surplus value extracted from peons' long workdays and from the exploitation of their families and of the peasant community. The remainder was achieved by the hacienda's adaptation to the market.

MARKETING

The hacienda emerged in order to satisfy the domestic demand created by the urban and mining-centre markets. Mexico City was the first market to give impetus to the formation of a belt of both agricultural and stock-raising haciendas around it. Later, its continuous population growth created a network of commercial channels supplying it with sugar, cotton, cacao, tropical fruits, and cattle from the north, the Pacific coast and Veracruz; wool, sheep, and lambs from the north-east; wheat and other grains from Puebla and the Bajío; and maize, the staple foodstuff, from the fertile lands of the areas surrounding the capital itself. The great mining centres of Zacatecas, Guanajuato, San Luis Potosí, Parral and Pachuca, along with other, smaller centres, were at first fed by the Indian agricultural areas of central Mexico, but in the late sixteenth century and during the two centuries that followed, they caused the development of agricultural and livestock haciendas in their own vicinities. In the Bajío and around Guadalajara, areas were settled with farmers and wide expanses were converted to growing crops and raising livestock intended primarily to supply the mining market.

Administrative capitals of provinces, such as Puebla, Guadalajara and

Valladolid (Morelia), were peopled by officials, members of the clergy and educational centres, and large groups of merchants, artisans and servants, and they, too, constituted important local and regional markets. But they never rivalled either in size or in importance the greatest market of all, the capital city itself. Mexico City was where the greatest number of people and the monetary profits of much of the economic activity of the viceroyalty were concentrated. Yet the capital city was no match for the dynamic mining markets, where the highest investments were made and the best salaries paid, and where the majority of the population used money or credit for trading. In other places where neither great investments nor important concentrations of wealth existed, where no great increase in population occurred, tiny markets barely provided sufficient outlets for small stock ranches requiring low investment and a minimal labour force. This was the case in Mérida, where the greater part of the foodstuffs that entered the city was provided by Indian farmers. The rest of the viceroyalty was a land of small farmers and of Indian villages where the population produced and consumed its own crops.

The commercial sector of agriculture in New Spain was thus concentrated around the two poles linking the colony to Spain: the mining complexes and the political and administrative centres. Agricultural production was conditioned not only by the area cultivated but also by frequent climatic variations. Droughts, frosts, hailstorms, and scarce or excessive rainfall substantially affected the volume of production and caused harvests to vary considerably in quality from year to year. As New Spain depended exclusively on domestic agricultural production to satisfy its needs, these tremendous cyclical fluctuations determined the volume of supply, the characteristics of demand, the level and variation of prices, and the market structure of basic staples such as maize, wheat, and meat. In years of abundant, regular rainfall the good yields brought a generous supply of grain and farm products into the markets. Although the owners of the large haciendas avoided selling in the months immediately following the harvest (November to April), the abundant supply provided by the Indians and the small and medium farmers pushed the price of maize down to its lowest level. It is important to note that maize was the basic foodstuff of the majority of the population as well as of draught and pack animals, livestock, pigs, and chickens. In these years of abundance, the grain trade in urban markets shrank considerably, because a large part of the native and mestizo population could rely on its own cereal production grown on tiny plots owned by families or individuals. A good harvest thus meant plentiful, cheap maize and the contraction of the market because of self-sufficiency, clear evidence that a considerable part of the urban population continued to possess small landholdings.

However, years of good harvests were interrupted by years of scanty rainfall, prolonged drought, early frosts, hailstorms, or a combination of those conditions. In the worst cases (1533, 1551–2, 1579–81, 1624, 1695, 1749–50, 1785–6 and 1809–10), the anticipated crop was reduced by half or more, sometimes throughout the whole agricultural zone, or in its main areas. Although bad weather afflicted all land equally, its effects were uneven. The great landowners' properties, rich lands, irrigated, well fertilized and sown with the best seed, were always the least affected. On the other hand, bad weather had fatal effects on the poor land, usually lacking in irrigation, animal manure, or selected seed, that belonged to Indians and smallholders. Because of this, and because the area of cultivation for commercial purposes was incomparably larger on the haciendas than on the lands owned by the native villages, the volume of grain that the hacienda had for sale in times of agricultural crisis would greatly exceed what the Indian communities or the small landholders could offer. Nonetheless, in years of agricultural crisis, the grain that arrived first in the urban and mining areas was that of native producers and creole and mestizo smallholders, bringing to the market what little they had salvaged from their crops to obtain cash with which to pay their tribute or their debts, or to repay loans incurred at the time of sowing. To do this they had to impose a strict diet on their own families for the rest of the year. The great landowners, on the other hand, hoarded their harvests in their granaries and sent grain to market only when prices were at their highest (May to October), when seasonal scarcity coincided with the crisis on the farms. Then, the opposite of what happened in the years of abundant harvest occurred; almost all the population became net consumers except the great landowners, whose volume of production and large storage capacity enabled them, as the only suppliers, to impose a 'seller's market'. In the severest agricultural crisis of the eighteenth century, prices of maize and wheat went up 100, 200, or at times even 300 per cent above the lowest price in the agricultural cycle. In other words, the great landowners obtained their highest profits in seasons when most of the population was suffering the onslaughts of soaring prices, hunger, and unemployment.

In every case of marked shrinkage in harvests, it was maize and wheat that led the rapid price rise, followed by meat, since both droughts and frosts destroyed the pasture and caused heavy mortality amongst cattle.

Years of bad harvests, then, meant a general scarcity of basic foodstuffs, a galloping rise in prices, and a swollen market of farm products. In such years, the volume of grain sales in city and mining markets would be two to three times what it was in years of good harvests. People who never purchased these products in times of plenty because they were self-sufficient producers consuming their own crops turned into full-scale consumers of the products of others in years of bad harvest. Moreover, in years of agricultural crisis, the whole supply system for foodstuffs operated to the advantage of urban and mining centres endowed with institutions whose function it was to buy up grain with municipal funds to maintain a constant cheap supply, and containing public granaries or municipal markets to which farmers were obliged to bring their grain for sale. These institutions' purchasing power, the authorities' pressure to make sure that crops were taken and sold there, the high prices, and the growing, urgent demand for food at these times combined to siphon the whole of the countryside's production into the chief cities and mining centres. In particular, high prices in the urban markets broke the barriers which normally made long-distance transportation of farm products unprofitable. This sequence of good and bad years, with its range of effects on the volume of production, supply, demand, and price levels, became a regular phenomenon, a recurring and immutable agricultural cycle with effects on the organization of the hacienda as a producing unit which was constructed precisely to counteract the most catastrophic effects of this cycle. In the short term, the hacienda's strategy was to extract the greatest possible profit from the seasonal changes in supply, demand, and agricultural prices by constructing enormous granaries which allowed hacendados to stockpile grain instead of having to sell it during the months of low prices. However, to combat the handicaps that arose from the variability of harvests, the restriction of markets, and the massive cheap supply from native producers and small landholders, the hacienda developed a more elaborate strategy which came to typify its characteristics as a producing unit.

Like every enterprise engaged in the sale of its products, the hacienda was organized so as to obtain a net surplus that its owner could treat as profit (that is, gross product minus the hacienda's own consumption requirements and minus the investment needed to renew its productive capabilities). To obtain this surplus, it was necessary to increase the volume of commercial production within the hacienda itself and extend the range of goods needed for home consumption and production, to avoid having to acquire these elsewhere. That is to say, the hacienda owners needed to increase their income from crop sales and to reduce their purchase of input goods to the minimum, so that they could devote themselves completely to maintaining their rank in society and to acquiring the European articles which they did not produce.

One way of attaining these objectives was to increase the size of the hacienda. As we have seen, the hacienda's losses or profits were unpredictable and depended on the vagaries of the climate and on the ups and downs of supply and demand. The owners therefore sought to equip their haciendas with the resources necessary to counteract the effects of these destabilizing factors. Within the boundaries of the hacienda, they sought to amass the greatest possible variety of land (irrigated or seasonal arable land and pastures) and of natural resources (rivers, springs, woodlands, and quarries) in an effort to create precisely the balanced economy which was lacking in the agricultural structure of New Spain. On the one hand this multiplicity of resources cut down the purchase of input goods from the outside, while on the other it protected the hacienda more adequately from the uncertainties of climate, with the availability of more extensive and diversified terrain. The most fertile and the best irrigated lands could be utilized for cash crops, and other areas planted with crops intended for home consumption, leaving the rest to lie fallow. All the haciendas of New Spain that have been studied show this characteristic of polyculture: alongside the cash crops (sugar-cane, maize, wheat, maguey, or live-stock) they produced an array of crops for their own consumption (maize, beans, peppers) and also exploited all other hacienda resources such as woodlands, lime-kilns, and quarries.

The acquisition of enormous expanses of land also helped the hacienda to fight off its competitors in the market. Every plot of land lost by the small farmer or the *ranchero*, and every piece of land wrested from an Indian village, reduced production for the hacendado's competitors and enlarged the market for his own production. The vast lands that the hacienda amassed and the many hectares that it kept lying fallow had, therefore, an economic logic. As we have already seen, robbing the Indians of their land came to be the best way of creating a labour force and also the best indirect way of multiplying consumers of the hacienda's products. For the dispossessed Indians there was no alternative but to hire themselves out to the hacienda as peons, to flock into the cities (and increase the number of urban consumers), or to flee to the most isolated areas of the country. However, in the jungle, the mountains, or the desert, Indian crops could not compete with those of the hacienda.

On the other hand, dividing the hacienda's extensive territory into areas for cash crops, areas producing for internal consumption, and areas lying fallow made a series of combinations possible whereby the owners could deal with the problems with which the agrarian and commercial structure of the colony presented them. Thus, in the sixteenth and seventeenth centuries, when markets were small, demand weak, and prices low, most of the growers concentrated on the fullest utilization of the areas reserved for internal consumption and on those left fallow, cutting back the area intended for cash crops. The area employed for home consumption exceeded that intended for cash crops so as to avoid low prices in the market and the purchase of commodities from outside. Also, the possibilities of polyculture were exploited to the maximum so that the fate of the hacienda did not depend on a single crop that could be ruined by bad weather. During these years of restricted demand and low prices, landowners often rented out a great part of the lands that the hacienda was not cultivating, with the dual purpose of securing another source of income and of having a reservoir of workers who tilled the hacienda land in return for the 'lease', without receiving any cash wages. Lastly, as the most important thing was to avoid money payment outside the hacienda, owners limited payment in money to expenditure that was really strictly necessary, that is, to advances in cash to attract workers.

In periods of demographic expansion, market growth, increasing demand, and rising prices, the mix and the use of the hacienda's resources were modified. As exemplified in the Bajío and the Guadalajara area in the later eighteenth century, the area intended for cultivation of cash crops and products for internal consumption was then enlarged at the expense of fallow lands, and it became necessary to lease or acquire new land. Land rose in value, and consequently, the most fertile was used for the more marketable products, while livestock and crops intended for internal consumption were moved to less fertile terrain. Use of marginal land increased, and the cultivated area generally was enlarged to meet the greater volume of products for the commercial market as well as for the growing number of hacienda workers. Owners then either raised rents or exacted more work from tenants, or simply evicted them so as to exploit the land directly and take advantage of the rise in prices in the urban market. It was at these times that pressure from the landowners on the territory of the Indian communities became stronger. When they failed to appropriate these lands, they were often leased, as happened in the Guadalajara area, where a great part of village land was leased to hacienda and ranch owners.

Consequently, in periods both of slackening and of appreciable rises in demand and prices, the hacendado always sought the maximum reduction in money outlay for incoming goods and an increase in his money income from direct sales in the market. Hence, the economic parameters of the hacienda were set by the monetary costs of inputs, on the one hand, and by the creation of monetary income through the sale of cash crops in the market, on the other. If the owner's lands were extensive and diversified, he could attract a labour force without having to spend great amounts of money, and through the proper blending of these resources he could produce at a cost low enough to be competitive in the market. However, if his land was scanty or infertile, or both, he was forced to seek labour and goods in exchange for money, and thereby raise his production costs, or else to increase the exploitation of family labour as the majority of ranchers and smallholders did. In the case of the owner of large expanses of diversified land, peons and seasonal day-labourers were made responsible for production for internal consumption as well as for sale in the market. A small farmer or rancher, however, would expect his own family to bear this burden.

Studies of colonial haciendas show that they all endeavoured to become self-sufficient in grain staples, especially maize, since corn rations were given in lieu of wages by all hacendados to both their permanent and their seasonal peons. A large number of the middle-sized haciendas and nearly all the large haciendas and latifundia were also self-sufficient in meat, dairy products, hides, and tallow, as well as in draught and pack animals. The great landed estates as well as the haciendas belonging to the religious orders, in addition to being self-sufficient in grain and animal products, were also self-sufficient in many basic consumer goods. There were carpenters and smiths right on the haciendas where agricultural implements and carts were made, and there were also small tanneries and soap and textile factories.

Haciendas also formed an interrelated and complementary production complex amongst themselves. In this way, anything that any of the haciendas did not produce in sufficient quantities was supplied by others without recourse to the open market. Likewise, in order to avoid the market, the miners of the north acquired extensive haciendas specializing in cereals and livestock, in order to provide food for their own workers, along with wood, charcoal, pack and draught animals, hides, tallow, and other materials required for the mining and refining of metals. Money was used as a measure of value, but it hardly ever actually changed hands. This practice became generalized in the seventeenth century. It regulated the relationships between the great hacendados and the powerful merchants of Mexico City, who cornered the greater part of the money supply, controlled the credit system, and had the monopoly of goods imported from Europe. Thus, for example, the owners of huge landed estates of the north, who had enormous herds of sheep and goats, sent livestock on the hoof, leather, and wool to the owners of the textile mills of Querétaro, San Miguel and Mexico City, receiving in exchange textiles, clothing, shoes, leather goods, and other merchandise. The balance in favour of one party or the other was accounted for by the Mexico City merchant, who acted for both sides as a credit institution and a clearing house. The procedure operated as follows: the textile mill owner opened an account for the livestock owner in a Mexico City mercantile house, where he credited him with the value of the livestock, leather or wool received from him. In turn, when the livestock owner received the textiles and other articles from the mill owner, he issued a receipt or *libranza* (letter of credit) in favour of the latter, likewise payable in the capital's commercial establishments or negotiable in exchange for other credits. This practice became common in transactions amongst hacendados and between hacendados and merchants. The latter, thanks to their experience and the power they had acquired over the money supply, credit, and imported goods, ultimately monopolized the dealings of the producers. Thus the lack of any effective monetary commercial exchange made producers dependent on merchants. Domestic producers of sugar, cotton, cacao, livestock, cereals, and other farm products sent their crops in great volume to the merchants in the capital, who sent them local and imported manufactures in exchange. The merchants, then, traded twice over, and hence their profits were substantial. On the one hand they resold the agricultural products at monopoly prices in the controlled markets of the capital and of the mining centres, and on the other they extracted great profits from trading foodstuffs and primary products for manufactures and imported goods. However, the large-scale producer of food, cereals, and basic agricultural products also stood to gain quite considerably. In the first place, although his trading with the merchant was not on an equal footing, the latter was a regular customer who was a sure outlet for his surplus production every year, and who could be relied on to pay immediately for it, or to give him merchandise or credit of an equal value. Secondly, the landowner resold the clothing, textiles, shoes and other manufactured goods that the merchant supplied him with to his own workers at a higher price, or frequently offered them as a part of their 'wages'. Sometimes, the hacendado himself opened a store in the area and dealt with other producers on the same terms as a Mexico City merchant did; that is, he took agricultural products in exchange for manufactured articles. Finally, the hacendado did not lose out because the cost of the inequality in trading was defrayed not by him but by his workers and by the Indian community. In the last analysis, since the profit resulting from these exchanges went to Spain, Spain stood to gain, together with the capital city and the middlemen. The losers were the small and medium-sized farmers and, above all, the Indian workers and the Indian villages.

Moreover, because they sold large amounts of their harvests to the merchants, the landowners used local markets to secure a year-round monetary income. Very soon, the great landowners' hoarding of the best lands nearest the urban markets, plus their access to credit and their family and economic ties with the officials responsible for supplying the cities with food, gave them monopoly control over the food supply. In the sixteenth century, native agriculture supplied the main cities of the central region, such as Mexico City and Puebla, but in the seventeenth and eighteenth centuries it was overtaken by the production of the haciendas that had grown up around them. The 200,000 *fanegas* of maize (one *fanega* equalled 1.55 English bushels or 55.5 litres) which Mexico City consumed each year came, at the end of the eighteenth century, for the most part from the haciendas of Chalco and of the valley of Toluca, owned by creoles, mestizos, and Spaniards. The same was the case in Guadalajara, where more than half the 80,000 *fanegas* of maize brought to market each year came from the haciendas of the great creole landowners. On the other hand, the share represented by native production, which between 1750 and 1770 already provided only about

25 per cent of the total of maize imported into the city, had fallen by 1810 to almost nothing. During the eighteenth century, every medium-sized and large city showed this concentration of the maize supply in the hands of the great hacendados. A further large share of Indians' and smallholders' production of maize and cereals was also hoarded by hacendados, merchants, and officials, who resold it in urban markets. This process was consolidated by a continual fusion of hacendados with city authorities, allowing the former to occupy the chief posts on the *cabildo*, with the result that regulations on food supply were favourable to the great landowners. Thus, although they were municipal institutions intended, in theory, to maintain a constant cheap supply of maize for the consumers, the granary and the corn exchange in fact came to work in the interests of the big producers from whom they purchased the greater part of their grain and who, as monopoly suppliers and sellers of grain, were able to act as a pressure group on the price levels.

The case of wheat and flour is a good example. From the late sixteenth century, hacendados (at first Spanish, but later creole) virtually monopolized the production of wheat sold in the cities. In the eighteenth century, the owners of large haciendas supplying the capital usually had a harvest averaging over 1,000 *cargas* of wheat (one *carga* equalled 149.5 kg), while the medium-sized haciendas could scarcely supply more than 200 to 400 *cargas*. The large landowners' pre-eminence in production induced them to build mills where wheat was ground, and these turned into markets and storage centres for the flour the cities consumed. Thus, in the eighteenth century, the chief mills around the capital had a combined storage capacity of 50,000 *cargas* of flour, some 40 per cent of the city's annual consumption. Two mills in the ownership of a single family controlled 30 per cent of the city's milling and storage capacity. What happened in the capital of the viceroyalty was repeated in Puebla, Valladolid, Oaxaca, Guanajuato, Zacatecas, and Guadalajara. Early in the eighteenth century, most of the wheat and flour entering the market in Guadalajara belonged to small and medium farmers, but by the end of the century these producers had almost disappeared, giving way to large hacendados who also owned the most important mills. Hence, the capacity for growing wheat and for producing and storing flour determined wheat prices in the urban market.

The slaughter and sale of cattle was also controlled by municipal authorities, whose chief officials included farmers and stock breeders.

The *abasto de carnes* (meat supply) was a municipal monopoly for the importation and sale of all the meat that was consumed in the city. The authorities leased it under contract to an individual, generally a stock breeder, who undertook to bring a given number of head of cattle during a given number of years. A few families were owners of the most extensive and numerous livestock haciendas around the viceregal capital, in the Bajío, and in the north, and therefore controlled the *abasto de carnes* and owned the three abattoirs that were licensed to operate. In Guadalajara in the late eighteenth century, one stock breeder alone, who was simultaneously *regidor y alférez real* (town councillor and royal standard-bearer) of the city, brought in 32 per cent of the livestock legally imported into the city for slaughter, and more than 70 per cent of the meat consumption was provided by five estates. The supply of sheep was even more concentrated, for just two haciendas sent Guadalajara more than 50 per cent of its total supply. In the second half of the eighteenth century, the hacendados of the Valley of Mexico also decided to exploit the enormous potential of the market that the capital, by then containing over 100,000 inhabitants, offered for the sale of pulque, the most popular beverage among the Indians and the castas (people of mixed race). In order to profit from this market, they converted into maguey fields the semi-arid lands north and north-east of the capital that were used for grazing and for the occasional growing of maize. Around 1760, the Jesuit estates concentrated in this area were producing 20 per cent of the pulque sold in the city; as much again came from the estates of the Conde de Jala, a powerful hacendado. At the end of the century the Jala family properties were incorporated with those of the Conde de Regla, and together they produced over half the pulque entering the viceregal capital. This monopoly of production was matched by control of the urban market: the same families that owned the haciendas had bought up the main shops in the city that were licensed to sell pulque.

Nevertheless, as the eighteenth century progressed, the monopoly of the large landowners disintegrated in Mexico City as well as in other principal cities of the colony. Almost every urban centre witnessed merchants taking over from producers the supply of meat, the marketing of maize, wheat, and flour, and the wholesale trading of sugar, cacao, hides, and wool. All the cases surveyed show that the great merchants displaced the large as well as the medium and small producers from marketing their products and from direct sale. This was done, on the one hand, through *habilitaciones* (loans) which the merchant advanced to the producer on the condition that most of the harvest be sold to him. On the other hand, with his command of cash resources, the merchant could exploit his position as the only potential purchaser; effectively, he was the only one able to make cash purchases of the bulk of the landowner's production. Whichever procedure was adopted, there can be no doubt that by the end of the eighteenth century the main commercial transactions in agricultural products were in the hands of merchants.

CREDIT

As we have seen, if a landowner did not combine in his own possession lands that were extensive, fertile, and diversified, or if he did not reduce to the minimum his cash expenditure, or if his cash reserves or his credit were not enough to permit him to ride out periods of falling demand and low prices, or to enable him to make rewarding investment in more land or equipment, his hacienda was simply not a good business. In other words, he was not producing any monetary surplus with which to obtain the goods and services which the colonial elite's urban lifestyle required. Conspicuous consumption was the essential manifestation of its power and status; however, it was very difficult for any one person to meet all the conditions necessary to ensure the stability of the hacienda. Recent studies have shown that very few families remained after two or three generations as owners of haciendas created by their ancestors.

The central problem in the formation of the hacienda certainly lay in the availability of ready cash to create, develop and maintain it. The history of the hacienda, therefore, is closely bound up with those individuals who possessed the scarcest resource of all, available capital and credit facilities. Everything we now know about the colonial economy of New Spain indicates that great estates did not arise from resources generated by agriculture alone, but from the investment in agriculture of income derived from encomienda, public office, mining, and commerce. The first Spaniards to accumulate land and cultivate it were the sixteenth-century *conquistadores–encomenderos* typified by Hernán Cortés; they were men who enjoyed a high annual income from public offices given to them as rewards for their exploits, who held hundreds of encomienda Indians yielding them free labour and tribute, and who, in addition to all this, had monetary incomes derived from commerce and mining. The founders of the enormous latifundia of the north were men of the same calibre: captains and governors of vast provinces which they had originally conquered and pacified, who became prosperous miners and finally owners of veritable territorial states where thousands of head of cattle grazed and where crops were grown to feed their mining and refining establishments. Later on, when the era of conquest and pacification was over, viceroys, judges, royal officials, magistrates, and officers of municipal councils acquired land. They used their official positions to obtain repartimiento Indians, credit, and special concessions enabling them to speculate in the market. The descendants of the original conquerors and encomenderos became united through marriage and economic and political ties to these powerful new men who handed out land and workers and who allowed access to the controlled urban markets. In this way, the luckiest retained and even extended their patrimonial estates. In the late sixteenth century and throughout the seventeenth, this generation of large landowners resisted the rise of a new generation of rich and powerful men: miners, merchants, and textile-mill owners. But they finally yielded and arranged new marriage, economic, and political alliances in order to survive.

The basis for the progressive symbiosis between landowners, officials, miners and the clergy was credit. The market characteristics already mentioned show that the chief difficulty faced by landowners was the availability of ready cash for seed, for purchasing and hiring implements, and for paying seasonal workers. Another problem was the need to borrow larger sums of money to build fences, granaries, and dams or to purchase more land. In these circumstances, the lack of liquid capital or the absence of cash transactions forced the landowner to seek loans. In the sixteenth and seventeenth centuries, in the absence of credit institutions, he obtained such loans from officials, mine owners, merchants, or the clergy. As security, he offered a socially prominent individual who was financially solvent or pledged rural or urban property. This meant that the landowners had to turn to individuals unrelated to agriculture in order to raise money or secure credit. This situation would give apparent support to the view that colonial agriculture was intrinsically incapable of yielding sufficient monetary profits to cover the running costs of the hacienda and to supply the owner with a surplus for savings, profitable investments, or for conspicuous consumption. Agricultural production did, in fact, produce a surplus, but it was diverted from the agricultural sector by the crown's economic policy and by the economic structure of New Spain.

The agricultural sector was affected by a political economy which impeded trade amongst the Spanish possessions in America. This worsened the effects of the cycles of good and bad harvests, of falling and soaring prices, and of the contraction and expansion of demand. That is to say, the impossibility of exporting grain when crops were abundant, or of importing it together with other foodstuffs in the years of agrarian crisis, made New Spain's agricultural cycle more extreme and the fluctuations in production and prices which so badly affected the economy more acute. Another economic policy decision which adversely affected the development of commercial agriculture in New Spain was the ban on the cultivation of certain plants, the processed products of which might compete with the manufactures exported by Spain. In reality, the enforced concentration on the growing of basic crops to feed the urban and mining areas meant that the agricultural sector was subsidizing silver production. However, most important of all was the crown's decision to appropriate almost all of New Spain's minted gold and silver. This action frustrated the development of a true mercantile economy, since it created a permanent outflow of the money supply. And the situation was further complicated by the fact that the monarch granted the merchant guild the monopoly of the now greatly reduced money supply.

Giving the merchants of the Mexico City *consulado* (merchant guild) the monopoly of trade with Spain, Asia, and – for a time – the Spanish possessions to the south and in the Caribbean enabled them to effect the greatest cash transactions, and reap the largest profits, in the unequal balance of trade between Spain and her colony. For example, manufactures were sold at monopoly prices in a captive market in exchange for precious metals and raw materials produced at low cost by exploiting the labour force, ensuring the predominance of the merchant over the producer. For the agricultural sector, this economic policy meant the transfer of its surplus production to the merchant, the permanent scarcity of money supply in the markets and the dependence on capital and credit monopolized by the merchant.

The relationship between the church and agriculture aggravated the distortions of agricultural development and made the situation of the hacienda more unstable. Unable to finance the immense effort of

indoctrination, pacification, social remodelling, and political legitimization undertaken by the church, the crown granted the latter the right
to collect and benefit from tithes. That is to say, the church extracted
10 per cent from agricultural and livestock production, the tithe being
a tax that had to be paid without any deduction allowed for 'seed, rent,
or any other expense'. No agricultural producer could evade the tithe,
not even the regular or secular clergy. Agricultural development was
further burdened by the innumerable and, at times, substantial monetary
donations made by the agricultural producers to churches, convents,
monasteries, confraternities, brotherhoods, hospitals, and other religious institutions. Since the landowners had no liquid capital, they
resorted to the procedure of taxing their estates with *censos* (mortgages),
which could be either redeemable or perpetually extended. In this way,
thousands of landowners burdened their holdings with *censos* payable
to the church. The mechanism consisted of burdening the hacienda with
a prescribed capital which was neither invested nor liable to total
repayment but on which the landowner undertook to pay an annual
interest of 5 per cent to the beneficiary of a pious donation. In other
words, without losing the ownership or use of his property, the
landowner diminished the annual income from the hacienda by payment
of 5 per cent interest on the amount donated to a religious institution.
This way of satisfying the pious feelings of the era was so massively
and so widely employed that at the end of the eighteenth century it was
said that there was no hacienda which was not burdened with one or
more *censos*.

The truth of the matter is that the unbridled multiplication of *censos*
on rural properties set up a process by which money was continually
drained from the producers' income. Ultimately, this situation helped
to destabilize the already precarious haciendas and ranches. As ecclesiastical and civil authorities alike recognized, hacendados and ranchers
were turned into mere administrators, leaving the religious institutions,
in effect, as the real landowners and beneficiaries of rural income.
Moreover, the accumulation of *censos* on haciendas brought about the
effective disappearance of the sale and purchase of rural property on the
basis of a cash transaction. Little money changed hands in the exchange,
since what actually occurred was the mere transfer of accumulated *censos*,
with the new owner incurring the obligation to pay the annual interest.
Through this process, rural land became 'property held in mortmain',
as Spanish liberals termed the accumulated ecclesiastical real estate

which never entered the market. In conclusion, even when agriculture did yield a surplus, this was channelled away by the continuous drain of capital which, added to the lack of cash-based commercial transactions, turned the hacienda, and especially the ranch, into a production unit highly vulnerable to the fluctuations of the agricultural and market cycles. The combination of these processes, in addition to the lack of access to credit, appears to provide the best explanation for the continual bankruptcies and divisions of ranches and haciendas.

Nevertheless, the great landowners did find effective ways to combat these ills and ensure the stability of the hacienda at the expense of the small and medium landowners. In the first place, they tried to secure the inheritance of the accumulated landed patrimony of the next generation. Every study of estates shows that after the death of most landowners their lands were divided among their children. The system of inheritance, then, became a further reason for the instability of the hacienda. Even when small or medium landowners did not inherit debts or mortgages with their properties, forcing their heirs to sell them, the division of land into small parcels determined the future loss of the patrimony since the *minifundio* and the tiny ranch were not suited to withstand violent climatic and price fluctuations. Faced with this threat, many hacendados in New Spain adopted the Spanish institution of the *mayorazgo* (entail) through which a family's rural and urban properties were made indivisible and had to be transmitted from one generation to the next through the succession of the eldest son. More than a thousand *mayorazgos* are known to have been created throughout the colonial period, many of them consisting of rural estates of modest proportions, instituted by farmers, the clergy, and members of provincial elites. Nevertheless, the most important *mayorazgos* formed vast estates in the ownership of a single family. These were originally founded by the descendants of the first *conquistadores* and encomenderos who had intermarried with rich miners and officials. Later on, in the eighteenth century, this group intermarried with the new rich families of merchants and miners, creating other important *mayorazgos*. The indivisibility and inalienability of the estates consolidated in a *mayorazgo* conferred economic stability on a landed patrimony that had been amassed over a generation and prevented its fragmentation or loss. On the other hand, it nullified individual aspirations nourished by the system of multiple inheritance, making the interests of every member coincide in the preservation of the wealth, power, prestige and distinction of the family as a unit through the perpetuation of a lineage. In the seventeenth and eighteenth centuries, titles of nobility were purchased by the richest hacendados, miners, merchants, and officials, who linked them to one or more territorial *mayorazgos*. Land, wealth, social prestige, and political power thus came together in a small nucleus of families who by the eighteenth century possessed the most extensive and fertile lands, monopolized the urban and mining markets, controlled the only sources of credit available, and derived the greater part of their money income by manipulating the network of external and internal trade.

The foundation of this oligarchy was the fusion of large landowner-ship with the monopoly of capital gained in the mining and commercial sectors. Credit was made available to the owners of large landholdings through the continuous marriage alliances that united their children with rich miners and merchants and through the accumulated land itself. Compared with the volatile fortunes made in mining and the hazardous adventures of commerce, the great landed estate came to be, in effect, the best way of preserving a patrimony and bequeathing it to succeeding generations, as well as constituting irrefutable proof of financial solvency. Furthermore, the new officials, miners, and merchants who had enriched themselves and who strengthened the landed patrimonies created by the early great landowners, were not alone. The church and the religious orders also turned rural (as well as urban) property into strong-boxes for the innumerable donations they received from private individuals. A portion of the money income received by way of *censos*, pious donations, bequests and chantries, was invested by the church and the religious orders in land and in urban properties. Another very substantial portion was given on loan to anyone who could pledge or mortgage rural or urban property, the best acceptable security of the period. In this way, the money that landowners, miners, merchants, manufacturers, and officials donated to the church in the form of pious donations returned to the richest families under the form of loans secured by their estates. These great landed families controlled the best and most valuable properties, its members also belonging to the religious orders that decided to whom the loans should be made. Recent studies of the amount of loans made by the religious orders and by the church to private individuals and the way in which these loans were made show that, without a doubt, the main beneficiaries of those funds were the principal families of landowners, miners, merchants, and officials. This small nucleus of interrelated families absorbed a large part of the available capital in New Spain as well as participating in the decision-making bodies of the various religious institutions.

The fact that merchants were inextricably bound up with an economic system which exported most of the surplus production to Spain prevented them from totally merging with the landowners, miners, and local manufacturers to form a colonial oligarchy with common interests. Moreover, the privileges that the Spanish crown granted to the merchants placed them at the apex of the dominant colonial economic system. Ultimately this new economic, political, and social status that the merchants gained during the eighteenth century was to put them at odds with the other members of the oligarchy. The concentration of credit and money supply in the hands of the merchants gave them greater political power than any other sector of the oligarchy. On the one hand, it made local, provincial, and viceregal officials dependent on them, because they needed cash securities to purchase public office. On the other hand, their enormous wealth allowed many merchants to buy public office for themselves and to preside over the main civil institutions. Furthermore, this same accumulated wealth began to finance the activities of municipal corporations, of the viceregal treasury, and even of the king of Spain.

Even though credit and the availability of liquid capital paved the way for the fusion of merchants with miners, the complete control that the former had over these resources made them the chief beneficiaries of mining. In exchange for the credit and commodities they provided the merchants appropriated the most substantial surpluses produced by the mining sector. The main measures by which agricultural producers were made subordinate to the merchants were the supply of credit and capital, and a greater monopoly over the external commercial sector. Merchants first deprived the agricultural producers of the marketing of export commodities and later displaced them from the domestic market. Throughout the eighteenth century and up to the time of New Spain's independence the great landowners depended on the capital and credit accumulated by the merchants.

7

RURAL ECONOMY AND SOCIETY
IN SPANISH SOUTH AMERICA

The Andean chain forms the warped backbone of South America. Its central ranges and plateaux constituted the heartland of the Inca empire. To a large extent, they maintained this role within the Spanish possessions throughout the colonial period, thanks to their enormous deposits of silver ore and their plentiful supply of hardy Indian workers. It is true that the northern and southern extensions of the Andes, with the adjacent basins of the Orinoco, the Magdalena and Río de la Plata, grew in economic importance. Yet colonial institutions and society bore above all the imprint of the Castilian conquest of the Inca realm.

Throughout the central Andean highlands (the sierra of present-day Peru, Bolivia, and Ecuador) vegetation, fauna and human conditions are determined primarily by the altitude. The percentage of cultivable land is exceedingly small. Also, the zone of pre-conquest agriculture was confined to between 2,800 and 3,600 metres above the sea. Here, after 1532, wheat and other Old World crops were added to the native maize and tubers. Above this zone, land can only be used for pasture. Here, European cattle and sheep gradually replaced the native llama as the chief resource. The eastern slopes (*ceja de montaña*) and also the deeper mountain valleys offer areas suitable for growing a wide variety of tropical products such as sugar, cacao, and coffee. The various vertical niches thus provide a surprisingly varied alimentary basis for human civilization, not only on a regional but often on a local level as well. Situated between the mountain barrier and cold water currents off-shore, the narrow Peruvian coastal strip (the *costa*) is a natural desert. However, in the course of the first millennium B.C., the construction of irrigation systems and the use of fertilizers allowed the development of agriculture

* Original text in English; revised and reduced in length by the Editor.

supporting a dense population and increasingly stratified societies. There was a continuous cultural interplay between costa and sierra until both merged under a common political structure, the Inca empire. Further north, the coast of Quito (Ecuador) comprises hot, humid lowlands suited primarily for plantation crops. The northern parts of the continent, New Granada (now Colombia) and Venezuela, defy simple characterization. The heartland of the former comprises the three north–south ranges of the Cordillera and between them the Magdalena and Cauca valleys. There is no easy access to either the Pacific or the Atlantic. In Venezuela, the highlands on the whole follow the northern coast. They are separated by vast grasslands (*llanos*) from the only major river, the Orinoco, which flows leisurely from west to east. Geographically and culturally, northern Colombia and all but the most western parts of Venezuela are very much a part of the Caribbean. South of the central Andes, Chile is a narrow strip along the ocean which stretches through three contrasting zones: desert in the north, a central 'Mediterranean' area with optimum conditions for agriculture and a forested, wet zone in the south. Across the Andes, the highlands of north-western Argentina form a continuation of the central Andean sierra, though the Tucumán and Mendoza areas form fertile and moist enclaves. Further south and east are the undulating grasslands of Paraguay, which were inhabited fairly densely by an Indian farming population. On the other hand, the grass-covered plains (the pampas) of Argentina were almost devoid of inhabitants at the time of conquest and would long remain so.

Even though each of these regions is immense and varied, we will use them to show some of the variations in colonial land tenure, labour systems, agricultural and pastoral production, and commercialization in Spanish South America.

LAND TENURE, CAPITAL, AND LABOUR

At the time of the conquest, the acquisition of land was not the main Spanish objective. Spaniards wanted primarily to re-establish in the New World the kind of urban-centred society they had left behind them in southern Spain. For provisions, these towns would rely on the surrounding native farming populations, subjected to a system of indirect colonial rule. The encomienda seemed to provide the ideal formula for this Spanish–Indian relationship. Entrusted to the protection and religious instruction of their encomenderos the Indians would deliver to them tribute in the form of commodities and/or labour service. As a legal institution, the encomienda did not imply rights to Indian lands. And in view of the density of Indian farmers in the nuclear areas as compared to the tiny clusters of European settlers, for a long time the demand for land was extremely limited.

Yet the legal instrument for land redistribution was an inherent feature of the very process of founding towns. Just as the householders (*vecinos*) received their ground plots by 'royal favour', they were entitled to receive larger or smaller tracts of land not cultivated already by the Indians for their own subsistence, as *mercedes de tierra* in the surrounding area. Depending on their prospective use, such land grants referred to farmlands (*mercedes de labor*) and grazing (*mercedes de estancias de ganados*) respectively. The type of grant used reflected the military reward character of the grants and the cautious approach of the crown: a *peonía* was originally a small piece of farmland granted to a foot-soldier; a *caballería*, the grant to a cavalryman, was about five times as much. A single *merced* often comprised more than one such unit, however. Grazing could also take place within the framework of town commons (*dehesas*) without giving rise to individual property rights.

Towards the middle of the sixteenth century Spanish immigration in the New World attained higher levels and some Spanish towns expanded quickly. Demand for food increased, particularly for products not yet readily supplied by Indian farmers, such as meat, wheat, sugar, and wine. Increasing numbers of Spaniards, encomenderos as well as others less privileged, took advantage of the land distribution machinery. Terminology for long remained vague but eventually land intended for grazing became known as *estancias*, while *chacras* were used for the cultivation of grains, vegetables or grapes. Various forms of labour were used for this expanding, but as yet small-scale, production. Some encomenderos used their Indians, although this was prohibited from 1549. Others secured part of the official allotment of paid Indian workers (*mitayos*), serving by turn to fill private as well as public labour needs. There was also a free, mainly Indian labour pool of day-workers (*jornaleros*). Another source of labour were Indian serfs (*yanaconas*) of a type existing under the Incas. African slaves, otherwise imported to be used as servants and urban artisans, also provided a growing share of rural labour in the neighbourhood of Spanish towns; but their high prices limited their use to clearly profitable agricultural enterprises.

Meanwhile, the encomienda, in the nuclear areas at least, steadily declined after the mid-century, not merely as a system of labour but also as an avenue to easy wealth and domination. This was, in part, a consequence of the drastic decline of the Indian population. Governmental rationing of labour (*repartimiento*) became increasingly necessary in view of the rapid expansion of the mining sector after the discovery of the rich silver mine of Potosí in Upper Peru in 1546. At the same time the concentration at Potosí in a most inhospitable environment, some 4,000 metres above sea level, of many tens of thousands of people, perhaps more than 100,000 at times, gave rise to a formidable demand for food, water, clothes (a very high priority in this chilly climate), stimulants (wine, liquors, coca leaves, yerba mate), fuel, construction materials, and beasts. Though declining in importance from the mid seventeenth century onwards, Potosí and other mines were to maintain their crucial role as centres of consumption until the very end of the colonial period.

The gradual growth of large-scale commercial agriculture and stock raising has to be seen in this context. There is little to sustain the view that the emergence of large-scale commercialized agricultural units and huge cattle ranches represents a seigniorial withdrawal from the larger economy to pursue the ideal of self-sufficiency on the early medieval model. As in New Spain, the great estates seem to have risen as integrated units within emerging regional markets surrounding mining and political–administrative centres. As the market for agricultural produce expanded the great landed estate expanded especially when land was readily available (as a result of Indian depopulation) and land prices were low. Thus, an element of speculation might creep into the building up of an estate. However, the prime incentive of landowners in acquiring more land was most probably to discourage competition from other landowners or to force the Indians, once deprived of their own lands, to provide them with cheap labour. For the large estates were formed through encroachments on the lands of neighbours, often Indians, as well as by means of *mercedes de tierra* and purchase. The legalization of this *de facto* situation took place as a consequence of the growing financial needs of the Spanish crown from the 1590s onwards. After due inspection, landowners were confirmed in hitherto questionable property rights after the payment of a fee (*composición de tierra*). This process obviously legalized many shocking abuses but it brought some order to a chaotic situation. The last *composiciones* took place in the course of the late eighteenth century.

Some landowners, especially larger ones, were absentees living in the towns who either let out their estates or had them run by *mayordomos*; but the large majority probably resided on their properties for at least a great part of the year. Some ensured that their estates passed from generation to generation without major divisions by taking advantage of the Spanish device of entailing their estates (*mayorazgo*). But recent research suggests that the opposite phenomenon of frequent changes in ownership by purchase was even more common. In the sugar-producing province of Lambayeque on the northern Peruvian coast between 1650 and 1719, only 22 per cent of estates changed hands by inheritance compared to 62 per cent by sale. *Composiciones*, donations, and dowries accounted for the remainder. Changes of ownership were facilitated by the often high level of indebtedness. In the case of Lambayeque we know that the debt burden of the haciendas totalled 36 per cent in 1681–1700, swelling to no less than 69 per cent a century later. By assuming the payment of various obligations – mortgage loans from the church (*censos*) or self-imposed obligations to the church to pay for masses or other religious services (*capellanías*) – the purchaser of an estate sometimes only had to pay a small sum in cash. At the same time, the large extent of these encumbrances made the division of properties more complicated and costly, and helped prevent excessive fragmentation. We do not know to what extent credits were also extended to landowners from non-ecclesiastical sources. But, in the eighteenth century at least, merchants sometimes ventured to give credit to landowners not solvent enough to receive church money but at higher rates of interest. One variety of credit was the *habilitación* (an institution combining the features of commission and loan), which was extended by merchants to, for example, owners of sugar plantations.

The size and relative importance of the great landed estates, usually called *haciendas* from the eighteenth century onwards, should by no means be exaggerated. First, most estates so called were probably quite modest and small with just a handful of workers. Secondly, Indian villages, reorganized as *reducciones* or *pueblos de indios* from around 1600 onwards, long controlled most of the land in the highland areas. They, too, became integrated to a degree within the emerging regional markets. With the decline of the Indian population discrepancies between the diminishing number of village Indians and their legally inalienable landholdings often arose. But non-Indian elements, notwithstanding legal prohibitions, quickly settled down among the Indians to cultivate part of their lands. Many former Indian *reducciones* were transformed into mestizo villages populated by small or medium-sized farmers. Others, albeit weakened, retained their corporative Indian character. They would become the communities (*comunidades*) of modern times.

During the colonial period the church, in particular religious orders such as the Jesuits, formed a more and more conspicuous element among landholders. The driving force behind Jesuit land acquisitions was the need to ensure a regular income for the upkeep of colleges and other urban activities. They were facilitated by gifts of land as well as cash from members of the elite. At times, land transfer to the church was also the consequence of individual landowners being unable to meet their financial obligations to some ecclesiastical body, these bodies being the main source of rural credit until at least the late eighteenth century. The land acquisition policy of the Jesuits was often strikingly systematic, so that properties specializing in different products complemented each other. They ran their holdings themselves, as a rule, while other ecclesiastics preferred to let them out. In Spanish South America, rural properties held by the church probably never constituted such a large share of total landholdings as in New Spain. Even so they often covered a great part of the very best lands, situated within a convenient distance of the main markets.

In 1767 the crown expelled the Jesuits from Spanish America and confiscated their extensive properties. Under state administration, these holdings became known as the *temporalidades*. Sooner or later, however, they were to pass into private hands, a process which remains to be systematically explored. It has been suggested that they were acquired by private owners 'almost always in the huge original units...at a fraction of their value'.[1] In the case of one district – Mendoza in Cuyo – we know, however, that the buyers were relatively modest people, not the existing local elite. In any event, the Jesuit loss meant a strengthening of the individual landowning sector, and the previous element of co-ordination, an important source of strength and profits, was mostly lost. In their pursuit of a regalist policy against the church,

[1] Arnold Bauer, 'The church and Spanish American agrarian structure, 1767–1865', *The Americas*, 28/1 (1971), 89.

the Bourbon governments also tried to reduce and regulate the ever increasing amount of landowner obligations to the church. In 1804 the redemption of self-imposed obligations (*obras pías*, *capellanías*) was decreed. Landowners would have to pay the capital value to the crown, which then would take over the financial responsibility towards the church. Although the effects of this revolutionary measure have been studied in the case of New Spain, where it cost many landowners their properties, almost nothing is known as yet as far as Spanish South America is concerned.

In the field of rural labour we also know much less about Spanish South America than New Spain. In the broadest terms African slave labour played an important role in the tropical lowlands, while Indians and mestizos provided the bulk of the labour force in the highlands. After the demise of the mita system rural labour there was legally free. The traditional idea of debt peonage as being the landowner's device for tying Indian labour to the estates has been increasingly undermined by recent research on New Spain. It is clear in the case of the viceroyalty of Peru that the opposite phenomenon, the withholding of wages, might have served exactly the same purpose. Probably, however, there were other reasons why landowners were able to compete successfully with miners and other employers for a supply of labour which, after shrinking steadily until the mid seventeenth century, slowly began to recover. The conditions of a hacienda worker, Indian or otherwise, given the usufruct of a parcel of land on which to grow food and some tiny wage in kind or cash, were simply less harsh than those of a mine worker. For that matter, they were also better than those of an inhabitant of an Indian village, continuously harassed by the authorities looking for mita labour, payment of tribute and fulfilment of other obligations.

On the Peruvian costa in the sixteenth century, while the Indian population declined and the income of the encomendero from tribute dwindled, the population of Lima, founded in 1535, grew quickly: in 1610 it numbered some 25,000 people, in the 1680s 80,000. Thus, a great many encomenderos and other Spaniards found it to their advantage to establish estancias and chacras on irrigated land in the valley of Rimac and neighbouring valleys with a view to supplying Lima's needs. The vanishing Indians were replaced as rural workers by imported African slaves. In the northern valleys, Spanish truck farms also appeared but, with less market stimulus, did not as a rule manage to thrive. Instead, they were absorbed or grew into larger units, some of which devoted themselves to ranching, others to the increasingly profitable cultivation of cotton or sugar. The territorial expansion of these haciendas was greatly facilitated by the steady decline of the Indian population which left community lands empty. For example, the community of Aucallama (Chancay), founded in 1551 with 2,000 people, had no Indians left in 1723 and its lands had little by little been auctioned off.

Side by side with the property of secular landlords, ecclesiastical holdings increased. In the valley of Jequetepeque, just north of Trujillo, the Augustinians maintained a virtual monopoly over the best lands for a couple of hundred years. Through contracts of perpetual lease (emphyteusis), however, their estates passed over to secular landlords from the 1780s onwards. In the valley of Chancay, on the other hand, several orders divided among them some of the best haciendas. The Jesuits possessed no less than eleven sugar haciendas in the northern and central valleys at the moment of expulsion in 1767. The growth of church properties, as well as the tapering off of the revenues of individual hacendados through *censos* and *capellanías*, was mainly a result of pious donations. But the Jesuits in particular also acquired many properties by purchase, financed either by profits or by loans obtained from inside or outside their order. The total value of 97 Jesuit haciendas in the whole of Peru in 1767 was 5.7 million pesos. On the southern coast properties tended to be smaller but more profitable than in the north. The great cash crop was wine. At first, Arequipa enjoyed an especially good location for diversified agriculture, being on the route from Lima to Potosí. In the surrounding valleys, encomenderos established prosperous estates. Later, however, from the 1570s onwards, the Upper Peruvian trade was channelled through the more southerly port of Arica and labour shortage also contributed to Arequipa's decline. This was not reversed until the mid eighteenth century, when Arequipa became a focal point on the trade circuit linking southern Peru, Upper Peru, and the Río de la Plata. African slaves formed an important part of the rural labour force on the Peruvian costa. The Jesuits in 1767 employed 5,224 slaves, 62 per cent on sugar plantations, 30 per cent in the vineyards. Slaves were often provided with plots on which to grow their own food. So were the permanent Indian workers (*agregados a las haciendas*). Gradually, the share of free black, mulatto, and mestizo labour also increased.

In the interior of northern Peru in the central Andean highlands, where sheep raising gave rise to numerous estancias as well as to textile workshops (*obrajes* and the smaller *chorrillos*), Spanish estates grew at the expense of Indian lands just as they did on the coast. Indians were the main labour force of sheep ranches as well as *obrajes*. At the same time, the non-Indian population steadily increased, so that at the end of the colonial period their numbers equalled those of the Indians, who had become peons on the great estates as their lands passed into the hands of the Spaniards.

Mines were often surrounded by haciendas which supplied them with their foodstuffs. To a degree Indian communities were also drawn into these local commercial networks. This was so in the case of Cerro de Pasco, north-east of Lima, where silver mining boomed towards the end of the eighteenth century. The mines of Huancavelica, the great deposit of mercury, were also surrounded by haciendas, which were character-ized by frequent changes of ownership by purchase. But in this case, they mostly served as reservoirs of labour for the mines. For consumption goods, Huancavelica had to rely on coastal producers.

Further south, the city of Cuzco constituted an important market and from early times was surrounded by *chacras*. By 1689, there were 705 haciendas in the region of Cuzco; in 1786, the number had decreased slightly to 647. Most were situated along the Camino Real, the road which, despite many difficult passages, connected Cuzco with Lima and Potosí. In 1689, a fifth of them were owned by gentlemen entitled to be addressed as 'don', 15 per cent by women (often widows) and no more than 7 per cent by the church and the religious orders. Ecclesiastical estates, though, included some of the largest and most profitable ones. The Jesuits owned the most important sugar estate, Pachachaca, located in a hot valley in Abancay, and the large *obraje*–hacienda of Pichuichuro in a higher, chillier part of the same province. Both were centres of networks of farming and ranching units, whose function was to supply the provisions needed by sugar and textile workers. Their ecological diversity clearly facilitated this type of economic integration. It also existed in the case of some huge *mayorazgos* such as that of the Marqués de Vallehumbroso. But most haciendas were probably quite modest and small. In 1689, a labour force of fifteen to twenty adult Indians seems to have been normal on Cuzco haciendas. Furthermore, most Indians were still living in their communities on the eve of independence. The non-Indian population of the Cuzco region increased slowly, from 5.7 per cent in 1689 to 17.4 in 1786.

In the cold region of Puno, Indian communities raising llamas and sheep were the main feature of rural society, though there were also scattered Spanish ranches. In Upper Peru, the valley of Cochabamba was one of the main granaries of Potosí. According to a seventeenth-century chronicler, the haciendas there were large and usually valued at 40,000–80,000 pesos. Only later did they begin to fragment as grain exports to Potosí ceased and landowners opted for letting out most of their lands to tenants.

The labour force of the haciendas in the central Andean highlands comprised three main categories. The mitayos (or *séptimas*) of the Indian villages served by turns in the same way as they did in the mines. The *yanaconas* constituted a permanent resident labour force, provided with the usufruct of small parcels of land for their subsistence but without pay and in fact tied to the estates. This category was of Inca origin but became more and more common in the course of the colonial period. Some free workers hired themselves out as *jornaleros*, paid mostly or wholly in kind and often indebted to the hacendado. Tenants or subtenants performed day work on the lands managed by the owner (*demesne*).

In the virtual absence of mining, the economic life of the Audiencia of Quito (present-day Ecuador) was geared to two major products: cacao in the wet tropical province of Guayas and woollen textiles in the highlands. On the coast, this gave rise to slave-based plantations; in the sierra both haciendas and, to a lesser extent, Indian communities tried to combine subsistence agriculture and sheep-raising with textile production. As in Peru, the haciendas of Quito were partly formed in extralegal ways, afterwards sanctioned by means of *composiciones*. In the case of the large hacienda of Gualachá, Cayambe, we know that it was transmitted by inheritance within the same family from the 1640s until 1819. But we do not know if this was typical or not. The ecclesiastical holdings were impressive. The Jesuits in 1767 possessed about a hundred haciendas, estancias and *obrajes*. They were valued at 0.9 million pesos, but were auctioned off at only 0.5 million. Some were taken over by creole aristocrats like the Marqués de Selva Alegre. Also in Peru, rural labour derived from the Inca institutions of *yanaconaje* and *mita*. But in Quito the *yanaconas* practically disappeared in the course of the seventeenth century. Instead, mitayos (here called *quintos*) came to form the bulk of the rural labour force. There was no competition in this case with the labour needs of mines. Through the concession of usufruct land parcels (here called *huasipungos*), however, and by making the mitayos incur debts, hacendados often succeeded in tying these temporary workers from the villages to their estates. Thus, their status became similar to that of the earlier *yanaconas*. Around 1740, two Spanish travellers gave a graphic account of this process on grain-producing haciendas and on cattle and sheep ranches. The shepherds are presented as possibly the least abused but much worse off than their counterparts in Spain. Worst of all were the conditions of those mitayos who were set to work in the prison-like *obrajes*. The Indians, of whatever origin, who were tied to the estates became known as *conciertos*, a somewhat ironic term because it means 'by contract'. Later, they would be called *huasipungueros*. By the end of the colonial period about half of the demographically stable Indian population of the highlands of Quito had become serfs of the haciendas.

In New Granada the encomenderos played a major role in the land appropriation process after the conquest (1537). In control of the town councils, they easily assigned themselves land within their encomiendas. The evolution of agrarian structures in New Granada offers considerable variety, however, because of the heterogeneous nature of the area.

Half of the high plateau called the *sabana* surrounding Santa Fe de Bogotá had passed into encomendero hands before the 1590s, when the Indians were gathered into *reducciones* (here called *resguardos*). The Spanish haciendas were consolidated through *composiciones*. One aristocrat got his 45,000-hectare property legalized for a mere 568 *pesos de oro*. *Mayorazgos* were few, however, and in the course of the seventeenth century some land was taken over by more modest landowners. The church was also able to acquire about half of the land. The Indian communities largely disappeared.

Until the 1590s encomienda Indians formed the chief source of labour in the *sabana*. After that the mita became the means of getting labour for agriculture as well as for mining and urban services. As in Quito, hacendados were often able to turn their six-month *concertados* into permanent, resident peons. A 'free' labour force also appeared in the eighteenth century, largely composed of mestizos, by now the majority of the population.

The *sabana* pattern was only different in degree from that of Tunja in the east. Here *resguardos* survived longer but were infiltrated by growing numbers of mestizo tenants. During the latter part of the eighteenth century the authorities allowed them to take over most of the land. The most humble, landless people in rural society, Indian as well as mestizo, became known as *agregados*.

Less populated regions presented a somewhat different pattern. In the Cauca valley, the control over the existing clusters of encomienda Indians was the point of departure for the formation of enormous latifundia soon to be filled with cattle. In the eighteenth century these holdings were divided up into more reasonable-sized hacienda units, largely devoted to the cultivation of sugar. They were worked by African slaves, in part transferred from the mining sector. Miners and merchants were conspicuous among landholders. The lands they acquired could be used as collateral for low-interest *censo* loans. Thus, the three economic sectors were variously intertwined and the decline of mining was to affect Cauca agriculture adversely towards the end of the eighteenth century.

The holdings of the Jesuits were scattered all over New Granada and comprised cattle ranches, grain-producing haciendas, as well as sugar, cacao, and banana plantations. They were valued at 0.6 million pesos in 1767. Plantations were worked by slaves, but they were fewer than on the more profitable plantations of the Peruvian Jesuits.

During the sixteenth century, the process of Spanish colonization in Venezuela was particularly disorderly and destructive. The Indian population, never dense, was severely reduced. In their unsuccessful quest for mines, or absorbed by the pearl industry, settlers were content to get their food supplies through encomienda tributes. But around 1600, with the cultivation of cacao, the structure of the Venezuelan economy was settled until the end of the eighteenth century. Cacao spread out from Caracas and the central coastal valleys. At the same time, cattle-raising was pushed southwards from the highlands into the northern parts of the llanos. *Mercedes de tierra* were, to begin with, given to very much the same individuals who received encomiendas.

We know how the increasing agricultural wealth was distributed among the citizens of Caracas in 1684. A quarter of these *vecinos*, 172 persons, held a total of 167 cacao plantations with 450,000 trees and 28 ranches with 38,000 head of cattle. By comparison, the wealth represented by wheat *labranzas* and sugar *trapiches* was insignificant. In the 1740s, when cacao production in the province of Caracas had multiplied by ten, the number of cacao proprietors had increased by only three. Some of them owned vast cattle ranches (*hatos*) as well. The process of concentration of land devoted to the overwhelmingly dominant commercial crop continued until the very end of the eighteenth century. More than 400 in the 1740s, by 1800 the owners of cacao plantations (*señores del gran cacao*) numbered no more than 160. They had benefited from *composiciones* and also deprived the small Indian pueblos of some of their land. The church controlled part of the landed wealth, about a fifth of the cacao area in the 1740s, but this was less than the properties of a single family, the Pontes. Absentee creole landlords concentrated in Caracas formed a homogeneous, ambitious elite which tenaciously fought royal functionaries and Spanish-born merchants, who from 1728 to 1784 monopolized external trade through the Caracas Company.

In Spanish American terms, landowners and their agricultural wealth in Venezuela toward the end of the colonial period had few counterparts. A French visitor was less impressed. In French Saint-Domingue, an infinitely smaller area, the value of rural production was ten times higher than that of the province of Caracas. What were the causes of this 'underdevelopment'? First, the well-known evils of *censos* and *capellanías*, in comparison with which tithes and sales-tax were less onerous because they adjusted to changes in production. There were also the price of absenteeism, greater costs to support often dishonest and inefficient administrators, as well as owners interested only in raising their socio-political status. Finally, the Frenchman also points at an external cause, the risky dependence on a continuous supply of African slaves, necessary because of their low fertility rate and the frequency of manumissions.[2]

Clearly, commercial agriculture in Venezuela had become increasingly dependent on slave labour. Apart from the extensive mission areas in the east and extreme south of the country, the remaining Indians had withdrawn into the age-old pattern of family units practising subsistence agriculture, based on manioc, maize, beans and plantains, and perpetuated through swidden. Also, many poor mestizos, free blacks and mulattos became *conuqueros* (smallholders) rather than hire themselves out for work. Slaves were therefore essential for cacao production and their productivity was relatively high. In stock-raising on the llanos, on the other hand, labour supply was never much of a problem. By the mid eighteenth century, there were a total of 3,500 peons, paid mostly

---

[2] Francisco Depons, *Viaje a la parte oriental de Tierra Firme en la América Meridional*, II (Caracas, 1960), 82–8.

in kind, and 400 slaves to take care of slightly more than 300,000 head of cattle in the areas of Guarico, Apure, and Cojedes.

In Chile, as the Indian population under Spanish control dwindled, a small number of encomenderos and other Spaniards were able to secure *mercedes de tierras* and divide most cultivable areas in central Chile among themselves. In 1614, Santiago was surrounded by about 100 chacras producing vegetables and grains and 350 estancias for cattle as well as grain production. Labour comprised a mixed lot of encomienda Indians, enslaved Mapuche prisoners from the south, Indian migrants from the other side of the Cordillera, blacks, and mestizos. But the small Spanish towns provided only a meagre market for agricultural produce. The main export was tallow, which could be sold at a profit in Peru, where it was used to make candles, a prerequisite for mining. The extensive cattle breeding with a view to providing tallow also had the advantage of requiring very little labour, a very scarce resource in seventeenth-century Chile.

After the earthquake of 1687 in hitherto wheat-growing districts on the Peruvian coast, a most promising market opened up for Chilean wheat. In response to external demand, wheat cultivation spread out from the ports, largely replacing stock raising. In the course of the eighteenth century, however, prices tended to slacken and, in some parts, yields also decreased. In this context, the subsequent concentration of landholdings, according to one scholar, should be interpreted as an effort to lower production costs.[3]

Also, a new way of securing labour was now tried. Within the framework of extensive cattle breeding, landowners often granted usufruct rights in marginal lots of land to Spaniards or mestizos of modest means in exchange for certain easily performed tasks, for instance in connection with rodeos. This was called a 'loan of land' (*préstamo de tierra*). With the increased value of land under the impact of wheat exports, coinciding with demographic growth, tenancy obligations (*arriendos*) were made more burdensome. Forced to pay heavy rents in kind or cash on their marginal terrains, tenants soon found themselves opting for rent in the form of day-work instead. By the end of the eighteenth century, in some parts such *inquilinos* already formed a more important source of labour than the ordinary farm-hands.

On the eve of independence, the landholding structure in the

[3] See Marcello Carmagnani, *Les mécanismes de la vie économique dans une société coloniale: le Chili (1680–1830)* (Paris, 1973).

Santiago region exhibited a high degree of concentration. There, 78 per cent of the number of units, worth less than 3,000 pesos, comprised less than 10 per cent of the total value. On the other hand, 11 per cent of the units, valued at more than 10,000 pesos, held more than 75 per cent of the total value. This structure also seemed quite stable. In the Valley of Putaendo in central Chile, the largest hacienda passed intact from one generation to another between 1670 and 1880. Sometimes, *mayorazgos* helped to keep the holdings within the family but usually they were not needed. Yet, in other cases, repeated divisions of properties initiated the process resulting in the minifundia of modern times. Finally, the composition of the landholding class was considerably modified in the eighteenth century when Spanish immigrants partly replaced old families of encomendero origin.

The immense region of the Río de la Plata proved disappointing because no mines at all were found there. In the north-west, colonization was merely an extension of that of Peru and Chile. Between 1553 and 1573 all the major towns had been founded and the sedentary Indian farmers distributed into encomiendas. Also, *mercedes de tierras* had been handed out in the areas around the towns. Meanwhile, direct expeditions from Spain only succeeded in establishing one permanent centre, Asunción, in 1541. Here in Paraguay, a rather dense Indian population was able to supply the Spaniards with farm produce – maize, manioc, and sweet potatoes. Paraguayan mestizos, a generation later, were the founders of Buenos Aires in 1580, but after the closing of its port fourteen years later, the city remained a sort of isolated island in the sea of pampa grasslands dependent on contraband for survival.

The north-western towns became linked, almost from the outset, to the Peruvian market, especially Potosí. First, they served as suppliers of textiles, based on wool in Córdoba and cotton in Tucumán and Santiago del Estero, later as suppliers of cattle and especially mules. In the seventeenth century, Paraguay also joined the Potosí network of trade as a supplier of yerba mate, the leaves of which were used to prepare a stimulating beverage. Yerba came from two sources, the citizens of Asunción and other towns using encomienda Indians for the harsh work of collecting it in faraway woods, and the Jesuit missions in the south and east of the area.

The other marketable products of the eastern Río de la Plata were pastoral. Towards the mid seventeenth century quickly formed herds of half-wild cattle (*ganado cimarrón*) appeared to constitute inexhaustible herds (*vaquerías*) to the south-west of Buenos Aires, in Entre Ríos and, on the northern shore of the Río de la Plata, Banda Oriental (now Uruguay). The way of exploiting the *vaquerías* was crude. *Vecinos* of Buenos Aires or of Santa Fe, up the river, asked the town council for a licence (*acción*) to round up and kill a certain number of beasts. Hides, tongue, and tallow only were of any commercial value. Indeed, external demand for them increased. It was only in the mid eighteenth century that a substantial number of estancias were set up by the Jesuit missions and around the Spanish towns, which now included Montevideo in the Banda Oriental. Often, previous *acciones* were taken as a basis for land property claims (*denuncias*). The minimum unit, a *suerte de estancia*, comprised about 1,875 hectares with a capacity of 900 head of cattle. Because land surveying was expensive, while land values remained exceedingly low, large areas were often held with doubtful titles. The owners as a rule lived in the nearest town. These estancieros were clearly subordinated to the rich merchant class. Around 1800, an estancia of 10,000 beasts was said to need no more than one overseer (*capataz*) and ten peons to run it. While urban labour was largely slave, cattle hands were usually free. Their wage level was high in Spanish American terms.

PRODUCTION

In the nuclear areas of advanced pre-Columbian agriculture, Indians used to produce not only for their own subsistence needs but also for those of non-productive upper strata with ceremonial and military roles. Conquest did not bring about any fundamentally new orientation of production. In peripheral areas, on the other hand, primitive farmers, hunters, and gatherers, if they survived conquest, had to be taught how to produce a surplus for their masters.

The basic pre-Columbian crops were tubers like manioc and potatoes, as well as maize, squash, and beans. Domesticated animals were scarce and supplied only a very small portion of dietary needs. Spaniards, however, refused to rely on native American crops. In 1532, every ship leaving for the New World was required to carry seeds, live plants, and domesticated animals to ensure the supply of all the food normally consumed by Spaniards. In the highlands, European crops were carefully fitted into the altitudinal scheme of pre-Columbian agriculture. Wheat could be grown up to 3,500 metres, barley to 4,000. In the case of a few commercial crops only, did the government at times discourage production in the New World because Spain's own exports of olives, silk, hemp, and wine were adversely affected. Spanish demands that Indian tributes in kind comprise wheat and other European crops made the natives learn how to produce them. The acculturation was obviously more rapid and thorough when the Spaniards were directing the production themselves, on chacras or haciendas. It was more difficult to change consumption habits, but just as in time non-Indians learned to appreciate native American produce, Indians began to grow some European plants for their own needs.

The spread of Old World domesticated animals was more revolutionary owing to the absence of New World counterparts, except for the llamas of the central highlands. Cattle multiplied with almost incredible speed in the South American grasslands. Sheep were accepted more easily by highland Indians due to their similarity with llamas. Horses were also accepted, even by the most bitter foes of the Spaniards, such as the Mapuches. Meat not only provided the main food of non-Indian populations but the free supply of meat also became a frequent condition set by Indian tribes for letting the missionaries gather them into *reducciones*.

The organization of production in highland Indian communities followed pre-Columbian patterns, in this respect only slightly modified by the introduction of Iberian municipal forms. On chacras, estancias, haciendas and plantations, naturally enough, European patterns prevailed. The plough was introduced but used almost exclusively on Spanish estates. On the steep slopes of the Andes the pre-Columbian foot plough (*chaquitaccla*) was clearly superior. The transfer of the European technology of the time was far from complete. While, for example, threshing with the use of beasts was introduced, irrigation with the help of a horse-drawn wheel (*noria*) was not. Due to the low level of technology, capitalization, and management, the sheer number of workers was the main determinant of agricultural production. There were also activities requiring special, usually more simple, varieties of productive organization, as in the case of the *vaquerías* of the Río de la Plata. Stimulants like coca and yerba were gathered in peripheral areas by Indians forced to do so by entrepreneurs and missionaries, often under very severe and dangerous conditions.

Little is known about the volumes of production, especially over time, even less about the rates of productivity. Furthermore, any data of this kind has to be related to similar information about other areas in or outside Latin America at the time, if they are to have any meaning. The fact that two-ninths of the tithes (*diezmos*) were entered in the records of the Royal Exchequer is one possible clue. It is very risky, however, to estimate volume of production on the basis of the monetary figures found in these accounts. The gathering of tithes was normally auctioned off to the highest bidder, which clearly implied a strong element of speculation in the transaction. The landed property of the bidder or of a guarantor (*fiador*) were used as security for these risky but sometimes very profitable ventures.[4]

In the Peruvian costa the process of change in agricultural production after the conquest was particularly profound. The major crops, like sugar and wine, domesticated animals, agricultural techniques, and the majority of the producers and consumers themselves came from abroad.

As early as *c.* 1550, Cieza de León commented upon the many sugar plantings of the district of Nazca. Towards the end of the eighteenth century, sugar production on the Peruvian coast totalled some 450,000 *arrobas* (1 arroba = 14.5 kg). However, the level of technology of the Peruvian sugar mills may have been lower than in other sugar-producing areas of the time. The cultivation of grapes and the resulting production of brandy and wines were concentrated in Ica and Moquegua on the southern coast. Ranching comprised the whole range of domesticated animals of the Mediterranean. Fodder crops like oats and alfalfa were also grown on a large scale. Although maize remained an important nutrient, white settlers preferred wheat. It was grown in great quantities despite a less than ideal climate. Towards the end of the colonial period, rice had also become an important food crop, grown especially in the Trujillo area. In Lambayeque, still further north, cotton was grown on a large scale from the seventeenth century onwards and used for the preparation of blankets.

The earthquakes of 1687 are said to have produced widespread sterility of the earth, thus bringing about a severe agricultural crisis. The destruction appears to have been limited to the environs of Lima, however, and the effects were probably only temporary. In the 1740s Lima was surrounded, two Spanish visitors wrote, by 'gardens, producing all the herbs and fruits known in Spain, and of the same

---

[4] By way of exception, the tithe collection was also entrusted to diocesan officials. Their estimates of actual harvest and livestock inventories (*tazmías de diezmos*) provide excellent sources on production, as is the case with the Cuzco diocese, 1781–6.

goodness and beauty, besides those common to America'. The extensive olive orchards, also, produced an 'oil...much preferable to that of Spain'.[5] Besides irrigation – by no means abandoned though probably less extensive than in pre-Columbian times – guano from the Chincha islands was still being used as a fertilizer, though this is often denied.

In the central Andean highlands considerably more pre-Columbian production patterns were retained than on the coast. A seventeenth-century chronicler stresses that in Upper Peru the Spanish scratch plough pulled by oxen and the native *chaquitaccla* were used side by side. The same blending of two different agricultural traditions was expressed by the dichotomies of maize and wheat, broad beans and potatoes, coca and sugar, llama and sheep. For each ecological niche, a choice could be made between Old or New World plants or animals. There was an element of disruption, however, when, for example, Spanish cattle invaded terrains hitherto reserved for farming. Also, the Indian networks of complementary, vertically integrated production units were often destroyed. On the other hand, the largest of the emerging Spanish estates often succeeded in incorporating different kinds of terrain in order to secure for themselves a wide range of products. Terracing and irrigation continued to be used, though to a lesser extent than in Inca times. Unirrigated tracts (*temporales*) gave inferior yields.

No overall picture of highland production can be obtained at the present time. For example, the parish of Ccapi (Paruro, Cuzco) produced, in 1689, an annual yield of 212 kg of grain per inhabitant. In another part of Cuzco, Calca y Lares, 148 kg of maize, 35 kg of wheat and 509 kg of potatoes were produced per inhabitant in 1786. These estimates compare favourably with present-day conditions, depressed due to overpopulation, erosion, and other factors. It is worth noticing that in Calca y Lares, in 1786, about a quarter of the wheat was grown by Indian communities, which also kept a third of the horses and half the cattle. On the other hand, Spanish haciendas produced 60 per cent of the maize and almost 30 per cent of the tubers. Apparently, the process of acculturation was advanced.

The oscillations of agricultural production were often violent owing to shifting weather conditions in a harsh environment where the extremes are very severe indeed. Droughts, early frosts, or floods would lead to famine and pave the way for epidemics which, in turn, might

---

[5] Jorge Juan and Antonio de Ulloa, *A voyage to South America*, ed. Irving A. Leonard (New York, 1964), 216–20.

cause crucial shortages of labour. It is interesting to note that harvest failure in 1782–3 caused a steeper rise in food prices in the City of Cuzco than the rebellion and siege by Tupac Amaru's Indians a couple of years earlier. Also, notwithstanding war destruction, the total tithe income of the diocese was higher in 1786 than in 1779.

A striking feature of highland rural society, in some of the northern as well as southern provinces, was the great extent of textile production based on wool from either llamas (vicuñas, alpacas) or sheep. Both the larger and smaller textile production units were, apart from a few towns, closely integrated with the rural economy, be it that of the haciendas or that of the communities. Where mining did not develop, textiles or perhaps the production of sugar, confined to deep hot valleys, or coca, carried out on the forested eastern slopes, provided the dynamics of rural society.

In the Audiencia of Quito the great variety and richness of tropical lowland production on the coast around Guayaquil, and in Esmeraldas, further north, never failed to impress visitors. First of all, there was the cacao tree producing 'its fruit twice a year, and in the same plenty and goodness'.[6] Also, the fertile but fever-ridden lands yielded cotton, tobacco, sugar cane, bananas, coconuts, manioc, peanuts, and many other fruits. In the highlands, production patterns hardly differed from those of the Peruvian sierra. In the case of the Guachalá hacienda, production stagnated during the late colonial period. This may have been a generalized phenomenon. There was, after all, very little stimulus for agricultural production in these isolated areas.

Bogotá, in the early seventeenth century, was considered a very cheap place to live, with an abundant supply of all kinds of provisions. This clearly reflected the great number of large and small producers in the *sabana* and also the proximity of higher as well as lower terrains, with their different crops. Looking at New Granada as a whole, the great variety of agricultural production is striking. There was no one dominant agricultural product. One would think that with the rapid decline of the Indian population throughout the region, the consumption pattern would be altered in favour of Old World crops. Yet a late eighteenth-century witness asserts that wheat consumption in Bogotá remained low because inhabitants preferred the indigenous maize. Wheat in the *sabana* was not merely produced for the people of Bogotá. It was also sent to distant markets along the Magdalena river and in

[6] *Ibid.*, 94.

the mining districts of Tolima and Antioquia. Thus, in the eighteenth century, agriculture in the *sabana* was adversely affected by the decline of mining and by competition, in Cartagena on the Caribbean coast, with imported North American grain. In fact agriculture in most of New Granada, beyond local subsistence, primarily functioned as an adjunct to mining. In the forested mining districts in the west, there were always plots where Indians or blacks cultivated maize, beans and manioc for the needs of some mining camp. Furthermore, the extensive cattle breeding in the Cauca and upper Magdalena valleys provided the mining and urban populations with abundant, protein-rich food. Tobacco was produced on a large scale and was subject to state monopoly from 1774 onwards. It was the single most important source of revenue in the viceroyalty of New Granada.

Venezuela's population remained relatively sparse throughout the colonial period. The urban centres were quite small and there was almost no mining sector. Thus, the question of subsistence was easily solved. The majority of the population derived their support from the swidden-based *conuco* agriculture of manioc, maize, and beans; and the abundant supply of meat from the cattle herds of the llanos made living fairly easy, even for the urban poor. In contrast to this extensively used rural landscape, the small areas devoted to cacao cultivation demanded a relatively big input of capital and know-how. The purchase of slaves alone represented a major investment. The question of labour subsistence was largely resolved by offering the workers space to grow their crops between the rows of trees entrusted to their care. Cacao requires an even water supply and towards the end of the colonial period elaborate irrigation and drainage works had been set up. To judge from export figures, production increased at an accelerated rate, from 1,000–2,000 *fanegas* (1 *fanega* = 110 *libras* = approx. 50 kg) in the 1630s to 125,000 *fanegas* in the 1790s.

In the shadow of cacao, other commercial cropps were late in developing. Only towards the very end of the colonial period did coffee, sugar, indigo, cotton, and tobacco expand in acreage and commercial importance. Tobacco was made a state monopoly in 1779. Unlike cacao, coffee, which would become Venezuela's next major crop, did not require irrigation and could thrive on slopes where drainage was not needed.

By the early seventeenth century in Chile, agricultural production in the area surrounding Santiago was already quite varied. Yet, for most items, such as grains, vegetables and wine, the city itself, still relatively small, and the troops on the Mapuche border were the only markets. In the Santiago area, some 40,000 head of cattle, and no less than 320,000 goats and 620,000 sheep, are reported. But on the whole, apart from tallow, which was exported, they served only local needs. The expansion of wheat cultivation for export towards the end of the seventeenth century naturally changed this pattern of production. To judge from tithe records, the value of production in agriculture and stock raising experienced a notable rise. In the area of Santiago, the yearly average has been estimated at 140,000 pesos in 1680–9, and at 341,000 in 1730–9, that is a yearly growth rate of 1 per cent, a considerable achievement in terms of a technically primitive economy. From the 1770s onwards, the rate of growth slowed down to 0.5 per cent. In the more southerly area around Concepción, the impact of external demand was felt with some delay and to a lesser degree. Further north, around La Serena, on the other hand, agriculture was mainly conditioned by mining, which experienced a recovery in the course of the eighteenth century. Thus here, the highest rate of growth in agriculture, 1.3 per cent, came as late as the 1790s. Still, Chile's productive capacity in agriculture was underutilized until the mid nineteenth century. Total demand was simply too limited.

Population in the Río de la Plata area remained exceedingly sparse throughout the colonial period. The major exception were the 30 Guaraní missions of the Jesuits, on and between the upper Paraná and Uruguay rivers. In the eighteenth century their population reached and occasionally exceeded 100,000. They were well organized economically and largely self-sufficient although they produced yerba mate largely for export. Overall the lack of domestic markets set very narrow limits on the production of most agricultural items. Those branches that did develop were geared to external demand. In the province of Tucumán, textiles were produced for Potosí until the Indian labour force declined in the early seventeenth century and better-situated producers took over that market. Then Tucumán became a mule-raising centre for Upper Peru.

The wasteful exploitation of the *vaquerías* of the pampas prior to the 1750s was geared to overseas demand. Production reached its peak during the period 1700–5, when 75,000 hides were exported each year. After 1750, when production was estancia-based, exports soon reached an even higher level, considerably more than 100,000 hides a year. Also, to some extent, not only fat and tallow, but also the meat was now exported. In the meat-salting plants (*saladeros*) of the Banda Oriental, jerked meat (*tasajo*) was prepared for overseas export too. In contrast, after the expulsion of the Jesuits in 1767, their vast estancias soon vanished. In the largest mission, Yapeyú, 57,000 head of cattle had been reduced to 13,000 and 46,000 sheep to 2,000 in 1798.

MARKETING

In view of poor overland communications and the great volume and bulkiness of most products of agriculture and stock-raising the distance to the centres of Spanish population was a crucial factor, largely responsible for the value of land and produce. When a mining boom subsided or a city lost population, the surrounding rural sector was inevitably affected adversely. On the other hand, specialized production of small-volume/high-value items like wine and sugar would lend themselves to long-distance trade and yet yield considerable profits. Also, the transportation of live animals, mules and cattle, though slow, could be a long-distance undertaking. Finally, water transport, if available, considerably reduced the problem of bringing agricultural produce to the market. Both the Pacific and the great rivers were used in this way. On the other hand, the existence of a great many excises and internal customs duties always hampered long-distance trade in comparison with the production costs of more local producers.

Price movements of agricultural products in colonial Spanish South America remain to be explored. Only a few series are known. One recent sample for late colonial Cochabamba suggests sharp seasonal and cyclical variations such as are known from New Spain. Prices probably also exhibited great local differences. Their impact was modified by the existence of a very large subsistence and barter sector. On the municipal level, efforts to regulate food prices in the interest of consumers as well as domestic producers were continually made.

Little is known about the ways in which marketing took place. Individual, very large-scale landowners, secular and ecclesiastical, sold the bulk of their products through their own agencies in Potosí and other towns (*remisiones*). Others preferred to sell their products on the spot or take them to the buyer's place (*ventas*). A system of regularly held fairs played a key role in some commercial activities such as the mule and cattle trade. Ecclesiastics, on the whole, seem to have preferred to sell their products direct to consumers rather than rely on merchants. Until legally suspended in the 1780s, the *reparto* or forced sale of merchandise to Indians and poor mestizos constituted a most important element of internal trade. In Peru, mules from the Río de la Plata and textiles from Quito and Cuzco constituted the main items of this trade. It has been estimated that *repartos* in Peru were more important as a means of transfer of Indian labour to the 'Spanish' sector of the economy than either the payment of tribute or mita obligations. *Reparto* implied a massive redistribution of Andean products like textiles and coca from producing to non-producing areas. The Indian administrators (*corregidores*) responsible for the *reparto*, were, however, probably to a great extent front men for professional merchants.

Inter-regional trade comprised a wide range of agricultural products as well as textiles. Perhaps a third of the sugar produced in the valleys of western Cuzco as late as 1800 found its way to the market of Potosí. The Peruvian sierra was supplied with continuous, large-scale imports of mules, bred on the plains and in the Andean foothills of the Río de la Plata area, and with yerba mate from Paraguay. Chile exported wheat to coastal Peru. On the other hand, agricultural products accounted for only a small, though increasing, share of Spanish South America's external trade. Exports of hides from the Río de la Plata region and cacao exports from Venezuela to Europe and New Spain, both expanded vigorously in the course of the eighteenth century. Otherwise, geographical isolation put South American producers at a disadvantage compared with those engaged in overseas trade in New Spain, so that imports into Spanish South America largely had to be paid for in specie.

The profitability of agriculture and stock raising can be measured only in relative terms against the backdrop of profitability in other branches of the economy. In eighteenth-century Spanish America a 'normal' yield in any activity would probably not exceed 5 per cent. We know that, for instance, Jesuit haciendas specializing in the growing of sugar and vines easily obtained much higher rates, but they were by no means typical. We do not yet have sufficient data to venture any generalization about the yield of privately owned haciendas. Available evidence suggests, however, that productive surplus was meagre. Furthermore, a great part of it was absorbed by obligations assumed to the church. For hacendados, the chance of making considerable profits depended on the exaction of exorbitant prices during harvest failures or on successful speculation through leases of tithe collection.

Around 1550, the chronicler Pedro de Cieza de León, deeply impressed by the fertility of the irrigated soils of the Peruvian costa and sierra, expressed the belief that the next generation would witness the export to other parts of Spanish America of 'wheat, wine, meats, wool, and even silks'.[7] This dream was not to be fulfilled, however, partly because these products were the same as those of New Spain. However, trade in agriculture soon developed on a considerable scale within the region. With a population of 25,000 in 1610 Lima, for example, consumed some 240,000 *fanegas* of wheat, 25,000 of maize, 3,500 head of cattle, 400 sheep, 6.9 tons of rice and 200,000 bottles of wine. These products came from areas as far away as Chile as well as from near-by. From the northern coast, sugar was exported to Guayaquil and Panama as well as to Chile. The ships bringing sugar to Chile returned with cargoes of wheat, thus reducing costs. In Lambayeque, where haciendas were few, even Indian communities learned to produce sugar for sale. Cotton was exported to the textile workshops of Quito. From the southern coast, Pisco brandy found markets in New Granada as well as Chile and wines even reached New Spain. Between the regions of Cuzco, Puno, and Arequipa another large channel of trade developed with Upper Peru and the Río de la Plata. In the 1770s the sugar producers of Cuzco and Arequipa are said to have competed on the Potosí market. The coca from Cuzco's *ceja.de montaña* also met with increasing competition from Upper Peruvian producers. But the greatest threat to Peruvian commercial interests was the gradual saturation of the new viceroyalty of Río de la Plata towards the end of the eighteenth century with English textiles and Brazilian sugar. The opening up of the port of Buenos Aires to legal overseas trade with Spain in 1776 was, indeed, a crucial watershed, even though the decline of trade across the southern sierra was far from sudden.

Commercial exchange at local and provincial levels was less directly affected by such shifting trends at a regional level. The districts suffering from a chronic shortage of grains or meat had to get these products from better-situated neighbours in exchange for the products of artisans or other items. There were also the scattered clusters of miners, and textile and plantation workers who had to be fed and clothed. Not merely the haciendas, big and small, but also Indian communities took part in this kind of trade.

Special needs grew out of the commercial exchange itself. Some

[7] Pedro de Cieza de León, *La crónica del Perú* (Buenos Aires, 1945), 27 (ch. 113).

districts specialized in supplying the mules and mule-drivers (*arrieros*) instrumental in carrying out the trade. They served the land routes between the northern port of Paita and the city of Lima and between Cuzco, Arequipa, Arica, and Potosí. Mules from the Río de la Plata were bought at the fairs of Salta, Jujuy, and Coporaque. A traveller's report from 1773 gives a very vivid picture of this gigantic trade, which brought 50,000–60,000 mules annually to the highlands to be used in transportation as well as in the mines.[8]

The city of Quito was described in the early seventeenth century as a lively centre of commerce and an obligatory point of passage for those travelling between New Granada and Peru. But it was extremely difficult to move and carry merchandise between Quito and the principal port, Guayaquil. The stretch from the highland village of Chimbo to Guayaquil was called 'the worst road in the world, because it always rains on these mountain slopes so that the mules fall into the mire'.[9] Such was the bottleneck through which exports from Quito of textiles and imports of Peruvian wines and brandy, Mexican indigo needed to dye Quito textiles, and the rice, fish, and salt from Guayas had to pass. Freight costs became exceedingly high. Only in the neighbourhood of Chimbo was it worth while to grow wheat for sale to the coast. Otherwise, sierra agriculture merely served local subsistence needs. The extreme dependence on textile exports led to a depressed economic climate towards the end of the eighteenth century. The cacao of the coast, on the other hand, held its own in southern markets. If inferior in quality to the products of New Spain and Venezuela, Guayaquil cacao was nevertheless cheaper. Exports totalled 130,000 *cargas* (11,310 tons) in 1820.

Coming from Peru and Quito the Camino Real crossed New Granada passing through Pasto, Popayán, and Bogotá before entering the Venezuelan province of Mérida. It was supplemented by pack trails, but even the sure-footed mules often slipped in the incredibly rugged terrain. Human carriers of both men and cargo were a common sight in the highlands of New Granada. Thus river navigation, whenever feasible, proved more attractive than travelling overland, despite the

[8] 'Concolorcorvo', *El lazarrillo de ciegos caminantes desde Buenos Aires hasta Lima* [1773] (Buenos Aires, 1942), 112–61.
[9] Quote from Antonio Vázquez de Espinosa, *Compendio y descripción de las Indias Occidentales* (Washington, D.C., 1948), 339, 346.

sluggishness of the pole-boats (*champanes*) on the Magdalena and Cauca rivers. In the mining districts food prices were often high. Nevertheless, and despite the immense environmental variety of New Granada, internal trade did not develop very much, owing to the difficulties of communication. Also it was hampered by the fact that the urban centres were relatively small. In the 1690s, to take an example, even the diligent Jesuits decided that it was of no use to cultivate some large haciendas in Pamplona in the north-east because there were no markets for their produce. Also, the predominance of gold exports discouraged agricultural production for the external market. In 1788, agricultural produce accounted for only 15 per cent of the value of exports from New Granada.

In Venezuela, unlike New Granada, little use was made of waterways such as the Orinoco for the purpose of trade, and land communications were very poor. Thus, in the interior, agriculture remained mainly subsistence-orientated. The export sector was confined to the coast and the adjacent mountain range. In the early seventeenth century, before cacao dominated the export economy, there were some attempts at producing for distant markets. Hides were exported to Spain, mules bred for export to New Granada and even Peru, small quantities of wheat and maize were sent to Cartagena, Havana, Santo Domingo. From the beginning cacao was exported to Spain and Mexico but also, through contraband trade, to Curaçao, occupied by the Dutch in 1634. The belated answer to the predominance of contraband trade in Venezuela was the establishment of the Caracas Company, which was given a monopoly of the purchase and export of Venezuelan products in 1728. By gradually lowering purchase prices on cacao, the company forced an expansion of production on the part of plantation owners eager not to see their income reduced. In the 1780s this odious monopoly was finally dismantled and Venezuela began to enjoy the Bourbon version of 'free trade'; but wars increasingly disturbed shipping. Cacao deteriorates rapidly when stored in humid conditions, and it was gradually replaced by more easily stored export articles like coffee, cotton, and indigo. There was a sharply rising demand for cotton and indigo from an England now in the throes of the early stages of the Industrial Revolution.

In Chile in the early seventeenth century, a primitive pattern of distribution of rural produce characteristic of the post-conquest years still prevailed in marginal areas. Goods were actually distributed in the town houses of the landowning encomenderos, reducing the business space of ordinary grocers (*pulperos*). On the other hand, the tallow export trade to Peru was controlled, towards the mid-century, by merchants who bought the produce from the estancieros. The value of yearly exports of produce from the area of Santiago to Peru rose from 280,000 pesos in 1690–9 to 1,350,000 in 1800–9. At the end of the seventeenth century, these exports were about evenly divided between the products of stock-raising and those of farming. At the beginning of the nineteenth century, the proportions were 40 and 55 per cent, with minerals making up the rest. Yet, even though labour costs were low, freight costs were high and the profits of most haciendas must have been rather modest. In one case from central Chile (Maule) in the 1790s, the profits attained 6.6 per cent. Peru was Chile's only market and the trade was carried out by Peruvian vessels. Until the end of the colonial period, Lima merchants were basically in control of the setting of wheat prices.

Until the mid-eighteenth century at least in the Río de la Plata area an external monetary economy co-existed with a 'natural economy' in the domestic sphere characterized by barter trade and even the use of 'money in kind' (*moneda de la tierra*). The development of north-western trade was clearly dependent on Upper Peruvian mining. The yearly exports of mules increased from 12,000 beasts in 1630 to 20,000 in 1700. It then dropped during the nadir of mining until the mid eighteenth century. Towards the end of the eighteenth century, a level of 50,000–60,000 animals was reached.

Meanwhile, the exports of hides and other products of stock-raising through Buenos Aires, though only partly hampered by legal restrictions, reached higher levels after the commercial–administrative reforms of 1776–8. The gradual conquest of the Upper Peruvian market was now confirmed and the already sizeable drain of silver via Buenos Aires grew in size. The population of Buenos Aires reached 22,000 in 1770, some 50,000 in 1810 and the prosperity of the city also rose. But if the prospective market value of the city for, let us say, inland producers of wine and wheat increased, the exceedingly high freight costs across the pampas now made it more convenient for the people of Buenos Aires to import their supplies. Communications in the Río de la Plata were slow. Besides mule-trains, caravans of ox-carts, able to defend themselves against Indian attacks, were the normal means. The very first stretch, from Buenos Aires to Córdoba, easily covered by a horseman in five days, took about a month. Traffic via Mendoza to Chile had to cross the forbidding, 4,000-metre-high Uspallata pass.

In the course of the conquest, the timing and duration of which varied from area to area, Old World plants and animals thoroughly changed the resource basis of the South American continent. After an initial period of reliance on Indian food supplied in the form of encomienda tribute, Spaniards moved out from the towns and established networks of truck farms and livestock estancias. Thus a European-type market economy, based on exchange value, was superimposed on the traditional Indian economy based on use value and functioning through barter and collective work. The rise of the great landed estate was closely connected with the decline of the native American population and the growth of the Spanish and mixed population, and above all with the expansion of mining. Long-distance exports (for example, wheat from Chile and cacao from Venezuela) also promoted the emergence of large estates. Towards the end of the seventeenth century the basic rural institutions had attained stability and the pattern for the remainder of the colonial period had been set. On the whole, the eighteenth century witnessed agricultural expansion: upward demographical trends widened markets despite the ups and downs of mining and ensured a steady supply of labour. Agricultural and stock-raising enterprises in Spanish South America during the colonial period were, however, seldom able to produce at their full capacity: market size did not allow it.

The landowning elite was neither homogeneous nor stable in its composition. Landed properties varied widely with respect to size, production, indebtedness, market access, and labour supply. Succession through inheritance appears to have been less normal than acquisition through sale. The relative importance of the hacienda as compared to small and medium-sized landholdings and Indian communities also varied with respect to time and space. Large landowners were often simultaneously public officials, merchants and miners. They exerted a great amount of local power but were themselves dependent on non-agricultural sources of income or on credit from the church or urban merchants. They were profit-orientated and their haciendas were integrated into the market. Their labour systems were coercive although often paternalistic. Their enterprises did not normally reach high levels of profitability and their wealth was to a great extent put to non-economic use.

8

ASPECTS OF THE INTERNAL ECONOMY

Colonies are structured by those who rule them to benefit the mother country and its ruling classes. To the extent that these rulers are successful in this aim colonies are, in Chaunu's word, extrovert. They are, at least in part, organized economically to send out to others significant portions of their most valuable or profitable raw materials and products. In colonial Spanish America much of the economic history which we know has emerged from studies of Spanish attempts to make the colonies serve metropolitan needs. One result has been an emphasis on the sea link, the *carrera de Indias*, and the fleet system. We know a fair amount about who went to the Indies and when, and what goods were carried in each direction across the Atlantic, more especially from Spanish America to Spain. Within Spanish America itself economic historians have allowed their interests to be shaped to some extent by what primarily interested the Spanish crown: above all, silver and gold mining and plantation agriculture, the bases of the great export trades, and the supply of labour to the mines and plantations. We know much less about the basic institutions, assumptions, systems and practices of the internal economy of colonial Spanish America. Drawing on the available secondary literature, which concentrates on a limited range of topics and regions, an attempt will be made in this chapter to examine three aspects of the internal economy: labour systems; taxation; and trade within the empire, both local and long-distance.

LABOUR

Colonial Spanish America began as a conquest society, and the first priority of the invaders was the extraction of wealth or capital from the conquered. During the conquest itself, and in the turbulent years which followed in each region, this extraction could be accomplished by direct seizure of previously accumulated surpluses of precious metals or stones. This took the form of looting or booty, an officially accepted way of paying soldiers or volunteer expeditionaries in the days before regularly paid standing armies. The best-known example is the ransom paid by Atahualpa to Pizarro's band of adventurers and the sharing out of this booty afterwards.

As the era of conquest came to an end and these surpluses were exhausted more systematic means of extraction were developed. One of the main methods became the direct exploitation of the native Americans themselves. Systems for utilizing local labour supplies varied quite widely over time and space in colonial Spanish America, but several underlying organizing forces and principles were at work. There was in the first place a close correlation between the socio-cultural organization of the Indian societies and the forms of labour organization that the Spanish settlers could impose on them. In complex stratified societies the invaders found existing conditions of slavery, servitude, and 'tied' labour. In many such cases they simply removed the apex of the social pyramid – the kings, royal houses, and rulers of large regions – and then governed using approximately the same labour systems, with lesser Indian rulers such as village chiefs as administrators. In areas where social organization was less advanced and stratified, where pre-Columbian labour had been less organized and disciplined, the conquering groups found labour much harder to employ systematically. This was especially true of nomads, unused to settled agriculture and occupying thinly settled areas. The regions where organized labour forces existed were also, of course, the areas of denser populations, such as central Mexico, highland Peru, and, to a somewhat lesser degree, the highland plateaux and valleys around Quito, Bogotá and Santiago de Guatemala (now Antigua). And along with dense, organized populations, themselves a form of accumulated capital, the first and succeeding generations of Spaniards found precious metals in Mexico and Peru, which were therefore heavily settled and became the core areas of the Spanish American empire. Regions of temperate climates and good soils like the pampas of the Río de la Plata and the ill-named Costa Rica were not settled heavily if they lacked aboriginal populations and precious metals or stones. Areas of relatively dense populations which held little other wealth sometimes attracted a modicum of Spanish settlement, but such areas could also be the most unfortunate of all after the conquest.

If they were fairly near to areas which had attracted Spaniards but which lacked a labour supply, then Indian slave exports became the main industry. In the second quarter of the sixteenth century many of the peoples of Nicaragua were sent as slaves to Peru, and above all to Panama. In a similar fashion the peoples of Trinidad, the Bahamas, Florida, Pánuco, and the Gulf of Honduras were used to restock the islands of the Caribbean. Perhaps the best known case was that of the pearl islands off the Venezuelan coast. Margarita and Cubagua attracted Spanish attention when beds of pearl-bearing oysters were discovered in their coastal waters. The pearlers imported Indians from Trinidad, the lesser Antilles, and points along the coast of Tierra Firme. This intensive exploitation soon depleted the oyster beds and the Indians of the pearl islands then became export material themselves. We find them in Panama and the islands of the greater Antilles. The European slave trade from Africa to the Americas is a larger version of this phenomenon, and it was also used at times as a way of installing replacement populations when aboriginal groups had disappeared.

Slavery was thus the first labour system almost everywhere. But it could not last and was soon for the most part brought to an end, although there were brief recrudescences of it, some legal, as after Indian rebellions, some illegal, as when labour-hungry settlers would advance into a nearby unconquered area to seize and bring out anyone they could catch. The crown, which opposed Indian slavery for humanitarian and political reasons, gradually asserted its authority. In regions such as Mexico and Peru, where sedentary village agriculture continued to be important, it was too disruptive. Spaniards who depended on village labour came to oppose the arbitrary removal of workers. Even in the rather anarchic Mexico of the 1520s and the turbulent Peru of the 1530s and 1540s the leaders of the invading Spanish groups recognized that they needed a rationing or distribution system which would provide labour for the powerful (and deny large quantities of it to the less powerful) in a way which would prevent too much strife – in this they failed notably in some cases – and which would be perceived as appropriate to the status of the individual. Castile of the *Reconquista* had known such a system. Kings had divided up conquered lands and peoples among those worthy of reward. Columbus brought this system of *repartimientos* or sharing out to the islands, although the rapid extinction of the local Indian populations prevented any great elaboration there. By the time Vicente Yáñez Pinzon negotiated a contract with the crown for the conquest of Puerto Rico (1502) the New World repartimiento was recognized by the crown. In that same year Ferdinand approved Governor Frey Nicolás de Ovando's grants of Indians to the settlers in Hispaniola. Later in Jamaica and Cuba similar grants were made as a matter of course. In Mexico and Peru, these labour repartimientos, later to be called *encomiendas*, became a way by which the most powerful and prestigious among the first settlers shared out the labour supply, more or less amicably, to the exclusion of those who did not have the power or position to do more than complain. Theoretically the crown was assigned the role of awarding encomiendas as a token of gratitude for the recipients' *hazañas* during the conquest or the subsequent early rebellions. In fact many *conquistadores* found themselves excluded from the early distributions whereas comparative latecomers who were better connected received handsome grants. In Peru and Nicaragua, for example, scenes of the exploits of the violent, rival gangs headed by the Pizarro, Almagro, Pedrarias and Contreras clans, grants of encomiendas were awarded, withdrawn, and reassigned as each new *adelantado* or governor was appointed, seized power, executed his predecessors, died, or fell from power. A man's military record during the conquest, or even his good behaviour in office or loyalty to the crown, were at best secondary considerations.

As time went on, nevertheless, it became apparent that in the core areas where the crown had vital interests most of the early settlers had made a tactical mistake in approving of the crown's assumption of primacy in the assigning of grants. The encomienda became, not a feudal fiefdom as Cortés had envisioned, but a contractual arrangement whereby a given number of Indian taxpayers was 'entrusted' to the material and spiritual care of a Spaniard and the cleric he was supposed to engage, in return for the right to extract certain roughly prescribed quantities of labour, goods or cash.

The crown was able to take gradual advantage of its regulatory position within the system and of its near monopoly of high patronage because the colonists, in addition to having an engrained loyalty reinforced by culture and status aspirations, needed the crown for prestige, titles, legitimacy, offices, and other emoluments. The royal government was under pressure too from humanitarians like Bartolomé de Las Casas. After one abortive and almost disastrous attempt to legislate the encomienda system out of existence, the so-called 'New Laws', which was a leading cause of the civil wars in Peru and of the

Contreras revolt in Nicaragua, the crown was able to restrict and manipulate the granting of encomiendas and of the rewards coming from them until encomiendas in the central densely populated areas were grudgingly recognized by all as belonging primordially to the crown, and as being temporary grants of income lasting for the recipient's lifetime and possibly, often in reduced form, throughout the lives of one or two of his successors.

Central government accomplished this by several avenues of attack. One was taxation and regulation. By a succession of laws the state seized more and more of the profits from encomiendas for itself and made the collection of these profits into a complicated series of stages. Some small encomiendas became more troublesome than they were worth and thus reverted to the crown. The state also made strenuous efforts to separate encomenderos from their charges. Encomiendas, it stressed, were grants of income, not of vassals. In the core areas encomenderos were prohibited from tarrying in or residing in their Indian encomiendas. *Calpisques*, *mayordomos*, village leaders, or other intermediaries collected the goods and money and delivered them to the absentee encomienda owners, thus increasing the legal and psychological distance between the two sides. The crown had swept away any vestiges of the lord and vassal relationship, and by the late sixteenth century the encomiendas in these central areas, heavily taxed and regulated, had become almost entirely part of the tributary tax, a pension system with many of the awards going to the widows and other dependants of poverty-stricken *beneméritos*, or to court retainers in Madrid who seldom if ever saw the Indies, far less the Indians 'entrusted' to them.

Other forces were at work to weaken the encomienda. One of the most important was population decline. Because of the lack of immunity to Old World diseases, and the economic and cultural disruptions caused by the conquest and the revolution which it brought, Indian populations disappeared by the million in the years after the conquest. The effect on the encomienda, composed entirely of Indian workers, was catastrophic. Encomiendas which had provided a Spanish family with an opulent living in the first generation could produce enough for a meagre existence two generations later, even if the nuclear Spanish family which lived off the early grant had not expanded into an extended family, as it usually had. Some encomiendas were vacated or abandoned in the late sixteenth century; the surviving Indians in them reverted to the crown.

For some early settlers the encomienda system became a trap. If a Spanish family had pretensions to nobility or a noble status the financial costs were heavy. A large seigniorial establishment was expected, including a large house, an army of retainers and hangers-on, a large family of spendthrift sons and dowry-consuming daughters, horses, arms, and expensive carriages and clothes. All this conspicuous consumption was carried out in a studied manner which placed high priority on an avoidance of the appearance of work and commerce. Such families, consuming all revenue, perhaps even destroying substantial amounts of capital, or at least converting it to poorly negotiable social prestige, were often destroyed by the shrinking, restricted encomienda if they waited too long. By the third generation they had fallen on relatively hard times, reduced to writing endless, bitter appeals to the crown containing inflated accounts of the merits and services of their conquest and first-settler ancestors, and wondering resentfully why so many rewards of the conquest had fallen to upstart latecomers.

In many of the central areas of the empire, however, the encomienda laid the base for many a fortune and thus contributed notably to economic development and the formation of elite wealth. It can be argued that the first encomiendas, at least in central Mexico, were so profitable and labour so plentiful as to distract attention away from land and land ownership. Some conquerors and first settlers, arriving in the New World with little of the world's goods, were astute enough to see this reward, this gift of more or less free labour and income, as a chance for a fresh start, an investment opportunity. Cortés and Alvarado, to name but two, used their encomiendas to pan gold, build ships, provision the shipyards, provision and crew the ships themselves, and provide porters and foot soldiers in the newly discovered lands. In the second and third generations, when the encomienda had become almost entirely a taxing system, astute encomenderos discerned that their grants were temporary and ultimately losing propositions. They extracted capital from them as fast as possible and diversified out of the dying institution, using it to invest in silver mines, commerce, herds of cattle, sheep, mules or horses, and above all land. Although there was no legal connection between the encomienda and land ownership, at least in the most important parts of the empire, the interrelationship is clear. In a number of cases the one financed the other.

Until recently, studies of the encomienda have concentrated on central Mexico, Peru, and the other important areas of the empire such as Quito and Bogotá. Later studies of more peripheral areas of the empire have had some surprising results. In areas such as Paraguay, Tucumán and perhaps even Chile – isolated, with little gold or silver and no dense agricultural populations, they were thinly settled by Spaniards and of slight economic interest to the crown – the encomienda survived in a fairly vigorous way until the end of the colonial period. Moreover, it either ignored or survived the impact of royal legislation and taxation, and retained some of its earliest attributes, including the right to commute tribute to labour and to use encomienda Indians as a labour force.

In central Mexico, Central America, Peru and Upper Peru, Quito, and New Granada the waning encomienda system was to some extent replaced as a major source of labour by various kinds of labour draft, although the two institutions coincided for many years. The emergence of a system of rotational labour drafts was closely tied to population decline. If the encomienda was, in part, a way for an emerging elite to control and share a major resource, labour, then repartimiento drafts were a way to ration an increasingly scarce supply. It is obvious from the names used for these drafts that in Mexico and Peru they were of pre-Columbian origin; the Mexican *coatequitl* and the Peruvian *mita* were further examples of the invaders' tendency to adopt existing functional institutions and to alter them slowly as circumstances demanded. In New Granada the labour draft for the mines also used the Quechua term but other drafts there were called *alquileres* or *concertajes*. In many parts of Central America people used the Castilian word *tanda*. In general the word *repartimiento* was used again, with its meaning of a sharing out or rationing of goods and services. Drafts were in use in Mexico by the 1550s, in Guatemala and the Andes by the 1570s, perhaps earlier, and in the highlands of New Granada by the 1590s.

In principle labour repartimiento was a paid labour draft in which a given percentage of the healthy, male, Indian population was obliged to travel away from home to work on assigned projects or at designated places. The time to be spent at this work was specified, as was the pay scale and, in general, the working conditions. In theory at least labour repartimientos were limited to public works projects or to industries or agricultures which were vital to public or state welfare. Certain tasks which the crown believed to be especially noxious to Indian health or well-being were specifically exempted from the repartimiento, at least in some places. Work on indoor sugar vats or on indigo plantations are two examples. Such legislation was often ignored or, as in so much else, its observance was brokered via a system of fines and bribes which, in effect, made the employment of Indians in some forbidden tasks subject to a royal fine or tax. Then, too, royal prohibiting legislation depended on the importance of the industry and on the availability of an alternative labour supply. Mercury mining at Huancavelica in Peru was almost certainly the most murderous repartimiento task of all, but it was essential after the use of the *patio* process for the refining of silver became important to the great mines at Potosí, and was granted large, organized repartimientos until late in the colonial period.

The labour repartimiento caused many complaints throughout its existence. Critics pointed out that proximity to a large city or to an intensive workplace, such as Mexico City and its *desagüe*, Potosí and its silver mines, the Huancavelica mercury mine, or even a new cathedral under construction, meant more frequent calls to the draft. The other side of the coin was that Indians called from a distance had to spend more time in travel to work and thus more time away from home. Both seasonal drafts, such as the ones for wheat farming around Mexico City and Puebla, and long-term ones for mining in Peru and New Granada, had important effects in Indian communities. Seasonal drafts for agriculture often coincided with the periods of intense agricultural activities in the villages – the harvest seasons for wheat and maize were almost exactly the same – so absent Indians found their crops ruined, partly harvested, or expensive to harvest because they had to pay others. There are some cases where Spanish landowners took advantage of these circumstances, offering to allow their Indian repartimiento workers to return home earlier if they would forgo the pay to which they were legally entitled. Anxious to return to their sowing, weeding, transplanting, or harvesting, some Indians were eager to accept. Long-term absences had even greater impacts. Some villages in Upper Peru were reported to be sad places of elderly men, women, children, and invalids. Men often returned ill to these villages, especially those men involved in the mitas of Potosí and Huancavelica. Other *mitayos* never returned. Some died at the mines of overwork, lung diseases, or toxaemia. Many more stayed at the mines as free labourers, petty traders, or petty smelters, becoming more or less acculturated to the mining or city societies where they found themselves, and some passing into the amorphous class called variously *castas*, *cholos*, *ladinos*, or *mestizos*. This consequent distortion of the sex ratio in Indian society may not have had much effect on fertility – there were many other more important factors, such as diet, spacing of births, and epidemics – but it did seriously affect some forms of production, family patterns, Indian government hierarchies, and morale. Within some villages in southern New Spain the seasonal agricultural draft (*coatequitl*) may to some extent have worked against the general flattening of the Indian economic and social pyramid, the elimination of Indian class differentiation brought about by the conquest and its consequences. Relatively wealthy Indians were able to buy their way out of their turn in the draft, in spite of some protests from parish clergy and royal officials. Indian village officials were able to exempt themselves, their family males, their friends, and others who could pay them or exchange favours with them. In villages where repartimiento judges insisted on a given number of workers for each rotation the village poor had to serve additional turns. The gap between the relatively wealthy and the destitute in the village seems to have widened accordingly.

The repartimiento provided a limited range of economic opportunities to some sectors of the creole class. The office of repartimiento judge (*juez de repartimiento* or *juez repartidor*) did not carry much prestige, with its involvement with lower-class Indians, work assignments, and petty officialdom, but it did provide opportunities for accumulation of cash and goods. Indians and Indian villages bribed these judges to obtain exemptions, Spanish town councils and wheat farmers paid them or offered them favours in order to obtain more than their allotted number of workers or to ensure the official's silence in the face of illegalities in such matters as pay, working conditions, and length of work spell. Lesser creoles competed fiercely for such posts, especially in times of economic difficulties, and because the salary involved was minimal, the term of office usually short, and the prestige of the office small, it is clear that the potential for cash in the job was uppermost in their minds. Creole and mestizo farmers, especially those who required only seasonal labour, benefited too. The system provided them with a subsidized labour force which, in spite of legal restrictions or the bribes to be paid to avoid them, was probably less expensive than going into the free labour market to hire workers. Local Spanish government and the urban creole class in general benefited from this labour subsidy. Street cleaning (when it was performed), the construction and cleaning of aqueducts and irrigation canals, street and road repairs, construction and upkeep of public buildings such as churches, *cabildos*, and gaols, and city beautification programmes all depended heavily on labour drafts in many parts of the colonies. Near some cities local villages were obliged illegally to provide wood, stone, provisions, or hay to public or private institutions. This *corvée* labour did not disappear in some of the predominantly Indian parts of Latin America until the fourth or fifth decades of the twentieth century. Small vestiges of it still appear. Above all, the royal government depended heavily on the mita in the Peruvian silver industry, in the mines of New Granada, and to a much smaller extent in New Spain.

The longevity of the labour repartimiento varied widely and depended on local factors. Inheriting a previous pre-Columbian system gave it an important start. Other factors of importance were the size and organization of the labour force – large numbers of people were needed to make the system worthwhile; the speed of the demise of the encomienda system; and the conjunction of silver or gold mines, a shortage of nearby labour or alternative systems of labour, and the degree of competition for available labour between individuals, and between individuals and the crown. In central Mexico the system started early, and the crown's *desagüe* consumed large numbers. The crown had two main rivals. Spaniards in private agriculture, although individually powerful, could not compete with it, and in fact the crown had abolished agricultural repartimientos by 1632. Spanish landowners were forced to move towards various forms of peonage and free wage labour as alternatives. The crown's other rival, the silver-mining industry of Guanajuato and further north, was more powerful and resorted to free contractual labour as a way of enticing workers out of the central area. By the end of the eighteenth century there may have been half a million or more Indians between Guanajuato and San Luis Potosí, many in mining. In peripheral areas of Mexico, where the crown's need for labour was less strong, the agricultural repartimiento lasted longer. It was still to be found in Oaxaca in 1700 or even later. In Central America the crown attacked the encomienda system vigorously, and in Guatemala at least, most Indians seem to have been 'in the crown' by 1550. The crown had little use for Indian labour, although it collected the tribute enthusiastically and royal officials extracted large quantities of work and goods by extralegal means. On the other hand Spanish agriculturalists, especially around Santiago, had a need for labour on wheat farms. Spanish cities also petitioned the crown for drafts for public works.

Because of these local characteristics, repartimientos survived much longer than in most of Mexico, and some local roadwork *corvées* were abolished there within living memory. In the highlands around Tunja and Bogotá the presence of some gold mines meant a mita which endured into the eighteenth century, but there was heavy competition for a declining labour force. In Quito's jurisdiction, because of the *obrajes*, a similar history seems to have occurred. The great home of the labour draft was, however, highland Peru and Upper Peru. There the silver and mercury mines, especially Potosí and Huancavelica, were the main preoccupation of crown and colonists, and consumed such large numbers of workers that the demand could be handled only by massive, organized drafts. Because the mines were so important to the crown and because it faced weak opposition from alternative employers, it hesitated to disrupt a functioning system. The great mita of Potosí survived until the eve of independence in spite of extensive debates and recriminations over its harshness and destructive nature.

At the beginning of the sixteenth century the invading Spaniards found many systems of 'tied', semi-servile labour. One such institution which they inherited was *yanaconaje* in the Inca empire. In the Inca system *yanaconas* had sometimes constituted a special class of serfs, tied to lands and households rather than to individual villages or groups. Some of their social and economic functions still remain vague. The term may also have been applied to many client relationships, even among high nobility. In any event, the Spaniards augmented the system and incorporated vagabonds and others into it. *Yanaconas* were not slaves in that legally they could not be sold individually. They and their families could be sold with the land to which they belonged, however, and in many ways those who worked in agriculture closely resembled serfs *adscripti ad glebam*. As in Roman times the landowners paid the head tax assigned to each *yanacona* head of family. The number of *yanaconas* grew throughout the Peruvian colonial period as debt peons and other kinds of tied or coerced workers were added to their numbers. Indian villagers, burdened by tribute and mita obligations, often escaped into *yanaconaje* by choice, finding it the lesser of two evils. In Mexico the *mayeques* found by the Spaniards on their arrival may have been somewhat similar in function. Many *mayeques* melted into the villages where they were, often their home villages anyway. Some officials sent them back to their villages of origin, where they became *tributarios*. *Naboría*, a term originating in the islands, was another category of

Indians outside the encomienda and the village. *Naborías* were a class of personal employees at first, but as the sixteenth century advanced the term was used loosely, the word often became *laborío*, to describe various forms of Indian 'free' labour, a category which grew in Mexico throughout the colonial period. *Laborío* was a common term for workmen in the eighteenth century. *Yanaconas, laboríos, gañanes*, and other categories of waged or free workers became important as sources of labour for the mines. There is evidence that the mines pulled Indian village labour towards them, thus changing their category to one of these just mentioned. In general in nearly all parts of the colony there was a leakage from tribute paying, encomienda and repartimiento village Indians towards the free-labour categories. No doubt many of these escapees from the villages also acculturated and classified themselves as mestizos, castas, or cholos as time went on.

In Latin America historiography until quite recently, peonage was almost synonymous with entrapment by debt and with forced servitude. This simple picture has now dissolved and a new synthesis, if one is any longer possible, has not yet emerged. Some studies of peonage have become so revisionist that it is well to begin by reaffirming that debt peonage and severe repressive conditions did exist in many workplaces. In northern Mexico, and in other places in Spanish America where there were isolated desert mining camps, *obrajes* (textile workshops) or quarries, the *tienda de raya* or some other variation of the company store were common. In New Spain as far south as Nicaragua some peons were kept on haciendas by means of debt. Often this debt was not large, nor was it used overtly as a coercive device. In some places debt or advances were used by villagers as a means of tiding them over until the maize harvest, the debt to be repaid by seasonal work on the nearby hacienda, *labor* or workshop, at the next period of intensive labour requirements. Similar devices were used in the islands once sugar began to dominate in the eighteenth century. *Adelantos* carried the sugar workers through the dead season and were paid off at the *zafra*, or cane cutting. In other words, debt was sometimes and in some places used to recruit and discipline a permanent labour force, often in mines or on haciendas, but advances against future work were also used to recruit village labour for seasonal work, or to sustain an incipient 'free' rural proletariat during the times of the year when it was not needed on the plantation.

Perhaps the commonest form of peonage in colonial Spanish America was an arrangement whereby peasants rented small plots on large estates. The peasant family would build a hut, grow staples such as maize, beans, and potatoes, and keep a few chickens (guinea-pigs in the Andes), and a pig if they were lucky. The rent for both land and water use was sometimes paid in cash, or in a portion of the produce of the smallholding, a form of sharecropping, although this nowhere reached the importance it had later in the south of the United States. More often the rent was paid by an agreed-upon quantity of work on the hacienda. Where agricultural land was scarce and the labouring population was growing, landowners could exact more days of work. This situation seems to have obtained in many parts of Mexico, Central America, Quito and Peru in the middle and late eighteenth century. When land hunger was not severe and labour was scarce the situation was more favourable to the labouring classes. The population trough of the seventeenth century and the years immediately following major epidemics throughout the colonial period would give rural workers these small opportunities. These land-renting arrangements, although they were contracts between very unequal partners, satisfied many economic requirements for both sides. Landowners obtained a workforce without paying wages and by allowing the use of marginal lands which they seldom needed. Indians and other rural landless people rented subsistence plots without surrendering cash, and sometimes obtained the patronage and even the physical protection of the landlord and his *mayordomos* against intruders such as village and royal officials, labour press gangs, brigands, and vagabonds.

Many of the arrangements which brought resident workforces of peons into being on haciendas, *labores*, *obrajes* and other workplaces have not yet been uncovered. Some of these were informal and unwritten, and involved various local customs and understandings. Paternalism was pervasive and embraced numerous economic and social linkages between peons and employers. Godfatherhood or *padrinazgo* was used by both sides to create binding ties. *Compadrazgo* or ritual co-parenthood served the same purpose. Paternalistic owners bound the workers by psychological ties. The workers obtained a vague form of social security for themselves, and especially their children. Much of this cultural aspect of peon–landowner economic relationships awaits examination. What we do know is that many peons did not have to be coerced. By the late sixteenth century, and certainly when population growth among the lower classes began to increase, from the mid seventeenth century in New Spain and the early eighteenth century in Peru, the Indian village became an oppressive place in many parts of Spanish America. Tribute payments, tasks such as the labour repartimiento and work on village common lands, payments to village *cofradías* and community chests, the exactions of passers-by and of the Indian village leadership, land hunger in the eighteenth century, all made the Indian village less of a place providing community and protection and more of a place from which to escape. Often the Indian voted for the hacienda with his feet. On a few occasions, and increasingly in the late colonial period, Indian village authorities would sue in court for the return of villagers who had departed for other work and residences. In some of these suits, when villagers had a choice they chose for the hacienda and against the village.

The slightly rosier picture of peonage presented above certainly did not apply to all categories. The horrible conditions in some mines caused death, flight, and other manifestations of misery and desperation. Equally bad were some of the textile obrajes in central Mexico, and in the valleys around Quito, Ambato, Latacunga, and Riobamba. There peons were locked in at night, sometimes chained to their work-benches, abused physically, overworked, and detained for years. Legal officials helped obraje owners, and sometimes conspired with them, by sentencing lower-class offenders to terms in the factories. Richer obrajes could also afford African slaves, sometimes as guards or overseers, so that some of these sweatshops, worked by slaves and convicts, resembled Mediterranean galleys more than anything else in their work atmosphere. In all these categories – slavery, encomienda, repartimiento, and the various forms of peonage – regional variation and custom were so diverse that all generalizations, such as those above, fail to cover many situations.

Free labour is a puzzling category, partly because some of it was relatively unregulated and unobserved, partly because the category was so diverse. The free labouring force grew throughout the colonial period and by independence was the largest segment of the working class in many areas. For most of the period free labourers were almost entirely composed of castas, i.e. people of mixed race, acculturated Indians, free blacks, and a few déclassé whites. Royal government and local officialdom were ambivalent towards this population. After 1580 the crown tried to collect tribute from free blacks and mulattos, but not from mestizos. This never began in many areas, and collected little where it did, such as in parts of central and western Mexico. Ambivalence towards the free poor extended to their work. Technically free, they were an important part of the workforce and had to work. Laws arising from this paradoxical situation stated that castas who could prove that they held regular and wholesome employment should remain un-molested; those who could not so prove should be arrested and put to work. Freedom, in other words, did not extend to a permission to ape the leisure activities of the elites. Castas, moreover, bore a burden of suspicion. Most of them were not of Spanish racial origin, and their intermediate status, much less than full citizens of the elite, led Spaniards to worry that some of them might become disaffected, lead rebellions, stir up trouble among Indians, or collaborate with pirates and foreign intruders. These paradoxical views pushed free castas towards certain categories of work. The skilled became artisans, an intermediate grouping which possessed such essential accomplishments, for example carpentry, silversmithing, wheelwrighting, or coopering, that they could not be ignored or severely oppressed. Some of these skilled artisans belonged to craft guilds which in their written constitutions resembled medieval European models. Guilds in the sixteenth- and seventeenth-century Spanish colonies were nearly all urban and in their governance and functions represented a very typical 'trade-off' for such a hierarchically organized society. On the positive side membership in a guild assured a craftsman and his apprentices some minimal working conditions, some freedom of action in the market-place as to location and employer, restraint or prohibition of possible competition, and access to recognized due process for minor infractions of the law or civil suits involving jurisdictional, work-related, or market quarrels. Guild membership also provided some degree of job security and life insurance. Guild artisans were enthusiastic joiners of *cofradías* or religious fraternities which acted as funeral societies and minor savings and loan institutions. *Cofradías* and guilds, their festivals and other ceremonies, gave skilled artisans a place in the world, a recognized modicum of prestige and a kind of deference, but there was another side to the coin. Officials made sure that craft guilds were not challenged by too many rivals, that membership was exclusive rather than inclusive, but in return wages and other emoluments, especially high profits, were quite rigidly depressed. Many fees, hourly rates and perquisites were strictly defined by superior authorities, thus slowing any great social mobility on the part of most skilled free workers, and subsidizing the artisan needs of the upper classes and the church. Much of this rested on the concept of a fair wage, as understood at the time. Nevertheless, some artisans were able to advance to a kind of middle-class status.

Unskilled free castas occupied similar intermediate places. Many were *mayordomos*, managers, foremen, tax and rent collectors. Manual labour in the fields or workshops was avoided, and work was done which elites found unacceptable. Many free castas became petty merchants, *tratantes* (small local dealers), and horse-traders. Some of them were the agents of bigger merchants in the cities, and many of them owed varying sums of money or obligations – another form of debt bondage. Cattle haciendas provided the free poor with employment opportunities while at the same time affording them an opportunity to escape from the suspicion and daily harassment of the cities and more disciplined workplaces. The unsupervised style of life of these early cowboys, semi-nomadic, skilled horsemen, familiar with lances, lassos and skinning knives, further fed the fears of city-dwellers.

Many free poor and runaway Indian villagers – and, in monocultural areas, seasonal labourers, Indians commuting between villages and plantations, and escaped black slaves – reinforced this unfavourable attitude by turning to more socially unacceptable life-styles. By the late sixteenth century vagabondage was growing, and it worried the authorities and Indian villages. As labour shortages appeared authorities made strenuous efforts to tie down these wanderers, but every economic pause or dislocation increased their numbers, and the vestigial police forces of the colonial centuries could do little. Vagabondage, at least in the eyes of the authorities, was related to brigandage, the final and most desperate resolution of their paradoxical status for the free poor and the castas. Impressionistic evidence, and recurrent waves of mass executions of delinquents, would indicate that rural robbery, often by large organized gangs, was common, and greatly hindered officials, merchants, and travellers and their movements.

Slaves from Africa arrived in Spanish America with some of the earliest expeditions. In the first and second quarters of the sixteenth century we find them at work panning on the more profitable of the gold-bearing rivers, and in other workplaces where profits were high or an Indian workforce was absent, or both. In general, because of the distances and costs involved, African slaves were more expensive to acquire and maintain than Indian villagers, and there was no self-sufficient agricultural village to which they could return during the slow season. The growth of a large working population of African slaves had to await the disappearance or decline of the native American population. In many parts of Spanish America African slaves, like the early Indian slaves from places such as the Bahamas and the pearl islands, were a replacement population. This was especially true on the Caribbean islands and coasts, but slaves were sent inland to the mountains, too. One estimate finds that over 100,000 of them arrived in Mexico before the middle of the seventeenth century. In the large cities such as Mexico City and Lima household slaves and liverymen were a sign of status and the ability to consume conspicuously. Slaves also worked in the textile obrajes, sugar plantations and silver mines.

The best-known examples of blacks replacing Indian workers are in coastal Venezuela and the Chocó area of Colombia, tropical areas of sparse Spanish settlement. In Venezuela encomienda Indians were at first sufficient for the low level of economic activity there and for the poor market demand. Venezuela seemed destined to be another Paraguay. The growth of the cacao monoculture and of exports to Mexico in the second quarter of the seventeenth century changed all this. Some planters extracted labour from their encomienda Indians, and slave-raiding for new manpower continued, indeed persisted until the 1640s and possibly beyond. But it was obvious that a replacement population and a new organization of manpower was necessary. Cacao provided enough surplus capital to permit the purchase of African slaves in the late seventeenth and eighteenth centuries. In the Chocó, unlike Potosí with its huge, well-organized mita, the local Indians in the gold mines never constituted an adequate workforce. By 1700 most had fled or died and the gold-miners imported black slaves as replacements via the port of Cartagena. As the mining industry prospered in the early eighteenth century sufficient capital accumulated to bring in an ever larger number of slaves. By the 1750s gangs of hundreds were not uncommon. Both the region around Caracas and the Chocó were areas with profitable export industries. Agriculture for local markets seldom produced large enough profits to afford slaves. In the second half of the eighteenth century, as European sugar prices rose, areas of Cuba formerly devoted to cattle ranching and a little sugar and tobacco were given over to large-scale sugar plantations (*ingenios*) worked by large armies of slaves.

It would be simplistic to present black slavery in colonial Spanish

America, or anywhere else, as a uniform condition of manual labour servitude. Many slaves became house servants, artisans, foremen, guards, petty merchants, and shopkeepers. Much depended on their skills and cultural attributes before enslavement in Africa. Peasants may have remained peasants, but some townspeople and artisans from Africa were able to seize opportunities in the New World. Manumission was common. Some slaves developed remunerative skills and accumulated the price of their freedom. Masters freed slaves for a variety of reasons ranging from old age, guilt, and gratitude to hard times. In periods of economic stress some slave-owners freed slaves rather than feed and clothe them, literally tossing them out. Unscrupulous masters sometimes 'freed' the elderly or the sick. Freedmen in Spanish America joined the large amorphous groups of castas, neither slave nor exactly free. In the eighteenth-century Caribbean islands they were especially important, providing what might be described as the articulative strata of the local societies. They were the brokers, artisans, local merchants, carriers of goods, and suppliers of goods and services scorned by the white elites and not permitted to most of the slaves. Out of this group at the end of the eighteenth century came the leaders of the Haitian revolt: Toussaint L'Ouverture and Henri Cristophe, Alexander Pétion and Jean-Pierre Boyer.[1]

TAXATION

The various labour systems represent one of the most important means of extracting wealth in the Spanish American colonial economy. The other leading form of capital extraction and accumulation was taxation. For almost the entire colonial period, and indeed until the late nineteenth century in some parts of Spanish America, the main tax imposed on the lower classes was the tribute, a head tax collected almost entirely from Indians as a symbol of their subject status. This capitation tax, which took no account of property or income, had its origins in late medieval European poll taxes such as the *moneda forera* paid by the peasants of Castile. In the New World it appears at a very early date: for example, there is a royal command for its introduction included in the instructions given to Governor Ovando of Santo Domingo in 1501. Regular tribute assessment and collection was introduced to Mexico in

---

[1] Further discussion of Indian labour can be found in ch. 5 above and ch. 9 below. For a detailed treatment of slavery in colonial Spanish America, see Bowser, *CHLA* II, ch. 10.

the early 1530s, although it had existed well before then, based on the pre-Columbian Aztec head tax which the Spaniards had inherited. In Peru tribute became universal, regulated and standardized during the regime of Viceroy Francisco de Toledo (1569–81). Thereafter it was a major component of Spanish colonial government and administration almost everywhere within the American empire. It showed great adaptability and longevity, especially in the more isolated and economically backward parts of South America. It did not disappear from highland Bolivia and some areas of Peru until the 1880s.

The early tribute was paid mostly to encomenderos who had been granted the privilege of receiving it and of benefiting from it. As encomiendas reverted to the crown, and as the productive Indian population declined, it became a more important source of revenue to the crown, which began to collect it more carefully and rigorously. After some early hesitancy and a few errors the tribute was finely tuned – sometimes explicitly in legislation, more often not – to push Indians towards certain kinds of work and crops. Moctezuma's and Huascar's tributes had consisted almost entirely of local products, the specialties of each tributary region, although basic staples such as maize, beans, and cotton cloth provided the bulk of the payments. At first the Spanish conquerors made few changes except for the elimination of Indian products, such as feathers, which were of little use to them. By the 1550s in Mexico, and two decades later in Peru, tribute regulations were beginning to discourage the intricate polyculture of the native American Indian, the almost oriental pre-conquest 'gardening' of Mexico's lake country and the coastal oases of Peru. The general policy was designed to thrust the Indian agriculturalists towards the production of the staples needed in the large centres of consumption. Maize, beans, and cotton cloth persisted, but in addition new items from the Old World such as wheat, wool, and chickens were introduced. The Spanish goal was to simplify tributary items to one or two per village, with a marked preference for staples, although some local specialties, especially those of great value such as gold dust or cacao, persisted for the entire colonial period. Thus the tribute played a major economic role in the dissemination of new and originally unpopular crops and animals. Wheat and silk cultivation, cattle-, sheep-, and swine-herding became widespread partly because Indians were forced to pay tax in these commodities, or to look after wheat fields or cattle as part of their village obligations.

Another purpose of Spanish tributary policy was to bring the severely disrupted Indian economy more into the European market-place. To this end, Spanish officials and encomenderos began to demand part of the tribute payments in coinage, thus forcing the Indians to sell their goods for cash or their labour for wages. Some Indians travelled long distances to far-off zones of economic activity, in order to earn the cash to pay their tributes. Many preferred to pay in coinage, and found it less onerous. Viceroy Toledo in Peru quickly understood that tributes in cash were needed to recruit large numbers of Indians into the Potosí and Huancavelica labour drafts, but in areas where economic activity was not quite so intense, and where such large numbers of workers were not needed, Spaniards who moved too precipitously towards a tribute consisting entirely of cash found that they had made an error. By drifting too close to a completely monetary tribute in some parts of central Mexico, given the falling Indian population and the consequent shortage of local foodstuffs, the authorities and encomenderos forced some Indians too much into the market, where their expertise and diligence began to compete too well for the taste of some Spanish merchants. Exactions in cash forced the Indians to flee from their oppressive villages and to turn to vagabondage or to the paternalistic protection of the haciendas, where, in at least a few cases, the owner would pay the tribute for them. Cash payments led to an ever steeper decline in agricultural production in the villages, with a resulting increase in price inflation in the cities. In Mexico the cash tribute, where it was imposed, was soon corrected to a mixture of agricultural goods, usually maize, and cash.

The way in which tribute was imposed, assessed, and collected caused a general levelling in the Indian social structure, a levelling which transformed the pre-Columbian Indians into tributary peasants, but which also, like the mita recruitment system, brought some social differentiation. Spanish authorities or their agents usually counted the villagers but tended to report the results of their counts as totals. They assigned the task of collecting the tribute to intermediaries, usually the hereditary, appointed or elected leaders of the village. This delegation changed the tribute from a direct capitation tax to one of communal responsibility. The encomendero or corregidor, usually following the previous census, would assign a total tax quantity to a given village and its *anexos* or subsidiaries. Village *principales* collected the tax from those below them as they wished or as circumstances permitted. Some were egalitarian, believed in community cohesiveness, and spread the load more or less fairly. More often, as many noted, village quota systems led to an ever greater weight on the poor and to local tyrannies.

Indian tribute maintained its severity until near the end of the colonial period, as the Indian population at first decreased and then only slowly revived, as the Spanish population grew, and as the financial needs and indigency of the royal government increased. Many of those originally exempted from the tax were added to the rolls, and temporary increases, many of which became permanent, were imposed. In Mexico, for example, an additional tribute was levied in 1552 to help pay for the construction of the cathedral, and lasted for almost two centuries. The *servicio real* and the *servicio del tostón*, a tax of four reales, were added at the end of the sixteenth century to help with royal expenses and with the costs of the ineffectual *barlovento* fleet for the suppression of piracy in the Caribbean. The *tostón* lasted nearly until the end of the colonial period. Other local additions to the tribute, often to pay for local public works, were numerous in the seventeenth century. There is no question that the tribute was a detested burden.

The tribute also caused problems for Spanish society. Encomenderos, and especially the crown, frequently received tribute in goods which they did not need but which could be resold to other segments of society. The solution, a very imperfect one, was a system of royal and private auctions, which enabled the royal treasury and cash-hungry encomenderos to solve this problem of convertibility by selling the maize and other goods collected for cash. Such a system, besides the obvious inefficiencies arising from the double transportation of bulky perishable goods, drove prices up because of the multiple transactions, without benefiting the crown or the encomendero class as much as might be supposed. These auctions were controlled by a class of middlemen – inevitably restricted in number, because few could afford the large quantities of cash needed to participate. There is evidence, too, that these auction entrepreneurs did not bid against one another and sometimes conspired to keep bidding low. At least so the crown complained. After they bought the staples, the middlemen sold them to those who needed them. Maize, for example, went to weekly urban markets, mines, stores, and (less frequently) back out to the Indian villages. These middlemen were accused of monopolizing and hoarding. Some would wait, keeping items such as maize from the market until prices were high. This occurred at least once a year just before the main harvest came in. Thus the redistribution mechanisms for tribute goods were wasteful and expensive and caused hardship and discontent.

Payments in cash also brought difficulties. The Indians and the poor, as in all hierarchically structured preindustrial societies, were the traditional dumping ground for inferior, shaved, or falsified coins. Merchants and the wealthy kept their good currency for long-distance trade or for hoarding against the possibility of bad times. The inferior coinage used to pay Indians or to buy goods from them then became tribute and was unloaded onto the royal treasuries, much to the disgust of officialdom. Some of this inferior coinage then went to Spain, at first sight manifesting an aberrant working of the law often falsely attributed to Gresham.[2]

Besides the tributes, two other systems of taxation – or rather extortion – were widely imposed on the rural poor. The commonest system in some of the poorer areas of Spanish America was the *derrama*. Under this practice, Indian villagers, usually women, were forced to work materials, usually wool or cotton, to the next stage or stages of elaboration. Thus raw cotton was turned to thread, thread to plain cloth, plain cloth to dyed cloth, and so on. The women subjected to this primitive 'putting-out' industry were usually underpaid or unpaid, and thus subsidized the price of the product to the final buyer and the costs of manufacture to the trader involved. The trader was often the local corregidor or *alcalde mayor*, himself wretchedly paid but with social status to maintain and enough local power to compel the poor to work for him. Such an individual seldom had the investment capital to intensify this process. The quantities of cotton or wool involved were usually quite small. The system did perform a useful economic function in poorer areas, for it depressed the price of clothing, thus enabling local townspeople to buy below the costs and freight charges of the clothing coming either from the obrajes or from Europe or the Philippines. Other goods which needed only one or two simple processing stages entered this system at times. Thus the *derrama* both augmented the salaries of officials (a sort of indirect subsidy to the crown's payroll) and depressed the cost of basic goods such as clothing.

The other form of taxation or extortion was the forced sale, the *reparto* (*repartimiento*) of *mercancías* or *efectos*. *Alcaldes mayores*, corregidores, and other officials in Indian areas, often at the beginning of their terms of office, travelled through the villages selling goods which they

[2] For further discussion, see ch. 9 below.

had bought wholesale in the city markets. At times such sales performed
a useful function. Staples came from one area to another where they
were needed and Indians were pleased to buy them even at inflated
prices. Often, however, these sales were exploitative, and unwanted
goods – silk stockings, olives, and razors are among those mentioned
– were foisted off on unwilling buyers, sometimes by force at exorbitant
prices. Indians resold these goods, or those of them which had not rotted
or spoiled, back into the Spanish market, often at lower prices than they
had paid, in the hope of recouping some of their losses. The transaction
involved here, besides the usual supplement to the salary and life-style
of the corregidor, was a subsidy, paid by the Indian society, which
lowered the cost of luxury goods to the Spanish society. Thus the people
of Lima were able to purchase some silk from China without paying
the full freight charge from Manila or all the profits of the middlemen
between Manila, Acapulco and Lima.

The predominantly Indian, rural poor also had to suffer the graft of
local officials. Salaries were little more than pittances, and by the time
of Philip II's death almost all local positions had to be purchased either
directly or indirectly by a gift to the royal coffers or to some royal
nominee. It was fully expected by both sides that the office-holder would
recover the cost of the office, augment his salary and probably increase
his income, investments and status by extracting from his clientele and
charges what the market would bear in the way of fees, bribes, gifts,
and illegal assessments. Would-be office-buyers understood this system,
and had a good sense of the price and value of individual positions. The
price of any given office rose or fell depending on its potential as a source
of income. Moreover, this understanding extended even to the lower
classes. Graft is frowned upon in societies with an egalitarian ethos
because it shifts capital upwards in the social structure in ways which
are classified as immoral. In colonial societies, however, where the lower
classes' access to power and decision-making was severely limited or
almost absent, graft payments may have played a strangely 'democratic'
role. They were one of the few ways in which the powerless, when they
had a little surplus cash or goods, could lessen the pressure of the law,
or even deflect its impact, not by participating in its enactment but by
softening or stopping its implementation by *ex post facto* payments.
Indians and castas recognized that graft payments to officials sometimes
helped them, and gave corruption a grudging acceptance as a way of
making colonial society, in at least a few instances, more humane. These

payments, made essentially from the poor or lesser local elites, are another instance of the state delegating to others its governmental powers. Graft saved the state the trouble and some of the expense of governing. It should be noted that lower classes, including Indians, exacted payments from those above, too, in return for promptness, satisfactory work, and care of machinery, livestock and other property.

Perhaps the most common perquisite of office among lower officials was simply that of living off the land, or unpaid billeting. Officials, and for that matter parish priests, did not expect to pay for food, lodgings, or fodder for their horses and mules when travelling. These visits were burdensome in rural jurisdictions, especially if the corregidor, priest, prior or bishop was an enthusiastic, frequent *visitador*. Furthermore, clergy took advantage of a brief stay in a village to baptize, confirm, marry, or say requiem masses for those who had reached the life stages represented by these ceremonies since the last clerical visit. Each of these priestly duties carried a prescribed fee, but many other casual functions, such as catechizing children, visits to the sick, extra prayers or sermons in the village church, attendance at and blessing of village feasts, chapels, images or monuments, did not. Some clergy began to exact regular fees for each visit, presumably to cover these extra tasks. In poor areas these fees, called the *visitación*, the *salutación*, and a variety of other local names, did not amount to much, but an energetic priest with a good horse could cover many villages, and return to them too frequently for the villagers' economic well-being. In the same vein a corregidor passing through might take the opportunity to check the account books of the *caja de comunidad*, inspect the wheat or maize fields set aside for tribute payments, make sure that the village council house was swept out and in good repair, attest to the fairness and legality of the most recent municipal election, and so on, all in the expectation of a monetary payment above and beyond food and lodgings for himself, his retainers, and his horses and mules.

Indian villagers and other rural poor groups in the eighteenth century attempted to accommodate, avoid or resist these constant acquisitive intruders and tax collectors. If levies, legal and illegal, were pushed beyond understood limits some complained, rioted or revolted, tactics which were seldom more than temporarily successful and often prompted severe repression. Individuals, and occasionally whole villages, fled either to unconquered frontiers or into vagabondage or the anonymity of the cities. Most villages tried to create their own 'broker' or 'barrier' institutions to enable them to adjust to Spanish economic pressure. One of these institutions, the *caja de comunidad* or community chest, was borrowed from Spanish society; it became part of Indian society in the second half of the sixteenth century and spread to many parts of the empire. The purpose of the *cajas* was to place Indian community finances on an organized basis. They were supported by assessments on villagers and by assigned lands. Part of the tribute was diverted to them for local purposes such as payments to local officials, repairs to buildings, or loans to local people. Some *cajas*, in spite of legal prohibitions, were raided persistently by local officials and the clergy, and thereby became one more burden on heavily taxed villagers. Because of these depredations many ran permanent deficits which had to be made up by forced levies on the villagers. Yet some *cajas* appear to have run annual deficits by design. These porous community treasure chests were leaking to some purpose. They may have been a collective device whereby Indians banded together to spread the cost of buying off intrusive forces and over-zealous scrutiny from royal officials or the clergy. Having deflected the attentions and pressures from beyond the village boundaries these communities were then at greater liberty to pursue their own cultural and communal priorities.

Cajas de comunidad financed village projects, including church restorations and repairs to the council house of the village, thus, presumably, bolstering village solidarity and community pride. Some of the money collected was returned to villagers as pay for work performed. Many villages in Mesoamerica were required to put aside certain fields where the quantity of wheat or maize needed to pay the tribute was grown. The local Indians who planted, weeded, irrigated, harvested and gleaned these plots received pay from the *cajas* in many cases. Higher village officials too obtained cash payments from them, and these disbursements may have been of some importance to the perpetuation of hierarchies and traditions. Taking a senior position in village hierarchies could be a costly proposition and many Indians were understandably reluctant to assume the financial burdens associated with *cargos*. Financial rewards from the *cajas* in the form of salaries helped to solve this problem, although much of this money went to the more prosperous villagers, no doubt. Some cajas became wealthy and acted as banks and lenders to Indians and even to Spaniards, owned haciendas, estancias, sugar and flour mills and workshops, and invested in trade far beyond the boundaries of their villages of origin.

Another major Indian institution, also adopted from Spanish society, the *cofradía* or religious confraternity, built up funds not only to pay for communal religious ceremonies (some seen by the authorities as idolatrous) but also to pay fees to priests and bishops on *visitas*. Some *cofradías* foundered under economic and religious pressures from outside; some played partly successful brokerage roles; and a few prospered, and invested in land, herds, mortgages, and other goods. These wealthy *cofradías* were then targets for outside opportunists once again.

Tribute and other impositions upon Indian society, and responses to these pressures, were a large part of the story of taxation in Spanish America, but by no means all of it. The crown and its representatives tried to tax other groups and activities, with great imagination but with rather less success. Government did not have the bureaucrats, accounting systems or technology to tax systematically, so it tried to impose general and simple taxes, hoping to obtain what was possible rather than the optimum from any given tax. Taxes upon trade were one obvious possibility, but in a time of little supervision of land routes, of rudimentary police forces, and of no standardized weights, measures and coinage, such levies had to be haphazard and approximate. One method was to make use of natural and mercantilist trade bottlenecks. Trade to and from Spain was supposed to enter and exit through just a few ports, such as Callao, Panama, Portobelo, Cartagena, Veracruz and Havana. It was fairly easy to levy taxes in these ports with the help of the powerful local *consulados* or merchant guilds, who liked to impose exit and entry taxes of their own, to the disgust of secondary provinces which did not have a legal port. Evasion was common through bribery of officials, contraband carried on board legal ships, and outright smuggling, but except for some of the very bleakest middle decades of the seventeenth century the royal treasury could expect a considerable income from *almojarifazgo*, as these customs fees were called. The treasury tried to impose fees on internal trade by placing customs houses on the royal highways and by ordering that certain trades travel along one permitted route. Two examples of this were the route from the area of Tucumán to Potosí, which brought mules, sugar and other foodstuffs to the silver mines on the barren altiplano, and the road from Guatemala through Chiapas to Puebla and Mexico City which, in its heyday, carried large quantities of cacao and indigo. The tendency towards monopolistic control of bottlenecks was apparent at lower levels of society also.

Strategically placed towns on secondary trade routes tried to emulate the *consulados* of Veracruz and Seville and to tax passing traders for their use of local facilities. Cartago, the colonial capital of Costa Rica, sat astride the route between Nicaragua and Panama, a route which brought the mules raised on the pastures around the Nicaraguan lakes to the *trajín* or transisthmian haulage system of Panama. The Cartago town council levied a small tax per mule while local ostlers and feed-store owners were accused of manipulating prices for their services while the mule-trains were in the town. From time to time clans and other cliques in cities such as Guayaquil and Compostela controlled cabildos and through them whole regions and their products.

Customs dues, both external and internal, legal and illegal, were not the only taxes on trade. The *alcabala* or sales tax had been used in Castile before the conquest and reached America in the late sixteenth century. At first it was thought of as a Spanish or European tax, and the Indian population was theoretically exempt except when it traded in European goods, although some Indians paid heavily, even on maize sales. It was set at 2 per cent of the sale price of goods, but rose to double that amount in the seventeenth century. In times of war or other emergencies higher rates were used, and often lasted, as taxes will, long beyond the emergency. Late in the eighteenth century it was raised to 6 per cent, which caused some dissatisfaction and disturbances. Some smaller Spanish towns delayed the imposition of the alcabala, merchants and cabildos banding together to resist the surveys and listing of merchants necessary to start up the system. Other towns pleaded difficulties or disasters to obtain temporary exemptions. In Quito, when it was finally forced upon the locals in 1591, it caused threats of riots and sedition. In Guatemala, where it was ordered to begin in 1576, the first real surveys began in 1602. In many towns it was assessed on the town in general as a lump sum. The town then assigned the collection to a tax farmer, who had to rely to some extent on sworn statements from encomenderos, hacendados, merchants and shopkeepers as to the volume and worth of their exchanges in the recently-completed tax period. Self-assessment for tax is a poor way to collect money. Many basic items, such as bread, arms, religious ornaments, horses, and all gifts and inheritances, were exempt from alcabala. What with fraud, intermittent collection, illegal buying and selling from Indians, and quarrels over which goods qualified and which did not, most alcabalas from minor cities must have been a disappointment to the royal treasury. Probably it was collected more zealously in the larger cities. In central Mexico, with the increased activity and trade of the mid eighteenth century, it became, like the crown's tobacco monopoly, one of the most financially important branches of the royal treasury.

Most government offices were purchased both in America and in Spain – those in very wealthy communities bringing bids many times higher than the same posts in poorer communities – but this tax in advance was not sufficient for the crown in that it did not allow access to the official's income, frequently high, after he had taken office. To remedy this situation the government instituted two very crude income taxes. The *mesada* was a payment of a month's income by every new official, secular and ecclesiastic, upon entering his new post. In civil offices this was difficult to assess because office-holders seldom revealed the truth about the monthly yield of their positions. Benefices were public knowledge and so clerics holding them were taxed more accurately. In 1631 the crown increased the tax for secular officials to half of the first year's salary, or a *media anata*. (Thus, in the seventeenth century the remaining mesada became known as the *mesada eclesiástica*.) By 1754 the crown was demanding, and the papacy was consenting to, a *media anata* on the salaries of the high clergy, but it took several years to put this change into practice and for most clergy the mesada was the tax collected for much of the eighteenth century. Sometimes the *media anata* was also collected on the first year's profits from purchases of crown lands.

Since the days of the *Reconquista* the crown had claimed and received a share of booty and especially bullion. In the New World this share became the *quinto real*, or 'royal fifth', and once the conquests were over the *quinto* became a tax on the production of precious stones, pearls, gold, and above all silver. Sometimes, to stimulate production, it was lowered to one-tenth, and in some places of marginal importance the local guild of miners or the city cabildo was able to persuade the crown to be satisfied with one-twentieth. This was the case for most of the colonial period in the silver mines of Honduras and in the gold mines between Popayán and Cali. The *quinto* was easier to collect in the large mines or in any mines which used a mercury amalgam for smelting. Mercury mining was a royal monopoly and, although the quality of the silver ore was an important factor, there was a rough correspondence between the quantity of mercury used and the amount of silver refined. Silver, however, is a considerable spur to human ingenuity, and fraud was rife in the silver mines. Silver was adulterated, bars were shaved, miners and officials stole ore, government officials from time to time conspired in vast schemes of defalcation of the treasury. Nevertheless, fraud at the mercury-using mines never reached the proportions that it did in the mines which continued to use the old fire and oven smelting, the *huayras*, as they were called in Upper Peru. In these mines, which in many cases were worked only for a few months or a year or two, even the royal tenth or twentieth was very difficult to collect. Nevertheless, in spite of these difficulties the *quinto* was one of the most important taxes in the Spanish New World, extracting large amounts of money from labour and production, and remitting much, perhaps most, of it to Spain, other parts of western Europe, and eventually the Far East.

Government monopolies such as the mercury mining mentioned above, early seventeenth-century copper mining at Santiago del Prado in eastern Cuba, and above all the very remunerative *estanco* or monopoly on tobacco, came to be of great importance as sources of revenue. In the late colonial period monopolies on 'necessities' such as salt, paper, gunpowder, and tobacco became extremely unpopular among all classes and led to outbreaks such as the Tupac Amaru revolt and the early struggles which led to independence. Government also rented out its monopolistic rights, sometimes rights to whole regions, although these were usually areas that the government had been unable to develop. The Guipúzcoa company and the Campeche company of the eighteenth century were two examples.

The crown was obliged by its status as patron of the church to act as a redistributive agency for one tax. It collected the ecclesiastical tithe or *diezmo* on the 'fruits of the earth', roughly speaking all agricultural and domesticated animal products. Usually Indians did not pay the tithe except on products introduced to them by Europeans. The crown probably found the collection, administration and disbursement of the tithe to be a losing proposition. It kept one-ninth of the proceeds to cover its costs, almost certainly not enough, and spent the rest on bishoprics, cathedral chapters, construction and maintenance of churches, hospitals, poorhouses, asylums and schools, and on the parish clergy. The *diezmo* was a transfer of wealth out of the agricultural sector to the church, but part of it was returned, not only to the extent that the church satisfied some of the psychological and spiritual needs of its adherents, but also to the poor and the sick in the form of primitive medical attention, charity and hospitalization, and to the wealthier in the form of education, loans, and ritual opportunities for displays of social prestige. The other ecclesiastical tax, collected by clergy but administered by the government, was the *santa cruzada*, a system of sale of indulgences every other year which brought in considerable revenue, especially in the eighteenth century. To a very limited extent there was an attempt to turn the indulgences into an income or wealth tax, with assessments varying from two to ten pesos depending on wealth, class and caste. Collection was farmed out to the clergy, in the towns usually to members of the cathedral chapter, and its efficiency and fairness, even by its own terms, varied widely.

These taxes, which became more complicated and numerous as the colonial centuries advanced – head taxes on the peasantry, the control of trade bottlenecks and the assessment of towns by the approximate value of their business transactions, confiscations from captive groups such as government officials and dependent clerics, government monopolies and the sale of government monopolies, levies to support the state religion, and the appropriation of a share of the product of the most spectacular wealth-producing industry, in this case silver mining – were all very old devices, the most obvious sources of revenue for early empires and direct descendants of Roman imperial taxation. No great bureaucracy was needed, since almost all these taxes were farmed out, that is to say, the right to collect a specific tax was purchased by a private individual who recouped the costs of the office by holding back part of the taxes which he collected, or who agreed to deliver a specific amount to the authorities. Sometimes the tax farmer's share was expressed as a percentage of the total collected, an incentive to collect enthusiastically and thoroughly. And, of course, tax farmers, all the way from hacendados, wealthy merchants, and indigent creoles to *calpisques* and Indian village *principales* and *alcaldes*, trimmed, overcollected, underreported, and held back excessive amounts, as much as was possible, while keeping a close eye on the degree of amiability, indulgence, sloth, honesty, and indigence of the treasury officials to whom they had to account and deliver. It was not until the reign of Charles III, the first promoter of a modern state bureaucracy, that vigorous efforts were made to cut down tax farming and to increase collection by state functionaries, *intendentes* and *subdelegados*.

The Spanish state, a transitional system seeking desperately for funds and trying to be modern about it, devoted considerable thought to the problem of how to take a share of capital and income from the wealthy, a class which had to be pampered because it performed so many social control and other functions for the government. *Composiciones* or *indultos*, ex post facto payments to the crown for overlooking irregularities and criminal activities (often abuses of the labour force) and granting titles to dubiously acquired (usually Indian) land, was a poor income producer, although often expensive to the individual concerned, and was more of a series of rewards to supporters on whom government depended.

The best that the government could manage, given its relationship with the upper class, was the *donativo gracioso*, a 'voluntary donation', which was really a system of involuntary, negotiated assessments or confiscations resembling English royal benevolences. The crown began this practice of elaborate begging, sometimes for gifts, sometimes for loans, in the early sixteenth century, often invoking the costs of an emergency or a special celebration such as a war or the birth of a royal heir, as an excuse, but by the reign of Charles II it had become a system, recurring fairly regularly every few years, and with a recognized procedure for assessment and collection. Local officials, often the *audiencia*, which would then delegate the responsibility to local corregidores, were ordered to assess the wealthy of each jurisdiction for a donation. Lists of such people were drawn up with appropriate, suggested amounts. The corregidor or town official then collected these sums, or some approximation to them, at times after a prolonged period of bargaining. Royal officials were not exempt, and they too paid up short, sending long and elaborate letters of excuse to Spain explaining the underpayment. The crown had some latent means of threatening royal officials, but was in a difficult position vis-à-vis its wealthy private citizens. As its demands for gifts became more frequent, abject, and desperate, the importuned developed more and more sales resistance and the indigent crown was obliged to offer inducements such as pensions, titles of nobility, future exemptions, and freedom from government regulations in order to collect. The results of these donations were contradictory. Some of them in the late sixteenth and early seventeenth centuries produced large sums which helped the crown to surmount real emergencies, such as the million pesos sent by the viceroy of Mexico in 1629 to compensate for Piet Heyn's capture of the silver fleet. But the donations were also a form of disinvestment, a removal of capital from the colonies, and in the long run alienated a class on which the crown depended. The crown's financial and bargaining position was too weak to turn these practices into real taxes on wealth or incomes, or to make them of any long-term utility or advantage.

DISTRIBUTION AND EXCHANGE

Colonial Spanish America had several overlapping and intersecting systems of production, distribution and exchange, which went through many phases of prosperity and decline, expansion and contraction.

At the lowest level was peasant agriculture and village exchanges. Maize, beans, tubers, some pulque and chicha, salt, fowls and other small domesticates, and handwoven cloth were produced by Indian smallholdings, more or less communal villages, and on the fringe areas of haciendas. To the extent that these basic goods were needed in larger markets such as Spanish cities the Indian community played the principal role in the early days of the encomienda, bringing large quantities of these staples for sale or, via the tribute, to auction in the cities. As the encomienda weakened and the Indian population declined, and as cities and mining centres became bigger and more attractive markets, local Indian producers and distributors were pushed aside to a considerable extent by Spanish farmers, owners of haciendas and obrajes, and Spanish or mestizo merchants. Indian production for the market was once more largely confined to the village level. The total quantity of goods involved certainly remained considerable, but individual quantities were small, moved about inefficiently, and lacked means of exchange. The system depended on the indefatigable industry and stamina of the Indian petty farmer and merchant, often the same person, and willingness to travel long distances with small quantities in search of meagre profits. Much of the exchange was by barter, or by substitute coinages such as cacao beans, cakes of brown sugar, or coca leaves. Money in its smallest denominations and falsified coinage were also common. The local *cabecera*, or sometimes a semi-vacant village which had been the pre-Columbian ceremonial centre, became the weekly market-place. People brought goods to these markets on their own backs or on the backs of mules or llamas. In the more 'Indian' areas such market days had cultural and religious functions which provided additional rewards to these merchants and made the profit margin slightly less important. In poor and marginal areas of Spanish America such as Paraguay, Tucumán, and rural Venezuela before cacao, areas with little Indian population and no important product to draw Spanish attention, the few Spanish settlers found that they had no alternative but to live off Indian production. It was in such areas that the encomienda lasted for most of the colonial period.

From time to time the emergence within the peasant economy of a desirable and profitable product (or, more frequently, the emergence within the European society of America, or in Europe itself, of a market for a previously ignored product) invited intrusion. Cacao, tobacco, cactus fibres, and in a slightly different way pulque and coca leaves are typical American crops which developed market values in the Europeanized economy because of changing patterns of distribution, changing tastes, or new ways of using products. Indian or peasant producers gradually lost control of the marketing system, and sometimes of the land and the productive process as well.

In some places and at some times Indian and other peasant groups were able to resist such intrusions and takeovers by displays of community solidarity. Usually peasant producers could limit, postpone, or prevent intrusion only by possession of a production or trade secret. A good example is cochineal, a dye which resulted from an intricate, skilled manufacturing process involving symbiotic relationships between humans, insects, and cactus. Spaniards, and even Indians from areas which did not produce cochineal, did not have the skills or patience to take over the production, and given its nature, the industry was difficult to rationalize or intensify. Economies of scale at the local level were counterproductive and led to declines in output. Production was in the hands of small producers – in this case Indian villagers in Oaxaca, the leading cochineal area – and so cochineal was delivered to many small village markets. Even at this stage it did not pay larger merchants or entrepreneurs to become involved. Petty merchants, Indians or castas, went around to these village markets buying up small quantities of the dye and delivering them to larger merchants. This is not to say that relationships in these local markets were fairer or more egalitarian. These petty traders, mule-skinners or more cosmopolitan Indian *principales*, often the main link between the peasant economy and the larger market economies, swindled, cajoled and coerced as much as they could. Both sides, Spanish above and Indian below, scorned them, as their common derisive names, such as *mercachifles* or *quebrantahuesos*, show. Thus Spaniards, through intermediaries, were able to profit from cochineal and to gather it together in sufficient bulk to make it a significant trade item as far away as Amsterdam and London, but they could not take over or fully control the production process, and the marketing system frustrated them until very late in the colonial period. Areas such as Oaxaca which had trade and marketing secrets which excluded non-Indians, were, of course, as a result able to remain more 'Indian'. Oaxaca, however, must be regarded as an exception. Most peasant areas which produced or marketed products which were of great value suffered massive intrusions, and major transformations in their production and marketing systems, and in their cultures, resulted.

By the early seventeenth century the expanding urban markets for meat, cereals (wheat as well as maize) and other basic foodstuffs in the more important parts of the empire were supplied for the most part not by Indian villages, except perhaps indirectly, but by large-scale, Spanish-owned estancias, sheep farms, pig farms, haciendas, wheat farms (*labores*) and market gardens. By the eighteenth century nine trade routes led to Mexico City, bringing into town hundreds of mule-trains and ox-carts laden with wheat, maize, cattle, pigs, hides, sugar, wines, and vegetables as well as textiles, dyes, and European goods. Several thousand mules entered the city each day, and Indian towns with grazing land near Mexico City became staging areas where cattle were rested and grazed until the city slaughterhouses were ready for them. Lima too was a big market, although the limited agricultural land near this desert oasis, and its coastal location, allowed Lima to draw some of its staples from a considerable distance, a luxury not logistically possible for inland, highland cities such as Mexico City, Bogotá or Quito. Lima's wheat came from the central valley of Chile and the northern oases of the Peruvian coast; its woods, cordage and pitch from Guayaquil or even from distant Nicaragua, and its maize and potatoes from the highlands of the hinterland. Lima was exceptional, however: most Spanish regional capitals of any size dominated interior highland valleys and created agricultural belts around them. The merchants who brought these staples to these cities were Spaniards or castas working for their own benefit, or as agents of Spanish farmers or larger city merchants. One exception was the Indian canoers in the canals approaching Mexico City from the south. The building, steering, and poling of canoes were skills or hard work which Spaniards scorned.

Distribution of staples within major cities was always a problem. Merchants, hacendados, wine growers and wheat farmers shared the basic colonial mentality which favoured monopoly and bottlenecks.

They tended to exclude competition and to withhold goods from the market to await shortages and higher prices. Groups of hacendados and wheat farmers quite obviously conspired towards these ends, and the result, if these monopolists were left unhindered, was shortages, even hardships, wild fluctuations in price, migrations among the poor, and chaotic market-places with outbreaks of looting and rioting. City authorities, *audiencias*, and even the viceregal governments intervened to make the system more just, to prevent shortages and exorbitant prices, and to preserve social tranquillity and the appearance of social control. The main devices used were the now familiar colonial ones which have already been discussed. Authorities ran monopolies themselves or auctioned off permission to monopolize and deliver a guaranteed quantity of goods. Government warehouses were called *pósitos* or *alhóndigas*. These institutions began in the New World in the late sixteenth and early seventeenth centuries and at first worked intermittently during times of shortages by confiscating and retaining Indian maize supplies brought into the city as tribute, and then redistributing the maize at set prices in the main city markets. In some cities the *alhóndigas* then became permanent features, buying up prescribed portions of the supplies of maize and other staples to depress the price and to control the profits of middlemen and monopolistic speculators. Cabildos themselves then became the monopolists to a certain extent, and some town councils, especially those controlled by tightly-knit cliques, played the market like true speculators. The town council, usually a far from affluent body in middle-sized and lesser Spanish towns, often borrowed heavily to buy staples for the alhóndiga, then found it tempting to recoup its outlays and perhaps even produce a small surplus for city reconstruction or beautification projects by holding up the redistribution from government warehouses until the price was just a little more favourable.

Some products such as meat, milk, and green vegetables could not be stored. In these cases the government could not monopolize purchase and redistribution and fell back on simply trying to ensure a dependable supply. This was done by auctioning the right to supply the city slaughterhouses or markets. A local hacendado would buy exclusive right to provision the city slaughterhouse, thus ensuring his monopoly and a right to charge high prices. The cabildo, abandoning fair prices to ensure a steady supply, was simply taking a percentage of his profits. The sufferers were those in the city who could not

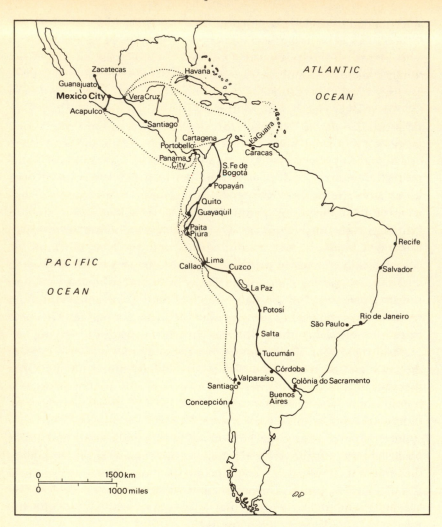

Internal trade routes

afford to pay the monopoly prices. Most cities supplied their own basic manufactures. In 1781 Buenos Aires, for example, had 27 bakeries, 139 shoemakers, 59 tailors, and 76 carpenters, all producing for the local market.

The larger cities and the concentrations of rural populations near them also provided the markets for long-distance colonial Spanish American trade in non-perishable items or perishables with a longer life.

These longer-distance trades and trade routes, together with the bureaucratic networks which moved office-holders from place to place, were the only real ties which brought the American empire together as a unit, and, as the results of the wars of independence and subsequent attempts at common markets were to demonstrate, they were rather ephemeral links at best. If Spain was the metropolis for colonial Spanish America, then to a great extent central Mexico was the metropolis for large parts of the Caribbean, for Venezuela, the northern and southern extremes of continental New Spain, the Philippines, and even, for many purposes, the west coast of Spanish South America and its immediate hinterlands. More specifically, Mexico City, to a lesser extent Lima, and, for much of the colonial period, Potosí were dominant economic centres, magnets which drew and held large and sometimes distant catchment areas. In the middle to late eighteenth century, as the colonial economy went through a profound adjustment from its *ancien régime* of mercantilism towards a renovated mercantile era, and as new raw materials and products such as sugar, tobacco, and animal products became major exports to Europe, Buenos Aires, Caracas, and Havana joined the list of major urban markets.

At all times until the very late colonial period long-distance Spanish American trades were regulated or limited by the same logistical determinants of time, distance, cargo space and freight rates that dominated the trades between Spanish America and Seville or Cadiz. In general trade by sea was less expensive and more expeditious, so sea routes could deliver goods with higher perishability and lower profit margins from greater distances. In a similar fashion, although the differences were usually less, routes via coastal plains, at least during the dry season, could carry more perishable bulk goods than routes through the mountains. Where foodstuffs were involved, routes through relatively temperate climates entailed less spoilage than those which ran through hot, arid or humid tropics.

For much of the colonial period, beginning as early as the lifetimes of Hernando Cortés and the Pizarro brothers, the colonial axis of all these routes ran from Potosí through La Paz and Cuzco to Lima-Callao, and thence by sea up the coast to Panama and Acapulco, and ultimately Mexico City. Goods moved southwards more than northwards, and bullion moved more northwards than southwards, but at both ends of the colonial axis there was, significantly enough, a supply of silver to fuel exchanges and to provide incentives, although there were long periods when Potosí and the mines north of Mexico City did an inadequate job of providing either.

The distances involved in this colonial axis and the attractiveness of its main markets and main product, silver, encouraged the growth of regional specialization. Some of these were based on pre-conquest products and trade wares which continued on an increased scale into the colonial period because they fitted into Europeanized patterns of demand. The potteries of Puebla and Guadalajara, of the Ica and Nazca valleys, provided not only the kitchenware of the cities, towns and villages, but also the *botijas* or flagons which carried wine, oil, brandy, and pulque over long distances. Cacao in Colima and Soconusco fed the Mexican market until more European plantations, first around Caracas in the late seventeenth century, then later Guayaquil, took over the trade. Some of these regional specializations arose because of significant lacks near large markets. Lima could not grow its own wheat and had to look to small oases nearby. Even these were not sufficient and in the first half of the eighteenth century the central valley of Chile, relatively closer than Cuzco, Andahuaylas and Abancay because of the sea link, became Lima's main supplier. The barren altiplano around Potosí grew little and could provide grazing for only a few hardy sheep and American cameloids. So the valleys around Cochabamba and Sucre became its granaries, and mules were reared in large numbers as far away as Mendoza and driven to the mines through the mountains. Some specializations came into existence because of the availability of raw materials and skilled artisans. The bells and cannon of the foundries of Arequipa and Puebla supplied the churches, forts, and ships of the cities, ports, and routes along the axis. Other specializations arose because of European inability to supply many essentials at a great distance. The infamous textile obrajes or large workshops of central Mexico and Quito, the vineyards and olive groves of central Chile and of the Peruvian coastal oases, were local suppliers at first but expanded rapidly when Spain proved logistically and economically incapable of filling the colonial demand for cheap textiles, wine, brandy and oil. As regional specialities grew they challenged Spanish products even in Mexico and the Caribbean. Peruvian wine, for example, undercut the price of supplies from Andalusia in the Mexico City market, even after the government protected Sevillian monopolists by banning Mexican imports of Peruvian wine, thus driving it into contraband and raising its costs.

The obrajes represent the outstanding success story of colonial Spanish American industry and long-distance, inter-American trade. They grew up in two centres: the valleys of Quito, Otavalo, Riobamba, Ambato, Latacunga, and Alausí in the Ecuadorean sierra, and central Mexico from Puebla to Mexico City. The Quito complex supplied much of Pacific South America to regions as distant as Potosí and Cartagena. Mexico supplied New Spain and some of the islands of the Caribbean. Both industries rose to prominence in the late sixteenth century and lasted in various stages of prosperity until just before independence. The obrajes around Quito depended on vast herds of sheep – the valley of Ambato alone held about 600,000 in the late seventeenth century – and were challenged by few rivals for their Indian labour supply. Slaves, free castas, and a few convicts were all employed in the Quito sweatshops, but most of the workers were recruited quite simply by the old devices of encomienda and repartimiento. By 1680 there were some 30,000 people involved in the Quito obrajes, and the average mill employed some 160 people. Mexico's textile mills faced stiffer competition, not only from European and oriental textiles, but also from the labour requirements of silver mines and much larger cities. As a result its obrajes made heavier use of slave and convict labour and free wage labour. Wool was the principal cloth woven, but cotton was also widely used. Some mills were large and employed hundreds of workers. In the first half of the eighteenth century renewed competition both from Europe and other colonial centres – Cajamarca and Cuzco in Peru, Querétaro in New Spain – undermined the prosperity of Quito and Puebla somewhat. By the end of the century, however, they had successfully found alternative markets and started new lines of manufacture, although at the very end of the colonial period European competition was again a major problem.[3]

The main axis between Mexico, Acapulco and Callao, with its spur to Potosí, also stimulated shipbuilding. Guayaquil was a principal shipyard, thanks to its supplies of hardwoods and pitch, throughout the colonial period. Smaller ports such as Huatulco, San Blas and Realejo helped from time to time. All along the main inter-American trade route were important spurs. Mexico City, via its Caribbean port of Veracruz, traded with the islands and mainland ports. Routes between Veracruz and Havana – and, although later in starting, between Veracruz and La

[3] For further discussion of obrajes in eighteenth-century Spanish America, see ch. 3 above.

Guaira – became important carriers of silver, cacao, hides, dyes, and sugar. Mexico City was a distribution point not only for the vast sparsely populated expanses to its north, but also for areas as far south as Chiapas and Yucatán. Ports along the sea route between Acapulco and Callao traded with large hinterlands. Acajutla and Realejo were the ports for Central America, not only exchanging local goods for silver and wine from Mexico and Peru, but also bringing ashore illegal goods from Peru and sending them by land to Mexico to evade customs, and loading ships for Peru with silks and spices from the Philippines which had been brought illegally by land from Mexico City and Acapulco. The ports of northern Peru performed similar functions. Piura and Santa were not only the ports for Paita and the Callejón de Huaylas, but also the landing-stages for illegal goods from Mexico and the Philippines via Mexico which were trying to evade the vigilance of customs officers in Callao. In a similar fashion Guayaquil was the port for the highlands around Quito, and La Serena, Valparaíso, and Concepción were the ports for northern, central, and southern Chile and for the interior provinces on the other side of the Andes around Mendoza and San Juan.

An even more important southern spur was the one which ran from the southern silver terminus of the axis, Potosí, down through Salta, Tucumán, and Córdoba to Buenos Aires and the Portuguese smuggling depot at Colônia do Sacramento. Some of the goods travelling northwards along this route, for example the horses, mules and cattle of Tucumán which were sent to supply the silver mines, were legal and open. But Buenos Aires, for some two centuries after its definitive settlement, was also the illegal back door to Potosí, a surreptitious route and a shorter one from Europe than the legal one via Panama and Callao. European manufactures and some of the luxuries which mining boom towns demand moved slowly along this long land route. Of greater worldwide import was the silver which moved illegally in the other direction. From Buenos Aires the silver of Potosí passed on to merchants in Sacramento and Rio de Janeiro, and thence not only to Lisbon but directly to Portuguese India and China to finance the spread of Western intrusion there. From 1640, when Portugal broke with the Spanish crown, until about 1705 this large exchange system suffered many difficulties and some nearly complete interruptions, but in the late sixteenth and early seventeenth centuries, and again as the Spaniards were forced to give the Buenos Aires slave trade concessions to foreign companies, first French, then English, after 1702 and 1713, the Potosí–Buenos Aires silver trade was of great international importance. American silver reached the Orient by another route. The longest spur on the Mexico City–Lima–Potosí axis was the route between Acapulco and the Philippines. This route exchanged silk and oriental spices for Mexican and Peruvian silver, and in spite of mid-seventeenth-century difficulties, seems to have produced great profits. Thus the silver axes of the main colonial trade route financed European activities and imperialism in the Orient: the Potosí end via Buenos Aires, the Portuguese, and other foreigners; the Mexican end via the Philippines and Canton.

Internal colonial trade, both the system which supplied staples to city markets and the long-distance system carrying silver, textiles and regional specialities, required means of articulation. We have already mentioned such institutions as governmental and private auctions, *pósitos* and *alhóndigas*, guilds of merchants and artisans, and minor merchants and traders who collected small amounts of valuable items in village markets for delivery to larger houses in the cities. The dominant exchange mechanism, however, just as in the village economy and in Western Europe, was the trade fair. The largest fairs were in the big cities and the place and time of their occurrence and their internal governance were regulated by law and local inspectors. Other fairs took place at crossroads where the various systems intersected. The most unique and famous fairs were the ones which linked the three internal trade systems which we have described with the official transoceanic trades carried by the fleets and the various licensed ships. These fairs took place in the great official ports or nearby, especially Veracruz, Jalapa, and Portobelo. In a curious way these fairs, right at the top of the hierarchy of trade systems, closely resembled those at the very bottom. Indian fairs often took place in vacant ceremonial villages which would fill up for the two or three days of the fair, then fall back to their usual tranquillity. So too with Portobelo and many other unhealthy tropical ports. While the fleets unloaded and reloaded people would pack into the ports, renting rooms and buying food, drink, and transportation at enormously inflated prices. Tent cities and temporary canvas warehouses would spring up on nearby beaches, and roaring commercial and social interaction would give these places the appearance of frenzied, round-the-clock activity for a few days or weeks. When the fleets sailed and the mule-trains toiled away inland these cities would sink back to small collections of huts, many of them vacant, as the merchants and administrators headed with indecent haste for more salubrious spots.

Much less is known of the merchants in the two intermediate systems which supplied the large internal markets than of the great merchants of the *consulados* of Mexico City, Veracruz, Lima, Seville, and Cadiz. The small group of merchants in Quito in the closing years of the sixteenth century has, however, been studied. Its main preoccupation was not distance but time, more specifically *jornadas* or days of travel. Its other problem was delays in payment and thus in collecting profits. Borrowing was limited, so the typical merchant often waited for his profit from a venture before he could reinvest in a new one. Textiles to Potosí and Popayán, and leather, sugar, and hardtack to various destinations were his principal exports. European goods, wine from Peru, and silver from Potosí were his imports. A few traders worked as individuals but most had to band together because of the shortage of private capital and the relative lack of credit. Sometimes non-merchants were brought into the *compañía*, providing capital, mules, or labour in return for a share of the profits. Lack of a standard series of weights and measures, fluctuations in rates and values, the impossibility of knowing the demand for certain items in distant markets, and above all the lack of a good and stable currency, caused disappointments, delays and losses. Some of these *compañías* of merchants spent months assembling the necessary capital and preparing for expeditions. Sometimes dozens of merchants became involved and the surrounding countryside had to be scoured for horses, mules, saddles, weatherproof containers, and fodder. Some of the caravans which left Quito were enormous, containing hundreds of mules. Failure rates among this generation of Quito merchants were low, and profits ranged between 10 and 30 per cent – good returns in a time of low inflation and fairly stable wages. The interest rates charged by lenders varied according to the destination, its distance in time, and its wealth as a market. Borrowing money for a trip to Guayaquil cost a merchant 10 per cent interest. The other extreme was Seville, for which lenders were unwilling to risk cash at less than 100 per cent. Potosí, with its high prices and wild spenders, cost less in interest than Panama. A loan towards sending goods to Cartagena by sea cost less in interest than a loan to send goods to Cartagena by land, in spite of the transhipments at Guayaquil and the isthmus. Merchants reinvested profits in the next venture, but even more in land, in consumption, and in the church. Businesses in this time and place seldom carried over to the next generation and ended with large distributions of assets when the merchant died. No doubt the Castilian laws of partible inheritance were much to blame in an era of large families. Merchants seem to have had no great feeling for their trade, did not found business 'houses', and did not hope that their heirs would follow in their footsteps. Their profits might be reinvested in another similar venture, or quite as easily in something entirely unrelated to trade. Merchants in very large commercial cities such as Mexico City and Lima were different. There some merchant families persisted over two or three generations and demonstrated a certain *esprit de corps* and status consciousness, partly because of the presence of the *consulados*. The merchants of Veracruz, Buenos Aires, Caracas, and Havana in the late eighteenth century were more professional and cosmopolitan than their earlier inland fellows. Nevertheless, there was always a marked inclination to get out of trade, to invest in land, and then to tie up fortunes in secure *mayorazgos* or entailed estates.

The history of prices and wages, another important aspect of production and exchange, has also perhaps not received the scholarly attention it deserves. Prices rose rapidly in the half-century or more after the conquest as the labouring population decreased, as silver mining monetized the economy quickly, and as the consuming population grew. This must have confused the calculations of producers and merchants considerably, but usually sixteenth-century inflation worked to their benefit, in the New World if not in the Old. Wages rose even more rapidly as labour not connected to slavery, encomienda and repartimiento/mita gained a comparative advantage because of its increasing scarcity. Producers, employers, and merchants had to balance off these increasing labour costs against the gains to be made from inflating prices. We do not know enough about this equation, but those who used large numbers of free labourers may have lost out slightly at the end of the day. Long-distance trades resulted in some wildly fluctuating prices because of the times and freights involved and because of the unevenness of supply. Famines, droughts, floods, volcanic eruptions, locusts, and epidemics brought temporary shortages and rapid price rises which were often worsened by eager monopolists. The price of Peruvian wine in Mexico, for example, varied greatly. We know little about wages, except for a general impression of stability in the seventeenth century which may have lessened in the eighteenth. Wages may have lagged behind prices, especially in late eighteenth-century Mexico, as the working population slowly increased, an additional long-term advantage to those who used wage labour.

Production and exchanges had to be financed. Credit sources included the church and its *capellanías*, or private endowments and benefices of the secular clergy, the royal exchequer, community chests, guilds and fraternities, and private individuals. Merchants themselves loaned money to other merchants and to miners and landowners. Speculators even played the market in the village economy by means of the *repartimientos de comercio*, advancing cash, equipment, horses, or mules in return for a share of the next harvest. Loans in general were fairly short-term and specific in purpose but land mortgages could last for years and the capital which such mortgages released was used for a wide variety of investments. Dowries were a very common means for transferring capital and financed many an enterprise or business expansion. In general credit instruments such as letters of credit and means of transferring capital and payments over distances and time were much poorer than in Western Europe. Because capital markets and the quantities of goods exchanged were relatively small, and because they were not backed by an extensive, widely understood and accepted system of credits and credit instruments, the system had to be backed by an agreed-upon valuable, which in this cultural context had to be bullion, especially silver. Not all of the marketing systems examined here needed the backing of a silver currency, at least not to the same extent. Village agricultural exchanges used barter or substitute coinages such as coca leaves or cacao beans. This is not to suggest that this economy was always a simple one. Studies of the various ecological niches and complementary zones of altitudes and specialization in the Andes and in Mesoamerica have demonstrated the existence of a 'vertical archipelago' of exchanges between different zones, governed by reciprocity and barter rather than calculated on strict and current market prices of the goods involved. Some of these barter exchanges could cover large distances, on rare occasions involving journeys taking weeks. Trade for the urban markets, however, especially long-distance trade and above all trade with Europe and the Orient, had to be backed by silver. There are several examples of ingenious traders relying upon alternative coinages. Cacao beans were used in Venezuela, Costa Rica, and in rural Mexico. Coca leaves were used in Upper Peru. There are even indications that the standard *botija* of wine or oil was understood as a measure of value, and thus became a sort of primitive money along the Pacific coast in the harder years of the mid seventeenth century. But in general, long-distance trades needed silver and when silver was scarce these trades languished.

Before 1535 the invading groups used barter or weighed pieces of gold and silver. The crown introduced a dangerous precedent by attempting to monetize the colonies and make some profit at the same time. It sent Castilian coins to the New World and declared them of higher value there than in Castile. Manipulation of the value of the coinage was a temptation to which the crown often yielded, with profitable, quick results and a disastrous impact on trading and on the confidence of the trading community in Spanish America.

Minting began in the New World in 1535 and for most of the colonial period the colonies produced their own coinage. From the beginning adulteration, falsification, and shaving of the coinage was rampant. Spaniards inherited an Aztec tradition of mixing gold with copper and this suspect *tipuzque* coinage circulated freely in Mexico past the mid sixteenth century. Thereafter Mexican coinage was considered more reliable. In Peru adulteration of silver with tin and lead pre-dated the conquest. Much early colonial Peruvian coinage was similarly mixed and Peruvian money remained an object of suspicion compared to that of Mexico for most of the colonial period. Potosí coins were a joke and were often rejected. At times falsified coinage was accepted in legal transactions, but at a discounted rate. Thus such coins were illegal technically but not in practice.

For much of the three centuries under discussion the standard coin was the *peso fuerte* or *peso de a ocho*, a silver coin divided into eight *reales*. In the lesser colonies this coin was often cut with a cold chisel, in two parts to make *tostones*, or in eight 'bits' or *reales*. *Moneda cortada* or *moneda recortada* did not inspire confidence. Cutting pesos often left *tostones* and *reales* of less than the correct size and weight. Clipping and shaving bits of coins reduced them to such shapelessness that coin weighing was a regular feature of small market-places. Good money was hoarded or exported and suspect *perulero* coins were the most common in America. To make matters worse the crown, Spanish merchants and foreigners drained the colonies of silver coinage with surprising efficiency, not only to Europe, but via Buenos Aires to Brazil and India, and via Acapulco to the Orient. Taxes were sent to Madrid, royal officers and merchants sent home substantial sums against the day of their retirement, and foreign smugglers preferred silver in exchange for the goods of north-western Europe or for African slaves. As silver mining declined in the mid seventeenth century, as the official Spanish fleet system deteriorated, and as smuggling and hoarding of good coinage increased, the colonies, especially the secondary ones of the circum-Caribbean area, suffered an intense currency shortage. And what remained was suspect trash. In the 1650s the state stepped in, tinkering with the debased coinage, devaluing the Peruvian *macacas*, and finally recalling them for restamping. None of these panic measures worked and the crown finally abandoned reform and left the situation to work itself out. Debased remnants were dumped on the Indian or free black communities and ended up in the treasury as payment of tribute and other taxes. Trade lost its main backing and stultified or became local. Barter grew but inhibited long-distance exchanges. Such monetary crises returned frequently after the mid seventeenth century. Southern Mexico was again troubled between 1700 and 1725. In 1728 the crown took over the mints, which had previously been leased to private companies, and tried to standardize coinage and stamping and to introduce the milled edge to discourage clipping – all seemingly to very little effect.

Coinage shortages and unreliability led to problems of convertibility, especially in rural or peripheral areas. Numerous complaints tell of powerful, wealthy regional figures who could not translate their capital to more desirable centres. A typical case would be that of a rancher in Mendoza or Sonora with thousands of head of cattle and countless hectares of land, trying to convert this obvious wealth into a move to Mexico City or even Madrid. How would such a man, or his widow, turn such holdings into a reliable coinage or its equivalent over long distances?

Currency and coinage, then, were a problem throughout the Spanish colonial period, an ironic situation given the wealth pouring out of the silver mines. In times of great shortages of coinage barter and substitute money returned, trade routes shortened because of lack of an agreed-upon means of exchange, and market confidence fell. When good coinage which enjoyed the confidence of traders was relatively abundant long-distance trade expanded and even local exchanges were quicker and easier. The state and quantity of silver coinage is one of the surest indicators of the general economic condition in such an early, unsophisticated money economy.

9

INDIAN SOCIETIES UNDER SPANISH RULE

In Spanish American studies Indian history of the colonial period is a relatively new topic. Throughout the nineteenth century and into the twentieth it was a widely held assumption that little or nothing of consequence in Indian life survived the conquests of the sixteenth century. The view was consistent with the classic writings on conquest, famous for their descriptions of massacres, tortures, and military victories unrelated to events before or after. The conquests appeared to be so concentrated, so cataclysmic, so dramatic in their confrontations of European soldiers with American natives, that no one questioned their power to annihilate. The classic writers knew that individual Indians survived to be utilized by the conquerors as slaves and labourers and tribute-payers. But the prevailing view was that none of the political, social, or cultural values of the American civilizations escaped destruction. The clear implication was that for Indians the aftermath of the conquests was deculturation and stagnation.

The view that no Indian culture persisted after the conquests was consistent with the Leyenda Negra (Black Legend), the tradition of anti-Hispanic criticism that developed in the sixteenth century, flourished in the seventeenth, eighteenth, and nineteenth centuries, and continued to exert an influence on interpretations of Spanish and Spanish American history in the twentieth century. The critics of Spanish colonialism argued that the *conquistadores* were inhumane and that an important consequence of their inhumanity was the unnecessary destruction of American Indian civilizations. Thus the Black Legend emphasized Spanish insensitivity, as if a less crude conqueror, or one with more appreciation for native American cultures, would have salvaged something for the post-conquest future. It is worth noting that the apologetic White Legend, in almost every other respect the reverse of the Black Legend, also emphasized the destructive character of the conquests. The defenders of Spanish colonialism took the position that the American civilizations, with their cannibalism, human sacrifice, and other barbarities, could deserve only to be destroyed.

In the nineteenth century, the same idea was reinforced by the literature of travel in Spanish America. The Indian described here was an impoverished and depressed person, essentially unchanged from the time of Cortés and Pizarro. Conquest had eliminated all that was good in Indian society and the remainder had been left to stultify. One of the earliest and most perceptive of the nineteenth-century travellers, Alexander von Humboldt, reported:

The better sort of Indians, among whom a certain degree of intellectual culture might be supposed, perished in great part at the commencement of the Spanish conquest... The remaining natives then consisted only of the most indigent race... and especially of those dregs of the people... who in the time of Cortés filled the streets of all the great cities of the Mexican empire.[1]

Later travellers used Humboldt's observations as their own. Their commentaries often took the form of rhetorical surprise that the Indians they encountered in Spanish America could be the descendants of the opulent, splendid Aztecs and Incas.

A hundred years after Humboldt, in the early twentieth century, much more was known about American Indians and about Spanish American history. But the knowledge was institutionalized and compartmentalized and in it the post-conquest centuries constituted a huge vacuum. One discipline, archaeology, concentrated entirely on the pre-conquest civilizations. In the archaeological view, Indian societies were 'pure' up to the time of white contact, after which they became contaminated and no longer fit for study. A second discipline, history, reported the details of conquest at length and proceeded to view the post-conquest period from an administrative and imperial perspective. Historians paid some attention to encomienda and the Christian mission, institutions in direct contact with the Indian population. But they had a very imperfect knowledge of post-conquest Indian societies themselves. Human history was understood to be a process involving change, and preferably progressive change, and although certain sectors of Latin America could be regarded as having undergone historic

---

[1] Alexander von Humboldt, *Political essay on the Kingdom of New Spain*, trans. John Black, ed. Mary Maples Dunn (New York, 1972), 53.

change these contrasted with the Indian sectors, which were seen as unchanged, unprogressive, and in some sense unhistorical. A third discipline, ethnology, picked up the Indian subject in contemporary times. Its preoccupation was with traits that might be identified as Indian or Spanish in origin, and the ratio between traits of supposedly Indian origin and traits of supposedly Spanish origin became a principal object of study. But this kind of taxonomic historicism was as far as ethnology was prepared to go in its recognition of the past. It paid minimal attention to real antecedents, and one of the discipline's conspicuous features was its contemporary orientation.

Thus, until very recently, knowledge of the American Indian remained fragmented and dispersed. The three disciplines continued to function separately, and none made intelligible the transition of Indian society from the conquest period to the present. The few individuals who were concerned with aspects of colonial Indian life were students of the codices, such as Eduard Seler, a leader in codical and epigraphical research in the late nineteenth and early twentieth centuries. Or they were students of native languages, such as Remi Siméon, who translated colonial Mexican annals from Nahuatl to French in the late nineteenth century. Or, in the aftermath of the Mexican revolution of 1910, they were *indigenistas*, such as Manuel Gamio, who advocated a comprehensive study of the Indian, combining archaeology, history, and ethnology, and whose great three-volume work, *La población del valle de Teotihuacán* (1922), was the first to examine a native community from its archaeological beginnings to modern times. In Peruvian studies a few dedicated persons – we think of Clements Markham, Hiram Bingham, and Philip Means – touched occasionally on colonial Indian subjects. But no one had as yet looked upon Indian post-conquest history as a topic worthy of separate treatment, with a character and identity of its own.

Serious research on colonial Indian history has been confined principally to the period since 1940. In Mexico it began as an extension of institutional studies concerned with labour and tribute, and demographic studies that used the statistics of tribute records. The demographic figures, or many of them, had been available for a long time, but it was only in the 1940s and 1950s that they were assembled and compared in a way that demonstrated a high population at the time of the conquest and a sharp decline thereafter. The studies focused new attention on local places and place-names, Indian family size, liability to tribute exaction, internal social structure, the decline of productivity, and the economy of the seventeenth century. In Peru, where colonial Indian studies for most topics began later and where they continue now in a less developed form, an important documentary stimulus has been the records of local tours of inspection (*visitas*). In both areas recent decades have witnessed the emergence of the intermediate discipline called ethnohistory. In Spanish American studies as elsewhere, social sciences have become more aware of a chronological dimension, and within all relevant disciplines the fashion for peasant studies, very evident in the 1960s and 1970s, has had a stimulating effect on research in colonial Indian history. The fact remains, nevertheless, that we are dealing with a new topic, still inadequately and unevenly known.

EARLY CONTACTS AND COLONIAL INSTITUTIONS

Indians first encountered Spaniards at the time of the discovery by Columbus in 1492. Thereafter for a period of 25 years Spanish expansion into new areas and additional Spanish contacts with Indians occurred only gradually, so that as late as 1517 the number of native peoples in direct or indirect association with Spaniards probably amounted to fewer than 10 per cent of the total aboriginal population of America. In the subsequent 25 years, between 1517 and 1542, with the rapid Spanish incursions into Central America, Mexico, Peru, northern South America, and northern Chile, and with the temporary Spanish penetrations into Amazonia and the region north of the Rio Grande, the percentage of Indians affected rose to 90 or more. After 1542 Spanish relations with Indians were modified in numerous ways, but few new contacts remained to be made, and those that were made occurred at a far slower pace.

In general, early Spanish–Indian encounters in the West Indies and mainland coastal areas resembled, and on the Spanish side were derived from, contacts with natives on the Atlantic coast of Africa and in the Canary Islands. The West Indian natives were sedentary agriculturists, distributed in small or medium-sized communities, with social classes, priests, a developed religion, warfare, a canoe-borne commerce, and local hereditary or elected rulers. The first island to become important in the West Indies was Hispaniola, where Indians of all classes were captured, enslaved, and put to work in farming, mining, carrying, construction, and related tasks. We lack reliable documentation on the coercion, the disruption of families, the illnesses, the mortality, and the economic dislocations of Indian society in the West Indies. But it is virtually certain that all these were present to an extreme degree, and we know that the population of the islands began at a very early date the precipitous decline that would end within a few generations in the total disappearance of Indians from this part of America. As the population dropped, Spanish slave raiding moved out into more distant islands, and an ever larger area fell under Spanish control. Miscellaneous military forays in other islands culminated in the organized military conquest of Cuba (1511), an event that served as precedent and model for the major conquests of the mainland. Conquest in its major phase terminated in 1542 with the Coronado expedition to the American West and the Orellana expedition down the Amazon. In general conquest proceeded most rapidly and proved to be most effective against the organized Indian states, for these fell to the Spaniards as unified entities. When an urban capital fell, the whole imperial area lost much of its power to resist. In the more loosely organized and weaker societies, on the other hand, Indians could fight on and each community could resist separately. Conquest was intense and disruptive, but its principal effect for the larger history is that it placed Indians under Spanish jurisdiction and rendered them liable to Spanish law and to the whole range of Spanish controls and influences, legal and illegal. Moreover, because Spanish imperialism was self-consciously monopolistic, conquest carried with it the implied or explicit rejection of other, non-Hispanic European influences upon Indians.

To these generalizations there were some significant exceptions. In parts of Spanish America (Hispaniola, fringe areas of the Aztec and Inca empires, California), where overt military conquest was absent or much reduced, its place was taken on the Spanish side by a force or threat of force sufficient to achieve an equivalent Indian subordination. Indians in some areas (northern Mexico, Florida, central Chile), resisted conquest for long periods, thereby postponing the imposition of Spanish rule. In a few places (parts of the Argentine pampas, southern Chile, remote and marginal regions everywhere) the native inhabitants were never conquered, and they remained effectively separate during the entire Spanish colonial period. Indian rebellions (Peru in the 1530s and the eighteenth century, New Mexico in the late seventeenth century, and many others) occasionally thwarted Spanish controls after they had been imposed, returning selected Indian societies, always temporarily, to an independent and hostile status. Individuals and groups, and in sixteenth-century Peru an entire Indian 'state', were sometimes able to flee from the areas of Spanish control and find refuge in remote regions.

Conquest was not a necessary preliminary to Christian conversion, but in practice in the Indian experience it was closely followed by conversion, and in both the Spanish and the Indian understanding there was a connection between the two. To Indians Christianity appeared to be what made the Spaniards strong. Christianity was especially impressive from the perspective of those whose own gods of war had failed them. On the Spanish side, Christian missionaries responded to the immense challenge of pagan America with a conversion effort unmatched in 1,500 years of Christianity. The principal campaign occurred in the early years, though subsequent efforts to extirpate remnant pagan idolatries were common in the seventeenth and eighteenth century. Conversion *per se* was restricted chiefly to the period of early contact in each area, for Spaniards were determined that Indians should be incorporated into colonial society as Christian vassals of the monarchy.

The most important early secular institution governing relations between Spaniards and Indians was *encomienda* or *repartimiento*. Its basic and universal feature was the assignment of groups of Indians to selected Spanish colonists (*encomenderos*) for tribute and labour. The terms *encomienda* and *repartimiento* referred essentially to the same institution, although the latter literally stressed the act of distribution and assignment while the emphasis of encomienda was on the responsibility of the encomendero towards his Indians. *Encomienda* was the preferred word in Spanish law and in ordinary metropolitan usage. The encomendero's responsibility included the Christian welfare of his Indians, and this meant that a resident or itinerant cleric was to be provided for. The basically secular character of encomienda was, however, never seriously questioned.

Encomienda developed in the West Indies during the second decade of the sixteenth century. It began as a substitute for slavery, or as an official compromise between the extreme enslavement practised by the first colonists and the free labour system theoretically approved by the crown. With respect to Arawaks, Caribs, and other Indians of the islands and mainland coast, from Venezuela north to Florida, early encomienda was a covering institution for the continuation of the armed raids, capture, removal, and enslavement practices of the first years. Encomienda in Mexico and Central America differed from the early insular prototype in its emphasis on the established Indian community as the assigned unit and in its dependence on community resources and social structures. Thus, on the mainland, sedentary Indian life was preserved in a more stable form than on the islands. In Peru encomienda followed the institutional model of New Spain, but it was delayed in its definitive establishment by the prolongation of conquest and civil war. Elsewhere in South America the institution might imply any of a number of degrees of assimilation. Where populations were sparse, where peoples were partly or wholly migratory, encomienda was inappropriate or appropriate only as a device for slave raiding. In Paraguay, where encomienda achieved its most stable lowland form, Indians served the encomenderos as labourers, servants, and polygamous wives. A mestizo society developed in Paraguay with kinship ties derived from Indian society. In extreme cases encomienda provided only a permit to trade with the designated Indian people. Thus the institution took a variety of forms, depending on the degree of Spanish pressure and the size and character of the Indian population. But the classic type, that which developed in the Aztec and Inca areas and their adjacent regions in western Mexico, Central America, Venezuela, Colombia, Ecuador, and northern Chile, was the large-scale exploitative institution involving an Indian society now fragmented into independent communities, each dominated by a Spanish encomendero and his staff.

The decline of encomienda in the second half of the sixteenth century was the consequence of a number of factors. Indian depopulation reduced the value of each holding. A progressively more effective royal legislation, motivated by Christian humanitarianism towards Indians and fear of a rising encomendero class in America, surrounded encomienda by ever more stringent regulations. Tribute and labour demands were progressively limited. Inheritance of encomienda from one generation to another was regulated or forbidden. Royal judicial authority established an effectual imperial law. By the late sixteenth century encomienda was well advanced in its long process of decline. In Yucatán, Paraguay, and a few other areas it persisted without major change, but elsewhere it gradually disappeared or was converted into a system of treasury grants to persons who were still called encomenderos but who exercised no control over Indian life.

As individual encomiendas reverted to the crown their Indians came officially under direct royal authority. This authority normally took the form of *corregimiento* (or *alcaldía mayor*), in which a royal official entitled *corregidor* (or *alcalde mayor*) was placed in charge of a local colonial jurisdiction. His duties included the exercise of local justice, exaction of Indian tribute, execution of royal law, and maintenance of order in the Indian community. Though sometimes aided by lieutenants (*tenientes*) and other staff members, the corregidor was regarded as the royal official in most direct control of local Indian areas. Corregidores represented royal rule in place of the personal, private rule of the encomenderos, and the intention was that they should treat Indians more humanely. In practice exploitation of Indians by corregidores in defiance of the law came to be accepted and institutionalized.

Beginning in the second half of the sixteenth century the private sector gained an immense new power, outside of encomienda, through land ownership, operation of mines, and commerce. This private sector was principally white, and it depended on Indian society for its raw materials and its labour. Royal officials, though forbidden to engage in the exploitative practices attendant on this development, did so with virtual impunity. Such practices were for the most part tolerated by the ineffective monarchy at least until the Bourbon reforms of the late eighteenth century, and they contributed to the classic types of Indian subordination, reorganization, and acculturation to which the main part of our discussion will now be devoted.

POLITICAL STRUCTURES

Spanish rule quickly fragmented all the larger political structures of native America. This was true of the Aztec and Inca empires as well as of the smaller and less developed Chibcha, Tarascan, northern Araucanian, and other political organizations. The largest Indian unit to survive the process of fragmentation was commonly the town, called *pueblo*, or the leading town, called *cabecera*. In theory at least, and to some extent in practice, the fragmentation re-established an Indian political society of discrete communities, the justification being that these units had existed prior to the creation of the Aztec, Inca, and other states and that they had been forced to join those states against their will. Thus the New Spanish state could be understood as a liberating agency rendering the rulers of local communities again 'independent'. Spanish theory postulated an alliance of king and local Indian ruler, each being understood to be a natural lord, a *señor natural*, in opposition to the illegitimate, and now rejected, imperial bureaucracies of Aztec and Inca and other Indian overlords.

The change from pre-colonial to colonial government involved a 'decapitation' of the native structure, with the cut coming just above the level of the native community. In place of Montezuma, Atahualpa, their councils, staffs, and aides, and the equivalents of these in other areas, the colonial organization introduced Spanish viceroys and the imperial apparatus down to the corregidor or his *teniente*. Only rarely did the colonial jurisdictions above the level of the town manifest a continuing Indianism. One might say, of course, that the two great colonial viceregal jurisdictions (*reinos*) themselves reflected the two great imperial areas of pre-conquest America. Other examples might be the early Spanish appointment of such 'puppet rulers' as Juan Velázquez Tlacotzin in Mexico and Manco Inca in Peru, or the area affected in a colonial labour summons, or a special political connection between one town and another. But all such survivals are interesting chiefly as isolated vestiges or as exceptions to the rule that Spaniards destroyed the larger native systems and concentrated on the unit town.

The term *cabecera*, principal town, is more specific here than the term *pueblo*, which may refer to any town, including a town subordinate to the cabecera. In the usual case, subsidiary political organizations below the level of the cabecera were permitted to remain. In Spanish terminology the smaller pueblos falling within a cabecera jurisdiction were its *sujetos*, and they were understood to owe allegiance to that cabecera and to be governed by it. *Sujetos* might be barrios, i.e., wards or quarters or subdivisions of the cabecera itself, or they might be estancias or ranches or *rancherías* situated at a distance. Other terms might be substituted for these, but the basic concept of the independent Indian town, subdivided into barrios and governing a local network of satellite villages or families, emerged as a fundamental and universal principle of colonial political structure. It was accepted by both Indians and Spaniards. In general it was this political unit, singly or in combinations of two, three, or more, that was granted in encomienda, that became a parish in the colonial ecclesiastical organization, and that became a corregimiento jurisdiction in the colonial political organization. It is true that the geographical jurisdictions of encomienda, parish, and corregimiento rarely coincided absolutely. But the differences among them were more the consequence of differing cabecera combinations and of minor deviations in boundary or structure than of any real change in the functioning of the cabecera–sujeto unit.

In theory the chieftains of these units – under the titles *tlatoani* in Mexico and *curaca* in Peru, and with other titles elsewhere – inherited

their positions in accordance with Indian succession rules. But even in
the early colonial period such chieftains were frequently interlopers.
This was because succession rules were flexible and manipulable,
because local dynasties came to an end in the conquest or the aftermath
of the conquest, and because encomenderos and other Spaniards had
an interest in inserting their own Indian protégés as local rulers. The
term *cacique*, an Arawak word brought by Spaniards from the West
Indies, increasingly displaced the various local mainland titles for such
chieftains. The new usage may well have been fostered by the many
usurpations of local dynastic offices, for a challenger could more easily
assume the borrowed title 'cacique' than the local title to which he had
no proper claim. Of course not all caciques were illegitimate rulers by
native standards. Nevertheless there is a certain irony in the Spanish
position that the regional caciques were to be identified as *señores
naturales*.

Local Indian leaders in the towns, with whatever title, were instrumental in promoting the Spanish institutions of church, encomienda,
and corregimiento. Clergy, encomenderos, and corregidores depended
on the local Indian rulers to implement the colonial institutions. In cases
of non-cooperation or outright resistance, clergy, encomenderos, and
corregidores were in a position to use compulsion or in extreme cases
to banish or kill local rulers and install more cooperative successors.
Such practices, to be sure, contributed to the usurpations and the
illegitimate *caciquismos* referred to above. But they also help to explain
how Spaniards in the post-conquest world were able to establish
Christianity, encomienda, and corregimiento, with so little opposition
from native peoples. Local caciques, even illegitimate ones, were
persons of tremendous power in their communities, and Spaniards
deliberately won them over by favours or by force.

Further political Hispanicization in the Indian towns occurred during
the middle and late sixteenth century. This began in New Spain where
the town were induced – by viceroys, clergy, encomenderos, and
corregidores – to develop the governing institutions of peninsular
Iberian municipalities. This meant *cabildos* (town councils), with *alcaldes*
(judges), *regidores* (aldermen), and various lesser officials, all Indians.
Indian towns responded positively to demands for such political
Hispanicization, and this also may reflect pressure exerted by Spaniards
upon key Indian leaders and a corresponding pressure exerted by these
upon the communities. By the late sixteenth century large cabeceras in

New Spain commonly supported councils with two or four Indian judges, and eight, ten, or twelve Indian aldermen. Smaller cabeceras might have only a single judge, and two or four aldermen. All would be members of the upper class within Indian society. As in peninsular Spain the *regidores* might be representatives of particular barrios or *sujetos*. The Indian judges heard criminal cases involving Indians, thus maintaining a distinct court in the first instance. Some of the remarkable intricacy and complication of the Spanish municipal prototype was reflected in Indian political institutions of the mid sixteenth century and after, as in representative and rotational schemes for election and service. Ordinarily the judges and aldermen were elected by the incumbent town council itself or by a core of Indian voters, the *vecinos* or *vocales* of the Indian community.

In the sixteenth century the new native government by cabildo came to serve as the principal intermediary between the Spanish state and the Indian population. In some places a new Indian officer, generally called *gobernador* or *alcalde mayor*, was chosen by the *vecinos* or by the town council at intervals of one or two or more years, or in some cases was appointed by viceregal authority for longer periods. This new Indian officer presided over the cabildo and rivalled and eventually outdistanced the cacique in local power and influence. That caciques increasingly lost out to town councils in the struggle for political control meant a decline in the principle of hereditary *cacicazgo* in Indian life. In the seventeenth century a cacique might still be an influential local figure by virtue of his lands and wealth, but his grandson or great-grandson in the eighteenth century might be almost indistinguishable from the mass of the Indian population. Thus in the internal Indian government in the towns, the adopted Spanish principles of institutionalized, elective, or appointive conciliar government did prevail over the original Indian principle of dynastic, hereditary, personal government. It was a process that in some cases was accomplished within a few years in the sixteenth century, while in other cases it required a longer time. Like much else introduced by the Spaniards it appeared in a more pronounced and effective form in the main communities of the heavily populated zones. In less developed, less densely populated, and more remote zones the original rule by local cacique continued to the end of the colonial period.

In the larger Indian towns of New Spain sixteenth-century political Hispanicization proceeded still further. The town councils were housed in *casas de cabildo* built in Spanish municipal styles and situated on the main plazas. They contained courtrooms and residence quarters, various chambers, an assembly hall for the Indian cabildo, and frequently a gaol. Judges and aldermen entered their hall ceremoniously after the manner of Spanish council members in cities of Spaniards. The Spanish procedures of call to order, roll, discussion, and vote were imitated in these Indian town councils. Minutes were kept, sometimes in the Indian language now transliterated into a written language. The *alcaldes* as a whole legislated on local matters, assigned plots, regulated markets, arranged celebrations, organized tribute collection and provision of labour, and ruled on the multitude of matters that required attention in municipal government.

But it should be remembered that an Indian cabildo, however Hispanicized, was never a truly powerful institution. Its authority was confined to the narrow range of options permitted it by the local clergy, encomendero, and corregidor, and these persons, singly or in combination, made the chief local decisions. In addition, as with so many other aspects of Spanish American colonial history, the seventeenth and early eighteenth centuries witnessed a stagnation or retrogression with respect to political Hispanicization. It does not seem to be a question of reversion to original Indian practices of community government, for these were largely forgotten by the seventeenth century. Town councils throughout the Hispanic world, in white society as in Indian society, lost some of their meaning in the seventeenth century and became still more formalized, conservative, and limited. The huge demographic losses suffered by Indian America and the depressed condition of Indian society as a whole were clearly reflected in a loss of status by local Indian governments. An increasing miscegenation began to call into question the very concept of 'Indian' governments in the towns. Caciques and cabildo members were required by law to be Indians. But here as elsewhere the concept of 'Indian' permitted a degree of interpretation, and mestizos acting as Indians are known to have infiltrated the offices of Indian government occasionally in the sixteenth century and with increasing frequency thereafter.

The funding of the Indian town governments was always precarious, and local councils were constantly on the lookout for sufficient sources of income. Community treasuries were *cajas de comunidad*, as in towns of Spaniards. They received revenue from each Indian family head, who contributed a fixed amount to support the local government, often by the same process as that by which tribute payments to the Spanish government were made. Indian towns sometimes required their residents to supply maize or other commodities, which the cabildo could then sell for a money income. Plots of town land might be assigned for this purpose. The herding of sheep or other animals on town properties and the rental or sale of community lands to Spaniards or to other Indians were additional methods by which towns obtained funds. It was assumed by Spanish administrators that the communities would use such funds for both municipal expenses – such as salaries for council members, construction of town buildings, or payments on outstanding debts – and, in the colonial phrase, the *ornato del culto*, or the maintenance of the church and the performance of religious services. The treasuries might be wholly accessible to the local corregidor or the local cleric, or both, and these Spanish officials could in effect dictate the disposition of funds. Town financial records of the seventeenth and eighteenth centuries show large expenses for church and fiesta supplies – wine, flowers, food, gifts to clergy, fireworks, costumes – as well as the normal and expectable expenses for secular political operations.

Indian town governments provided additionally a structure for the maintenance of Indian class systems. In central New Spain the distinction was between upper-class Indians, generally called *principales*, and lower-class Indians, generally called *macehuales*. The *principales* were the descendants of a pre-conquest Aztec upper class whose members were called *pipiltin* (singular, *pilli*). The many special military and other titles of the *pipiltin* fell into abeyance or disappeared entirely during the sixteenth century. But in the Hispanicized municipal governments only the *principales* were eligible for positions in the cabildo. *Principales* did serve in council offices in the mid sixteenth century and after, and for the most part the holding of such an office was testimony to the upper-class rank of the individual concerned. But the restriction of office holding to *principales* was soon subjected to strain, for Spanish rules also required annual elections and forbade re-election of the same person to a council office. With population decline, particularly in the smaller towns, it became impossible to abide by these inconsistent regulations, and the usual solution was not the admission of *macehuales* to office-holding, as might be supposed, but rather a vigorous defiance of the rule against re-election. Thus a local Indian aristocracy successfully controlled the town governments for a time, and the same persons year after year occupied the new offices despite the law.

But the *principales* of central New Spain were unable to maintain their position in the deteriorating circumstances of later colonial times. Increasingly, in one cabildo after another, and in the society at large, the distinction between *principales* and *macehuales* faded away. Spaniards had at first emphasized the distinction between them, not only in council offices but with respect to other kinds of privilege, exemption, and status. The decline of the cabildos in the seventeenth century paralleled the decline of the *principales* and the elimination or neglect of their privileges. Some lost their lands and retainers and wealth and became indistinguishable from *macehuales*. Others left the Indian community, migrated to the city, and entered the company of mestizos, mulattos, Negroes, and the urban proletariat. Mestizos, mulattos, and Negroes meanwhile infiltrated the cabildos, contributing to the breakdown of the concept of 'Indian' town government, but particularly jeopardizing the traditional role of the *principales*, for they were the ones who had dominated the offices of that government.

In Peru the *curacas* emerged as powerful local authorities in the post-conquest world, and they filled the universal cacique role of puppet ruler in mediating Spanish and Indian society. In the sixteenth century their colonial territories commonly retained the pre-conquest sub-divisions and the subordinate officials in an unbroken continuity. Like their equivalents in Mexico, the Peruvian *curacas* were then threatened by the new Hispanicized, institutionalized Indian governments. Indian cabildos, first formulated for the principal towns in the mid sixteenth century, proliferated rapidly. By 1565 the city of Lima had three, one for the Indian residents, one for those who had migrated from elsewhere, and a third for the inhabitants of the immediately surrounding area. The cabildos' powers related to properties, markets, gaols, and other local affairs, of course under the superior jurisdiction of Spanish authorities. The Indian *alcaldes* exercised justice in the first instance and the Indian *alguaciles* constituted a local police force. Most communities had two *alcaldes*, but Cuzco had eight in the early seventeenth century, and Huancavelica had eighteen *alcaldes de minas* in the eighteenth century.

The *curacas* were able to take advantage of their situation in ways that were not available to their counterparts in Mexico. Beginning in the 1560s the Indian nobles in Peru petitioned for and received titles as *alguaciles* and *alcaldes mayores*. A typical petition described the aristocratic lineage and the services that the Indian author had contributed to

Pizarro or some other *conquistador*. A successful candidate for the position of *alcalde mayor* had the authority to appoint annual judges and aldermen and to administer local justice in the name of the king. Some were given charge of the maintenance of the roads, bridges, and way stations that had survived from Inca times. By 1600 Indian *alcaldes mayores* had been installed through the whole Incaic area from Quito to Potosí. The offices came in effect to be monopolized by *curacas*, who were able to prevent their falling into the hands of lesser Indians. The Peruvian institution thus served to support and prolong the class of *curacas* more than other classes. But by the end of the colonial period this also had deteriorated. Spaniards and mestizos pre-empted some of the offices of the council and even the office of *alcalde mayor*.

A subject that is still poorly understood and that requires intensive comparative research concerns the *calpulli* and the *ayllu*. These terms refer to the basic social units above the level of the family, in Mexico and Peru respectively. Students have debated the character of these units, whether or not they represented kin groups, whether or not they may be translated as 'barrio' or 'ward', the extent of the jurisdiction that they exercised. The terms need to be accurately differentiated from other terms, e.g. *tlaxilacalli*, which in Mexico appears to have had a meaning very similar to *calpulli*. The distribution and usage need to be studied (it appears that in the sixteenth century the term *calpulli* was more commonly used in Guatemala than in central Mexico). The point of special interest here, however, once we learn what the units really were, concerns their durability in the colonial period and thereafter. It has been argued that they were the essential Indian social elements, without which Indian life and culture could not have survived to modern times.

RELIGION

It was with respect to religion that the Spaniards made their most determined effort to modify Indian society. This was because many features of Indian religion were offensive from the point of view of Christianity and because Christianity was held by the Spaniards to be the only true religion. Spaniards were willing to use force on occasion to destroy temples and idols, extirpate human sacrifice and other practices, and punish recalcitrants. But in principle Spaniards believed in non-coercive Christianization, and the missionary effort, despite its intensity and its universality, was in most respects a peaceful operation.

In this it differed, and Indians could readily see that it differed, from the military conquests that immediately preceded it.

Native American religions were far from uniform, but they may be characterized as fundamentally polytheistic and animistic, with the worship of celestial bodies and natural phenomena, propitiation of deities, shamanism, and a participatory ceremonial. The most sophisticated American religions included cult objects, intricate calendars, temples and similar religious buildings, priestly classes, and rich astrological and narrative literatures. Some became celebrated among Spaniards for their inclusion of elements similar to those of Christianity, especially baptism, confession, marriage, and the symbol of the cross.

Serious, large-scale conversion efforts began in the 1520s in Mexico and spread rapidly through native America in the aftermath of the conquest armies. The missionaries' first task was to eliminate the outstanding evidences of paganism and to terminate or reduce the power of the native priests, and for the most part these steps were successfully accomplished during the first generation. Thereafter the missionaries placed a strong emphasis on the essential tenets, and the most visible features, of the Christian religion. Here the assumption was that the finer points of faith and doctrine could reasonably be postponed. Few active missionaries could devote time to the prolonged training necessary for full conversion. Especially at first the missionaries concentrated on mass baptism and rudimentary sacramental instruction. We have evidence from various parts of native America that Indians assembled willingly and enthusiastically for mass baptism. But other evidence suggests that the reports of enthusiastic early Indian attendance at mass baptism may have been exaggerated by the optimistic missionaries. The elements of native religion that resembled Christianity were sometimes utilized as aids or guides in Christian instruction, but it is also true that missionaries feared the similar pagan practices as the work of the devil, designed to trap the unwary and distort the Christian purpose. As time progressed, the need and occasion for mass baptism and initial learning of course diminished.

With respect to Indian religious belief the end result was syncretism, or the fusion of pagan and Christian faiths. The fusion appeared in a number of forms. Indians might retain a fundamentally polytheistic position by accepting the Christian deity as one additional member of a pantheon, or by giving first attention to the Trinity or the community of saints rather than to the Christian God. The crucifixion might appear as a form of human sacrifice. Indians who seemed to be worshipping in the Christian manner might place idols behind the altars, as if in the hope of a response if the Christian religion should fail. Particulars of the Christian faith might be incorporated into an essentially pagan world view. Clergy throughout the colonial period sought out and discovered evidence of surviving paganism in hidden cult objects or covert practices.

The first missionaries moved from town to town and area to area, but as their numbers increased an orderly episcopal and parochial system developed, with resident clergy in the larger Indian communities. Indians in outlying areas were then reached by regular or irregular visitation. Missionaries gave special attention to the sons of upper-class Indians, in the knowledge that these would become the leaders of the next generation and would be in a position to exert a Christian influence upon the community in the future. By the same principle, upper-class Indians who resisted Christianity or reverted, after conversion, to pagan forms of worship were liable to severe punishment. Numerous cases of whipping and imprisonment and occasional cases of execution for these causes are recorded. Clergy conducted Christian services in the towns, at first in temporary buildings or open chapels, subsequently in churches, often large and impressive churches, built by Indian labour. Local clergy in the sixteenth century frequently functioned within the institution of encomienda. This circumstance sometimes determined the location of churches or in other ways influenced the course of the Christianization programme.

In an Indian community of the seventeenth century anywhere in Spanish America, Christianity played a leading role. The church was the largest and most imposing structure in every town. It dominated a complex of subordinate buildings, sometimes including a monastery. All had been built by Indians, often in voluntary and unrecompensed labour, and maintenance and repair had likewise been Indian work. Unless it were a large community it would ordinarily have only one resident white priest. Indians were forbidden ordination as priests, but all minor church tasks were performed by Indians, and an Indian hierarchy of officials was basic to the maintenance of the religious community. The principal religious rites, including baptisms, marriages, and funerals, were conducted in the church and provided a predictable and orderly ritual for Indian lives. The day of the town's patron saint, often the saint after whom the town was named, was a great local festival day, distinguishing one Indian community from its neighbours, sometimes in an atmosphere of competition. Certain saints' images were locally celebrated for bleeding, sweating, talking, or healing. A few locations – Guadalupe in Mexico and Copacabana in Peru are outstanding examples – became Indian pilgrimage sites. In every community fiestas were semi-religious occasions, providing release from routine and promoting collective loyalty to church, state, and society.

A Christian institution to which the Indians of Spanish America came to give special attention was the *cofradía* (sodality). *Cofradías* appear not to have been established by the early missionaries, nor were they considered appropriate for Indians during the first 50 years or so of Christianity in the colony. They grew up in Indian society in the late sixteenth and seventeenth centuries, and they then multiplied and spread. No student has yet catalogued the history and distribution of these sodalities in the Spanish colonies. But there can be no question that by the mid seventeenth century a large number had been established in the Indian towns. An individual parish, depending on circumstances, might have from one to six or more. Each had its functions in the maintenance of the church and in the fulfilment of the Christian life. *Cofradías* financed and managed chapels, Masses, ecclesiastical festivals, charities, and certain landed and other properties of the church. Indian members supported the *cofradía* treasury with initiation fees and regular dues, the funds then being allocated by the sodality's majordomo to meet the designated expenses. In some cases membership conferred plenary indulgence, and the funds were used to provide for shrouds, coffins, Masses, vigils, and burials when members died. Thus in addition to their other functions, *cofradías* might be institutions of individual insurance, guaranteeing favourable conditions for both body and soul after death. Their communal features reflect the developed, pervasive, institutionalized Christianity of the seventeenth and eighteenth centuries. They provided an organized mode of life, and Indians were perhaps the more attracted to them as the secular institutions of Indian society increasingly failed to provide equivalent satisfactions. The sodality records sometimes reveal a deliberate Indianism, a sense of the Indians' separation from and distrust of white society.

TRIBUTE

That Indians should pay tribute was one of the earliest and most fundamental of Spanish convictions in the colonial world. The tradition derived from Spain, where peasants were *pecheros*, payers of *pecho* or tribute. In America, where colonists paid no *pecho*, the tribute obligation fell on the new, non-Spanish lower class. In theory Indians paid tribute as the obligation of 'vassals' (this term was used in the colonial period) to the crown, and in return for the benefits or supposed benefits of Spanish civilization. Many Indians had paid tribute in their pre-conquest state, a fact that facilitated both the theory and the practice of Spanish tribute exaction.

Spanish seizures of goods, especially gold, in the early, Caribbean phase of conquest and settlement came gradually to be regulated in encomienda, by which the king granted to an intermediary, the encomendero, the privilege of receiving the tribute that Indians otherwise owed to the crown. Tribute became one of the principal devices of control exercised by encomenderos over Indians, and their tribute collectors, themselves commonly Indians, were among the most feared of the encomenderos' agents. A large part of the contemporary commentary on encomienda to the mid sixteenth century concerns excesses in tribute collection.

As in other aspects of encomienda, excesses in tribute collection were made possible by the encomenderos' reliance on local Indian leaders. Tribute was delivered first to the cacique in the early period, and a portion was then extracted under the cacique's direction to be turned over to the encomendero. In the absence of such co-operation from caciques or their equivalents, Spaniards had no reliable means of requiring tribute payments from Indians. But this co-operation also permitted caciques to drain off large parts of the Indians' tribute for their own enrichment. Early criticisms of the encomenderos, to the effect that they were extortionate in their demands, often failed to allow for the Indian caciques, who might be even more extortionate. The situation provides one of our most telling examples of colonial oppression within Indian society itself.

Royal efforts to curb the encomenderos meant that fixed amounts of tribute, ordinarily based on counts or estimates of the Indian population of the encomiendas, were now legislated. Given the methods of collection, which were well known, the crown was obliged to set limits both on the encomenderos' and on the caciques' incomes from tribute, and this was done. As local Indian governments increasingly drained power from caciques, tribute payments became more regularized and confined within an approximation of the legal limits. Caciques' incomes, like other evidence of caciques' authority, declined in the late sixteenth and the seventeenth centuries. The substitution of cabildo government for cacique government was a significant step in the process of establishing royal control over tribute exaction. In places where the town councils did not come into being Spaniards used other methods, including coercion, reward, and substitution, to ensure that caciques could both receive and pass on tribute without excessively exploiting the system to their own advantage.

Family heads were full tributaries in colonial Indian society. Widows, widowers, bachelors, and spinsters were half-tributaries. Encomiendas in the second half of the sixteenth century were legally limited to a tribute computed by multiplying the number of tributaries by the unit amount that each·was to pay. The figure constantly changed, for the Indian tributary population declined, a fact that explains why we have so many recorded population counts in the second half of the sixteenth century. But the familiar irregularities and complications persisted. Because Indians were still the collectors, i.e. the persons who visited the individual tributaries and received their payments, a basically Indian system of assessment could frequently be retained under the guise of a uniform capitation tax. This meant the covert perpetuation of group exemptions, computations based on land or wealth, embezzlement of funds, and additional practices that Spaniards were in no position to control. On the Spanish side also many obstacles stood in the way of an equitable system of payments by Indian tributaries. The unit tributary amount was still ordinarily made up of a money payment and a payment in kind, and the values of these varied markedly from place to place. In addition, the Spanish government, ever more in need of funds in the later sixteenth and the seventeenth centuries, imposed a number of new taxes on Indians, under such special titles as *servicio*, for naval defence, and *ministros*, for the costs of Indian litigation. Like the original 'tribute' these were also subject to local variation. Indian liability to the taxes designed for Spaniards, such as the *alcabala* (sales tax), likewise differed in time and place, and many local exactions, originally imposed temporarily and arbitrarily by agents of the state or the church, came to be permanently established by custom. It is not simply that Indians in Chile paid different amounts from those paid by Indians in Mexico. The inhabitants of two neighbouring towns in either colony might also pay quite different amounts. The Spanish effort to arrive at uniformity in assessment was never successful.

The tribute practices described above relate to encomienda, but it should be noted that the escheatment of encomiendas to the crown did nothing to halt irregularities in tribute exaction. Contemporary observers often found corregidores to be more demanding than encomenderos. Corregidores, like encomenderos, relied on the caciques or cabildos and conspired with them to reward the Indian tribute takers with a portion of the excess taken. They enforced illegal exactions in money, food, or other goods, and arranged tribute sales at illegal prices, with secret payments. They demanded *derechos* (fees or bribes) for population counts, investments in office, approval of council legislation, and other functions that by law should have been performed gratis. Corregidores found willing accomplices in malfeasance in Indian council members, who charged illegally for fiestas, voted additions to their own salaries, and in various ways used their offices to increase and divert tribute funds for their own profit.

Within the Indian community the exactions of tribute had some important influences upon local productivity. Many Indian goods – maize, cacao, native textiles, and numerous others – continued to be paid in tribute. Sometimes the tribute requirements were for payment in European goods, such as wheat, woollen textiles, money, chickens, or eggs. Indians raised or made European goods in order to sell them for the money that would be paid in tribute. Undoubtedly the cultivation or manufacture of European products constituted a step in the direction of Hispanicization. Yet it is clear that goods were frequently raised or made by Indians exclusively as tribute goods, without any intent or desire to adapt them into Indian life.

LABOUR

Legal and illegal enslavement of Indians for purposes of labour occurred principally in the West Indies and in the adjacent mainland from Central America to Venezuela. In Mexico and Peru the *conquistadores* were more concerned with encomienda than with outright slavery, but they did make slaves of Indians captured in the wars, justifying the action by the *Requerimiento* (which threatened slavery for Indians who

refused to surrender and receive the Christian gospel) or by the principle
that captives taken in a just and Christian war could be legitimately
enslaved. *Conquistadores* also argued that Indians who were slaves in their
own native society should continue to be slaves after the conquests,
since this involved merely perpetuation of a pre-existing status and not
a new act of enslavement. For a time the crown permitted Indian
enslavement in cases of rebellion and as punishment for particular
crimes. Throughout the sixteenth century and on into the seventeenth
we find instances of Indian slavery among captives taken in frontier wars
and among individuals sentenced for crime. But in general, after the
Laws of Burgos (1512), the prevailing principle was that Indians were
free persons and not slaves.

Information on the Spaniards' use of Indian labour in the West Indies
after the establishment of encomienda leaves much to be desired. Critics
charged, probably accurately, that encomienda labour hardly differed
from slavery, and that Indians continued to be overworked and
mistreated as they had been during the first years. Encomienda Indians
were sometimes sold or rented out by their encomenderos in defiance
of the law; little was done to ensure the labourers' Christianization or
to provide for their welfare in the way required by law. Mining,
transportation, agriculture, building, and military service were the main
categories of work. In the West Indies the encomiendas came to an end
within two generations through the extinction of the native population.
But it should not be assumed that the severe conditions of labour either
in slavery or in encomienda constituted a direct cause of this extinction.
As elsewhere, diseases introduced by Spaniards may be supposed to
have been the chief cause. It is true, of course, that the diseases may
have had more lethal consequences because of the fatigue, malnutrition,
and other conditions attending Spanish labour practices.

Encomienda on the mainland was an onerous institution for Indians,
but in the principal areas its labour component was limited to the first
colonial generations. For central Mexico we have an abundant
documentation on the subject, including some critical views by Indians
themselves. It is quite clear the encomenderos exploited their Indians
with respect to labour as they did with respect to tribute. As in tribute
they depended on caciques or other Indians as intermediaries and local
bosses. From the start the crown regarded the labour portion of
encomienda as a temporary and unsatisfactory expedient pending the

establishment of free wage labour, and it was this royal position that resulted in the removal of Indian labour from the encomenderos' control. The removal took place in the mid sixteenth century in central New Spain and a generation later in the central Andes. Thus by the late sixteenth century in the densely populated areas encomienda had become an institution for the exaction of tribute and could no longer be regarded as a source of private labour. Encomenderos desiring Indians as workers in these areas were now obligated to rely upon the new institution of labour *repartimiento* or *mita*.

Again we have a difference between the central and the outlying zones. Outside the central areas, in regions where the encomenderos were less numerous, encomienda continued to be an institution for regulating labour as well as an institution for collecting tribute. Even in the very late colonial period, surviving encomenderos still exercised this labour power in Chile, Paraguay, Yucatán, and elsewhere where the encomienda itself survived. The marginal survivals may perhaps be explained as instances of default. They were not important enough, from the metropolitan perspective, to constitute a threat to the crown or to provoke repressive legislation. In addition these were regions where the native social structures did not lend themselves to large-scale, organized labour drafts for agriculture or mining. The small-scale labour encomienda was the more appropriate institution in these areas because the local societies were fragmented or because they lacked the markets and mines and resources to sustain a comprehensive tribute or labour organization.

Labour *repartimiento*, as it was called in New Spain, or *mita*, the term used in Peru, was the new institution designed to regulate the work of Indians in the public sector following the separation of this work from the private or encomienda sector. Repartimiento was a response both to the increased number of Spaniards and to the reduced number of Indian labourers. It was a more economical system for the distribution of Indian labourers following the excesses and waste of manpower of encomienda. In repartimiento, each Indian community at periodic intervals became responsible for releasing a fraction of its able-bodied male population for labour. Each labouring group worked for its employer for a given period, ranging from a week to four months or more. The Indian workers then received a modest wage and returned to their communities while a new contingent, recruited and assigned in the same manner, took their places. As we have seen, encomenderos in the principal areas were now obliged to request repartimiento workers in the same way as other Spaniards.

The mita labour for the Peruvian mines at Potosí represents repartimiento in its most impressive form. Here in the late sixteenth and seventeenth centuries the flow of workers to and from the mine assumed the proportions of mass migrations. Local Indian officials directed the selection and organization. When the appointed day came the labourers formed a huge procession, with their families, llamas, food, and other supplies. From a distant province the journey required several months. In the seventeenth century many thousands of persons and animals were constantly wending their way to and from Potosí. Workers and their families might be away from their communities for a year or more. No other labour draft of the colony compared with this one for numbers of persons, duration, and intensity. The closest rivals in Mexico were for the rebuilding of Tenochtitlán in the sixteenth century and for the drainage of the Valley of Mexico in the early seventeenth century.

Repartimiento served the labour needs of the colony more effectively than encomienda had done, but it was increasingly subject to strain as the Indian population continued to decline. An Indian community of 400 tributaries, one that might originally have been required to supply eight or twelve or sixteen workers for each repartimiento draft, inevitably found itself less and less able to meet the quota as its population fell to 200 or 100 or even less. Spanish officials made some effort to adjust the quotas downward, but adjustments were commonly in arrears of the population loss, and in any case a lowering of the quota necessarily reduced the effectiveness of repartimiento as a means of labour recruitment. Indian communities now sought to hire outside workers or to send youths, the aged, or women to the repartimiento in order to fulfil their obligations. The strain on the communities and their Indian governments became severe, especially in those agricultural and mining areas where population loss was greatest.

In central New Spain the agricultural employers, no longer able to secure the workers they needed through repartimiento, made private labour contracts with individual workers, loaned money to Indians for repayment in labour, and in other ways defied or circumvented the system. The agricultural repartimiento deteriorated further and was finally abolished in 1633. The mining industry in New Spain had already ceased to depend on it, and this meant that only a few state-controlled operations, notably the drainage of the Valley of Mexico lakes, continued to receive such workers in substantial numbers.

Thus in the later seventeenth and eighteenth centuries, in central New Spain, most Indian labour was 'free'. As the native population again increased, conditions in the rural labour market became the reverse of what they had been. There were now too many workers for the number of jobs. Unemployed workers overflowed their pueblos and roamed the countryside. Because of the competition for employment the rural labourer's wage, having risen steadily from the early sixteenth century to the mid seventeenth century, remained almost constant for the next 150 years. The situation was advantageous for the hacendados, who kept a core of workers on their premises for year-round labour and could hire any number of additional labourers for seasonal needs.

In the central Andes a different situation prevailed. Here the mita remained the principal instrument for assembling the labour at Potosí and at other Peruvian mines throughout the colonial period. The mining technology was far behind the Mexican. In the eighteenth century great hoists were lifting the ore to the surface in Mexico, while in Peru Indian labourers were still climbing tiers of ladders carrying ore on their backs. In agriculture the Peruvian employers found many of the same deficiencies in the labour system that Mexican employers found. But the agricultural estates of Peru accommodated a special class of workers, the *yana* or *yanaconas*, formerly servants and workers for the Inca upper class. The *yanaconas* grew in number, relatively if not absolutely, in the sixteenth century as other Indians escaped the pressures of community life to join them. They were protected by law, favoured by the Spaniards, exempted at least in theory from tribute and mita, and bound to the land. The detailed history and further implications of the differences in labour conditions between the Andean highlands and central Mexico, both densely settled areas attractive to Spanish estate holders and employers, require further study and explanation.

Students have frequently identified peonage as the classic labour form of rural Spanish America. The supposition has been that hacienda owners and other landed employers characteristically compelled Indians to work by advancing them money and requiring repayment in labour. 'Classic' peonage assumes (1) an authoritarian hacendado unable or unwilling to maintain a labour force of hired workers, and (2) a group of impoverished Indian labourers desirous of escaping from their predicament but held through the circumstance of their debt. Through a series of subsequent loans, the hacendado then ensured that the debt would never be repaid in full. In extreme cases, after the original peon died, the still unredeemed debt was inherited by his son, and thus generation after generation whole Indian families were obligated to remain on the hacienda and commit themselves to lifetimes of labour. Peonage has been understood as an institution through which unscrupulous employers extracted the maximum of service from a controlled labour force at minimal expense. But recent studies suggest that peonage in these terms was less extensive in the colonial period than has been believed. The colonial record provides many instances of peonage in agriculture, mining, and other labour. But in particular areas the complex of pressures on Indian livelihood was such that Indian labourers did not need to be held by debt. An Indian of the seventeenth century, landless, unable to pay his tribute, without the resources to feed his family, willingly moved from his village to the hacienda. He might count himself fortunate to arrive and remain there, to work a plot of land, to receive a wage or a payment in advance of a wage, and to have the protective patronage of the owner. The hacienda sometimes assumed responsibility for his tribute payment, and it functioned further as an institution of credit, allowing him to fall into arrears in his obligations without incurring punishment or losing his job.

In the Spanish American cities, as in rural areas, Indians performed most of the labour. But the urban conditions were quite different from those of the countryside. Repartimiento labour for urban tasks was common in the sixteenth century, and it persisted intermittently, sometimes with long interruptions, throughout the colonial period. Food, fuel, fodder, and other goods for the city's officials and other residents were often supplied in a repartimiento institution that combined tribute in kind with the tasks of transporting and storing it. Some labour was for the construction or expansion of the urban zone. A class of Indians skilled at masonry, carpentry, and related occupations came quickly into being to serve as the teachers and bosses of the unskilled mass. The cities constantly needed workers. Houses had to be constructed and kept in repair. Churches and cathedrals were under construction for decades. Shops and public edifices, streets and bridges, water supplies and sewage systems all required labour, first for construction, then for repair, and finally for rebuilding. Indian residents of the towns and of the cities' environs were always regarded as the appropriate labourers for these tasks. They were summoned by repartimiento, and even after the formal repartimientos for these tasks were abolished, as they were for some cities, new ones kept the Indian labourers at special work.

An important difference between Indian labour in the cities and in the towns and countryside relates to crafts and craft guilds. Crafts in rural areas focused upon the utilitarian arts of native domestic and agricultural life: weaving of textiles, manufacture of pottery and baskets, fashioning of simple tools. Crafts in the city were far more complex. Spaniards expressed amazement at the rapidity with which Indians acquired the skills of Spanish manufacturing. In Mexico City Indians quickly learned to make gloves, shoes, saddles, glassware, and ironware. Within a generation following the fall of the Aztec capital, Indians were turning out doublets, waistcoats, breeches, and all the Spanish garments for sale in the Spanish markets of the city. The competition was acutely felt by Spanish tailors, shoemakers, silversmiths, and other craftsmen, who organized themselves in guilds and sought to resist or control the new Indian production. But by degrees Indians were admitted into the guilds as apprentices and journeymen and even as masters of some of the trades, and they progressively fused at these and all other social levels with Negroes, mestizos, and mulattos in the dense, mixed, crowded conditions of the city.

One more urban labouring institution is relevant to Indian life. This is the *obraje*, a workshop designed particularly for the production of woollen cloth. Obrajes began in the sixteenth century, with Indian labour. The chief tasks were washing, carding, spinning, and weaving. By the seventeenth century the obrajes had developed into exploitative sweatshops, and they became famous for their low wages and disreputable conditions. Indians and others found guilty of crimes were sentenced to obraje labour for periods of months or years, and Indians in this condition were known as slave labourers throughout colonial times.

LAND

In theory the Spanish imperial government respected Indian landholding and sought to confine Spanish lands to vacant areas or tracts whose transfer to Spanish ownership would not prejudice Indian interests. But in practice this principle was not adhered to. Spaniards naturally assumed possession of the valuable urban zones conquered in Tenochtitlán and Cuzco, and Indians were quite unable to resist the property pre-emptions in these and other cities by Cortés, Pizarro, and their *conquistador* followers. The land-granting authorities of the Spanish colonial government – cabildos, viceroys, and their agents – characteristically gave higher priority to Spanish interests than to Indian interests. Spanish colonists argued that they required more land for large-scale agriculture and cattle grazing than Indians did for their intensive, small-scale crop cultivation. To Spaniards the lands that Indians used for hunting or other community purposes seemed 'vacant' and hence available to them. There is a sense in which all the lands in America that ultimately came into Spanish possession were usurped from Indians. But the 'usurpations' were of many kinds, including purchase, trade, and voluntary bestowal by individual Indians, and the question of conflicting Spanish and Indian 'claims' is one of great complexity.

Historical attention has been directed in large part to the alienated 'village lands', lands that formerly fell under the jurisdiction of Indian communities and were then lost, usually to white hacendados or other property owners. In extreme cases all of a community's lands might be lost, for a hacienda could completely surround a town-site, causing the community in effect to be incorporated within the hacienda's jurisdiction. But the more common outcome in the colonial period was the loss of a portion of the community lands. This permitted the survival of the community in a politically independent status, but it increased the likelihood of its economic subordination to the hacienda. The relationship of political separation and economic domination served the interests of the hacienda, for the hacendado was relieved of the obligation of providing for the town and the continued availability of a nearby labour supply was assured.

Spanish colonists were originally attracted to the densely settled zones of central Mexico and the central Andes less for land than for booty, labour, and tribute. These zones were accordingly the areas of the major conquests and of the earliest and largest mainland encomiendas. Encomienda was the appropriate early institution here, and significantly it involved not a grant of land but a grant of Indians for tribute and work. In the Spanish peninsular heritage land ownership had traditionally provided economic profit and social status. But the transplanting of this tradition to the New World was delayed in the central zones of the colony precisely by the large, dense, landholding Indian population. Only with the decline of this population in the sixteenth century would quantities of land become available. One of the first and most consistent consequences of Indian demographic decline was the taking over of abandoned lands by Spanish colonists.

The process was not a simple one. In the Indian tradition a parcel of land vacated by the death of its occupant normally reverted to the community for reassignment to a new occupant. It was not understood to be available for occupation from outside. If there were no candidate within the community to whom the parcel might be assigned, the elders, the cacique, or the Indian cabildo might hold it unassigned as community property, pending the appearance of an appropriate holder. The holder in any case would have only the usufruct of the property. He could occupy it so long as he raised crops on it and used it to support his family. This characteristic communal Indian understanding of land use conflicted with the Spaniards' sense of absolute property and complicated any simple substitution of Spanish for Indian ownership when land became 'unoccupied' through death.

The community's capacity to retain its land, on the other hand, was severely strained under colonial conditions. Indian communities were weakened, not just reduced in size, by depopulation. When the difficulties became severe enough, Indian communities were forced to yield. If the Indian cabildo needed money to pay the town's tribute, it seemed preferable to rent out or sell property to Spaniards than to go to gaol for arrears in payment. The council members might further withhold properties from persons in their own community in order to have properties to rent or sell. The problems usually grew more pressing over time. Though they might be relieved to some extent by a year of abundance, they became progressively more critical in years of shortage. It was especially in periods of stress that Indian communities lost land and Spaniards gained it. In such periods, Indian communities were the more willing to sell land to Spanish colonists, and the colonists were the more anxious to buy, especially at reduced prices. Spanish colonial law, derivative as always from European precedents, tended to regard sale as a legitimate contractual arrangement between two willing persons irrespective of the surrounding circumstances.

Spanish law, at first supportive and protective of Indian landholding, subsequently provided new means for the transfer of Indian land to Spanish hands. In both Mexico and Peru the state policy of *congregación* (*reducción*) in the late sixteenth and seventeenth centuries meant that whole Indian town sites were destroyed, their occupants moved ('congregated' or 'reduced') to other places, and their lands sequestered. The justification was that Indians should live in compact units for the sake of social and political order, religious instruction, municipal control, and an acceleration of the civilizing process. In principle all Indian landholders resettled in *congregación* were to retain their landed possessions, or, if the resettlement were at too great a distance, to be compensated with equivalent lands near the new location. Spaniards always denied that *congregación* was designed as a means of land transfer. But this was its universal consequence.

When *congregación* was further implemented by the legal devices of *denuncia* and *composición*, the result was still more damaging for Indian land. *Denuncia* permitted any Spanish colonist to claim vacant land and, after some formalities and the payment of a fee, to hold it as legal owner. *Composición* permitted him to gain full legal possession of ('compose') any portion of his property that suffered from defective titles. *Denuncia* and composition· were particularly appropriate to the seventeenth century, the period of reduced Indian population, for this was a time of vacated land and weakened Indian resistance. Land rendered unoccupied by depopulation could be denounced or simply seized and held, and later composed. It is true that Indians, and not simply whites, were authorized to employ both these means for securing property. But in fact very few Indians did so, for Indians in general remained ignorant of the law, lacked the requisite funds, and had relatively few opportunities for turning the situation to their advantage. Even the increase in Indian numbers in the eighteenth century failed to stimulate any appreciable native recourse to *denuncia* or composition, both for the reasons stated and because by this time so much of the land, and especially the productive and usable land, had passed to other owners.

Apart from legal transfers the records of colonial land transactions are filled with evidence of falsification, threats, and other illegal practices. Individual Indians were persuaded to 'sell' portions of the community's common land to Spaniards. Spaniards negotiated for the sale of one property and received, or took, a more desirable one. Spaniards bribed or forced Indians to donate land. Indians rented out land to Spaniards and after receiving rent for a period of years were given to understand they had been receiving instalments on a sale and that a full transfer of ownership was now required. Against such practices the Indian community was sometimes able to offer short-term resistance or to blunt or delay the effect. Indians are known to have surreptitiously moved boundary markers, presented forged documents of title, and sought to deceive Spaniards in other ways. Indian communities able to afford the expense could bring legal action, and we know of many cases in which Indian communities won lawsuits in colonial courts against Spanish colonists who seized their land. But the long-term advantage lay on the Spanish side, for the Spaniards were wealthier and stronger, could offer higher prices and bribes, could employ more skilful lawyers, and could afford to await the next favourable opportunity. For the most part it was a process that proceeded in one direction. Lands that came under Spanish control rarely reverted to Indian possession.

ACCULTURATION

Most educational institutions established by Spaniards for Indians were associated with the campaigns for religious conversion. This was the case in the areas of dense Indian population during the early period, and it was the case afterwards on the frontiers, where missionaries continued to come into contact with unconverted Indians. In addition to the religious training, mission schools made some effort to provide the rudiments of a secular education. Selected members of the Indian upper class, especially sons of caciques, did emerge from such schools with a knowledge of the Spanish language and the ability to read and write. At the one outstanding and exemplary school of this type, the Colegio de Santa Cruz de Tlatelolco (part of Mexico City), upper-class Indian students learned Latin and were offered a humanistic education roughly comparable to that provided by aristocratic *colegios* in Spain. But the effective period of Santa Cruz de Tlatelolco was confined to the mid sixteenth century, and although the seventeenth-century Colegio del Príncipe in Lima had some of the same objectives, nothing quite like Santa Cruz is known elsewhere or at any other time.

One of the leaders of the sixteenth-century missionary work, Vasco de Quiroga, sought to establish utopian Indian societies in two small communities, both called Santa Fe, in New Spain. His regulations called for a literate Indian population, common property, rotational office holding, and an economy based on agriculture and craft skills. His purpose was to realize in practice the idealistic society conceived by Thomas More and to demonstrate the doctrine of Indian perfectibility.

Quiroga's work is of importance for what it reveals of the missionary mentality and the philosophy of Christian humanism in a New World form. But in practical terms its implications for change in Indian society were very slight.

The histories of Santa Cruz de Tlatelolco and of the two communities of Santa Fe suggest that large-scale Indian acculturation, where it occurred, was not the result of Spanish efforts at formal education. Rather it was the result of other kinds of interaction between Spaniards and Indians. Native adaptations in speech, dress, social activities, economic productivity, and daily life depended on Indian class and status, Indian proximity to centres of Spanish population, and the character of the relevant relations between Indians and Spaniards. Only with respect to religion do we find widespread teaching on the Spanish side and an acceptance, or partial acceptance, of that teaching on the Indian side.

In the sixteenth century, members of the Indian upper class, particularly the caciques, had the foremost opportunities for Hispanicization. Caciques knew that the role of local puppet ruler would win them privileges, and they were quick to exploit the possibilities. Caciques and other members of the Indian upper class were permitted to carry firearms, wear swords, dress in Spanish clothing, ride horses, and fraternize with white colonists. In the sixteenth century a surprising number of upper-class Indians travelled to Spain to present themselves at the royal court, where they requested additional privileges, titles of nobility, and coats of arms in official recognition of their rank and of the supportive role, real or assumed, that they or their fathers had played in the Spanish conquests. Caciques lived in houses constructed in Spanish styles and furnished with Spanish beds, tables, chairs, tapestries, and similar accoutrements otherwise unknown in native life. They were landholders, sometimes on a large scale, with servants, labourers, flocks of sheep, and agricultural enterprises. A few even became encomenderos. They owned Negro slaves, made large charitable donations to Spanish institutions, bought and sold expensive things, and notarized their contracts. They married within the Indian upper class and willed their estates to their successors.

The decline of the cacique class in the seventeenth and eighteenth centuries was the result of the many new circumstances in the later history of the colony. Caciques lost their native retainers to disease, to the repartimiento, or to the estates of Spaniards. Their political power suffered under the competition of the Hispanicized cabildos in the towns. Their communities no longer supported them, and they lost out to white or mestizo entrepreneurs. A limited number of cacique families, especially in Peru, survived with their wealth, power, prestige, and economic enterprises intact at the end of the eighteenth century. But many others failed, preserving only a memory of the family's past and an ineffective claim to status. A crucial factor seems to have been that Spanish society now had no further use for the caciques and no longer needed them to perform a puppet role.

For the mass of the Indian population the adoption of Spanish traits and products was a much slower and more selective process than it was for the caciques or other Indians of the upper class. Most Indians did not learn the Spanish language. The native languages came to include a number of Spanish terms, but these were chiefly loan-words for which the languages had no equivalents. Most Indian houses and methods of house construction in the eighteenth century differed little from those of the fifteenth. In dress some Indians adopted trousers, shirts, hats, and woollen cloth, while others preserved the original Indian clothing in whole or in part. European chickens were widely accepted through Indian America, and chickens and eggs were frequently included among the tribute goods that Indians paid to Spaniards. Wheat, often required in tribute also, played a lesser role in native life than did chickens. Some products that had been confined mainly to the Indian ruling classes in pre-conquest times came to be much more generally consumed in the colony, the outstanding examples being pulque in Mexico and coca and chicha in Peru. Indians raised pigs and sheep on a limited scale. The raising of horses and cattle seems to have become more an Indian practice in Peru than in central Mexico, perhaps because the native llama served as a psychological preparation. In the settled agricultural zones of Mexico, where Spaniards established haciendas and ranches, cows and steers were feared and hated by Indians, at least partly because of their destructive intrusions into agricultural lands. But, as is well known, horses became an important adjunct to the migratory Indian life beyond the Mexican frontier, among the Navajos and Apaches, where they facilitated raiding, theft, and contraband. A similar Indian adoption of horses, for similar reasons, occurred in Venezuela, Chile, the eastern Chaco, and other locations where Indians could retain attitudes of hostility around the edges of the settled zones and live a migratory, marauding life.

The reasons for the various acts of acceptance and rejection are quite complex, and they remain inadequately studied. In the case of the caciques, we have perhaps a sufficient explanation in their strong motivation for Hispanicization and in the absence of any material obstacle or preventative. In the case of the large, sedentary populations of Mexico and Peru we may postulate both a less powerful motivation and a much larger number of obstacles. The Indian masses, unlike the caciques, did not need motivation to preserve power and status, for they had no power or status to preserve. They were prevented from taking steps towards Hispanicization by Spanish prohibitions, by their own poverty and low estate, and by their often fierce loyalties to traditional Indian society. Mass Indian society continued to function by its own rules, and the pressures of these rules inhibited a single individual from moving in the direction of Hispanicization. Spaniards forbade ordinary Indians to carry swords or firearms. But for most of those who lived in Indian society carrying swords or firearms would have been an antisocial act. Moreover, most could not have afforded swords or firearms if they had wanted them. On the other hand Spaniards did not forbid Indians to use ploughs, and Indians could have constructed the simple Spanish ploughs readily, using only a few pieces of wood. But the obstacles were many. Ploughs would have meant draft animals, together with the problems of feeding, storage, and maintenance, with which Indians were for the most part unfamiliar. A plough agriculture would have meant changing the assignment of properties in the areas of small agricultural plots. It would have meant abandoning the existing intensive agricultural methods and adjusting further to this change. The plough would have modified the rhythm of the agricultural calendar, on which individual and collective life depended. Agricultural practices for Indians were closely bound up with traditional ceremonies and group behaviour. Given the total situation it is not surprising that Indians in the sixteenth century preferred the familiar native digging-stick.

The Indian community itself was a conservative institution, impeding acculturation. Nostalgia for the vanished splendours of the native past was more characteristic of the towns of Peru than of those of Mexico, for the Inca rulers continued to be remembered in drama, pageantry, portraiture, and impersonation in the life of the former Inca empire. Incaic ideology was present to some extent in the foremost of the eighteenth-century Indian rebellions, that of Tupac Amaru. But even in the absence of this kind of reminiscence the Indian community characteristically and positively asserted Indian values. It could absorb a Hispanicized Indian government and the Christian religion and some other powerful influences from the Spanish world and still retain its integral, pervasive, controlling Indian character. Indian godparenthood (*compadrazgo*) and the Indian *cofradías* may perhaps both be understood as defensive institutions. They promoted solidarity and a closing of Indian ranks against outside pressures of all kinds. Against both Spaniards and other Indians an Indian community could proclaim its identity and assert its superiority by the character of its patron saint, the size of its church, or the brilliance of its fireworks at fiesta time. Saints, churches, and fireworks, like godparenthood and the *cofradía*, were Spanish introductions, and they therefore represent a degree of acculturation. But they reinforced the sense of Indian communality in the same way as did the dances and costumes and masks and the other genuinely Indian means of accomplishing the same thing.

An important late colonial instrument of forced acculturation was the *repartimiento* (or *reparto*) *de efectos*. In this the corregidores, though forbidden to engage in commercial activities, were the promoters and main agents of economic distribution among Indians. In some cases they took over this function from Indian merchants, or from white middlemen or itinerant sellers, whose practice in the sixteenth and seventeenth centuries was to visit Indian communities and distribute goods in native markets. In the seventeenth and eighteenth centuries corregidores were able to dispose of surplus goods and goods in general by requiring Indians to purchase them. In some districts corregidores were the covert partners of private merchants in these operations; in others they held an effectual and illegal monopoly on the Indian trade, controlling supplies, sales, and prices. The forced-sale repartimiento was designed to liquidate any produce in the Spanish exchange economy at the expense of the Indian and to extract from Indian hands any money remaining after tribute, ecclesiastical fees, sodality dues, and other expenses had been paid. The Indians were compelled to accept, and pay exorbitant prices for, animals, household goods, clothing, and luxuries such as silk stockings and jewellery that were totally superfluous in Indian life. In the late colonial period some legalization of the *repartimiento de efectos* occurred, but the practice itself continued and the legal limits placed on the amounts and prices of the distributed goods were never restrictive.

It should be observed that changes over time had an important bearing on Indian acculturation. The obstacles, whether physical or psychological, that prevented the adoption of particular Spanish products in the sixteenth century might disappear or change appreciably during the ensuing 200 years. Indians did gradually gain familiarity with Spanish agricultural methods in the labour repartimiento of the sixteenth century and the haciendas and plantations of the seventeenth century. Each type of Spanish enterprise induced a new or incremental acculturation. The two classic types were the wheat farm and the sugar plantation, but there were many others. Apart from agriculture, the accelerated migration to the cities, the further penetration of Spaniards into the hinterland, the unrelieved extension of *mestizaje*, the many Spanish goods that found their way into Indian markets, were all factors inducing a progressive Indian acculturation. The process was slow but it was a cumulative and an accelerating one. Backward steps in the direction of a return to pure Indianism were extremely rare. Acculturation proceeded most rapidly where Indians were few and where whites, Negroes, mestizos, and mulattos were numerous, and the tendency was always for Indian populations to shrink in relation to the other populations. Acculturated Indians ceased to *be* Indians culturally or in the understanding of the time, and eventually much of the Indian population loss could be attributed to the acculturation itself, the siphoning off of individuals into other groups, the departure of Indians from their towns, and the 'passing' of persons who ceased to behave like Indians and began to behave like mestizos. In time those who left the village and spoke Spanish were understood to be mestizos, and those who stayed and spoke Indian languages were understood to be Indians. Thus the cultural criteria superseded the biological criteria, and the society that was called 'Indian' remained as a residue in constant process of diminution. Again and again the traits of this residue, even those of European origin, were identified as Indian traits.

During the centuries following the conquests Indian community life tended to be overtly peaceful. But local rebellions sometimes erupted, directed against specific controls, such as new taxes, labour demands, *repartimientos de efectos*, and land usurpations. Women and children as well as men characteristically participated. Like so much else in Indian life the rebellions were community enterprises, expressing a corporate Indian protest. They were emotional, intense, and short-lived, often lasting only a few hours. The typical uprising did no serious injury to

Spanish government and was quickly suppressed. The most celebrated uprising, that of Tupac Amaru in Peru in the 1780s, had numerous community implications but differed from others in affecting a larger area, the central and northern Andes, and extending over a longer period, from 1780 to 1782.

Generalizations about Indians under Spanish rule frequently do violence to the variety of conditions in colonial Spanish America. Important differences distinguished one area from another, and in each the situation changed over time. Students of this subject have identified as especially relevant determining factors: the density and social organization of the original Indian population; the proximity of that population to mines and Spanish cities; and the suitability of the area under consideration for Spanish haciendas and plantations. Even in regions at great distances from each other, if conditions such as these were similar, the historian may expect to find approximately similar relations between Spaniards and Indians. Thus the densely populated areas of Mexico and South America reveal a number of points in common, and the same may be said of the lowlands of both coasts. The Chichimeca on the northern frontier were more like the Araucanians on the southern frontier than either people was like any of the intermediate peoples in the 5,000 miles that separated them.

The populous and organized societies of the Mexican and Andean highlands strenuously resisted Spanish conquest, but they succumbed relatively intact. They came into Spanish hands with their internal structures and institutions still in working order, at least at local levels. This meant that families and individual Indians rarely came into direct contact with Spaniards. Indian families and towns survived and individuals retained their relations with their families and their towns. The society's capacity to deliver tribute and labour was not basically modified by conquest. Indians had delivered tribute and labour to their own rulers, and they continued to do so after suffering drastic depopulation and the pressures of the late sixteenth and the seventeenth centuries. Both the depopulation and the pressure were roughly parallel in the central areas of the two viceroyalties, and the Indian responses remained basically similar. From conquest times on we can identify a chronological lag between Mexico and Peru, and we have spoken above of some particular points of difference, but even in the seventeenth and eighteenth centuries central Mexico and central Peru may be classified together and contrasted with other areas.

In the coastal zones the original populations were less dense and the demographic losses more severe than in the highlands. Indian agriculture tended to be 'slash-and-burn' and Indian towns to be less structured and less able to protect their lands. This meant an earlier and larger opportunity for Spaniards to pre-empt fertile valleys and establish haciendas and plantations. Indian agriculture and Indian technology were insufficient to provide the surpluses that were necessary if tribute collection were to be successful. Labour shortages also were more acute. Spaniards dealt directly with Indians as individuals and imported Negro slaves to supplement the declining labour force. Other Indian workers migrated from the highlands and formed new communities or lived on the Spanish estates. Epidemics, forced labour, peonage, racial mixing, and eventually the virtual obliteration of the Indian population characterized Central American and South American coastal areas. The lowlands ceased to be Indian and became mestizo. Similar processes affected large parts of northern Mexico, where the original Indian population was sparse and where Spaniards were attracted by the silver mines. In northern Mexico Indian workers, imported from the south, became labourers in haciendas or mines and eventually disappeared in the mestizo–mulatto mixtures.

Highland and lowland areas, because of their differing climatic and ecological conditions and because of the different types of native society they supported, may thus be broadly distinguished with respect to Indian history under Spanish domination. But a number of other solutions should also be noted. The Jesuit congregations in the Guaraní region of South America provide one of history's foremost examples of benevolent tutelage under ecclesiastical auspices. The Jesuits imposed a strict supervisory control and a communal regimen for which Indians had no alternative after the Jesuits were expelled in 1767. Likewise, in the Yaqui region of northern Mexico a mission society was maintained by communal agricultural labour. The proceeds supported both Indians and Jesuits in the seventeenth and eighteenth centuries. In these marginal mission areas acculturation proceeded in the absence or virtual absence of encomienda, corregimiento, tribute, hacienda, mining, and a lay Spanish population, all of which were so instrumental in the processes of acculturation in other places. The cases are not important in terms of numbers of Indians, for only minuscule populations, in contrast to the large and thickly settled population of the Aztec and Inca empires, were involved. But they indicate something of the typological variety among Spanish influences and Indian responses.

What survived of Indian culture in Spanish America may be identified mainly at the level of individual, family, and community life. The tendency was for communities to become independent of one another, to resist Spanish pressures in community forms, and to survive as depositaries of a remnant Indianism. Upper-class native culture disappeared, not, as Humboldt thought, through death in the conquests, but more gradually over time, and through historical processes of extirpation or adaptation. With some exceptions the caciques, the original leaders in Hispanicization, abandoned Indian society in their own private interests. Others who were not caciques, and not even *principales*, left the villages to join haciendas, plantations, mines, or cities, or to hide in the forests, or to wander the country roads. But the village survivors supported one another in resisting change. They retained, so far as they could, their own forms of activity in agriculture, dress, daily life, food, and local customs. It is a mistake of course to conceive of what happened in Indian America exclusively in terms of what survived and what did not. We are dealing with a complex of relationships, within which mere survival is only one of the significant features of any trait. Others are the place of that trait in the total configuration, its origin and meaning, the emphasis or de-emphasis accorded it, and its convergence or interaction or deviation with respect to other traits. These subjects, and the modifications of all of them over time, we are still in the early stages of understanding.

BIBLIOGRAPHICAL ESSAYS

ABBREVIATIONS

HAHR   *Hispanic American Historical Review*
HM   *Historia Mexicana*
JGSWGL *Jahrbuch für Geschichte von Staat, Wirtschaft und Gesellschaft Lateinamerikas*
JLAS   *Journal of Latin American Studies*
LARR   *Latin American Research Review*
RHA   *Revista de Historia de América*

1. THE SPANISH CONQUEST

Charles Julian Bishko, 'The Iberian background of Latin American history: recent progress and continuing problems', *HAHR*, 36 (1956), 50–80, is an admirable introduction to the essential bibliographical tools and identifies the areas in which more research is needed, as well as those in which valuable work has been done. The *Indice histórico español* (Barcelona, 1953–), which may be regarded as a sequel to Benito Sánchez Alonso's indispensable *Fuentes de la historia española e hispano-americana*, 3 vols. (3rd edn, Madrid, 1952), with the additional advantage of including brief comments on the books and articles which it lists, has unfortunately shown signs of flagging in recent years. There is now a good selection of general books on the Iberian peninsula in the later Middle Ages and the Early Modern period, although Spain is much better served in this respect than Portugal. The classic work of Roger B. Merriman, *The rise of the Spanish Empire in the Old World and the New*, 4 vols. (New York, 1918–34, reprinted 1962) is still useful, particularly for political and institutional history, but has at many points been superseded by more recent work. It is weakest in the areas of economic and social history, where it should be supplemented by Jaime Vicens Vives, *An economic history of Spain* (Princeton, 1969), and vols. II and III of the *Historia social y económica de España y América* (Barcelona, 1957), a collaborative enterprise edited by Vicens Vives. Medieval Spain as a frontier society is surveyed by A. MacKay, *Spain in the Middle Ages* (London, 1977), and later medieval Spain is examined in much greater detail by J. N. Hillgarth, *The Spanish kingdoms, 1250–1516*, 2 vols. (Oxford, 1976–8). For the sixteenth and seventeenth centuries, see Antonio Domínguez Ortiz, *The Golden Age of Spain, 1516–1659*

(London, 1971); J. H. Elliott, *Imperial Spain, 1469–1716* (London, 1963); John Lynch, *Spain under the Habsburgs*, 2 vols. (2nd edn, Oxford, 1981). *Spain. A companion to Spanish studies*, ed. P. E. Russell (London, 1973) offers a useful up-to-date introduction to Spanish history and civilization.

There exist a number of good surveys of the colonial period in Spanish America which begin with the conquest and early settlement and which offer helpful bibliographical guidance: C. H. Haring, *The Spanish Empire in America* (New York, 1947); J. H. Parry, *The Spanish Seaborne Empire* (London, 1966); Charles Gibson, *Spain in America* (New York, 1966); Richard Konetzke, *Süd- und Mittelamarika, 1. Die Indianerkulturen Altamerikas und die spanisch-portugiesische Kolonialherrschaft* (Fischer Weltgeschichte, XXII, Frankfurt, 1965); Francisco Morales Padrón, *Historia general de América* (2nd edn, Madrid, 1975); Guillermo Céspedes, *Latin America: the early years* (New York, 1974).

To these general works should be added more specialized studies of particular aspects of the relationship between Spain and America. In the area of law and institutions, J. M. Ots Capdequí, *El estado español en las Indias* (3rd edn, Mexico, 1957), and Silvio Zavala, *Las instituciones jurídicas en la conquista de América* (Madrid, 1935), remain very useful investigations of the juridical foundations of Spanish rule. The same theme is explored with great richness of detail by Mario Góngora, *El estado en el derecho indiano* (Santiago de Chile, 1951). Mario Góngora's *Studies in the colonial history of Spanish America* (Cambridge, 1975) brings together a number of his essays on different aspects of Spain in the Indies and reveals how much the understanding of Spanish society and institutions can add to the understanding of the historical development of Spanish America. For many years, Earl J. Hamilton, *American treasure and the price revolution in Spain, 1501–1650* (Cambridge, Mass., 1934) was the starting-point for all discussion of the economic relationship between Spain and America, and, in spite of criticisms which reflect changing trends in the study of economic history, it remains a work of fundamental importance. Its theme, however, has been amplified and in many respects transformed by the massive study of Pierre and Huguette Chaunu on Seville's Atlantic trade, *Séville et l'Atlantique, 1504–1650* (8 vols., Paris, 1955–9). Different aspects of the relationship between Spain and the Indies are briefly examined and summarized in J. H. Elliott, *The Old World and the New, 1492–1650* (Cambridge, 1970), which pays particular attention to the cultural interplay between the two. Some of the themes discussed in this book, along with many others, were explored at an international conference held at the University of California in Los Angeles in 1975. The conference papers, which include some important pioneering essays, were published under the title of *First images of America*, edited by Fredi Chiappelli, 2 vols. (Los Angeles, 1976).

The literature on the discovery and conquest of America is enormous. One possible way of approaching it is through two volumes by Pierre Chaunu, *L'Expansion européenne du XIIIe au XVe siècle*, and *Conquête et exploitation des Nouveaux Mondes* ('Nouvelle Clio', vols. 26 and 26 *bis*, Paris, 1969). These not only contain long bibliographies, but also discuss some of the problems which have dominated recent historical debate. The Iberian maritime empires are set into the general context of European overseas expansion in G. V. Scammell, *The world encompassed* (London–Berkeley, 1980). See also the works of J. H. Parry, most recently *The discovery of South America* (London, 1979).

A great deal of time and energy was invested, especially in the nineteenth century, in the publication of documentary collections of material on the discovery, conquest and colonization of America. A great corpus of documentation is therefore available in print, although the editing of it often leaves much to be desired. Major collections include *Colección de documentos inéditos relativos al descubrimiento, conquista y organización de las antiguas posesiones españolas de América y Oceania*, ed. Pacheco, Cárdenas and Torres de Mendoza, 42 vols. (Madrid, 1863–84), and its sequel, *Colección de documentos inéditos relativos al descubrimiento, conquista y organización de las antiguas posesiones españolas de Ultramar*, 25 vols. (Madrid, 1885–1932). For both of these series, Ernst Schäfer, *Indice de la colección de documentos inéditos de Indias*...(Madrid, 1946), is an indispensable guide. Another great Spanish series, the *Colección de documentos inéditos para la historia de España*, 112 vols. (Madrid, 1842–95), also contains important American material, which is best located through Julián Paz, *Catálogo de la colección de documentos inéditos para la historia de España*, 2 vols. (Madrid, 1930–1). Richard Konetzke, *Colección de documentos para la historia de la formación social de Hispanoamerica, 1493–1810*, 3 vols. (Madrid, 1953–62), is an extremely valuable selection of documents relating to the theme of government and society in the Spanish colonial world.

The discovery, conquest and colonization of the New World can also be approached through printed contemporary accounts. An important new bibliographical guide to this material is now being prepared at the John Carter Brown Library of Brown University, Providence, which contains extensive holdings of early works on the Americas: *European Americana: a chronological guide to works printed in Europe relating to the Americas, 1493–1776*, ed. John Alden. Vol. I, covering the period 1493–1600, was published in 1980, and vol II, covering 1600–1650, in 1982. Many of the early histories and descriptions of the Americas are discussed in Francisco Esteve Barba, *Historiografía Indiana* (Madrid, 1964), while Colin Steele, *English interpreters of the Iberian New World from Purchas to Stevens, 1603–1726* (Oxford, 1975) is a bibliographical study which lists and describes English translations of Spanish and Portuguese books on the New World.

During the nineteenth and early twentieth centuries a great deal of scholarly effort was devoted to narrative and descriptive accounts of the discovery and conquest of America and to biographical studies of individual explorers and *conquistadores*. In the second half of the twentieth century interest has tended to shift towards such questions as the social background of the *conquistadores* as a collective group, and the organization and financing of voyages of discovery and colonization. But the old tradition was maintained in particular by Samuel Eliot Morison, both in his classic biography of Columbus, *Admiral of the Ocean Sea*, 2 vols. (Boston, 1942), and his *The European discovery of America*, of which the volume dealing with the southern voyages (New York and Oxford, 1974) is concerned with the Iberian New World. J. H. Parry, *The age of reconnaissance* (London, 1963) is a comprehensive survey of the history of European overseas discovery and colonization, and the collection of essays by Charles Verlinden, *The beginnings of modern colonization* (Ithaca and London, 1970) contains important information on the transfer of colonial techniques from the Mediterranean to the Atlantic, and on the role of the Genoese in the early stages of colonization. Further useful information on the role of the entrepreneur in colonial enterprises can be found in Guillermo Lohmann Villena, *Les Espinosa. Une famille d'hommes d'affaires en Espagne et aux Indes à l'époque de la colonisation* (Paris, 1968).

Wilcomb E. Washburn, 'The Meaning of "Discovery" in the Fifteenth and Sixteenth Centuries', *HAHR*, 68 (1962), 1–21, is a suggestive exploration of what discovery meant to contemporary Europeans. A somewhat similar inquiry was undertaken by Edmundo O'Gorman in his controversial work, *The invention of America* (Bloomington, 1961), which, as its title suggests, replaces the concept of 'discovery' by that of 'invention'.

The best introduction to the 'island' period of discovery is Carl O. Sauer, *The early Spanish Main* (Berkeley, Los Angeles and Cambridge, 1966). Ursula Lamb, *Frey Nicolás de Ovando, gobernador de las Indias, 1501–1509* (Madrid, 1956), is an important study of trial and error in the first Spanish attempts at settlement in the New World. The later story of the Caribbean is admirably told by Kenneth R. Andrews, *The Spanish Caribbean. Trade and plunder, 1530–1630* (New Haven–London, 1978); and, as always, much fascinating information can be gleaned from the Chaunus' *Séville et l'Atlantique*, cited above.

For the Spanish movement into mainland America, Mario Góngora, *Los grupos de conquistadores en Tierra Firme, 1509–1530* (Santiago de Chile, 1962) is an important examination of the background and composition of bands of *conquistadores*. Juan Friede, *Los Welser en la conquista de Venezuela* (Caracas–Madrid, 1961) looks at the role of commercial considerations in the process of conquest and colonization, as also does Enrique Otte, *Las perlas del Caribe: Nueva Cádiz de Cubagua* (Caracas, 1977). Murdo J. MacLeod, *Spanish Central America. A socioeconomic history, 1520–1720* (Berkeley, 1973), traces similar themes far into the colonial period.

Richard Konetzke, *Descubridores y conquistadores de América* (Madrid, 1968), leads up to the conquest of Mexico by way of the Caribbean and the first probing of the mainland. For the conquest of Mexico itself the letters of Cortés, and Bernal Díaz del Castillo's *Conquest of New Spain*, provide a superb record of events from the Spanish point of view, but need to be read with caution. The most convenient compilation of Cortés' letters and papers is Hernán Cortés, *Cartas y documentos*, ed. Mario Hernández Sánchez-Barba (Mexico, 1963), but a critical edition is badly needed. Hernán Cortés, *Letters from Mexico*, translated and edited by A. R. Pagden (Oxford, 1972) is a modern unabridged English translation, and has the advantage of notes and commentary. In recent years there has been a growing interest in the conquest from the standpoint of the conquered, stimulated by Miguel León-Portilla's anthology of texts compiled from indigenous sources, *Visión de los vencidos* (Mexico, 1959; translated as *The broken spears*, London, 1962). As yet, there is no comprehensive study of the conquest of Mexico from this standpoint comparable to Nathan Wachtel's *La Vision des vaincus. Les Indiens du Pérou devant la conquête espagnole, 1530–1570* (Paris, 1971;

translated as *The vision of the vanquished*, London, 1977). For a full discussion of this theme, see *CHLA*, 1, bibliographical essay 7. As far as the military aspects of conquest are concerned, Alberto Mario Salas, *Las armas de la conquista* (Buenos Aires, 1950) provides a detailed discussion of the weapons and methods of warfare of conquerors and conquered, while C. H. Gardiner examines the important theme of *Naval power in the conquest of Mexico* (Austin, 1956).

For warfare and conquest in other parts of Mexico and Central America, the following works are particularly useful: Robert S. Chamberlain, *The conquest and colonization of Yucatán* (Washington, D.C., 1948), and, by the same author, *The conquest and colonization of Honduras* (Washington, D.C., 1953); and for northern and north-western New Spain, Philip Wayne Powell, *Soldiers, Indians and silver. The northward advance of New Spain, 1550–1600* (Berkeley and Los Angeles, 1952), and Edward H. Spicer, *Cycles of conquest. The impact of Spain, Mexico and the United States on the Indians of the South-west, 1533–1960* (Tucson, 1962).

The literature on the conquest of Peru is on the whole less satisfactory than that on the conquest of Mexico, but two contributions to volume II of the *Handbook of South American Indians* (Washington, D.C., 1946), provide an admirable starting-point: J. H. Rowe, 'Inca Culture at the time of the Spanish Conquest', and G. Kubler, 'The Quechua in the colonial world'. John Hemming, *The conquest of the Incas* (London, 1970) is a splendid narrative in the tradition of Prescott, and is particularly good on the continuation of Inca resistance once the 'conquest' was over. James Lockhart provides a prosopography of the conquerors in *The men of Cajamarca* (Austin, 1972), which may be regarded as a prelude to his *Spanish Peru, 1532–1560* (Madison, 1968). For the Araucanian wars in Chile, see Alvaro Jara, *Guerre et société au Chili. Essai de sociologie coloniale* (Paris, 1961). See also *CHLA* 1, bibliographical essays 5 and 7.

George M. Foster, *Culture and conquest* (Chicago, 1960) is a suggestive anthropological study of problems of acculturation in the Spanish colonial world, a theme which is impressively pursued for the Indian population of Mexico by Charles Gibson in his *The Aztecs under Spanish rule* (Stanford, 1964). José Durand studies the transformation of conqueror into colonist in *La transformación social del conquistador*, 2 vols. (Mexico, 1953). The hopes, fears and concerns of the early colonists are vividly revealed in their letters, selected, edited and translated by James Lockhart and Enrique Otte, *Letters and people of the Spanish Indies. The sixteenth century* (Cambridge, 1976). Richard Konetzke, 'La Formación de la nobleza de Indias', *Estudios Americanos*, 3 (1951), 329–57, is fundamental for the evolution of a new social elite in the Spanish Indies.

On population, land and towns in the immediate post-conquest period, see *CHLA* II, bibliographical essays 1, 5, 6 and 3, and on the church, see *CHLA* I, bibliographical essay 14. For the theme of 'spiritual conquest' Robert Ricard, *La 'Conquête spirituelle' du Mexique* (Paris, 1933) and John L. Phelan, *The Millennial Kingdom of the Franciscans in the New World* (2nd edn, Berkeley and Los Angeles, 1970), deserve special mention.

2. SPAIN AND AMERICA BEFORE 1700

In addition to the general studies by Domínguez Ortiz, Elliott and Lynch, listed in *CHLA* I, bibliographical essay 6, there are a number of more specialized studies of Spanish government and society which ought to be taken into account by anyone interested in following the relationship between Spain and its American possessions in the sixteenth and seventeenth centuries. The best brief account of the reign of Charles V is by H. G. Koenigsberger, 'The empire of Charles V in Europe', in vol. II of *The New Cambridge Modern History* (Cambridge, 1958). There are two recent biographies of Philip II: Peter Pierson, *Philip II of Spain* (London, 1975) and Geoffrey Parker, *Philip II* (Boston and Toronto, 1978). But incomparably the most important study of the age of Philip II is by Fernand Braudel, *La Méditerranée et le monde méditerranéen à l'époque de Philippe II*, 2 vols. (2nd edn, Paris, 1966); translated as *The Mediterranean and the Mediterranean world in the age of Philip II*, 2 vols. (London, 1972–3), which is especially useful for tracing the shift in the centre of gravity of Spanish power from the Mediterranean to the Atlantic during the course of Philip's reign. I. A. A. Thompson, *War and government in Habsburg Spain, 1560–1620* (London, 1976), is a pioneering piece of research into Spain's organization for war, and the strains imposed by warfare on the Spanish administrative system.

Problems relating to the decline of Spain are discussed by J. H. Elliott, 'The decline of Spain', and 'Self-perception and decline in seventeenth-century Spain', in *Past and Present*, 19 (1961) and 74 (1977) respectively, and there is a brilliant treatment of this theme by Pierre Vilar, 'Le Temps du Quichotte', *Europe*, 34 (1956). The reign of Charles II, the least-known period in the history of Habsburg Spain, is discussed by Henry Kamen in *Spain in the later seventeenth century* (London, 1980), while R. A. Stradling surveys the vicissitudes of Spanish power in *Europe and the decline of Spain* (London, 1981). Vol. II of John Lynch, *Spain under the Habsburgs*, 2 vols. (2nd edn, Oxford, 1981), has the great merit of relating the history of seventeenth-century Spain to that of Spanish America, but there is a crying need for a systematic and comprehensive study of this relationship over the sixteenth and seventeenth centuries as a whole. Pierre and Huguette Chaunu's *Séville et l'Atlantique*, 8 vols. (Paris, 1958–9), does this on a massive scale for the commercial relationship, but many other aspects of the relationship, at both the institutional and the personal level, have scarcely begun to be explored. Some indication of the possibilities is suggested by the uncompleted, and in many respects flawed, work of Manuel Giménez Fernández, *Bartolomé de Las Casas*, 2 vols. (Seville, 1953–60), which places under a microscope the crown's policies towards the Indies between 1516 and 1523 and the role of its advisers and officials in formulating and implementing those policies, but which is distorted by its obsessive hatred of Ferdinand the Catholic and his men. For the reign of Philip II, the title of José Miranda's *España y Nueva España en la época de Felipe II* (Mexico, 1962) promises well, but the book consists of two separate sections, one on Spain and the other on New Spain, and while each constitutes an excellent essay in itself, the connection between the two is never developed.

In view of the dearth of studies examining simultaneous developments in the metropolis and the colonies, the bibliographical suggestions which follow will include works on both Spain and Spanish America.

J. H. Parry, *The Spanish theory of empire in the sixteenth century* (Cambridge, 1940) and Silvio Zavala, *La filosofía política en la conquista de América* (Mexico, 1947) are helpful introductions to the Spanish theory of empire, as also is chapter 2 of Mario Góngora's *Studies in the colonial history of Spanish America* (Cambridge, 1975). J. A. Fernández-Santamaria, *The state, war and peace* (Cambridge, 1977) is a close examination of Spanish political theory in the first half of the sixteenth century, which includes discussions of attitudes to the Indies, while Venancio Carro, *La teología y los teólogo-juristas españoles ante la conquista de Indias* (Seville, 1945), directly addresses the problem of the conquest of America in scholastic thought.

H. G. Koenigsberger, *The practice of empire* (Ithaca, 1969), although concerned with the government of Sicily under Philip II, raises issues of general importance for the understanding of Spanish administrative practice. The most important organ for the administration of the Spanish New World was the Council of the Indies, and the composition and institutional history of this council are examined in detail in the classic work by Ernesto Schäfer, *El Consejo Real y Supremo de las Indias*, 2 vols. (Seville, 1935–47), to which should be added the volume of essays by D. Ramos and others, *El Consejo de las Indias en el siglo XVI* (Valladolid, 1970). Aspects of financial administration are discussed by Ismael Sánchez-Bella, *La organización financiera de las Indias, siglo XVI* (Seville, 1968).

A splendid mass of documentation for the study of the viceroys of Mexico and Peru during the Habsburg period has now been made available by Lewis Hanke, in his *Los virreyes españoles en América durante el gobierno de la casa de Austria*, Biblioteca de Autores Españoles, vols. 233–7 (Madrid, 1976–8) for Mexico, and vols. 280–5 (Madrid, 1978–80) for Peru. A number of viceroys have received individual studies, of which the following are especially noteworthy: Arthur S. Aiton, *Antonio de Mendoza, first viceroy of New Spain* (Durham, N.C., 1927); Roberto Levillier, *Don Francisco de Toledo, supremo organizador del Perú*, 2 vols. (Buenos Aires, 1935–40); María Justina Sarabia Viejo, *Don Luís de Velasco, virrey de Nueva España 1550–1564* (Seville, 1978).

The best study of an *audiencia* is J. H. Parry, *The Audiencia of New Galicia in the sixteenth century* (Cambridge, 1948), but in general far too little is known about Spanish judges and officials in the Indies. Peggy K. Liss, *Mexico under Spain, 1521–1556* (Chicago, 1975), besides synthesizing a complicated period in the history of Mexico, shows how the crown gradually imposed its authority on *conquistador* society. Richard L. Kagan, *Students and society in early modern Spain* (Baltimore, 1974) is a pioneering study of the educational background of the men who administered Spain and America, but too few of these men are yet known as individual personalities. This makes all the more valuable John Leddy Phelan's *The kingdom of Quito in the seventeenth century* (Madison, 1967), which examines the contrasts between the ideals and the practice of the Spanish bureaucracy through a study of the career of Dr Antonio de Morga, president of the *audiencia* of Quito from 1615 to 1636. Another approach to these judges and officials is by way of their own writings, of which Alonso de Zorita's *The lords of New Spain*, translated and edited by Benjamin Keen (London, 1965) and Juan de Matienzo's *Gobierno del Perú*, edited by Guillermo Lohmann Villena (Paris and Lima, 1967) are especially revealing.

Other useful studies of different aspects of Spanish colonial administration are Guillermo Lohmann Villena, *El corregidor de Indios en el Perú bajo los Austrias* (Madrid, 1957), and J. H. Parry's examination of *The sale of public office in the Spanish Indies under the Hapsburgs* (Berkeley, 1953), a theme which is also considered in Mark A. Burkholder and D. S. Chandler, *From impotence to authority. The Spanish crown and the American Audiencias, 1687–1808* (Columbia, Mo., 1977). For a fuller discussion of the literature on urban development and municipal administration, see *CHLA* II, bibliographical essay 3, and, on the church, see *CHLA*, I, bibliographical essay 14.

The Spanish treatment of the Indians was a source of controversy to contemporaries and has remained so ever since. As Sverker Arnoldsson showed in his *La leyenda negra. Estudios sobre sus orígenes* (Göteborg, 1960), the 'black legend' of Spanish cruelty pre-dated the conquest of America, but the reports of the massacres and maltreatment of the Indians did much to determine the image of Spain in the European consciousness. This in turn called forth from Spain and its defenders a 'white legend'. Charles Gibson examines both in his anthology, *The black legend: Anti-Spanish attitudes in the Old World and the New* (New York, 1971).

Spanish theory and practice as regards the treatment of the indigenous peoples of America has been the source of intense study and heated debate in the historiography of the past 50 years, a debate focused particularly, although not exclusively, on the controversial figure of Bartolomé de Las Casas. The bibliography on Las Casas is now enormous, as can be seen from the selection of titles at the end of Juan Friede and Benjamin Keen, *Bartolomé de Las Casas in history* (DeKalb, 1971), a selection of essays on different aspects of his career and reputation. A central figure in the Las Casas controversy has been Lewis Hanke, who has done more than anyone else to bring the aspirations and achievements of Las Casas to the attention of the English-speaking world, and whose *The Spanish struggle for justice in the conquest of America* (Philadelphia, 1949), and *Aristotle and the American Indians* (London, 1959) have breathed new life into the sixteenth-century debate for twentieth-century readers. The great French Hispanist, Marcel Bataillon, whose monumental study of the influence of Erasmus in Spain, *Erasmo y España*, 2 vols. (Mexico, 1950) also has important implications for sixteenth-century America, wrote a number of carefully argued essays on Las Casas and his writings, which were collected under a single cover in his *Études sur Bartolomé de Las Casas* (Paris, 1965). Out of a massive bibliography two other books besides the work of Giménez Fernandez (*B. de Las Casas*) deserve special mention: Juan Friede, *Bartolomé de Las Casas; precursor del anticolonialismo* (Mexico, 1974), which pays close attention to the context in which Las Casas was operating, and Angel Losada, *Fray Bartolomé de Las Casas a la luz de la moderna crítica histórica* (Madrid, 1970). A recent biography which takes account of modern research is Philippe-Ignace André-Vicent, *Bartolomé de Las Casas. Prophète du Nouveau Monde* (Paris, 1980). Angel Losada also devoted himself to studying and editing the works of Las Casas' rival, Sepúlveda. Las Casas and Sepúlveda, however, are only two of the many sixteenth-century Spaniards, some well known and others scarcely known at all, who discussed the capacities and status of the Indians and the treatment they deserved. The works of some of these figures are only now becoming accessible for study, thanks to the efforts of scholars like Ernest J. Burrus, whose *The writings of Alonso de la Vera Cruz*, 5 vols. (Rome, St Louis and Tucson, 1968–76) shows the possibilities. Other contemporary documents of great interest are published by José A. Llaguno in *La personalidad jurídica del indio y el III Concilio Provincial Mexicano (1585)* (Mexico, 1963). Joseph Höffner, *Christentum und Menschenwürde. Das Anliegen der Spanischen Kolonialethik im goldenen Zeitalter* (Trier, 1947), remains a useful survey of sixteenth-century Spanish theories about the Indians, but the source material and studies that have appeared in recent years suggest the need for a new synthesis.

One of the major problems in the study of the controversy over the Indians is to determine what effects, if any, the theorizing had on colonial practice; and here a work like that by Juan A. and Judith E. Villamarin, *Indian labor in mainland colonial Spanish America* (Newark, Delaware, 1975) serves as a salutary reminder of the gulf that separated ideals from reality. The effectiveness, or otherwise, of theory and legislation on behaviour in the Indies and the general question of the relationship between settler society and the *república de los indios* still requires much study at the local level, of the type undertaken by Juan Friede in his *Vida y luchas de don Juan del Valle, primer obispo de Popayán y protector de indios* (Popayán, 1961), or Eugene E. Korth, *Spanish policy in colonial Chile. The struggle for social justice, 1535–1700* (Stanford, 1968).

On the sea link between Spain and the Indies, the *carrera de Indias*, and colonial trade, see *CHLA* I, bibliographical essay 10.

Problems of war, defence and taxation must loom large in any attempt to chart the changing relationship between metropolitan Spain and the Indies in the later sixteenth and seventeenth centuries. A. P. Newton, *The European nations in the West Indies, 1493–1688* (London, 1933; reprinted 1966), remains a useful outline survey of the incursions of North Europeans into the Spanish colonial world. This should be supplemented by Kenneth R. Andrews, *The Spanish Caribbean. Trade and plunder, 1580–1630* (New Haven and London, 1978) and by the same author's excellent re-assessment of *Drake's voyages* (London, 1967). Peter Gerhard, *Pirates on the West Coast of New Spain, 1575–1742* (Glendale, 1960) examines the growing threat posed by piracy in the Pacific. For reactions to these attacks, Roland D. Hussey, 'Spanish reaction to foreign aggression in the Caribbean to about 1680', *HAHR*, 9 (1929), 286–302 is still of value. The defence of the Panama isthmus is examined by Guillermo Céspedes del Castillo, 'La defensa militar del istmo de Panamá a fines del siglo XVII y cominezos del XVIII', *Anuario de Estudios Americanos*, 9 (1952), 235–75, while Günter Kahle, 'Die Encomienda als militärische Institution im kolonialen Hispanoamerika', *JGSWGL*, 2 (1965), 88–105, traces the decline and fall of the military role of the *encomendero*. Detailed examinations of defence problems at a local level, and also of the consequences of enemy attack, may be found in J. A. Calderón Quijano, *História de las fortificaciones en Nueva España* (Seville, 1957); Enriqueta Vila Vilar, *Historia de Puerto Rico, 1600–1650* (Seville, 1974); Frank Moya Pons, *Historia colonial de Santo Domingo* (3rd edn, Santiago, Dominican Republic, 1977); and C. R. Boxer, *Salvador de Sá and the struggle for Brazil and Angola, 1602–1688* (London, 1952). Olivares' scheme for the Union of Arms is briefly discussed in J. H. Elliott, *The revolt of the Catalans* (Cambridge, 1963), ch. 7, while Fred Bronner examines attempts to introduce it in Peru in 'La Unión de Armas en el Perú. Aspectos político-legales', *Anuario de Estudios Americanos*, 24 (1967), 1133–71, but the scheme still requires a comprehensive treatment. For the introduction of the *alcabala* into the Indies, Robert S. Smith, 'Sales taxes in New Spain, 1575–1770', *HAHR*, 28 (1948), 2–37, is fundamental.

The seventeenth century is the least well known, and the least studied, of any century of Spanish-American history. Thanks to the pioneering work of Woodrow Borah, *New Spain's century of depression* (Berkeley and

Los Angeles, 1951), the more sombre aspects of the century have tended to be emphasized, at the expense of its more creative and formative characteristics. The Borah thesis is examined in the light of more recent research by P. J. Bakewell in his introduction to the Spanish translation, *El siglo de la depresión en Nueva España* (Mexico, 1975). J. I. Israel, *Race, class and politics in colonial Mexico, 1610–1670* (Oxford, 1975), discusses some of the processes at work in seventeenth-century Mexican society, as does José F. de la Peña, *Oligarquía y propiedad en Nueva España, 1550–1624* (Mexico, 1983), which examines the important theme of the consolidation of an elite, on the basis of rich new documentation. An important aspect of the creole question is analysed by A. Tibesar in 'The Alternativa: a study in Spanish–Creole relations in seventeenth-century Peru', *The Americas*, 11 (1955), 229–83, but in general more work has been done for New Spain than for Peru on the formation of a settler society with its own growing sense of identity. Irving A. Leonard, *Baroque times in Old Mexico* (Ann Arbor, 1959) and Jacques Lafaye, *Quetzalcóatl and Guadalupe. The formation of Mexican national consciousness, 1531–1813* (Chicago, 1976) are the outstanding recent contributions to a subject of fundamental importance for understanding the eventual break with Spain.

3. BOURBON SPAIN AND ITS AMERICAN EMPIRE

For Spain at the start of the Bourbon period there is John Lynch, *Spain under the Habsburgs*, 2 vols. (2nd edn, Oxford, 1981) and two works by Henry Kamen, *Spain in the Later Seventeenth Century* (London, 1980), and *The War of Succession in Spain 1700–15* (London, 1969). The best general accounts of the eighteenth century are Gonzalo Anes, *El antiguo régimen: los Borbones* (Historia de España Alfaguara IV, Madrid, 1975) and Antonio Domínguez Ortiz, *Sociedad y estado en el siglo XVIII español* (Madrid, 1976). The impact of the Enlightenment is discussed in Richard Herr, *The eighteenth-century revolution in Spain* (Princeton, 1958), Luis Sánchez Agesta, *El pensamiento político del despotismo ilustrado* (Madrid, 1953) and Jean Sarrailh, *L'Espagne éclairée de la seconde moitié du XVIIIe siècle* (Paris, 1954). On Jansenism read Joël Saugnieux, *Le Jansénisme espagnol du XVIIIe siècle, ses composantes et ses sources* (Oviedo, 1975). On the economy there is Jordi Nadal and Gabriel Tortella (eds.), *Agricultura, comercio colonial y crecimiento económico en la España contemporánea* (Barcelona, 1974), Gonzalo Anes, *Las crisis agrarias en la España moderna* (Madrid, 1970) and David R. Ringrose, *Transportation and economic stagnation in Spain 1750–1850* (Durham, N.C., 1970), and his 'Perspectives on the economy of eighteenth century Spain' in *Historia Ibérica* (1973), I, 59–102. Trade with the American empire is dealt with by Geoffrey J. Walker, *Spanish politics and imperial trade 1707–1789* (London, 1979), and Antonio García-Baquero González, *Cádiz y el Atlántico 1717–1778*, 2 vols. (Seville, 1976), and his *Comercio colonial y guerras revolucionarias* (Seville, 1972). See also Barbara H. and Stanley J. Stein, 'Concepts and realities of Spanish economic growth 1759–1789', *Historia Ibérica*, I (1973), 103–19.

For the Revolution of Government see the first part of D. A. Brading, *Miners and merchants in Bourbon Mexico 1763–1810* (Cambridge, 1971). Other studies are Luis Navarro García, *Intendencias de Indias* (Seville, 1959), John Lynch, *Spanish colonial administration 1782–1810. The intendant system in the viceroyalty of the Río de la Plata* (London, 1958), and J. R. Fisher, *Government and society in colonial Peru. The intendant system 1784–1814* (London, 1970). For its impact in New Granada see John Leddy Phelan, *The people and the king. The Comunero Revolution in Colombia, 1781* (Madison, 1978). Céspedes del Castillo, *Lima y Buenos Aires* (Sevilla, 1956), is still useful. On creole participation in *audiencias*, see Mark A. Burkholder and D. S. Chandler, *From impotence to authority. The Spanish crown and the American audiencias 1787–1808* (Columbia, Miss., 1977). The campaign against the Church is dealt with by Nancy M. Farriss, *Crown and clergy in colonial Mexico 1759–1821. The crisis of ecclesiastical privilege* (London, 1968). No less than three books are available on the military: Christon I. Archer, *The army in Bourbon Mexico 1760–1810* (Albuquerque, 1977), Leon G. Campbell, *The military and society in colonial Peru 1750–1810* (Philadelphia, 1978) and Allan J. Kuethe, *Military reform and society in New Granada, 1773–1808* (Gainesville, 1978).

On the colonial economy the starting point must always be Alexander von Humboldt, *Essai politique sur le Royaume de la Nouvelle-Espagne*, 2 vols. (Paris, 1807–11), and *Voyage aux régions equinoxiales de Nouveau Continent fait en 1799, 1801, 1802, 1803 et 1804* (Paris, 1807). Both these works present a mass of information and have been translated into both English and Spanish. For Mexico there is E. Arcila Farías, *El siglo ilustrado en América. Reformas económicas del siglo XVII en Nueva España* (Caracas, 1955). Brian R. Hamnett, *Politics and trade in southern Mexico 1750–1821* (Cambridge, 1971) covers repartimientos de comercio and D. A. Brading, *Miners and merchants in Bourbon Mexico*, the export economy.

For Cuba, apart from Humboldt's *Voyage*, there is Manuel Moreno

Fraginals, *The sugar mill. The socioeconomic complex of sugar in Cuba 1760–1860* (New York, 1976), but see also Javier Ortiz de la Tabla Ducasse, *Comercio exterior de Veracruz 1778–1821* (Seville, 1978). On Central America, consult Robert S. Smith, 'Indigo production and trade in colonial Guatemala', *HAHR*, 39 (1959), 181–211; and Troy S. Floyd, 'Bourbon palliatives and the Central American mining industry 1765–1800', *The Americas*, 18 (1961), 103–25 and his 'The indigo merchant: promoter of Central American economic development 1700–1808', *Business History Review*, 39 (1965), 466–88. For Venezuela,. E. Arcila Farías, *Comercio entre Venezuela y Mexico en los siglos XVII y XVIII* (Mexico, 1950) is all-important. On Colombia, see John Leddy Phelan, *The people and the king. The Comunero revolution in Colombia, 1781* and A. D. Macfarlane, 'Economic change in the viceroyalty of New Granada with special reference to overseas trade 1739–1810' (Ph.D. dissertation, London University, 1977). On Ecuador, the coast is covered by Michael T. Hammerly, *Historia social y económica de la antigua provincia de Guayaquil 1763–1842* (Guayaquil, 1973).

On silver-mining in Peru, J. R. Fisher, *Silver mines and silver miners in colonial Peru 1776–1824* (Liverpool, 1977), gives the chief series of production. For a comparative view see D. A. Brading and Harry E. Cross, 'Colonial silver mining: Mexico and Peru', *HAHR*, 52 (1972), 545–79. For a fuller discussion of the literature on eighteenth-century mining, see *CHLA* II, bibliographical essay 4. For Chile the best introduction is Marcello Carmagnani, *Les Mécanismes de la vie économique dans une société coloniale: le Chili 1680–1830* (Paris, 1973). Equally important are Sergio Villalobos, *El comercio y la crisis colonial* (Santiago de Chile, 1968), and Mario Góngora, *Origen de los 'inquilinos' de Chile central* (Santiago de Chile, 1960). For the Río de la Plata area the introductory chapter of Tulio Halperin-Donghi, *Politics, economics and society in Argentina in the revolutionary period* (Cambridge, 1975), is invaluable; a supplement is Susan Midgen Socolow, *The merchants of Buenos Aires 1778–1810. Family and commerce* (Cambridge, 1978). For the literature on eighteenth-century population growth, see *CHLA* II, bibliographical essay 1. Similarly, on urban growth *CHLA*, II, essay 3, on agriculture *CHLA*, II, essays 5 and 6, and on the internal economy, including the *obrajes*, *CHLA*, II, essay 7.

4. URBAN DEVELOPMENT

Collections and guides

Proceedings of the eight Symposia on Latin American Urbanization from Its Origins to Our Time, held from 1966 to 1982 at meetings of the International Congress of Americanists, yield a broad view of contemporary research on Latin American urban history. They include more than 150 papers from many disciplines, ranging from pre-Columbian times to the present and from case studies to broad conceptual statements and bibliographic reviews. At least 50 deal with colonial Spanish America. The published proceedings are: J. E. Hardoy and R. P. Schaedel (eds.), *El proceso de urbanización en América desde sus orígenes hasta nuestros días* (Buenos Aires, 1969); J. E. Hardoy, E. W. Palm and R. P. Schaedel (eds.), 'The process of urbanization in America since its origins to the present time' in *Verhandlungen des XXXVIII. Internationalen Amerikanistenkongresses*, 4 (Stuttgart and Munich, 1972), 9–318; R. P. Schaedel *et al.*, *Urbanización y proceso social en América* (Lima, 1972); J. E. Hardoy and R. P. Schaedel (eds.), *Las ciudades de América Latina y sus áreas de influencia a través de la historia* (Buenos Aires, 1975); J. E. Hardoy and R. P. Schaedel (eds.), *Asentamientos urbanos y organización socioproductiva en la historia de América Latina* (Buenos Aires, 1977); J. E. Hardoy, R. M. Morse and R. P. Schaedel (eds.), *Ensayos histórico-sociales sobre la urbanización en América Latina* (Buenos Aires, 1978); W. Borah, J. Hardoy and G. A. Stelter (eds.), *Urbanization in the Americas: the background in comparative perspective*, special issue, *Urban History Review* (Ottawa, 1980); R. M. Morse and J. E. Hardey (eds.), *Cultura urbana latinoamericana* (Buenos Aires, 1985). Publication of the Ninth Symposium is planned. English versions of 21 papers from the first four Symposia were published in R. P. Schaedel, J. E. Hardoy and N. S. Kinzer (eds.), *Urbanization in the Americas from its beginnings to the present* (The Hague, 1978). Six papers from the Sixth Symposium appeared in English in *Comparative Urban Research*, 8/1 (1980), and four from the Eighth Symposium in *Journal of Urban History* 10/4 (1984). Other collections: R. Altamira y Crevea *et al.*, *Contribuciones a la historia municipal de América* (Mexico, 1951); F. de Solano (ed.), *Estudios sobre la ciudad iberoamericana* (Madrid, 1975); and D. J. Robinson (ed.), *Social fabric and spatial structure in colonial Latin America* (Ann Arbor, 1979).

The basic bibliography for urbanization is F. de Solano *et al.*, *El proceso urbano iberoamericano desde sus orígenes hasta los principios del siglo XIX, estudio bibliográfico* (Madrid, 1973–4), listing over 1,800 items for the pre-Columbian and colonial periods (also in Solano, *Estudios*, 727–866). J. E. Hardoy *et al.*, *Urbanización en América Latina, una bibliografía sobre su historia* (Buenos Aires, 1975), the first of three projected volumes, covers pre-Columbian urbanization and the colonial period to 1540. For municipal sources see A. Millares Carlo, *Los archivos municipales de Latinoamérica: libros de actas y colecciones documentales, apuntes bibliográficos* (Maracaibo, 1961).

Backgrounds

The volumes by Solano *et al.* (*El proceso urbano*) and Hardoy *et al.* (*Urbanización*) cover pre-Columbian research. J. E. Hardoy, *Pre-Columbian cities* (New York, 1973) is a good conspectus with extensive references.

For the Spanish background: E. A. Gutkind, *International history of city development*, vol. III: *Urban development in Southern Europe: Spain and Portugal* (New York, 1967); A. García y Bellido *et al.*, *Resumen histórico del urbanismo en España* (2nd edn, Madrid, 1968); L. García de Valdeavellano, *Sobre los burgos y los burgueses de la España medieval* (Madrid, 1960); J.M.Font y Rius, 'Les villes dans l'Espagne du Moyen Age' in Société Jean Bodin, *La ville* I (Brussels, 1954), 263–95; J. Vicens Vives, *An Economic History of Spain* (Princeton, 1969), section on 'Urban Economy'; J. A. Maravall, *Las comunidades de Castilla* (2nd edn, Madrid, 1970); A. Alvarez de Morales, *Las hermandades, expresión del movimiento comunero en España* (Valladolid, 1974); R. Ricard, 'La *Plaza Mayor* en Espagne et en Amérique Espagnole', *Annales, Économie–Sociétés–Civilisations*, 2/4 (1947), 433–8; R. Pike, *Aristocrats and traders, Sevillian society in the sixteenth century* (Ithaca, 1972). Some of the themes introduced in the first section of this chapter are expanded in R. M. Morse, 'A prolegomenon to Latin American urban history', *HAHR*, 52/3 (1972), 359–94.

Cartography

J. E. Hardoy surveys published and manuscript sources in 'La cartografía urbana en América Latina durante el período colonial. Un análisis de fuentes', in Hardoy, Morse and Schaedel, *Ensayos*, 19–58. Also: D. Angulo Iñiguez, *Planos de monumentos arquitectónicos de América y*

Filipinas existentes en el Archivo de Indias (3 vols., Seville, 1933); F. Chueca Goitia and L. Torres Balbás, *Planos de ciudades iberoamericanas y filipinas existentes en el Archivo de Indias* (2 vols., Madrid, 1951).

General studies

If one construes urban history to include 'settlement patterns', if one accepts the central role of towns in Spanish colonization, and if one views urban centres as linked to regional and transatlantic economies, then the sources for urban history become almost coextensive with those for Spanish American history in general. The bibliographies cited above list some of this material.

Various general issues are mapped out in R. M. Morse, 'Some characteristics of Latin American urban history', *American Historical Review*, 67/2 (1962), 317–38; G. A. Kubler, 'Cities and culture in the colonial period in Latin America', *Diogenes*, 47 (1964), 53–62; C. Sempat Assadourian, *El sistema de la economía colonial* (Mexico, 1983); S. M. Socolow and L. L. Johnson, 'Urbanization in colonial Latin America', *Journal of Urban History*, 8/1 (1981): 27–59; and J. K. Chance, 'The colonial Latin American city: preindustrial or capitalist', *Urban Anthropology*, 4/3 (1975), 211–28. One can follow the urbanization process to 1630 in J. M. Houston, 'The foundation of colonial towns in Hispanic America', in R. P. Beckinsale and J. M. Houston (eds.), *Urbanization and its problems* (Oxford, 1968), 352–90; and J. E. Hardoy and C. Aranovich, 'Urbanización en América Hispana entre 1580 y 1630', *Boletín del Centro de Investigaciones Históricas y Estéticas* (Universidad Central de Caracas) [*BCIHE*], 11 (1969), 9–89. G. Céspedes del Castillo traces the Lima– Buenos Aires rivalry in *Lima y Buenos Aires* (Seville, 1947). K. Davis takes a comparative hemispheric view in 'Colonial expansion and urban diffusion in the Americas', *International Journal of Comparative Sociology*, 1/1 (1960), 43–66, while R. R. Reed shows how Spain's New World experience influenced urbanization in the Philippines in *Colonial Manila, the context of Hispanic urbanism and process of morphogenesis* (Berkeley and Los Angeles, 1978).

C. Bayle gives an informed survey of municipal life and institutions in *Los cabildos seculares en la América Española* (Madrid, 1952). M. Góngora examines the legal context of municipal government in *El estado en el derecho indiano* (Santiago de Chile, 1951) and, more succinctly, in *Studies in the colonial history of Spanish America* (Cambridge, 1975),

98–119. J. M. Ots Capdequí, *España en América, el régimen de tierras en la época colonial* (Mexico, 1959) shows the importance of the municipality in controlling land distribution. For cabildos see also A. Muro Orejón, 'El ayuntamiento de Sevilla, modelo de los municipios americanos', *Anales de la Universidad Hispalense*, 21/1 (1960), 69–85, and F. X. Tapia, *El cabildo abierto colonial* (Madrid, 1966).

W. Borah reviews the voluminous literature bearing on the accommodation of Indians to urban life under Spain in 'Aspectos demográficos y físicos de la transición del mundo aborigen al mundo colonial', in Hardoy, Morse and Schaedel, *Ensayos*, 59–89. Also: C. Bayle, 'Cabildos de indios en América Española', *Missionalia Hispánica*, 8/22 (1951), 5–35; M. Mörner, *La corona española y los foráneos en los pueblos de indios de América* (Stockholm, 1970); F. de Solano, 'Urbanización y municipalización de la población indígena', in Solano, *Estudios*, 241–68.

W. Borah also assesses the often controversial literature on Spanish American urban design in 'European cultural influence in the formation of the first plan for urban centers that has lasted to our time', in Schaedel *et al.*, *Urbanización*, 157–90. See also G. M. Foster's chapter, 'Cities, towns, and villages: the grid-plan puzzle', in his *Culture and conquest* (Chicago, 1960), 34–49; G. Guarda, *Santo Tomás de Aquino y las fuentes del urbanismo indiano* (Santiago de Chile, 1965); E. W. Palm, 'La ville espagnole au nouveau monde dans la première moitié du XVIᵉ siècle', *La découverte de l'Amérique*, 10ᵉ *Stage International d'Études Humanistes* (Paris, 1968); L. Benevolo, 'Las nuevas ciudades fundadas en el siglo XVI en América Latina', *BCIHE*, 9 (1969), 117–36; L. M. Zawiska, 'Fundación de las ciudades hispanoamericanas', *BCIHE*, 13 (1972), 88–128; D. P. Crouch and A. I. Mundigo, 'The city planning ordinances of the laws of the Indies revisited', *Town Planning Review*, 48/3–4 (1977), 247–68, 397–418; G. Kubler, 'Open-grid town plans in Europe and America', in Schaedel, Hardoy and Kinzer, *Urbanization*, 327–42.

Other topics: F. Domínguez Compañy, 'Actas de fundación de ciudades hispanoamericanas', *RHA*, 83 (1977), 19–51; R. Archila, 'La medicina y la higiene en la ciudad' in Solano, *Estudios*, 655–85; F. de Solano, 'An introduction to the study of provisioning in the colonial city' and G. Gasparini, 'The colonial city as a center for the spread of architectural and pictorial schools', both in Schaedel, Hardoy and Kinzer, *Urbanization*, 99–129 and 269–81.

Regional studies

Antilles

C. O. Sauer presents a coherent account, with good maps, of Spanish town-founding in the Antilles and Tierra Firme to 1519 in *The early Spanish Main* (Berkeley and Los Angeles, 1966). J. M. F. de Arrate y Acosta, *Llave del Nuevo Mundo* (Mexico, 1949) is a descriptive and historical account of Havana by a town councillor, written in the 1750s and first published in 1830. E. W. Palm, *Los monumentos arquitectónicos de la Española, con una introducción a América* (2 vols., Ciudad Trujillo, 1955) is near-definitive for the topic and deals broadly with the origins of New World urbanization. Also: J. Pérez de Tudela, 'La quiebra de la factoría y el nuevo poblamiento de la Española', *Revista de Indias*, 60 (1955), 197–252; J. Artiles, *La Habana de Velázquez* (Havana, 1946); I. A. Wright, *Historia documentada de San Cristóbal de la Habana en el siglo XVI* (2 vols., Havana, 1927), *Historia documentada de San Cristóbal de la Habana en la primera mitad del siglo XVII* (Havana, 1930), and *Santiago de Cuba and its district (1607–1640)* (Madrid, 1918); Adolfo de Hostos, *Ciudad murada, ensayo acerca del proceso de la civilización en la ciudad española de San Juan Bautista de Puerto Rico* (Havana, 1948); M. A. Castro de Dávila, 'The place of San Juan de Puerto Rico among Hispanic American cities', *Revista Interamericana*, 6/2 (1976), 156–73.

Mesoamerica

C. Gibson treats the reorientation of pre-Columbian cities and settlement patterns under Spanish rule in Mexico in *Tlaxcala in the sixteenth century* (New Haven, 1952), *The Aztecs under Spanish rule* (Stanford, 1964), especially the chapters 'Towns' and 'The City', and 'Spanish-Indian institutions and colonial urbanism in New Spain', in Hardoy and Schaedel, *El proceso*, 225–39. This theme also features in studies of Mexico's three main regions in I. Altman and J. Lockhart (eds.), *Provinces of early Mexico* (Berkeley and Los Angeles, 1976). A. Moreno Toscano and E. Florescano, 'El sector externo y la organización espacial y regional de Mexico (1521–1910)', in J. W. Wilkie, M. C. Meyer and E. Monzón de Wilkie (eds.), *Contemporary Mexico* (Berkeley and Los Angeles, 1976), 62–96, relates changing urban systems to economics, public policy and transportation. G. Kubler, *Mexican architecture of the sixteenth century* (2 vols., New Haven, 1948) has much to say on demography and urban form. M. Giménez Fernández, *Hernán Cortés y su revolución comunera* (Seville, 1948) shows Cortés' strategic use of municipal organization. P. W. Powell studies the special challenge of urban settlement on the Chichimeca frontier in *Soldiers, Indians, and silver, the northward advance of Spain, 1550–1600* (Berkeley and Los Angeles, 1952). Central American urbanization is treated in M. J. MacLeod, *Spanish Central America, a socioeconomic history 1520–1720* (Berkeley and Los Angeles, 1973) and, more explicitly, by S. D. Markman, *Colonial architecture of Antigua Guatemala* (Philadelphia, 1966), and several of his papers for the Symposia on Latin American urbanization, cited above.

On Mexico City: M. Toussaint, F. Gómez de Orozco and J. Fernández, *Planos de la ciudad de México, siglos XVI y XVII* (Mexico, 1938); E. W. Palm, 'Tenochtitlán y la ciudad ideal de Durero', *Journal de la Société des Américanistes*, N.S. 40 (1951), 59–66; S. B. Schwartz, 'Cities of empire: Mexico and Bahia in the sixteenth century', *Journal of Inter-American Studies*, 11/4 (1969), 616–37; E. Poulain, *Vie économique et sociale à Mexico d'après les 'Actas del cabildo de la ciudad de Mexico', 1594–1616* (Caen, 1966); R. E. Boyer, *La gran inundación, vida y sociedad en la ciudad de México (1629–1638)* (Mexico, 1975); L. S. Hoberman, 'Merchants in seventeenth-century Mexico City: a preliminary portrait', *HAHR*, 57/3 (1977), 479–503; R. Feijóo, 'El tumulto de 1624' and 'El tumulto de 1692', *HM*, 14/1 (1964), 42–70 and 14/4 (1965), 656–79; G. Poras Muñoz, *El gobierno de la ciudad de México en el siglo XVI* Mexico, 1982).

On other towns and cities: J. McAndrew, *The open-air churches of sixteenth century Mexico* (Cambridge, 1965); F. Chevalier, 'Signification sociale de la fondation de Puebla de los Ángeles', *RHA*, 23 (1947), 105–30; F. Marín-Tamayo, *La división racial en Puebla de los Ángeles bajo el régimen colonial* (Puebla, 1960); J. Bazant, 'Evolution of the textile industry of Puebla, 1544–1845', *Comparative Studies in Society and History*, 7/1 (1964), 56–69; M. Carmagnani, 'Demografía y sociedad: la estructura social de los centros mineros del norte de México', *HM*, 21 (1970–1), 419–59; P. J. Bakewell, *Silver Mining and Society in Colonial Mexico: Zacatecas 1546–1700* (Cambridge, 1971); J. K. Chance, *Race and Class in Colonial Oaxaca* (Stanford, 1978); E. Chinchilla Aguilar, *El ayuntamiento colonial de la ciudad de Guatemala* (Guatemala, 1961).

Northern South America

J. A. and J. E. Villamarín trace the reworking of native settlement patterns on the *sabana* of Bogotá in 'Chibcha settlement under Spanish rule: 1537–1810' in Robinson, *Social Fabric*, 25–84. Other regional studies: A. Castillero, *Políticas de poblamiento en Castilla del Oro y Veragua en los orígenes de la colonización* (Panama, 1972); C. Martínez, *Apuntes sobre el urbanismo en el Nuevo Reino de Granada* (Bogotá, 1967); G. Gasparini, 'Formación de ciudades coloniales en Venezuela, siglo XVI', *BCIHE*, 10 (1968), 9–43; A. Perera, *Historia de la organización de pueblos antiguos en Venezuela* (3 vols., Madrid, 1964).

On particular towns and cities: C. Verlinden, 'Santa María la Antigua del Darién, première "ville" coloniale de la Tierra Firme américaine', *RHA*, 45 (1958), 1–48; A. Rubio, *Esquema para un análisis de geografía urbana de la primitiva ciudad de Panamá, Panamá la Vieja, 1519–1671* (Panama, 1947); G. Gasparini, *Caracas colonial* (Buenos Aires, 1969); P. M. Arcaya, *El cabildo de Caracas* (Caracas, 1965); J. V. Lombardi, 'The rise of Caracas as a primate city' in Robinson, *Social Fabric*, 433–72; S. Blank, 'Patrons, clients, and kin in seventeenth-century Caracas', *HAHR*, 54/2 (1974), 260–83; E. Marco Dorta, *Cartagena de Indias, puerto y plaza fuerte* (Madrid, 1960); G. Arboleda, *Historia de Cali* (2nd edn, 3 vols., Cali, 1956); V. Cortés Alonso, 'Tunja y sus vecinos', *Revista de Indias*, 25/99–100 (1965), 155–207; P. Marzahl, *Town in the empire: government, politics, and society in seventeenth century Popayán* (Austin, 1978).

South America: West Coast and Andes

J. Basadre made a classic analysis of changing settlement patterns and their political implications from Incan to modern times in *La multitud, la ciudad y el campo en la historia del Perú* (Lima, 1929). G. Lohmann Villena studies the *corregidor*'s key role in *El corregidor de indios en el Perú bajo los Austrias* (Madrid, 1957). Newer scholarship offers further clues in: J. V. Murra, *Formaciones económicas y políticas del mundo andino* (Lima, 1975), especially the chapter entitled 'El control vertical de un máximo de pisos ecológicos en la economía de las sociedades andinas'; N. Wachtel, *Sociedad e ideología* (Lima, 1973); and K. Spalding, *De indio a campesino* (Lima, 1974). Administrative studies include J. P. Moore, *The Cabildo in Peru under the Hapsburgs* (Durham, 1954) and J. Alemparte, *El cabildo en Chile colonial* (2nd edn, Santiago de Chile, 1966). G. Guarda stresses military determinants for Chile in *Influencia militar en las ciudades del Reino de Chile* (Santiago de Chile, 1967); M. Carmagnani features economic factors in 'Formación de un mercado compulsivo y el papel de los mercaderes: la región de Santiago de Chile (1559–1600)', *JGSWGL*, 12 (1975), 104–33, and *Les mécanismes de la vie économique dans une société coloniale: le Chili, 1580–1830* (Paris, 1973); and M. Góngora treats social structure in 'Urban social stratification in colonial Chile', *HAHR*, 55/3 (1975), 421–48.

On particular cities: J. C. Super, 'Partnership and profit in the early Andean trade: the experiences of Quito merchants, 1580–1610', *JLAS*, 11/2 (1979), 265–81; M. L. Conniff, 'Guayaquil through independence: urban development in a colonial system', *The Americas*, 33/3 (1977), 385–410; J. Bromley and J. Barbagelata, *Evolución urbana de la ciudad de Lima* (Lima, 1945); M. Colin, *Le Cuzco à la fin du XVIIᵉ et au début du XVIIIᵉ siècle* (Paris, 1966); B. Arzáns de Orsúa y Vela, *Historia de la Villa Imperial de Potosí* (3 vols., Providence, 1965); L. Hanke, *The Imperial City of Potosí* (The Hague, 1956); A. Crespo R., *Historia de la ciudad de La Paz, siglo XVII* (Lima, 1961); M. Beltrán Ávila, *Capítulos de la historia colonial de Oruro* (La Paz, 1925); J. Urquidi Zambrano, *La urbanización de la ciudad de Cochabamba* (Cochabamba, 1967); R. Martínez Lemoine, 'Desarrollo urbano de Santiago (1541–1941)', *Revista Paraguaya de Sociología*, 15/42–3 (1978), 57–90; A. de Ramón, *La ciudad de Santiago entre 1650 y 1700* (Santiago de Chile, 1975).

The Río de la Plata Region
J. E. Hardoy and L. A. Romero provide a synthesis of Argentine urban history and a critique of sources in 'La ciudad argentina en el período precensal (1516–1869)', *Revista de la Sociedad Interamericana de Planificación*, 5/17 (1971), 16–39. J. Comadrán Ruiz supplies demographic context in *Evolución demográfica argentina en el período hispano (1535–1810)* (Buenos Aires, 1969). A classic study of colonial Buenos Aires, first published in 1900 and influenced by Le Play's sociology, is J. A. García, *La ciudad indiana*, in his *Obras completas* (2 vols., Buenos Aires, 1955), I, 283–475. See also A. Razori, *Historia de la ciudad argentina* (3 vols., Buenos Aires, 1945); R. Levillier, *Descubrimiento y población del norte de Argentina por españoles del Perú* (Buenos Aires, 1943); R. Zorraquín Becú, 'Los cabildos argentinos', *Revista de la Facultad de Derecho y Ciencias Sociales*, 11/47 (1956), 95–156; R. Zabala and E. de Gandía, *Historia de la ciudad de Buenos Aires* (2 vols., Buenos Aires, 1936–7); N. Besio Moreno, *Buenos Aires, puerto del Río de la Plata, estudio crítico de su población 1536–1936* (Buenos Aires, 1939); J. Comadrán Ruiz, 'Nacimiento y desarrollo de los núcleos urbanos y del poblamiento de la campaña del país de Cuyo durante la época hispana (1551–1810)', *Anuario de Estudios Americanos*, 19 (1952), 145–246; J. Álvarez, *Historia de Rosario (1689–1939)* (Buenos

Aires, 1943); L. E. Azarola Gil, *Los orígenes de Montevideo, 1607–1749* (Buenos Aires, 1933); F. R. Moreno, *La ciudad de Asunción* (Buenos Aires, 1926); R. Gutiérrez, 'Estructura urbana de las misiones jesuíticas del Paraguay', in Hardoy and Schaedel, *Asentamientos*, 129–53.

Late colonial period

General: Two concise syntheses are W. Borah, 'Latin American cities in the eighteenth century: a sketch', in Borah, Hardoy and Stelter, *Urbanization*, 7–14, and D. A. Brading, 'The city in Bourbon Spanish America: elite and masses', *Comparative Urban Research*, 8/1 (1980): 71–85. Surveys and statistics for Latin America and for eight countries from 1750 to 1920 are found in R. M. Morse, *Las ciudades latino-americanas* (2 vols., Mexico, 1973), vol. II; urban statistics are also given in Borah's paper just cited and in R. E. Boyer and K. A. Davies, *Urbanization in 19th-Century Latin America: Statistics and Sources* (Los Angeles, 1973). E. M. Lahmeyer Lobo studies urban merchant guilds in *Aspectos da atuação dos consulados de Sevilha, Cádiz e da América Hispânica na evolução econômica do século XVIII* (Rio de Janeiro, 1965). C. Esteva Fabregat quantifies urban and rural racial composition in 'Población y mestizaje en las ciudades de Iberoamérica: siglo XVIII', in Solano, *Estudios*, 551–604.

Antilles and Mexico: M. Nunes Dias, *O comércio livre entre Havana e os pôrtos de Espanha (1778–1789)* (2 vols., São Paulo, 1965); A. R. Caro de Delgado, *El cabildo o régimen municipal puertorriqueño en el siglo XVIII* (San Juan, 1965); Jean Saint-Vil, 'Villes et bourgs de Saint Domingue au XVIIIème siècle', *Conjonction*, 138 (1978), 5–32; A. Moreno Toscano, 'Regional economy and urbanization: three examples of the relationship between cities and regions in New Spain at the end of the eighteenth century', in Schaedel, Hardoy and Kinzer, *Urbanization*, 399–424; D. A. Brading, *Miners and merchants in Bourbon Mexico 1763–1810* (Cambridge, 1971); F. de la Maza, *La ciudad de México en el siglo XVIII* (Mexico, 1968); E. Báez Macías, 'Planos y censos de la ciudad de México 1753', *Boletín del Archivo General de la Nación*, 7/1–2 (1966), 407–84; A. Moreno Toscano and J. González Angulo, 'Cambios en la estructura interna de la ciudad de México (1753–1882)', in Hardoy and Schaedel, *Asentamientos*, 171–95; D. B. Cooper, *Epidemic disease in Mexico City 1761–1813* (Austin, 1965); R. Liehr, *Ayuntamiento y oligarquía en Puebla, 1787–1810* (2 vols., Mexico, 1971); L. L. Greenow, 'Spatial dimensions of the credit market in eighteenth-century Nueva Galicia', in Robinson (ed.), *Social fabric*, 227–79; E. Van Young, 'Urban market and hinterland: Guadalajara and its region in the eighteenth century', *HAHR*, 59/4 (1979), 593–635; D. E. López Sarrelangue, *Una villa mexicana en el siglo XVIII* (Mexico, 1966); M. L. Moorhead, *The Presidio* (Norman, 1975).

South America: A. Twinam, 'Enterprise and elites: eighteenth-century Medellín', *HAHR*, 59/3 (1979), 444–75; J. P. Moore, *The cabildo in Peru under the Bourbons* (Durham, 1966); V. A. Barriga (ed.), *Memorias para la historia de Arequipa, 1786–1796* (3 vols., Arequipa, 1941–8); G. Guarda, *La ciudad chilena del siglo XVIII* (Buenos Aires, 1968); G. O. Tjarks, *El consulado de Buenos Aires y sus proyecciones en la historia del Río de la Plata* (2 vols., Buenos Aires, 1962); J. L. Moreno, 'La estructura social y demográfica de la ciudad de Buenos Aires en el año de 1778', *Anuario del Instituto de Investigaciones Históricas* (Universidad Nacional del Litoral) [*AIIH*], 8 (1965), 151–70; S. M. Socolow, *The merchants of Buenos Aires 1778–1810* (Cambridge, 1978); L. L. Johnson and S. M. Socolow, 'Population and space in eighteenth century Buenos Aires', in Robinson, *Social fabric*, 339–68; F. J. Cervera and M. Gallardo, 'Santa Fe, 1765–1830: historia y demografía', *AIIH*, 9 (1966–7), 39–66; P. S. Martínez Constanzo, *Historia económica de Mendoza durante el virreinato, 1776–1810* (Madrid, 1961); D. J. Robinson and T. Thomas, 'New towns in eighteenth century Argentina', *JLAS*, 6/1 (1974), 1–33; R. Gutiérrez, *Estructura socio-política, sistema productivo y resultante espacial en las misiones jesuíticas del Paraguay durante el siglo XVIII* (Resistencia, 1974); three articles in *Revista Paraguaya de Sociología*, 15/42–3 (1978): R. E. Velázquez, 'Poblamiento del Paraguay en el siglo XVIII' (175–89), M. Lombardi, 'El proceso de urbanización en el Uruguay en los siglos XVIII y XIX' (9–45), and J. Rial Roade, A. M. Cocchi and J. Klaczko, 'Proceso de asentamientos urbanos en el Uruguay: siglos XVIII y XIX' (91–114).

Much information on late colonial urban conditions in northern South America and Mexico is found in: F. Depons, *Voyage à la partie orientale de la Terre-firme dans l'Amérique Méridionale (1801–1804)* (3 vols., Paris, 1806), A. von Humboldt and A. Bonpland, *Personal narrative of travels to the equinoctial regions of the New Continent during the years 1799–1804* (7 vols., London, 1814–29), and Humboldt's *Political essay on the kingdom of New Spain* (4 vols., London, 1811).

5. MINING

No adequate general book on colonial Spanish American mining yet exists. The only attempt at such a work, Carlos Prieto's *Mining in the New World* (New York, 1973) ignores important topics. The best introductory guide must therefore be the perceptive article by D. A. Brading and Harry E. Cross, 'Colonial silver mining: Mexico and Peru', *HAHR*, 52/4 (1972), 545–79. Modesto Bargalló, *La minería y la metalurgía en la América española durante la época colonial* (Mexico, 1955) concentrates on technical aspects of mining and refining, on which it is the best study available.

The fundamental bibliography is Eugenio Maffei and Ramón Rua Figueroa, *Apuntes para una biblioteca española de libros, folletos y artículos, impresos y manuscritos, relativos al conocimiento y explotación de las riquezas minerales y a las ciencias auxiliares* (2 vols., Madrid, 1871), reprinted VI Congreso Internacional de Minería, vols. 2 and 3 (León, 1970). This is updated by Justo García Morales, *Apuntes para una bibliografía minera española e iberoamericana* (1870–1969), VI Congreso Internacional de Minería, vol. 4 (León, 1970).

Only one significant collection of colonial documents specifically on mining exists: Modesto Bargalló, *La amalgamación de los minerales de plata en Hispanoamérica colonial* (Mexico, 1969), indispensable on its topic. Various colonial treatises and histories on, or dealing with, mining are available. Among these are, for New Spain: Francisco Xavier de Gamboa, *Comentarios a las Ordenanzas de Minas* (Madrid, 1971), translated into English as *Commentaries on the Mining Ordinances of Spain* (2 vols., London, 1830), good on technical as well as legal questions; Fausto de Elhúyar, *Memoria sobre el influjo de la minería en...la Nueva España* (Madrid, 1825) and *Indagaciones sobre la amonedación en la Nueva España* (Madrid, 1816); Jose Garcés y Eguía, *Nueva teórica y práctica del beneficio de los metales* (Mexico, 1802); Alexander von Humboldt, *Political essay on the Kingdom of New Spain* (4 vols., London, 1811–22), translated into Spanish as *Ensayo político sobre el Reino de la Nueva España* (Mexico, 1966). For South America, Luis Capoche, *Relación general de la Villa Imperial de Potosí* (Biblioteca de Autores Españoles, CXXII, Madrid, 1959), which is fundamental for Potosí up to *c.* 1585; Alvaro Alonso Barba, *Arte de metales* (Madrid, 1640; Eng. trans. London, 1923), a remarkable seventeenth-century refining treatise by a priest of Charcas; Bartolomé Arzáns de Orsúa y Vela (1676–1738), *Historia de la Villa Imperial de Potosí*

(3 vols., Providence, Rhode Island, 1965); Pedro Vicente Cañete y Domínguez, *Guía histórica, geográfica, física, política, civil y legal del Gobierno e Intendencia de la Provincia de Potosí* [1787] (Potosí, 1952). Also important is Georgius Agricola, *De re metallica* (Basle, 1556; Eng. trans. London, 1912), a highly influential work in Spanish America.

Of all regions of Spanish America, it is New Spain that has most attracted the attention of modern mining historians. Henry R. Wagner, 'Early silver mining in New Spain', *RHA*, 14 (1942), 49–71, studies the early decades. P. J. Bakewell and Robert C. West examine important northern districts, particularly in the seventeenth century, in, respectively, *Silver mining and society in colonial Mexico, Zacatecas 1546–1700* (Cambridge, 1971) and *The mining community of northern New Spain: the Parral mining district* (Ibero-Americana 30, Berkeley and Los Angeles, 1949). Clement G. Motten, *Mexican silver and the Enlightenment* (Philadelphia, 1950) surveys the eighteenth century. D. A. Brading's fundamental *Miners and merchants in Bourbon Mexico, 1763–1810* (Cambridge, 1971) deals particularly with Guanajuato but also embraces other centres and multifarious topics related to mining. Walter Howe, *The mining guild of New Spain and its Tribunal General, 1770–1821* (Cambridge, Mass., 1949) is thorough. Humboldt's *Political essay* is indispensable for the late eighteenth century. See also, in general, Miguel León-Portilla *et al.*, *La minería en México* (Mexico, 1978).

Central American mining is treated by Murdo J. MacLeod in *Spanish Central America. A socioeconomic history, 1520–1720* (Berkeley and Los Angeles, 1973). For New Granada see especially Robert C. West, *Colonial placer mining in Colombia* (Baton Rouge, 1952) and Germán Colmenares, *Historia económica y social de Colombia, 1537–1719* (Medellín, 1976); also William F. Sharp, *Slavery on the Spanish frontier. The Colombian Chocó, 1680–1810* (Norman, Oklahoma, 1976). On Quito little is available, but Aquiles R. Pérez, *Las mitas en la Real Audiencia de Quito* (Quito, 1947) has information on mining as well as labour. The most thorough work for Peruvian mining is John R. Fisher's *Silver mines and silver miners in colonial Peru, 1776–1824* (Liverpool, 1977). Josep María Barnadas, *Charcas, 1535–1565: orígenes históricos de una sociedad colonial* (Centro de Investigación y Promoción del Campesinado, La Paz, 1973), is informative on early mining in that mineral-rich province. But Potosí still awaits a general study. Most comprehensive to date, among multitudinous shorter ones, are the introduction by Lewis Hanke to Capoche's *Relación general*, and that by Hanke and Gunnar Mendoza to

Arzáns' *Historia.* For Chile, Ernesto Greve, 'Historia de la amalgamación de la plata', *Revista Chilena de Historia y Geografía,* 102 (1943), 158–259, is broader than it sounds. Marcello Carmagnani, in *El salariado minero en Chile colonial. Su desarrollo en una sociedad provincial: el Norte Chico, 1690–1800* (Santiago de Chile, 1963), describes mining and labour in an important gold district.

For mercury mining, see above all M. F. Lang, *El monopolio estatal del mercurio en el México colonial (1550–1710)* (Mexico, 1977) and Guillermo Lohmann Villena, *Las minas de Huancavelica en los siglos XVI y XVII* (Seville, 1949). For eighteenth-century Huancavelica, see Arthur P. Whitaker, *The Huancavelica mercury mine* (Cambridge, Mass., 1941); and for Almadén, A. Matilla Tascón, *Historia de las minas de Almadén,* vol. 1: *Desde la época romana hasta el año 1645* (Madrid, 1958).

Good brief studies on specific topics are Alberto Crespo Rodas, 'La "mita" de Potosí', *Revista Histórica,* 22 (Lima, 1955–6), 169–82; for legal and moral aspects of the mita, Jorge Basadre, 'El régimen de la mita', *Letras* (Universidad Mayor de San Carlos, Lima, 1937), 325–63; and Alan Probert, 'Bartolomé de Medina: the patio process and the sixteenth-century silver crisis', *Journal of the West,* 8 (1969), 90–124.

6. THE HACIENDA IN NEW SPAIN

The study of the hacienda as a productive unit in the creation of new forms of exploitation of the soil and of labour is a relatively recent phenomenon in Mexico. Lesley B. Simpson, *Exploitation of land in central Mexico in the sixteenth century* (Berkeley and Los Angeles, 1952) illustrates with quantitative data the impressive, early conversion of Indian lands into agricultural and stock-raising enterprises owned and run by Spaniards. François Chevalier, *La formation des grandes domaines au Mexique* (Paris, 1952; Sp. ed. 1956; Eng. ed. 1963) continued the traditional interest in forms of land tenure – for example Helen Phipps, *Some aspects of the agrarian question in Mexico* (Austin, 1925); George McCutchen McBride, *The land systems of Mexico* (New York, 1927); Silvio Zavala, *Las encomiendas y propiedad territorial en algunas regiones de la América Española* (Mexico, 1940); Jesús Amaya Tapete, *Ameca, protofundación mexicana* (Mexico, 1951) – and gave a new dimension to studies on land ownership and agriculture. Using a wide variety of private and official archives, Chevalier reconstructed the main processes which influenced the formation of the latifundia, traced their development over time, and related the expansion of the hacienda to the general development of the colony and in particular to the establishment of a new economic structure.

Although the dominant theme is still that of land ownership, most recent studies include an analysis of production and productivity, systems of labour, technology, administration, the market, and other micro- and macro-economic aspects. A detailed exposition of the themes and standpoints of such studies may be found in Magnus Mörner's review of recent literature ('The Spanish American hacienda: a survey of recent research and debate', *HAHR*, 53/1 (1973), 183–216), and in Reinhard Liehr, 'Orígenes, evolución y estructura socioeconómica de la hacienda hispanoamericana', *Anuario de Estudios Americanos*, 33 (1976), 527–77. Equally recent is the attempt to define more precisely the economic characteristics of the hacienda and to pinpoint the differences between it and the latifundium, the plantation and other institutions. This attempt to arrive at a more rigorous definition was begun by Eric R. Wolf and Sidney W. Mintz in 'Haciendas and plantations in Middle America and the Antilles', *Social and Economic Studies*, 6 (1957), 380–412. This has been followed up, albeit irregularly, in recent years. See, for example, James Lockhart, 'Encomienda and hacienda: the evolution of the great estate in the Spanish Indies', *HAHR*, 49/3 (1969), 411–29; Robert G. Keith, 'Encomienda, hacienda and corregimiento in Spanish America: a structural analysis', *HAHR*, 51/3 (1971), 431–46, and his introduction to the collective work he edited, *Haciendas and plantations in Latin American history* (New York, 1977), 1–35.

Since 1970, the analysis of agricultural problems during the colonial period has taken the form of regional studies, and in particular of monographs devoted to one or more haciendas. Over these years, a number of monographs have appeared which, apart from describing the formation of this type of landed estate, have tackled more deeply the growing problems of production, labour, the market and the influence of landowners on the social and political life of the region. Charles Gibson, *The Aztecs under Spanish Rule: a history of the Indians of the Valley of Mexico, 1519–1810* (Stanford, 1964) created a model for scholarly analysis at a regional level which has been adopted by many researchers interested in agricultural issues. The collective work, *Haciendas, latifundios y plantaciones en América Latina* (Mexico, 1975), edited by Enrique

Florescano, brought together a series of essays which consider issues of property, production, labour and market outlets in various privately owned estates and in Jesuit haciendas, the latter being preferred for the richness and accessibility of their archives. In 1970, Ward Barrett published one of the best studies on the economy of the sugar hacienda, *The sugar hacienda of the Marqueses del Valle*, in which he paid special attention to the technical and administrative aspects of the hacienda, as well as to labour costs and productivity. However, the vast majority of studies have concentrated on the Jesuit-owned haciendas: Ursula Edwald, *Estudios sobre la hacienda colonial en México. Las propiedades rurales del Colegio Espíritu Santo en Puebla* (Wiesbaden, 1970); James D. Riley, *Hacendados jesuitas en México* (Mexico, 1976); Herman W. Konrad, *A Jesuit hacienda in colonial Mexico: Santa Lucía, 1576–1767* (Stanford, 1980).

Also numerous are studies which examine the formation and development of one or more haciendas over extended periods. See, for example, Jan Bazant, *Cinco haciendas mexicanas* (Mexico, 1974); Edith Boorstein Couturier, *La hacienda de Hueyapán, 1559–1936* (Mexico, 1976); Enrique Semo (ed.), *Siete ensayos sobre la hacienda mexicana, 1780–1880* (Mexico, 1977). These monographs and other economic studies have stimulated the analysis of agrarian problems region by region. William B. Taylor, *Landlord and peasant in colonial Oaxaca* (Stanford, 1972) is an important study which points to a sharp contrast between the development of Indian and Spanish properties in this region and the findings of Chevalier, Gibson and other authors with regard to the centre and north of Mexico. On the vast northern cattle-raising region, Charles H. Harris has written a fundamental work which traces the economic, social and political history of a large family-owned latifundium: *A Mexican family empire. The latifundio of the Sánchez Navarro family, 1765–1867* (Austin, 1975). The Puebla–Tlaxcala area has been the subject of continuing scrutiny by a group of German scholars, who have published such studies as that of Ursula Edwald, already cited, and Hans J. Prenn, *Milpa y hacienda. Tenencia de la tierra indígena y española en la cuenca del Alto Atoyac, Puebla, 1529–1650* (1978). Among these, particularly worthy of note is Herbert J. Nickel, *Soziale Morphologie der Mexikanischen Hacienda* (Wiesbaden, 1978), which gives us a general model of the Mexican hacienda and compares this with that of the Puebla–Tlaxcala area. One of the best analyses of the origin and development of the hacienda in a particular region is Robert Patch, 'La formación de estancias y haciendas en Yucatán durante la colonia',

Boletín de la Escuela de Ciencias Antropológicas de la Universidad de Yucatán (July–August 1976).

On the Bajío, the main grain-producing region in the seventeenth and eighteenth centuries, David A. Brading's *Haciendas and ranchos in the Mexican Bajío. León 1700–1860* (Cambridge, 1978), is one of the first studies on the formation of the ranches. In his unpublished doctoral thesis, 'Creole Mexico: Spanish elites, haciendas and Indian towns, 1750–1810' (University of Texas, 1976), John Tutino examines the social stratification of landowners and the relationship between haciendas and villages in Central Mexico. Claude Morin examines these relationships, agricultural production and the situation of Indian workers in *Michoacán en la Nueva España del siglo XVIII* (Mexico, 1979). One of the best studies on the regional agricultural economy is Eric Van Young, *Hacienda and market in eighteenth-century Mexico: the rural economy of the Guadalajara region, 1675–1820* (Los Angeles, 1981), which considers production, labour, the market and the hacienda system in the region of Guadalajara. Ida Altman and James Lockhart (eds.), *Provinces of early Mexico* (Berkeley and Los Angeles, 1976), brings together a series of regional essays describing agrarian processes, the formation of haciendas and the relations between them and the Indian villages in Yucatán, Oaxaca, Toluca, Tlaxcala, the Valley of Mexico, Querétaro, Zacatecas and Coahuila.

The books by Chevalier and Simpson mentioned above provide the best information on the expansion of cattle raising and the formation of cattle estancias and haciendas in the sixteenth century. William H. Dusemberry, *The Mexican mesta. The administration of ranching in colonial Mexico* (Urbana, 1963), provides an overall analysis of the organization created by cattle breeders in order to regulate seasonal migration, grazing rights, legal matters and the slaughter of cattle. Ramón Ma. Serrera, *Guadalajara, ciudad ganadera. Estudio regional novo-hispano, 1760–1805* (Seville, 1977), contains an analysis of the breeding of cattle, horses, mules and sheep, of the economic function of these activities in the region, and of the great ranching families.

Changes in the agrarian landscape brought about by the development of the haciendas and ranches and by the introduction of new crops and animals are treated in some of the works already mentioned. Alejandra Moreno Toscano offers us a general panorama of these changes in her *Geografía económica de México. Siglo XVI* (Mexico, 1968). Peter Gerhard has studied in some detail the effects of policies which obliged Indian villages to merge into larger units: see 'Congregaciones de indios en la Nueva España antes de 1570', *HM*, 26 (1976–7), 347–95, and 'La evolución del pueblo rural mexicano: 1519–1975', *HM*, 24 (1974–5), 566–78.

The transformation of large tracts of Indian land into private estates owned by Spaniards gave rise to new forms of soil exploitation based on new systems of labour, which in turn created a new pattern of relations between workers and landowners. Between 1929 and 1950, several studies presented an initial view of the chronological development of the systems of agricultural labour and some of their principal characteristics: Lesley B. Simpson, *The Encomienda. Forced native labor in the Spanish Colonia, 1492–1550* (Berkeley and Los Angeles, 1929), *Studies in the administration of the Indians in New Spain* (Berkeley and Los Angeles, 1938 and 1940), and *The encomienda of New Spain* (Berkeley and Los Angeles, 1950); Silvio Zavala, 'Los orígenes coloniales del peonaje en México', *El Trimestre Económico*, 10 (1943–4), 711–48; S. Zavala and María Castelo (eds.), *Fuentes para la historia del trabajo en Nueva España, 1552–1805* (8 vols., Mexico, 1939–46).

Based on these studies and on those of Gonzalo Aguirre Beltrán on the importation of black slaves (*La población negra de México, 1519–1810* (Mexico, 1940)), of George Kubler on the effects of the demographic crisis on the supply of Indian labour (*Mexican architecture in the sixteenth century* (2 vols., New Haven, 1948)), and on the research into the epidemics and demographic catastrophes of the sixteenth century he himself had carried out with S. F. Cook, W. Borah's important study *New Spain's century of depression* (Berkeley and Los Angeles, 1951) showed the devastating effects of the decline of the Indian population on agriculture, mining and the activities of Spanish settlers. According to Borah, the loss of the labour force which was one of the props of colonial society caused a general economic crisis, the organization of labour along different lines, namely the creation of a landless peasantry, and new forms of production and circulation of agricultural produce.

In *The Aztecs under Spanish rule*, Charles Gibson produced the most comprehensive study currently available on Indian labour in any one region. The analysis of systems of agricultural labour in the Valley of Mexico led him to suggest that debt peonage was no longer predominant in this region at the end of the eighteenth century, and that the methods of coercion used initially to retain workers had changed owing to the transformation of the hacienda into an institution which offered regular wages throughout the year and attractive living and social conditions for the Indians who had lost their lands or had cut their links with their community of origin. This hypothesis has been raised in almost all recent studies on the haciendas and agricultural labour, but none has proved convincingly that debt peonage and political coercion ceased to be important as methods of retaining labourers on the haciendas. The studies mentioned above on the haciendas rather confirm that the practice of retaining wages persisted, and prove that the worker did not usually receive payment in cash, but in credit facilities and goods, all of which demonstrates the presence of political and social pressures which curtailed the worker's freedom of movement and employment.

More recent studies (see, for example, John Tutino, 'Life and labor on north Mexican haciendas: the Querétaro–San Luis Potosí region: 1775–1810', and E. Florescano, 'Evaluación y síntesis de las ponencias sobre el trabajo colonial', in *El trabajo y los trabajadores en la historia de México* (Mexico, 1979), 339–77 and 756–97), show that the permanent labourers on the haciendas, the peons, constituted a new social grouping, a product of racial mixture, acculturation and the economic changes of the sixteenth and seventeenth centuries. On the other hand, the majority of seasonal labourers were from Indian villages (E. Florescano, Isabel González Sánchez *et al.*, *La clase obrera en la historia de México. De la colonia al imperio* (Mexico, 1980)).

Until the 1960s the predominant assumption in agrarian studies was that the hacienda was a self-sufficient unit of a feudal rather than commercial type. This thesis has been replaced by new interpretations which show that the hacienda originated in the introduction of the mercantile economy and that its development ran parallel to the growth of mercantile exchange and market outlets. In *Precios del maíz y crisis agrícolas en México, 1708–1810* (Mexico, 1969), E. Florescano examined the principal mechanisms which regulated the demand for and availability of grain on the urban market, and related fluctuations in the price of maize to agricultural crisis and seasonal shortages. Later studies have confirmed the presence of such mechanisms in various regions (see the works by D. A. Brading on León and Eric Van Young on Guadalajara cited above), and in the mining area (Richard L. Garner, 'Zacatecas, 1750–1821. The study of a late colonial Mexican city', unpublished doctoral thesis, University of Michigan, 1970).

The theoretical basis which permitted a deeper economic interpretation of the relationship between agriculture and the market and the dominant economic system was provided by recent Marxist studies, in particular the work of Witold Kula, *An economic theory of the feudal system* (original Polish edition, 1962; Buenos Aires, 1974; London, 1976). Inspired by this and other Marxist studies, Carlos Sempat Assadourian and Ángel Palerm, among others, have treated in a different way the problem of the articulation of the colonial economy with the world system, the characteristics which forged the development of the mercantile colonial economy and the subordinate role played in this by agriculture compared with mineral production. On this issue, see the studies by both authors in E. Florescano (ed.), *Ensayos sobre el desarrollo económico de México y América Latina, 1500–1975* (Mexico, 1979).

The dependence of primary producers in the face of the seasonal and cyclical fluctuations of the market (see Florescano, *Precios*; Brading, *Haciendas and ranchos*; Van Young, *Hacienda and market*; Garner, 'Zacatecas, 1750–1821') produced an even greater dependence among farmers and cattle raisers on commercial capital. During the eighteenth century this expressed itself, in the main urban and mining centres, through the domination of the mechanisms of circulation of agricultural produce and the control of market outlets by the merchant sector; for this, see the already mentioned study by Van Young and Harris, *A Mexican family empire*; Tutino, 'Creole Mexico', and Marco Bellingeri, *Las haciendas en México. El caso de San Antonio Teochatlaco, 1800–1920*, forthcoming. The studies by Asunción Lavrin on the credit extended by religious institutions to producers and merchants ('El capital eclesiástico y las élites sociales en Nueva España a fines del siglo XVIII', paper presented at the V Simposio de Historia Económica de América Latina, Lima, April 1978), R. B. Lindley on credit and family relations within the colonial elite ('Kinship and credit in the structure of the Guadalajara oligarchy, 1800–1830', unpublished Ph.D. thesis, Austin, 1976), Gisela von Wobeser on the contraction of debts among the owners of haciendas (*San Carlos Borromeo. Endeudamiento de una hacienda colonial, 1608–1729* (Mexico, 1980)), J. Tutino on the concentration of wealth and land within the commercial sector ('Creole Mexico') and Doris Ladd on the colonial aristocracy (*The Mexican nobility at Independence* (Austin, 1976)), all demonstrate the gradual erosion of the power of primary producers in the face of the credit and capital accumulated by merchants, and the formation of a small but powerful oligarchy of great families, predominant among which were merchants.

7. RURAL ECONOMY AND SOCIETY IN SPANISH
SOUTH AMERICA

The rural history of Spanish South America finally began to receive some attention from scholars during the 1970s. Even now, far more research is devoted to the large estates than to smallholders and *comunidades*. See Magnus Mörner, 'The Spanish American hacienda. A survey of recent research and debate', *HAHR*, 53/2 (1973), 183–216; articles by Reinhard Liehr in H. J. Puhle (ed.), *Lateinamerika. Historische Realität und Dependencia-Theorien* (Hamburg, 1976), 105–46, and H. Pietschmann in G. Siebenmann (ed.), *Die lateinamerikanische Hacienda. Ihre Rolle in der Geschichte von Wirtschaft und Gesellschaft* (Diessenhofen, 1979), 37–48. Interesting perspectives are provided by Cristóbal Kay, 'Desarrollo comparativo del sistema señorial europeo y del sistema de hacienda latinoamericano', *Anuario de Estudios Americanos*, 31 (1976), 681–723. Agricultural productivity and technology during the colonial period have until now received very little attention. An older but still important study of the legal aspects is J. M. Ots Capdequí, *El régimen de la tierra en la América española durante el período colonial* (Ciudad Trujillo, 1946).

A general survey of Peruvian rural history is provided by V. Roel Pineda, *Historia social y económica de la Colonia* (Lima, 1970). Recent monographs include R. G. Keith, *Conquest and agrarian change: the emergence of the hacienda system on the Peruvian coast* (Cambridge, Mass., 1976); M. Burga, *De la encomienda a la hacienda capitalista. El Valle de Jequetepeque del siglo XVI al XX* (Lima, 1976); K. A. Davies, 'The rural domain of the city of Arequipa, 1540–1665' (Ph.D. dissertation, University of Connecticut, 1974); S. E. Ramírez-Horton, 'Land tenure and the economics of power in colonial Peru' (unpublished dissertation, University of Wisconsin, 1977); and M. Mörner, *Perfil de la sociedad rural del Cuzco a fines de la colonia* (Lima, 1978). The valley of Chancay has been studied in several contributions by J. Matos Mar and others. In vol. II of *Trabajos de historia* (4 vols., Lima, 1977) Pablo Macera studied Jesuit haciendas and the history of sugar production. See also Nicholas P. Cushner, *Lords of the land: sugar, wine and Jesuit estates of coastal Peru 1600–1767* (Albany, 1980). For labour see Frederick P. Bowser, *The African slave in colonial Peru, 1524–1650* (Stanford, 1974); for the role of the Indians as labour and in trade, K. Spalding, *De indio a campesino. Cambios en la estructura social del Perú colonial* (Lima, 1974). Food supply is discussed in O. Febres Villaroel, 'La crisis agrícola en el Perú en el último tercio del siglo XVIII', *Revista Histórica*, 27 (Lima, 1964), 102–99, and Demetrio Ramos, *Trigo chileno, navieros del Callao y hacendados limeños entre la crisis agrícola del siglo XVII y la comercial de la primera mitad del siglo XVIII* (Madrid, 1967). Irrigation is studied by H. Villanueva U. and J. Sherbondy (eds.), *Cuzco: agua y poder* (Cuzco, 1979).

The most serious work so far on the rural history of Upper Peru (Bolivia) is B. Larson, 'Economic decline and social change in an agrarian hinterland: Cochabamba (Bolivia) in the late colonial period' (unpublished dissertation, Columbia University, 1978). Labour aspects are dealt with by N. Sánchez-Albornoz, *Indios y tributos en el Alto Perú* (Lima, 1978). Articles by S. Rivera Cusicanqui and others have appeared in the journal *Avances* (La Paz, 1978–), and D. Santamaría has published two interesting articles on hacienda production and Indian land property rights from 1780 to 1810 in the journal *Desarrollo Económico*, 17 (Buenos Aires, 1977).

Mario Góngora has been the pioneer in the field of Chilean rural history. His works include: *Origen de los 'inquilinos' de Chile Central* (Santiago, 1960); (with J. Borde), *Evolución de la propiedad rural en el valle del Puangue*, I–II (Santiago, 1956); *Encomenderos y estancieros. Estudios acerca de la constitución social aristocrática de Chile después de la Conquista, 1580–1660* (Santiago, 1970); *Studies in the colonial history of Spanish America* (Cambridge, 1975). See also R. Baraona, X. Aranda and R. Santana, *Valle de Putaendo. Estudio de estructura agraria* (Santiago, 1969). An important and unique contribution is that of M. Carmagnani, *Les mécanismes de la vie économique dans une société coloniale: le Chili 1680–1830* (Paris, 1973).

For short surveys of the rural history of the Río de la Plata see C. S. Assadourian, G. Beato and J. C. Chiaramonte, *Argentina. De la conquista a la Independencia* (Buenos Aires, 1972); H. C. Giberti, *Historia económica de la ganadería argentina* (Buenos Aires, 1961); A. R. Castellanos, *Breve historia de la ganadería en el Uruguay* (Montevideo, 1971). Pedro Santos Martínez, *Historia económica de Mendoza durante el Virreinato, 1776–1810* (Madrid, 1961), is an important regional history. See also his *Las industrias durante el Virreinato (1776–1810)* (Buenos Aires, 1969). C. Garzón Maceda, *Economía del Tucumán. Economía natural y economía monetaria. Siglos XVI, XVII, XVIII* (Córdoba, 1968), is another penetrating study of general interest. Rural history is also dealt with in J. L. Mora Mérida, *Historia social de Paraguay, 1600–50* (Seville, 1973).

On the Jesuit missions, see M. Mörner, *Actividades políticas y económicas de los jesuitas en el Río de la Plata. La era de los Habsburgos* (Buenos Aires, 1968), and his article on the rivalry of Uruguayan *ganado cimarrón* in *Revista Portuguesa de História*, 9 (Coimbra, 1961). See also E. A. Coni, *Historia de las vaquerías de Río de la Plata, 1555–1750* (Buenos Aires, 1956) and the articles by J. C. Garavaglia and T. Halperín Donghi in Enrique Florescano (ed.), *Haciendas, latifundios y plantaciones en América Latina* (Mexico, 1975). S. M. Socolow, 'Economic activities of the *porteño* merchants: the viceregal period', *HAHR*, 55/2 (1975), is also useful.

The Audiencia of Quito (Ecuador) is still little explored. More data on rural and social history than the title suggests can be found in C. Moreno Yáñez, *Sublevaciones indígenas en la Audiencia de Quito, comienzos del siglo XVIII hasta finales de la Colonia* (Bonn, 1976). See also E. Bonifaz, 'Origen y evolución de una hacienda histórica, Guachalá', *Boletín de la Academia Nacional de Historia*, 53 (Quito, 1970), and U. Oberem, 'Contribución a la historia del trabajador rural de América Latina: "conciertos" y "huasipungueros" en Ecuador' (Universitätsschwerpunkt Lateinamerikaforschung, Bielefeld, 1977, mimeo). On the coast, see M. T. Hamerly's excellent *Historia social y económica de la antigua provincia de Guayaquil, 1763–1842* (Guayaquil, 1973), and M. Chiriboga's article on the history of cacao plantations in *Estudios Rurales Latinoamericanos*, 1/1 (Bogotá, 1978).

In Colombia, the sociologist O. Fals Borda was the pioneer in rural history. See his work *El hombre y la tierra en Boyacá* (Bogotá, 1957), and his article on Indian 'congregations', 1595–1850, in *The Americas*, 13/4 (1957). On the Indian communities see also an article by T. Gómez in *Cahiers du Monde Hispanique et Luso-Brésilien*, 27 (Toulouse, 1977). The main contributions by G. Colmenares include *Haciendas de los jesuitas en el Nuevo Reino de Granada, siglo XVIII* (Bogotá, 1969); *Historia económica y social de Colombia, 1537–1719* (Bogotá, 1973); *Cali: terratenientes, mineros y comerciantes. Siglo XVIII* (Cali, 1975). See also J. A. Villamarín, 'Haciendas en la Sabana de Bogotá, Colombia, en la época colonial: 1539–1810', in Florescano, *Haciendas, latifundios y plantaciones*, and contributions by different authors in *Anuario Colombiano de Historia Social y de la Cultura* (Bogotá, 1963–).

In his pioneering work, *Economía colonial de Venezuela* (Mexico, 1946), E. Arcila Farías dealt mainly with commercialization. For a broader approach see, Federico Brito Figueroa, *Estructura económica de Venezuela colonial* (Caracas, 1963), an analysis in strictly Marxist terms. A fine study on the late colonial and early national periods is M. Izard, *La agricultura venezolana en una época de transición* (Caracas, 1972).

8. ASPECTS OF THE INTERNAL ECONOMY

There are no satisfactory surveys of the Spanish American colonial economies. A provocative, thoughtful, but dated Marxist interpretation is Sergio Bagú, *Economía de la sociedad colonial: ensayo de historia comparada de América Latina* (Buenos Aires, 1949). Also somewhat dated is Emilio A. Coni, *Agricultura, comercio e industria coloniales (siglo XVI–XVIII)* (Buenos Aires, 1941). A more modern but less stimulating study is Demetrio Ramos, *Minería y comercio interprovincial en Hispanoamérica (siglos XVI, XVII y XVIII)* (Valladolid, 1970). Much useful material on economic institutions can still be found in C. H. Haring, *The Spanish empire in America* (New York, 1947). A study with a very different emphasis, as the title suggests, is the short book by Stanley J. and Barbara H. Stein, *The colonial heritage of Latin America: essays on economic dependence in perspective* (New York, 1970). For the Atlantic sea link, Atlantic trade and the Atlantic economy in general, see *CHLA* 1, Bibliographical Essay 10.

Labour

A convenient summary of Indian colonial labour systems is by Juan A. and Judith E. Villamarín, *Indian labor in mainland colonial Spanish America* (Newark, Delaware, 1975). The evolution of such labour systems may be grasped by reading in sequence the introductions to the several volumes by Silvio Zavala and María Castelo (eds.), *Fuentes para la historia del trabajo en Nueva España, 1552–1805* (8 vols., Mexico, 1939–46). Readers should also consult Zavala's *El servicio personal de los indios en el Perú (extractos del siglo XVI, XVII, XVIII)* (3 vols., Mexico, 1978–80), which has extensive discussion of the Peruvian encomienda, mita and peonage. The encomienda, how it declined because of population loss and royal legislation, and how some entrepreneurs used it as a device for capital accumulation and diversification, are discussed in José Miranda, *La función económica del encomendero en los orígenes del régimen colonial (Nueva España, 1525–1531)* (Mexico, 1965). The link between the encomienda and land tenure in general is discussed in two very different essays: James Lockhart, 'Encomienda and hacienda; the evolution of the great estate in the Spanish Indies', *HAHR*, 49/3 (1969), 411–29; and Robert G. Keith, 'Encomienda, hacienda and corregimiento in Spanish America: a structural analysis', *HAHR*, 51/3 (1971), 431–46. The pioneer of studies on peonage is, once again, Silvio Zavala, in his 'Los orígenes coloniales del peonaje en México', *El Trimestre Económico*, 10 (1943–4), 711–48. See also Genaro V. Vázquez, *Legislación del trabajo en los siglos xvi, xvii y xviii* (Mexico, 1938); Samuel Kagan, *Los vagabundos en la Nueva España, siglo XVI* (Mexico, 1957); Richard Konetzke, 'Los mestizos en la legislación colonial', *Revista de Estudios Políticos*, 112–14 (1960), 113–30, 179–215; and Karen Spalding, *De indio a campesino. Cambios en la estructura social del Perú colonial* (Lima, 1974). For the literature on black slavery, see, *CHLA* II, Bibliographical Essay 10.

Taxation

Gabriel Ardant is the main authority on systems of taxation. See, for example, his massive *Théorie sociologique de l'impôt* (2 vols., Paris, 1965). José Miranda surveys the history and economies of Indian tribute in Mexico, in his *El tributo indígena en la Nueva España durante el siglo XVI* (Mexico, 1952). Nicolás Sánchez-Albornoz covers a later and longer period, including the post-independence tributes of the nineteenth century, in *Indios y tributos en el Alto Perú* (Lima, 1978). Ronald Escobedo Mansilla, *El tributo indígena en el Perú, siglos XVI y XVII* (Pamplona, 1979) is thorough but lacks interpretation and imagination.

Derramas and *repartimientos de mercancías* await detailed history and analysis. Meanwhile, a good study of the late colonial repartimientos in Peru is H. Moreno Cebrián, *El corregidor de indios y la economía peruana en el siglo XVIII. (Los repartos forzosos de mercancías)* (Madrid, 1977). We are equally lacking in definitive works on the specific institutions which Indians adopted so readily, the *caja de comunidad* and the *cofradía*. There are two unpublished dissertations containing extensive information: Francis Joseph Brooks, 'Parish and *cofradía* in eighteenth-century Mexico' (Ph.D. thesis, Princeton University, 1976); and Gary Wendell Graff, '*Cofradías* in the new kingdom of Granada: lay fraternities in a Spanish-American frontier society, 1600–1755' (Ph.D. thesis, University of Wisconsin, 1973). See also Gonzalo Aguirre Beltrán, *Formas de gobierno indígena* (Mexico, 1953); Pedro Carrasco, 'The civil religious hierarchy in Mesoamerican communities; pre-Spanish background and colonial development', *American Anthropologist*, 63 (1961), 483–97;

appropriate parts of the impressive study by Pierre Duviols, *La lutte contre les religions autochtones dans le Pérou colonial* (Paris, 1971); and José Miranda and Silvio Zavala, 'Instituciones indígenas en la colonia', in A. Caso (ed.), *Métodos y resultados de la política indigenista en México* (Mexico, 1954), 29–167.

Distribution and exchange

On the *consulados* see, for example, Germán O. E. Tjarks, *El consulado de Buenos Aires, y sus proyecciones en la historia del Río de la Plata* (2 vols., Buenos Aires, 1962) and the older Robert S. Smith, *The Spanish guild merchant. A history of the consulado, 1250–1700* (Durham, N.C., 1940). Government *estancos* or monopolies are the subject of a series of works from the Escuela de Estudios Hispanoamericanos in Seville. The most recent is by José Jesús Hernández Palomo, *La renta del pulque en Nueva España, 1663–1810* (Seville, 1979). The crown's revenues are studied exhaustively in Francisco Gallardo y Fernández, *Orígen, progresos y estado de las rentas de la corona de España, su gobierno y administración* (8 vols., Madrid, 1805–8).

The Indian economy and market system are discussed in such well-known works as Charles Gibson, *The Aztecs under Spanish rule: a history of the Indians of the Valley of Mexico, 1519–1810* (Stanford, 1964); Josep M. Barnadas, *Charcas, 1535–1565: orígenes históricos de una sociedad colonial* (La Paz, 1973); and Magnus Mörner, *La corona española y los foráneos en los pueblos de indios de América* (Stockholm, 1970).

For long-distance commerce, routes and markets, the following should provide an introduction: Woodrow Borah, *Early colonial trade and navigation between Mexico and Peru* (Berkeley and Los Angeles, 1954); Marcello Carmagnani, *Les mécanismes de la vie économique dans une société coloniale: le Chili (1680–1830)* (Paris, 1973); Manuel Moreyra y Paz Soldán, *El comercio de exportación en el Pacífico a comienzos del siglo XVIII* (Lima, 1944); and María Encarnación Rodríguez Vicente, *El tribunal del consulado de Lima en la primera mitad del siglo XVII* (Madrid, 1960). Lawrence A. Clayton reviews some works on Pacific trade in 'Trade and navigation in the seventeenth-century viceroyalty of Peru', *JLAS*, 7 (1975), 1–21, and gives us a good picture of a colonial shipyard and port in *Caulkers and carpenters in a New World: the shipyards of colonial Guayaquil* (Athens, Ohio, 1980). The Potosí–Buenos Aires route has a large but scattered bibliography. Helpful are Mario Rodríguez, 'Dom

Pedro of Braganza and Colônia do Sacramento, 1680–1705', *HAHR*, 38 (1958), 180–208; and Sergio Villalobos R., *Comercio y contrabando en el Río de la Plata y Chile, 1700–1811* (Buenos Aires, 1965). An amusing account of the journey between Buenos Aires and Lima is 'Concolorcorvo', *El Lazarillo, a guide for inexperienced travelers between Buenos Aires and Lima, 1773*, tr. Walter D. Kline (Bloomington, 1965). Fairs are discussed in Manuel Carrera Stampa's 'Las ferias novohispanas', *HM*, 2 (1952–3), 319–42, which also contains maps of trade routes, and in Allyn C. Loosley, 'The Puerto Bello fairs', *HAHR*, 13 (1933), 314–35. Carrera Stampa also wrote a pioneering work on craft guilds, *Los gremios mexicanos: la organización gremial en Nueva España, 1521–1810* (Mexico, 1954).

The literature on merchants is extensive, especially for the eighteenth century. Two articles on the less well-known early groups are John C. Super, 'Partnership and profit in the early Andean trades: the experiences of Quito merchants, 1580–1610', *JLAS*, 2 (1979), 265–81, and Louisa Schell Hoberman, 'Merchants in seventeenth-century Mexico City: a preliminary portrait', *HAHR*, 57 (1977), 479–503. Work on colonial industries has also been voluminous. For recent studies of the textile *obrajes*, see John C. Super, 'Querétaro *obrajes*: industry and society in provincial Mexico 1600–1810', *HAHR*, 56 (1976), 197–216; Robson Tyrer, 'The demographic and economic history of the Audiencia of Quito: Indian population and the textile industry, 1600–1810' (Ph.D. thesis, University of California at Berkeley, 1976); Javier Ortiz de la Tabla Ducasse, 'El obraje colonial ecuatoriano. Aproximación a su estudio', *Revista de Indias*, 27 (1977), 471–541; G. P. C. Thomson, 'Economy and society in Puebla de los Ángeles 1800–1850' (D.Phil. thesis, Oxford, 1978); Richard J. Salvucci, 'Enterprise and economic development in eighteenth-century Mexico: the case of the obrajes' (Ph.D. thesis, Princeton University, 1982).

Other colonial industries have interested scholars such as Eduardo Arcila Farias, who described Venezuela's cacao in *Economía colonial de Venezuela* (Mexico, 1946), and the trade in it to Veracruz in *Comercio entre Venezuela y México en los siglos XVI y XVII* (Mexico, 1959); Manuel Rubio Sánchez, *Historia del añil o xiquilite en Centroamérica* (2 vols., San Salvador, 1976–7); and John E. Kicza, 'The pulque trade of late colonial Mexico City', *The Americas*, 27 (1980), 193–221. There is a census of the small manufacturers of Buenos Aires in Lyman L. Johnson, 'The entrepreneurial reorganization of an artisan trade. The bakers of Buenos Aires, 1770–1820', *The Americas*, 27 (1980), 139–60.

Sixteenth-century price inflation was the object of a study by Woodrow Borah and Sherburne Cook, *Price trends of some basic commodities in central Mexico, 1531–1570* (Berkeley and Los Angeles, 1958). Enrique Florescano covered the same problems for the last century of the colonial period in his *Precios de maíz y crisis agrícolas en México, 1708–1810* (Mexico, 1969).

For opposing views on the seventeenth-century crisis, see Woodrow Borah, *New Spain's century of depression* (Berkeley and Los Angeles, 1951), and volume II of John Lynch's *Spain under the Hapsburgs* (2 vols., Oxford, 1965, 1969). The colonial boom of the eighteenth century and the partial setbacks which took place in the years before independence have been studied in many of the works already cited. The other side of the eighteenth-century economic boom is nowhere better summed up than in D. A. Brading's *Haciendas and ranchos in the Mexican Bajío: León, 1700–1860* (Cambridge, 1978). See also Eric Van Young, *Hacienda and market in eighteenth-century Mexico: the rural economy of the Guadalajara region, 1675–1820* (Berkeley and Los Angeles, 1981).

9. INDIAN SOCIETIES UNDER SPANISH RULE

A bibliography of Spanish American ethnohistory up to 1967, by Howard F. Cline, is contained in section B, pp. 117–48, of Charles C. Griffin (ed.), *Latin America. A guide to the historical literature* (Austin, 1971). The section provides references to some 300 basic works relating to both pre- and post-Columbian ethnohistory, with evaluative commentary. Many of the entries are original in the *Guide*. Others are taken from the *Handbook of Latin American Studies*, which initiated a section on the ethnohistory of Mesoamerica by Henry B. Nicholson in no. 22 (1960), and a section on the ethnohistory of South America by John V. Murra in no. 29 (1967). The *Handbook of Latin American Studies* is the foremost bibliographical work for continuing reference. The sections on ethnohistory are now published as part of the Humanities volumes, issued every other year. The student should note that works bearing on Indian history in the colonial period may sometimes be found in sections other than Ethnohistory, especially in History and Ethnology.

A major work of reference for the ethnohistory and particularly the ethnohistorical bibliography of Mesoamerica is the *Guide to ethnohistorical sources*, which comprises the four final volumes (12–15) of Robert Wauchope (ed.), *Handbook of Middle American Indians* (Austin, 1964–75). The four volumes were edited by Howard Cline and they contain articles on the relevant bibliographical materials, the *Relaciones geográficas*, the chronicles and their authors, the pictorial manuscripts (codices), materials in the native and in the European traditions, and much else. There is no comparable guide to the ethnohistorical source material of South America, but two summary articles survey the bibliography and the current state of research: John V. Murra, 'Current research and prospects in Andean ethnohistory', *LARR*, 5 (1970), 3–36, and Karen Spalding, 'The colonial Indian: past and future research perspectives', *LARR*, 7 (1972), 47–76.

Basic works on Spanish institutional controls over Indians include Clarence Haring, *The Spanish empire in America* (revised edn, New York, 1963), which is still the most satisfactory one-volume general summary, and a series of writings on special topics: Alberto Mario Salas, *Las armas de la conquista* (Buenos Aires, 1950) on conquest, warfare, and weapons; Silvio Zavala, *La encomienda indiana* (Madrid, 1935) and *Las instituciones jurídicas en la conquista de América* (Madrid, 1935; revised edn, 1971); L. B. Simpson, *The encomienda in New Spain* (revised edn, 1950); Guillermo Lohmann Villena, *El corregidor de indios en el Perú bajo los Austrias* (Madrid, 1957); Constantino Bayle, *Los cabildos seculares en la América española* (Madrid, 1952); and many others. Peter Gerhard, *A guide to the historical geography of New Spain* (Cambridge, 1972) is fundamental for the history of encomiendas, corregimientos, town foundations, and local institutions and events. Special note should be taken of Lewis Hanke, *The Spanish struggle for justice in the conquest of America* (Philadelphia, 1949), on the campaign for fair treatment of Indians, and of Edward H. Spicer, *Cycles of conquest. The impact of Spain, Mexico and the United States on the Indians of the South-West 1533–1960* (Tucson, 1962), an examination of white–Indian contacts in northern Mexico and the south-west of the United States.

The classic treatment of Indian conversion in Mexico to the 1570s is Robert Ricard, *La 'conquête spirituelle' du Mexique* (Paris, 1933; also in Spanish and English translation). The historical literature on northern Mexican and borderlands missions is too extensive to summarize here. For South America see especially Fernando de Armas Medina, *Cristianización del Perú* (1952); Antonine Tibesar, *Franciscan beginnings in colonial Peru (1532–1600)* (Seville, 1953); and Pierre Duviols, *La lutte contre les religions autochtones dans le Pérou coloniale.* 'L'*extirpation de l'idolâtrie*' *entre 1532 et 1660* (Lima, 1971).

Important writings on tribute, land and labour, largely from the Spanish administrative point of view, are José Miranda, *El tributo indígena en la Nueva España durante el siglo XVI* (Mexico, 1952); L. B. Simpson, *Exploitation of land in central Mexico in the sixteenth century* (Berkeley and Los Angeles, 1952); François Chevalier, *La formation des grands domaines au Mexique. Terre et société aux XVIᵉ–XVIIᵉ siècles* (Paris, 1952; also in Spanish and English translations); and the series of introductions to the volumes of Silvio A. Zavala and María Costelo (eds.), *Fuentes para la historia del trabajo en Nueva España* (8 vols., Mexico, 1939– 46). All relate to Mexico, and again there are no comparable studies for South America. An important recent work on the hacienda in Peru is Robert G. Keith, *Conquest and agrarian change. The emergence of the hacienda system on the Peruvian coast* (Cambridge, Mass., 1976). A general survey of labour is Juan A. and Judith E. Villamarín, *Indian labor in mainland colonial Spanish America* (Newark, Delaware, 1975). On relations between Spaniards and Indians the article by Elman R. Service, 'Indian–European relations in colonial Latin America', *American Anthropologist*, 57 (1955), 411–25, and the general treatment by Magnus Mörner, *Race mixture in the history of Latin America* (Boston, 1967), are worthy of attention.

The study of Indian society under colonial conditions owes much to the seminal work of the California demographers L. B. Simpson, Sherburne F. Cook and Woodrow Borah, beginning in the 1940s and continuing to the present, and published principally in the Ibero-Americana series. See Bibliographical Essay 1, above. Borah especially has developed the original demographic materials in studies of Indian social organization, tribute payment, labour and prices. Pioneering work in the analysis of Nahuatl texts and codices for what they yield on Indian social structure and social history has been accomplished by Pedro Carrasco, Joaquín Galarza, Hanns J. Prem and others. Frances Karttunen and James Lockhart have also examined the colonial history of the Nahuatl language in *Nahuatl in the middle years. Language contact phenomena in texts of the colonial period* (Berkeley and Los Angeles, 1976). Treatments of colonial Indian society in particular areas of Mexico include Delfina López Sarrelangue, *La nobleza indígena de Patzcuaro en la época virreinal* (Mexico, 1965); Charles Gibson, *Tlaxcala in the sixteenth century* (New Haven, 1952) and *The Aztecs under Spanish rule* (Stanford,

1964); William B. Taylor, *Landlord and peasant in colonial Oaxaca* (Stanford, 1972) and *Drinking, homicide and rebellion in colonial Mexican villages* (Stanford, 1979); Ronald Spores, *The Mixtec kings and their people* (Norman, Oklahoma, 1967); and the collection of studies edited by Ida Altman and James Lockhart, *Provinces of early Mexico* (Berkeley and Los Angeles, 1976).

In South America comparable work began later and the studies are not so far advanced as in Mexico, but current research is making rapid headway. A pioneering survey was George Kubler, 'The Quechua in the colonial world' in vol. II (1946) of the *Handbook of South American Indians*, ed. Julian H. Steward. Most of the recent contributions are in the form of specialized articles. But see Nathan Wachtel, *La vision des vaincus* (Paris, 1971; also in English translation), a wide-ranging, imaginative, structuralist analysis of Indian life and thought in Peru. Articles and special studies by Waldemar Espinosa Soriano, Alvaro Jara, Udo Oberen, María Rostworowski de Diez Canseco and Karen Spalding examine Indian social organization, labour, *curacas*, *visitas*, *señoríos* and related topics, especially for the sixteenth century.

INDEX

445